LIFE ON AIR

Life on Air

A History of Radio Four

DAVID HENDY

OXFORD
UNIVERSITY PRESS

OXFORD

UNIVERSITY PRESS

Great Clarendon Street, Oxford OX2 6DP

Oxford University Press is a department of the University of Oxford.
It furthers the University's objective of excellence in research, scholarship,
and education by publishing worldwide in

Oxford New York

Auckland Cape Town Dar es Salaam Hong Kong Karachi
Kuala Lumpur Madrid Melbourne Mexico City Nairobi
New Delhi Shanghai Taipei Toronto

With offices in

Argentina Austria Brazil Chile Czech Republic France Greece
Guatemala Hungary Italy Japan Poland Portugal Singapore
South Korea Switzerland Thailand Turkey Ukraine Vietnam

Oxford is a registered trade mark of Oxford University Press
in the UK and in certain other countries

Published in the United States
by Oxford University Press Inc., New York

© David Hendy 2007

British Library Cataloguing in Publication Data

Data available

Library of Congress Cataloging in Publication Data

Data available

Typeset by SPI Publisher Services, Pondicherry, India
Printed in Great Britain
on acid-free paper by
Clays Ltd, St Ives plc

ISBN 978–0–19–924881–0

1

For Henrietta, Eloise, and Morgan.

Preface

This book attempts to reveal as fully as possible the 'inside' story of Radio Four's history, and to set it against the backdrop of changing cultural life in Britain during the last decades of the twentieth century.

It is a story built largely on unprecedented access to the BBC's extraordinary collection of written archives. But this is *a* history of Radio Four, not *the* history: it is large but, of necessity, selective. Selective, in part, because the sheer output of Radio Four has been so vast—some 13,000 or so separate programmes a year, every year, for forty years: one can only pick examples and hope the choice proves fruitful. Selective, chronologically, because while it touches briefly on events back in 1939 and as recently as 2006, it concentrates overwhelmingly on the period from 1967 to 1997: the first thirty years of Radio Four's forty-year existence.

The basic reason for focusing on this period is that access to the BBC's archives is not unlimited. It has been possible for a vast range of documents between 1967 and 1987, for a smaller number between 1987 and 1997, and for none at all after that date. There are newspaper cuttings galore, of course, and they tell a good story. Indeed, newspapers have been vital to an understanding of events: they made or broke the reputation of programmes, they set the climate of critical debate, they shaped public attitudes, they stirred controversies. I make no apology for using them liberally: what they said mattered at the time. But to rely *only* on newspapers would be to tell only half the story. Something approaching a rounded version of events comes by reaching deep inside the BBC itself, by talking to those who worked there, and by seeing what they really said—and meant—in their dealings with each other at the time. Many of these dialogues have been captured for us in the BBC's voluminous written documents. Jean Seaton, who now wears Asa Briggs's old mantle as the Corporation's historian, says of its archives that they 'illuminate contemporary history more vividly than any other'. And so they do. Indeed, they tell far more than half the story: they take us to the heart of the BBC's thinking, and to its view of the wider world. I have not wished to tread too far beyond the firm grounding they provide.

Despite the enforced cut-off date, what remains is by far the largest part of Radio Four's story. Many of us have listened to Radio Four during this same period; we *think* we know a great deal about it. In a sense we are right: listening gives us what Seaton calls 'a kind of map'—a *feel* for the programmes that worked, or did not work, that gave pleasure, or irritated. But memory is selective; sometimes it misleads; occasionally it is shaped by second-hand opinions and popular mythology imbibed unconsciously. Even at its best, it succeeds at telling us *what* happened rather than answering the more interesting questions of *why* something happened and *how*.

This book attempts some answers to those 'why' and 'how' questions: why Radio Four has survived despite so often being viewed as an anachronism, why it is that so many listeners claim it is stitched into the very fabric of their being, how it has been coaxed or cajoled into reflecting the changing times, how exactly it came to establish its reputation as a national institution or as an emblem of middle-class Britishness. The individual and combined thinking of those who actually worked for Radio Four on such matters has, up till now, been invisible. This is my attempt to bring it into the public domain.

Although this is not an 'official' history, the whole project would have been impossible without access to the BBC's archives. My first debt is therefore to Jacqueline Kavanagh, Jeff Walden, and other staff at the BBC Written Archive Centre in Caversham. Robin Reynolds of BBC Heritage helped me to secure access to post-1979 material and the BBC's invaluable collection of oral history interviews with past employees. Shampa Hussein and Richard Jeffery at BBC Research Central also gave invaluable assistance with picture research.

For access to other material I must also thank: the British Library Sound Archives, Edinburgh University Library Special Collections, the Mass-Observation Archive at Sussex University Library, and the Bodleian Library, Oxford University. I am grateful, too, for access to the private papers of Monica Sims, Joy Whitby, and John Gray, and for access to unpublished work by John Grist, Hugh Chignell, and Matt Thompson.

I have spoken to a large number of BBC staff, and others indirectly connected with Radio Four, both on and off the record. I wish to thank, especially, those who agreed to be interviewed formally, at some length, and sometimes repeatedly: Gerard Mansell, Joy Whitby, Ian McIntyre, Monica Sims, David Hatch, Michael Green, Helen Boaden, Mark Damazer, Philip French, George Fischer, Michael Mason, Jock Gallagher, John Tydeman, Richard Wade, Piers Plowright, Matt Thompson, Caroline Millington, Nick MacKinnon, and Gillian Reynolds.

I am especially indebted to Gillian Reynolds for reading early drafts of the book and making so many helpful comments. Others who did the same included Jean Seaton, Andrew Crisell, Hugh Chignell, Sally Feldman, Matthew Linfoot, John Tydeman, Gerard Mansell, Ian McIntyre, Monica Sims, David Hatch, Michael Green, Richard Wade, Caroline Millington, Joy Whitby, Liz Forgan, James Boyle, and Matt Thompson. They all saved me from error and offered valuable suggestions.

Several years of researching and writing depended on funding and personal support. I would therefore like to acknowledge the help of the following: the Leverhulme Trust, for the award of a Research Fellowship and Grant 2002–3; the Arts and Humanities Research Council, for granting a period of research leave in 2005–6; the Scouloudi Foundation in association with the Institute for Historical Research at the University of London, for a Historical Award in 2003; and, at the University of Westminster, Colin Sparks, Annette Hill, Peter Goodwin, Sally Feldman, Matthew Linfoot, and members of the Communication and Media

Research Institute, who all, in different ways, helped relieve me of normal teaching and administrative duties at points between 2001 and 2006.

Throughout, I have benefited hugely from the intellectual stimulation, encouragement, and inspiration that comes from working in close proximity to Jean Seaton and the team she has assembled to help prepare the next volume of the BBC's authorized history. Jean Seaton herself has been an enduring source of encouragement and advice. I also owe a large debt to my friend and colleague, Paddy Scannell, who first got me interested in media history and kept me to the current task during moments of doubt.

At Oxford University Press, the book has been managed with professionalism and patience, first, by Ruth Parr, who originally commissioned the book, and then by Anne Gelling, Rupert Cousens, Zoë Washford, Samantha Skyrme, Kate Hind, and Edwin Pritchard, who saw it through to completion. I must also thank the Press's own external readers for their constructive comments.

The process of researching and writing a book draws many people into its orbit, if only temporarily. But it is always those closest to an author who become trapped in its gravitational pull. For enduring half a decade of mental or physical absence and irritable or obsessive behaviour, I wish to thank more than anyone else my wonderful family: Henrietta, Eloise, and Morgan. The cliché holds true: they have been a tower of strength. My gratitude is boundless, and it is to all three of them that I dedicate this book.

D. H.

Acknowledgements

All extracts from British Broadcasting Corporation documents are published with the permission of the BBC and its Written Archives Centre. The BBC has also licensed the use of 'Radio Four' in the title of this book. Extracts from the Papers and Correspondence of Michael Meredith Swann are published with permission and by courtesy of Edinburgh University Library; those from the Mass-Observation Archive in University of Sussex Special Collections, with permission of Curtis Brown Group Ltd., London, on behalf of the Trustees of the Mass-Observation Archive (Copyright © Mass-observation Archive).

Quotations from various private letters have been included with the kind permission of the following: Professor Evelyn Barish, Joy Whitby, and Caroline Millington. Unpublished papers have also been quoted with the permission of Monica Sims, Michael Mason, John Grist, Matt Thompson, and Hugh Chignell.

The extract from 'Prayer' is taken from *Mean Time* by Carol Ann Duffy, published by Anvil Press Poetry in 1993.

All photographs are copyright of the BBC and are reproduced with its permission, except for the following: photograph 3 (by permission of Joy Whitby and *Radio Times*); photograph 20 (copyright Press Association).

Contents

List of Plates

1. Gerald Mansell, Chief of the Home Service then Controller of Radio Four, 1965–9.
2. William Hardcastle, the presenter of *The World at One*, 1965–75.
3. Tony Whitby, the Controller of Radio Four, 1969–75.
4. Robin Day and his producer Walter Wallich preparing an edition of *It's Your Line*, 1975.
5. Gerald Priestland and Jacky Gillot getting ready to present *Newsdesk*, 1971.
6. Clare Lawson Dick, Controller of Radio Four, 1975–6, shown in the top bunk of her sleeping quarters in Broadcasting House, 1941.
7. Three *Today* presenters of 1974: Robert Robinson, John Timpson, and Des Lynam.
8. Sue MacGregor presenting *Woman's Hour* in 1973.
9. Ian McIntyre, the Controller of Radio Four, 1976–8.
10. *The Hitchhiker's Guide to the Galaxy* is put together in the studio, 1978.
11. Cast members from *The Archers* on location in 1980.
12. Michael Hordern, John Le Mesurier, and Ian Holm reading their scripts for *Lord of the Rings*, 1981.
13. Roy Plomley and the Conservative leader, Margaret Thatcher, discuss *Desert Island Discs*, 1978.
14. Roger Cook in the *Checkpoint* office, chasing a story in 1983.
15. Monica Sims, the Controller of Radio Four, 1978–83.
16. Nicholas Barnes as Nigel (later Adrian) Mole, in January 1982.
17. David Hatch, the Controller of Radio Four, 1983–6, pictured rehearsing *I'm Sorry I'll Read That Again* in 1968.
18. Brian Redhead, photographed in Manchester in 1976, scans the papers ready for *Today*.
19. The *Rollercoaster* presenters in 1984.
20. The cast of *Citizens*, 1987.
21. Michael Green, the Controller of Radio Four, 1986–96.
22. Gerry Anderson, the presenter of *Anderson Country*, 1994.
23. Prunella Scales, Joan Sanderson, and Gerry Cowper: the three stars of *After Henry*, 1985–9.
24. John Humphrys in the *Today* office, Broadcasting House, on the occasion of the last edition made in the building before the move to White city in 1998.

A Note on Terminology

I refer to both 'Radio' and 'radio'. Where capitalized: a reference to that managerial division within the BBC responsible for Radio Four and the other national radio networks. Otherwise: a reference to the medium of radio more generally. Similarly, 'Light Entertainment' is a department, 'light entertainment' a genre. And so on, for 'Religion', 'Current Affairs', 'News', etc.

Introduction

In May 1988 an elderly woman caught a bus from Blackpool to London, marched into Broadcasting House, pulled a revolver from her handbag, and shot at a BBC commissionaire standing in the reception. Her gun turned out to be a replica and her bullets turned out to be blanks. No one was hurt. But it was the cause of her complaint that struck many observers as most worthy of comment: she had been driven to violence, so she said, by her inability to receive Radio Four. Less than a year later another sad tale reached the pages of the newspapers. This time, a retired vicar in Surrey bludgeoned his wife to death with a radio set. His wrath was roused, we later learned, by the choice of music on *Desert Island Discs*.[1]

These personal tragedies provide unsettling evidence of a fundamental truth: no other radio station in Britain, perhaps in the world, generates such passion as Radio Four. For the most part, thankfully, it is a passion that falls short of violence. But feelings undoubtedly run high. There is unbounded respect or devotion from its admirers, and ridicule, even cynicism, from its doubters. Radio Four is repeatedly described as a source of intelligent companionship for the 9.5 million or so British people who tune in at some point or another every week—many of whom measure their domestic routines of getting up, preparing meals, and going to bed by the passage of its landmark programmes. Quite a few of them go further, declaring that life without Radio Four would be utterly unbearable.

Perhaps the nation would be different without it too. According to the novelist Sebastian Faulks, Radio Four's 'humane, upper-middlebrow seriousness has done more both to define British society and to hold it together than any political or artistic movement of the last 100 years'. For some observers it is 'a guide to the heart of English culture', by which is meant a mixture of pragmatism, understatement, mild eccentricity, and a willingness to laugh at oneself. For others it is a guide not to English culture, let alone British culture, but to something narrower and less appealing: a mouthpiece for the middle class and the middle-aged—for suburbia, for 'Middle England', and for everything that goes with such rhetorical and social terrain: a narrow, nostalgic, complaining, inward-looking conservatism. Most agree that it is the favoured station of the chattering classes and opinion-formers, listened to by Prime Ministers, bishops, civil servants, campaigners, business leaders, and—so we are led to believe—the Royal Family itself. Its highest-rated programme, *Today*, has been called 'a sort of organ of our constitution' for its impact on British politics and journalism. For much of its life Radio Four has supplied more news than any other service in Britain, commissioned more drama than any other organization in the world, and held a virtual national monopoly in the production of radio comedy. The press reviews more of its programmes, scrutinizes more of its policy decisions, and publishes more letters of complaint from its listeners, than for any other station in Britain. If nuclear war begins, so rumour has it, Radio Four will even be the last voice of authority we hear before Armageddon arrives, its continuity announcer ensconced in a bunker, offering crumbs of comfort in hushed but elegant tones when all other broadcasters have been atomized into silence. Until then it remains in the minds of its most ardent admirers and in the words of at least one newspaper critic, quite simply 'The world's greatest broadcasting channel'.[2]

Perhaps Radio Four's most striking characteristic of all is the extent to which we have come to expect so much of it—and perhaps come to expect more than it can ever deliver. The weight of history and tradition bearing down on Radio Four is immense. Here is something that traces its ancestry in a direct line back to the Home Service; through that, in turn, to the BBC's pre-war National and Regional Programmes; and, travelling further back in time, to the very first broadcasts from Studio 2LO in London at the start of the 1920s. It belongs, in short, to the rootstock of British broadcasting: as Asa Briggs put it in his magisterial history of the BBC, it is, indirectly at least, the 'rock on which all else was founded'.[3]

When listeners and critics and broadcasters draw attention to this lineage, they invariably speak of Radio Four as 'the heartbeat' of the Corporation or 'the keeper of its soul'. The choice of words is hugely significant. It forges a link with the BBC's founding father, its first Director-General, John Reith, and to the ethos of public service broadcasting he propounded in the 1920s and 1930s—and which still, to some extent, conditions the way in which the BBC views itself, and is viewed by us. This 'Reithian' ethos is sometimes lazily defined as straightforwardly elitist, patrician, authoritarian, stifling. But it was always more complex than that. When Reith talked of bringing to British people 'the best' of things— ideas and culture and information they did not know they wanted but which he, at least, knew they *needed* in an era of mass democracy—he undoubtedly played the neo-Victorian paternalist to perfection. What could be grander, after all, than his quintessential claim that broadcasting should give a lead to public taste rather than pander to it? 'He who prides himself on giving what he thinks the public wants is often creating a fictitious demand for lower standards which he himself will then satisfy.'[4] Yet Reith went on to say very clearly that the whole point was to bring the best 'into *the greatest number* of homes'. If broadcasting was a force for the improvement of taste and knowledge and manners, as well as a means of promoting social unity, the task was to enable men and women throughout the country to take an interest in things from which they had previously been excluded. And if *all* British people were to be led on to higher things, the BBC needed to attract a mass audience. It *needed* to be truly popular.[5] Hence the classic formulation of the BBC's mission being to 'inform, educate, and entertain': in part, an expression of the desire to build rounded, enlightened citizens by exposing them to the broadest range of material; in part, a recognition that only through the enticement of popular programmes would decently sized audiences ever be secured for all the tougher, more 'improving' fare.

The result, in any case, was this: that the National and Regional Programmes, then the Home Service, and finally Radio Four—none were *ever* designed to provide *only* those worthy programmes which other media have generally found unprofitable. Reithianism held firmly to the idea that for a public service to do its work—for it to complete its cultural mission—it had to be witnessed by the public at large. Broadcasting was always *for* listeners, not producers—and for listeners in sizeable number. This was why Reith never reconciled himself to the Third Programme, introduced long after he had left the Corporation. He found it 'objectionable' precisely because it ring-fenced culture for a tiny minority, rather than diffusing it in the generality of the BBC's services.[6]

For Reith's heirs, then, it has always been Radio Four that really mattered. It is the Reithian service par excellence: perhaps not as avant-garde as some would wish, certainly overcautious at times; but, through its 'mixed' programming, generally committed to the old BBC project of nurturing rounded citizens and forging a 'common culture'. The very range of its schedule, stretching from news and classic drama through features, quizzes, religious services, discussion programmes, and consumer magazines, all the way to comedy and popular serials, has represented the coming together in one place of the Corporation's three defining tasks: informing, educating, entertaining. The language with which it generally speaks—not quite fully literary, not quite fully colloquial—sits profitably somewhere between the 'instant' and the 'academic'. And the claim by one of those charged with running it, that it is 'like a friend who has read a few more books, seen a bit more of the world', provides a resonant declaration of the surviving desire to improve—but gently, even surreptitiously. Indeed, it is precisely these achievements that have ensured Radio Four's special place in the British broadcasting ecology: never the most popular service in sheer ratings terms, but *sufficiently* popular while remaining *sufficiently* committed to quality for it to become extraordinarily influential—indeed, for it to become, as much as any part of the BBC could, a kind of 'civil power' fundamental to British character formation during the later twentieth century.[7]

Yet few things work as they should, and nothing stays the same forever. When a broadcasting institution is as entangled in national life as Radio Four, warm rhetoric keeps coming up against cold, complex, maddening reality. Methods, values, ideas: all these mutate. To view Radio Four's historical development since its birth in 1967 is to see a network constantly bending under the strain of wider forces, both internal and external—and to see, too, a network trying desperately to hold on, through everything, to its essential sense of purpose.

Tensions abound. And they can be destructive as well as creative. Take, for instance, the goal of maintaining both popularity and quality. Exactly how 'improving' can Radio Four be before it strikes listeners as preachy or 'difficult' and loses its audience? Exactly how 'accessible' can it be before a sense of authoritativeness evaporates and credibility is lost? Or take the commonly declared goal of accurately reflecting the world in all its social, cultural, and political complexity—a task so vast that selectivity is unavoidable. When time is limited, whose culture is featured? Whose beliefs? Whose problems? Whose solutions? When the world shows itself to be fractious, insolent, or rude, what then of the BBC's tradition of leading rather than following? If it describes does it condone? If it avoids does it lie? In letting us hear what *is*, as opposed to what *ought to be*, is the BBC abandoning its historic claim to maintain standards in thought and language and behaviour? Or is it fulfilling its duty to be truthful? In short, is it to be prescriptive or descriptive?

Once upon a time, the BBC navigated such tricky questions by presuming a social, cultural, and political consensus whose values were widely shared in British life. Even that was not easy. For as long as a consensus was seen to exist there was always the acute problem for broadcasters of defining how wide that consensus was—and of maintaining a delicate balance of voices and opinions within it. But the problem has worsened. As the twentieth century unfolded we found consensus to be a steadily more elusive quality. Viewpoints harden, tastes diversify, verities crumble. In the circumstances, there is a paper-thin line for broadcasters between successfully resolving—or, at least, *managing*—these tensions, and falling headlong into the chasm that opens between rhetorical positions accelerating further apart.

An organization such as the BBC is stuffed with plenty of clever, creative people, and Radio Four is no exception. But even they cannot always resolve matters rationally and calmly. At least since the War, the Corporation has operated neither as a perfect monolith nor on the basis of strict compliance with top-down commands. There are hierarchies, naturally, as well as proper procedures and mechanisms for editorial supervision. But, as Reith acknowledged, even in his day what the BBC did was 'not what one individual thinks', but came instead 'from a consensus of opinion and experience' among managers and producers.[8] The business of programme-making has proceeded by a kind of case law ever since, and, as the sociologist Tom Burns noted, differences of opinion are precisely what constitute much of the Corporation's 'internal business and social life'.[9]

When the BBC's culture of internal debate and collaboration is working smoothly, discussion generally proceeds in articulate, intelligent, and civilized ways. Consequently, as the BBC's current historian Jean Seaton suggests, programmes are like 'icebergs': the exposed tip of a chain of thoughts, where sometimes the thought process is more important—or at least, more revealing—than the programmes themselves.[10] Sometimes, of course, the process of internal debate goes awry. Tom Burns, and, more recently, Georgina Born—two academics who have immersed themselves in the BBC for extended periods of observation—have both concluded that in place of free-flowing debate there has often evolved in BBC culture a recalcitrant belief that things are as they are simply because this is the way that things 'are done': in place of open debate there is *habit* reinforced by mutual defensiveness.[11] Sometimes, too, there are sharp divisions of opinion *within* the Corporation—unsurprisingly, perhaps, given that the Corporation encompasses a vast range of professions, each holding to its own 'tribal wisdom'. Talk to anyone in the BBC and they speak endlessly of 'powerful baronies' and 'warring factions', territorial disputes or philosophical rows between journalists and dramatists, television people and radio people, Governors and managers, managers and producers, prescriptivists and descriptivists, traditionalists and experimenters, young and old—any number of whom believe that it is they, and they alone, who understand what the BBC is all about.

We can see how these internal strains impinge on the normal business of broadcasting when we turn to the inner workings of Radio Four itself. Clearly, Radio Four exists as far as the listeners are concerned. But, curiously, within the BBC it is almost a chimera—institutionally no more than the collated effort of many entirely separate organizational units. The only people who explicitly work *for* Radio Four are the Controller and the small handful of people who assist him or her in preparing a schedule of 'output'. Programmes themselves are made in semi-autonomous 'supply' departments scattered throughout the BBC—departments such as 'News', 'Drama', 'Light Entertainment', and so on, all of which usually recruit and manage their own producers and all of which serve several different radio networks at once. Indeed, since the departments have generally been allowed to get on with the daily business of making programmes and deciding what to offer to each network, some who worked in them have, in the past, viewed Controllers as little more than glorified schedulers. Controllers, on the other hand, have always had editorial responsibility for the overall composition of what goes out on their network. They act as the 'buyer' in the relationship and inevitably wish to exert the power this status confers: departments 'offer' programme ideas, Controllers accept or refuse with a view to the overall impact on the schedule 'mix'. Formally and informally, they have the stronger hand. But it is a relationship that betrays all the usual imperfections of the marketplace. Departments come to assume territorial rights and guard them jealously; Controllers come to be wary of disturbing good working relations with the 'factory floor'; a balance has to be found in commissioning that will ensure a fair distribution of resources between departments and across the BBC; a balance has to be maintained in the genres and formats that listeners demand; and every now and then Controllers have to respond to changes in editorial policy that trickle down from above. In short, the schedule of programmes on Radio Four takes on its character not so much through the whim of an individual Controller, but through that Controller's efforts—successful or otherwise—to superimpose a personal vision of the right overall 'mix' onto a palimpsest of tradition and precedent and common sense and deal-making.

Controllers are central to the history of Radio Four, then, not because they are all-powerful, but because they are nonetheless highly influential. And from the late 1960s onwards, we can see them exerting more and more of their power to review the editorial mix, and to reassign programme-making territory between the departments accordingly. Their relationship with the departments was usually one of partnership, but they always had the last word. Increasingly, they used it.

Controllers are also central to the history of Radio Four because it is *through* them that we witness the coming-together and the weighing-up of so many competing pressures for change. One recurring tension is between those who see Radio Four as first and foremost a place for news and topical debate, and those who see its special virtue in the wide range of genres that it embraces. This is not *just* a battle between journalists and, say, dramatists: it is also an intellectual battle over the nature of broadcasting itself—over whether it is to be about 'mixed' programming, which carries with it the Reithian project, or 'generic', specialized programming, which appears to fragment the listening public into special interest groups and which thus, apparently, abandons an aspiration to enlarge our cultural horizons.

A debate like this will be shaped by other pressures. Two among them are money and ratings. Radio Four has to justify its share of the BBC's finite resources. In general, radio is cheaper to make than television by quite some margin: hour by hour it costs, at most, a tenth, and often as little as a fiftieth of what goes onto the screen. In radio terms, however, Radio Four is extraordinarily expensive. In 2005–6 it cost just over £71 million to run—more than four times as much as Radio One, which had roughly comparable audience figures, and three times as much as Radio Two, the most popular British radio station of all that year. This is public money. So there is always the awkward matter of why a licence fee paid by almost every British household is spent disproportionately on a network fewer than one in ten of the population uses each day, and only one in five of the population uses over the course of a week.[12] The classic defence is that both *quality* and *range* costs—and this is obviously true. The nature of the beast—encompassing journalism, documentaries, comedy, and drama—draws it into producing the most labour-intensive and highest-cost forms of speech radio. Doing it on the cheap would never be easy. But exactly *what* constitutes 'quality'—and *what* range of programming genres is practicable—will always be open to vigorous debate. Hence, for example, the recurring tussles behind the scenes over whether Radio Four needed to commission so much drama. As for ratings, Radio Four's history coincides with a steady proliferation in the number of television channels and radio stations, the growth in cassettes, compact discs, and, latterly, the Internet: with these rival attractions, the underlying trend in Radio Four's own share of the available audience would appear, at least on the face of it, to be destined to travel ever downwards. The question of how many people listen—and what kind of people listen—consequently becomes an omnipresent source of anxiety for those running Radio Four: the fear being that a point might one day be reached where ratings become so low—or so skewed, socially and geographically—that spending on a reasonably generous scale is regarded as indefensible.

Then there is the intrusion of politics. The BBC, it has been pointed out, is perpetually involved in political wrangles of varying degrees of seriousness. Inevitably so. It is a body aligned, if not quite with the 'State', then certainly with the 'Nation'. The licence fee and the Royal Charter by which it exists are both matters decided in Parliament, and governments establish the parameters within which broadcasters operate. It is important to remember, too, that individual politicians listen and watch. The relationship emerging from this close embrace is tense and fallible, and affects the climate within which programmes are made. Radio Four's role in this is paradoxical. MPs get a great deal of their news from it, so they value programmes such as *Today* enormously. On the other hand, since for them Radio Four *is* the BBC, the Corporation's general health will be judged— fairly or not—on the basis of what the network transmits. Those at the top of the Corporation know, therefore, that any rows concerning Radio Four will never be parochial: they become symbolic, and, with a press likely to take a keen interest, easily capable of spinning out of control. They need managing. The response can be assured or flat-footed; but it is always utterly alive to the political and the public mood.

Finally, and perhaps decisively, there are the listeners. Such is their loyalty to Radio Four that they fight hard to protect it—and sometimes, too, they smother it with love. For those running the network they are a blessing and a curse. Only a minority ever complain; but they are well connected, articulate, and generally dislike change of any kind. Their attachment can be deeply affecting: a humbling sign of Radio Four's importance in their daily lives, and also, for an older generation especially, a legacy of the close rapport with a Home Service many grew up listening to during and after the War. But it is an attachment that exercises a powerful constraint. As one recent observer of Radio Four put it, 'the clammy breath of suffocating approval blows over it like the dank air in an undertaker's parlour'.[13] For a network required by all those other pressures to find new listeners and, of course, deliver that Reithian commitment to expose the British public to ideas and information and culture which might otherwise pass them by, this is a problem. Programme-makers are people for whom creativity and topicality are meat and drink. Their job, as they see it, is to measure the mood of the times, to restlessly turn over social issues, spot trends, nurture new talents—and then to place the fruits of their labours in the public domain. In so doing, they know full well that public attitudes and tastes are more varied than many Radio Four listeners allow, but they also know that it is the Radio Four listeners who will judge their work—and who will turn off if it all becomes too much. Compromises are therefore required. How Radio Four moves with the times, how it reflects the culture and ideas and opinions of any given time while also keeping faith with its most dedicated listeners: this is the most fascinating and complex power struggle of all.

So this history of Radio Four is a *cultural* history by necessity. It describes an institution constantly being shaped by the world outside: by programme-makers seeking to reflect our shifting preoccupations and anxieties; by pressures to protect ratings without 'dumbing down'; by tactical considerations of politics and money and public opinion. It is impossible to explain its evolution without acknowledging something of the creative milieu in which the BBC operates—what was happening in the arts, in journalism, in thought, between 1967 and the end of the century–or, indeed, without acknowledging that Radio Four, in turn, helps to *give* shape and direction to some of these trends. Radio Four is deeply symbolic of aspects of British life, because it is part of British life, and no history of, say, dramatic writing, or of popular reading habits, or of television comedy, or of political communication, or of middle-class identity in the last decades of the twentieth century, can be complete without recognizing this. Even when we restrict ourselves to examining life within the Corporation, we discover that departmental rivalry and the clash of personalities leads us towards matters of psychology and anthropology, of gossip and of networking as much as of high-minded engagement with policy. So while the old cliché has it that radio is all about sound, Radio Four, it turns out, is about almost everything *except* sound. Briggs claimed perceptively that 'To write the history of broadcasting in the 20th century is in a sense to write the history of everything else.' At times, writing about Radio Four seems more challenging still: like trying to define something that is so much a surrogate for other things, so weighed down with contradictory expectations, so taken for granted, that it feels rather like pinning down something as complex as, say, Britishness itself: reductive to the point of meaninglessness.

Where on earth do we start? For me, it begins with one of Jean Seaton's characteristically astute observations: that at one level the BBC's story is a history of men and women 'trying to make programmes that people like and that also— not in a preachy way (well only occasionally in a preachy way)—do them good'.[14] This simple definition captures something of the Corporation's eternal challenges: to inform, educate, and entertain—that is, to do what commercial broadcasters do *and* more; then to find the right 'tone' with which to pull off the trick. It is also a definition that balances our proper concern for the infrastructure of politics and culture with a recognition of the centrality of people and programmes. Individual managers, producers, or presenters make a difference: television is complex, with each programme involving tens, perhaps hundreds, of specialized workers; in radio, a programme can be the work of just one producer or presenter, or at most a small handful—and the simplicity of production makes these people more fully the author of their own work. There is the possibility of individual sensibilities making a difference, and creativity is at the heart of the story. As for the programmes, they matter more than anything else because it is in them that we find the myriad pressures—aesthetic, institutional, personal, political—metabolized and illuminated. Programmes tell us how programme-makers thought about their audiences—that is, about *us*—and how they responded to those thoughts.

What follows, however, is not a definitive history of programmes, for Radio Four is clearly greater than the sum of its parts. When so much happens simultaneously, this can only be conveyed by attempting some sort of thematic assessment, without, I hope, losing a sense of the network's overall evolutionary direction. The structure of what follows is therefore neither fully chronological, nor fully thematic. Generally, I try to address issues at the most appropriate point in the timeline, which means, for example, that while rows over bad language undoubtedly recur throughout Radio Four's history, they are discussed most fully when attempting to portray the heated debates over permissiveness in the early 1970s. Conversely, anyone wishing to trace, say, the development of comedy will need to dip into the narrative at several points. By and large, I try to begin and end the three main parts with chapters that look at issues and events that affected Radio Four as a whole, while sandwiched between are two or three chapters focused on narrower terrain. There is consequently a pattern of sorts, since the plot proceeds in a kind of three-steps-forward, two-steps-back fashion. But as far as possible, each new chapter begins a little bit further along the historical timeline, so that the underlying structure gradually takes us through from 1967 to 1997 and a little beyond.

Two themes weave in and out more than any other: the ability, or otherwise, of Radio Four to accurately reflect the times within which its producers and listeners have lived; and the struggle to maintain a variety of programmes and styles rather than succumbing to a tidier, sleeker, more *singular* kind of broadcasting. These themes particularly dominate the first two parts of this book, and, in a sense, they define their respective themes: in Part I, the casting-off of the Home Service legacy amid the cultural turmoil of the 1960s and early 1970s; in Part II, the growing tension in the years 1976 to 1983 between those advocating a 'rich mix' and those wishing to see an all-news network.

There is, however, another theme slowly gaining momentum during both these periods, and which, in turn, dominates Part III: the central role of Radio Four's listeners in shaping the network's development. 'Listener Power', as the final section is called, was there all along, of course, since the BBC was intrinsically conscious of its public role, and therefore of public opinion. But only from 1983 did the audience mobilize itself and become a force to be reckoned with. This collective 'ownership' is important. But so, in the end, are the private and personal meanings of Radio Four. They consequently form the subject of the very last chapter.

This, then, is the structure and the scope of what follows. As for an argument, I wish, as Asa Briggs once advised, to 'let people of the time—and institutions—speak for themselves'.[15] But the evidence of their testimony is cumulative, and three conclusions will strike me as inescapable. First, that, unusually in media history, we can talk of a service that ends up being generally more *up*market than when it began.

Second, that Radio Four's wider impact on British broadcasting and culture unfolds in all sorts of predictable *and* unforeseen ways. And finally, that little of this has been easily achieved. If there was progress, it proceeded in fits and starts and after the occasional wrong turn. Radio Four is taken for granted as an irreplaceable part of daily life for millions of Britons, but it has only ever existed as part of a unique and fragile public service system. Its survival has never been inevitable: history shows it needed to be fought *for* as well as fought over. Sometimes, as we shall see, the battle came close to being lost altogether.

PART I
REFORMATION:
C.1963–1976

'A broadcaster is in all decisions involved with the moral life of his society, with its patterns of values, with the stresses and changes those patterns of values are undergoing at any particular time'

Richard Hoggart, Radio Four, 1971

1

September 1967

'The Sixties seem to stand in the centre of it all, sucking in the influences of the past, creating the touchstones of the future'

Jonathon Green, *All Dressed up*

DIES MIRABILIS

At ten to midnight on Friday 29 September 1967, the Home Service reached the end of its nightly weather forecast for coastal waters around Britain and went quiet for the very last time.

As he sat in his darkened studio in Broadcasting House that night the continuity announcer on duty, David Dunhill, retained a firm sense of decorum in the face of history. But keen listeners would have detected that he was more concerned with the passing of the old than the beginning of the new. 'This is the end of the Home Service for today and for all days,' he told them, 'So, goodbye Home Service—two of the best words in the British language.' 'We're like a bride on the eve of her wedding,' he added: 'we go on being the same person, we hope, but we'll never again have the same name.' At 6.35 the following morning *Farming Today* took to the air, and the Home was reborn as Radio Four.[1]

Actually, the old name *did* survive for a year or two more. Until the shock of change was thought to have passed there would be an announcement on air once a day that this was indeed 'Radio 4, *the Home Service*'.[2] But the fact remained that the Home as such had gone forever and a new service had taken its place. More striking still was the fact that, apart from Dunhill's brief valediction, there was little public fuss or ceremony over the whole affair. The simple truth was that Radio Four's birth was a sideshow. If newspapers mentioned broadcasting at all that weekend it was to report on another far more spectacular arrival—that of the BBC's brand new music station, Radio One. From the moment Tony Blackburn opened proceedings with a blast of 'Flowers in the Rain' by The Move, it was pop's official debut on the staid old BBC that caught the journalists' attention. Here, the *Sunday Telegraph* declared overexcitedly, was the Corporation, with its 'disc-jockeyed, jingle-packed, gimmick-ridden, "pop" music programme', promising, at long last, to send the nation's teenagers into orbit.[3]

The attention being given to Radio One at the end of September 1967 spoke of a new dawn in British broadcasting. The role of radio within the BBC's range of services seemed to be changing in fundamental ways, and the Corporation's historic commitment to speech radio suddenly looked vulnerable. 'Death to the Home Service' was the provocative slogan stamped across a T-shirt worn by one of the new DJs as he cavorted in front of the cameras that weekend. It reeked, not just of the ascendancy of pop and the confidence of unruly youth, but of the implicit belief that a whole tradition in programming was about to be swept away in its wake.

There was good reason to be fearful. After all, the BBC's reorganization of its services, with the Light, the Third, and the Home all simultaneously giving way to Radios One, Two, Three, and Four, had been prompted in the first place by the exigencies of pop. The offshore pirates that had sprung up in the early 1960s, and which had captured several million listeners in the face of the BBC's inattention to new musical tastes, were being scuttled in 1967. The creation of a new pop music service on the BBC was the reward (or price, depending on one's view) offered by the Wilson government. BBC thinking about the name for this new service had been tortuous: 'Radio Elizabeth' and 'Melody Radio' were just two names among many doing the rounds. The most functional approach gradually presented itself as the easiest solution: each service would simply be numbered. In the circumstances it seemed sensible for the new pop service and the residual Light Programme from which it emerged to be paired—making Radios One and Two; and sensible, too, for echoes of the old Third Programme to be carried in the title Radio Three. By a process of elimination—and no more—the Home Service had become Radio Four.[4]

To those who believed the Home was a long-established flagship, this was an ominous inversion of the proper hierarchy. The *Observer*'s radio critic, Paul Ferris, pointed out that at the end of the 1950s the *Radio Times* had reversed the order of its pages so that television's schedules were placed before radio's for the first time. That had symbolized a decisive swing in the balance of power between the two media. Now, by turning the Home Service into programme number four, 'the planners are starting to prepare to think about easing themselves into a position to get ready, one day when they hope nobody's looking, to kill it'.[5]

Behind the sense of doom lurked a sneaking suspicion that whatever name it had, the new service looked like an anachronism before it had begun. Its umbilical link to the past was obvious. Glancing at its schedule of programmes we find, for example, *Saturday Night Theatre*, which had been running since 1943, *Radio Newsreel*, which had first run on the BBC's Overseas Services during the War, *The Archers*, which had started on the Light Programme in 1951, *Desert Island Discs*, which had been going since 1942, the *Daily Service*, which had first appeared in 1928.[6] Take all these, and add the miscellany of magazine programmes, comedies, and documentaries, as well as about three hours of music a day. The sheer range and mix of programmes was impressive. But it was a menu barely distinguishable from that published a week before under the Home Service moniker—barely distinguishable, indeed, from anything printed in the *Radio Times* a decade or more before.

The world outside, by way of contrast, was not just momentarily distracted by pop: it was going through what appeared to be an extraordinary period of cultural turmoil. In September 1967, a 'summer of love' was reaching its psychedelic close. Hippies were following Timothy Leary's famous instruction to 'turn on, tune in and drop out'; The Pink Floyd had just released their debut studio album and The Beatles had released *Sergeant Pepper*; counter-cultural luminaries, such as Alan Ginsberg, Herbert Marcuse, and the American Black Power leader Stokely Carmichael had gathered at the Roundhouse in London before an audience camped out like a spontaneous commune; the scatological underground newspaper *Oz* had been launched, to take its place alongside *International Times*. If one looked in the right places there was a dizzying kaleidoscope of drugs, flower-power, love-ins, teach-ins, and freak-outs. In music, theatre, film, fashion, literature, and politics, it seemed as if public and critical attention was being hypnotized by the experimental, the outspoken, the irreverent, and the young.[7]

There seemed, in short, to be an unbridgeable chasm between Radio Four and the world into which it was born. One stressed continuity with the past; the other, novelty and upheaval. It was understandable that the BBC would wish its new service to inherit several million Home Service listeners by reassuring them that Radio Four remained largely unchanged. But in its dying days even *The Spectator* had described the Home as 'an arthritic old groaner' that to a large part of its audience had come to stand for 'the last yellow streak of a golden age'.[8] It was hardly the kind of legacy that seemed to sit well with the times. If Radio Four was to catch up before it was too late, one critic concluded, what was needed was 'a bloody revolution'.[9]

But did it *want* to catch up? And if it did, could it do so without offending those who rather liked the arthritic old groaner just as it was? Could it do so without upsetting some of the traditional ways of doing things inside the BBC? Or, the most urgent question of all: was a 'revolution' required in the first place?

Certainly, if those running Radio Four in September 1967 looked around them, it was not hard to detect plenty of faddishness in some of the counter-cultural fervour. It was there on the West End stage, for example, where, despite the lingering shadow of the Lord Chamberlain's censorship, one could watch a *Midsummer Night's Dream* with its Bottom clad in motorcycle leathers and what one critic called an endless array of 'runaway young couples, swapping infatuations and trading insults throughout a night-long rave-up'. Alternatively, in the fashion pages: advice to raid second-hand stalls for Indian cloth, Greek beads, and Moroccan jewellery—'anything bright and beautiful' to be piled on however one wanted. It was all so 'very contemporary', as the *Sunday Telegraph* put it. And so very silly, too, went the barely suppressed reproach. All this 'pansied-up' dressing, this titillation, this desire to baffle and unbalance audiences, this wilful indulgence in 'avoiding a commitment to a point of view': as Anthony Burgess wrote after watching the gyrations of a kaftan-wrapped Jimmy Savile on *Top of the Pops*, it was just so much 'ignoble descent into mindlessness'—so obviously phoney that, mercifully, it would surely not last long.[10]

Obviously, much *was* froth and nonsense. But much, too, was beginning to feel like part of a more enduring shift in popular attitudes and intellectual life. First, as historians of post-war Britain remind us, many of the features of the late 1960s drew strength from a deep-rooted set of social changes stretching back to the 1950s and beyond. The desire to provoke and unsettle was merely the latest manifestation of that slow but unshakeable 'decline of deference' which seamlessly connected Jimmy Porter's 1956 debut at the Royal Court to the growing disillusionment—post-Suez, post-Profumo—with those in positions of authority. By 1967, an indifference to received opinion and a willingness to speak out permeated social attitudes more generally.[11] What gave this older phenomenon a new impetus and a harder edge was the coming of age of the post-war baby-boom: a younger generation not just enjoying unprecedented spending power—and expressing it through self-consciously 'different' clothes and music—but one utterly sundered from the hardship their parents had experienced in the 1930s, one attending university in greater numbers than ever before, one more questioning of the conventions of society, more willing to demonstrate when roused to anger.[12] In the autumn of 1967, the first flurry of campus sit-ins and protest marches showed how some of the heat of the civil rights and anti-Vietnam War movement was drifting across the Atlantic to give focus to this inchoate rage—and providing a foretaste of what might follow. Little of this felt superficial.[13]

There was, of course, another Britain, where old habits and a faith in old institutions was refusing to die: where men still 'devoted their weekends to gardening, bowling and fishing', where families 'decamped on holiday to Scarborough and Skegness', where portraits of the Queen were proudly displayed behind the bar of dilapidated pubs.[14] Here, any decline of deference was something to be deplored rather than celebrated: seen, perhaps, as just one more symbol of a larger British decline, starting with the loss of Empire and culminating—or so it seemed—in uncontrolled immigration, endless economic crisis, industrial militancy, and recurring devaluation. Even when the Wilson government could point to dramatic progress in social reform there was little agreement on its merits. While the Home Secretary, Roy Jenkins, talked of creating a 'civilized' society, conservatives accused him of having encouraged the 'permissive' society and threw up their hands in horror at the moral decay.[15] This popular and instinctive conservatism, soaked in the rhetoric of loss, found its intellectual voice among critics worrying away at the abandonment of strict cultural standards. George Steiner, for example, argued in his newly published book, *Language and Silence* (1967), that all sense of value and hierarchy was being swept aside by the democratization of feeling.[16] It was obviously becoming more and more difficult in the 1960s for people like Steiner 'to see a future for a society which could not take a coherent or self-restraining view of itself '.[17] This was, perhaps, the one thing upon which both conservatives and radicals could agree: that, far from being skin-deep and ephemeral, the counter-cultural postures of 1967 embodied a direct challenge to social and conventional norms. If there really were 'no rules' in fashion or music or art or sexual behaviour, if commentators were right to talk of the pyramid of high and middle and low culture crumbling to dust as 'the three great classes melt and mingle', if informality was 'in' and authority was 'out'—if all this was true, then there had, indeed, been a cultural revolution of some substance.[18]

The central dilemma facing Radio Four in September 1967 was therefore embodied in Steiner's lament. It spoke of a growing conservative anxiety—and recognized, at precisely the same time, that the drive for a society less in thrall to tradition had further to run. It was as though the dividing line between those who believed in dispensing with the past and those in favour of preserving it seemed to sharpen. The implications were slow to unfold. So slow, indeed, that it has sometimes looked as if the 1960s left few enduring monuments to a ferment that felt so momentous to those caught up in it at the time. But as Tony Judt points out in his survey of the post-war period, the changes it brought were 'so all-embracing as to seem natural, and, by the early-Seventies, wholly normal'. If there was one overarching theme that could be detected in Britain—as, indeed, in much of the western world in 1967—Judt believes it was probably the generational redistribution of authority—and with it the questioning of authority itself. A decade earlier everything had been run by and—so it seemed—*for* old men. 'Authority, whether in the bedroom, the home, the streets, educational establishments, workplaces, the media or politics, passed unquestioned.' By the end of the decade, a new generation—more questioning, more vocal, less tied to tradition—was starting to weave its way into the organizational fabric of the nation. 'Authority had either been withdrawn from most spheres of social life, or else acknowledged only in the breach.'[19] Culture, meanwhile, was everywhere. It was ordinary and it was plural. Matthew Arnold's famous mid-Victorian description—that it was 'the best which has been thought and said in the world'—had been eclipsed by Raymond Williams's more recent assertion that it was 'a whole way of life'.[20]

In the circumstances there seemed less and less room for an agreed canon of great art and literature, or for received wisdoms based around an objective truth—or, indeed, for any 'expertise' in the traditional sense at all. In short, the division of labour that had put some people in charge of interpreting the world on our behalf seemed increasingly suspect. And if the idea of an 'official' culture no longer rang true, then the institutions that once traded in it—the galleries, the concert halls, the universities, the Arts Council, the Church and, of course, the BBC—all now faced one fundamental question. If they could not—or would not—adapt to this new world, what on earth were they *for?*

THE BBC IN 1967

In principle, the question demanded the swiftest of responses from those in charge of broadcasting, because it was television and radio that brought the vast majority of Britons face to face with the world around them. Indeed, such was the pervasiveness of broadcasting that it had already started to arouse academic scrutiny. Television, especially, had caught the attention of Raymond Williams, who was now studying its power to shape cultural values and identities—for good or ill. The Canadian media guru Marshall McLuhan was also spending time on the matter, and concluding, rather gloomily, that the organic processes of cultural inheritance human society had enjoyed through most of its history— with beliefs, traditions, and moral standards being passed carefully from generation to generation—were now being destroyed by broadcasting's overpowering immediacy. When subjected to closer scrutiny, many of McLuhan's ideas crumbled into a mass of contradictions. Yet he was canny enough to lard his theorizing with attention-grabbing phrases such as 'the medium is the message'. His themes seemed to resonate. In September 1967 even the *Radio Times* was ruminating in McLuhanite fashion, wondering about the social implications of televising the rioting in America that summer. Soon, it warned, 'with communications satellites poised above every continent, the graphic details of every racial incident, wherever it may occur, will be instantly available to everyone with a television set.' A ceaseless flow of disruptive images, it was now feared, might distract us from the general stability of the world. It might even create its own momentum for change: for the media did not just symbolize—they contained the potential to amplify.[21]

When it came to the BBC, anxiety multiplied. In the Corporation's hands broadcasting was more than a matter of delivering programmes to people's homes as if they were gas or electricity: it was a matter of Culture, of Morality, of Politics. The BBC had too much historical baggage for it to be otherwise. It had been forged by Reith precisely on the basis of Matthew Arnold's conception of culture as a unifying force, and in an age coming to terms with the implications for public opinion of mass democracy. Reith held that only those with 'a claim to be heard above their fellows' were worthy of being put on the air; that the public were to be offered programmes 'slightly better than it thinks it likes'; that broadcasting was above the petty world of politics and controversy; that the appropriate tone was of rational and gentlemanly discourse—and decency throughout.[22] Much had changed since of course. Reith's departure, the War, the arrival of ITV in 1955—all had helped push the BBC slowly and steadily in the direction of loosening up its style, of becoming more topical and less didactic.[23] What nevertheless endured was the Corporation's sense of national *purpose*—and with it the public's assumption that here was an important organization from which certain standards and values were expected. Working out precisely what that purpose was, and which particular standards and values applied, was the tricky part. Instinctively, conservatives of all persuasions looked to the BBC as a bulwark against the worst aspects of modernity: a bastion of cultural conformity and decent values in a world of cultural pluralism for some; a bastion of public service in a world of rampant commercialism for others. Yet broadcasters themselves were generally people of a progressive and liberal mien. They were instinctively curious about novelty and about the world outside. If topicality and controversy and irreverence and experimentation really were all in the air, they would be ready and willing to inhale.

One decisive lead had come right from the top—and right at the beginning of the decade—with the appointment of Hugh Carleton-Greene as Director-General in 1960. Greene was one of the BBC's own, having run the German Service during the War, the entire Overseas Service, and, more recently, the whole of its news and current affairs output. He was perfectly familiar with the old ethos—he had even declared his pride in being 'one of Reith's successors'. As far as he was concerned ITV's claim to be more 'democratic' in offering popular programmes was beside the point, since ratings in themselves proved nothing about the *quality* of the experience for the viewer or listener.[24] He talked the Reithian talk. But his experiences had shaped him into a very different creature from Reith. Before the War, he had soaked up the atmosphere of Germany's decadent nightlife; after it, he had seen the damaging effects of totalitarianism. He carried with him a sceptical attitude to authority and a deep regard for individual liberties. When it came to broadcasting his attitude to programme-makers was generally to let them get on with their business with as little editorial interference as possible. And when he took overall charge he declared that the BBC under him should be fully alive to the temper of the times. He wanted to 'open the windows and dissipate the ivory tower stuffiness' that he thought still clung to parts of the organization.[25] He wanted to encourage programme-makers to take risks. He wanted the microphone and the television screen to be 'available to the widest possible range of subjects and to the best exponents available of the differing views on any given subject' so that those with differing views might thus come 'to know and understand each other's attitudes'. And in one of his most important statements of intent he declared this: 'I believe we have a duty to take account of the changes in society, to be ahead of public opinion, rather than always to wait upon it.'[26] It was a hugely significant change of emphasis. As Asa Briggs points out, 'What mainly distinguished this time from others in the history of broadcasting was that the BBC itself as an institution—with Greene as its Director-General—considered it necessary to align itself with change and to spotlight its own preoccupations with it.'[27]

This realignment had already shaped the BBC's television output. The defining programmes since 1960 had been gritty, questioning, and satirical in equal measure. There was, for example, *Z Cars*, set in a northern police force and subjecting its working culture to fierce critical scrutiny. There was also *The*

Wednesday Play, described by its creator Sydney Newman as dramatizing 'the turning points in contemporary Britain', memorably tackling abortion in *Up the Junction* (1965) and homelessness in *Cathy Come Home* (1966). Most famously of all, there was *That Was the Week That Was* (1962–3), with its live late-night mix of satire and topicality.[28] For many, this last programme had become *the* symbol of the BBC's new ethos. Greene himself described it as 'frank, close to life, analytical, impatient of taboos and cant and often very funny'. It certainly influenced many subsequent programmes—not just drama and light entertainment, but also current affairs, which now felt freer in taking a more anti-authoritarian tone. 'Nothing', the Director-General said, 'could ever be the same again.'[29]

He was right. For in September 1967 BBC Television retained a distinctly modish feel. Take the new arts series on BBC 2, *Release*. Its first edition began by intercutting snippets of Marshall McLuhan with pop-art style film montages in an attempt to probe twenty topical themes, for which the *Radio Times* had helpfully provided viewers with a cut-out-and-keep list. In no apparent order the subjects tackled were: James Bond, Volkswagen, Renaissance Art, Twiggy, Baseball, The Cavern Club, Earth, The Space Capsule, Diplomacy, Sex, Guilt, God, LSD, The Negro, Art, The Beatles, Education, Success, Vietnam, and 'The Electric Age'. People at home were invited to send in their list, marking where they thought McLuhan had scored a 'hit' or a 'miss'.[30] The programme evidently embraced popular culture without apology and treated it with vim. Significantly, it refused to declare its own position on the relative merits of each theme—a conscious effort to avoid judgement. Other BBC programmes in the schedules that month took less frivolous—but no less topical—journeys. One documentary, called *The Colour War*, examined 'White-Negro' relations all over the world in order to answer three questions about the rioting in America: 'Why is it happening? Will it get worse? Will it happen here?' Another had Alan Whicker hanging out with the Love Generation of San Francisco.[31]

More traditional fare had by no means disappeared. In the last week of September alone viewers could catch *The Good Old Days*, *Animal Magic*, *Jackanory*, and a new six-part adaptation of a very old BBC favourite, *Pride and Prejudice*. Even *Dixon of Dock Green* was about to return, bringing with it a cosy image of British policing that had been going strong since 1955.[32] Behind the scenes, meanwhile, producers were busy preparing what was to prove an iconic example of improving television when it was finally broadcast in 1969—Kenneth Clark's *Civilization*. This was to be expensively produced, erudite in an unashamedly patrician manner, and blithely uninterested in anything other than the highest cultural artefacts of western art. Technical polish and colour film aside, it was the kind of series that would not have felt out of place in the 1950s.

Yet if the coexistence of the reassuringly traditional alongside the highly contemporary confirmed anything, it was the new level of confidence BBC

Television displayed in its ability to serve all sections of the British public at one and the same time—mixing as it did the popular with the esoteric, the highbrow with the lowbrow, the entertaining with the informative, the mischievous with the respectable. It was Reithianism, but with a modern face. And it was the perfect embodiment of the Director-General himself—like 'the best kind of Uncle', as one newspaper put it: 'the kind who isn't stuffy, prefers chuckles to a frown; wants his nephews and nieces to treat serious things seriously, but doesn't wish to spoil anyone's fun'.[33]

Whatever the precise impact of Greene himself, the BBC's Television service was certainly riding high in 1967. Everything seemed to be working in its favour. Audiences were growing steadily as people spent more hours watching television. Income was rising as more programmes were transmitted in colour and more viewers bought higher-priced colour licences to pay for them. Even the competition offered by ITV had been contained, with the BBC coexisting in a stable duopoly that shared out the spoils roughly equally. The opening of a brand new Television Centre in 1960 had been a potent symbol of where creative and institutional priorities appeared to stand in the new era. And those who worked there knew that after a succession of men at the top who had regarded radio, not television, as the real business of broadcasting, there was at last a Director-General who gave them the kind of support they craved. Television producers now felt there was an unstoppable creative buzz about their profession—the kind of buzz that could be heard at its loudest in a place like Current Affairs. This was the department that had been responsible for *That Was the Week That Was*, and now made a whole array of other lively and topical series, such as *Gallery*, *24 Hours*, *Panorama*, and *The Money Programme*. It enclosed a considerable pool of talent, too, with people like Paul Fox, Jeremy Isaacs, Robin Day, Anthony Smith, and Alasdair Milne all working there around this time. It was a confident generation that had imbibed the cultural mood of 1960s Britain in full. Its members questioned authority, disdained bureaucracy, and believed, as one of them put it, that 'it was only a matter of time' before they would be in charge. If one of them moved on countless others were only too willing to move in, since many of the Corporation's brightest and most ambitious recruits now avoided Radio and aimed straight for a career in Television instead. Lime Grove, which housed Current Affairs, provided the most exciting place to be in the BBC, if not the whole of British broadcasting. Here, creating a stir was almost regarded as part of one's duty. As a BBC manager told the Director-General in September 1967, it was 'no good broadcasting if you can't catch people's attention'. And Lime Grove was certainly catching people's attention. By all accounts, BBC Television as a whole was doing it too. And behind this success lay its ability to reflect on screen what one of its habitués called 'the world in which we lived and the people who made it'.[34]

RADIO IN A TELEVISION AGE

Those who travelled a few miles east from Television Centre or Lime Grove to attend the occasional meeting at Broadcasting House would find themselves breathing an altogether different atmosphere. Here, where Radio resided, it was not just the physical presence of BBC managers and administrators that made life feel more constrained; it was also the immense weight of tradition—and the sense of entering a place forgotten by the passage of time. As one memoir recalls, it was as if 'the adventurers, the innovators, the challengers of the establishment' had all flown west, leaving behind only the aged, the nostalgic, and the timid.[35] A few new recruits still washed up, of course. But even they were generally under-whelmed by what they found. Take one young journalist who had joined in 1966, the 22-year-old John Simpson. When he arrived at the front doors of Broadcasting House for his first day's work, he eyed up all the other radio staff hurrying in and out. 'Slightly older versions of myself: tweedy, brief-cased, polite, earnest, conscientious, middle-class, slightly arty, nonconformist, yet distinctly conformist as well.' Once inside, he walked along the building's gently curving, dimly lit corridors, past shut doors belonging to the kind of programmes he had listened to all his life—*The Critics, Lift up Your Hearts, Radio Newsreel.* Every-where he sensed Reith's 'gloomy influence'. When he eventually got to the newsroom, Simpson found a large, low-ceilinged, rather sepulchral space with 'a preponderance of grey hair and cardigans and a distinct scarcity of women'. Here, journalistic standards turned out to be exacting but unadventurous. Sub-editors would seize whatever he had written and wield a 6B pencil 'like a US infantryman used his automatic rifle in a Vietnamese village' and lay waste to whole sentences so as to erase all signs of stylistic excess or individuality. One or two other youngsters lurked in the yellow half-light—among them a 25-year-old Will Wyatt, who had joined just the year before. Wyatt thought the atmosphere peaceful, studious even. Apart from the various sub-editors, one of whom needed a bottle of whiskey to get through the night shift and another of whom was writing a study of Victorian churchmen, there were the Home Service newsreaders drifting in and out: 'distinguished looking gents with Adam's apples that looked like a swallowed walnut'. Simpson noted that they no longer had to wear dinner jackets to read the evening news, but thought 'most of them looked as though they wanted to'. Unsurprisingly, it was a place from which these two young recruits planned to escape as quickly as possible. 'They were good people. It was a job that needed doing. But the newsroom was an island away from the world, not in it.'[36]

And so it sometimes felt in other parts of the building, too. Occupants remember an air of 'nervy perfectionism and essential dullness', a predilection for formality that unfolded in countless ways. People spoke to one another differently, for a start. In Television, secretaries were on first-name terms with their editors; in Radio, most still felt it proper to use surnames. Departmental boundaries, meanwhile, were rigidly patrolled. The various programme-making divisions—News, Talks, and Entertainment (which included Music, Features, Drama, Variety, Children's Hour, Gramophone Records, Outside Broadcasts, and Recorded Programmes)—all regarded each other as 'strange tribes' with little reason to mingle. To make matters worse, each department had firm expectations as to how many, and which, programmes it should be allowed to make—and would defend its 'quota' to the death. Baronialism of this kind was common enough throughout the Corporation, but people felt its weight more intensely in Broadcasting House, where meetings often descended into Machiavellian man-oeuvrings between rival factions, and where too many doors remained resolutely closed.[37] Naturally, each department thought of itself as unique, but there were unspoken hierarchies. Talks producers, for example, traditionally regarded them-selves as first among equals—'like being in the fast lane of the Civil Service', as one of them put it. They saw their job as constituting the essence of the BBC's public service mission: 'First came the word and in the BBC it was "the spoken word" and here was the eternal flame of the BBC—the Talks producers tended it.' When Robin Day joined the Talks department after a spell in Television, he found the experience to be rather like joining a good regiment—'dark suits during the week, tweeds on Friday'. It all seemed 'very stiff and starchy and hidebound', according to another émigré from Television, who was particularly struck by the number of programmes still being heavily scripted and studio based. Apart from anything else, it was a style of production that made every-thing much more subject to scrutiny from above.[38]

Inevitably, all this fed through to the kind of programmes being heard on air. A young Libby Purves, just off to university, remembers tuning into the Home Service during its dying days and deciding the BBC had recoiled from the Cultural Revolution in maidenly horror 'like a comedy spinster leaping on a chair to avoid a mouse'. What stuck in her mind were 'dreary High Anglican Sunday services with a lot of chanted psalms . . . classic plays suitable for doing the ironing to on wet afternoons, and pat little detective dramas'.[39] Many of the professional critics formed similar impressions in their first judgements on the new Radio Four. The *Listener*, for instance, grumbled about the 'totalitarian status' it accorded to Christianity and about the *Today* presenter Jack de Manio's 'tiresome' habit of railing against men with long hair. The *Spectator* suspected that it was being treated by the BBC as a kind of village magazine, 'suitable for the physically or mentally subnormal, but in no sense central to our own lives, except at moments of low resistance, such as early in the morning or when cooking or motoring'.[40] Even its most ardent admirers were a little exasperated. One, a young American academic who had lived in Britain on and off through the 1960s, wrote to the Director-General in September 1967, saying first of all how much she had enjoyed it in general and then going on to complain of the 'vast array of stereotypes and prejudices' she had been forced to put up with over the years. In programme after programme, she wrote, 'the message is that foreigners, if they are different, are wrong and unpleasant'. 'If it is trying to keep England insular, it is making a good job of it. But if it thinks it is neutral, the situation is serious.'[41]

It was the direct comparison with television that threw apparent failures into sharpest relief. One reviewer was cruel enough to contrast David Frost's performance on his new ITV series, *At Last the 1948 Show*, with Freddy Grisewood's chairing of *Any Questions?* Frost, he thought, was always relaxed and assured with his audience: 'he confides in it, consults it, takes his cue from it without, so far as I can tell, any cynicism or any condescension'. Grisewood, on the other hand, was a man clearly stuck in his ways—inevitably, perhaps, for someone who had joined the BBC as an announcer in 1929 and was now fast approaching 80. All he seemed capable of producing from his guest panellists and town-hall audience was a succession of 'smug little capsule judgments' followed by 'monstrous applause for each glib sentiment'.[42]

It all seemed to reflect badly on the listeners as much as it did on Radio Four—as if both parties had agreed to turn their backs on the contemporary world so as to avoid glimpsing its real horrors and to keep an illusory, nostalgic, version alive in its place. In many ways it was the perfect 'fit' between a conservative medium and a conservative constituency. But even marriages of convenience could not survive forever, since neither party was immortal. The problem was put at its most extreme by Peter Black, writing in the *Daily Mail*. 'When I listen to *Any Answers?*' he confessed, 'I seem to see this listener':

About 92 years old; lives alone and has enough money though not as much as he had; is in fair health except that the way things are going make him sick and tired, and he suffers from boiling blood. His patron is Freddie Grisewood, to whom he writes letters beginning: 'Why, oh why?' 'When will the powers that be...' 'How right you are, Sir Cyril Osborne!' etc... The letters echo discontent and disapproval. For the writers, the world has become a bus rolling past them full of yelling teenagers and spattering them with mud as it goes.[43]

It was a devastating portrait. If it was in any way accurate—and there were too many critiques in similar vein for there not to be at least a grain of truth—then it was a sorry state of affairs, and did not bode well for Radio Four's future health. What on earth had happened over the years to produce such alarm and despondency?

THE HOME SERVICE LEGACY

To find some of the answers we have to go back to the beginning of the Home Service in 1939 and trace the outline of its own slightly tortured history over the following quarter-of-a-century. This was a period that has been called the 'greatest era' of BBC Radio—an era when the Home Service played its part in providing the British people with an array of programmes that embedded themselves into the national consciousness for a whole generation.[44] This was also a period during which the Home faced two fundamental challenges to its existence: increased competition from other radio services and increased competition from television. Exactly how it responded to these two external challenges was crucial. It did not just shape the kind of radio heard on air; it also shaped the working culture of Broadcasting House—the climate in which radio producers went about their daily business and thought about their craft. In neither case were the best interests of the Home Service—or even the kind of radio it stood for—always at the heart of Corporation thinking. Nor were the right people always in place to take the decisions necessary to survival. One person who recognized this more than anyone was Clare Lawson Dick. As part of the team planning the Home's wartime broadcasts, and then as Assistant or Chief Assistant, Lawson Dick acted as its second-in-command right through to the early 1970s. From this position at the heart of it all she observed what she described later as a 'strange succession of chances' governing the evolution of the Home Service. For her, and for others working behind the scenes, this was not quite the golden age it seemed to those listening at home. It was, as she put it instead, more like an age of 'troubled times'.[45]

It had all started well enough, because the Home had had a good War.[46] It had been created on Friday 1 September 1939, just two days before Chamberlain made his famous announcement on the outbreak of hostilities. For security reasons, the BBC had merged its only two domestic radio services—the National Programme, broadcast from London, and the Regional Programme, broadcast from Manchester, Birmingham, and other major cities. Since continental commercial stations such as Radio Luxembourg had been swept off air and—for a short while at least—theatres, cinemas, and concert halls had also been closed, the new Home Service had a virtual monopoly of the public's attention in the early stages of the conflict. It was an opportunity almost blown right at the start, as the BBC quickly overloaded its schedules with serious music, uninformative news bulletins, and dour Ministry of Information talks on fuel economy, food rationing, or national savings, with the inevitable result that millions of listeners either turned off completely or retuned their wireless sets to catch Lord Haw-Haw's dark ruminations. From 1940, the Home also had to compete with the BBC's Forces Programme and its successor the General Forces Programme, which millions of civilian listeners preferred for its undemanding and entertaining mix of series such as *Music While You Work* and *Forces Favourites*. Even so, the national mission to boost home-front morale demanded of the BBC as a whole that it learn the virtues of being less aloof and more in touch with the various moods of its audience. This new ethos worked its way through to the Home Service, which soon established star attractions of its own. Indeed, to recite a list of its biggest successes is to conjure for many who lived through the War some of the most memorable pleasures that were experienced amid the deprivation and horror. There was, for example, *ITMA*, which set news standards in the range and tempo of light entertainment, *War Reports*, which supplied up-to-date and generally accurate news from the battle fronts, the Sunday-evening *Post-scripts*, which offered effective, if somewhat sentimental, reassurance in the form of talks from the likes of J. B. Priestley, and *The Brains' Trust*, which mixed informal education with knockabout conversation in a combination that appealed across classes and ages. Such programmes attracted a huge proportion of the British population: 17 million regularly for the *Nine o'Clock News*, 14 million for *ITMA*. In time, even lengthy dramas on *Saturday Night Theatre* were attracting some 10 million listeners. By the last year of the War, the Home actually had a bigger share of the national audience than the General Forces Programme, attracting sixty out of every hundred listeners.

Success like this took years to dissipate. Having become a part of the deeply felt wartime experience of the British people, the Home's public reputation was sustained through the 1940s and 1950s. In drama and features, there was critical approval for landmark productions such as Louis MacNeice's *The Dark Tower* (1946) and popular approval for the regular diet of middlebrow adaptations on *Saturday Night Theatre*, the *Monday Night Play* and Sunday evening serials. In light entertainment, panel games such as *My Word!* and *Round Britain Quiz* secured their own devoted audiences, while *The Goon Show*, which ran for more than 200 episodes between 1952 and 1960, was to achieve extraordinary cult status—and influence a later generation of writers, performers, and producers— for what has been described as its 'fusion of the crass and the clever, of naivety and knowingness'. For most *Goons* fans, enjoyment depended on regular listening: long-term immersion in the characters and their catchphrases imbued the show with what one reviewer called 'the glow of recognition'.[47] And when the *Goons* disappeared, there were other series that managed to inherit something of the same glow—series like *Round the Horne*, which in 1965 melded the comic talents of Marty Feldman, Barry Took, Hugh Paddick, Betty Marsden, Bill Pertwee, Kenneth Horne, and Kenneth Williams to create a series of sketches dripping with innuendo—most involving the two camp characters Julian and Sandy. Its com- mand of euphemism was perhaps the best example of the way in which the BBC's notoriously strict 'Green Book' guidelines (which banned jokes on, among other things, lavatories, honeymoon couples, chambermaids, and 'effeminacy in men') acted unintentionally as a stimulus, rather than as a barrier, to creativity.[48]

No current affairs or talks programmes on the Home Service were ever listened to with such affection as these comedies. But there were certainly enough series in the 1950s and early 1960s to ensure that its reputation for solid, decent, reliable reportage and analysis was reinforced. One, launched in 1954, was *At Home and Abroad*, which pulled together interviews and talks from around the world to create a twice-weekly magazine. Since each of its items was relatively short and up to date, and running orders were only finalized on the day of broadcast, *At Home and Abroad* restored a sense of urgency and topicality that had largely disappeared since the end of war-reporting in 1945, and which subsequently survived on *Ten o'Clock*, when it started running on the Home in 1960.[49]

It was programmes such as these, enriched as they were with a regular leavening of classical music, which helped establish the Home's *de facto* status as the flagship network of the BBC during the post-war era. The service was generally reliable, informative, uplifting without being didactic, and reasonably varied. If it was sometimes a little stolid or cosy, then countless diaries and autobiographies and personal recollections from those who grew up listening to the Home during these decades suggest that this was precisely what many people expected—and wanted—from the BBC.[50]

It was, however, not quite what the BBC, or indeed some of its producers, had had in mind when the post-war Home Service was being planned back in 1944. It was then that the Director-General William Haley and his senior lieutenants had developed a scheme for radio in which the Home would be just one of three services. The expansion of listener choice and the desire for a little internal competition within the BBC itself were two motivating forces; so too was Haley's wish to 'provide for all classes equally' and to continue the BBC's aim to improve cultural and ethical standards.[51] What emerged was a 'pyramid' of services through which it was hoped listeners would slowly move upwards in a steady process of cultural improvement. At the bottom was the Light Programme, clearly modelled on the Forces programme, with light music and variety dominating. At the top, there was the Third Programme, devoted to classical music, drama, and talk of the highest quality. And in the broad middle there was the 'Home Service', defined in planning documents as *the* staple BBC service:

The real Home programme of the people of the United Kingdom, carefully balanced, appealing to all classes, paying attention to culture at a level at which the ordinary listener can appreciate it; giving talks that will inform the whole democracy rather than an already informed section; and generally so designed that it will steadily but imperceptibly raise the standard of taste, entertainment, outlook and citizenship.[52]

The intentions were all well and good. But since the BBC's most entertaining and popular programmes were hived off to the Light and its most challenging now belonged to the Third, the Home was faced, by default, with becoming a rather narrower, more 'middlebrow' service than it had been in wartime. It was true, as Haley protested, that each of the three services would overlap and that each would be to some extent 'mixed'. The BBC, he said, had no intention of putting all its 'cultural eggs into one basket'. Even so, the basic diet of the Home had changed subtly, and it was possible to envisage it being outflanked by the sheer popularity of the Light on one side and by the glittering cultural prestige of the Third on the other.

The dangers in this were not immediately apparent, for at first the Home gave as good as it got—especially when competing with the Light Programme. In

January 1947, for instance, some 40 per cent of the Home's output consisted of music—more than half of which was 'light' or 'dance', rather than classical. It also put out twice as much 'variety' as 'talks or discussion'. In the longer term, however, the BBC's managers were intent on pushing the Home and the Light into becoming more and more distinctive. This was an easy enough task for the Light, which was told in 1957 simply to devote itself more fully to popular entertainment and music.[53] But even the BBC's managers admitted that it was 'hard to define' what the contents of the Home Service were to be, beyond the general dictum that it was to serve 'the broad middle section of the community and the range of taste and interest falling between high-brow and low-brow'. It could still have music, they said, ranging perhaps from Gilbert and Sullivan to 'prom-type symphony music', and it could still have drama ranging from *Wednesday Matinee* fare through to Ibsen. But the nearest they came to giving it a clearly defined identity was to suggest that it provided 'the main news and information services of the BBC', and that it might accordingly take over a few Light Programme series such as *Any Questions?*[54]

All this left the Home with the lion's share of what one of its Controllers called 'sober' programmes designed to honour most of the Corporation's public service obligations. This was fine for its reputation. It was not so helpful for ratings. And as the Light Programme went on to win a larger and larger share of the radio audience, so the Home's own share started to slide alarmingly. By the end of the 1950s, Clare Lawson Dick wrote, listeners were draining away 'like the bath water when the plug is pulled out'. 'None of us knew if, in the end, the bath would not empty entirely.'[55]

Television made it much, much worse, of course. From the mid-1950s, both the number of viewers and the hours spent watching television rose spectacularly. The Coronation in 1953 and the start of ITV two years later produced notable surges in public interest. By March 1958 the number of combined television-and-radio licences in Britain's fifteen million homes overtook the number of radio-only licences for the first time. By 1964, there were some thirteen million sets in British households, and television had become the cornerstone of many a family's evening entertainment. Indeed, it was quite normal to find about half the country's population clustered around the screen on any given evening—for anything between three and five hours on average. Naturally watching more television meant listening to less radio. Evening listening was falling at a particularly fast rate. Between 1955 and 1960 the share of the adult population tuning into the Home for *Saturday Night Theatre*, for example, fell from 14 per cent to just under 4. The future for the whole of what the BBC still called 'sound broadcasting' was starting to look desperate, since the implications of television's ascendancy were obvious enough. The Corporation had been spending the largest share of its budget on television since 1958. It had also declared that 'we must soon begin to look upon it as playing the major part in the general task of broadcasting for the home audience'.[56] For radio, it looked as if the best that could be hoped for was a future of managed decline. For the Home Service, which had very much the same mix of programmes as television, it looked as if the decline to be managed would be the steepest of all. After all, if there now seemed little point in *listening* to drama or comedy or documentaries when they could be *seen* instead, then it was not altogether unreasonable for BBC managers, or politicians, or critics, or indeed ordinary members of the public, to wonder what exactly the point was in making these programmes for radio in the first place.

In the circumstances, one might have expected the Home Service to have applied the best creative thinking to working out a survival plan. Yet its three post-war Controllers, Lindsay Wellington, Andrew Stewart, and Ronald Lewin, were all cautious men by instinct and drew heavily on the past. None seemed well adapted to the role of competing with television or finding a role for the Home that would complement it. Wellington, who was Controller between 1945 and 1952, was a man who had joined the BBC back in 1924. He was cultivated and approachable, though not inventive. He worked, Clare Lawson Dick felt, 'more by way of comment on the action of others than by architectural designing of his own'.[57] The documentary producer Geoffrey Bridson described him rather caustically as a man who 'walked' rather than ran the Home. He was genial enough and disposed to any idea—'provided it was politically and in every other way innocuous'.[58] When Wellington was elevated to the post of Director of Sound Broadcasting, the job of Controller fell to Andrew Stewart, who had joined the BBC in 1926, and was, if anything, even more soberly cautious than Wellington himself. Some who knew Stewart found him to be 'firm and principled', and admired in particular his concern for high standards, both morally and intellectually. Lawson Dick, on the other hand, found him both authoritarian and narrow. She noted the large photograph of Reith that he kept on his desk.[59] Like his mentor, Stewart was what Bridson called 'a very proper Scot'—a man, indeed, for whom 'the script of Sir John Reith was still the only legal tender':

When I once suggested changing the name and image of the Home Service, he gazed at me in astonishment as though I had suggested changing the shape of the British Isles. Home, I pointed out, was what all bright boys and girls were eager to get away from: the label was middle-aged and losing us a generation of up-and-coming listeners. And was it really necessary to deaden every programme gap with the dulcet pealing of Bow Bells? His Grace the Archbishop of Canterbury, he solemnly assured me, would be deeply disturbed if we didn't![60]

The demanding task of detailed planning fell to Ronald Lewin, who in turn took over from Stewart in 1957. Lewin was 'highly educated and academically brilliant', Lawson Dick conceded, but otherwise a disastrous choice. Despite the accumulating evidence of television's hold over the audience in the evening, he seemed uninterested in shifting more effort to the Home's daytime schedule. For Lewin, it was the evening—when journalists, MPs, academics, and business people, and not just housewives, were listening—which remained the best time for placing radio's biggest or most interesting programmes. 'Don't you realise', he once told Lawson Dick, 'that the Master of the House doesn't get in until about seven-thirty?'[61] Unsurprisingly, he failed to reverse Stewart's decision to give away large parts of the Home's daytime schedule to Schools Broadcasting—a worthy enough gesture, but hardly one guaranteed to boost the ratings. Lewin was also physically and psychologically fragile, and it was not long before he was forced to take long periods off work. He eventually succumbed to debilitating depression and a nervous breakdown. In this leadership vacuum, the Home's journalists did at least have a separate editorial chain of command within which to work. For them, however, the problem was one of overmanagement, not undermanagement. In News, overall responsibility lay with Tahu Hole, a massive bloodhound-like New Zealander, described by one of his staff as a figure out of some black-and-white Hitchcock movie—'a monster in every sense'. 'I am sure he was kind to his wife and his dog, but amongst his staff he inspired nothing but terror, exuding a sinister aroma of power as if he knew something to the discredit of each of them.' Here was a man who spent hours brooding over scripts that had already been transmitted, looking for errors and heresies, discouraging scoops, establishing News as a service like the gas, water, or electricity—'useful, but unremarkable'.[62]

As far as Clare Lawson Dick was concerned the main consequence of all this was administrative drift. By the mid-1960s, the machinery for running the Home had broken down completely—and none of the BBC's senior managers seemed to have noticed. For producers at large the problem was about creativity, or the lack of it. Instead of energetic showmanship and a flow of ideas from those in a position to set the tone, there had been timidity, sobriety, and enervation. Over time, producers had learned to adjust their ideas to what they knew to be acceptable. Bridson, for example, never bothered the Home Service with his most complex and imaginative features ideas, which he gave straight to the Third. He did try offering the Home a series of trenchant documentaries on subjects such as nuclear armament, Soviet Russia, McCarthyism, poverty, or racial conflict, but soon found that even these were rejected, mostly for being 'too controversial or too political'. The BBC, he concluded, had come to regard the Home as the place 'to reflect the most respect-ably orthodox opinion as it already existed'. It had become a victim of its own sterile sense of decorum. Instead of moving heaven and earth to improve its wilting image, loudly calling attention to itself or infusing its programmes with glamour and star quality, it was fighting shy of anything that might 'give offence or get itself talked about or give rise to a question in the House of Commons'. It was reduced to offering programmes that 'never affirmed anything, they merely balanced points of view until all finally cancelled out'. In short, it had been slowly but inexorably getting 'drearier and more derivative'.[63]

Regular listeners were largely unaware of these anxieties among BBC insiders. But the combined effect of competition from the Light, critical attention being devoted to the Third, television's steady ascendancy, a long period of administrative drift, and an atmosphere far from conducive to original programme ideas—this was all real enough. The problem was not merely that the audience size was diminishing, though that in itself was dispiriting. It was also that those who had stood by the Home were less and less representative of the British population as a whole and steadily more representative of a rump section of its middle third. In the long run, Haley's pyramid of radio services had tended to entrench cultural differences based on class and age, rather than transcend them. All that talk from 1944 about the Home Service 'appealing to all classes' had been quietly replaced by talk of it appealing to those who were 'not necessarily middle-class, though predominantly so', who were 'more middle-aged and elderly than young', who were 'not at all interested in culture or the intellect'. The typical listener was now described as someone who liked plays 'which are not what they would call either morbid or silly' and who preferred 'light music to either symphony music or jazz'.[64] True, the number of people who fell into this category was by no means insignificant. But it was hardly the audience profile of a station fully in kilter with the youthful, questioning, eclectic spirit of the 1960s.

By September 1967, then, there was within Broadcasting House and among astute observers of the broadcasting scene a palpable sense of uncertainty over what sort of role Radio Four might be able to create for itself out of this inheritance. The highbrows, once dedicated to the old Third Programme, now had Radio Three—an expensive indulgence, but one that kept obvious faith with the BBC's commitment to music, drama, and talk of the most stretching quality. The teenagers now had Radio One, which only seemed to emphasize that younger listeners might turn their back on the spoken word forever. Many of their parents, meanwhile, seemed perfectly content with the melodic pleasures of Radio Two. In the face of the cultural turmoil of 1967, the really important question that had to be asked was this: did a 'middlebrow' radio service offering a quaint mix of talk, shot through with a middle-aged and Establishment flavour, make sense any more? The omens were not good. Once, at the end of the 1940s, a wit had called the trio of Light, Home, and Third, the 'Slight, Drone and Weird'. In September 1967, the *Guardian* was offering an even more brutal mnemonic for what was now a quartet. In numerical order, it suggested, they might be remembered as 'pop, bop, fop and sop'.[65] And it was the poor old 'Sop' that looked to be in the biggest trouble of all. If it was to remain the BBC's flagship radio service, it seemed as if only an overhaul of the most radical kind would save it.

UNDERCURRENTS OF CHANGE

Yet if one looked hard enough behind the scenes and below the surface there *were* already signs of change. Attitudes, people, working cultures, programmes: none of these were quite as fixed as the doomsayers thought. One source of instability lay in the fact that the pre-War generation of producers and managers in Broadcasting House was now reaching retirement—and being replaced by those who had reached adulthood as the decline of deference had taken hold. A second factor was that programme-makers were starting to absorb for themselves—and starting to recognize a need to reflect back to the audience—at least a flavour of a country in cultural turmoil. As Philip French, a producer at the time, recalled, even gloomy, Reithian Broadcasting House now 'seethed with liberal guilt'.[66] A third was the pragmatic, indeed desperate, realization that unless speech radio moved with the times its extinction might be imminent.

Whatever the precise chemistry of change, 1967 represented a tipping point delicately poised between past and future. One year before, John Simpson had been arriving at Broadcasting House dressed in tweeds. By the beginning of 1968 he was turning up in yellow cords and a dashing red scarf. 'The times were changing', he explained. Now when he went to meetings, managers who had once patronized him were listening to him patiently. 'Young people', it was assumed, had 'much better ideas than older ones.'[67] Young people, it was assumed, could also be courted as Radio Four listeners, and not just fobbed off with Radio One. Stephen Bonarjee, who had worked under Greene to reshape Television news, and had recently taken over responsibility for *Today*, was busy telling his producers about the new ethos. 'We should aim', he said, 'to be more interesting to younger working class people living in the regions.' The tactics? More items on fashion, sport, bringing up children, and 'money matters which directly affect their pockets'; fewer 'cranky' items of 'elderly and middle class' appeal.[68]

The names of many programmes remained fixed, but their content could be fluid and contemporary. In one season alone, the weekly current affairs programme *Focus* tackled, among other themes, drug addiction, illegitimacy, Welsh nationalism, the rise of the far Right, and race relations—hardly a list that could be called cosy or uncontentious. At the same time *The Critics*, which had been providing a commentary on the arts since 1947, was rejuvenating its regular guest panellists, making use, for example, of Stuart Hall, a rising star of British cultural studies. The science programme, *Scientifically Speaking*, was featuring the 29-year-old 'young lion' Steven Rose, who talked about the iniquities of Vietnam as well as the mechanics of memory. Elsewhere, Malcolm Muggeridge was still holding forth, a true relic of the Home Service era. But even he was talking to the Maharishi Mahesh Yogi.[69]

The *Listener*'s critic was gracious enough to acknowledge what was happening, and declared that a service once 'in the doldrums' had, in its dying days, become 'thoroughly interesting and lively'.[70] But as a rule, little of this quiet revolution grabbed as much attention in the pages of the press, or in the public imagination, as the more self-conscious flowering of television. Radio was, in a very real sense, a background medium, heard but not always listened to, taken for granted and unspectacular. Radio, the wireless, the 'dear' old Home Service: to many a journalist, it was all far too convenient a metaphor for an older, archaic Britain to be dispensed with just yet. Even some of those who worked for it seemed to have talked themselves into such a mood of despair that they failed to notice what was happening. For those who listened carefully and watched events in Broadcasting House closely, however, September 1967 provided a snapshot of an institution in gradual thaw—one reaching tentatively toward a less dowdy, harder-edged style more in tune with the age.

For the new Radio Four, there were as many dangers in this rejuvenation as there were in sticking with the old ways, for it raised all sorts of fundamental questions. Should it, for example, be trying to reach a wider, younger, more socially mixed audience in order to survive, or concentrating instead on shoring up the loyalty of existing listeners? The trick, naturally, was to attract new listeners *and* retain existing ones. But given the fissiparous nature of contemporary culture, and especially the sharpening divide in taste between the generations, it seemed highly likely that a crude attempt to modernize would risk the rude displeasure of those who had been most loyal to the old arrangements. For many of these listeners, the fast-changing world they could witness on their television screens was not necessarily what they wanted to hear on their radio sets. For them Eliot spoke true: humankind really could not bear very much reality. And so in their expectant minds Radio Four was no mirror turned on the world but a safe haven in a stormy sea of change.

There were other dangers to be faced within. Even if they wanted to, the people running Radio Four could not simply change everything through an act of will. For one thing, they were part of an organization where creativity and decision-making was widely dispersed. Programme-makers in a whole range of departments, both in London and around the country, would have to be persuaded of the need for change—something that was only likely to happen if they believed that it was change in the right direction. Given that BBC Radio was just as fissiparous as the world outside in 1967 this would not be easy. Old habits and production practices might need to be challenged; suspicions might need to be allayed; competing ideas about what constituted 'good' broadcasting might need to be resolved. And all the time, nothing could be done in isolation from the wider debates affecting the BBC. This was a Corporation that liked to act as one whenever possible in order to protect the idea that it had a distinctive and united public service mission. It was also a Corporation that faced a formidable agenda of managerial, financial, political, and editorial challenges in 1967. It was, for instance, an institution founded on the notion of consensus, now faced on one side with a survey of public opinion which showed a large proportion of the British public thought it 'toffee-nosed', and on the other with a campaigner like Mary Whitehouse who was convinced that the BBC—or at least its Director-General—was more responsible than any other body in Britain for what she saw as the 'moral collapse' of the time.[71] The Corporation could sensibly counter that such views exaggerated and misled—that while the BBC was less remote than some claimed it was also not nearly as permissive as others feared. But it knew that inflated rhetoric had a habit of taking hold and shaping the whole political climate within which it operated. If it were to do so, this wider debate over standards and taste—in essence, over whether or not reflecting social change amounted to collusion with social change—would hardly pass by without infecting more parochial debates over the direction of Radio Four.

Not all change at the BBC posed grand questions of taste or culture. There were more practical issues to be faced in 1967, though ones no less serious in their implications. The Corporation's finances were deteriorating for a start, since there had been a less than generous licence fee increase in 1966. There were many inside Broadcasting House who suspected that the continued expansion of television, the launch of Radio One, and the BBC's imminent move into local radio would all deplete resources for what they saw as the most important part of the BBC's work, namely running Radios Three and Four.[72] Long-serving producers such as Rayner Heppenstall now complained of Radio being invaded by 'cost accountants, time-and-motion-study experts' and turning into a place where men 'whose breast-pockets bulged with pens and coloured pencils' invented more and more forms for producers to fill in.[73] Heppenstall was notoriously acerbic about most aspects of the modern world, but he was certainly right on this score. BBC records show that by 1967 managers were indeed worrying at inefficiencies in the system, busy quantifying the work rate of producers and bemoaning any duplication of effort.[74] Part of this represented a more general professionalization of working life at the BBC: not just the adoption of new systems of financial accountability, but also the general drift away from a culture where long and bibulous lunch-breaks could be taken at the *Stag's Head* or *The George*, or where endless hours could be spent in studios editing tape recordings into polished perfection, and closer to one where time was money and where editorial decisions needed to be justified and minuted. The precise effect of all this on the programmes to be made in the coming years was a matter of intense debate in Broadcasting House. Pessimists had worried for years about creative juices drying up in Radio. But what many of them had had in mind as a solution was more money, more freedom, and more respect from those above them in the BBC hierarchy. Talk of rationalization of effort and new systems of control did not bode so well. It was a brutal reminder that 'catching up with the times' cut two ways: a requirement to sharpen up as well as loosen up.

The new regime was given symbolic force on 1 September 1967, with the arrival of a new Chairman at the BBC. He was Lord Hill of Luton, known to many ordinary Britons as the wartime Radio Doctor—and to those who worked in broadcasting as a commercial television man with well-known Conservative sympathies. His appointment was seen by many at the BBC as a bizarre act of spite by a Prime Minister who could never get over the feeling that the Corporation had been out to get him and therefore needed to be taken down a peg or two. Hill's arrival was accompanied by real feelings of foreboding. His task, everyone assumed, was to inject yet more discipline into the Corporation's editorial and production activities. He quickly made clear he was his own man by talking directly to BBC staff and doing what the Director-General had always refused to do, namely to meet Mary Whitehouse and listen to her complaints.[75] This, in itself was an omen of change. Greene considered Hill's appointment a personal insult and never felt comfortable working with a Chairman obviously much more interventionist than any of his predecessors. In less than a year Greene was to announce his own retirement. Soon, there would be a new Director-General as well as a new Chairman. It was not altogether clear in which direction these changes would take the BBC. But there was no doubt that the Greene era, with its characteristic stamp of confident liberalism, was coming to an end, and that what was to follow had the smell of something more controlling. As one radio producer put it so memorably when reflecting on the BBC in this era, it was as though an organization run by bohemians disguised as civil servants was gradually being taken over by civil servants disguised as bohemians.[76]

Inevitably, some of those who had always believed radio should have a future were already beginning to feel a little nostalgic for the past. Others were impatient to embrace the new regime and, if necessary, reinvent the medium from scratch. In this respect, the events and the debates of 1967 had started to draw into the open some of the great cleavages in British life—and shown, too, that they ran through the BBC just as much as they ran through society at large. It was, however, the social cleavages that were most visible at the time. Greene described what he saw as an age-old division—'Cavalier versus Roundhead, Sir Toby Belch versus Malvolio' as he put it—being overlaid by another, newer one: 'the split between those who looked back to a largely imaginary golden age, to the imperial glories of Victorian England and hated the present, and those who accepted the present and found it in many ways more attractive than the past'. 'It was not', he went on, 'a split between old and young or between Left and Right or between those who favoured delicacy and those who favoured candour. It was something much more complicated than that, and if one could stand back a bit as the brickbats flew it provided a fascinating glimpse of the national mood.'[77]

The BBC's problem was that it could not stand back and remain a fascinated observer of the national mood. People who worked for it, members of the public, politicians, campaigners—all wanted to know where it stood on matters of culture, morality, and politics. When it came to programmes the full range of viewpoints would somehow have to be understood, then absorbed, and finally reflected back to the country. If there were any gaps, there would have to be a rational explanation. In an era of rapid cultural change, many of those building the new Radio Four knew that their greatest challenge was to keep something of the Home Service heritage whilst moving with the times. There were others— and many of the listeners to the old Home Service were among them—who distrusted deeply the motives for change, and who would contest almost every departure from tradition. 'The convulsions currently affecting the BBC', the *Guardian* concluded, 'are really a crisis of middle age':

To this, for individuals, there are two possible responses—to pretend one is still young, or to practise the serenity of recognising one must die. For institutions it is harder: they have to seek some middle way, some compromise between ageing and mortality. BBC Radio has evidently not yet found this balance.[78]

The *Guardian* was right. September 1967, though it marked the official birth of Radio Four, was really neither an end nor a beginning. If it marked anything, it marked a moment of transition, a moment that crystallized the acute dilemmas of balance it faced—between change and continuity, between the energy and creativity of youth and the wisdom of age and precedent, perhaps even between the two cultural nations which the critic Edward Shils had defined in the 1950s, one metropolitan and sophisticated, the other provincial and 'petit-bourgeois'.[79] Caught between these alternatives, the 'new' Radio Four, even more than the old Home Service that went before, could probably only evolve through messy compromise. There had been much talk of revolution in the world at large that year—not so much a political revolution, but a revolution in lifestyles, in manners, in music, in morals. For Radio Four the year marked not so much a revolution as the midway point in a gradual, but no less dramatic, reconstruction.

2

Reconstruction

'There is a little civil war seething below the surface of radio. It is between the Mods and the Ancients, between those who see radio as the keeper of traditions that BBC TV has basely surrendered, and those who believe radio can only survive by competing in the modern world of communications and meeting it not only in speed but in style.'

Daily Mail, 16 September 1967

The Home Service's reconstruction began in earnest several years before the excitements of September 1967, with the arrival in 1963 of a new man at the top of Radio determined to tear apart many of Broadcasting House's settled habits. It was to reach a climax in 1969 with the publication of one of the BBC's most controversial blueprints for change in its entire history, *Broadcasting in the Seventies*. The six years between these two dates, and the internal rows that accompanied them, provide the theme for this chapter.

Much was done in a relatively short space of time. Reconstruction entailed the dismantling of several venerated radio institutions, the appointment of a vigorous new Controller, and concerted attempts to introduce a new degree of informality and topicality onto the air. There was also a steady growth in the amount and range of news and current affairs offered to listeners. Changes were designed, so their advocates claimed, to produce a sharper, more relevant, more authoritative, Radio Four. But by the end of the process the arguments were being muddied by wider debates and deeper resentments. Money—or the lack of it—was one complication. Worry over the kind of journalism being created was another. But perhaps the most serious of all concerned the attempt to make Radio Four and the other three national radio services more 'generic'—that is, more consistent and predictable in character. Planners saw this as the best—perhaps the *only*—response to television's relentless conquest of the mass audience. Many producers and critics thought 'generic radio' too high a price—that it robbed the medium of the kind of fluidity and serendipity and creative self-confidence that had once made it a cultural force in its own right. As to

Broadcasting in the Seventies, before the ink on the document was dry Geoffrey
Bridson spoke up for many of his colleagues in BBC Radio when he claimed that
it 'proved to most thinking people that the seventies were for the Yahoos'.[1]

THE GILLARD AXE

The first stage in building something new was the demolition of old structures.
And when the BBC appointed its latest Director of Sound Broadcasting in 1963, it
found a man brave enough—or, at least, thick-skinned enough—to do the dirty
work involved. This was Frank Gillard, who had a distinguished career behind him
as a BBC war correspondent covering Montgomery's North African campaigns and
the D-Day landings, and who had worked since at the BBC's West Region based in
Bristol, as head of programmes and later as Controller. Experience of reporting in
the field and a deep commitment to regional life had both left their mark. His
policy in Bristol, he once explained, had always been 'to get away from the artificial
atmosphere of the studio...and take the microphone among the people'.[2] *Any
Questions?* was his proudest creation, though he knew large parts of Broadcasting
House had always looked down on it. When he took over the whole of 'Sound' in
1963 he cast himself as an outsider able to see with uncommon clarity 'the dead
hand of the centre'. Things, he decided, had 'not changed a bit' since the end of the
War. He wanted to see the BBC establish local radio, he wanted the BBC to
provide more popular music, and he wanted listeners to know what to expect when
they switched on their sets. There were existing parts of the system standing in the
way of achieving these goals—departments and programmes that had, as he put it
'outlived their natural span of life'. He grumbled in particular about too many
scripted programmes, and he echoed the sentiments of Television staff by describing Broadcasting House as having been 'left with an awful lot of burnt out people'.
Unlike his predecessor Lindsay Wellington, he was quite prepared to confront these
obstacles without flinching at the unpleasantness involved.[3]

Gillard's first moves were also his most infamous: the ending of *Children's
Hour* and the closure of the Feature's Department—both in 1964. It was the
move against *Children's Hour* that came first, with rumours circulating within
weeks of Gillard's arrival in Broadcasting House. By then the *Children's Hour*
name had already disappeared: since April 1961 the programme had been billed
as *For the Young*. The name change, unfortunately, had done nothing to arrest the
dramatic decline in listening, and by the end of 1963 as few as 25,000 people
were tuning in to each edition, most of them, Gillard reckoned, being 'middle-
aged and elderly ladies who liked to be reminded of the golden days of their
youth'. The vast majority of children, meanwhile, were either watching television, listening to *Saturday Club* on the Light, or tuning into one of the pirate
stations. In other words, the target audience had deserted. The decision in

January 1964 to end its run by the following Easter therefore made perfect managerial sense. But it closed forty-two years of broadcasting history, and prompted a torrent of complaints from listeners as well as questions being raised in Parliament. The public outcry, Hugh Greene later admitted privately, represented 'a greater storm than anything that ever happened in television or radio throughout the whole of his term'. Even Gillard described his move against *Children's Hour* as 'heartbreaking'.[4]

The new Director of Sound had no such misgivings about closing the Features Department, one of the true sacred cows of BBC mythology. The 'feature' was seen as a classic form of radio that had been developed by the BBC before the War, and was generally understood to be a programme broadly factual or literary in subject matter, but which was also imaginatively executed. In the description of one distinguished producer, Douglas Cleverdon, the aim was to 'combine any sound elements—words, music, sound effects—in any mixture of forms', and with very few rules determining what could or could not be done. The creative possibilities opened up by this wonderfully loose definition had been demonstrated by the distinguished output of the Features Department over the years: at the dramatic end of the spectrum, Dylan Thomas's masterpiece *Under Milk Wood* (1954); at the documentary end of the spectrum, Geoffrey Bridson's *The Bomb* (1962), which analysed with brutal clarity the consequences of a nuclear attack on Britain; and, typical of the broad middle ground, the ballad opera *My People and Your People* (1959), about the love affair between a young West Indian immigrant in London and a young Scottish skiffle musician.[5] *The Times* described the department that had produced these programmes as 'the growing-point for pure radio, the one department which ensures that the medium is explored and exploited'. 'Broadcast talks', it went on, 'have their affinities with conversation and with public speaking. Radio drama often belongs to the stage. The Features Department is concerned with broadcasting pure and simple—or pure and complex.'[6] With notices like this, Features Department had long been regarded both within the BBC and without as the epitome of creativity, and the producers who worked there—figures such as Louis MacNeice, Rayner Heppenstall, Francis 'Jack' Dillon, its head Laurence Gilliam, and Geoffrey Bridson himself—had long been regarded (and undoubtedly regarded themselves) as an elite cadre in the Corporation.[7] By the end of 1963, however, their great days were undoubtedly over. MacNeice had died of pneumonia in September; Gilliam was on his deathbed with cancer of the kidneys; no one was being recruited to replace them; and those who survived in the department were drinking heavily. The kind of torpor that had settled on the department was described vividly by Heppenstall, who told of how he would only arrive at his office after two lunchtime gin-and-tonics, a large glass of Bulgarian wine, and a drink or two at both the BBC staff club and *The George*. He was, he admitted, 'inclined to sleep in the afternoons', and even when he was awake he regarded his work for the Home Service as merely a series of 'fill-ins'. Inspiration, he said, left him whenever he entered the doors of Broadcasting House, and depression drove him to keep a cocktail of barbiturate poisons close to hand. In the circumstances, it came as no surprise to Gillard to discover the department's productivity had been sliding as demand for its work had dwindled. Drama was usurping it in the market for imaginative work; the expanding empire of Talks and Current Affairs was squeezing it out of the market for straight documentaries. By now Features' lapidary treatment of subject matter came at too high a price for an increasingly cost-conscious BBC. Even the cheapest of their productions cost the BBC roughly double the price of a conventional documentary.[8]

Having decided that Features was costing too much, producing 'very inferior' work, and had little hope of redemption, Gillard swung the axe. On 10 February 1964 the sixteen surviving Features producers were called to a special meeting, and told their department would close within the year. At the meeting, Heppenstall recalled Gillard looking embarrassed, but he noted, too, that he 'spoke as though with justified defiance'. The Director's decision, in any case, was final. Over the next few months, the department's staff were redeployed—some joining Drama, others joining Talks. Few of the individuals concerned were surprised at the turn of events but all were upset at the ending of a certain *esprit de corps*. Most also agreed with Bridson's gloomy prediction that in their new, dispersed existence 'the feature programme itself, the spearhead of creative and controversial writing on radio, would not survive for long'.[9]

The ending of *Children's Hour* and the closure of the Features department gave back to Gillard some badly needed money. But even more useful was the room this created for fresh initiatives in programming. In one of his first interviews on taking up his post, Gillard had spoken about being 'keen on radio developing patterns, with more definite groupings'. He no longer wanted to hear what he thought of as the incongruous spectacle of poetry readings sandwiched between two pop programmes. 'A radio network nowadays is of the greatest value to its listeners if its output is consistent in character', he stated baldly.[10] As to the kind of consistency that would be demanded of the Home Service in particular, that, too, was becoming a little clearer. Gillard saw the two growth areas for radio as, first, information, particularly at the local level—a need he felt would be fulfilled by the BBC starting local radio on a large scale before the commercial broadcasters moved in—and second, popular music, a need he felt would be provided in the long run by the introduction of a wholly separate fourth service, and in the short run through increasing the amount of music on the Light.[11] It was this short-term reshaping of the Light that now influenced decisively the future shape of the Home, for in practice the Light could only play more music if it was cleared of some of its existing speech programmes, and it was the Home, already a predominantly speech service, that seemed to be the obvious place to accommodate these surplus items.

A gradual but decisive shuffling of the programme pack therefore took place over the following two years: first *Woman's Hour* was repeated on the Home during the summer months when schools programmes were off the air; then *Radio Newsreel* and *The Archers* made the switch permanently. At much the same time the Home took responsibility for one or two of the Third's speech programmes, such as *In Your Garden*, while a tranche of the Home's own music programmes—*Record Review, Music Magazine, Music in Our Time*—travelled in the opposite direction—or, to be more accurate, went to the new 'Music Programme', which henceforth ran in place of the Third during the daytime.[12]

Gillard's main aim in all this restructuring had been to enhance the popular appeal of the Light and the Third through expanding the amount of continuous music at the heart of their output. So far, however, the Home Service's new focus on speech looked more like a by-product of these manoeuvres than an act of visionary design intended to enhance its own appeal. This created difficulties. What, for instance, might the Home eventually become in this new dispensation? It was not yet clear. On the one hand, the abolition of the Features Department seemed to suggest that a blander definition of what constituted 'speech radio' might soon prevail. As far as *The Times* was concerned the department had been *the* guarantee that radio would not 'degenerate into a mere purveyor of music and information'.[13] In its absence, the Home faced nagging doubts about its ability to furnish listeners with programmes of quality—or at least with programmes of demonstrable creativity. And, having been the one to swing the axe, Gillard himself would never escape entirely the label of cultural philistine as far as some in Broadcasting House were concerned. On the other hand, having taken over programmes from both the 'lowbrow' Light and the 'highbrow' Third, the Home's schedule had, in the main, become much *more* 'mixed' than ever before—at least in the genre of speech. Gillard thought this politically advantageous. Whatever happened elsewhere in his domain, he implied, the Home represented a vestigial commitment to the Reithian principle of offering listeners a less predictable schedule in order to lead them into experiences they might not have chosen for themselves.[14]

It was the kind of thinking that people such as Bridson, who had moaned about the Home's concentration on dull and worthy programmes during the 1950s, should have welcomed. Times had changed, however. Now that the two radio services on either side of the Home were more 'generic', its own thoroughly mixed output looked increasingly anachronistic—and harder to sell to the listening public. After all, did comedy and news really have anything in common, any more than, say, pop and classical music, simply because they both happened to be forms of speech? Or, to put it more practically, would the 'mixed' schedule of the Home find its own audience—or merely a ragbag of listeners with different, and sometimes contradictory, expectations and demands? The question turned on whether or not the service could forge an identity capable of pulling together its many tones and flavours. To simply call it 'middlebrow' no longer seemed adequate. At the very least, it needed the kind of strategic thinking that had been lavished on the Light and the Third over the past year or so. Hence, when Gillard finally moved Ronald Lewin out of the Home Service in May 1965, he told the new man in charge to 'sort it out'.[15] If the large-scale adjustments he had effected since 1963 were to make any sense where they mattered most—that is, on air—more subtle changes would have to be introduced in the very heart of the operation.

THE MANSELL ERA

The man who took charge of the Home from 1965 was, in one sense, very much a Gillard appointment. Like his Director, Gerard Mansell was an outsider unafraid to bring radical change to Broadcasting House. Yet he brought to his new job a more subtle and cosmopolitan approach. His background was intriguing, for a start. With an English father and a French mother, he had been born and educated in Paris, and spent the War in army intelligence, being awarded the Croix de Guerre in 1944. He had joined the BBC's foreign news department in 1951, working his way up the Overseas Service's features and talks section—though only after four years at Chelsea School of Art and exhibiting at the Royal Academy. Quite apart from writing a book about Algerian history, or making the occasional speech on foreign policy at Chatham House, he continued to paint, to read the French papers, and listen to the *France-Inter* radio service from Paris. He was, the *Guardian* suggested, a man with both artistic ability and an analytical mind.[16] Mansell described himself by claiming that he 'wasn't a narrow-fronted chap at all': the cultural luggage he carried to his new job was 'in no way populist'. He would, certainly put his 'foot on the accelerator' of change, but he explicitly rejected the idea that radio should simply chase ratings or merely concentrate on what television could not yet do, namely provide music and up-to-date information. He wanted what he called 'a complete service' for his listeners, with 'mature talks, good plays, music, discussions, and so on'. He was also keen to shake off the nickname 'the good old Home', since it carried with it what he regarded as too burdensome an expectation of nostalgia. Whatever the precise prescription for achieving these formidable ambitions, he clearly had the ideas and energy that just might carry them through. For Clare Lawson Dick, who had been struggling to hold the Home Service together during Lewin's declining months, his arrival came as 'an immense relief'.[17]

Once in place, Mansell made it clear that one of the things he most wanted to hear on the Home Service was a greater sense of informality.[18] There had been tentative experiments on this front already. The Home's long-serving signature tune, *Bow Bells*, had, for example, been replaced with Handel's *Water Music* in March 1963 in an attempt to offer a 'lighter and brighter sound', and later the same year newsreaders had started to name themselves on air for the first time since the War in order to provide 'more informality and friendliness'.[19] Mansell, who thought the very name Home Service rather too dowdy for the 'climate in which we are now operating', decided to take matters further by root-and-branch reform—not just of the way news was introduced but also of the announcements between programmes, since it was these that helped to set the whole tone of the output.[20] Hence, for example, in 1967 he floated the idea of using the Home's relaunch as the new Radio Four as an excuse to drop Big Ben at ten o'clock, on the grounds that it was 'too formal'—a proposal promptly rebuffed by producers, who pointed out that ITV's *News at Ten* had recently adopted the chimes and thus demonstrated their popular appeal. A compromise was subsequently reached in which Big Ben stayed but the headlines at the start of the news bulletin were read by a programme presenter rather than a newsreader—so as to give the occasion a more 'personalized' touch. A few months later Mansell oversaw the introduction of musical jingles during some awkward gaps between programmes and during the run up to bulletins. He even discussed the possibility of Radio Four dispensing altogether with playing the national anthem on the occasion of every royal birthday—a plan which met with wide agreement in the summer of 1968 on the basis that the practice 'corresponded less and less with the mood of the public'.[21]

The crucial arena for change, though, was not in the interstices between programmes but in the presentation of the programmes themselves. And it was here that the more informal approach to be found on other radio services had an impact—especially after 1967, when the unscripted banter of the disc-jockeys at Radio One made its debut on the BBC. Theirs was a style often condemned as inane by their colleagues on Radios Three and Four, but it was also acknowledged, if sometimes reluctantly, as the kind of style that better reflected the informality of the times.[22] Gillard had always thought heavily scripted programmes rather ponderous and liked the idea of anything 'looser' getting onto the air. Mansell, too, listened to what was happening either side of him—not just at Radio One but at the various French stations he liked to monitor regularly—and professed himself to be after 'the raw stuff' of spontaneous talk rather than what he called 'the slightly stiff, slightly buttoned up formats which existed up to that point'.[23]

One example of the sort of old Home Service programme that disturbed him most was *The World of Books*. This had usually consisted of three scripted talks followed by a formal interview—a menu Mansell thought both 'lumpy' and lacking flow. His suggestion now was that it be turned into an entirely unscripted programme—much to its producer's initial horror.[24] In a similar spirit, he asked if the people hired to read out listeners' letters in the feedback programme *Listening Post* could be 'younger-sounding' and have a more 'neutral, classless style'.[25] The kind of tone that could be achieved, Mansell thought, was best reflected in something like *A Word in Edgeways*, the Saturday-evening discussion programme from Manchester chaired by the young Northern Editor of the *Guardian*, Brian Redhead. This was a programme with a solid reputation among the newspaper critics for its lively and freewheeling discussion and for introducing to the airwaves a notably young and cosmopolitan group of academics, journalists, and writers. It was here as much as anywhere that what Mansell called 'the great diversification of opinion . . . the breakdown of deference' was reflected on air during his time in charge of Radio Four. It was not just a matter of which guests had been chosen, nor the issues that were under discussion, but the whole relaxed, lively, intelligent—and sometimes provocative—way in which people addressed each other in the course of their encounters. None of this was meant to be populist: as far as Mansell was concerned most of Radio Four's output was, as he put it, 'serious stuff—and meant to be'. But *A Word in Edgeways* undoubtedly demonstrated a more youthful, more questioning style of the kind he dearly wished to hear percolating through as many programmes as possible over the coming years.[26]

Introducing this 'more youthful, more questioning' flavour to news programmes involved Mansell in rather more delicate negotiation. Journalists working on bulletins or a programme such as *Today* did not answer directly to the Chief of the Home Service but to their own Editor of News and Current Affairs. In the circumstances, Mansell could only suggest in the broadest terms what he, as a commissioning editor, would like to hear. This much, however, he did with zeal. And it was clear that he wished to see a twofold revolution in style. First, he wanted the introduction of more 'actuality' of the kind that *Radio Newsreel* had pioneered: the sounds of the outside world, recorded interviews with people in the news, telephone reports from correspondents in the thick of events—anything other than an endless succession of beautifully scripted and lovingly recorded 'voice reports' from the soulless depths of the Broadcasting House newsroom. Second, he wanted these 'inserts', as they were called, to be introduced in a more spontaneous and flowing manner by those presenting in the studio. 'We are still basically operating on the assumption that the proper way to present news is for an announcer to read it at the microphone in a totally impersonal manner, and that voice-casts and explanatory and background material should be kept separate from "straight" news', he told the Editor of News and Current Affairs in August 1967. An entirely new approach was now in order:

We should seek to break down these barriers, which are largely artificial, and move towards an integrated 'news show' formula in which all these ingredients are fused, as I am sure they can be without losing either the well established authority and reputation of BBC news or the all important separation of news and comment. I took the opportunity of my recent stay in Paris to listen again to the ORTF 7pm bulletin, and what struck me most, leaving aside all question of quality of content and news values, was that the two newscasters were speaking informally and conversationally as people and sounded like well-informed journalists who knew what they were talking about and had themselves been involved in the collection and preparation of their material. The style was relaxed, informal and matter of fact, and gave the listener the feeling that he was in close contact with the news collecting and processing machinery . . . *Newsreel*-type material was woven in in a completely natural manner without the somewhat formal cues in and out which we so often use.[27]

The Editor wrote back seeking assurances that if a change in this direction were to be made presenters would still be encouraged to sound 'authoritative and dispassionate', not 'excited, shocked, disapproving or delighted'.[28] Once Mansell's assurances had been given on this point agreement was soon reached, and over the following years more and more voice-reports from correspondents out in the field were inserted into bulletins, while the *Six o'Clock News*, once rigidly tied to a fifteen-minute slot, also became more flexible in length and format. It was the start of a wider revolution in radio news at the BBC, which saw a wholesale shift to more textured news bulletins and news programmes, and the steady disappearance from the airwaves of announcers' unadorned 'straight-reads'.

Progress in this direction was never entirely smooth, though, if only because the BBC's news and current affairs operation was a many-headed beast: it was impossible to get every part of it to think and act in the same way at the same time. Awkward changes of gear sometimes became apparent, such as when reports filed by overseas correspondents trained in the old style were included in the faster-paced and more personalized bulletins being forged in London. Indeed, the Editor of the Radio Newsroom thought their dispatches now sometimes sounded 'as much out of place as a *Times* leader stuck in the middle of the *Daily Mirror*'.[29] Similarly, moving away from scripting everything encouraged more off-the-cuff remarks, and that brought its own risks. Dissonance of this kind was taken seriously at the BBC. Historically, it had always liked to speak with one voice—especially when it came to news. Consistency and an air of detachment: these were two important protections against accusations of bias or editorializing. Yet it was obvious that in the second half of the 1960s the range of voices and presentational styles on Radio Four was starting to multiply, just as it had been doing on television for some time. Presentation was therefore never a neutral matter, never *just* about style. It also raised complex questions of journalistic value—questions that multiplied further as the amount and range of news and current affairs continued to expand in the course of Radio's Four's reconstruction.

THE WORLD AT ONE AND THE RISE OF NEWS AND CURRENT AFFAIRS

Mansell had realized back in 1965 that Gillard's restructuring of the three-network system gave him a singular opportunity—the chance to make the Home Service *the* main provider of news and current affairs for the whole of the BBC. So quite apart from his desire to introduce more informality across the board he had a second objective, which was to find room for more journalism. News and current affairs had been the BBC's biggest area of growth since the War, and the process had accelerated under Hugh Greene. Supplying the Home with a greater quantity of news would therefore not be difficult: both Gillard and Greene were on side. The real problem was to determine what *kind* of journalism should reach the airwaves. On the Home, different imperatives seemed to clash. Mansell favoured liveness and immediacy—which technology now made easier to achieve than ever before. But he also saw the Home as having the role of bringing broadsheet standards to the widest possible audience: the aim, he said, was to ensure 'the public got a proper assessment of what was going on' amid the social, political, and cultural turmoil of the time.[30] Could broadsheet quality and tabloid 'immediacy' coexist on the same service? Might some way be found of combining the best features of both in a new format? Or should there be a decision simply to opt for one style of journalism or the other?

   The arguments in favour of retaining a sense of old-school decorum were undoubtedly strong. There was a reputation to protect—not just the BBC's, but specifically BBC Radio's. The MP Richard Crossman had written in 1963 about the politicians' humiliating discovery that 'what they say in a television interview is quite unimportant...what matters is how they say it—the "image" they create'. Television, he argued, was 'relying more and more on the tricks of interviewers, snapshots of men in the street, carefully staged rows between experts, and other visual gags, in order to retain the viewers' half attention'. Radio was different: liberated from the need to find pictures it could focus on ideas and issues. And the Home Service was best of all. 'Anyone who really wants to obtain the maximum information about current news', Crossman concluded, 'must prefer the *Ten o'Clock* news each evening to any news programme available on either television channel.'[31] It was an argument that gained in appeal as the decade progressed, not least because politicians on all sides seemed to be worrying more and more over the motives of those who worked behind the screen. The television studio—where they had very little control—was displacing Parliament as the main crucible of national debate. But they suspected that the confrontational discussions and persistent interviewing conducted in front of the cameras was designed to sharpen differences between politicians purely for the benefit of broadcasters in search of drama. An innate distrust was building up, and certain flashpoints pushed it to new heights. The Tories objected to what they felt was unfair treatment in BBC Television's coverage of the 1964 General Election. Labour was even tetchier, disappointed, no doubt, that it was not getting the positive treatment it felt it deserved from the BBC in order to counterbalance the habitual iniquities of Fleet Street. As Ben Pimlott pointed out, Harold Wilson came to see television as 'the instrument of a conspiracy against the Labour Party, and especially against himself'. In the face of this accumulating disgruntlement, it came as no surprise that Mansell was ready to extol the virtues of his own rival attractions. Thus, for example, he boasted of the Home's *Ten o'Clock* as being a

place for 'thoughtful quality coverage designed for the more politically sophisticated segment of the audience'.[32]

One institutional response to the disgruntlement of politicians was for the
BBC to step back a little from the politicians' gladiatorial bouts. The Director-
General's Chief Assistant, Oliver Whitley, warned of the need to respond to a
distinct change in the public mood. Given the evident inability of either Labour
or the Conservatives to tackle Britain's underlying economic weaknesses, he told
the BBC's Board of Management in 1965, the public was getting tired of hearing
about Parliament and politicians and their 'party games'. Out of disillusion there
would come 'an impatient desire to examine more radical causes', and if so the
BBC should turn its spotlight away from 'purely political argumentation' and
begin to explore the underlying trends in government, industrial relations,
technology, and society. It should also do so in new and more analytical ways.[33]

This was just the kind of manifesto to which Radio could respond magnificently—if it were so inclined. First, when it came to providing 'analytical'
treatment radio could boast, just as Crossman had suggested, that it was the
medium of ideas. Second, when it came to moving away from the studio debate
and heading off to explore the world at large radio was infinitely lighter and
fleeter of foot than television. If television wanted to go outside, it was always
encumbered by the need to assemble crews, process film, and find tortuous ways
to transmit material back to base. In radio, the mechanics of getting a news story
onto the air were often simply a matter of finding a microphone or a telephone
and a voice to speak. Even if a radio programme required recorded material this
was easy enough: hand-held 'midget' portable recorders were now widely available and tape could be edited quickly.[34] Radio, in other words, could gather news
faster and more widely. And, for now at least, its allocation of the BBC's
collective newsgathering resources reflected this. The Six Days Arab–Israeli War
in June 1967, for instance, was a radio event—simply because a programme like
the Home's *Ten o'Clock* could draw on up to twelve radio correspondents in the
field, while Television News had to make do with just four camera crews.[35]

In the later 1960s it was this second characteristic of radio news—its advantage
over television in covering unfolding events—that seemed to be gaining momentum. More and more scheduled programmes were being scrapped at short
notice in order to transmit live 'up-to-the-minute' coverage of dramatic events;
reporters filed more of their voice pieces for bulletins over the telephone in order
to break news that much faster; and the once-sedate documentary series *Focus* was
revived with a noticeably more urgent style, like that of *Radio Newsreel*, with
sharply edited actuality and brisk narration from Edgar Lustgarten—an
approach the *Listener* praised for its 'rasping candour' and 'rare sense of immediacy'.[36] One of the factors behind this drive towards immediacy was simply that
more and more Fleet Street journalists were arriving at Broadcasting House.
According to John Timpson, who had been working in News Division for several
years, the transitional moment was in 1966 or 1967. It was about then, he

noticed, that the majority of recruits became hard news men from the popular dailies—people used to working fast and sometimes ruthlessly against competition. 'An Oxbridge accent was no longer as important as a good contacts book, a shrewd eye for a new angle, and a skin like a rhinoceros', he recalled: the reporters' offices 'no longer had the leisurely atmosphere of a club smoking room'. John Simpson, who was also still around, reckoned that by 1968 the only reporter who would get recruited was one who convinced the editor he was 'the kind of man who would walk into a brothel'.[37]

There was one programme in particular that stood at the centre of these changes—and at the centre of any debate over journalistic style and journalistic values: *The World at One*. This had been launched in 1965, and had, controversially, blended the previously free-standing one o'clock news with its own commentary to create an integrated half-hour of news *and* current affairs. It thus broke down one of the defining boundaries within journalism at the BBC. The Corporation had always insisted that the reporting of facts and the interpretation of facts were two quite separate matters—indeed, were two quite separate professions: News Division had always been responsible for bulletins; Current Affairs had taken charge of any interpretive programming that followed. *The World at One* did nothing to disturb this division behind the scenes. But, by allowing the programme presenter to write and deliver the headlines, it did appear to blur it on air. Moreover, it played fast and loose in all sorts of other ways. The programme that had previously occupied the lunchtime slot was called *This Time of Day*, and the fact that Mansell wanted the new programme to be given what he called a 'harder, terser title' reflected his desire for it to be 'quite substantially more "newsy" and altogether brisker'.[38] Mansell's other key decision was that instead of the programme being produced by staff drawn in general from the Talks and Current Affairs Group, as would have been expected, it was entrusted to a small group of producers from the closely knit *Radio Newsreel* team, led by Andrew Boyle. Theirs was a very different culture, less hidebound by questions of balance, correctness, and deference, and much more inclined to be controversial. Boyle himself, ruddy-faced in appearance but cool and contained in manner, an intellectual interested in history and keen on ideas, was, Mansell thought, 'a very non-establishment, very inventive, very bold character'. Around him he quickly gathered an able team of reporters, including Jack Pizzey, Nick Barratt, Nick Woolley, Wendy Jones, Sandra Harris, and, a little later, Roger Cook and Sue MacGregor. As a team, they were, in Mansell's own description, 'a bit of a crowd of buccaneers . . . I liked that'.[39]

To complete the sense of adventure, Boyle had in turn hired as the programme's main presenter William Hardcastle, who had been a Washington Correspondent for Reuters and had edited the *Daily Mail*. 'Bill' Hardcastle was a large, beetle-browed, untidy person, cigarette-smoking, hard-drinking, and shirt-sleeved, and he brought to *The World at One* some of the urgency and heat of Fleet Street. His breathless delivery mangled the conventions of measured speech that still held sway across most of the Home Service, and prompted a regular flow of complaint by disappointed listeners. 'Why', one typical letter-writer asked the BBC, 'is this pompous man allowed to race and gasp his way through the programme, making innumerable mistakes and frequently stumbling over words?'[40] The simple answer was that Hardcastle's relentless pursuit of news communicated itself in a way that made journalism suddenly sound exciting to the vast majority of those who tuned in. He may have sounded as if he was about to choke on his own quick-fire speech during many of his combative political interviews, but he also had what one reviewer called 'a witty authority that never declines into flippancy'. 'Crisp informality' the *Financial Times* called it—a quality it thought might also derive from the programme being put together in just three hours each morning, leaving no time for long conferences about balance and respon-sibility in the traditional BBC manner. Perhaps this accounted, too, for the *Guardian* labelling it as 'invariably, if discreetly, on the side of the angels'.[41] The programme certainly distinguished itself by a quick-witted response to the dramatic events of the time and by the ability of its reports to capture the feel of what was happening through a rich brew of actuality and the voices of ordinary people: vivid accounts from the streets of Paris in May 1968, complete with the sound of uprooted cobbles being smashed and the klaxons of the riot police; three months later, the recordings of a Czech radio journalist who had hung his microphone out of a hotel window in Wenceslas Square to capture the rumble of Soviet tanks crushing the Dubček regime; intimate portraits of people in Britain struggling to live in poverty or coping with homelessness. On each occasion being as up to date as possible became a matter of principle. The programme team took a legendary delight in tearing up running order after running order as the programme edged closer to transmission. Hardcastle, in particular, spiked any story that turned out to be boring. 'If Bill didn't think a story "had legs", then it didn't make it on air', Sue MacGregor recalls. '"WGAS", Bill would mutter as a doubtful story was explained to him. These were the initials one of his Washington stringers used to put at the end of a particularly boring wire story. They stood for "Who Gives a Shit?"'[42]

One measure of *The World at One*'s success was the large audience it attracted in only a matter of weeks. By the end of 1965 more than two million people were tuning in, a dramatic rise on the numbers listening at the same time of day before its launch. Over the next few years, the figure would rise to four million.[43] These were the kind of ratings that seemed to establish beyond doubt that tough journalism could find a substantial audience, even among the supposedly delicate devotees of the Home. And since *The World at One* offered a less stilted tone without any apparent compromise in journalistic standards, it represented a hugely enticing formula for those working there. 'I think many of us began to copy Bill—however unconsciously', Sue MacGregor later admitted. Soon enough, all sorts of programmes—not just news programmes, but features, documentaries, magazines—were being presented in a manner described by one critic as 'that brisk, man-of-the-world style, slightly journalistic in the Harmsworth manner'.[44] And from September 1967 the *World at One* was duplicated directly in *The World This Weekend*, a new enterprise which Mansell had also entrusted to Boyle and his team. This was designed quite explicitly as a Sunday-newspaper-of-the-air, complete with the wide range of perspectives and subject matter that description implied. Hardcastle, again, was the presenter, and he promised a 'not-always-reverent' interpretation of events.[45] *The World This Weekend* therefore represented more than an act of colonization for journalism *per se*. It also represented the growing preference within the BBC for a particular *kind* of journalism. And it represented the growing ambition of Current Affairs as a departmental grouping within Broadcasting House.

One of the areas of Radio Four that proved far more resistant to reform was *Today*, which had been running as a low-key operation since 1957. It was, as John Timpson recalls, 'not so much a programme, more a way of telling the time'. Even in the mid-1960s it tended to consist—as he put it—of 'eccentric octogenarians, prize pumpkins, and folk who ate lightbulbs and spiders'.[46] It suffered from serious structural problems, too, since it was broadcast in two separate twenty-five-minute editions on either side of the 8 a.m. news, with some Home Service regions—such as Wales and the West—choosing to opt out of the second edition. These opt-outs, combined with the rival attractions of breakfast-time music on the BBC's other radio services, meant that *Today*'s daily audience, though a respectable four million, had been declining gently since the end of 1965. The man now in overall charge, Stephen Bonarjee, was clearly anxious to arrest the trend—and not just by gearing the programme towards younger listeners. Like Andrew Boyle, he saw virtue in being as up to date as possible and in creating a greater sense of immediacy. From 1968, he therefore encouraged a pattern of staff working through the night, arranged for the first editions of newspapers to be delivered to the production office by midnight so that any press stories could be followed up swiftly, and invested in equipment that allowed reporters to send tape recordings down phone lines rather than having to travel back to Broadcasting House.[47] All this amounted to the beginning of a long, slow effort at toughening up—and speeding up—the journalism on *Today*. But there was as yet no appetite for getting rid of the programme's main presenter, Jack de Manio, and this set firm limits to how far the essential character of the programme could be altered. De Manio was about as different from William Hardcastle as it was possible to be: *The World at One*'s anchor every inch the tough, worldly newsman, *Today*'s presenter a Bentley-driving habitué of Chelsea and the clubs of St James, complete with a rich gin and tonic voice.[48] When his contract was renewed for a further two years in August 1967, it was a sign that the programme's general air of amiability would survive the rest of the decade. *Today*, the BBC declared, 'does not seek to be "important"', but to be a 'newsy miscellany' held together by the 'friendly personality' of de Manio himself.[49] Only when de Manio took his summer break in 1969 did the programme's editors experiment with the idea of presenters joining the night shift of producers instead of arriving at a leisurely 6.30 a.m., so that they could be fully involved in preparing their programme, as Hardcastle had been doing on *The World at One* since 1965. Soon after, De Manio's contract was renewed again—though this time, ominously, only for six months.[50] His era at *Today* was about to draw to a close.

BROADCASTING IN THE SEVENTIES

By the end of 1967, news and current affairs had more prominence than ever in the schedules. The introduction of *The World at One* and *The World This Weekend*, the first signs of reform at *Today*, the brisker news bulletins, and the sharper edge to news and current affairs programmes such as *Focus*—all this had also infused Radio Four with a stronger sense of topicality. Whatever the merits in programmes of entertainment or diversion, news and current affairs, taken together, now amounted to about a quarter of the overall output. As Clare Lawson Dick now claimed, it was this coverage, above all, that made Radio Four 'an essential service in the life of the nation'.[51]

Within Broadcasting House, however, the strain of expansion was soon beginning to tell. The main news studio, '3B', was already handling three times as much programming as in 1960, and a hastily convened working party agreed unanimously that the situation 'was already critical'.[52] In 1968 there were increasingly desperate pleas for more studios and equipment, more staff, and more money to help meet the demands of the invigorated schedule. Very little could be done, however, because there were too many other claims on BBC Radio's resources at precisely the same time. Radio One needed financing, and so too did the new chain of local radio stations that the BBC had committed itself to building. The expenditure on local radio, in particular, was bitterly resented by many producers in Broadcasting House, who knew full well it meant a smaller slice of the financial cake for them. 'There was no popular demand for it; there were no resources to pay for it; and once committed to the policy, there could be no turning back from it', Bridson grumbled. 'The whole future of serious radio was undermined.'[53]

What made the situation acute was that income had been static for some time. Radio still drew its revenue from a separate 'radio-only' licence, which fewer and fewer people were choosing to buy and which successive governments had been reluctant to raise by more than a few shillings.[54] Even before the tight 1966 licence-fee settlement was announced, producers had been warned to cut down the length of time spent in studios editing tape and that 'cost would have to be regarded as a prime factor in assessing the viability' of any programme ideas. In November 1966 technician support was cut back and new regional production centres planned for Birmingham and Manchester were postponed. The following year, producers were asked to 'economise on electricity whenever possible'. By April 1968, even John Snagge's radio commentary on the Oxford–Cambridge Boat Race was affected when he found that the launch he had been given by the BBC was simply too old to keep up and he had lost sight of both teams.[55] It was a rather comic sign of a more serious problem—an accumulating deficit in the replacement of old equipment. During the second half of the decade, the amount of money being spent on each hour of network radio as a whole dropped by over a quarter, and producers were in no doubt that programme quality was beginning to suffer.[56]

There was, then, plenty of evidence of penny-pinching within Broadcasting House. But with a Prime Minister convinced the BBC needed taming, and the country in the midst of an austere deflationary economic policy, it remained politically expedient for the Corporation to demonstrate rather more publicly both its good housekeeping and its firm editorial grip. It was for this reason that the new Chairman, Lord Hill, decided in 1968 to invite the McKinsey consultancy firm to investigate whether or not BBC Radio was being run efficiently. Representatives from the firm started their work in the spring, producing an initial report in September and a final report in February 1970. On administrative structures, they recommended that the title of Gillard's post should be changed from Director to one of *Managing* Director, with similar changes in Television and the External Services. This not only made Gillard, or his successors, directly responsible to the Director-General, but also imbued the post with a stronger responsibility for the control of resources, as well as programme output. As for finances, McKinsey's initial report suggested that most economies so far had been achieved merely by increasing the proportion of cheap programmes in the schedules, and there was now a need to make 'real' economies through savings in the regions and through cutting the cost of live music from the BBC's orchestras.[57]

All such recommendations would eventually have to be considered by the BBC's Board of Governors, but Gillard had already instituted a parallel in-house 'Working Group' of his own, meeting every Friday morning, under the chairmanship of his deputy, Dick Marriott, and with Mansell and the other network Controllers among its members. This Group was not looking directly at economies but rather at the BBC's use of medium wave and long wave. Wavelength frequencies were allocated by international agreement, and the BBC suspected it would soon be asked to relinquish one or more of those it currently used. Marriott and his colleagues were therefore charged with finding ways of rationalizing the BBC's use of the frequencies by its four national networks and the various regional services. One of the Group's conclusions was that each network should recognize more decisively the difference between daytime and night-time radio. The early evening junction was vital, it suggested, because it was at this point that listeners might be persuaded to stay tuned for a little longer, provided the programming was right. This was significant, because Mansell had already done much to strengthen the appeal of the 6 p.m.–7.30 p.m. slot on Radio Four, through changes to the *Six o'Clock News*, and the introduction of *Radio Newsreel* and *The Archers*, and he now wished to see fewer Regions opting out at this time in favour of their own news programmes. The idea pointed towards a Radio Four that would be much more 'centralized' in its schedules, and in which the Regions would no longer necessarily need medium wave frequencies of their own. In effect, the Group seemed to be saying this: with local radio now in existence, regional broadcasting might cease, and this would ensure there could still be four national networks in which the whole range of programming, from drama and news through to music and light entertainment, was provided.[58]

It recognized, nevertheless, that in the face of television radio had 'lost its compulsiveness', and that few listeners any longer bothered to look at the printed schedules in their daily papers or in the *Radio Times*. In the face of this strictly casual approach to radio, it argued that each of the four networks needed to offer services 'with a definite and recognisable programme character', so that listeners could tune in with a 'reasonable expectation' of getting *what* they wanted, and knowing *when* they could expect it. If Schools and Further Education pro-grammes, as well as the forthcoming Open University programmes, could be put into a separate educational VHF network, then Radio Four could be left free to be a 'spoken word' service for the 'average sensible citizen' as well as 'the opinion-forming section of society'. A small group of journalists suggested that Radio Four should simply make way for a continuous news service, 'free in form, without rigid time-slots'. But this idea was swept aside by Bonarjee. The danger, he thought, was of creating 'broiler house' journalism 'unable to lift its sights beyond the next half-hour segment'. He also pointed out that there was no sign of audience figures increasing whenever Radio Four had offered extra news coverage. The Group's official position therefore remained that while Radio Four might in the future have *most* stress on news and current affairs, its output should be leavened by the continuation of mainstream classical music, drama and serials, comedies, and panel shows.[59]

Marriott's Working Group was making good progress. But at the end of October 1968 it was announced that it was to be replaced by a new 'Policy Study Group', chaired by Mansell himself, which would work more closely with the McKinsey consultants. In itself this seemed sensible enough, since it meant the programming ideas of the Working Group and the new plans for resources and administration could be brought together more logically. Yet the new Group was ordered to work in total isolation. This, Mansell felt, was a profound tactical error. 'We had to operate in secret, we were not allowed to talk to anybody, to discuss what we were proposing.' It therefore 'created a climate of suspicion among the staff, particularly in the Talks department and in Drama and Music— all the things which carried the stamp of high cultural value'. What really frustrated Mansell was that most of his Policy Study Group's proposals drew heavily on the work of the preceding Working Group, which had worked openly and consulted widely, and had come up with a scheme which pushed to its logical conclusion many of the changes he and Gillard had already been introducing gradually—and with little fuss—since 1963. Now, coming as they did out of a Group required to work in secret, any further proposals looked as though they were part of a sinister plot.[60]

Mansell had no option, however, but to push on. Detailed schedules for each of the networks had to be drawn up, and areas for cutting costs identified. It became clear that music costs would have to be reduced through closing some of the BBC's orchestras. There might be economies in foreign news coverage. Perhaps a thousand jobs would go altogether, and there would have to be improved productivity from those remaining, pushed through by tougher management in each programme-making department. But much could be done by shifting resources—from regional services to local radio, and from evening programmes, which were a minority attraction, to daytime, when far more people were listening. At breakfast time, it was decided, Radio Four should offer its listeners a 'morning newspaper of the air'—a phrase that clearly suggested *Today* would have to become much more journalistic in its mission.[61]

The Group produced its final report in May 1969. It was at this point, however, that matters became more complicated by the involvement of a new figure parachuted into BBC Radio: Ian Trethowan. The previous year, Trethowan had been phoned up by the man about to replace Hugh Greene as Director-General, Charles Curran, and asked if he would be interested in succeeding Gillard as Managing Director of Radio. Trethowan had been a political journalist in Fleet Street and an editor at ITN before spending several years presenting political programmes such as *Gallery* on BBC Television. He was also a man with many political contacts, particularly within the Tory Party, and who knew both the Chairman Lord Hill and Curran, whom he thought 'simply liked the idea of my being around'.[62] What Trethowan knew less well was the culture of Broadcasting House—or, indeed, how to manage the 4,000 or so staff that would be under his control. Nevertheless, he got the job—and was immediately told by Hill to write up the Group's work.

After all the spadework of Marriott and Mansell, it was therefore Trethowan who put his stamp on what finally emerged: *Broadcasting in the Seventies*, the eleven-page manifesto unveiled to staff and the Press on 10 July 1969. This was certainly a different document to the one Mansell might have proffered. Most of the proposals—more consistent programme genres on each national network, a shift from regional radio to local radio, and the loss of several orchestras—were on familiar lines. But the tone of the published pamphlet sought to highlight change, where Mansell might have stressed continuity. In place of detailed schedules, it also made sweeping statements, such as its declaration that radio services would become more 'specialized', and that Radio Four would carry more news. But *how* specialized? How *much* extra news? *Which* programmes would have to disappear to make way for the new ones? Staff inevitably thought the worst.[63]

Protest escalated rapidly, both within the BBC and beyond. In Bristol, 150 staff from West Region passed a resolution deploring *Broadcasting in the Seventies*, and the Head of Programmes in North Region, Graham Miller, warned the Director-General that there was anger and 'a sense of betrayal' among his Manchester staff.[64] Simmering discontent reached a climax on 14 February 1970, when 134 producers or ex-producers signed a letter published in *The Times* which denounced the whole affair as an act of philistinism: 'What we object to is the abandonment of creative, mixed planning in favour of a schematic division into categories on all four programmes; and, above all, the refusal to devote a large, well-defined area of broadcasting time to a service of the arts and sciences.'[65] By this stage, there was also the threat of industrial action from the broadcasting unions and an extremely articulate public lobby building up a head of steam. The Campaign for Better Broadcasting had been launched in September 1969, with signatories including Sir Adrian Boult, Jonathan Miller, George Melly, Frank Kermode, and Henry Moore, arguing that the BBC was abandoning the unique role it had long played in the country's cultural and intellectual life. Even members of High Table in King's College, Cambridge, had their own letter published in *The Times* in January 1970, reminding the BBC that there was 'no such thing as public taste', because it was '*you*', the BBC, that made it.[66]

Very little of the fuss concerned plans for Radio Four—at least directly. Apart from Regional staff fearing for their own jobs, the loudest complaints came from those aghast at what was to happen on Radio Three. *Broadcasting in the Seventies* suggested that in order for it to be more consistently focused on music it should lose many of the speech programmes—features, serious drama, and criticism of the arts, for example—that had constituted its vestigial Third Programme element. What BBC managers were at pains to make clear was that very little of this would actually be lost at all—it would merely move to Radio Four, which was, after all, now the proper home for speech. Moreover, any programme shifted to Radio Four would immediately enjoy a much larger audience. In the 1968 Proms season, they pointed out, Radio Four's coverage had attracted nearly two-and-a-half times as many listeners as Radio Three's. If this were to be replicated across the board it would mean *more* people listening to serious or 'quality' programmes, not fewer—a truly Reithian measure of success.

It was a persuasive argument, but trust between producers and management had broken down badly by the start of 1970, and the BBC would have to work hard to mollify its critics. Despite Mansell's four-year programme of sharpening up Radio Four's output and giving it a more contemporary feel—perhaps *because* of it—there was a lingering feeling that Radio Four was too 'bread-and-butter', too 'matter-of-fact', frankly too middlebrow still, to offer a safe enough home for the old treasures of the Third. That Mansell had decided to end *The Critics*, which had supplied the old Home with elevated arts debate for some twenty-two years, just as the *Broadcasting in the Seventies* furore was reaching its climax only seemed to add weight to their fears. By now, as one young reporter at Broadcasting House recalled, BBC Radio was not just 'hierarchical, intellectual, and pulsating with creative energy': it was also 'full of people at war with each other'.[67]

The sense of dramatic change at the end of the decade suited Lord Hill, who had told Gillard that he had wanted a great milestone to mark his regime as Chairman and was looking to Radio rather than Television to provide it. But it certainly made *Broadcasting in the Seventies* needlessly provocative. Gillard felt that just as the McKinsey consultants 'didn't tell us anything we didn't know before', everything that *Broadcasting in the Seventies* set out to do 'could have been done by stealth without causing any disturbance whatever . . . As it was, it was regarded as a cover-up plan for the debasement of the serious side of radio.'[68] Even Trethowan, who had contributed to the sense of crisis, admitted later that the BBC's mistake was to allow arguments to become polarized, when change was more a matter of 'a nudge on the tiller' than anything 'as drastic as a change of tack'. What generated heat, he felt, was that a whole decade of frustration had built up among radio producers. They had felt unloved and neglected in the face of television's rise, and unsure whether radio could—or should—be maintained as a creative medium produced to the highest quality for a national audience or simply adapted to a series of clearly defined and targeted services of pop, news, or classical music, 'increasingly on a local basis'.[69] Emotions remained raw. The whole situation, Gillard concluded, 'aggregated into a most uncomfortable, miserable year or two for the BBC'.[70]

In truth, people in Broadcasting House should have been feeling modestly optimistic in 1969, since, amid the years of dislocation, a steady decline in radio audiences through the 1950s had been quietly reversed. True, fewer were listening in the evenings. But numbers listening during the daytime had actually increased, and there were more than twice as many radio sets being bought in 1967 as nine years earlier. Not all of these extra listeners were tuning to the new pop service, as the success of *The World at One* had proved. And, once the smoke of battle over *Broadcasting in the Seventies* had cleared, it became apparent that it was Radio Four that might stand to benefit most in the future. Through inheriting some of the old Third Programme output, it would, if anything, be providing more plays, documentaries, and serious discussion programmes— perhaps two or three hours more each evening—which would surely, somehow, enrich its character.[71]

Yet there were huge difficulties to be faced, too. The licence-fee increase of 10 shillings announced by the government in August 1969 was welcome, but it was not due to take effect for two years. And while the BBC had been given permission to expand local radio, it had also been forced by the outcry into keeping its orchestras. For now, there would be no savings in the BBC's music costs. Though Mansell protested that there was 'no question of milking the

Networks to pay for local radio', it was obvious that money, to say the least, would be tight—particularly if inflation were ever to send costs spiralling upwards.[72] There was also no sign from the government that the much needed new educational channel that *Broadcasting in the Seventies* had envisaged would be created. That left Radio Four with the responsibility for accommodating most Schools programmes, together with whatever Open University programmes would be required from 1971. The duty to broadcast extra highbrow programmes of the kind ejected from the Third Programme, also coincided with a duty to broadcast more popular speech programmes to be ejected from Radio Two, such as *Any Questions?* and, eventually, *Woman's Hour.* The mix on Radio Four was to be broader than ever. Would it hold together?

The answer would not come from Mansell. While he had been ensconced in the preparations for *Broadcasting in the Seventies*, it was his deputy, Clare Lawson Dick, as on so many occasions before in her long career, who had been left with the task of drawing up the new schedules for the 1970 relaunch, and trying to make everything fit. She knew that, officially, Mansell would be expected to return when his work was done. 'But as he walked briskly and cheerfully out of his office on his way to start the new job, I thought to myself, "He won't come back".' And she was right. By the time the programme changes wrought by *Broadcasting in the Seventies* were implemented, on 4 April 1970, Mansell had been promoted to the new post of 'Director of Programmes, Radio'—in effect Trethowan's deputy. The new pattern for the new decade would have to be the responsibility of a new Controller. Lawson Dick, who had served Radio Four for so long was an obvious candidate and applied for the position. But in October 1969 it was announced that the new Controller would, instead, be Trethowan's nominee, the 39-year-old Secretary of the BBC, Tony Whitby. When Lawson Dick went to Whitby's office to congratulate him, 'He flew across the room, kissed me and still holding my hand said: "You will be asking yourself why him? And you'll be asking yourself why not me? And I don't know what to say." It was done so naturally and with such high spirits that I really loved him for it and we worked together in complete accord from then onwards.'[73]

3

Three in One

'Radio 4 is not a homogeneous network trying to please a homogeneous public.'

BBC Handbook, 1976

THE WHITBY ERA

For those still smarting over *Broadcasting in the Seventies*, Tony Whitby's appointment as the new Controller of Radio Four seemed to rub salt into raw wounds. As one recalled, it looked as though 'a carnivore had just descended among the herbivores'. Their own world—the world of Broadcasting House and of BBC Radio—they saw as 'having a civilizing mission': 'residually Christian, something of the navy, of the civil service, of showbiz, something of variety, of the universities—an extraordinary mixture'.[1] It was a world in which Talks producers such as Philip French and Michael Mason—the two men who supplied these rich descriptions and who had both been among the signatories of that famous letter to *The Times* in February 1970—had been able to pitch ideas for serious speech programmes to the Third Programme, run by Howard Newby, who was one of their own, a former Talks producer and an accomplished novelist, a mild-mannered intellectual's intellectual. Now, with Radio Three largely devoted to music, they would have to get the largest part of their work broadcast on Radio Four. Their ideas would henceforth be evaluated by Whitby—who had spent most of the past decade as a television journalist. His world—the world of Lime Grove and Television Centre—was more streamlined, more competitive, more aggressive. To make matters worse, the new Controller was taking up his post just as Ian Trethowan—another Television man—was taking overall charge of Radio as its Managing Director, and while there was still widespread distrust among staff of the Chairman, Lord Hill, someone doubly tainted by his background in commercial television. Distrust of these new men lurked just beneath the surface of the *Broadcasting in the Seventies* debate, a feeling that they would prove to be rather contemptuous of radio's hidebound ways of doing things.[2] 'We took a rather cynical view of our new bosses', Mason recalled:

They regarded themselves as sort of Nietzschean supermen, coming among a lot of poor old people who were only in Radio because they hadn't got the guts or they hadn't got the ability to make it into Television... They always had this paradigm in their minds of themselves as brutally tough people forcing some wittering old lady in Tunbridge Wells to face the brutal facts of life.[3]

Over the next five years Mason, and at least some of his fellow doubters, learned to see Tony Whitby in a rather different light. The new Controller showed himself to be a much more complex man: forceful, decisive, and tough, certainly, in the Nietzschean way Mason suggests, but also with a strong mind of his own about what made a programme good or bad, and with more than enough enthusiasm and charm to persuade most people to come round to his way of thinking.

Like his predecessor, Gerard Mansell, Whitby had spent his time at the BBC in current affairs. He had joined the BBC in 1958, working first for the Home Service series *At Home and Abroad*, then moving to Lime Grove when he was spotted by Grace Wyndham-Goldie, who had an eye for brilliant young men. There, he had worked at *Panorama* and the Westminster political programme *Gallery* when Ian Trethowan had been one of its regular presenters, before rising to become Editor of *24 Hours*. At Lime Grove he worked alongside Stephen Bonarjee, Anthony Smith, Phillip Whitehead, Robin Day, Alistair Burnett, and Robert Kee, and was immersed in the world of political journalism. Since both *Gallery* and *24 Hours* were self-consciously ideas-based and took politics ser- iously, there were academics around too, such as David Butler and Robert McKenzie, with whom he got on well. Whitby's career in the civil service prior to joining the Corporation no doubt instilled in him something noticed by another of his Lime Grove colleagues: an ability to be 'self-contained and reserved in public'. He was shrewd, analytical, and cool, yet also boyish and cheerful when among friends.[4] If he could be impatient with those he thought foolish or pompous most BBC colleagues found that he was rarely lost for words and always witty when he felt in the mood.

Whitby also had a private passion: the stage. He had already written a successful musical play of his own under the pseudonym Anthony Lesser— *Meet Me by Moonlight*, performed at the Aldwych Theatre in London in 1957, and starring Jeremy Brett. The play was set in the drawing room of a house in an English provincial town in 1884, and sought to dispel the myth that the Victorians were humourless and self-satisfied. In his programme notes Whitby asked the audience not to laugh *at* the Victorians, but *with* them, showing sympathy and affection. 'It should be played straight and true, letting the fun arise out of the characters and the situations... Sincerity is, therefore, the keynote to the playing of all the characters.'[5] Whitby certainly knew his Victor- ians, having done a thesis on Matthew Arnold while at Oxford. As Asa Briggs observed, 'he knew what Philistines were'.[6] He had been born and brought up in

Bristol by parents with little wealth or formal education. But his national service had been spent in the Intelligence Corps in Vienna, and it was there that he had revelled in the arts, dabbled in army theatrical life, and had begun to collect pictures. His wife, Joy, felt his time there 'opened up a side of himself that he was absolutely intoxicated with'. And playwriting was to remain a private passion that ran parallel to his career in the BBC. 'He would literally come back and go straight upstairs and spend the evening writing . . . He always felt that an alternative would have been, if he could have afforded it, to become a writer and to get out of it all.' When asked what his idea of paradise was, he replied that it would be to be in heaven looking down on a theatre full of people rocking in the aisles at his jokes.[7] His later plays—*Love by Appointment* (1966), *The Chicken Girl* (1967), and *The Bedwinner* (1974)—were all contemporary farces in the Ray Cooney manner, often set in the London suburbs and dealing with suburban mores and the infidelities and domestic strains between men and women.[8] To Whitby, so it appeared, comedy was a serious business and its effect on the audience profound. He thought the science of laughter—the rigorous timing and structure a farce demanded—endlessly fascinating; he also believed firmly that one learned more by laughing than by being lectured at.[9]

There was, then, as much of the theatrical impresario about Whitby as there was the serious mandarin or the dedicated political journalist. And his three careers—as civil servant, as current affairs producer, and as private playwright— evidently coalesced into shaping his distinctive professional style. Briggs points out that in his brief spell as BBC Secretary in 1969, he was noticeably conciliatory towards staff rebelling against *Broadcasting in the Seventies*. 'These people', Whitby told Lord Hill, 'wanted to get off the hook, and should be helped to do so.'[10] The civil servant in him may have encouraged a certain predilection for public neutrality, but his wife believed he found life at its most interesting when there was some vigorous debate to be had. Like his intellectual hero, Matthew Arnold, 'dialectic was what he loved . . . he was very interested in extremes and the way they rubbed off against each other'. Clare Lawson Dick saw in him a special flair for picking out the ideas of other people and embellishing them by throwing out his own thoughts and suggestions. His office, she noticed, 'was often visited by producers who wanted, not so much his guidance—for guidance can be stultifying—as the stimulation of his conversation.'[11]

One of those who called in regularly was David Hatch, a graduate of the 1963 Cambridge Circus show who had been working in BBC Radio's Light Entertainment department since 1964, writing, producing, and performing in series such as *I'm Sorry I'll Read That Again*. Hatch thought Whitby was 'as brave as anything' in supporting new ideas: he would not just commission a programme, but talk it through at each stage of development, providing the producer with a 'critical but constructive dialogue'. He could hate a programme 'but encourage the artistic spirit of the producer'.[12] Another who visited his office was the Talks producer George Fischer, a Hungarian émigré of the 1956 vintage who was to become head of radio Talks and Documentaries in 1972. As with many central European refugees from Communism, Fischer was politically conservative—certainly more so than the liberally inclined Whitby—but he became a valued friend and admirer. He admired Whitby for listening to as many programmes as possible, and always having 'very, very pungent points' to make about them afterwards. Producers just finishing a live programme in the studio came to expect a phone call from him within minutes of the transmission, relaying a stream of comments, good or bad. As a Controller, he would be among the twenty or so senior producers and managers meeting every Wednesday morning for a quintessential BBC occasion, Review Board. It was here that selected programmes from the previous seven days would be discussed, and the editorial issues they raised would be argued over at some length and ferocity in conditions of strict confidentiality. Given Whitby's sharp tongue and quick mind he was made for such gladiatorial combat. 'At the beginning', Fischer recalled, 'I could see some eyebrows shooting up—"who the hell is he to say this?" ' But producers soon learned that they needed to respond on his terms: 'if you tangled with Tony, you had better have your ammunition ready... he ruled supreme'.[13] Fischer also noted Whitby's ability to summon his powers of diplomacy and charm to keep senior managers like Gerard Mansell and Ian Trethowan happy—and therefore largely away from the day-to-day work of the production departments. Mansell, now Trethowan's deputy, recalled that 'Tony was so obviously competent, that I didn't worry very much about what he got up to.' 'He was a bright, intelligent, perceptive chap with a strong sense of what Radio Four should be.'[14]

What, though, *was* his sense of what Radio Four should be? The idea that he would make any radical departure from the Mansell era was quickly dispelled when he told the *Radio Times* in March 1970 that it would be 'cruel and silly' to construct a totally new format from scratch. 'We have got an audience who have grown accustomed to it as it was over the years.'[15] Lawson Dick detected in his caution the workings of a deeply calculating mind, since he would only make a change in the schedule after studying intensely the audience figures for each programme. He did, in any case, inherit three clear obligations dictated by *Broadcasting in the Seventies*, and it was these that now set the framework for the next five years on Radio Four. That document required him, in effect, to offer serious programmes of a Third Programme type *and* to continue with programmes of popular entertainment *and* to establish even more emphasis on news and current affairs. To constrain him further, he was expected to fulfil all three of these simultaneously so as to ensure that no single obligation was seen to triumph over the others.

Given the almost impossibly broad remit, Whitby talked very little about Radio Four as the 'middlebrow' network, perhaps recognizing the difficulty of knowing where in this expanded terrain the middle could now be found. Instead, he offered a model that seemed wonderfully apt for a man of his own tastes and background. From April 1970, he said, Radio Four would be a 'more catholic medium than hitherto', rather like a 'well-labelled library that has a few surprises in it'. In short, he declared, it would be 'three-networks-in-one'. First, almost a third of each day would be news and news related—an increase of about a fifth, achieved largely through lengthening *Today*, introducing a new 'commuter magazine' at 5 p.m. (*PM*), and a new spot at 7 p.m. for a commentary on the day's events (*Newsdesk*). *Ten o'Clock* was also changed into *The World Tonight*, which was designed to be 'more thoughtful' than the other so-called 'sequence' programmes. *The World Tonight*, which *The Economist* thought might provide 'a few sops for aggrieved dons displaced from the Third', was a bridge to the second category in Radio Four's output, namely speech programmes of such evident seriousness that they would dispel any lingering doubts about BBC Radio's commitment to high culture and intelligent debate. Whitby alluded to the kinds of programme in the pipeline: regular documentaries on subjects such as Bertrand Russell or Renoir, as well as a new weekly current affairs series for 'the thinking man' that would be intellectually uncompromising.[16] The third strand of programmes—general entertainment—was inevitably the most eclectic of all in both brow level and style, ranging from parlour games such as *Twenty Questions* and old favourites such as *The Archers* and *Desert Island Discs*, through to comedy such as *The Men from the Ministry*, all the way to drama, with a play every weekday afternoon, and poetry, in the form of *With Great Pleasure*, which invited well-known figures to perform and discuss their favourite verse before a theatre audience.

There was, in fact a fourth 'network' lurking within Radio Four, since two hours every weekday morning and another hour every afternoon were still devoted to schools programmes during term time, and from January 1971 the Open University acquired rights during the weekends. Only after June 1973, with the imminent arrival of commercial radio competition, did the BBC restrict its educational programmes to Radio Four's VHF output, freeing up Radio Four's medium wave to become, for the first time, a service to the 'general listener' throughout the day.

The summer of 1973 therefore marked a second wave of change, following on from those made in 1970. It was then that *Woman's Hour* could finally be shifted permanently from Radio Two to Radio Four, as *Broadcasting in the Seventies* had always envisaged it would be. It was then, too, that Whitby introduced two new phone-ins, *Checkpoint*, a new consumer magazine presented by Roger Cook and produced by the *World at One* team, as well as hourly news bulletins throughout the day, and even a new 'signature tune' for the network—an orchestral arrangement by Fritz Spiegl of a traditional skipping tune to replace the familiar church bells. The overall impact of his changes in 1973 was to increase further the total amount of news, current affairs, and topical talk: from a third to just over a half of Radio Four's output. Of the 'three-networks-in-one', this was clearly the one in the ascendant.[17]

Beyond such immediately visible recasting of the Radio Four schedule, however, there lurked a more subtle task for the Controller to perform: to define the style, the tone, the *feel* of this new, more catholic entity. Was it enough to allow the three strands of programme to develop in their own ways, or could there be enough of an exchange of ideas, enough of a collective sense of what defined a 'good' Radio Four programme, for Whitby's 'well-stocked library' to become more than the sum of its parts?

THE THIRD INHERITANCE

Politically, the most pressing task in 1970 was to silence those voices that had been raised in defence of the old Third Programme. Suspicions lingered over whether Radio Four's professed commitment to programmes of distinction was reliable, and these had to be dispelled.

In this respect, Whitby's treatment of existing gardening series had already set alarm bells ringing. In the run up to *Broadcasting in the Seventies*, Radio Four was regularly broadcasting two gardening programmes: the popular *Gardeners' Question Time*, produced in Manchester, and the more elevated *In Your Garden*, inherited from the Third Programme in 1966. *Gardener's Question Time* clearly treated the subject as leisurely enjoyment; *In Your Garden* regarded it as a serious professional affair. The new schedules from April 1970 only had room for one of them—and Whitby had opted to keep *Gardeners' Question Time*. The decision made sense in many ways. *Gardeners' Question Time*'s audience was five times that of *In Your Garden*—one million or so, as against 200,000. Most tuned in simply because it was 'attractive listening', not because they were actively interested in gardening—though, as Gerard Mansell pointed out, 'some of them may well have developed an interest in gardening as a result'.[18] Indeed, the aim, as the editor in overall charge of *Gardeners' Question Time* made clear, was 'to inform (in an entertaining way) the many millions of amateur gardeners in this country, and not the comparatively small number of specialist experts (professional or amateur)'. The programme was therefore 'doing the job allotted to it'.[19] For others, however, the loss of *In Your Garden* was appalling. Archie Gordon, the head of Arts, Science, and Documentaries in London, saw gardening not as passing entertainment, but as 'the greatest of the English arts'. This he did with some personal feeling. He was, after all, *Lord* Archie Gordon, the second son of the third Marquess of Aberdeen and Temair, a full-blooded member of the landed class, who had helped run the Council for the Protection of Rural England before the War. He loathed *Gardeners' Question Time*: its panellists treated the subject 'as a show', offering listeners lame music-hall jokes. Radio Four failed in its public duty, as he saw it, if it did not provide specialist authorities giving accurate advice to the 'gullible sheep' among its audience.[20]

Whitby resisted Gordon's attack, and *Gardeners' Question Time* survived. He did, however, recognize the clear need to compensate elsewhere by showing that his schedules included at least some programmes of cultural and intellectual élan. And the solution, as far as he was concerned, lay in the field of documentaries. In

February 1970, four days after the letter of mass protest from staff against *Broadcasting in the Seventies* had been published in *The Times*, Whitby held a meeting to discuss a project that both he and Michael Mason, one of the letter's signatories, were keen to develop: a large-scale history of 'the British Common Man' from prehistory through to the Sixties.

Over the next eighteen months, Mason worked with his co-producer Daniel Snowman to make what turned out to be the epic twenty-six-part series *The Long March of Everyman*. By the time it was first broadcast in November 1971, this had turned out to be the most expensively produced and marketed programme in BBC radio history. Its aim, Mason said, was to take 'the great commonplaces' of most people's lives—'daily bread, keeping warm, working conditions, sexual morality, enjoyment, children, attitudes to THEM—Government, boss, vicar, etc'—and use them to rediscover the roots of British popular identity. Listeners, indeed, would be allowed 'to think of the past, not as a forced diet of "Them", but as a banquet of "Us" '.[21] It was a pitch timed to perfection, since the contemporary taste for 'history from below' had by now filtered through to a wide range of adult education groups and local history societies and had forged fresh links between economic history, anthropology, and the new traditions of cultural studies being established in British universities. There was a keen appetite for history that took seriously the experiences and the feelings of people in the past, and academics such as Asa Briggs, Christopher Hill, Barry Cunliffe, Stuart Hall, and Raymond Williams were all happy to advise on the project.[22]

But *The Long March*, while careful to display its academic credentials, was intended less as a study of the past than as 'an attempt to evoke some aspects of it'—what Mason called 'a work of art composed out of the findings of scientific research'. Mason had therefore made it clear from the outset that, as far as he was concerned, 'good straight documentary is not enough' and that a spectacular approach was needed. It was only through something grand in scale and manner that Radio Four could achieve for itself what BBC Television had achieved in 1969 through Kenneth Clarke's *Civilization*, and was already planning to achieve again through Jacob Bronowski's *The Ascent of Man*, namely a sense of occasion 'which we can hope to get the listener to make a date with'. Such an event, Mason hoped, might even have the fortuitous effect of prompting a revival in the Features tradition that had been 'destroyed' in 1964.[23]

Mason's chosen strategy was to draw on the complex 'montage' style of two earlier epic features he had produced for the Third Programme, *A Bayeux Tapestry* and *Rus*. They adopted what he called a 'total audio' approach, with 'all kinds of sound in principle, but speech as the string section of the orchestra'.[24] He now called this 'the Great Music of audio', a new art form to be deployed in the service of radio, and drawing on an eclectic mix of raw ingredients:

Ordinary talk of ordinary people; poetry; prose fiction; folk-song; historical documents; natural sound; 'art music'; radiophonic sound; the reflection and analysis of the learned;

drama; the expertise of actors, instrumentalists, singers; radiophonically treated speech. All these things can be orchestrated to create a 'new sound' which is something more than all its components taken separately.[25]

To achieve this heady brew involved a production effort of Herculean proportions throughout the rest of 1970 and most of 1971. Mason spent hundreds of hours in the studios of the BBC's Radiophonic Workshop, working with engineers to produce a vast library of sound effects and musical sequences, or manipulating countless voice recordings to add echoes and stereophonic wizardry. Actors were employed to recite the words of established political figures and writers, while the voices of 'the people' were provided by ordinary men and women around the country, in recordings gathered by Charles Parker, the features producer from the Midlands Region who had made his name with the celebrated 'radio ballads' of the late 1950s and early 1960s, and later—after it was realized Parker was taking too long—by a team of volunteers and students recruited throughout the BBC's regional centres.[26]

When the first episode was finally broadcast, it gave listeners an accurate taste of just what they were in for. Celtic and Roman Britain was evoked through the words of Julius Caesar and Tacitus, or of Boadicea—with a Welsh accent—addressing her crowd of followers. Against chanting and marching, the clash of swords and the fierce cries of battle, historians described the struggle for power; against the sounds of wind and sea, and trees being felled, they described the taming of the landscape. The importance of climate, the routines of domestic life, and the wheels of commerce were all discussed, and enveloped in a lovingly woven tapestry of music and location atmosphere, the whole experience lasting a full forty-five minutes.[27]

Twenty-five episodes and six months later, when the series was over, John Carey passed judgement in the *Listener*. He was not impressed:

Root-seeking underdogs... who switched on at one of the *March's* more radiophonic moments may well have suspected some fault in their sets. Others perhaps concluded they were tuned in to a private carouse in the sound-effects department... Scraps of plays, letters, diaries, poems, swept by in the radiophonic effluent. But who wrote what, why, where—even whether he intended fact or fiction—were details repeatedly obliterated... That the programmes intended thought-provoking 'collage' plainly can't be urged. To the majority of listeners, the chopped documents they contained would be quite mysterious, so no accurate thought could arise from their conjunction. Rather, *The Long March* should be seen as a contribution to the determined modern effort to discredit knowledge and replace it by pure sensation—a movement entailing, in other quarters, drugs, and outcries against school and university exams.[28]

Carey only paused in his withering critique to commend Christopher Hill's programme on the Civil War for being 'the sharpest witted' of the series—though ironically, it was Hill who wrote privately to Mason and Snowman to express his own disquiet over the whole affair. 'The idea of the programme was magnificent,' he told them. But the general effect had been to suggest that 'Everyman had marched through history uttering incomprehensible noises of protest'.[29]

Whitby, who had invested a great deal of Radio Four's reputation in the series, was stung into an immediate public response to Carey's assault. Between 500,000 and 1 million people had listened to *The Long March*, he wrote back: there were clearly plenty of people around who had not just wanted 'a history lesson' but were prepared to 'open their ears and their hearts'. He backed the series at Review Board too, telling colleagues that it was getting better and better as it progressed, while Mansell praised it for its 'dream quality'. As for the new Managing Director, Trethowan, his ears were more attuned to political debate than to the arts. He merely said, rather grudgingly, that he 'had had to concentrate very hard, but perhaps that was no bad thing'.[30]

The Long March's real problem, though, as Gillian Reynolds suggested in the *Guardian*, was that being placed on Radio Four rather than on the old Third Programme, it had 'the difficult problem of selling whole fresh salmon to a public grown accustomed to battered fish fingers'.[31] 'The programmes have evidently been compiled with great enjoyment', another reviewer suggested. But the pertinent question was this: 'Are Them enjoying it as much as Uz?' 'There are, as we know, producers' productions and listeners' productions, and occasionally they don't coincide.'[32] This cut to the heart of the matter, because as it so happened *The Long March* had indeed left a section of the Radio Four audience cold. There was, for a start, the simple problem of technology. Mason had spared no effort in making his multi-layered stereo extravaganza sound beautiful. But more than ninety out of every hundred Radio Four listeners were tuned to low-fidelity, monophonic medium wave, not high-fidelity, stereophonic VHF—and most were doing so on cheap portable transistors. As a result, the subtly differentiated layers of Mason's careful mix frequently poured into the kitchens of Britain as an undifferentiated fog of noise. Hence the anguished complaint from one listener with 'an average radio in an ordinary house'—typical of others who wrote in— that 'so many voices and accents', so much 'ghastly banging of the cymbal' amounted to nothing more than a destructive gimmick.[33] But it was not *just* a problem of technology. For many Radio Four listeners, the whole design of the programme was intrinsically baffling. Its 'montage' technique of piecing together actuality and music and sound effects without the comforting presence of a narrator was something that did not sit easily with them, coming as it did on a network dominated by more conventional and restrained programming styles. Whitby was sensitive enough to this undercurrent of anxiety to warn his producers that montage demanded 'a special attitude of mind', and would thus remain a minority pursuit.[34] He remained a loyal supporter of Mason's *Long March*, arguing vociferously that 'it was more honourable and more important to fail in an attempt to do something new and difficult than to score a safe success'.[35] But he knew too that the kind of programme Mason offered could never occupy more than a specially protected corner of Radio Four. And it was no coincidence that the one series of Mason's that *was* hugely popular with both listeners and BBC colleagues was *Plain Tales from the Raj* (1974–5), which consisted of the largely unadorned personal recollections of British army and civil-service personnel, speaking in what one colleague described as a 'profusion of voices of the type to be heard nowadays only in Harrods'. Mason was congratulated on that occasion for his use of 'background sound, subtle, discreet and never intrusive'. And when the series was revived in 1975 as *More Plain Tales from the Raj*, he was told it 'demonstrated the strength of the spoken word alone to convey experience'.[36]

The Long March had, at least, fulfilled its main task as far as Whitby was concerned, which was to draw loud attention to itself. In the ill-tempered aftermath of *Broadcasting in the Seventies* it had offered a necessary token of faith in Radio Four's ability to accommodate imaginative and ambitious work of a Third Programme type. It was clear, though, that both Whitby and his colleagues throughout News and Talks and Current Affairs more often put their faith in programmes they could describe as 'unpretentious' or 'simple and straightforward' in structure. They usually welcomed the presence of an uncluttered voice, and offered most praise when they could also detect in it a 'sober' and 'cool' tone. Whitby thought that two other qualities were also highly desirable: first, voices that could speak with 'authority' on a given subject, and second, the chance for listeners to hear, as he put it, 'from the horse's mouth'—to hear from the people actually making the news, or formulating the original ideas of the time, rather than from, say, journalists who would only be representing them second hand. It was these qualities that he wished to capture in a new weekly current affairs series for 'the thinking man': *Analysis*. If *The Long March* had been intended to demonstrate that imaginative work had survived on Radio Four, *Analysis* was intended to demonstrate that so, too, had serious discussion.

The very first edition, broadcast on the evening of Friday 10 April 1970, was typical of the programme's unashamed cleverness. The title, *The War for Jenkins' Ear*, alluded to that evening's topic, the forthcoming budget of the Chancellor of the Exchequer, Roy Jenkins. The presenter, Ian McIntyre, began with an elegantly crafted introduction:

Next Tuesday sees the annual enactment of a classical piece of British folk ritual. Budget Day ranks with the Grand National or a deciding Test against Australia. Not everyone is altogether clear about what's going on, but most people feel a vague sense of involvement. One of the most important things about ritual is that it shouldn't change. There will, therefore, be the traditional speculation about what the Chancellor is going to drink at the despatch box. Mr Leo Abse will, as always, give sartorial expression to his inflamed Celtic imagination, and the inevitable Sir Gerald Nabarro will excite controversy as to whether he is doing a commercial for a well-known firm of Covent Garden outfitters or rehearsing for an amateur revival of *East Lynn*.[37]

Such was the style that McIntyre's narration created more of an essay than a report. He quoted not newspaper cuttings but primary sources, such as a report on the British economy by the American Brookings Institution. Lengthy extracts from an interview with its author, a Harvard professor, followed. Later, there were similar extracts from the heads of the International Monetary Fund, the Trades Union Congress, the Confederation of British Industry, and the Managing Director of Rothschilds in Zurich. These were self-evidently 'important' people who could speak with undoubted authority in their respective fields. It was all very much 'from the horse's mouth', just as Whitby had wanted it to be.

At the following week's Review Board, Whitby said that *Analysis* had met his highest hopes. And over the next few years it continued to keep him largely happy through a series of impressive coups: interviews with Ian Smith, King Hussein, the Shah of Iran; documentaries about the Organization of African Unity, the Strategic Arms Limitation Talks, the campaign trail of Willi Brandt in West Germany. During this time, McIntyre, who continued to be the main presenter, was heaped with praise for his writing, both from inside the BBC and through the columns of the radio critics. In 1972 there was even talk of his being groomed as Alistair Cooke's eventual replacement, since it was naively thought that Cooke 'couldn't be expected to keep on broadcasting forever'. McIntyre's main achievement, it was generally agreed, was avoiding the sin of oversimplification in either ideas or language—a sin some thought had set in elsewhere.[38]

McIntyre later characterized *Analysis* as defining a fundamental difference between the work of journalists and the work he was engaged in as a 'current affairs broadcaster'. 'The business of journalists', he said, 'was to get the news and present it.' '*Our* business was to get behind the news and dig and illuminate and go a bit further': 'they were very, very distinct disciplines.[39] This was a familiar enough rhetorical distinction in the BBC, even if Bill Hardcastle and the *World at One* team had done much to blur the boundaries. But *Analysis* went further than merely attempting to restore the old bifurcation—it implicitly asserted its *superiority* over what it regarded as the sloppy habits of instant and superficial reportage now pervading the rest of BBC current affairs. Within its own small and rather self-contained unit, protected by Whitby and Trethowan and under the rigorous watch of George Fischer, *Analysis* quickly elevated the use of primary sources into a creed. Its producers and presenters were required to immerse themselves in books, copies of speeches, Hansard, Acts of Parliament, academic reports, or official statistics on any given subject before going anywhere near the recording studio. When the programme was criticized for being insufficiently combative—as it was in July 1970 for an edition featuring the Israeli Prime Minister Golda Meir—Fischer stressed that its aim had been 'to present a portrait of Mrs Meir through the medium of conversation', and that not all broadcasters were 'briefed to reduce everything to the Procrustean bed of the Arab-Israeli conflict'.[40]

Inevitably, there were dissenting voices, not least from the rest of the current affairs staff in Broadcasting House, who resented the new programme's aspirations to flagship status. Arthur Hutchinson, who was in overall charge of Talks and

Current Affairs, thought McIntyre's approach 'mannered' and never warmed to it. He thought it odd, too, that McIntyre was allowed to present an edition of *Analysis* about the war in Vietnam without ever having visited the country. Whitby replied that McIntyre could be trusted to display 'derived authority', but even Mansell felt the overall tone had on this occasion ended up a little too detached. There was also irritation at *Analysis* broadcasting the first major interview with Heath after he became Prime Minister, and doing the same with Wilson when he returned to Downing Street in 1974. Both interviews were reported extensively in the broadsheet press, to the delight of Whitby, Trethowan, and Fischer, though not, it would seem, to Hutchinson and many of his producers, all of whom, Fischer believed, 'couldn't stomach' the fuss. Probably, the only notice they did enjoy was that provided by Radio Moscow. It used one of its broadcasts to rail against McIntyre as a 'bourgeois London pen-pusher'.[41]

Analysis was certainly what producers would call a 'hard listen', and every Friday evening when it began, two out of three of those who had been tuned in to *Any Questions?* just before switched off. But with 200,000 listeners *Analysis* was doing no worse than mid-evening programmes on any other night of the week, and, crucially, it was attracting the attention of politicians, broadsheet journalists, civil servants, and academics—in short, the opinion-forming class.[42] For a network keen to establish its intellectual credentials this was a valuable constituency. Whitby recognized that the programme's appeal would never be wide: he had predicted a small audience, and was content with it. But courage on this front was intimately connected with progress elsewhere in the schedule: achieving success with other, very different programmes, which reliably fulfilled the task of being popular and accessible.

MORE TOPICALITY, MORE VOICES

Whitby was described by those closest to him as very democratic in temperament. 'He'd come from the grassroots, and he was therefore very much in touch with what ordinary people without academic qualifications really wanted—and it wasn't necessarily trivia', his widow believed.[43] If so, this would certainly have fitted nicely with BBC thinking at the time. Quite apart from the strictures of the 1965 document *Broadcasting and the Public Mood*, which had urged a widening of political debate from the narrow confines of Westminster, there was now the example of local radio, with its 'access' programmes and its interest in putting the citizen 'in touch, as never before, with the issues of the day'.[44] People's opinions also mattered to the BBC because its traditional air of detachment seemed to be getting progressively harder to sustain. 'If the BBC were to be objective, and nothing else', the Director-General Charles Curran warned, it would have to 'exclude in its account of the world every expression of debatable opinion.' Since, whatever else it was accused of, the BBC was certainly 'biased in favour of parliamentary democracy', it had to guarantee that a plurality of opinions could be expressed freely and widely.[45]

Radio could steal a march on television here, for the simplest way of disseminating popular opinion was through putting ordinary people's voices directly on the air. 'How can we influence the men and women who shape our world?' was the rhetorical question one Talks producer posed in October 1969. 'I propose a grassroots dialogue, a telephone democracy': '45-minutes a week "live" between 8 and 10 in the evening, when we invite a public figure to be interviewed by the presenter, by a suitable specialist *and* by listeners at home'. Her model was the French radio programme *Europe Soir*, where 'the questions listeners ask are remarkably cogent and penetrating, just the sort of questions one longs to pop into a pompous *Panorama* interview'. The following month, Whitby suggested that this idea of a 'telephone-your-question-to-the-victim' show should be pursued. Two months later, the Post Office, which had long worried about the stress that this kind of thing might place on telephone exchanges, finally gave its technical approval.[46] No one at Broadcasting House was yet using the term 'phone-in', but the phenomenon had been born.

Radio Four's first example of the genre, *It's Your Line*, ran on Tuesday evenings from October 1970. Robin Day presented whenever his television commitments allowed, with George Scott regularly filling in. Guests, Whitby promised, would range from 'Prime Ministers to Pop Stars'. In fact, the first guest turned out to be the trades unionist Hugh Scanlon, who attracted some 8,000 calls, a figure which more than satisfied Whitby and the programme's producer, Walter Wallich. For every call put on air, Wallich claimed, there were ten others which would have been just as good. 'The great majority of those who had telephoned were obviously informed and intelligent people.' The programme, Mansell thought, had finally 'put paid to the myth that opening telephone lines to the public was a recipe for inanity'.[47]

Things did not always go so smoothly. A special 'People to People' edition in August 1972 focused on the arrival in Britain of Asian families ejected by Uganda's Idi Amin. Eighty per cent of the phone calls had been against admitting them. Since any attempt to create a balance of voices would have misrepresented this weight of opinion, the producer felt duty bound to put on air a large number of anti-immigrant views.[48] 'One after another rang in with arguments so rooted in frightened prejudice that all objectivity departed', Gillian Reynolds reported in the *Guardian*. 'It felt like keeping watch at the bedside of a people in the last stages of spiritual sickness. I listened only to the first 40 minutes and after that total despair engulfed me.' Privately, many in Broadcasting House felt much the same. Mansell suspected that certain subjects 'touched off a deeply irrational response', and since only the 'emotionally committed' would bother to phone, the programme had risked reinforcing 'undesirable' attitudes. 'Bigot to Bigot' might have been a better title for the programme, suggested another member of Review

Board. The *Daily Telegraph* nevertheless saw some merit in the whole affair. Its reviewer had been shocked by the undisguised prejudice of the callers. But, he argued, it 'only goes to show how conditioned I am by the liberal consensus to which I belong and which is so well aired through broadcasting': the occasional airing of a different, 'lower middle-class, reactionary consensus' was a useful corrective. Stephen Bonarjee concluded that *It's Your Line* 'illustrated how wide the gap was between the communicators and the public at large', though since the programme's goal was to ventilate the public's views, 'it was irrelevant whether or not professional radio people happened to like them'.[49]

Whatever the anxieties caused by that particular edition, *It's Your Line* had secured its place in the Radio Four schedules for some years to come. Whitby felt the intelligence of the audience usually produced 'a really good current affairs programme without generating heat or tension'. And the audiences were respectable: 1–2 per cent of the population, or between 500,000 and 1 million listeners most weeks. Another measure Whitby watched closely was the so-called 'Reaction Index', which tried to gauge actual levels of satisfaction from those who tuned in to a given programme. On a scale of 1–100, an 'RI' of 60 or so was acceptable, and anything above 70 good. Most editions of *It's Your Line* hovered around the 65–70 range, though, naturally, success varied according to the choice of guest. Enoch Powell, for instance, prompted an exceptional RI of 72; Barbara Castle broke the record by receiving 21,000 calls during one especially combative appearance in 1971.[50] Germaine Greer also delivered a virtuoso performance in 1970, answering hostile questions on promiscuity, Miss World, Mary Whitehouse, lesbianism, virginity, and the difference between animal and human sex. Inside Broadcasting House they were thrilled with her. The programme, Review Board agreed, 'had provided an admirably frank discussion of sexual relations and other matters not usually discussed on Radio Four'. To Whitby, the programme's pleasure derived from Greer's quality of mind and verbal fluency. She had 'displayed a mastery of words not excelled in many scripted programmes'. The audience, however, was less enamoured, and gave a low reaction index of 55. 'It doesn't mean to say they hated the programme', the producer protested: just that 'so many listeners hated her and her views'.[51]

The success of *It's Your Line* encouraged Whitby to explore other ways of using the phone-in format on Radio Four. From December 1971, a new Sunday lunchtime programme chaired by Cliff Michelmore, *Whatever You Think*, sought to update the old *Brains Trust* idea of a panel of experts answering listeners' queries. The aim was 'to provide civilized (though not too rarefied) conversation', and to avoid strictly political subjects in favour of being 'agreeable and entertaining'.[52] Eighteen months later, two new phone-ins turned up in morning slots vacated by the schools programmes shifted to VHF. *Tuesday Call* and *Friday Call*, both designed it was said to appeal particularly to women, often steered clear of current affairs completely and stuck to practical advice. In the first few months *Tuesday Call* tackled poetry, standards of English on radio, problems of middle age, how to get published, and tips for gardening, DIY, and cookery. The Head of Talks and Current Affairs was very positive, particularly about its young presenter from the *Woman's Hour* team, Sue MacGregor. *Friday Call*, on the other hand, he found to be 'an odd miscellany', with hugely erratic standards of questioning and presenting. Esther Rantzen, for instance, was praised for her sensitivity with callers, but when the Radio Two presenter Jimmy Young chaired an edition in September 1973, the Controller of Radio Three, Stephen Hearst, lambasted his apparent reluctance to pronounce on serious matters. The result, Hearst said, was a programme guilty of 'turning the common-ness of the common man into a fine art'. 'To take refuge in the great undistinguished majority was not to act as a civilising influence.' A year later, when the programme had been shifted to Birmingham and renamed *Voice of the People*, the Head of Radio Drama, Martin Esslin, launched an even more vicious attack. Listeners' views on Rhodesia, for example, had struck him as no more than 'the kind of talk one heard in Salisbury hotels, a collection of untested and untestable old wives' tales'.[53] He loathed the whole style, and, although his distaste was extreme, he had evidently touched a nerve, since Howard Newby, now the Director of Programmes, reminded his colleagues that 'it was surely one's duty to serve truth and not merely to expose prejudice, especially if callers were continually and vehemently in the wrong'. The format worked best, it was agreed, when instead of airing the clash of ill-informed generalities callers were invited to speak about their own experiences—experiences that might otherwise never be broadcast on national radio. One example, much praised at the time, was a *Friday Call* devoted to the subject of loneliness, in which one caller, an insurance agent, described movingly the isolation he witnessed every day when collecting payments from people living in tower blocks.[54]

As for Whitby, he was increasingly uneasy over some of the grander claims being made for phone-ins. His interest in them was not so much as acts of participatory democracy, nor as a scientific measure of public opinion. He knew that callers were, as he put it, 'more typical of the Radio Four audience than of the country as a whole', and as such 'tended to be mainly middle-class and to represent the "Disgusted, Worthing" point of view'. What such programmes *did* give him was a new and different 'texture' to his schedules—one in which voices and experiences rarely heard elsewhere on the network would find their moment in the sun. In that sense he believed them to be in the same noble tradition as the social documentaries the BBC had been making for decades.[55]

'Texture', then, was a defining concern; varying it, an important means of creating the catholic feel the Controller was after. But there were dangers here. To begin with, listeners were highly sensitive to the audibility of voices—especially ones speaking over the phone. There had already been a rumbling public campaign over the use of phones in news bulletins, with listeners writing in to complain that the more reports there were on the phone the more incomprehensible the news became, and unfavourable comparisons being drawn in the press between the 'crackly phone-calls from BBC men on the spot and gurgling introductory electronic music' on Radio Four and the 'clear solo-voiced, perfectly enunciated, plainly written news bulletins' of the World Service. By 1972 the BBC was very much on the defensive, admitting publicly that the proper balance between sound quality and immediacy had not yet been struck.[56]

The Corporation's problem, however, was that once again it was not just dealing with a simple matter of technical clarity. What seemed to annoy Radio Four listeners most was what one complainant called 'the endless irritation of *changing* voices'—too many jumps from one speaker to another, a pervasive tone of urgency, a blurring of what was thought to be inviolable 'fact' with more contentious 'comment'.[57] These were listeners who had grown up with a BBC that had spoken with *one* voice. Now they were confronted with a bewildering array of *different* voices, and could see no reason for the change. Someone like Whitby, on the other hand, knew full well that the proliferation of voices and styles was a natural—indeed a desirable—consequence of the proliferation of journalism. Since April 1970, Radio Four had been carrying over five hours a day of the stuff, and if each of the so-called 'sequence' programmes—*Today, The World at One, PM, Newsdesk, The World Tonight*—was forced to justify its presence, one way of doing so was by claiming to offer not just the latest news but a qualitatively different approach to its interpretation.

Even if we were to examine just three of these programmes, we would be struck by the extent of stylistic divergence. *The World Tonight*, for example, was adopting an even more serious tone and an even more international outlook than its predecessor, *Ten o'Clock*, and attracting warm comments in the press for having done so. As a late-evening programme it was particularly well placed to report on developments in the United States, and its coverage of the Watergate affair and the final agonies of the Vietnam War were regarded as distinguished. Review Board ascribed to its first presenter, Douglas Stuart, 'impartial-sounding, statesman-like qualities'.[58] *Newsdesk*, by way of contrast, had Gerald Priestland and Jacky Gillot as its regular presenters—both much more assertive personalities. Priestland described his approach as giving early-evening listeners a dose of 'news with a human voice':

It was fun to see how close to the wind one could sail. I wasn't interested in pushing any particular line, but in exposing folly and pomposity, sometimes evoking pity, even confessing hilarity or boredom. I reckoned that the franker I was about personal feelings, particularly when rooted in some experience of the subject, the readier listeners would be to take them in the spirit in which they were offered: as a contribution towards understanding and not as laying down the law or pretending total objectivity. The motto, frequently announced, was: 'We hope it's the truth. We know it's not the whole truth. It'll be a miracle if it's nothing but the truth.'[59]

PM had a much more prosaic sense of purpose. It had been conceived with an eye to the growing number of commuters listening to their car radios as well as women at home preparing evening meals while 'awaiting the return of their

menfolk'. The preferred style was therefore described officially as loosely constructed, wide ranging, with plenty of 'gaiety and fun' for an audience thought
unlikely to be listening too attentively. Its presenters—Bill Hardcastle and Derek
Cooper in the early days—presided over a quick and eclectic succession of items,
including personality interviews, previews of evening television highlights, summaries of the evening papers, and letters from listeners. There had even been the
suggestion, quickly scotched, that a regular horoscope might be featured.[60]

There were undoubtedly pressures for each of these programmes to conform
to some ill-defined, middling BBC tone. Douglas Stuart on *The World Tonight*
was often judged, for example, to be a little *too* low-key; Priestland, though
usually given more leeway on account of his stature as a foreign correspondent,
was regularly ticked off for being biased, sarcastic or 'sneering'; *PM*, meanwhile,
was thought to have succumbed to stylistic excess in its manic presentational
style—irritating listeners ('Two men spouting forth news in turns') and the
Director of Programmes ('too much formalised gimmickry'). Whitby, however,
was usually more tolerant. He believed the only alternative to these idiosyncrasies
and inconsistencies was to have what he described with distaste as 'long periods of
bland, homogeneous current affairs broadcasting'. When interviewed by the
Guardian in 1971 he said plainly that 'I don't think we've decided what our
style is yet.' But this foot-dragging may well have been a deliberate fudge. All
Whitby's comments to fellow producers suggest he was quite happy to let a
diversity of approach survive on air for as long as possible. And for the time being
he had hard facts on his side: audiences for Radio Four were up noticeably by the
end of 1970, and rose further in 1971. As for *PM*, which had received the fiercest
critical maulings in the Press: it had increased Radio Four's audience for the late
afternoon by nearly 80 per cent in a matter of months. Listeners appeared to like
the new programmes more than they were willing to admit.[61]

'PLEASURE IS THE POLICY'

While the BBC's own data suggested that Radio Four's news and current affairs
programmes were winning listeners, there remained a vociferous minority who
were fed up with them. 'This is the dullest and most frustrating week I have ever
spent since I first listened to radio more than 50 years ago', wrote one listener in
1970. 'It has been words, words, words, news, news unceasingly.' 'Whenever we
sit down to relax we have News, more News ad nauseam', wrote another, asking
'How long will it be before Radio 4 broadcasts to many thousands of aerials
rendered deaf because of boredom?'[62]

In truth, there *was* a lot of news about. Not only were the sequence programmes gaining more extensive squatters' rights across the schedule, but every
turn of events in the world now seemed to demand more and more coverage.

Quite apart from reporting the General Election in 1970—and two in 1974—there were special programmes for the Budget, for local elections, and for debates on Common Market entry, as well as extra news services at key moments in the accelerating industrial turmoil under the Conservative government of Edward Heath. Whitby thought this coverage had a virtuous cycle of effect for Radio Four. It was, he suggested, 'creating a greater interest in what was going on in the world and this must at least help to maintain the willingness of the audience to turn to Radio'. He also recognized that much of the news was unremittingly grim—not just wave after wave of industrial conflict at home, but war in Vietnam, Cambodia, and the Middle East, violence in Northern Ireland, the unravelling of Nixon in America. As the BBC's main bearer of news, Radio Four was becoming the main bearer of *bad* news. Quantity and quality conspired. Further doubts were raised by *The Times*'s radio critic, David Wade, who referred to Radio Four's 'newsmongering'. 'Such is the pressure of events, of the incessant way in which things go on happening', he warned, 'that news runs people, not vice versa.' Too many people in Broadcasting House, another critic added, seemed to take it for granted that 'Radio Four as a main news wavelength was henceforth immutable.'[63]

Since Whitby seemed as anxious as the columnists were to avoid Radio Four becoming unremittingly gloomy, he was quick to declare in 1971 that he would start to bring more 'predictable pleasure' to the audience, particularly those he described as 'the traditional Home Service listeners'.[64] One means of doing this was to guide producers away from ideas that risked making the network sound so relentlessly downbeat. In 1973, for instance, he rejected a proposal from Manchester for a programme on what he described as the 'searing and miserable' tale of the Lancashire Famine on the simple grounds that Radio Four already had to put on so many sad and depressing programmes about contemporary life.[65] A second strategy was to ensure that whatever downbeat fare did manage to make its way on air was more than counterbalanced by highly visible slices of popular entertainment—much of it infused with a sense of nostalgia. Thus, at the end of 1971, *The Classic Serial* was extended from thirty minutes to one hour, beginning with a new production of Dickens's *Nicholas Nickleby*. There were also repeats of the original wartime *Brains Trust*, the return of some music at the weekends in the form of *Music to Remember* and *These You Have Loved*, and even the reuniting of Peter Sellers, Spike Milligan, and Harry Secombe for *The Last Goon Show of All*—which, after months of overheated press coverage, ended up as a big critical disappointment but nevertheless secured nearly four million listeners.[66]

Such was the impression of playing safe that even the *Daily Telegraph* thought the schedule sometimes had a 'distinct air of looking backwards, of offering nostalgia for the middle-aged and elderly'.[67] As far as Whitby was concerned, this was precisely the point. Radio Four, he kept telling his colleagues, simply had to carry on providing 'middle of the road entertainment for the more conservative listeners'. He might not always share these listeners' tastes, but had to acknowledge that whatever else they were they were unshakeable. *Top Team*, the schoolchildren's panel game, for example, struck him as a 'boring' programme that appealed 'mainly to those who inhabited a never-never land in which children were bright, polite and attentive and the problems with which one was faced were purely factual'. Despite this—or, more likely, *because* of it—*Top Team* remained, in Whitby's words, 'remarkably successful with the Radio Four audience'.[68] Other popular series, such as *Desert Island Discs*, *Top of the Form*, *My Word*, *Just a Minute*, and *Dr Finlay's Casebook* were talked of inside Broadcasting House simply as 'well-loved'—a phrase that usually meant they were distinctly *un*loved by a large proportion of those gathered at Review Board, but recognized as 'pre-sold' titles which it would be pointless to criticize. They were, in short, the kind of programmes that, whatever their aesthetic merits, offered reassuring continuity to a section of the audience feeling overwhelmed by change elsewhere. Whitby had a term for these programmes. They were, he said, what constituted 'the tide of the familiar bringing in the unfamiliar'.[69]

The balancing act was a delicate one, though. After all the effort at rejuvenation since 1963, Broadcasting House was terrified by the prospect of radio appearing to be a thing of the past. Even under the broad umbrella of entertainment, therefore, the need for something genuinely novel and challenging was acknowledged. As Whitby put it, Radio Four had a duty to reflect the views of the 'young disenchanted' as well as the 'aged nostalgic'.[70] It had done so before with the mixture of manic parodies and corny jokes in *I'm Sorry, I'll Read That Again*. As the writer Matt Coward recalled, 'When I was a kid, every cool person I knew loved *I'm Sorry I'll Read That Again*, and every prig hated it.'[71] By 1970, though, this particular series had been running for five years and Whitby felt the time was right for something completely new. He consequently announced that he was after a 'light' Saturday night show as part of the new schedules—and gave a clear signal to the Light Entertainment department that what he meant by this was satire.[72]

The request came at just the right time for Light Entertainment. Only a few years before, none of the department's producers had been under 30 years old. Even now most were in their fifties: a cohort once stereotyped, only half-jokingly, as 'ex-bomber pilots'—men who had done wartime or post-war national service and shared the tastes and common experiences of their generation. The Head of Light Entertainment in 1970, Con Mahoney, was an archetypal member, having joined the BBC in the 1930s straight after leaving school and slowly working his way up. Like his peers, he was more at home with the *Goons* than the *Pythons*, and even seven years after *That Was the Week That Was* he was distinctly suspicious of satire as a genre. Nevertheless, he had had the professional sense to acknowledge changing fashion, and since 1963 he had regularly dispatched producers to the universities in order to recruit fresh talent and keep a particular eye on the Cambridge Footlights. John Cleese, Bill Oddie, Tim Brooke-Taylor, and Graeme Garden were among the first to be spotted this way; Cleese was even offered a contract as a writer-producer.[73] Now, at the beginning of 1970, it was two other members of this new generation, David Hatch and Simon Brett, who together came up with a response to Whitby's request. Their proposal was *Weekending*, a studio-based show which looked back at the week's news through a succession of short comic sketches: not so much an escape from Radio Four's heavy diet of news as a satirical engagement with it.

As soon as the show was first broadcast, at 11.15 p.m. on Saturday 4 April 1970, it was clear that it would have a decidedly political edge and be prepared to risk accusations of bad taste. Since each edition was put together in the studio in only two hours and proceeded at a breathless pace, it also had a roughness and immediacy that seemed to mark it out from some of the more stately programmes elsewhere on Radio Four. 'This programme is *supposed* to go beyond the normal bounds or it would have no bite', Hatch told Mahoney when defending one of its sketches. One running joke that caused jitters from BBC management was Execution Corner, in which a public figure would be named just before the audience heard sound effects signalling their imagined death. Tony Benn was featured for several weeks in a row. Trethowan, who took politics enormously seriously, was frequently aghast at the series' scurrilous approach to the Great and Good. When a Sunday lunchtime repeat was mooted in 1974, the minutes of Review Board noted only a two-word response from Trethowan: 'God forbid.' Another unreconstructed doubter was the news editor, Peter Woon, who loathed *Weekending*'s irreverence towards news and current affairs and accused it of being rather old-fashioned. The Head of BBC Radio's religious programmes, on the other hand, was usually supportive. Like Whitby, he argued forcefully that there needed to be a permanent place on Radio Four for a programme that did not take news seriously.[74]

Ratings proved stubbornly low for *Weekending* during its first year. There were also some crucifying reviews in the press. But those who did listen to it over the following eighteen months recorded a measure of appreciation that crept up slowly from a truly terrible 'RI' of 38 to a much more satisfactory 60. By the mid-1970s, when it had become something of a minor cult among younger Radio Four listeners, and especially among university students, the audience reaction figure had risen to as high as 77.[75] As long as *Weekending* was reaching the small but devoted audience Whitby thought likely for late-night listening, he was inclined to give it the benefit of his doubt. He knew, too, that the programme was the work of a young and highly talented group of actors, producers, and writers who could at any moment be lured away from Radio Four to the more lucrative world of television. He therefore offered them a kind of personal protection against managerial ire whenever they occasionally lapsed, in much the same manner as he was doing for *Analysis* within the area of current affairs. Whitby lost a battle with Trethowan for the show to stay on air through the first General Election campaign of 1974, but he was invariably willing to speak up for it at Review Board, praising its verbal wit and defending its use of controversy at a time when so much of the news seemed so grim. In holding up a mirror to the topical events which dominated Radio Four's output, *Weekending* seemed to help make the events themselves more bearable. Being funny, Whitby believed, was intrinsically life enhancing, and so something to be valued in itself. But he also had an eye to its effect on the Radio Four schedule as a whole: it provided a moment in its stream of overarching seriousness when listeners might switch on with a sense of pleasure and anticipation, rather than a sense of duty.[76]

'MAGAZINISMUS'

Whitby's measured attention to each of his 'three-networks-in-one' ensured that, despite the gloomy predictions made amid the heated rhetoric over *Broadcasting in the Seventies* in 1969, Radio Four, half a decade on, still retained the Reithian ideal of mixed programming it had inherited from the Home Service. Indeed, with programmes such as *The Long March*, *Analysis*, *It's Your Line*, and *Weekending*, it was easy to argue—and convincingly—that the 'new' Radio Four was offering its listeners a wider range of programmes than ever before. True, news, current affairs, and topical programmes, such as phone-ins and discussions, now spread collectively across nearly half the schedule. But this was a schedule that also genuinely reflected something of the old Third Programme taste for placing intellectually or aesthetically demanding programmes before its audience. And it was a schedule that simultaneously found more than a little room for nostalgia, popular drama, comedy, even a little music—the sort of popular pleasures the old Light Programme had once done famously well. Each programme had its own task to fulfil: here, to offer a window on considered and expert thinking; there, to let one hear the raw responses of the suburbs and the regions; elsewhere, to articulate the scepticism of youth, or to carry the echo of the past for an older generation sated with contemporary reality. It was, so the *Sunday Times* judged in April 1973, a Radio Four 'at once more cultured and more catholic' than ever before.[77]

No doubt, the Reithian ideal would have been for each listener to experience the whole of what Radio Four had to offer in order to become the rounded citizen of the BBC's dreams. But Whitby had to operate on the basis that few listeners actively behaved like this. Audience Research showed a mere handful staying with Radio Four for hour after hour. At any given time, three out of every 200 Britons were listening to Radio Four—and these were *different* people opting in and out of the network at *different* times. For Whitby the conclusion was clear:

While it would be foolish to assume that each programme has a completely different set of listeners, it is no more foolish than to assume that any two programmes have the same set of listeners. The truth lies somewhere between the two and it is safe to assume that it lies nearer the former than the latter... The main objective of our network strategy must be that each programme caters as well as it can for the listeners whom it knows it has.[78]

Radio Four, in other words, was not a network with a single identity, middlebrow or otherwise. Nor did it have a single audience. In one sense it was little more than a shared wavelength in which at least three different audiences might find their own preferred programmes and styles lurking within.

Yet, at the time many radio producers and broadsheet radio critics, with the battles over *Broadcasting in the Seventies* still on their minds, were far more alert to signs of a general levelling down than to signs of a network spreading its wings. They tended to focus not on variety but on the powerful centripetal forces at work in Whitby's scheduling strategies. As Controller, he naturally wanted to persuade listeners to any given programme to return week after week, and perhaps stay tuned for the next programme on air. After all, only in that way could his station's audience figures rise overall.

Whitby therefore looked for ways to build links between the different parts of the output, by grouping together disparate programmes under new 'umbrella' series titles. He also replicated tried and trusted formulae, especially the 'magazine' format—which consequently became more pervasive under his regime. With both strategies, Whitby's confidence in his rationale was fully matched by the disquiet of those who were opposed. What they sensed was not variety and range, but signs of uniformity and blandness.

Whitby's instinct, that disparate programmes pulled together under a new title could attract a bigger audience, was put to the test in October 1970 by the launch of *You and Yours*. This swallowed up four previous 'service' programmes, *Can I Help You*, *Listening Post*, *In Practice*, and *You and Your Money*, and promised to give listeners advice five lunchtimes a week 'on everyday affairs from savings to sex, from holidays to health'. It seemed to work. Within a matter of months, the programme was attracting about a million listeners each day, and consistent praise inside Broadcasting House for the way it dealt with the daily concerns of 'ordinary people' in a practical and down-to-earth manner.[79] A similar strategy was used in 1972, when Whitby created a sequence of programmes back to back on Saturday mornings, collectively labelled *Saturday Briefing*. This included *From Our Own Correspondent*, *The Week in Westminster*, ad hoc documentaries, and a review of the political journals in *The Weekly World*. The programmes themselves were not new, and their formats changed only imperceptibly, but in their new slots they were flagged in the *Radio Times* as offering a new and more unified theme: the place where 'Radio 4 fills you in on the political scene at home and abroad'. Whitby claimed that the whole sequence was 'much appreciated by MPs and opinion-formers generally, a group for whom BBC Radio took satisfaction in catering'.[80]

Falling somewhere between the general appeal of *You and Yours* and the more specialized nature of *Saturday Briefing* was the broad—and harder to categorize—area of the arts. When the old Home Service's best-known arts programme, *The Critics*, had been dropped in 1969, it had been replaced by a patchwork of new series: *Options*, launched in 1970, followed by *Scan* in 1971, both general programmes about the arts, and *Now Read On*, which dealt with literature. Few BBC insiders were altogether satisfied with this solution. Philip French, for instance, thought *Scan* 'schematic' and 'intolerably middlebrow', and although he was clearly still smarting over the loss of *The Critics*, his assessment was no crueller than most being offered in Review Board. By 1972, Whitby was also becoming increasingly uneasy: none of these programmes, he felt, had quite made up their minds whether they were addressing a knowledgeable 'specialist' audience or a less well-informed 'general' one. Clearly, one solution would be for them to recognize their limited appeal and to get on with speaking intelligently to their own, narrowly defined community of listeners. That, he suggested, 'would at least make it possible to get the tone of such programmes right.' His own inclination, however, was to strengthen their appeal to a general audience by grouping them together 'under a general heading in much the same way as the programmes in *Saturday Briefing*'. He also thought the new programme should attempt to cover both arts *and* science, in the hope that Snow's two cultures might once more be reunited. His only other prescription was a rather revealing request to the Talks department: 'I don't care what you call the programme', he told its producers, 'as long as the word "art" or "critic" isn't in the title.'[81]

Whitby got his way, or at least most of it: the new programme was called *Kaleidoscope*, and included science—though only half-heartedly, and then not at all after 1974. First broadcast at 10.30 p.m. on Monday 2 April 1973, *Kaleido-scope* was to prove one of the archetypal Radio Four magazine programmes of the era. Whereas programmes such as *The Critics* had served up sustained conversation for the length of each edition in the classic 'Talks' manner—and followed what French had described as 'Leavis's and Eliot's idea of the common pursuit of True Judgement'—*Kaleidoscope* offered a more fragmented and less lofty approach in its opening week: three-minute interviews with Joan Baez, short studio discussions about Quasars or Picasso, musical excerpts from Diana Ross. This was typical of the magazine format's busy mélange of content and style. It was also, at its most basic, exactly the same technique employed in *You and Yours*, *Woman's Hour*, and a news sequence such as *PM*. In each case, the presenter would weave a number of disparate elements into some sort of unity; the overall 'shape' of each programme would be familiar enough to regular listeners, but the content ever-changing, each 'item' a self-contained three or four minutes that could be placed in almost any part of the running order, or dropped altogether if a better story came along close to transmission. Magazines allowed more to be covered in less time, and could be produced in something approaching an 'assembly-line' style, where well-oiled routines ensured no pro-gramme had to be built entirely from scratch every day.[82]

To Whitby, the advantage in such techniques was this: that in offering speech in a series of short, loosely connected items, instead of in a 'piece of continuous thought and argument', a magazine-style treatment fitted the way in which radio was now listened to at home. It was, indeed, the daytime format par excellence.

Thus, when *Start the Week with Richard Baker* was launched in 1970, featuring in its first edition a succession of disparate items on pigeons, tax reform, Wordsworth, and cookery (to be joined in subsequent months by Monty Modlyn's 'roving microphone' and a satirical calypso), it was shaped like this precisely because it was conceived as a cheerful 'accompaniment to morning domestic chores' and not as something that might demand concentrated attention.[83]

The trouble was that magazines sometimes felt rather too much like the speech-radio equivalent of all those disc-jockey programmes on Radios One and Two: symbolic of radio's 'secondary' status as a background medium in the television era, and consequently a convenient target for critics who felt the BBC was giving up the battle to nurture serious and creative radio. There was something troublingly *industrial* about a magazine: it consumed a vast and endless amount of raw material, and, unlike 'ad hoc' documentaries or features, it had to fill preordained slots on the schedule that often stretched well into the future. Instead of being an idea in search of an outlet, it appeared to be an outlet in search of ideas: an inversion of what was perceived to be the proper precedence of content before style. The well of suspicion ran deep, since the format itself long pre-dated Whitby's tenure. It had been heard first during the daytime schedules of American radio in the 1920s and 1930s, and was then pioneered on the BBC through various 'kitchen front' programmes broadcast on the Home Service during the War and then, more permanently after 1946, through *Woman's Hour*.[84] That particular series quickly established a solid reputation for bringing serious issues before a large working-class audience. But *Woman's Hour* had been the exception that seemed to prove the rule about magazines. From a British perspective, the format's American origins confirmed the worst suspicions. The Leavisite view of American culture as vapid, populist, and without value persisted stubbornly in critical circles. Richard Hoggart had carried the tradition forward through his classic of 1957, *The Uses of Literacy*, which laid into the kind of damage wrought by popular—for which, read *Americanized*—print magazines. He decried their brevity and superficiality, and especially their bittiness—the ' "dolly mixtures" pleasures' they offered, of a 'constant diet of odd snippets, of unrelated scrappy facts, each with its sugary little kernel of "human interest" ':

There must be no connected sequences of any length; everything is interesting, as interesting as the next thing, if only it is short, unconnected, and pepped-up. The rain of undifferentiated anecdotes pours down . . . Today new sensations by the dozens have to be found daily. So there has to be a continuous straining, a vast amount of sleight-of-hand to pass off what is really thin tack as strong and meaty stuff, and endless inflation and distortion of angle so that the tiny shall appear immense.[85]

Hoggart revived his own theme in 1971 when he delivered the *Reith Lectures* on Radio Four, and talked of the pressure in broadcasting to 'trivialize serious things, the trivial material relentlessly produced, the unspoken but clear assumption that most people are capable of responding to very little'.[86]

By this time, Hoggart was being dismissed by Review Board as 'an original' whose ideas were now more than a decade out of fashion.[87] But many of the newspapers' radio critics clearly disagreed, for there were uncanny echoes of Hoggart (if not quite Leavis) in their increasingly barbed comments on some of Radio Four's own magazines, phone-ins, and discussion programmes. *The Times*'s David Wade led the assault in September 1971, when he wrote that 'idiot showbiz and magazinismus in equal parts have taken over... the rule appears to be what cannot be said in ten minutes or less will never be said at all'. Two years later, he attacked Radio Four's use of generic series titles to group together disparate programmes: the *You and Yours* model writ ever larger. Passing judgement on *The Spellbinders*, six programmes looking at magnetic personalities of the twentieth century ranging from Goebbels to James Dean, he suggested that the series' only unity lay in its title 'which has been as it were hastily wrapped round a job lot of documentaries like a tatty old sheet of brown paper': a blanket title was 'reckoned to be one way of inducing people who tuned in at 8pm last week to do so again next like a row of Pavlovian rabbits'.[88] Paul Ferris, meanwhile, suggested in his *Observer* review of *Kaleidoscope* that its magazine format reflected 'the great ragbag of our times'. 'What is at fault', he argued, 'is the relentless assumption that seven minutes here, eight minutes there, night after night, cheaply produced item after cheaply produced item, is going to amount to something more than a convenient way of providing two-and-a-half hours of radio a week.' Gillian Reynolds, meanwhile, looked across the schedule and detected a creeping blandness in the whole presentational style of Radio Four. 'It seems to have stratified itself down to a highly predictable pattern', she suggested:

The thinking seems to be, if its news or argument then it must be George Scott. If the topic is musical, the man to say the words between the tunes must be Richard Baker. Both Mr Scott and Mr Baker are, of course, highly acceptable broadcasters but the way in which they are currently being used does make me rather feel like Pavlov's bitch.[89]

Pavlov again. Invoking the Russian scientist cut to the heart of the problem as far as Whitby's critics were concerned. 'The more educated the listeners are', argued one BBC producer, 'the more readily they consult a guide.' 'We neither shall nor should wish to destroy this element of choice.'[90] Discerning listeners, it was implied, were selective, not slavish: it was a measure of their quality of mind that they switched the radio *off* from time to time.

This was the kind of thinking that went beyond Hoggart and straight back to Reith. In the 1920s, what was then called 'tap listening'—listening continuously from one programme to the next—was abhorrent to official BBC policy, precisely because it implied the listener was hearing, rather than listening: being passive rather than truly attentive.[91] Grumbles from producers within the BBC about the spread of magazines on Radio Four in the 1970s were therefore infused with the potent rhetoric of loss. The end of *The Critics*, for example, was seen as the end of a particularly influential tradition. Joan Bakewell, who had listened as a teenager, claimed that, for her, the patient erudition of *The Critics*, with its 'semi-academic thoughtful mode...governed by good manners in an old-fashioned way' had laid down 'patterns of civilized discourse'. As one of the programme's regular contributors, Al Alvarez, pointed out, it had been an example of how people thought good conversation should be. Philip French and Lorna Moore, both of whom had produced *The Critics* before it was dropped, distrusted *Kaleidoscope* because, as a topical magazine, its inevitable duty was to concentrate on news *about* the arts rather than offering the stuff itself. This, they feared, left an intellectual void in a network where extended criticism and serious reflection should have been given houseroom.[92] Other producers were inclined to agree with this as a matter of general principle. 'Are there not listeners who would appreciate "continuous thought and argument" if it were broadcast in the daytime?', one asked Whitby pointedly. 'And where else can they get it but in Radio Four?'[93] Even some of the *Woman's Hour* team were getting jumpy. Once upon a time their programme had stood out, they told him; now the style they had pioneered was so pervasive that *Woman's Hour* faced being lost in the crowd.[94]

Much of this was needlessly gloomy. As with Hoggart, it expressed a fear of advancing conformity where 'the only duty is to keep to the middle of the crowded road'.[95] But there was less and less of the middlebrow about Radio Four under Whitby, and more and more of a teasing out of *different* audiences, programme styles, and brow-levels.

The main dividing line usually coincided with the difference between daytime and evening programmes. After early evening, the popularity of television ensured that radio was left with the minority of diehards: small in number, but people who had evidently made a positive choice to listen rather than to view. Programmes for this discerning group could be demanding. Hence the evening placing for programmes like *Analysis* and *The Long March of Everyman*, as well as for the 'continuous thought and argument' of *A Word in Edgeways*. They could not be expected to get large listening figures: when the television audience was borne in mind, Whitby calculated that any Radio Four programme which might be of interest to half the British public would be doing well if it ended up with about 500,000 listeners—or about 1 per cent of the population. Such programmes would be judged on their ability to impress their small and knowledgeable audience with their authority on the chosen topic. Indeed it was a mantra of George Fischer, whose department made many of these programmes, that producers should be able to talk to the artists or scientists with whom they dealt 'on equal terms'.[96] Daytime was a different matter. Between breakfast and supper radio was still a majority medium. During these hours there was a much bigger—but less devoted—audience to be won, and Whitby expected any programme to be 'adequately appreciated by listeners inevitably distracted by other things'.[97]

This distinction was not new, but competition sharpened it in the early 1970s. Quite apart from the rival attraction of BBC local radio, there was afternoon television on ITV after 1972. Even before the first commercial local radio stations came on air in the autumn of 1973, Radio Four's rising audiences of 1970 and 1971 had given way to a noticeable decline in 1972 and 1973. Whitby, tutored as he was in the ways of television, confronted fiercer competition with an aggressive attention to his own daytime schedule. The proliferation of phone-ins and magazines, and the use of familiar big-name presenters between 1970 and 1974 was part of this larger battle. For some, it was simply too big a part. The BBC's most senior editor in Manchester grumbled that with more and more regular long-term series in the schedules—more and more of them, it seemed to him, planned and executed in London—he and his fellow producers found it harder to get their ideas accepted for Radio Four. 'I—and they—do think that you put too much emphasis on the pursuit of majorities at the expense of minorities', he told Whitby in August 1973.[98] His complaint echoed those from other BBC centres in Birmingham, Bristol, Cardiff, and Glasgow, as well as the rows during 1969 and 1970 over the loss of the Third Programme. The sense of distrust left by *Broadcasting in the Seventies* provided the filter through which many managerial changes to Radio were seen by BBC staff and public commentators over the following five years.

What irked Whitby was that this somehow rendered invisible much that had been done since 1970 to drive Radio Four more upmarket than ever before. It was not just a matter of symbolic programmes such as *Analysis* or *The Long March* that infused Radio Four with something of the old Third. It was also that there had been a toughening up in other parts of the schedule. By the end of 1973, heavyweight financial news had been introduced in the evenings, specifically to serve, in Whitby's words, 'the opinion-formers and the late-to-bed middle-classes'. *Today* had eased Jack de Manio out of its presenter's seat in 1971: for the next three years, Robert Robinson presented alongside John Timpson. In Robinson the programme had found a man of sly, dry wit who 'used words to fashion lexicological *objets d'art*'. He, even more than Timpson, helped transform *Today* into a much less frivolous affair. And those at the top of BBC Radio regarded some loss of audience as a price worth paying for this transformation. Their own audience research showed that Robinson was unpopular with 'a very large minority' of listeners. During his stint as presenter, *Today*'s audience figures started to decline after several years of growth. 'Faced with a *Today* presenter who quotes Milton', Trethowan told the Governors in 1973, 'some listeners may have fled to the more homespun ways of Terry Wogan on Radio Two.' Similarly, he pointed out, the predilection of *The World Tonight* to include lots of foreign news, including, on one memorable occasion, a forty-minute interview with Albert Speer ('something of a connoisseur's item'), probably contributed to the decline in Radio Four's evening audiences in 1972 and 1973. Trethowan, though, was not disheartened. 'It is beyond dispute', he said, 'that by lightening

Radio Four we could increase its audience.' 'We believe, however, that this would be a betrayal of everything we have set out to do since *Broadcasting in the Seventies*. Far from watering down serious radio, we believe we should seek ways of making it more authoritative.' The broadsheets, he pointed out, appeared to like Radio Four best when it was at its weightiest. 'There is', he deduced, 'no critical encouragement to lighten the content.'[99]

Trethowan concluded his report to the Governors in 1973 by declaring that there was now a considerable sense of pride and confidence in radio:

The troubles of three years ago are now matters of the past. There are still philosophical arguments within radio, and there are inevitably a few scars which will be part of the BBC's history. But time and experience has largely banished two of the most serious wounds of 1970—suspicion of the new management and a pervasive sense of being forgotten and unloved in a television world.[100]

This papered over some serious cracks. Unease over the spread of magazine programmes and the apparent ubiquity of phone-ins, disappointment over the lack of considered criticism of the arts, the difficulty of convincing sceptical listeners to stick with complicated montage features, the fear of boring listeners with too much news: all these were real enough in the first half of the 1970s. But Trethowan was right in one sense. The wounds *were* healing, if slowly. Even the listeners were getting used to the new schedules. There had been thousands of letters of complaint about the new Radio Four schedule in 1970, and above all about the sudden increase in the amount of news and current affairs. When extra hourly bulletins were introduced in the summer of 1973, however, complaints amounted to barely a trickle. 'The dog has not barked', Whitby told colleagues. 'It has not even whimpered.'[101]

Perhaps, in his mastery of scheduling tricks and audience statistics, Radio Four's Controller had been a Pavlov in disguise after all. Perhaps, too, listeners had fewer niggles about the form and style of Radio Four's programmes simply because they had more substantive concerns in the early 1970s. For, as one type of complaint died away, two even more divisive ones had been growing in both volume and intensity: complaints over the question of how sex and politics should be reflected on the national airwaves. Popular anxiety over form and style, it seemed, was giving way to a more enduring anxiety over taste and bias.

4

Politics and Permissiveness

*'I suppose you're trying to be "with it", with decadence and communism and
complete lowering of all standards.'*

Letter from a Radio Four listener, 1970

THE END OF CONSENSUS?

The 1970s was, by most accounts, a peevish decade in the conduct of public
affairs in Britain. Looking back, the journalist Christopher Booker, who had once
written of the expansiveness and sense of possibility that marked the 1960s,
described the prevailing mood that followed as 'a somewhat weary, increasingly
conservative, increasingly apprehensive disenchantment'. The international collapse of the fixed exchange-rate system and OPEC's dramatic oil price rises in
1973 knocked a widespread faith in gradual material progress and replaced it
with economic stagflation and talk of 'diminishing expectations'. There was a
new climate of brooding introspection, as much cultural and political as it was
economic. And it was tangible well before 1973. The Conservative election
victory of June 1970 had ended more than half a decade of Labour rule and
promised a less emollient relationship with the trades unions—unions which
were, in turn, increasingly militant in the face of accelerating job losses. It also
indicated a more receptive attitude to the 'moral majority', represented by,
among others, Mary Whitehouse and her National Viewers' and Listeners'
Association. The social conservatism she represented was not new, and it did
not entirely displace the progressive spirit of the previous decade. But Sixties
attitudes, even if they were still percolating through society, now had to contend
with more vocal opinions hardened against them. Just as the old assumptions of
the Establishment had been questioned in the 1960s, those of the liberal elite
now no longer went unchallenged. And there were few signs of compromise or
understanding. The novelist Martin Amis, then in his first day job at the *Times
Literary Supplement*, recalled the slowly unfolding consequences of the previous
decade's destruction of formal hierarchies in matters of taste and judgement. By
the 1970s, he wrote, 'nobody's feelings or opinions appeared more authentic, and
thus more important than anybody else's'. The problem, he thought, was that

such feelings were rarely indicative of a new freedom in thought: they were 'admixtures of herd opinions and social anxieties'. Hence what followed was not the tolerant exchange of ideas but an increasing determination to close one's ears, speak one's mind, and draw a line. Questions of sex, language, taste, and morality were all connected, all politicized, and all polarized.[1]

Whether or not there had *ever* been a firm consensus on such matters, many within the BBC, whose job it was to hunt down public taste and measure the temperature of high politics, felt—indeed behaved—as if something had changed. The new government's determination to legislate for local commercial radio was a sign that the Corporation would not be having it all its own way and needed to be on its guard. Perhaps, too, the appointment as Director-General in 1969 of the committed Catholic, Charles Curran, in place of Hugh Greene, encouraged the belief among some campaigners that they could be pushing at a half-opened door—that a less wilfully progressive era at the BBC was within reach. Curran warned them that it was not the job of broadcasters to 'adopt a particular morality as their own and then to use the broadcasting medium in order to persuade everybody else to follow that morality'. Yet he talked also of 'moral responsibility' and of a BBC that 'depends fundamentally on the general assent of the public for its continued existence'. The Corporation, he argued, always needed to take account of 'the general climate of opinion in which we live, assessing what is within the bounds of a widely tolerant amalgam of views'. As for what was being said about the BBC in Parliament, Curran understood well that 'whether or not what is said is true and justified, the salutary effect is to produce a precautionary vigilance'.[2]

The BBC, an organization founded on the very notion of consensus, was not just faced with the need to bend to public opinion or to reflect its growing fractiousness. It was also caught in the crossfire. Its stated mission, 'to inform, to educate, to entertain' was accepted on most sides. But to inform *of what*? To educate *to what*? To entertain *with what*? There was little agreement on these questions. Curran himself dismissed 'common sense' as an appropriate guideline, since there was too little common sense to be found: 'the plurality of moral standpoints seems to be moving further from uniformity, or even consistency'.[3] From 1970, the BBC was being attacked with a new ferocity from both Left and Right, by progressives and reactionaries, by those disdainful of its caution and those offended at the liberties it seemed to be taking in matters of politics, taste, and decency. There was, so the former producer Antony Jay warned in 1972, 'a greater unity of opposition to the BBC in Parliament and among people of authority and influence outside than there has ever been before'. In return, there was also what *The Times* called 'an air of pugnacious insecurity' among BBC staff.[4]

In these circumstances of mutual distrust almost everything the BBC said and did mattered. A poll in 1972 of a cross-section of men and women listed in *Who's Who* showed they regarded the BBC as more influential than Parliament or the Church.[5] This no doubt proved to many MPs what they already feared: that power was slipping remorselessly away from Westminster and towards the broadcasting studios. The Corporation was caught in a paradox. It liked to claim that its task was to reflect society as it was, but there seemed little point in being the national instrument of broadcasting unless its programmes somehow made a *difference* to people's lives. And how could the Corporation claim that its programmes had the power to make things better without also admitting that they might, in some cases, have the power to make things worse? There were certainly plenty of people trying to put it right on the matter. Roughly a quarter of a million letters and phone calls a year poured into the BBC throughout the early 1970s, and very many of them were complaining about its programmes' harmful effects: too much sex, too much politics, too much triviality, too many left-wing voices, too many right-wing voices, too much bad language, and so on. Were listeners and viewers merely becoming more sensitive? Or were programme standards actually deteriorating?

What was Radio Four's role in this fractious debate? Against a background of what he called 'an ungovernable weariness at the problems of the world', Raymond Williams wrote in 1972 of how television was 'so pervasive that we project onto it many of our feelings about quite other things'.[6] But what he wrote of television applied equally to radio—perhaps more so: for throughout most of this period at least half of the letters and phone calls of complaint to the BBC concerned what was heard rather than what was seen. Among these, the vast majority were about programmes on Radio Four. One producer, writing about *The Archers*, complained that when the programme had switched from the Light Programme to the Home, it had swapped an easy-going audience for an 'acid', perennially whinging one. Radio Four listeners it seemed were more likely than any other section of the BBC audience to complain. They would complain about almost anything, too. But in the early 1970s there were two subjects that seemed to attract their attention more than any other: language and bias.

Often, complaints over language—usually about 'bad' language—were quite separate from those about bias. But just as often the two subjects were brought together, with particular lapses interpreted as indicative of a general sloppiness within the Corporation. The Radio Four audience included a great many people who had been listening to the BBC since the War, or earlier. To them, culture and politics were not matters of ephemeral taste but of eternal standards: any slip by the BBC was not just a fall from the glory days of Reith but easily regarded as an index of the nation's decline.[7] Indeed, it was the Radio Four audience that presented the BBC with conservative thinking in its strongest manifestation. For a BBC confronted by sharp differences *within* public opinion, and by sharp differences in attitude *between* its own liberal inclinations and its more cautious audience, deciding 'what went' was to be as fraught on Radio Four as anywhere. The wider context of what was happening in Television was important because in a single Corporation it often had a direct bearing on debates in Broadcasting House. But there were differences, too—not just as a result of the different nature of Radio Four's own audience, but because of the peculiar characteristics of the radio medium. Sometimes, Radio Four would seem like a place apart.

POLITICS AND BIAS

The period began with Labour politicians brooding over the BBC's June 1970 General Election television coverage. Wilson, already inclined to be suspicious, was now grumbling about the choice of topics on *Panorama* and what he thought had been a larger amount of time devoted to Heath in news reports.[8] Any lingering trust was destroyed by *Yesterday's Men*, a *24 Hours* documentary broadcast in June 1971. Its stated intention had been sensible enough: to explore what it was like to lose high office suddenly and unexpectedly. But it had poked fun clumsily at Wilson's expense, and succeeded in alienating not just Wilson but the Labour Party at large. Eighteen months later, the Conservatives were similarly affronted by another television programme, *A Question of Ulster*. This was originally planned so as to be scrupulously balanced between Protestant and Catholic, Loyalist and Republican, Right and Left. The Director-General was also adamant that its purpose was to reveal 'the complexity of the task which faced any Government in dealing with the Irish question'. Yet backroom man-oeuvring by the Stormont government and scaremongering reports in the *Daily Telegraph* ensured that when the programme was transmitted in January 1972 during a period of intense street fighting in Northern Ireland, it was in a climate where the expression of radically opposed views, no matter how calmly expressed, was regarded as the height of journalistic irresponsibility.[9] The Corporation successfully resisted pressure from within the government to stop the broadcast, but paid the price of further entrenching Conservative opinion against it. For the next year or two, the BBC's coverage of civil disturbances in Northern Ireland brought constant attacks from politicians and members of the public, who could not understand why the BBC did not explicitly support 'our' troops. They expected the national broadcaster to be partisan: neutrality, it seemed, smacked of disloyalty.

The reporting of industrial conflict followed a similar pattern. Against the background of an oil crisis, spiralling inflation, and the government's attempts to curb trade union power and enforce a statutory prices and incomes policy, 1973 saw a rising tide of strikes by miners, train drivers, and power workers that eventually tipped Heath into introducing the three-day week and announcing a General Election in February 1974 on the question, 'Who Governs Britain?' The country seemed deeply divided and the politicians' electoral rhetoric sharper than ever. When Labour returned to power, entrenched by a second narrow General Election victory in October, wounded Conservative opinion wondered if the BBC's journalism had exaggerated the economic and industrial crises of 1973–4.

Had it, for instance, given too much time to strike leaders such as Joe Gormley, Mick McGahy, and Arthur Scargill, and too little to managers such as Derek Ezra from the Coal Board? Members of the BBC's own General Advisory Council, which sought to represent lay opinion, certainly thought so. When it met in February 1974 the Council recorded widespread agreement that on industrial matters 'BBC news tended to stoke the fires rather than quench them'. For a Director-General who believed the BBC was 'the child of parliamentary democracy', this was a disturbing accusation: if it was biased, Curran stated, it should be biased in favour of 'the resolution, in circumstances of tolerance, of the differences of view which will then arise'. The real difficulty, as far as the Chairman was concerned was more basic still: the risk that the audience would simply cease paying any attention 'if one went on too long about the nation's problems'.[10]

Behind the flashpoints lay more fundamental concerns about the BBC's journalism. The anxieties of those on the Left were articulated most influentially in an article in *New Society* by Stuart Hall, then Richard Hoggart's deputy at the Centre for Contemporary Cultural Studies in Birmingham University. The problem, Hall thought, was not one of devious reporters deliberately slanting news, but an inbuilt, almost unconscious bias towards the status quo in the way in which news was produced. All sorts of entirely separate stories, he argued, were lumped together in catch-all categories such as 'law and order', obscuring political complexities; too much 'heady, breathless immediacy' prioritized superficial action over a discussion of root causes; shop stewards, civil rights activists, or strikers faced noticeably sharper interviewing, and on themes defined by politicians or industrialists invoking a spurious national interest.[11]

In the early 1970s, however, it was the anxieties of those on the Right that benefited from both political momentum and the weight of public opinion—or, at least, the opinions expressed by those who wrote letters of complaint. One of the opening shots had been fired in October 1968 by the distinguished former BBC reporter Charles Gardner, who wrote to the Chairman to grumble about a 'Knock 'em all' attitude and an 'inverted McCarthyism' having taken over since his time. Arrogant young producers, he complained, pursued flimsy propagandist stories to contrive confrontations 'in a hostile atmosphere bristling with false questions more devised to show off the personality of the questioner than to elicit the truth'.[12] The nub of the matter, he believed, was internal discipline—a theme quickly picked up by many in the Tory Party. In 1972 one of their backbenchers, Nicholas Ridley, was given the chance to inspect the BBC's operation at close quarters, and he later reported back to Lord Hill that too many staff indulged anti-establishment ideas. Since it was 'not for the BBC', but for politicians, to seek to influence people's views, Ridley suggested, the Corporation should ruthlessly eliminate 'propagandists' among its staff, give the Board of Governors more control over programmes, ensure that each programme was vetted by a senior manager before transmission, and either appoint a politician to advise on which news items were to be covered or accept the growing pressure for some sort of

Broadcasting Council to provide public accountability.[13] No one at the BBC could have accepted such an absurdly interventionist prescription, but the diagnosis was becoming something of a broken record. The problem, Antony Jay believed, was not so much with News staff, who were often recruited from Fleet Street and therefore reflected, if anything, a moderately reactionary political stance, but with Current Affairs, where a more questioning ethos prevailed, and one that had attracted the brightest of the graduates of the early 1960s—men and women who reflected the progressive consensus of their generation but not necessarily 'the views of most of the country'. On top of this, Jay suggested, the sudden expansion of journalism in the BBC since the 1960s had caused a serious break in the continuity of folk wisdom and editorial control: young recruits had been 'given their heads before they had found their feet'. The Prime Minister's Chief Press Officer told the BBC Chairman Michael Swann much the same thing in a private meeting at Downing Street in February 1973. Too many current affairs producers, he complained, were simply 'immature'.[14]

The BBC's response to such criticism was that it did indeed have a very clear system of editorial control, though its workings were complex and largely invisible. Journalism, the BBC argued, did not lend itself to Mosaic laws of conduct. The sheer number of programmes and bulletins meant that no senior manager could hope to view or listen to every programme before transmission. If producers were in any doubt they were required to 'refer up' to their departmental heads who might in turn refer up again, and so on, as far as Director-General or even the Board of Governors. But Directors-General had no wish to be inundated with referrals, and still less a wish to involve Governors in editorial matters. 'The merits of reference upward', the BBC stated, 'must be set against the depression of the morale of a creative team if it feels too heavy a hand on it.' Producers, then, were given a large degree of freedom to exercise their own editorial judgement, and this is where corporate professional experience was supposed to be influential in developing within staff 'a sense' of what was right. Criticism of programmes was usually by retrospective review. Policy evolved through the clash of debate in regular meetings—such as the news editors' meeting with the Director-General every Friday, and the meeting of senior producers, editors, departmental heads, and network controllers in Review Board every Wednesday. At each of these meetings, programmes broadcast during the previous seven days were reviewed, policy options aired, decisions made on a case-by-case basis, and minutes then circulated to about 150 senior staff so that policy filtered down through the various layers of the organization. Such gatherings were the beating editorial heart of the BBC's operation, where the talk could be funny, irreverent, cruel, and intelligent in equal measure, where egos battled for advancement, where front-line staff could challenge the decisions of their betters, where the 'peer group' set the standards. They were also, the BBC believed, proof of its collective and constant self-questioning.[15] The challenge it now faced was to convince a sceptical public that this, in itself, was still good enough.

This, then, was the wider context. But what impact did such anxiety over the BBC's journalistic standards have on Radio Four's own reporting of politics? During the 1960s, as we know, the fierce criticism of Television current affairs had always carried with it the implication that Radio was somehow more responsible and refined. In the 1970s it looked as if something of this feeling survived. After all, when Harold Wilson grumbled privately to the BBC Chairman in 1973 about the 'political inexperience' of BBC television producers, he made a point of contrasting their alleged inadequacies with the skill of Ian McIntyre on Radio Four's *Analysis*.[16] The audience for *Analysis* was tiny, of course. But it was an influential one, and like other programmes on Radio Four it gave politicians a greater opportunity to state their case at length without the unflattering gaze of cameras or the seeming inevitability of confrontational set-ups. Robin Day, who presented *Panorama* on BBC 1 as well as *It's Your Line* on Radio Four—and was therefore in a position to make a comparison between the two media—wrote of radio's superior ability to allow for the 'exchange of ideas'.[17] Managers in Broadcasting House invariably flattered themselves that Radio Four's coverage of a whole range of set-piece political events was 'cooler' and 'more authoritative' than Television's. And their satisfaction was complete when, in 1975, a systematic comparison between the *Nine o'Clock News* on BBC 1 and the 10 p.m. bulletin on Radio Four showed the latter's selection of stories—with a preference for issues over events—was more akin to that of *The Times* than to its television counterpart.[18]

Yet some of the mud thrown at BBC journalism in general was bound to stick to Radio Four. It was, for a start, the Corporation's largest single outlet for news, talks, and current affairs. In 1972 it broadcast 2,828 hours of it, compared with a mere 839 on BBC 1. And if one measure of the scale of its political coverage was the number of times MPs appeared, then here too it easily surpassed television: just over a thousand appearances in the second half of 1972—compared with below 300 on screen.[19] With political reporting on this scale, irritation was unavoidable. A great deal of it, however, was concentrated on one programme, namely *The World at One*. This, ironically, was the very programme Stuart Hall had chosen to identify as most typical of the BBC's in-built bias *towards* the status quo. Almost everyone else—including many of those who worked for it—saw it as virulently *anti*-establishment. One reason, no doubt was the pugnacious style of its presenter, Bill Hardcastle. Another was the programme's habit of putting outspoken newspaper journalists on air in preference to the BBC's own more cautious correspondents, in order to achieve what the editor unashamedly called a 'punch-up'. In any event, measured in terms of volume and stridency, it was *The World at One*'s free-wheeling mixture of news and comment that reaped the biggest whirlwind of public disapproval. Hardcastle himself was persistently charged with a bullying tone; the programme was regularly assailed in correspondence from listeners for being pro-Communist, anti-Rhodesian, anti-Ulster, anti-monarchist. One woman who wrote from Harrogate in 1973 was typical of the ire it faced: 'you, who live in the atmosphere of long-haired disaffection which now represents the BBC, are no doubt reflecting that hotbed of disloyalty... but you forget that you are NOT representing the British people'.[20]

The programme also attracted attention at a more political level. It was, for example, an early target of Mary Whitehouse, who, prompted by its coverage of debates over abortion in 1967, had accused it of being a 'platform for extreme, secular, humanist views'. And, according to the Conservative politician, Iain Macleod, it ranked alongside BBC Television's *24 Hours* as the Corporation's worst offender for left-wing bias. What caused most aggravation was its reporting of Northern Ireland. In August 1971, for example, when Lord Carrington wrote to the BBC's Chairman accusing the Corporation of 'daily sniping' at the army, he named *The World at One* as a prime offender. More disapprobation followed in September—this time from the public—when the programme broadcast an interview with the Provisional IRA's Joe Cahill.[21]

On the specific question of Northern Ireland, the BBC's anxiety was such that it moved quickly to protect its own flanks. At first within Broadcasting House there was talk of ensuring that moderate or conciliatory voices in Northern Ireland were given more prominence so that 'whatever the BBC did should appear to be constructive'. When it became obvious that events were sliding rapidly away from any conciliatory centre ground, the BBC decided that only tight top-down editorial control would do. In December 1971, having declared that it 'was not prepared to conduct a propaganda campaign... on behalf of the Army and the Stormont Government and against the Roman Catholic community', it unveiled new procedures. From now on, producers were told, each item about Northern Ireland on *The World at One* and its sister programme *The World This Weekend* would be heard before transmission by the Head of Talks and Current Affairs.[22] This was an extraordinary breach of the Corporation's usual editorial conventions, and left staff feeling distinctly queasy. For some listeners it went nowhere near far enough. To their ears, the 'unpatriotic' coverage of Northern Ireland was merely one example of a deeper and wider imbalance that needed addressing. Why, they asked, was the programme 'biased in favour of immigrants'? Why was Enoch Powell being unfairly treated? Why were Palestine Liberation Organization 'terrorists' being referred to on air as 'commandos'? Why was the Angry Brigade being given a platform for its views? Why had its sympathizers been allowed to be offensive to the Employment Secretary, Robert Carr? And why, when apologizing for the incident, had William Hardcastle been allowed to refer to the minister as simply 'Carr'?[23]

On these wider questions, editors in Broadcasting House generally stood their ground. Accusations about left-wing bias, the Director of Programmes said in 1971, usually came from those 'who failed to register the expression of opinions which coincided with their own and noticed only those which were opposed to them'. Often, these were listeners who had caught one programme, rather than the whole range of programmes on a given topic. Sometimes, they were reacting to a critical article in a newspaper, rather than the original programme: complaints always tended to double or triple in number once an alleged lapse in standards had been reported by Fleet Street. And sometimes, Review Board decided, they complained simply because journalists, whose job it was to 'reflect the world as it was', had revealed to them some of the unpleasant truths of contemporary life. There was certainly evidence that those who bothered to write letters represented the most reactionary elements of the Radio Four audience rather than the public as a whole. In the month of the June 1970 General Election, for instance, official complaints of left-wing bias received by the BBC outnumbered those of right-wing bias by about five to one. A much larger survey the following spring suggested that a majority of the uncomplaining audience believed there to be more Conservative than Labour sympathizers among the Corporation's presenters and newsreaders.[24]

All this made it easier for the steady stream of 'predictable' complaints to be heavily discounted as irrational displays, reflecting, if anything, the listeners' own biases. And whenever allegations seemed a little more convincing—or at least whenever they seemed to demand a fuller response—that, too, was usually managed relatively painlessly. Thus, when Enoch Powell complained in March 1971 of a left-wing bias in the selection of magazines reviewed in *The Weekly World*, its producer was asked to dig out the statistics. The two magazines most frequently quoted, he discovered, had been *The Economist* and the *Spectator*, followed by the *New Statesman*, then *Punch* and *Tribune*, while the distinctly leftish *New Society* trailed in last place: hardly evidence, as Powell had alleged, of marked political bias.[25] As for maintaining a balance in the number of MPs appearing on air, that was a little trickier. For much of the time between 1970 and 1974 the Conservative government struck many at the BBC as overly reluctant to make Ministers available for interview when requests were made; Labour, meanwhile, seemed to have a disproportionate number of better speakers—Wilson himself was described as having a 'dazzling mastery of technique'. In these circumstances, programmes like *The World at One* and *The Week in Westminster* had to be told at regular intervals that the left was being too heavily represented and that more effort was needed to put right-wing contributors on air. This 'touch on the tiller' was perfectly in line with BBC doctrine as formulated by its previous Directors-General, William Haley and Hugh Greene in 1949 and 1968, respectively. This allowed for equality of treatment *over time* so that the stultifying effects of having to balance points of view within a single programme could be avoided.[26]

Few of these internal mechanisms were visible to the outside world, however. And political life was becoming too fraught to allow even the *impression* of editorial laxity—no matter how exaggerated—to take hold. Something had to be done to allay the sense of public distrust. One important measure came from Ian Trethowan in January 1973, when he used his authority as Managing Director of Radio to recommend that, as far as possible, both sides of an issue were reflected within a single programme—a significant revision of the Haley–Greene doctrine.[27] There were all sorts of other minor adjudications that spoke of a more cautious editorial climate emerging between 1971 and 1974. It was agreed at Review Board, for example, that, while giving airtime to supporters of the Angry Brigade had been acceptable, allowing them to make gratuitous remarks was 'an error of editorial judgement'. Similarly, a feature on the Underground Press in *The World Tonight* in January 1971, timed to throw some light on the anarchic fringe in the week that the Brigade bombed the Employment Secretary's house, led to a ticking off for the reporter, who had apparently displayed 'a degree of enthusiasm for these publications not entirely appropriate'. When Nixon resumed US bombing of North Vietnam in 1973, the Director-General, having sensed a great deal of comment against the war and very little exploration of American thinking, laid down a general principle: 'whenever there was an emotional outcry or campaign', he said, 'the BBC's journalists must stand back from the fray and ask themselves whether they had paid sufficient attention to the other side's point of view'. As for the apparently more trivial matter of William Hardcastle referring to the Employment Secretary as 'Carr', this, it was agreed, had probably been an unintended slip in which perfectly normal newsroom jargon had leaked into the public arena, but the lesson was clear: 'more care needed to taken' if unnecessary offence was to be avoided.[28]

Trethowan's statement to a Review Board that 'one false note could cause untold damage' was typical of the smoke signals emanating from editorial meetings during this whole period. Week in week out, the language used on air was examined for any hints of partiality, interviews with politicians scrutinized for any unevenness in treatment, the selection of items in bulletins measured against the choice of stories in the national press. Often, discussion was highly defensive, consisting of retrospective justification for decisions taken: when, for example, politicians complained of too much gladiatorial combat on air, editors were keen to point out that if the tone on programmes such as *Any Questions?* was now more rancorous it was because the politicians themselves had become more adversarial, not the broadcasters.[29] Just as often, though, editorial discussions exhibited a rational spirit of self-questioning, and a willingness to change tack. And if it was true, as many politicians and members of the public suspected, that the natural instincts of many current affairs producers were left of centre—or perhaps more accurately anti-establishment—it was also true that the complex system of editorial control in Broadcasting House was, by and large, keeping such instincts in check.

Indeed, if anything, it seemed by 1974 as if the pendulum may have swung a little too far in the other direction. Edward Heath had indicated through his press spokesman that the government now had fewer causes for complaint, while accusations of bias from Conservative politicians in general had eased off noticeably.[30] This no doubt made life easier for a harassed Corporation, but it also raised new suspicions. It was already understood, both within the BBC and without, for example, that *Analysis* was in a broad sense 'right leaning'—not overtly biased as such, but exhibiting an intellectual fascination with much new thinking on the

Right: neo-liberal economics, Cold War politics, the damning testimony of
Alexander Solzhenitsyn (who had just been expelled by the Soviets).[31] However,
there were now accusations of more sinister forces at work. In the early months of
1974, the political journalist Tony Howard used the *New Statesman*'s 'Crucifer'
column to goad the BBC, hinting that Trethowan's Conservative sympathies had
led to improper editorial interference in his Radio directorate. Howard offered
only hints about what this meant. However, Ian McIntyre and George Fischer,
both men with known Conservative sympathies of their own, have since described
Trethowan's role in a programme they were making at the time. 'We knew',
McIntyre said, 'that people in the Party picked up the phone to Trethowan and
tried to lean on him, and that he did occasionally—as we thought—"sell the
pass".' On this occasion, McIntyre and Fischer had agreed that Maurice Cowling,
the conservative Cambridge historian, would be among the contributors to an
election edition of *Analysis*. 'When Trethowan got to hear about this', McIntyre
recalled, 'he called George up and said, "I'm not having that man in the programme, he's a fucking Powellite".' Fischer's defence was that Cowling was being
used as a historian rather than for his political beliefs, and the programme went
ahead as planned. McIntyre remembers Trethowan 'foaming at the mouth' and
instructing Fischer to cancel Cowling's contract for a future edition.[32]

The politics behind this intervention were convoluted. Enoch Powell, it is
worth recalling, had urged the electorate to vote Labour in February 1974 as a
protest against his own government's enthusiasm for joining the Common
Market. Clearly, at this precise moment, to be a 'Powellite' was not a badge of
honour in respectable Tory circles. Yet despite Trethowan's own antipathy, Powell
remained a figure of the Right—and certainly remained a politician in great
demand among other programme-makers on Radio Four. Even before his
infamous 'Rivers of Blood' speech in April 1968, calling for the voluntary
repatriation of immigrants, he had become a valued commodity for his articulate
outspokenness and unorthodox thinking, appearing with remarkable regularity
on programmes such as *Any Questions?*, *It's Your Line*, *Friday Call*, and *A Word in
Edgeways*, as well as all the usual sequence programmes. Indeed, no Liberal or
Labour politician came close to matching Powell's Stakhanovite ubiquity on
Radio Four: in 1972, for example, he appeared more often than any other
politician, except for Robert Carr and Harold Macmillan. This made for a
striking contrast with BBC Television, where in the same year it was David
Steel and Tony Benn who appeared most regularly. Powell's success on Radio
Four was helped, no doubt, by his willingness—unusual enough at the time—to
furnish producers with copies of his speeches well in advance. He also rarely
failed to come up with some highly quotable comment. As one editor confessed,
he was 'more skilful than any other politician at manipulating the media'. The
effect, however, was starting to look embarrassing. In 1973, the *Observer* used a
leading article to argue that Radio Four might just be giving Powell a little too
much coverage, while the *Guardian* accused the Corporation of being secretive

about the number of times he had appeared. By then, some within Broadcasting House were also finding his novelty wearing a little thin. He had, for instance, been a regular contributor to one of Radio Four's major documentary series that year, *Politics in the Seventies*. The series was a tour de force presented by Robin Day, winning plenty of praise at Review Board and in the press for its detailed and sophisticated analysis of British politics. But, one editor wondered, might it not have been more accurately called 'Powell in the Seventies'?[33]

These niggles were symptomatic of a much wider issue with which the BBC now had to grapple: for Powell was just one among many political figures who had come to be regarded as part of an overexposed 'Stage Army'. Balancing between parties had done nothing to remove the wider impression among listeners that there was simply too much political debate on air, that too much of it was being conducted in polarized terms, and that it always involved the same old voices. The problem seemed especially urgent after the February 1974 Election, since the BBC's own post-mortem suggested that audiences had been put off by both the sheer quantity of coverage, especially on television, and by its confrontational nature. The Chairman was convinced that, once again, the behaviour of politicians had been crucial in repelling the electorate: their positions had hardened and sharpened, he thought, 'to an extent at which resistance had set in'.[34]

It was possible, of course, for the BBC to help listeners by placing political debate in a wider context, adding explanation and interpretation. Yet when it did so it invariably faced the accusation that it was editorializing. So another solution, very much in the opposite direction, now commended itself. The BBC, the head of radio current affairs said, should stand *further* back from the fray and 'do no more than allow the combatants to make their points on the air'.[35]

One way of doing so was to allow the public to question the politicians themselves through a phone-in. This had indeed been tried with election coverage for the first time during the February campaign, when Robin Day chaired a new series, *Election Call*, every weekday morning on Radio Four. Each edition featured a senior politician from one of the three main parties, so that for the first time since the hustings had gone out of fashion, ordinary voters were able to question prominent candidates directly during a campaign, live, and with the possibility of entering into a brief subsequent discussion. It became the BBC's hit programme of the whole election. Between one and one-and-a-half million listeners tuned in to each edition—a much higher audience than for Radio Four's regular phone-ins. Every day, somewhere between 5,000 and 11,000 people tried to call; in most cases about 400 managed to get through and an average of eighteen callers were put on air. There were the inevitable complaints from listeners who had not been put on air, and from others who thought Day had been too rough with his guests. But the Director-General found the presenter 'friendly but firm', and he heaped praise on the voters for asking 'apposite' questions. What most thrilled managers in Broadcasting House, however, was that after several years of television supremacy, *Election Call* re-established radio as a considerable force in the BBC's election coverage. The programme had also been broadcast during the daytime, rather than reserved for the minority evening audience: an act of faith in the mainstream audience that had clearly paid off. Audiences dipped slightly when *Election Call* returned for the October campaign, but its reputation remained intact. 'Honours for the best bit of broadcasting democracy', the *Daily Telegraph* argued, 'must once again go to Radio Four's daily phone-in programme': Robin Day was now the 'champion of the people'.[36]

Election Call only provided half a solution to the BBC's difficulties, though. Its main limitation was that it never ranged beyond the familiar terrain of the three established Westminster parties. It certainly could not introduce to the airwaves any of the more radical voices or ideas that were beginning to make their presence felt in British political life. There remained, as Steven Bonarjee had told the Controller of Radio Four back in 1970, 'a whole host of minority views, causes and pressure groups, not all of them "round the bend" '.[37] The tetchy reaction to the Angry Brigade's opinions being broadcast on *The World at One* had been a warning of how objectionable many Radio Four listeners found the expression of such voices: listeners persisted, it seemed, in believing that all the voices they heard were somehow 'the BBC' speaking to them. Yet something had to give, for politics had not just hardened—it had diversified. The National Front's sudden intrusion into the 1974 campaigns showed how race had returned as an issue; the founding of the Gay Liberation Front and the Women's Liberation movement in 1970 symbolized a new vigour to sexual politics, and in particular, a new sensitivity among campaigners as to how they were represented on air. As the range of opinions stretched sideways, Radio Four had to confront this phenomenon, just as it had to deal with the manoeuvrings of the main political parties. And the central questions were these: who among the hitherto voiceless could speak? How often? And on what terms?

One test case came in 1971, when Vanessa and Corin Redgrave introduced a selection of their favourite literature for an edition of *With Great Pleasure*. There was inevitable shock from some listeners that such avowedly radical left-wing campaigners had been allowed on air. But, as Tony Whitby pointed out, neither of them had expressed support for a political party on the programme itself: they had merely identified with the underdog; it would be perfectly legitimate, he argued, to hear an equivalent broadcast from the Right extolling the virtues of tradition and the wisdom of elders. The Editor of the Radio Newsroom was inclined to agree. The BBC had an obligation to provide an opportunity for the expression of views held by any 'substantial section' of the population, he thought. Therefore the views represented by the Redgraves should be reflected in all sorts of other programmes 'from time to time'. 'So long as the alternative society existed in any strength', the Director of Programmes concluded, 'the BBC could not properly ignore it or refuse it some share of air-time.'[38]

Good intentions were one thing; practical results quite another. Take, for example, sexual equality. In a BBC still overwhelmingly 'masculine', it was inevitable that some women felt as if they, too, were members of the 'alternative society'. True, there were plenty working behind the scenes in BBC Radio, and there was the iconic presence of *Woman's Hour*, where women—and women's issues—were treated seriously on a daily basis. But even here the emphasis was still sometimes weighted unduly towards domestic subject matter, and younger producers on the team had to push hard to get more attention paid to what they described tentatively in meetings as 'changing attitudes to women's role'.[39] Elsewhere, the survival of a programme such as *Petticoat Line* seemed to say it all. Here was a programme conceived in 1965 as a 'mildly feminist' forum for the light-hearted discussion of listeners' problems, but which, in the hands of its regular presenter Anona Winn (who had first broadcast for the BBC in the 1920s), sounded more like a showcase of arch 1950s-style femininity. Winn's faithful following among older listeners protected the programme from the Controller's axe since, as Whitby put it, he would be hanged 'from the lampposts of Bond Street' if she were removed. That did not stop others in Broadcasting House from damning the programme as 'unendurable', and its contributors as 'female dinosaurs' who 'belonged not to the last generation, but to the generation before the last'. Something of the new spirit in feminism did finally reach the airwaves in January 1971, in a short series called *Militant Women*. Its presenter, Sue MacGregor, had read Germaine Greer's *The Female Eunuch* (1970), describing it as 'a trumpet blast of defiance', and had even attended a Women's Liberation rally in Trafalgar Square. Thus inspired, she included in the programme not just interviews with leading figures such as Greer and Eva Figes, but a whole range of radical voices urging a revolution in relations between the sexes.[40]

A separate battle to revolutionize employment practices was still to be won. Over the next year or so, Joan Bakewell and Mary Marquis both had stints presenting *Today* and Jacky Gillot presented *Newsdesk* alongside Gerald Priestland. But women newsreaders were nowhere to be heard. This was an oversight now being pursued vigorously by the pressure group 'Women in the Media', and it achieved a minor victory of sorts in September 1972 when one of its members, Hylda Bamber, along with Barbara Edwards, was asked to join the all-male team of continuity announcers responsible for newsreading on Radio Four. The *Daily Mail* marked the occasion by announcing that Radio Four had 'fallen' to Women's Lib. But two continuity announcers out of twelve still looked a rather dismal concession, and in 1974 Women in the Media entered a bad-tempered dispute with the man in charge of Radio Four's announcers, the Presentation Editor, Jim Black, over the need to go further. As it happened, the proportion of women auditioned for newsreading jobs had just reached exactly half; the number working as announcers was also about to expand to four, with the addition of Sheila Tracey and Jean Challis; two more were in training. Tony Whitby joined the fray by claiming that Radio Four's attitude to women newsreaders was by now entirely straightforward: 'I want only the best newsreaders and if that should lead to 100% women that's fine by me.' 'If it leads to 100% men', he added, 'that's fine also, except in so far as one has any reason to suspect that it may be due to prejudice.' Prejudice, of course, was precisely the problem he faced, and it was usually stronger among listeners than among colleagues: every appearance of a woman newsreader had been followed by a small but persistent flow of complaints in the postbag. It was, Whitby decided, a question of unfamiliarity. And the only solution to that, as he himself made clear, was to proceed even further in the direction now set.[41]

Once women had reached the airwaves, there were the inevitable accusations of editorializing. Jacky Gillot, for instance, came unstuck when she opened an edition of *Newsdesk* in November 1971 by drawing an analogy between the tarring-and-feathering of a woman in Derry and the treatment of contestants on that evening's Miss World competition—women who would, as she put it, 'have their faces smothered, their hair scissored and torn through metal, be almost stripped, be made to turn in unison so that an even larger crowd can laugh at—or look more lecherously at—their backsides'. This, one listener complained, was a 'most biased, bigoted and unnecessary string of comments'.[42]

Whitby suspected this reaction reflected 'anti-feminism prejudice'. But it was telling in more ways than one. For, as the range of opinions and voices on air steadily widened during this period, it was the 'tone' of presenters like Gillot— and for that matter, of men such as Gerald Priestland, Robin Day, Bill Hardcastle, and the rest—which gradually became *the* central issue in discussions of bias: *how* they discussed a subject was seen to reveal their own attitudes and prejudices more clearly than anything else. Signs of aggressiveness, irony, scepticism, even faint cynicism: all were seized on by disgruntled listeners as signs of partiality.

To senior programme-makers in Broadcasting House, however, the issue was whether this behaviour was being meted out in all directions equally. The 'sceptical' tone had an innate usefulness. According to one former Talks producer, Krishan Kumar, this was a direct consequence of the BBC's steady reinvention of itself as 'the "great stage" on which all the actors, great and small, parade and say their piece'. By playing the plain man, a presenter ensured that the BBC's willingness to accommodate such voices was never mistaken for sympathy towards them. The ubiquity of those skilled in the technique on Radio Four during the 1970s was therefore no accident. It was, Kumar believed, precisely the means by which, in times of sharp political differences, the BBC could 'give the appearance of allowing expression to every tendency, every movement, in British society—while at the same time ensuring that basic control is still in trained and trusted hands'.[43]

Kumar possibly imputes rather too much forethought into a process taking hold only gradually. It was also a process that cut both ways: plain man speaking prompted more rather than fewer complaints, probably because it reinforced the impression of the BBC being *anti*-establishment rather more than it did the desired impression of the BBC being neutral. Indeed, in the end there seemed very little Radio Four could do to escape all criticism of bias in its coverage of politics. True, many of its journalists tended, as the *Guardian* put it, 'by inclination and experience to be natural sceptics, distrustful of authority, interested in minority causes, prickers of Establishment and Whitehall balloons'. But, as it went on to argue, this was 'not the same as party political bias'.[44] The BBC had in any case taken some of the heat out of political attacks by demonstrating that its editorial supervision had become more watchful since 1970. Giving politicians direct access to the airwaves in the form of programmes such as *Election Call* had probably also helped in overcoming their suspicions about broadcasters' intentions. Assuaging the anxieties of the general public, however, was trickier, since ordinary listeners remained unfamiliar with the inner workings of the BBC. The Director-General claimed that all of what was said in letters from the public had already been said much earlier in discussions among the professionals. Yet it was difficult for listeners to appreciate the constant process of debate that attended most editorial decisions. The BBC kept trying to explain that when it aired each and every viewpoint it was simply showing its natural enthusiasm for the circulation of ideas. Yet to some people outside the BBC such tolerance was, in itself, a troubling Sixties concept. The Corporation had evidently not won over its audience to the idea that airing an opinion was not the same as subscribing to it. As the Director-General admitted, 'it is not the tolerance of the BBC which is an issue'. 'It is that of the audience.'[45] And theirs was a tolerance already being tested, so they felt, on too many other fronts—above all, perhaps, on matters of 'bad' language and decency.

'BAD' LANGUAGE AND THE PERMISSIVE BACKLASH

One of the great British social taboos had already been breached on 13 November 1965 when Kenneth Tynan used the word 'fuck' on the late-night television show *BBC-3*. Asked during an interview if he would allow the National Theatre to stage a play in which there was sexual intercourse, he had replied 'Oh, I think so'—and then added with characteristic mischief, 'I doubt if there are very many rational people in this world to whom the word "fuck" is particularly diabolical or revolting or totally forbidden.' It was, a *Daily Express* columnist declared with predictable irrationality, 'the bloodiest outrage' he had 'ever known'.[46] Others harrumphed that this was not the kind of language one wanted to hear in one's own home, and certainly not the kind of language that the BBC, as the historic guardian of spoken English, ought to be peddling. Over the following decade, language—'bad' language—was a perennial subject of dispute, both between the BBC and its audience, and within the Corporation itself.

Tynan's offence was bound to have attracted attention, coming as it did through the mass medium of television, watched by millions and written about almost every day in Fleet Street. Had he been speaking on radio, he would certainly have been heard by far fewer people. And, as producers in Broadcasting House endlessly complained, much of radio's output simply went unnoticed by journalists looking for a story. In principle, this relative obscurity offered the tantalizing freedom to speak to the committed minority in a way unacceptable to the great majority. In practice, however, since radio was invited into people's own homes, it was also expected—no less than television—to conform broadly to domestic standards of behaviour. It was all very well to go to the theatre to hear bawdy humour, or go to the cinema to watch an X-certificate film: one knew what one was getting. But broadcasting, with its mixed schedules, always had a certain unpredictability that risked taking people by surprise. As the Director-General reminded his staff, it therefore required an additional element of courtesy: 'the protection of bodily privacy from even verbal assault', he argued, 'is a reasonable claim on the broadcasters'.[47]

In some respects radio was in a *more* sensitive position than television. Drama producers, for example, had learned that the absence of visual clues in radio plays sometimes misled listeners into hearing something that had not taken place in the studio. A kiss and a sigh and a rustle of crinoline could mean something—or nothing: the action really was in the ear of the beholder. This ability to be infinitely suggestive was precisely the joy of radio to many dramatists. But it could—and did—lead to trouble. Several listeners complained of profanities they were sure had been added to the 1975 radio versions of the popular television drama *The Likely Lads*, though they had been mistaken: the original scripts were unchanged.[48] The message was clear enough. Words were *the* raw material of an aural medium. They reached listeners without the distraction of visual images and were thus fully exposed. In a service devoted to speech, the choice of words would rarely go unnoticed.

Naturally enough, therefore, the BBC had always exercised a tight rein on what could and could not be uttered on air. Indeed, the risk of something appalling being said was one of the motivations for the Corporation's historic preference for recorded and scripted programmes. In Reith's day, and even during the first years after the War, a producer who wished to put on air the voice of the ordinary British man or woman could never give a true rendition of the demotic style. Speakers were interviewed, their comments transcribed, then worked into scripts that were subsequently handed back to be 'performed' by the original interviewees in as spontaneous a style as was possible in the circumstances. This undoubtedly contributed to the BBC's reputation in some quarters for sounding unbearably prissy and stilted, exuding what had once been called 'finicking, suburban, synthetic, plus-fours gentility'.[49] Whatever changes there were in the 1950s and the early 1960s in making BBC Radio more informal, more colloquial, and more personal, the limits on inappropriate words had been immutable. The convention as it existed at the beginning of the 1960s has been described by one producer thus: 'the word "damn" was frequently deleted from Home Service and Light Programme plays, the word "bloody" had to be "referred" and the word "bugger" (and worse) was totally proscribed'.[50]

By the early 1970s, however, something was shifting. As the same producer put it, ' "damn" ceased to be damnable and the use of the word "bloody" was left to the discretion of producers'.[51] Even the classic four-letter expletive made its Radio Four debut—though not without considerable anguish behind the scenes. What, then, had happened?

Clearly, one long-term pressure for change had come from a general move towards decensorship in the arts. The mass sales of Penguin's unexpurgated *Lady Chatterley's Lover* following the failure to prosecute it for obscenity in 1960 meant, as John Sutherland put it, that even by 1961 'the novelty of seeing "fuck" in print was passed'; it had also established 'artistic merit' as a proper defence for publication. At much the same time the film industry had started to feel the liberating effect of having relinquished family viewing to television, with film censors adopting a more liberal attitude as the 1960s progressed. The cult films of the early 1970s—films like *The Devils* (1970), *Straw Dogs* (1971), *A Clockwork Orange* (1971), and *Last Tango in Paris* (1972)—provided ample proof that cinema had become much more explicit in a dramatically short space of time. Stage plays remained subject to the scrutiny of the Lord Chamberlain, whose decisions appeared arbitrary and, increasingly, untenable—so untenable, indeed, that by 1968 even his powers of censorship were abolished. This ushered in an age of new theatrical opportunities for writers wishing to comment on contemporary issues and shock audiences verbally and visually, or, as Kenneth Tynan himself demonstrated with his 'erotic revue' of 1970, *Oh Calcutta!*, for anyone wishing simply to titillate. Against the background of Roy Jenkins' liberalizing legislation, all this decensorship showed that the notion of individual consent was pulling ahead of the old imperatives of a uniform public morality.[52] And this set a clear challenge to broadcasters. The BBC could not work in isolation from the standards being set elsewhere: television and radio drew much of their source material from literature, cinema, and the stage. Their worlds were intertwined. Some accommodation with them seemed unavoidable.

Another pressure for change had come from within BBC Radio, and specifically through the appointment of a new Head of Radio Drama in 1963. The previous occupant, Val Gielgud, had been in place since 1929. During his thirty-four-year reign, he had allowed a few of his producers—notably Donald McWhinnie and Barbara Bray—to nurture the avant-garde and to dabble with Brecht and Pinter. But he had also remained resolutely unconvinced by much recent dramatic writing, and his tastes were deeply conservative: a preference for good plain stories, the classics, Shakespeare.[53] The new man was very different. Martin Esslin had been born in Budapest and educated in Vienna before fleeing the Anschluss and joining the BBC's European Service upon his arrival in Britain.

His learning was catholic, his reading voracious, and he spent much of his time at Bush House translating and producing hundreds of previously inaccessible European plays. In the process he established himself as the world's leading authority on what he called 'The Theatre of the Absurd', a category which encompassed the work of, among others, Brecht, Ionesco, Beckett, Frisch, Artaud, and Pinter. Esslin's 1962 book on the Absurdists, which became one of the seminal theatrical texts of the decade, signalled belated recognition by the BBC for a whole stream of dramatic writing that the British theatrical establishment had generally overlooked. 'All theatre managers are illiterate', Esslin said decisively on his appointment. 'None of them reads even French.' And he was determined that the Radio Drama department would now change all that.[54] Whereas Gielgud declared Pinter 'incomprehensible', Esslin was determined to offer patronage to 'difficult' plays, including, inevitably, plays by those who often used language in deliberately challenging ways.

If there was to be a dramatic avant-garde on BBC Radio, its natural home before 1970 was the Third Programme. It was here, for example, that Pinter's *Landscape* was broadcast in April 1968, having been denied a stage production by the Lord Chamberlain in one of his last acts before abolition. In the play, a middle-aged couple sit in a kitchen, the woman totally withdrawn from the outside world and recalling delicately her memories of making love by the seaside, the man raging coarsely at her, but apparently going unnoticed. The dialogue contains a few carefully placed expletives—ranging from the occasional 'shit' to a more explosive 'fuck' in the final scene. The Lord Chamberlain's Office had moaned about its 'ornamental indecencies' and demanded that Pinter made seven small cuts—which the playwright subsequently refused to do. Esslin, on the other hand, knew his Pinter. He argued forcefully that since only through the playwright's careful choice of words was the elusiveness of human personality conveyed, that the drama lay 'entirely in the language', the play should be performed uncut or not at all—and that BBC Radio should do it if the British stage could not. After careful consideration by the then-Controller of the Third, Howard Newby, and referral right up to the level of Director-General, there was general agreement that Pinter's work had artistic merit and approval had duly been given.[55]

Pinter was undoubtedly being treated as a special case, so there was no sudden flood of explicit language on the air. But a precedent had been established, and very soon other difficult plays were in the pipeline, threatening to stretch the boundaries of what might be permissible on air: one was *After Liverpool* by Jamie Saunders, which had several four-letter words; another was David Rudkin's *Cries from Casement as His Bones are Brought to Dublin*, which combined explicit language, gay sex scenes, and Irish nationalism in one magnificently provocative brew.[56]

As of April 1970, and the removal of many of the speech programmes from the old Third Programme required by *Broadcasting in the Seventies*, it suddenly became Radio Four's responsibility to handle linguistically explicit, sexually suggestive, and difficult plays of this kind. Indeed, there appeared to be something of an obligation to do so, if only to prove that the BBC's commitment to demanding work had survived the Third's death. Tony Whitby declared his plan in a memo to Ian Trethowan, on 6 March 1970:

The rather conservative attitude which the Home Service and Radio Four have taken in the past to what should be heard on the air in the delicate area of sex might have to be modified a little in the direction of permissiveness. One instance cropped up very soon after my arrival in the shape of a play which would formerly have been placed on Three without any objections from Howard about the language in it but which now falls naturally to Radio Four. It is a Danish play of some international repute called 'Brother of the Bride'. In order to establish our future policy I instructed that it should be rendered into idiomatic and probably dialectic English in our Northern drama factory so that we could see exactly what we were being faced with. It hasn't yet come back but will shortly and I will submit it with a recommendation that we should transmit it when we have reduced every unnecessary concept and expletive from it. This may well crop up from time to time in other areas. I should emphasise that I am not by any means advocating a relaxation which would go as far as the standards which Television permit themselves. But I think we can modify a little, and should.[57]

The Brother of the Bride was essentially a meditation on class, but it had at its dramatic core the sexual fumbling of two young people during a wedding. Whitby thought it 'brilliant and moving'. When the script changes had been made in Leeds he recognized, however, that they would still not be enough to avoid 'considerable protest' from the Radio Four audience. He was forced, in this instance, to cancel.[58]

Nevertheless Whitby had signalled a move, as he put it, 'a little in the direction of permissiveness', and producers of all types, not just those in Drama, were keen to test what exactly this meant. Might a documentary about the generation gap include a family discussion in which the son tells the father to 'fuck off', one producer asked in June 1970? The family was liberal minded, she explained, and the phrase fell perfectly naturally into the programme. 'I would only agree', Whitby replied, 'if it was absolutely impossible to cut without totally ruining the sequence.' In this case, it was eventually decided to 'fiddle the editing' so that the word itself was inaudible.[59] Ten months later, Michael Mason, then preparing *The Long March of Everyman*, wrote to his head of department, Lord Archie Gordon, requesting permission to keep in the phrase 'Roll on my fucking demob' for the programme covering the Second World War. It reproduced, he suggested, an archetypal *cri de cœur* of the time. 'The programme can undoubtedly be made without the word', he conceded, 'but if we do omit that one instance I think we do withhold a deep historical and emotional truth which the voice of Everyman himself did in fact choose to convey by using.' The reply, again, was a polite refusal.[60] A more equivocal response came in 1974, when the BBC's New York producer mooted the idea of reconstructing key scenes from the infamous Watergate-era White House Transcripts. One of the minor revelations of the Watergate scandal had been that Nixon and his entourage had displayed a prodigious appetite for swearing, but the transcripts themselves had blanked out their precise choice of words. 'To be most effective and life-like', the producer argued, 'we should substitute the most likely American expletive for each blank, e.g. "son of a bitch", "fucking bastard" etc.' 'After all the steamy words from Casement's diaries broadcast on Radio Three', he went on, 'a few "fucks" from Nixon might seem quite normal.' 'I am considering it as a possibility', Whitby wrote back, though there was no sign in the end of an unexpurgated re-enactment being produced.[61] Indeed, agonized procrastination or outright refusal was far more common than acceptance. The only—and possibly the first—fully sanctioned appearance on Radio Four of the f-word in this period came late in 1970, not in a drama, but in a discussion programme in which the director Lindsay Anderson used it, after 'due consideration upwards'.[62]

Despite all the anxiety generated, the offending word proved to be less of a problem for Radio Four than Whitby once feared, simply because it remained sufficiently extreme to prompt immediate referral up the editorial chain of command and for managerial caution to hold sway. The bigger problem by far was the infusion of *less* extreme language that, so to speak, slipped under the radar: the 'bloodies' and 'damns' of much ordinary speech. These were the kind of words that did not require automatic referral upwards, but which nevertheless caused real offence to some of Radio Four's most loyal listeners—particularly for the more religiously sensitive among them, who interpreted 'bloody' as a blasphemy to rank alongside 'Christ'.

It should all have been familiar to anyone who had witnessed the kitchen-sink plays of British theatre in the 1950s, or indeed to the millions who had been watching the 'realist' television dramas of the past decade, such as *Z Cars*, or Alf Garnett in *Till Death Us Do Part*. These were programmes rich in the linguistic verisimilitude deemed necessary to any portrayal of British working-class life. Yet while television had pushed ahead, like theatre and literature before it, radio's accommodation to dramatic grit came late, and by the early 1970s a dangerously pent-up desire for greater artistic licence had been created in Broadcasting House. Martin Esslin raised his own concerns at a meeting of Review Board in September 1971. 'It would be difficult for radio to adhere to its present standards', he suggested, 'as long as television continued to assume a much more ready acceptance of permissiveness on the part of the public.' Already, he declared, some of his producers 'had expressed fears that they would be regarded as "fuddy-duddies" if they turned their backs on some of the trends in this direction set by television.'[63]

Given the strength of British regional theatre in the early 1970s, it was inevitable that the BBC's own regional production centres led the way in introducing more gritty realism to Radio Four. From Leeds, the producer Alfred Bradley continued to supply the network with a wave of plays by northern writers, such as Stan Barstow, Barry Collins, Barry Hines, and Alan Plater. Birmingham, meanwhile, supplied productions such as *Filthy Fryer and the Woman of Maturer Years*, an early play from Andrew Davies, who two decades later went on to adapt several classic dramas for BBC television. *Filthy Fryer*, broadcast on a Saturday afternoon in October 1970, painted a rambunctious picture of contemporary teenage life in Britain. The dialogue avoided the usual four-letter expletives, and had therefore not been referred to London prior to broadcast. But it turned out to be peppered with the language of a schoolboy obsessed with sex. In the course of one hour, listeners heard seven 'bloodies', four 'Gods', three 'sods', three 'Christs', and two 'arses'—as well as plenty of lusty talk about 'milk white thighs', masturbation, and even animal sex. It did, however, also mention Hamlet, Sartre, Camus, and Marcuse. It therefore demanded, at one level at least, to be taken seriously. Esslin defended it as 'a very funny play and a completely harmless one'. Its conclusions, he said, 'were highly moral and it contained nothing to which anyone accustomed to television could take exception.' Whitby agreed that the play was funny and that it ought to have been transmitted, but he thought that in handling the subject of sexual fantasies indelicately, it was 'equally true that it caused gross and unnecessary offence which ought to have been avoided'. Howard Newby concluded a post-mortem by stating that he did not see 'any need to retreat from recent advances in frankness', but that the play highlighted 'the dangers broadcasters ran in dealing with what to many people were still delicate subjects'.[64]

This appeared to sanction a moderate relaxation in attitudes—coupled with a warning to tread carefully: a classic hedging of bets that left plenty of room for disagreement and confusion. How, for instance, could a programme such as *The Archers* adapt to the new taste for frankness? As a self-proclaimed 'everyday story of country folk' it was an obvious place to reflect the riches of demotic speech. Yet its status as a fixture of popular and utterly familiar escapism made any attempt at renovation fraught with danger. As Norman Painting, who played Phil Archer and wrote many scripts under the pseudonym Bruno Milna, made clear, *The Archers* was emphatically *not* 'full of the things newspapers are full of '. 'We don't reflect 100 per cent the permissive society', he suggested, 'I think we much more represent the silent majority... so you won't find sex and violence and rape and abortion and the pill thrust down your throat.'[65]

In fact, despite itself, *The Archers* had reflected something of the spirit of the 1960s. There were the libidinous intrusions of Paddy Redmond, the occasionally out-of-hand antics of young dancers at the Arkwright Hall social events, Jennifer Archer's tempestuous passage from beatnik teenager to unmarried mother. But while the plots tried to be 'with it' the dialogue had usually been hopelessly archaic. When Polly Perks and Lilian Archer fantasized about a sexual encounter with Sean Connery, they talked coyly about what it would be like to 'go away' with him. Such 'mincing language,' as audience researchers put it, appeared to have upset the elderly without convincing younger listeners.[66] More radical attempts to inject realism were only taken between 1970 and 1972, with a change of gear imposed from above. In 1970, the Director-General, along with Trethowan and Whitby, had expressed considerable misgivings about the quality of recent scripts by the programme's ageing creator Ted Mason, and word filtered through to Birmingham. Editors there were told bluntly by Trethowan that the series would be axed if it was not improved within six months. They, in turn, ordered *The Archers'* producer, Tony Shryane to make the series 'less cosy' and ensure it reflected 'current behaviour in society'.[67] Once Godfrey Baseley had been eased out of the editor's chair in 1972, and replaced with Malcolm Lynch, a scriptwriter from ITV's *Coronation Street*, storylines offered action of previously unimagined sensationalism. As the *Observer* noted incredulously, in one week alone Ambridge experienced 'a plane crash, a train crash, a quasi-rape and the church bells fell down'.[68] The dialogue, throughout, remained chaste. But amongst the torrent of letters and phone calls of complaint from listeners aghast at the new brutalism was a strangely large number accusing the series of allowing 'too much swearing'. Between ten and twenty formal complaints arrived at the BBC each week through much of the autumn of 1972, rising to more than forty a week in November. At one stage, the programme's editor was required to offer Review Board a 'firm assurance that the word "bugger" had not been used'. At first, BBC managers were mystified: no one in either Broadcasting House or Pebble Mill could recall ever hearing any offending words. After much scratching of heads, it was reckoned that complaints arose not from any decline in standards so much as the difference in style. Heightened drama was simply unattractive to the many people whose preference was for a quiet, friendly style of life. Like the real world, *The Archers* appeared to have become in some intangible way 'coarser'.[69] What was wanted was something a little *un*like the real world. Change, managers agreed, had been made too quickly and too dramatically and would have to be taken in hand. From the end of 1972, the serial reverted to a gentler pace and tone.

Trouble over *The Archers* was symptomatic of a wider lesson being drawn in Broadcasting House. While many producers wanted radio to catch up with television in matters of language and taste, many listeners apparently wanted Radio Four to go in the other direction entirely—to offer something of a safe haven in the stormy sea of social change all around. 'We don't want the standard of radio plays to sink to those of TV's' wrote one listener revolted by a *Midweek Theatre* production in 1970. The complaint was typical, and it was tempting to conclude, as many in the BBC now did, that the *more* Television pushed the boundaries, the more Radio Four might have to hold the line. Regular listeners thought the prescription was clear. One now wrote to complain of the general tone of irreverence and crudity he felt had gripped the network since the late 1960s. Every producer, he suggested, should be forced to remember the famous dictum: 'The more the times appear in revolt, the greater is the need for people of firm character who recognize the possibilities for good, to resist all evil and serve as a model for others.'[70]

How could Radio Four balance the desire of most producers to reflect a more permissive attitude to language in other media with the equally evident desire of many of its listeners to turn their back on it? Many members of the public no doubt imagined that the BBC had clear and unimpeachable rules, and that it was simply guilty of a breakdown in editorial control whenever they heard something on air that offended them. But beyond the requirement to 'refer up' when clearly offensive or controversial material was in prospect, producers were allowed a large degree of freedom in reaching their own judgement on questions of taste. And language, as far as producers were concerned, *was* more a matter of taste than of standards. While the latter implied firmly agreed boundaries, the former was something that shifted with the temper of the times and was always a matter for dispute. Staff constantly had to work out for themselves what was permissible and what was not. Their difficulty in the early 1970s, as one Light Entertainment producer put it, was that 'it had now become much more difficult to decide what was generally acceptable'.[71] Clearly, tastes *had* changed. But how much? And had they changed for everyone? More pertinently, had they changed for the Radio Four listener? Could some middle ground be reached, somewhere between the point where linguistic attitudes at large now stood and where Radio Four listeners believed them—or wished them—to be? This was the fundamental question that hung over much of the discussion about taste and language at the time, and it admitted of no easy answer. Whatever tribal wisdom existed on the matter was formed less through prescriptive rules than through the endless clash of opinion, the ongoing discussion of experience, a certain amount of trial and error—and perhaps, too, that 'liberal guilt' that Philip French had identified as characterizing all BBC discussions on culture at the time.

Take, for example, the acceptability of particular words such as 'bloody' or 'bugger'. George Bernard Shaw had declared as early as 1914 that 'bloody' was 'in common use' by 'four-fifths of the English nation'. By 1966 sociologists reckoned that about half the nation's youth were happy to use far more obscene words in everyday conversation. Yet in 1971 the Assistant Head of Radio Drama was still wondering aloud 'whether the coarseness of working-class life was not a figment of middle-class imagination'. Surely, he suggested, 'swearing was more common in middle-class families?' If he was right, the danger, as one of the BBC Governors pointed out, was that the relaxed attitude of all those middle-class producers at the BBC would be 'too easily transferred to the programmes' for which they were responsible.[72] The problem seemed particularly acute when it came to blasphemy. Radio Four, shot through as it was with threads of Christian worship, had about it what one drama producer called 'a vague moral Christian aura'. Consequently, for a small minority of listeners, religious expletives—and 'bloody' was put into this category by many—caused more offence than anything else. Producers, actors, and writers, though, did not have a natural sensitivity in this area, since few were avowedly Christian. Esslin, for example, insisted that '"bloody" had passed into normal speech'; others, that the word was not in itself blasphemous to begin with.[73] 'Bugger', by way of contrast, involved calculations of geography rather than theology. An *Afternoon Theatre* play in May 1972 that drew several complaints prompted Whitby to conclude that many correspondents 'had apparently failed to draw a necessary distinction between the North country term of affection pronounced "booger" and the abusive Southern term "bugger"'. That would not stop people in the south being offended, Howard Newby replied, though he agreed that the distinction might be valid.[74]

One way of navigating through the minefield of taste was to recognize that complaints over language were often about more than words alone. The BBC's Secretary, Colin Shaw, argued that there was probably in the British public 'a tendency to condemn changes in the use of words less for the changes themselves than for other changes in society which they may reflect'. If only the rude words would go away, they seemed to be thinking, then society would be different, that is, better.[75] One change that evidently rankled was the appearance on air of a wider range of accents than ever before. Some Radio Four listeners were particularly put off by Northern Irish voices, especially after the Provisional IRA's bombing campaign in England had begun in 1974. Quite apart from anti-Irish sentiment, the accent often led to charges of bad language where none had in fact been uttered. Non-'RP' English accents still caused trouble. Even *Thought for the Day* was attacked on this basis in 1973, when the Londoner Sir Bernard Miles was the contributor. Apparently, the Director-General noted sarcastically, it was somehow irreligious to talk about Jesus in anything other than standard southern English. In the face of such evidence, Whitby once declared in frustration that he thought the whole obsession some listeners had with bad language was simply an excuse for 'ventilating their marked bias' against any programme featuring the working classes.[76] Shaw's famous observation, nearly sixty years old, that it was impossible for an Englishman to open his mouth without making some other Englishman hate or despise him, seemed as pertinent as ever.

As for the portrayal of sex, it was recognized that here, too, listeners were often reacting against the subject matter itself. Homosexuality appeared to be an issue of extraordinary sensitivity. In April 1975, one play, which had centred on a lesbian relationship, prompted complaints that Radio Four was condoning 'depraved and revolting females'. Another, broadcast later the same month, was accused by one incensed listener of being 'filthy, disgusting, lesbian tripe'. Both dramas were defended vigorously at Review Board for being truthful, sensitive, and harmless. The Drama department, no doubt, was particularly alert to the nuances of human emotion on this theme: its Assistant Head was Hallam Tennyson, the old-Etonian, Marxist, pacifist, great-grandson of the poet—and a man in the process of declaring publicly his own homosexuality. But, as Howard Newby now told Tennyson and his colleagues, the standards that counted were external: 'what would cause not a ripple in Hampstead might give offence in Bolton'. Two months later, when *Afternoon Theatre* included another play about homosexuality, written by a clergyman and praised at Review

Board for being both responsible and sincere, Newby stated baldly that 'he did not wish to see too much about homosexuality for the rest of the year'.[77]

The best that could be said of this episode was that overt talk of heterosexual behaviour was treated with almost as much nervousness. *Stop the Week* featured in listener correspondence in 1975 when Kenneth Tynan reviewed an autobiography that recounted a young girl's rape. A vicar wrote from Tonbridge in Kent to deplore what he called the pornographic filth entering his house, and argued that the BBC was giving in to immorality and promiscuity. The outcry prompted one member of Review Board to ask whether 'a discussion which mentioned such matters as "loss of virginity" and "penis envy" was entirely suitable at 6.15 p.m.'. The Head of Current Affairs Magazine Programmes, Alan Rogers, offered his defence: the idea had been to bring a *Punch* magazine style of witty conversation to Radio Four, and 'if programmes were structured in such a way as to not raise the eyebrows of the most conservative listener then we should quickly cease to be of service to the younger listeners, who on the whole, find this programme an interesting one'.[78]

The mention of younger listeners pointed to a generation gap in attitudes opening up—one that many in the BBC realized they might not always be able to span. They knew from the statistics that, just as with the issue of political bias, complaints tended to be indicative of the letter-writing temperament—an older and more conservative temperament—rather than the mood of the public as a whole. A survey by the *Sunday Times* in 1973, for example, showed that fewer than two out of ten people in the public at large thought that swearing and bad language was a problem on the radio—though the figures rose to three out of ten for those over 65.[79] Given this evidence Martin Esslin suggested that the BBC's letter-writers were just 'cranks'. In any case, he argued, eight or ten complaints about any given play out of an audience of, say, half a million seemed perfectly acceptable.[80]

The letters could not be dismissed entirely, however. For one thing, they set a numerical benchmark. If the average radio drama attracted somewhere between five and ten complaints, it could be assumed that a boundary had been crossed whenever a dramatically larger number arrived. Andrew Davies's *Filthy Fryer* play attracted thirty-six complaints—four or five times the average. In the aftermath Whitby pointed out what he regarded as a crucial lesson, namely that any discussion of language and decency was not about some abstract standard but about what genuinely caused offence: 'If people were disgusted by a phrase then that phrase was by definition disgusting.'[81]

The point was crucial, because it showed that whatever Esslin believed, and whatever anyone in Broadcasting House might have wished, the Controller of Radio Four knew he had to work with the audience he had, old-fashioned, intolerant, and curmudgeonly though it might be. 'It would be wrong', Whitby told his colleagues, 'to broadcast *only* the kind of plays' of which complainants would approve. On the other hand, he made clear that their views could not be ignored. The task, in fact, was to ensure that Radio Four had programmes in tune with the more relaxed attitude of the time *and* programmes old-fashioned enough to reassure the more conservative members of the audience.[82] This reflected a classic compromise of the kind being articulated elsewhere in the BBC at the same time. In June 1971, for instance, David Attenborough, the Director of Programmes for BBC Television, suggested that 'while the BBC need feel no obligation to be in the van of those dedicated to knocking down verbal conventions in the belief that in some way this is a blow for freedom, neither must it allow itself to become permanently wedded to a particular set of conventions so that it is unable to include common demotic speech in its plays'.[83]

Here then was the consensual BBC view of the matter at its most delicately balanced. The BBC would not be in the business of causing deliberate offence, and it had no wish to go as far as cinema, theatre, or publishing in pushing the boundaries of language and decency. But if it ignored the changes in attitude of recent years, it would, as its Secretary Colin Shaw put it, 'quickly present a distorted picture of reality, and would invite rejection'. Above all, as the Director-General Charles Curran argued, though the BBC claimed to be neutral between the different sections of British society it was also committed to a 'Miltonic freedom of opinion and its expression'.[84] Such a broadly liberal view, magnified further down the editorial chain by a generation of producers inclined to favour a more relaxed attitude to language and taste, allowed the BBC to push the boundaries of the permissible gently forward, absorbing some of the pressure for more radical change while never quite neglecting the sensitivities of those most alarmed by the turn of events.

It was a pleasingly rational position. But as Curran and other senior managers in the BBC knew well enough, it was a position that had to bend to the circumstances of political reality. And in this respect, the moment for consensus had passed. By 1971 there were already plenty of signs that a backlash against the permissive trends of the late 1960s was gathering pace. There had been growing uneasiness for two or three years from those who called themselves the silent moral majority, but a series of set-piece events now seemed to give them momentum. During the summer, *Oz* magazine, one of the symbolic organs of 1960s liberation and iconoclasm, was charged with obscenity. When its Editor, Richard Neville, was sentenced to fifteen months in prison, the redoubtable Mary Whitehouse declared that it was 'a very good thing that the line has been drawn'.[85] In September, there was a rally in Trafalgar Square by the new Christian campaigning group, The Festival of Light, in which Mrs Whitehouse played a prominent role again. Afterwards, its leaders sent a delegation to the BBC to argue that 'broadcasting is not the place for any and every social experiment' and urging that 'the conventions of two or three years back be restored'.[86]

There was certainly a new urgency to debates within the BBC over taste and decency that autumn. In October, BBC plans for its own programme complaints commission emerged—to fend off gathering demands for a powerful external

Broadcasting Council to be established in order to keep an eye on the Corporation. At the beginning of November, Lord Hill held a special Colloquy of Governors and senior managers in the board room of Broadcasting House for a full and frank discussion of the whole issue. Two more Colloquies were held in February and July 1972. Throughout, the drift of the Governors' position was clear: there was a backlash against permissiveness and the BBC was 'underestimating' its power; if the BBC was trying to reflect current morality, 'the danger lay in reflecting only metropolitan morality'; if the London stage was happy to tolerate bad language and nudity, then perhaps the BBC should 'opt out of what seemed to be the mainstream of entertainment'. Against this rising swell of concern, managers argued that if the BBC still stood for freedom of speech and thought, people would occasionally have to put up with hearing things that they did not like; years before, the Managing Director of Television pointed out, the BBC spoke as with one voice, but 'nowadays the BBC was a platform upon which a great many people appeared to speak in their own way'; the BBC could not opt out of the mainstream, since it had to have the best artists, the best writers, the best directors; broadcasting, because of its nature, would in any case remain 'miles on the right side of that which was currently available in novels, plays and the cinema'. And so the argument raged. Curran concluded that the BBC's Governors and the BBC's managers were divided on the matter and could never agree on a single set of moral standards. He added that it was nevertheless their duty to apply their individual consciences in order to produce a consensus. And, given the atmosphere of criticism among politicians, campaigners, and sections of the Press, the overriding necessity would have to be caution. 'The BBC's greatest asset was its freedom', he told those assembled. 'It was necessary to behave in the present so that freedom was preserved for tomorrow.'[87]

What this amounted to was an admission that the BBC would do whatever it took to fend off a broadcasting council, and that some restraint on artistic freedom might be the appropriate sacrifice. This was bound to have a chastening effect at the programme-making end of the machine. Curran's words were instantly taken to heart by Trethowan, who was already jumpy about matters of language and taste, and who now used his position as Managing Director of Radio to rein in what he regarded as the worst excesses. With unfortunate timing, only a week after the Director-General had urged caution, *Woman's Hour* (still on Radio Two, but with highlights repeated on Radio Four) broadcast a pre-recorded interview with a 16-year-old boy, who had been condemning the paucity of ideas in the underground press: they could do nothing except 'fucking this and fucking that', he had said. All ten of the programme's producers, their editor Wynn Knowles, and the head of their department, Stephen Bonarjee, had considered the interview and found it acceptable, particularly in the light of its condemnatory tone. When it was broadcast, the BBC received a fairly muted twenty-four phone calls of complaint within the first twenty-four hours. The following morning, however, both the *Daily Mail* and the *Daily Telegraph* reported the broadcast in detail, and within a few days the number of complaints had risen to over 200. Trethowan put it about that the matter should have been referred up and that if it had been he would have vetoed it. Publicly he defended the programme, but privately he castigated all the staff concerned. 'As we learnt over *Yesterday's Men*,' he told them, 'the damage is done by the second wave of reaction—the people who did not hear the programme and fasten on the newspaper mythology.' Given the current climate of opinion, he went on, 'it was entirely predictable that the Press would seize on the incident, blow it up out of all proportion, ignore the admirable quality of the programme as a whole, and give the public the impression that even *Woman's Hour* had climbed on the BBC's well-known permissive band-wagon.' It was, he confided in Curran, 'a good example of the BBC getting involved in an unnecessary controversy', and he told him about the stark warning he had issued to heads of departments:

I took your theme—'preserving tomorrow's freedom'—and warned them that if we were to fight off the threats to our editorial independence over the next two or three years, it was essential to avoid incidents of this kind. I told them we cannot avoid controversy but we must endeavour to make sure that we fight on grounds of our own choosing, ground which we really believe to be worth defending.

Trethowan mentioned the BBC's reporting of Northern Ireland as a case in point. Producers attempting to push the limits of taste, he concluded, needed to see that 'we are not trying to avoid battles but rather to limit ourselves to the ones that really matter'.[88]

The BBC's wider reputation for its news coverage was what counted, he seemed to be saying, even if the price to be paid was playwrights and producers muttering about censorship. Hence Trethowan's choice of words, when, six months later, he vetoed a four-letter word in a Radio Four documentary about violence in schools: whatever the merits of the individual case, he decided, 'it simply is not worth the inevitable row'. Archie Gordon offered much the same reasoning when he denied Michael Mason his four-letter words in *The Long March of Everyman*. The outstanding argument against the use of the term, he argued, was one of political expediency: 'if excision is thought to save the body of the BBC, let us not be soulful.'[89]

A sense of tactical retrenchment was palpable as 1971 drew to a close. Review Board had already discussed the 'current reaction against so-called permissive-ness' as 'the new phenomenon' in September. There was, Howard Newby told his colleagues at one meeting, 'an undercurrent of unease among many normal, balanced people' about standards in radio programmes.[90] Having absorbed this analysis, Radio's senior managers sought to rise to its challenge. One response was to show to the public that boundaries did indeed exist within the BBC by producing a new, and widely advertised, set of guidelines for its staff. Drafts of a formal policy paper had been in preparation since the middle of 1971; what finally emerged was a manual circulated to producers—what the Press quickly labelled a Swearing Code Book. Its provisions made fascinating reading. Taste and standards, the guidelines stated, held 'different meanings for different people'. The use of swear words was therefore defended on artistic grounds: permissible when, for instance, 'any substitute would diminish the author's intentions without justification'. On the other hand, any gratuitous use would be indefensible, and the automatic need for 'referral up' was stressed with new vigour. Producers were reminded that drama should involve 'more than commissioning contemporary dramatists to write as they choose': the audience should be offered 'a balance of productions, the optimistic as well as the pessimistic, the provincial as well as the metropolitan'. Above all, listeners should have their expectations met.[91]

This last point was crucial, since it recognized that offence was usually caused when listeners were taken by surprise. One way round this was to encourage writers and producers to ensure that the style of each play was established in its opening minutes, so that listeners could quickly get the measure of what they were letting themselves in for. Scheduling was another tool. *Saturday Night Theatre* and *Afternoon Theatre* were both 'popular' and 'straight-down-the-middle' slots unsuitable for strong meat. Over half of the audience for the Saturday play was usually made up of women over 50—precisely the part of the population that surveys showed were most concerned with 'bad' language. *The Monday Play*, on the other hand, was a place where more demanding plays could be accommodated: its minority audience, Whitby believed, 'was well used to tough material'.[92]

Taste, it was reckoned, grew to match that upon which it was fed. But all tastes needed to be catered for. The more demanding kind of drama was possible, it was implied, only because Radio Four could claim to be offering plenty of popular and pleasurable output elsewhere: the one acted as a shield for the other. Some material, of course, had to be kept off Radio Four entirely, and placed on Radio Three. Readings from Pamela Hansford Johnson's *The Honours Board*, for example, were ruled out, on the grounds that there was simply too much sexual frankness in it. 'A satyr, a lesbian and a dipso all in one school is too much to take', a producer decided, though he confessed to having read it 'with some pleasure' himself.[93]

By February 1974, Mary Whitehouse was able to tell her supporters in the National Viewers' and Listeners' Association that 'constant pressure of public opinion has had its effect' on broadcasting.[94] She articulated a quiet satisfaction among campaigners for the 'moral majority' that the liberal instincts of the 1960s, once apparently running amok in the BBC under Greene, had been held in check.

Yet they had not quite had things all their own way. Radio Four, though more cautious in its handling of language in 1974 than in 1970, had by no means reverted to the standards of an earlier generation. If there were fewer 'bloodies' on air, it was as much to do with the natural dissipation of that pent-up thirst for social realism and bawdiness which had erupted in the late 1960s as it was to any prevailing climate of censorship. Dramatists and producers had got the desire to shock out of their system. Meanwhile, even some of the more popular strands, such as *Saturday Night Theatre* and *Afternoon Theatre* were transmitting plays on the sort of intimate themes that would once have been unthinkable on the old Home Service. The transmission in June 1974 of Bill Naughton's *All in Good Time*, which charted a couple's inability to consummate their marriage, was just one example of the sort of drama now considered perfectly suitable for the old family slot—provided that 'excessive' bad language was avoided. Later the same year, David Niven read extracts from his memoirs, *The Moon's a Balloon*, much to Mary Whitehouse's disgust, since they referred quite explicitly to his earliest sexual exploits. The Controller defended the broadcasts on the grounds that they had been told in a witty and highly moral manner. Even the formal guidelines issued to staff in 1973, while setting clear boundaries on the use of offensive words, had invited producers and writers 'to approach contemporary life in a contemporary way'.[95]

There was, in other words, plenty of evidence that the liberal instincts of the 1960s had been gradually absorbed by Broadcasting House, and were even surviving the more cautious atmosphere of the 1970s. The contradictory mixture of bravado, self-doubt, and anxiety over matters of language displayed by programme-makers was a vivid example of what Arthur Marwick called 'measured judgement'—the British Establishment's ability to tolerate change by taming it, rather than choosing to embrace it or to reject it wholesale.[96] It was an example, too, of what Harold Perkin called 'the professional ideals of rational discourse', which, since the 1960s, had come to oppose ancient taboos and moral obfuscation.[97] Tony Whitby demonstrated this magnificently when he came to defend a programme under attack for its detailed discussion of unwanted pregnancies:

We should not allow ourselves to be put in the position of having to demonstrate that broadcasting a certain programme does no damage of any kind; with the implication that if it creates one pennyworth of harm it should therefore not be transmitted. This is an utterly false proposition. *Not* broadcasting certain types of programme is also damaging and the good that we do by airing certain subjects in a responsible way, though it may well be immeasurable, must be set in the balance against any incidental harm . . . A broadcasting service which avoids difficult subjects because they create difficult questions of public relations or because they can be shown to have damaging effects in some ways, may be shirking its public responsibilities. Certain questions need to be aired and discussed in a responsible society if that society is to grow in a healthy way.[98]

This was a defence that cut to the heart of the BBC's sense of moral purpose. But not everyone saw things that way, for just as Radio Four's treatment of 'bad' language demonstrated 'measured judgement' and 'rational discourse' it also demonstrated the strength of the permissive backlash in the early 1970s. Indeed, Radio Four was the kind of institution where the forces of conservatism could be seen at their most vivid. Any progress had to face the pressure of unending complaint from a small but vociferous letter-writing public devoted to the idea of a BBC enforcing eternal standards, rather than reflecting the shifting sands of taste. Behind this protesting vanguard, the Radio Four audience at large was disproportionately middle-aged and middle class, and, as Trethowan had put it, 'a shade more authoritarian than the country as a whole'.[99] 'Measured judgement' of what would go and what would not was therefore destined to find a median point of compromise somewhere just to the right of the cultural centre ground. A gauging of public opinion and the impact of press coverage: this was never entirely absent from deliberations in the BBC—at least, not in Broadcasting House. Indeed, knowing 'what goes and what does not' had always been an essential task of the BBC producer. It undoubtedly meant that many programmes were made with staff looking over their shoulders. There could be a thin line between measured judgement and paralysing caution.

Above all, measured judgement and rational discourse was mired in political calculation: a need for the BBC to keep its powder dry for what it saw as its more important battles: its fights with politicians and the public over accusations of bias in its journalism, and its efforts to keep external regulation at bay. Sometimes these forces seemed powerful enough to overwhelm what had been achieved. By the summer of 1975, Martin Esslin, whose Drama Department had faced so much of the criticism over the years, was expressing deep frustration. BBC Radio, he complained, was *still* applying much more rigid standards on questions of language and permissiveness than those in Television. To accept different standards was 'to perpetuate the myth that radio was designed for old ladies in Littlehampton'. It was, he concluded, in danger of becoming 'the medium of the nostalgic people'. Almost a year later, and just before his retirement, he appeared to lose heart completely. Radio Four, he told colleagues, 'had not really adjusted to the contemporary world': should the BBC not simply declare that Radio Four was 'the old people's channel' and keep it that way? No, the Controller replied, reminding him of all the progress of the past ten years. But given the natural tendency of people to want to escape from 'present troubles' one conclusion was inescapable: a little nostalgia was a harmless, even desirable, thing. Modernity, it appeared, would have to be handled with caution for a little while longer.[100]

5

Crises

'Everywhere there are new developments, new indignities; the intelligent people survey the autumn world, and liberal and radical hackles rise, and fresh faces are about . . .'

The History Man, Malcolm Bradbury, 1975

TO LEAD OR TO FOLLOW?

On Friday 10 January 1975, various BBC panjandrums—Governors, Advisory Council members, members of the Board of Management, and a small handful of programme-makers—all made their way to Ditchley Park, a secluded country house in the heart of the Cotswolds where Winston Churchill had spent time during the War. There, they were joined for the weekend by a select group of newspaper editors, clergymen, trade unionists, and academics, all concerned in one way or another with broadcasting. Safely ensconced amid the marble grandeur, they spent three days asking themselves one deceptively simple question: was it the BBC's role to reflect or to lead?

Everyone agreed that it was a question too big to provide an easy answer. Yet it seemed to get to the heart of all the agonizing of the past decade: agonizing over accusations of politics and bias, over permissiveness and bad language, over whether the right balance had been struck between programmes that demanded attention and those that could be heard inattentively in the background, over the need to move with the times while respecting the yearning for familiarity. It was perhaps inevitable that the discussions at Ditchley were inconclusive. The Chairman of the General Advisory Council, Lord Aldington, made clear his position from the outset. 'I have always had the view', he told guests, 'that the BBC should lead.' By this he meant that the BBC should be seeking to increase understanding, 'which includes tolerance', and if it was partisan, it was only in the sense of preferring 'truth to falsehood, and peace between men and women'. It was a classic statement of good liberal intentions. But it was one neatly balanced by a different, more calculating assessment of the BBC's public role. Broadcasting, it was also pointed out, 'existed by gift of Government.' The BBC, though infused with principles of free and rational debate, could never stand apart from the climate of public and political opinion. It was the BBC's eternal predicament that both these statements were right. And therefore hardly surprising that the nearest the weekend's discussions came to finding an answer was this: that the BBC should reflect *and* lead. As for the practical implications of such a prescription, that too was opaque and perceptive in equal measure: 'There is no consensus . . . but you ignore it at your peril.'[1]

Given the presence of debates like this, the way in which Radio Four was developing by the middle of the 1970s could never simply be an internal Broadcasting House matter, nor even solely a BBC matter. It depended on a wider relationship with society and with politics, with the drift of cultural debate and the tenor of intellectual life. It also depended on pragmatic matters: money, vested interests, personalities, the competition for listeners. No matter how decisive a Controller such as Tony Whitby could be, so much remained beyond his grasp and so much remained unresolved. It was clear, for example, that he had wanted Radio Four to be a more varied network than the old Home Service, and one with a more popular touch. He had wanted it to be entertaining as well as informative, intellectually demanding at times and sometimes even prepared to cause offence. But new programmes depended on money, which might not always be forthcoming. New ideas depended on good working relationships with the various programme-making departments—outside London as well as in Broadcasting House. Yet there was no guarantee that the pain of *Broadcasting in the Seventies* had yet been forgiven, that production departments could deliver, or that strengthening regional demands for autonomy could be contained. And the desire to be intellectually demanding had to compete with the desire to be more inclusive and to protect audience ratings at a time when there was more competition in prospect.

In all these respects, the outlook was unpromising. Indeed, by 1975 matters had conspired to create a series of crises within Broadcasting House that left Radio Four feeling less sure of itself than at any time since 1970. This uncertainty defined a transitional period between the reconstructions of 1963–73 and a 'Counter-Reformation' that was to follow in the late 1970s. To capture the sense—and the complexities—of this transition, we need to move away from the Controller's office and the arguments over the qualities of individual programmes that have dominated the last two chapters and look at Radio Four through different lenses. We need to examine the underlying intellectual debates about the whole purpose of Radio Four—debates that were conducted among a network of programme-makers and production departments throughout the BBC. We also need to set these grand debates against more mundane, but no less decisive, concerns over resources—concerns that could never be absent when discussing something as expensive and labour intensive as Radio Four but which undoubtedly reached a new intensity as the middle of the decade arrived.

THE REGIONS

One underlying assumption of the BBC's was that Radio Four was a national service. And, technically speaking, so it was: a service, as it had been since 1939, for the whole of the United Kingdom and its people. But beyond the confines of Broadcasting House this particular claim started to unravel—and did so at a faster rate the further north and west one travelled.

One of the reasons for this was that ever since Reith's days the Corporation had shown a remarkable tendency both to centralize its administrative powers and to assume that 'the best of everything' was in London. As for where matters stood in 1971, we have the words of the head of BBC Radio's current affairs programmes, Stephen Bonarjee, in a memo to Tony Whitby: 'It is notorious that most producers and programme executives are more familiar with the Costa Brava than with Birmingham and Manchester, let alone Cardiff and Glasgow. Few of them have been north of Barnet.'[2]

Bonarjee exaggerated. But he also repeated a widespread suspicion: that Radio Four remained dangerously aloof from the English regions and the Celtic nations. In a place such as Manchester the general sense, as one of the producers working there put it, was of 'a highly metropolitan, southern-orientated network that took a certain amount of output from outside London, but, one felt, only on sufferance'. Hence the awkward questions that kept arriving at Broadcasting House. Why did Radio Four not cover the Eisteddfod as the Home Service had done, asked a Welsh listener? Why, when the Arts Council had done so much to develop interest in regional culture, was the BBC failing in its 'similar duty' to the people of the North, asked one of the BBC's advisory councils? Why, indeed, did Radio Four sound 'so alien' to most of the country, asked one of its own producers?[3]

If Radio Four was steadily becoming too metropolitan—or, as Bonarjee put it, 'too London suburban'—the obvious question was this: what could, or should, be done about it? In an age of rising nationalist sentiment in Scotland and Wales, and at a time when the BBC was itself extolling the virtues of devolution through its commitment to local radio in England, it seemed that any hint of metropolitanism would be stamped out. After all, as Philip French pointed out, such was the perceived virtue in all things regional by now that 'the word "provincial" was banned' as unnecessarily demeaning, even obscene.[4] For many in Broadcasting House, however, there were perfectly good reasons for arguing that unless the centre of gravity in Radio Four was kept firmly in London, the regional tail would soon be wagging the national dog—a horrible inversion that threatened efforts to give the network a stronger overall identity, threatened programme standards, and—quite apart from anything else—threatened the London departments' dominance over limited resources. There would therefore be firm limits on whatever devolutionary tendencies Radio Four might wish to pursue in an ideal world. Whether the result would be a workable compromise, or the worst of both worlds, remained to be seen.

Structures certainly strove for a reasonable balance. But they were complicated and were, in any case, in flux. During the 1950s and 1960s the main guarantee that a national service reflected more than the life of the capital had come through a 'federal' arrangement. The Home Service, and then Radio Four, was broadcast not right across the country from one single powerful transmitter on one fixed frequency, but through a series of medium wave transmitters, each with a limited 'footprint' of transmission. These transmitters were linked for most, but not all, of the day. Millions of people therefore listened, not to 'the Home Service' or 'Radio Four', but to a Scottish, Welsh, Northern Irish, North of England, West, or Midland Region variation of it, with several hours a day of locally produced programmes interlaced with others supplied from London. Controllers in London could decide that a programme made in one Region might be of interest to listeners elsewhere and rebroadcast it as part of the 'Basic' service. Equally, Controllers in, say, the 'Scottish Home Service' or 'Radio 4 Scotland', were free, just like those in Wales and in Northern Ireland, to 'opt out' of almost all of the basic London service if they wished. The financial resources available in Glasgow, Cardiff, and Belfast, however, were never sufficient to fill the schedules with more than a modicum of truly popular home-made programmes. Series such as *The McFlannels*, *Caniadaeth y Cysegr*, or *The McCooeys* remained exceptional, rather than the norm. As in the English Regions, a large quota of London-made programmes continued to make up the overall mix.[5]

Some critics, such as the Scottish Talks producer John Gray, had complained that much of regional programming did little in any case to reflect contemporary identities: Scottish broadcasting, he argued, 'consistently looked backwards' and was often tartan wrapped.[6] There was some agreement, too, that whatever their programme achievements since the 1930s—and they were many—the English Regions made little geographical sense. Their borders were based not on any real social or cultural logic but on the 'reach' of the various transmitters. Hence North Region extended deeply into the Midlands and Lincolnshire, Midland Region stretched from the Welsh border to East Anglia, and West Region came as far east as Brighton. Each, as Briggs has pointed out, was capable of feeling isolated in terms of 'staff, professionalism, operations, and general thought from the central body of the Corporation'.[7]

Yet despite all this, the federal structure had one important and jealously guarded dimension. Control over scheduling, technically at least, was vested in the regional editors, and this allowed them to add their own flavour to the raw ingredients of the 'Basic' service. In the language of Broadcasting House this was called 'opting out'; from the regional end of the machine it was regarded more as a selective process of opting *in* to London. Either way, it was a system that allowed the Regions, not London, to determine precisely how 'metropolitan' or otherwise Radio Four sounded to a listener in any particular part of the country.

Broadcasting in the Seventies forged a different relationship. After 1970, Radio Four in Scotland, in Wales, and in Northern Ireland continued much as before, drawing heavily on Radio Four in London but inevitably including more and more of their own programmes as the desire for separate national identities strengthened. English regional diversity, on the other hand, was supposed to be reflected through a chain of some forty self-standing local radio stations: the old English Regions were abolished, thereby creating a more uniform, 'national' Radio Four. Or rather, the Regions were *almost* abolished. As Radio Four was still distributed through a series of medium wave and VHF transmitters, the technical possibility remained of different parts of the country 'opting out' of Radio Four at agreed times of the day. It allowed those parts of the country still without their own BBC local radio station to continue receiving a local news service via the Radio Four transmitters. Other parts of the country also persisted in claiming a minimal opt-out. Listeners in the South-West, for example, were offered *Today from the South and West*; those in the North had *Talkabout*; Midlands listeners could hear *Regional Extra*.[8] Over time, more and more of these bespoke programmes disappeared. But even in 1975 a rump remained in Plymouth and Norwich, the two largest urban areas in England still lacking a BBC local station of their own.

Such residual opt-outs were a constant headache for network schedulers in London. To avoid messy 'junctions' on air, each had to occur at a precisely agreed time. And this meant that just when programme-makers were keen to create more flexibility, and, in particular, to create more space for live coverage, Radio Four was forced to retain certain fixed points in its schedule. Northern Ireland, for instance, wanted to opt out of *Today* for its own news service. *Today*'s editor in London complained this had 'bedevilled' his producers for years, preventing them from ever letting a report or interview run beyond what he called the 'notorious "25 past opt-out"'. Other regional editors demanded that the 'first edition' of *Today* should never trail any items featured in its 'second edition', so that they too could opt out of the programme halfway through without confusing their own listeners.[9] To any presenter trying to hold it all together in the London studio, it felt, as John Timpson once put it, like presiding over 'a series of hiccups'.[10] To BBC managers seeing large parts of the country deserting the 'second edition' of *Today*, what was most disturbing was the effect on audience ratings. There was an editorial consideration, too. As the Director of Programmes saw it, anyone catching only half of Radio Four's main breakfast programme would miss 'important new material, particularly in times of major national or international crisis'. From the Broadcasting House perspective, then, the piece-by-piece extinction of regional opt-outs was a brutal necessity and a consistent long-term goal.[11]

This drive to centralize control of the schedule had to be balanced by some other guarantee of a regional dimension to Radio Four's programmes. And after 1970, this was supposed to be achieved through the recasting of Birmingham, Manchester, and Bristol as 'Network Production Centres', rather than as headquarters of large regional hinterlands. The change was not just nominal. Instead of filtering output *from* London, their task now was to provide a steady flow of programmes and ideas in the other direction—*to* London for broadcasting nationwide. In this way, perspectives on life outside London might be woven into the overall fabric of output. This sounded a reasonably fruitful solution. But it put Controllers and Departmental Heads in Broadcasting House in the position of being powerful customers who could pick and choose between different suppliers—and the Network Production Centres were therefore nervously dependent on the tastes of those running affairs in London. Each Centre had some staple properties of its own, providing a toehold on the schedule. Bristol produced *Any Questions?* and *Any Answers?* and had a tradition of making natural history programmes; Birmingham had suzerainty over *The Archers* and farming programmes; Manchester looked after *Gardeners' Question Time* and *A Word in Edgeways*. These were the bread-and-butter commissions, and the loss of any one of them would have been a deathblow. As one Network Centre editor put it, 'you needed a focal point out of London: you needed to huddle around something for warmth'.[12]

But these programmes were never going to be enough to keep the small group of producers under the Centres' control in gainful employment. Each was therefore engaged constantly in pitching to London a stream of ideas for the limited number of 'ad hoc' programmes on the Radio Four schedule. Success in this arena was far from guaranteed.

Bristol, for instance, had a very mixed record. It did well enough in securing extra commissions for book readings, partly, no doubt, because of the presence of Pamela Howe, who had first worked in the London Features Department in the 1940s and had become celebrated for her literary acumen. She had been the first to spot the appeal of Winifred Foley's handwritten memoir of a 1920s childhood in the Forest of Dean, and turn it into a *Woman's Hour* serial and subsequently the best-selling book, *A Child in the Forest*. She also produced Martin Jarvis's reading of Richmal Crompton's *Just William* stories and continued, alongside Philip Larkin, to champion a revival in the reputation of Barbara Pym. Most programme proposals with her name attached—literary quizzes and documentaries, as well as readings—were assured of a good reception in London.[13] Attempts by Bristol to offer archaeology programmes went less smoothly. *The Changing Past*, which first ran in 1968, had coincided nicely with a surge in 'rescue' archaeology. But by 1975 it was getting audiences of fewer than 100,000. A new series, *Origins*, was offered the following year with the professed aim of 'attracting a wide lay listener-ship'. Guidance from London had been quite specific: the new programme needed to 'include drama, romance and excitement'. As one manager urged, listeners were 'keen to learn—provided no one implies that they are being taught'. The first editions of the new programme, however, were savaged at Review Board for consisting of 'archaeologists speaking to archaeologists'—a damning phrase that echoed the old criticism of the Third, namely that it consisted of 'dons talking to dons'. The series was relaunched and eventually earned warm praise for having hit 'the right level'—'avoiding the pitfalls of being either too popular or too academic'—but only after dark hints that responsibility might be handed over to London.[14] Negotiations had left little room for doubt as to where the balance of power now stood.

Manchester, which as the headquarters of the old North Region probably had the most distinguished history of all the English Regions for its pioneering documentaries of the 1930s, seemed to find life even harder under the new regime. Cricket coverage at Headingley and Old Trafford, along with the local presence of several distinguished orchestras, ensured it was rarely underemployed on Radio Two and Radio Three. Its ad hoc commissions for Radio Four were more restricted. High spots were provided by Alfred Bradley, busy directing a stream of drama productions from the Leeds studios, and by the Centre's persistent flair in producing quizzes and panel games such as *Round Britain Quiz*. But its problem was that what it did best—fashioning informative, delicately scripted, beautifully crafted documentaries mixing narration and actuality in the 'classic' style, and especially ones focused on examining social conditions—no longer coincided with what its most important customer, Tony Whitby, was necessarily looking for. As Controller, he had made clear he wanted fewer 'searing and miserable' documentaries on the schedule. He had also raised fundamental doubts about the kind of techniques being deployed in their making. Of Charles Parker—a Birmingham-based producer, rather than a Manchester-based one, but someone who nevertheless represented the same finely woven documentary tradition at its most elaborate—Whitby had said this: that his programmes were 'so intensely edited, and shaped and polished that while they were great works of art, they *didn't necessarily represent anything real out there*'.[15] If a programme could not be popular, Whitby implied, it should at least be 'raw'. If it could be popular *and* raw, then so much the better.

In the short term it was Parker's old stamping ground, Birmingham, which found it easier to rise to this challenge. Its editor, Jock Gallagher, had an urgent need to widen his Centre's portfolio of commissions beyond *The Archers*, because, Charles Parker aside—and, increasingly he *was* left aside, as simply too expensive and too pernickety to fit in—there was little ongoing tradition of documentary-making in Pebble Mill to draw upon.[16] As a consequence, Gallagher had no vested interest in observing existing programme boundaries: 'Up until then there had been "Talks" and "Features" and "Drama" and so on … and I just came in with the idea "let's make programmes".' 'I didn't have a label … but wanted a kind of mix between talks *and* features *and* documentaries.' Gallagher defined Birmingham as a 'barony without portfolio'. The approach was scattergun, but it also had the virtue of adaptability, and by 1975 his unit was providing Radio Four with 446 hours of programmes a year—106 more than Bristol and 188 more than Manchester. Among its achievements was a steadily expanding output of factual programmes of every variety, such as the magazine series *Parents and Children*, the medical series *New Lifelines in Medicine*, and a vast number of one-off programmes on subjects such as anorexia nervosa, the role of the secretary, market research, and the ethics of transplant surgery. It also produced the first BBC chat show by Terry Wogan, *Wogan's World*, which ran for several series on Radio Four from the middle of 1974, and a Sunday lunchtime politics series, *From the Grassroots*, which had begun in 1970.[17]

One way or another, all these commissions kept the three English Network Production Centres afloat throughout the 1970s. In part, they were acts of positive discrimination by a Controller in London who had the power to shift the volume of work a little in favour of one part of the BBC and then another according to the latest dictates of his schedule. But room for manoeuvre was terribly limited. He had no desire to see producers left idle or made redundant, and he knew that if he were ever to shift his favours decisively towards one part of the BBC it would always be at the expense of another. Chiefly, of course, it would be at the expense of London, for whereas Bristol, Manchester, and Birmingham supplied Radio Four with a combined total of just over 1,000 hours of pro-grammes a year, the London-based production departments supplied over 5,000 hours. They were hardly likely to give away this valuable hoard without a struggle. Fairness, protectiveness, and, sometimes, simple inertia combined in equal measure.

Here, then, was the managerial argument for moving at no more than glacial speed when it came to embracing 'regionalism' on Radio Four. But there were aesthetic considerations, too, and it was possible that these might just force the pace a little. In particular, there was the matter of deciding what *kind* of programmes one was after when shopping around outside London. It was obviously desirable for programmes bought from Bristol, Manchester, or Birmingham to sound at least a *little* different from the standard fare—less 'metropolitan', as it were. But how different could they be without succumbing to a patronizing caricature of provincial life? And how different could they be without disturbing the expect-ations of Radio Four's fiercely conservative, predominantly southern English, audience?

The answers to these questions were never consistent. Take, for instance, the difference between the three programme areas of drama, programme-presenting, and topical debate. Drama, it seemed, had the greatest leeway in expressing a regional identity. Under the *ancien régime* of Val Gielgud, some of the BBC Regions had felt they were being called upon simply to supply local repertory talent to reproduce a West End success for the *Saturday Night Theatre* slot. But Alfred Bradley, who defined his role in Leeds as a catalyst 'bringing together talents which have not yet been recognised at the centre', sensed a change for the better in the 1970s: a genuine desire in London to hear not just northern voices but northern voices articulating northern dramatic visions. 'The members of the script unit in London showed perception and sensitivity in the way they considered regional submissions', he claimed. Instead of the old system, where staff in the North produced plays for their own region and then offered the tapes to London 'for them to pick out the ones which were worthy to be heard on the network', a creative dialogue now began at the commissioning stage and continued through to transmission. Writers whom Bradley had supported over the years, such as Stan Barstow, Alan Ayckbourn, Barry Collins, Barry Hines, and Alan Plater, continued to get regular exposure on Radio Four; newer, younger ones were also nurtured.[18] Bristol, meanwhile, was assured of support for regular dollops of classic Hardy—such as the *Far from the Madding Crowd* it produced to much acclaim in 1974. Accents had to be handled carefully: there was constant anxiety that some were simply too strong to be understood by a national audience, and frequent suggestions in London that the taste for linguistic realism needed restraint.[19] But in drama, at least, identity was recognized to be what much writing was all about in the 1970s. Difference was everything. It spoke of authenticity—and authenticity was something that grew by distance from London.

Presenting programmes, and, in particular, reading the news, was a much more circumscribed affair. On one side, there was constant sniping from the growing number of BBC local station managers faced with commercial competitors busy adopting a colloquial—if rather mid-Atlantic—style of address. They saw no reason why the 'over-carefully structured and rigid' language of Radio Four should not be abandoned henceforth in favour of what was called 'the vigorous, vulgar, human, compassionate, non-grammatical language' of the regions.[20] On the other side, Radio Four faced constant harrying from those for whom 'Received Pronunciation' was still the gold standard. And it was on this second front that pressure now seemed to be mounting. In 1972, for instance, the Education Secretary, Margaret Thatcher, set up the Bullock Inquiry into the influence of language on schoolchildren. In the following year, the broadcaster Ludovic Kennedy got a great deal of attention in the press for accusing his fellow professionals of making 'moronic grunts'. As the Managing Director of Radio told senior producers, the whole question of the influence of language was once again in the air.[21] Certainly it was a constant source of irritation among Radio Four's own listeners, who deluged Controllers with niggles over grammar, pronunciation, and accents. Older listeners, especially, were of the generation who had learned to parse a sentence and expect punishment if the rules were not obeyed. As one writer to the BBC put it, the rules—and the sanctions—were clear: 'one split infinitive, one whack; two split infinitives, two whacks; and so on'. Since the BBC was seen as a sort of kennel-maid extraordinary to the Queen's English, any perceived failure to enforce this highly prescriptive approach on its own newsreaders and presenters smelled like another failure of nerve in the permissive BBC. 'I would gladly endure all your left-wing propaganda, your continued mangling of foreign names, your hells, damns, short and curlies, etc', wrote one complainant, 'if you would only master "who", "whom", "like", "as", "me" and "I".'[22]

The gut response of many in Broadcasting House was to regard such people as linguistic hangers-and-floggers. English, it was generally agreed, was living, richly varied, and constantly changing: the public might look to the BBC for correctness, but the Corporation surely risked losing touch with 'the broad mass of listeners' if modern usage was ignored entirely. Public anxiety, however, was real and it needed to be appeased. Some of the listeners' complaints were also judged to be well founded. Review Board consequently started featuring a regular 'Clanger's Corner' where offences against 'good' spoken English were admonished. The pronunciation of 'garage' as 'garridge', the intrusive 'r' in the middle of words such as 'drawing', the pronunciation of 'the' as 'thee', and a forward shift in emphasis—as in '<u>re</u>search', '<u>di</u>stribute', and even '<u>re</u>port': these were typical of the errors that most offended BBC managers.[23] Whatever the warm rhetoric about adopting a descriptive approach to language, these were criticisms that smacked of old-fashioned prescriptiveness of a southern persuasion. And the desire for codification on precisely these terms had further to run. By the end of the decade BBC Radio was commissioning Robert Burchfield, the Editor of the Oxford English Dictionary, to produce new staff guidelines in order to enforce greater conformity. After acknowledging carefully that English was protean and that most versions spoken on Radio Four were 'in broad terms acceptable', Burchfield ended up reverting to guidance strikingly similar to that articulated under Reith, namely that 'the form of speech recommended is that of a person born and brought up in one of the Home Counties, educated at one of the established southern universities, and not yet so set in his ways that all linguistic change is regarded as unacceptable'.[24] It was true that the hee-haw tones of the upper class were spurned: Burchfield ruled the *ors/-orf* sound in words like *cross* and *off* to be obsolescent. And it was true that this was a trend already reinforced by Radio Four's own Controllers—not least Tony Whitby, who had, for instance, rejected one programme idea from Manchester in 1973 because it had as its presenter someone he thought 'quite extraordinarily plummy—like Margaret Dumont in the Marx Brothers films'.[25] But the conclusion to be drawn from the whole obsession with language was clear enough: any widening in the range of voices and accents that had crept in among Radio Four's plays, or among contributors in its documentaries or news programmes, had not yet been fully extended to those employed directly by the BBC to speak on its behalf as news readers. There was clearly more work to be done to end 'metropolitanism' on the linguistic front.[26]

The third programme area, topical debate, was perhaps most emblematic of the contradictory expectations placed on regional Centres. Birmingham's *From the Grassroots*, for example, had been explicitly designed 'for the general listener with an interest in politics outside the Westminster square mile'. In the programme, a presenter would interview appropriate experts 'down the line' in various local studios, putting to them comments phoned in by listeners. The idea, according to Jock Gallagher, came from a conversation with Whitby 'about what they weren't doing in London'—local issues, such as road-building, housing, or pollution, being argued over by local people. Whitby and Mansell were taken by its vigour and vitality: it threw up 'questions which had been overlooked and voices which it was good to hear'; it was 'unmannered' and 'totally non-metropolitan' in feel. Indeed it provided exactly what one internal policy document said was needed most from the *British* Broadcasting Corporation—a demonstration that it had 'not one circle of acquaintances radiating from London, but a number each radiating from a different part of the country'.[27] Yet there was an equal measure of unease in London over what was called 'parish pumpery' creeping onto the air. Success was still measured against the old benchmarks—as one backhanded compliment for *Grassroots* revealed. So good were its speakers, one member of Review Board said, that it had sounded 'as if it might have come from London rather than from the provinces'.[28] Even Whitby, who was an enthusiast for experiments of this kind, acknowledged that tokenism could be damaging. When, for instance, a listener had complained that *Kaleidoscope* went on and on about London's theatre scene, he responded bullishly. He was, as he put it, 'not against having a new bit of theatre from Dundee' in the programme. But: 'there must be a reason for that item beyond the fact that it's opening tonight and is in Dundee'. Indeed he went further: 'If the duty/worthy items have been getting in because of exaggerated respect for topicality and for non-metropolitan happenings, then to hell with topicality and the provinces.'[29]

Given this prescription, it is clear that the English Network Production Centres rarely thrived when they offered programmes of a full-blooded regional flavour. That, in any case, was the kind of stuff local radio was supposed to be providing for the licence-fee-paying public. What sold the Centres' work to Radio Four Controllers was a more subtle quality altogether: a bit more colour, a bit more variety, a bit more of a *worldly* outlook than might be found from those working in the relatively claustrophobic corridors of Broadcasting House. There was acute awareness, even in London, that if all programmes ended up being made by people living in the same ten or so square miles of the capital, they might end up sounding the same, and reflecting the same prejudices and passions. As a Manchester producer stated proudly, 'we weren't part of the college of Radio Four... we let the air in'. Which indeed they did—though in the form of a gentle breeze rather than a full-blown storm.[30]

Producers in Scotland, Wales, and Northern Ireland were in an even more awkward position. In a period of rising devolutionary sentiment they were expected to play a full part in building the various national cultures. A National Region's first responsibility must be to its own audience they told colleagues in London. Much of their programming, far from being universal in appeal, was therefore deliberately—though moderately—separatist in tone and subject matter. This made it all the more difficult for the rump of producers whose job it was to 'sell' programmes to a national network based in London. The effects of this were striking. In April 1977, the Controller of Radio Three, Stephen Hearst, grumbled that in five years he had not had one offer of a Talks programme from

BBC Wales, and that many of their programmes, like those from Scotland, were 'below network standards'. A senior Welsh editor protested that Radio Four's Controller had shown little interest in his programmes either, but that in both cases 'the reason why more programmes were not offered . . . was not lack of talent but of time'. Scottish representatives pitched in by complaining that Radio Four's taste for grouping more and more of its programmes into series—each under the editorial control of a London department—made it harder anyway for them to break into the market for commissions.[31] Against this backdrop, the total contribution to Radio Four from the three National Regions was minis-cule—some 139 hours in 1973—considerably less than the total from just one of the three English Centres. Two years later, the collective total was just 126 hours: an absolute decline, rather than growth.[32]

The solution to this imperfect relationship was either to strengthen it further or to sever it altogether—and circumstances now forced the BBC on a path towards the latter. What complicated matters was that the BBC still had no proper tier of local radio in Scotland, Wales, or Northern Ireland, as it had in England. When commercial operators started appearing in the national regions after 1974 it was therefore 'Radio Four Scotland' and its counterparts that had to carry the entire burden of competing for audiences on behalf of the BBC. But as one manager pointed out, the kind of programmes supplied from London were hardly of sufficient popular appeal to compete with commercial disc-jockeys serving up pop music interlaced with a patter rich in local references. In the short term, the Celtic nations could do no more than press hard for the right to opt out of 'Basic Radio Four' as much as possible, and subtly reinvent themselves as being a little closer in flavour to Radio One or Radio Two. There was, though, a limit to how much they could be allowed to do this before Radio Four's ability to provide what the Director-General called 'a coherent news and information service to the whole of the United Kingdom' was destroyed. The obvious solution was to run two services in parallel: to create fully separate stations—Radio Scotland, Radio Ulster, Radio Wales, and its Welsh language service Radio Cymru—while at the same time finding some way to make 'Basic Radio Four' available across the whole of the United Kingdom as a full-scale alternative. Technically, the simplest way of doing this would be to switch Basic Radio Four from medium wave to the all-powerful 1500 metres long wave transmitter. This, however, was subject to ongoing international discussions over wavelength allocations. Nothing could happen until November 1978. Until then, Scotland, Wales, and Northern Ireland were never entirely free to go their own way: they were obliged to carry a minimum of London-based programming for those listeners who still wanted Radio Four but could not hear it on VHF or from a medium wave signal drifting across the English border.[33] These interim arrangements were messy, and ensured that hardly anyone was fully satisfied. The lack of outright independence frustrated nationalist sentiment, while the twitching after-life of the old-style 'opt-outs' frustrated those who wanted to listen to

Basic Radio Four programmes and nothing else. It was an arranged marriage, and for most of the decade there was little love or understanding on show from either partner.

Radio Four's relationship with the BBC's Regions was, then, rich in potential but awkward to manage. A Controller like Tony Whitby could see the tactical advantages in nurturing production staff who existed beyond the direct control of the big London departments: it allowed him to cut through some of the rigid conventions that had accumulated in Broadcasting House, and it offered some guarantee that the world as portrayed on Radio Four would, every now and often, be seen through 'non-Metropolitan' eyes. What exactly 'non-Metropolitan' meant was, of course, as blurred as the editorial lines of responsibility that now criss-crossed the land. And it proved impossible to agree whether the Regions were getting too much work, or too little. Some in London wondered touchingly—perhaps mischievously—whether Glasgow, Cardiff, and Belfast had enough 'critical mass' to offer a creative working environment for producers. At the same time, staff everywhere blamed each other for a lack of resources. The Broadcasting Council for Wales argued in January 1976 that 'The BBC Wales radio service has expanded in the last few years far beyond the actual development money made available'; the BBC's director of public affairs in London stated that 'the concentration of resources on regional development in recent years has weakened the BBC centrally'.[34] No one dared suggest that either the National Regions or the English Network Production Centres should be closed down completely. The 'climate of the day', as Whitby noted, was irrevocably against expansion in London. Even so, there was now open muttering in Broadcasting House that national networks such as Radio Four might have lost as much as they had gained from regional growth. And, unsurprisingly, money—or the lack of it—lay behind much of the squabbling.[35]

CUTBACKS

Towards the end of 1974, the BBC as a whole was facing a deepening financial crisis. The root of the trouble was inflation. The licence fee had not been increased since 1971, but wages and prices had been leapfrogging at an accelerating pace ever since. By January 1974, with the added effect of the 1973 oil price rise, the Retail Price Index stood at 25 per cent above its 1971 level.[36] The BBC had been cushioned from the worst effects of rampant inflation by borrowing money, through the growing number of colour television licences, and by government controls keeping a lid on salary bills. But by the end of 1974 the rise in sales of colour sets was slowing down, pay controls had been removed, and in just one year electricity and phone bills had risen by some 30 per cent. Overall, the BBC calculated that its income had risen by about 20 per cent while its total costs had risen by somewhere between 40 and 50 per cent. The 1974–5 financial year would leave the BBC an unprecedented £19 million pounds in deficit. Pending any new licence-fee settlement—and political uncertainty throughout 1974 made any quick agreement unlikely—a downward spiral could only be avoided by hasty cutbacks in spending.[37]

Those at the top of the BBC were usually generous to the Radio directorate: despite the far greater costs of production in Television, it was still being allocated something between a quarter and a third of the Corporation's total revenue.[38] Trethowan, who had to fight Radio's corner at Board meetings, recalls colleagues from Television Centre such as Hugh Wheldon and David Attenborough being 'really pretty tolerant' of his demands. The Governors, too, were generally biddable. 'The archetypal BBC Governor is a sort of Radio Four listener, and I am afraid I did somewhat play on this', he admitted.[39] Even so, it was clear that Radio would have to bear its share of the BBC's pain. It had extra strains of its own, too. The 1969 McKinsey Report had assumed that Radio's growing deficit would be cut by £1 million a year by halving the number of BBC orchestras. In the troubled negotiations that followed *Broadcasting in the Seventies*, this had proved politically impossible. In 1974, Radio was therefore still carrying the cost of maintaining twelve of its own orchestras. At the same time, 'needletime' payments had been rising in dramatic jumps, the cost of magnetic tape (a staple of radio production) was rising exponentially, extra programmes and staff had been required to end programme-sharing by Radio One and Radio Two, and millions of pounds had been spent on expanding the number of local radio stations.

These outgoings had demanded a frantic effort to save costs elsewhere. In the short term, a little money was saved by delaying long-overdue repairs to studios, and more still by asking producers to spend less time editing and to make shorter phone calls. Soon, production offices were ordered to return old tape for recycling—with the unfortunate result that many unique recordings were erased. Productivity rates were also monitored closely.[40] This last measure particularly alarmed some in Broadcasting House. It was noted, for example, that while staff in Current Affairs Magazine Programmes each made an average of forty-five minutes of programmes a week, those working on *Analysis* supplied no more than eight hours a year. As far as George Fischer was concerned, this imbalance merely reflected his own producers' need to devote time to primary research: if they were now required to match the same level of productivity as their colleagues the result, he claimed, would be more and more superficial programmes, and the eventual outcome would be a BBC losing its status as a 'highly authoritative body that can really talk profoundly about things'. The solution he suggested to Trethowan— 'let's get rid of bloody local radio'—did not endear itself to the Managing Director, who was a committed advocate of the new tier in broadcasting.[41] In any case, by December 1974 it was clear that further, and more drastic, economies were needed, and that enough money could only be saved by cutting whole programmes. One target was *Down Your Way*, which had first appeared on the Home Service in 1946. Whitby said that he hated the idea of cutting it, 'and wouldn't be if I could see any equally effective way of saving the money we must'.[42] Its removal, however, was an integral part of an even more far-reaching economy measure: the merging of Radio Three and Four during parts of the weekend. *Weekend Woman's Hour, Afternoon Theatre*, and the Saturday edition of *You and Yours* all had to go, replaced by recorded music programmes from Radio Three. Radio Four's audience on Saturday afternoons very quickly suffered a sharp decline.[43]

By the end of January 1975, hundreds of listeners a week were writing to complain about this turn of events. Cuts were now tangible, rather than hidden, and press coverage made a hitherto indifferent public more aware of quite how precarious the Corporation's finances were.[44] When the new licence was finally announced at the end of January, it was set at a level the BBC Chairman thought 'not bad' given the conditions of national economic crisis. It was, though, less than the Corporation had been asking for. The worst of the planned cutbacks could be modified, though only a little. Inflation also remained unpredictable: the Director-General warned that some 'pretty severe' precautionary measures would have to remain. Most emergency measures would not be reversed until much later in 1975.[45]

The financial crisis, though hardly terminal, was an important moment in the history of Radio Four during the 1970s. It represented the point when half a decade or more of almost continuous expansion and renewed self-confidence in BBC Radio had faltered. True, there were some rows over *Broadcasting in the Seventies* that had never been completely laid to rest: many producers, especially those who had worked for the old Third Programme, were still not convinced that Radio Four was quite making up for a perceived gap in the BBC's cultural provision; staff in Birmingham, Manchester, Bristol, Glasgow, Cardiff, and Belfast still had an uneasy relationship with Broadcasting House in London. But BBC Radio as a whole had done more than survive, it had grown—and more than anyone in the mid-1960s would have imagined. Between 1970 and 1975, the yearly output of the four national radio networks had risen by 8 per cent to over 25,000 hours a year. Radio Four was part of this growth. It had managed to clear its morning schedules of the Schools programmes, and expanded its general programmes and news bulletins across the entire daytime—on medium wave at least. Though there was now less 'regional' radio being made in England, local radio was broadcasting nearly 70,000 hours a year—three times more than five years earlier—and Wales, Scotland, and Northern Ireland between them were broadcasting 4,000 hours a year, an increase of 25 per cent. In the 1950s, radio listeners had had a choice of just two services for most of the daytime—the Home and the Light—with the Third added in the evenings; now they had four national networks, possibly a local radio station to listen to, and schools kept on VHF—in effect, six services in all.[46]

The man in overall charge of this expanding empire, Ian Trethowan, believed firmly that range and quantity mattered, and that nothing could be removed without destroying the effectiveness of the whole:

One of the prime advantages which radio still enjoys over television is its ability to offer a far larger number of simultaneous alternatives; pop music, light music, news, plays, serious music, education, local programmes and a range of variations within each service... We have not in this country, gone as far towards specialisation as they have in North America, nor are we likely to do so. Even if we had enough money, we could not conceivably have sufficient frequencies. Each service, therefore, incorporates a number of compromises, which together should ensure that there is no type of pro- gramme—or indeed individual programme of merit—which cannot find a broadcasting home somewhere. But each service still maintains its own distinctive character and together they provide the listener with what he seeks: a reasonably clearly-defined range of alternatives.[47]

Broadcasting in the Seventies had always envisaged that as each individual BBC radio network became a little more specialized, the existence of an overall 'family' of services was vital: it was the guarantee that the BBC still allowed each licence-fee payer the opportunity to widen their horizons. The range was also 'self-supporting': the expensive minority tastes of Radios Three and Four justified by means of the counterbalancing popularity of local radio and Radios One and Two. It was all part of the 'One BBC' philosophy, which the Corporation had tried to sell vigorously whenever political smoke-signals threatened the Corporation with dismember- ment. It argued that the licence fee impelled the BBC to serve the whole public, not just part of it. 'An organisation concerned exclusively with minorities', it argued, 'would be in danger of losing touch with the generality of people' and become more insulated and remote; a comprehensive output allowed the BBC to open up for everyone 'prospects hitherto denied and to share pleasures otherwise unknown'; the sheer size of the operation was also a guarantee of its strength to resist short-term political pressures from all sorts of directions.[48]

So the philosophy went. But rarely had it been so unfashionable to be so large. The international publishing phenomenon of the moment was Ernst Schuma- cher's *Small is Beautiful*. Its central proposal, for radically reduced units of production in large corporations, tapped into the commonly suspected link between size and wastefulness. In July 1974 Trethowan was telling his staff 'the view that '"Small is beautiful" had gained a good deal of popular currency'.[49] The Press was certainly now seizing upon any example of BBC profligacy. In January 1976, three Sunday papers revealed that, incredibly, ten spiders needed for a scene in a television drama had been brought to the London studios from Kent by taxi. The BBC's explanation, that if the spiders had travelled by more economical means the costs of holding up filming would have been greater, made little impact on the damage that had been done.[50] Worse came in July when Radio was implicated in accusations of extravagance at the Democratic Party convention in New York. The *Guardian* reported that an 'army' of fifty-nine BBC people were there to cover the event. BBC managers felt that they could justify the numbers by the large range of programmes they would be required to service. But, again, the criticism took its toll. Ambitious plans for staffing at the forthcoming Republican Party convention, as well as the British party conference season that autumn, were hastily revised downwards.[51]

From inside the BBC, financial problems did not appear to stem from profligacy so much as from finite resources being spread too thinly. More local radio stations, extra services for the National Regions, longer broadcasting hours all round, separate output on Radio Four's medium wave and VHF frequency for much of the morning: all this had been done on a fixed income. The point appeared to have been reached where expansion would have to cease, perhaps even for contraction to begin. Some programme cuts would have to stay, and some jobs remain unfilled. More radical still—and with ominous implications for Radio Four during the next five years—was the possibility that the 'six' BBC Radio services might have to become five, or perhaps even four. On 10 June 1975 Trethowan wrote to various Controllers and department heads inviting them to a meeting to discuss whether one long-term plan should be 'a merging of one network with local radio'.[52]

It was only a partial consolation, therefore, when the short-term cutbacks to Radio Four were eased, and in some cases reversed, in the spring of 1975. By then, in any case, the outlook seemed gloomier than before, because on top of Trethowan's talk of structural mergers a new and unexpected blow had struck.

A SUDDEN DEATH

On the night of Tuesday 25 February 1975 Radio Four's Controller, Tony Whitby, died after a long struggle with liver cancer that he had concealed from everyone except his wife, Joy. He was just 45. Fifteen months earlier, in November 1973, he had seen a doctor and been told he might only have three weeks to live. The following month he went into hospital to have a tumour removed, but it had already spread. 'We never knew how long it would take', his wife recalled, 'and there was just the off chance that he would get cured...so he went on regardless, as if life were open-ended.' At home, he carried on playing toy-soldiers and football with his three young sons, taking them to see Crystal Palace matches whenever possible, taking short breaks at his cottage in the Sussex Downs when the need to rest was particularly acute.[53] At work, he tried to attend meetings as normal. But throughout the following year, it became harder and harder to conceal the effects of illness. Most of those who worked with him assumed he had some form of hepatitis. Only his closest colleague, the long-serving Chief Assistant Clare Lawson Dick, suspected something more was amiss.

As I watched him lose weight and turn yellow, and spend ever more time having distressing treatments in Westminster Hospital, and ever more time on sick leave, I could not do anything but recognise what was happening ... It was a strange experience, heart-rending but a privilege, to work with him and to see the courage and resource with which he dealt with his mortal illness. He was looking to the future and planning for it to the last, although he knew he would not take part in it.[54]

One of Whitby's last plans for the future had been to arrange his own memorial service. He wrote to Michael Mayne, then BBC Radio's Head of Religious Broadcasting, telling him that 'If anyone is to say anything about me, I'd like it to be you.' When it was time for Mayne to make his address, he told of how Whitby had combined in his role as Controller the personae of judge, encourager, scourge, and impresario. He had been 'both introvert and extrovert, gentle and abrasive, self-disciplined and emotional', but above all impatient with 'the pretentious': ' "I think you know what makes me tick", he wrote in his last letter to me. "I've had two objects in life: to undermine nonsense and to make people laugh". He was irreverent about authority and very, very funny.'[55] In his radio column for *The Times*, David Wade paid tribute to the way in which Whitby had contrived to infiltrate his network with more and more good programmes, though with very little of the public thanks that he had deserved:

With no other section of the output is it so hard to please more than a fraction of the audience at once ... There is always a difficult obligation on Radio 4 not only to satisfy its mass audience but to provide more than most of it asks for or knows it wants. It is an obligation which, slowly but surely, Mr Whitby was fulfilling before his untimely death.[56]

The *Listener* reminded readers that since it had fallen to Whitby to implement *Broadcasting in the Seventies*, his task had been to synthesise innovation with the demand for continuity. Of the three enjoinders on the BBC, to inform, to educate, to entertain, he had put the last first: the other two he had interpreted 'in a noticeably personal way to mean an enlarging ... of listeners' capacities and satisfactions'. Among the BBC's most senior ranks as well as among ordinary producers, it concluded, his 'great talent' would be sorely missed.[57] And so it was. A year later Michael Mayne wrote to Joy Whitby, telling her that her husband's name was often mentioned at Review Board 'in connection with some policy decision or programme idea he initiated'. But, he added, 'that meeting is so much duller without his devastating wit'.[58]

By then, Whitby's place as Controller had been taken by his deputy, Clare Lawson Dick. Hers had been one of the longest apprenticeships imaginable. She had been Chief Assistant at Radio Four for eighteen years, planning the Home Service since the War, and had joined the BBC in 1935 when Reith was still in charge. By the time she took control at the beginning of April 1975, she was 62 years old—already past official retirement age. No one expected her appointment to last more than a year or so: it was clearly both an overdue reward for long service and a stop-gap forced by the suddenness of Whitby's death. Nevertheless, Lawson Dick was not quite the ageing aunt, since she evidently brought an inimitable style to the job. 'When she glides into the office', the *Observer* reported, 'the tall, slender Miss Lawson Dick looks more like a fashion house *directrice* in her late forties. She has an extraordinary youthful face and uses her long hands expressively as she talks.' Tony Whitby's widow, Joy, who had got to know her well over the years, thought of her as 'very like Queen Elizabeth I', with her hooded eyes, her wit, and assurance. She had spent much of the War at the BBC's hideout near Evesham, rubbing shoulders with Drama and Features producers, orchestral musicians, and what she called 'a bevy of exotic foreigners' from the monitoring service, all of whom had been moved from London for their own safety. Later, when her own London flat had been bombed in the Blitz, she moved into Broadcasting House. 'When the sirens went as dusk fell', she recalled, 'we moved down into the basements, and there we worked, ate, drank, played— sometimes quite childish games—and slept until the morning.' She was, Joy Whitby thought, 'very much one of those War-time BBC people who had an artificially exciting life . . . and she had many known and unknown private love-affairs with the Great and the Good'.[59]

What Clare Lawson Dick brought to the post professionally was supreme mastery over the Radio Four schedule, which she knew how to manipulate better than anyone. Not that she planned major change. She was, she admitted, 'already exhausted emotionally and physically' from day-to-day management of the network during the last months of Whitby's illness. She also had little inclination to change a pattern with which she had been so intimately involved in construct-ing. 'The job', she told the *Daily Telegraph*, 'is chiefly to keep the present programme pattern running well.' This entailed a commitment to maintaining the precarious balance Whitby had achieved between his three-networks-in-one—news and current affairs, popular entertainment, and serious debate. 'I have always believed', she later wrote, that Radio Four 'should appeal not only to the intellect but also to the emotions.' News, she said, made it an essential service in the life of the nation, but its programmes would 'be a failure if the listeners did not look on them with affection': 'listeners should turn to them for relaxation and to be "taken out of themselves"'.[60]

It was, of course, impossible not to make *some* alterations in the course of the next few months. During the summer, Lawson Dick responded to public pressure and the slight easing of finances by bringing back *Down Your Way*. Autumn also saw the return of some Saturday afternoon programmes hit by the merger with Radio Three, namely regular drama and *Weekend Woman's Hour*. One casualty was *4th Dimension*, a children's programme that had run intermit-tently for three years but signally failed to capture more than the tiniest of audiences.[61] There were, however, no big initiatives that had not already been contemplated at the beginning of the year. If there was any overarching change to Radio Four under Clare Lawson Dick, it was merely this: that after Whitby life simply became slightly less exciting in Broadcasting House. There was, for the time being, no new vision for the network. Programme cuts had also affected the whole mood of planning. A Review Board meeting in September 1975 captured the sense of pessimism. It discussed fresh audience research that showed the average listener was now tuning in for an hour less each week than at the same time the year before. The Director of Programmes, Howard Newby, asked assembled staff whether they felt network radio programmes needed revitalizing. Were some programmes becoming stale? Was there a lack of stimulating, radical ideas? What could be done to encourage new thinking? His own instinct was that 'a radical review' was indeed needed—'a need', George Fischer added, 'to recapture the stimulating atmosphere that existed in 1971 and 1972'. The Radio Four schedule built by Mansell in the late 1960s, and then by Whitby since 1970, had served it well, most agreed. Perhaps, though, the time had come to refresh it again. There was now an old-fashioned feel to it, a tendency to play safe and to 'stick to the proven formula'.[62]

Such honest criticism opened the floodgates. Doubts were now raised about a whole range of Radio Four's programmes. An 'autumnal melancholy feel' was detected in *The Archers*: 'The characters seemed more worried and sadder than they did six months ago.' Perhaps it was because the series' writers 'lived in the real world and were perhaps merely reflecting the uncertainty of the present economic and political situation'. Perhaps, a drama producer ventured, it was just difficult with a long-running programme to maintain the enthusiasm and creativity of its writers and producers. *Gardeners' Question Time*, fast approaching its thirtieth anniversary, was another programme now seen as in desperate need of regeneration. David Hatch, who had taken control of the Manchester Network Production Centre near the end of 1974, described its regular panellists—Alan Gemmell, Bill Sowerbutts, and Fred Streeter—as a 'very elderly trio'; they might be replaced on occasions, he suggested, as a salutary lesson to 'a rather self-satisfied team'. As it happened, Nature acted on his behalf: Streeter died that autumn aged 98 after breaking his hip, while Gemmell was struck down with shingles early in 1976. *Today*, meanwhile, was judged by a range of opinion to be 'trivial', 'facetious', and lacking in authority. As for Radio Four's phone-ins, which had always attracted mixed reviews, it was generally agreed that they needed scaling back, with programmes such as *It's Your Line* to be mounted only on special occasions. 'So many series', George Fischer believed, had 'tended in time to become space-filling exercises.'[63]

On all fronts, it appeared, the mood in Broadcasting House by the end of 1975 was in favour of a radical injection of new voices and new programmes, a loosening-up of the schedule. Only a timely clear-out of established properties, though, would be able to create enough room for novelty. Significantly, several key members of staff were also on the move at the beginning of 1976. Ian Trethowan left Radio to take charge of Television; Howard Newby, who, as Director of Programmes, had been serving as his deputy, now became the new

Managing Director; his old post was filled, in turn, by the Controller of Radios One and Two, Douglas Muggeridge. The founding producer of *The World at One*, Andrew Boyle had already left his small empire, which also included *PM* and *The World This Weekend*, to join the BBC in Scotland; his departure initiated a complex reshuffling of the men in charge of Radio Four's other current affairs sequences. Boyle's long-time presenter, William Hardcastle, had died in November 1975 after a massive stroke; Gerald Priestland, too, had disappeared from the airwaves, at least for the time being, after suffering a debilitating nervous breakdown which he blamed on the cumulative effects of war-reporting. In the Drama Department, Martin Esslin was retiring after nearly thirteen years in charge and having established a colossal international reputation. As for the key post of Controller, Clare Lawson Dick could not hold onto the post for more than a few more months. The next task was to get a new person in place, and tackle the programmes themselves.

COMPETITION AND CULTURE

At the start of the second half of the decade, Radio Four appeared poised for a period of radical upheaval. But exactly what *kind* of change was needed? If there was one question that had hung over every debate since the 1960s as to what Radio Four should be, it was this: how could it carve out a role for itself in an age of expanding competition for audiences? It was not altogether clear that a satisfactory answer had yet been found.

Competition itself was hardly a shock: the Home Service had had to stand its ground against the Forces Programme during the War and the Light Programme thereafter. Nevertheless, October 1973 is usually seen as a significant moment in the history of BBC Radio because it was then that its monopoly was legally broken for the first time with the arrival in London of LBC (the London Broadcasting Company) and Capital, the first two of a rapidly expanding chain of commercial local radio stations. In fact, the crucial point had been three years earlier, since it was in 1970 that a Conservative Party pledged to legislate in favour of commercial radio had come to power. The BBC's collective task of anticipating exactly what form commercial radio would take began *then*, not in 1973. So, consequently, did all the anxiety over exactly how a network such as Radio Four should respond.

Until the new government's plans were actually published in 1971, there was speculation, for example, that the minister responsible, Christopher Chataway, wanted to establish a national commercial station specifically to rival Radio Four. Even after that idea had evaporated, it was widely assumed before it went on air that LBC might steal Radio Four's valued audience of opinion-formers in the capital through providing upmarket financial news. 'If we do not get ahead of them now', the head of current affairs told Trethowan, 'we shall be forced by

competition to follow the Commercial All-News station into such an enterprise.'
'And following the "opposition" is always an ungraceful posture.' The commercial operators also hinted that they would be scheduling drama, especially soap
operas, prompting an anxious debate in 1972 about whether *The Archers* was
sufficiently up to date in style and content to retain its audience, and whether
Radios One and Two ought to develop some soap operas of their own. The
biggest fear of all was that a slick breakfast-time news programme on LBC would
hit the audience for *Today*. It was the imminent arrival of commercial competition in 1973 that finally pushed the BBC into confining Radio Four's Schools
programmes to VHF, allowing general programmes on medium wave during
weekday mornings for the first time, as well as doubling the number of news
bulletins, introducing signature music, and starting *Today* earlier.[64]
    As it turned out, the immediate impact on Radio Four of the first two
commercial stations in London was small. Much to BBC managers' surprise,
LBC chose not to adopt an American 'rolling' all-news format, with straight news
being repeated and updated every twenty minutes or so. A crucial opportunity,
Trethowan thought, 'had been missed beyond recall'. Instead, LBC's mix of
phone-ins and news magazines was not so very different from that already on
offer, though, in Trethowan's opinion, 'certainly offering no challenge to the BBC
in terms of prestige or authority'. Newspaper critics also gave the two London
commercial stations distinctly mixed opening reviews. Both *The Economist* and
the *Financial Times* dismissed Capital Radio's phone-ins as 'an embarrassment'.
As for LBC, it was 'amateur and lacking in authority'—a crashing mistake
according to the *Daily Telegraph*. BBC Radio's own publicity manager was
delighted. Perhaps, he suggested, 'many newspapermen were now coming to
realize for the first time that good radio broadcasting was not so easy to achieve
as professionals sometimes made it appear'. The first hard statistics on listening
figures also gave Radio Four no immediate cause for alarm. By the end of the first
month of competition, Capital had only just overtaken Radio Three in the
London area, while LBC had half Capital's audience—and not much more than
a tenth of Radio Four's: not a cause for complacency, perhaps, but certainly one for
quiet satisfaction. As was the news, at the end of April 1974, that Capital Radio
was ditching drama productions in order to save money. There was speculation,
too, that LBC faced life-threatening financial difficulties of its own.[65]
    Commercial radio stations posed a stronger threat when they started opening
outside London on medium wave frequencies the government had snatched from
Radio Four. In Scotland, Radio Clyde was acknowledged by the BBC as an early
success in critical as well as popular terms, because for now at least it was required
by the Independent Broadcasting Authority to support a whole range of public-
service programmes, including opera and local election coverage.[66] Over the next
few years it was commercial stations such as Radio Clyde, Radio Forth, Swansea
Sound, and those in Liverpool and Manchester, which succeeded best in stealing
listeners from the BBC, playing as they did on strong local identities and popular

suspicion that the Corporation was still too London orientated. The main losses, however, were sustained not by Radio Four but by Radios One and Two, simply because the commercial stations gradually circumvented their public-service obligations and closed down current affairs, drama, or general entertainment in favour of pop music. Radio Four found it had less and less to fear on that front.

Instead, it faced competition elsewhere. It was no coincidence, for instance, that the size of the Radio Four audience was shrinking at almost exactly the same rate as the BBC's own local radio stations were expanding in number. Each new station was broadcasting a mix of middle-of-the-road music, chat, phone-ins, and news, and appealing mainly to older listeners. In other words, they were crowding onto some of Radio Four's traditional territory. Meanwhile, the fact that the decline in Radio Four's audience was most marked during the afternoons pointed to another competitor: the start of full-scale daytime broadcasting by ITV. Neither the BBC nor the ITV companies had bothered much with daytime television before, not least because the hours of broadcasting were regulated by government, and because they naturally preferred to concentrate their firepower on the large family audiences available each evening. This had allowed radio to survive longer than anyone had predicted as the main medium of the daytime, while slowly coming to terms with its loss of the mass audience after suppertime. From January 1972 everything changed, with the government's decision to 'de-restrict' the total number of hours that operators could broadcast. It was the beginning of the end of radio's monopoly during the daylight hours. That summer, daytime television coverage of the Munich Olympics became a compulsive attraction for millions of British people. ITV also started scheduling popular dramas, panel games, and talk shows. By the middle of 1973, Trethowan was forced to admit that commercial television had 'established an attractive pattern of afternoon entertainment, aimed particularly at housewives— the same audience at which Radios Two and Four had for years set their caps'. Soon, there was even more alarming talk—of 'breakfast television'. When this arrived a few years later it would represent a rude intrusion into radio's primetime. For the moment the mere prospect was enough to stir Radio's anxieties further.[67]

Quite apart from any damage inflicted on Radio Four's audience figures, television seemed to be shaping the older medium in all sorts of ways throughout the early 1970s. The question, in essence, was not simply one of counting heads, or even of grabbing a decent share of diminishing resources. It was also about how to compete with the newer medium for critical attention. There was, as there had been for years, much resentment in Broadcasting House over television's greater share of column inches in the newspapers. The radio medium was somehow too invisible, too transitory, too functional, too faceless, too passé to have a measurable impact on public life—yet simultaneously too 'mass' in appeal to be treated, alongside film or theatre, as art. Many of the new men running BBC Radio were former television people accustomed to making a public impact with their programmes. They had wanted radio to draw more attention to itself, to garner critical attention, perhaps even to create a sense of occasion or glamour.

The question remained: whether this could be done by making Radio Four *more* like television, or *less* like it—by competing with television on its own terms, or by occupying whatever ground was left over.

One response had been simply to import successful television formats into the radio schedules. Wogan's chat-show for Radio Four had been one example of this. There was also talk in 1972 of evolving a programme like BBC 1's *Nationwide* and in 1975 of developing 'a *Panorama* of Radio'. Another strategy was to bring to radio some of the fame and excitement that attached to individual personalities whose careers had been forged on the screen. Hence the arrival of presenters such as Robin Day, Robert Robinson, Cliff Michelmore, Richard Baker, Michael Barratt, and Joan Bakewell, as well as comedians such as Ronnie Barker—described as 'currently one of the biggest box-office attractions in light entertainment' during his 1971 series *Lines from My Grandfather's Forehead*. There was little doubt that individuals like these, already well known to the British public through television, could raise the ratings and catch the eye of the press. But getting them—or indeed anyone of eminence—to appear on radio was never straightforward. As Trethowan pointed out, once upon a time, appearing on *The Brains Trust* would have been 'the most important event of the week' for those on the team: nowadays, with radio no longer 'at the centre of the nation's life... producers often found themselves fielding a Second XI'. Even those who *were* secured came at a price. For a start, Television set what Radio staff could only consider an inflated rate for talent. But there was also the question of mismatched styles. When Michael Parkinson hosted a Sunday evening chat-show on Radio Four in 1976, many at Review Board judged the programme guilty of trivializing its subject matter: as entertainment it was tolerable, but 'it could hardly be considered distinguished'. As for politicians, schooled in the combative, image-conscious terrain of the television studio: they now seemed to *perform* rather than to argue whenever they appeared on *Any Questions?* Indeed, as one BBC Radio manager put it, 'every broadcaster now put on an act and tried to be a populariser in front of the microphone'.[68]

Television producers, naturally, saw the world rather differently. Their Drama Department, Martin Esslin complained, looked down on Radio. Such rivalry was not just infuriating: it was damaging. Esslin pointed to the example of *Far from the Madding Crowd*, which had been on Radio Four and BBC Television at exactly the same time, creating a horrible competition for the same actors. The situation was wasteful in money, resources and expertise. Worse, 'animosity was such that if Radio Drama recommended a writer he was finished as far as BBC Television was concerned'.[69] This was not a relationship of equals, and deep down radio producers knew it. When Stephen Hearst arrived from BBC Television to take charge of Radio Three he sensed what he called a 'stockade mentality' in Broadcasting House. It was perverse, he thought, for Radio to attempt to cover any and every event, and to carry on producing programmes in every genre: like it or not, television already did many of them so well, and there was something a little demeaning in radio's refusal to strike out on its own.[70] This was a message that resonated with those in Broadcasting House who dearly wished radio to be recognized as an art form *sui generis*, to be able to claim to be doing something quite *different* from—but of equal artistic value to—practitioners in television, cinema, the theatre, or literature. Indeed, it was partly this that had driven managerial support for the large-scale productions of Michael Mason, such as *The Long March of Everyman,* or the various efforts to match television's adoption of colour with radio's own box of aural tricks—'radiophonic' effects, stereo, and so on.[71]

As far as most listeners were concerned, radio was not meant to be spectacular, or an art form: it was something simply 'there' at the press of a button, something they wished to take for granted. Its future therefore had to be reconceived in less grandiose terms. And it was this more pragmatic thinking that now shaped most planning in Broadcasting House. The BBC's own official *Handbook* declared bluntly that radio was important simply because it was 'available everywhere'. This alluded not just to its portability, but to its essentially democratic nature. Whitby, for example, had written to the editor of the *Radio Times* in 1973, asking him not to 'overdo' publicity for stereo, because its image was 'that of a complicated and expensive medium of reception'. The Controller wanted instead to convey an image of something 'cheap, instant and simple'.[72]

The challenge for programme-makers and editors was to balance this vision of radio's ubiquity and simplicity—a vision that could so easily carry the unfortunate hint of banality—with something more fitting for a national institution dedicated to cultural leadership. Inevitably, the issue that arose was about exactly how approachable programmes could be before they became vacuous, or, alternatively, how demanding they could be before they left their audience behind. As so often, the argument came down to one about tone: not just *who* was speaking, but *how* they were speaking, and, crucially, whether or not anything of importance was thereby conveyed.

The difficulty for Radio Four was that two trends in programme-making appeared to collide on this point. On the one hand, the search for 'access', the voice of common experience and opinion, the desire to avoid being sneering, elitist, cold, or detached, and to be warm and friendly instead, threw up programmes like *Voice of the People*, from Birmingham. It was, its editor Jock Gallagher declared, essentially a chance to hear 'ordinary folk rambling on a bit', and it was generally agreed that, whatever the merits of what was said on air, the participation of so-called 'non professionals' gave Radio Four a new texture. On the other hand, Trethowan had declared his wish for Radio Four to be 'more authoritative'. And this was an approach that demanded detachment, rather than intimacy, and an emphasis on the significant rather than the mundane. But which of these trends should be encouraged more? People like Martin Esslin, George Fischer, and Stephen Hearst generally approved of the latter, of pushing the audience as far as they would go, and perhaps a little further—making regular appeals for more 'informed' opinion and 'cool analysis'. During one heated

Review Board held in the Council Chamber of Broadcasting House in August 1975, they all rounded on a documentary, coincidentally produced in Birmingham under Gallagher's watch, for representing what they felt to be the worst features of modish *vox populi*. The programme, *Going into Uniform*, was a portrait of life in the armed forces, featuring a collage of interviews with people talking about why they had enlisted and whether the job had measured up to their expectations. The recordings had been gathered on location with the portable tape recorder most in use at the time, the 'Uher', before being mixed back at the Pebble Mill studios. Hearst condemned the final product as offering 'chit-chat of the most banal kind'. It had, he thought, 'been all surface impression.' Gallagher responded by arguing that those interviewed had said what they meant: 'One could not put words into their mouths.' Esslin was not impressed. 'The fact that nowadays one could record anyone with a Uher meant that the BBC was in danger of filling the air with nothing but empty chat.' 'Rigour was needed: there had to be some analytical framework.' As for Hearst, he was aghast at what Gallagher appeared to be suggesting. He 'detected an implication...that anyone who talked without thinking was real, while anyone who thought first and then talked was not'—'hardly a thought to voice in the presence of a portrait of the late Lord Reith'.[73]

It was, perhaps, no coincidence that the three men most articulate in their defence of an intellectually ambitious approach to broadcasting were all European refugees—part of what some in Broadcasting House referred to loosely as the 'central European mafia'. Martin Esslin, born as Martin Julius Pereszlenyi, was a Hungarian Jewish intellectual to his core, who had benefited from bookish, cultured parents, and what he called 'an excellent, fully rounded education'. At school in Vienna he had studied Latin and Greek; no modern languages were offered, so an aunt taught him French, while he taught himself English, Italian, and Spanish. Since lessons finished at 1 p.m., the afternoons were free to roam bookshops; in the evenings, his father took him to the theatre and the opera. He had his own puppet theatre, and used it to act out the plays of Shakespeare, Goethe, and Schiller, as well as folk plays, operas, and operettas. At university, Esslin studied English and Philosophy, and attended classes given by the great director Max Reinhardt. When he fled to Britain during the War, and joined the BBC's European Service at Bush House, he found himself working in what he described as 'a real spirit of fraternity' alongside countless other refugees such as Ernst Gombrich and George Weidenfeld in a microcosm of European intellectual life. But, like many refugees of his generation, Esslin also wanted to fit into British life. He made a point of reading the leading newspapers and journals every day, such as the *Spectator* and *New Statesman*: 'the less interested I am in the article', he had decided, 'the more important it is that I should read it'. Soon enough, he understood the niceties of the leg-before-wicket rule and the arcane politics of the Church of England as fully as the dramatic virtues of the leading continental playwrights.[74]

Stephen Hearst, who beat Esslin to the post of Controller of Radio Three in 1972, had been raised in Vienna, too. Schooled, like Esslin, in all aspects of classical culture and the arts, he had also put on dramatic productions in his youth, and read both *Mein Kampf* and *Das Kapital*. After fleeing to Britain, and brief internment, he studied at Oxford and later worked as Head of Arts Features in BBC Television alongside people such as Huw Wheldon, Ken Russell, and Jonathan Miller. At Review Board, Hearst was sometimes crushing, and rarely less than mercurial. Many colleagues in the Radio directorate thought he remained a television executive at heart, 'constantly pouring out ideas for the momentous, the dramatic, the spectacular and the expensive'. To dispel any hint of being an Establishment old fogey, he once told a young producer to 'come up with a series of programmes in which the brightest people—no matter who or where they are—argue the most heterodox views you or they can think of '.[75]

George Fischer was part of a second wave of refugees who had left Hungary in 1956. He had trained as an accountant and a basketball player in his native country, and when he arrived in Britain he studied Economics at Manchester University before joining the BBC's Hungarian Section. When he shifted to Broadcasting House as a Talks producer under Archie Gordon, Howard Newby noticed at once his 'energy, intelligence, and perseverance'. Others soon noticed his readiness to savage any programme that had not met his own exacting standards. Gerald Priestland, for one, described how Fischer 'hovered over one's shoulder like a thunder cloud complaining about "self-indulgence" and "insufficient rigour"'. He was certainly abrasive, Philip French remembers, but 'he made no demands on others that he did not equally make upon himself'. 'I can think of no one I met during my 30 years with the Corporation who was more dedicated to the ethos of the BBC and to public service broadcasting.'[76]

What all three men had in common, besides a strong, though rather waspish, respect for British life and culture, was a European breadth of learning and a deeply felt distrust—nurtured through bitter personal experience—of philistinism, ignorance, and prejudice. 'The English educational system', Esslin grumbled, 'doesn't produce universalists.' Yet, as far as he was concerned, 'diversification' was *the* 'principle of progress'. Daniel Snowman, a producer who worked with many of them, suggests that their presence near the top of the BBC was less important for the importation of European ideas than for symbolizing the seriousness and broadmindedness of those in the Corporation who recruited and promoted them.[77] But they *did* add something. Esslin, Hearst, and Fischer, along with their fellow émigrés, reinforced an intellectually cosmopolitan approach to the whole business of judging programmes. The idea that a drama producer had nothing to contribute to a discussion about the news or that a documentary producer had no insight on matters of music was anathema to them. Broadcasting House, they thought, should be a Republic of Ideas. They carried over to another generation something of what Noel Annan described in *Our Age*, his recollection of the British poets, writers, dons, and politicians of the inter-war years. What that group shared, Annan claimed, was a delight in general ideas, a concern for morality and manners, a belief in a pluralism in which people of goodwill should 'sit down together and work out sensible solutions to their problems', and a belief, too, in 'spreading Arnold's sweetness and light'.[78]

For those rubbing up against the BBC's émigrés there was another, rather tougher, characteristic to be reckoned with. Their formidable intellects and a shared devotion to rigour set the bar high for the level of debate at forums such as Review Board, and their intolerance of ignorance could sometimes verge upon the oppressive. Jock Gallagher, who regularly attended Review Board, recalls the meetings as 'just mind-blowing': 'I had no idea what they were talking about.' He shared with Fischer an accountant's training, but had never been to university, let alone immersed himself in the classics of European culture. Having worked his way into the BBC via photography during National Service and a career in regional newspaper journalism, Gallagher saw himself as 'a little working-class lad with no education worth talking about':

I suddenly found myself hopelessly and utterly out of my social depth, not to mention intellectual depth . . . I'd known these people, and I'd heard and not really understood a lot of their programmes . . . I was one of the common herd, who, I thought, was in touch with the listeners more effectively than they were. And I kept trying to make that point: 'If I don't understand then the listeners won't be able to understand'. They were interesting conversations . . . because I was in a massive minority of one.[79]

But Gallagher was not quite alone, since he fitted well Annan's description of that newer generation of public servants coming after 'Our Age'—one in which 'the manners of the grammar school boys became ascendant'; one formed by popular culture and palpably more streetwise.[80] It was a description that certainly matched many of the other producers and journalists working on programmes for Radio Four—people who approached their task more pragmatically, who felt more comfortable reflecting the world as it was than trying to lead it towards a higher plane of civilization. For this group of broadcasters, events and people loomed larger than ideas and abstractions. Phone-ins, magazines, and practical advice programmes—many, such as *You and Yours* and *Woman's Hour*, produced by the 'Current Affairs Magazine Programmes' unit—were central to their conception of the public service function of the BBC. It was the voices and opinions of ordinary people that took centre stage in their programmes. One in 1975 on illiteracy, for example, came with a very clear manifesto from its producer. 'I do not want this to be yet another investigation of "why Johnny did not learn to read",' she wrote to Clare Lawson Dick, 'but to convey in the words of the people affected how it feels to be an illiterate . . . So much can be conveyed by juxtaposing different voices without the need for elaborate interpretations by an expert.' 'I hope to edit in such a way that narration is kept to a minimum or even excluded altogether.'[81]

Those in favour of this more instantly accessible and informal style undoubtedly had momentum on their side by the middle of the decade, since those urging the BBC to speak with authority sensed one overriding deficiency in their cause: an apparent absence of suitably qualified experts to do all the interpreting and analysis they were after. 'Fifteen years ago', Hearst argued in 1975, *Any Questions?* had 'always contained a wise man who would speak for three minutes or so and leave a kind of silence in the air.' Now, as even Clare Lawson Dick agreed, there were elders in abundance but 'no betters left'. People confident in their own authority were 'no longer to be found', and even if a programme attempted to question a contemporary thinker, where was the guarantee that anything of substance would emerge? Sometimes, a producer lamented, when one probed too hard, 'your spike went right the way through and came out the other side into thin air'.[82]

In the circumstances, a series such as *The Reith Lectures* seemed an anachronism, its survival puzzling. The programme's roll call had been impressive since 1948. Bertrand Russell, Nikolaus Pevsner, John Kenneth Galbraith: these were but three among many distinguished guests. By 1972, however, it seemed difficult, according to Whitby, 'to find lecturers capable of living up to the concept'—and even more difficult to imagine people at home taking notice of anyone who did. The problem, according to Stephen Bonarjee, 'was to find a way of talking to people that they would be prepared to accept': the very concept of lectures seemed hopelessly didactic and one-way. After Reith himself died in 1971 there was much speculation that the series would be abandoned completely.[83]

Yet in the end *The Reith Lectures* were retained. And the manner of their survival showed just how persistent—and how wonderfully adaptable—the Reithian forces within Broadcasting House were. First, the *Lectures* were given a more inclusive style: a studio audience of journalists, industrialists, sociologists, and politicians to represent the audience at home and 'able to answer back on his or her behalf'. Then, having adapted the format to modern democratic sensibilities, there was a renewed effort to stiffen the programme's intellectual content. Lecturers, it was agreed, should always have stature and they should always have something to say—which usually meant something that had not yet been said or thought elsewhere, or something that flew against received opinion. They were also to be appointed with eighteen months notice rather than just nine or ten, so that they had more time to prepare their scripts. The results seemed pleasing: a succession of lecturers in the mid-1970s—people such as Alistair Buchan, Ralf Dahrendorf, and Edward Norman—praised inside Broadcasting House for their great authority, their 'important' ideas, or, in the case of Norman, simply for providing a spiky and unpopular assault against 'trendy Christianity'. This was not just old-style lecturing dropped into a new format. Some melding of form and content had been necessary. Buchan, it was pointed out, did well because he had '*natural* authority' and his lectures made an impact because they were 'updated close to broadcast for topicality'; Dahrendorf was praised not just for the importance of his ideas, but because over time his ability *as a broadcaster* had improved. Intellectuals thus survived on Radio Four not just because of the strength of their ideas, important though they were, but because they recognized their ideas had to be expressed in a more accessible style—and because there were producers around who helped them to find it.[84]

Indeed, in many ways *The Reith Lectures* were emblematic of Radio Four's central aesthetic challenge, since most programme-makers found that rarely was there a simple choice between informality and formality, between hearing from ordinary people or experts, between hearing human experiences or the considered analysis of ideas. Wherever possible, producing programmes for Radio Four was about trying to find a workable coincidence of the different approaches—a middle ground that might capture some of their virtues but none of their vices. Hence the measured praise for a 1975 programme about childlessness in which 'there had been enough scientific information, but not too much', in which 'no necessary details had been shirked, but there had been no embarrassment', and in which the presenter 'had been sympathetic without being maudlin'. Hence, too, the praise for any Radio Four programme acting as a bridge between those in the audience who were 'vaguely interested' and those who were already knowledgeable. *Kaleidoscope*, for example, reconciled what George Fischer called 'the need to satisfy the connoisseur with the need to involve the uninitiated'. And hence the praise for those individuals with the gift of alchemy, who could speak with authority *and* warmth—those such as the journalist James Cameron, complimented for offering depth and objectivity, but also compassion and sympathy, what Review Board called 'just the right touch'.[85]

Clearly not every programme could fulfil these hopes and ambitions. But there was a palpable sense of public purpose to broadcasting on Radio Four. True, there was no longer much talk in Broadcasting House about 'uplift', or about programmes for 'improving' listeners' minds: vertical hierarchies were clearly out of fashion. But there was plenty of talk about something very similar, which also sounded appropriately egalitarian: a desire to *widen* listeners' horizons. This desire had been articulated at its most forbidding by Radio's radically tough central Europeans, with their firm commitment to rigour and intellectual diversity. Yet it was exactly what Whitby had been after with his somewhat gentler talk of Radio Four offering 'the tide of the familiar bringing in the unfamiliar'. Certainly, it was behind his original desire for *Kaleidoscope* to be a programme not just of the arts but of the arts *and* sciences—what he called an 'intellectually stimulating' juxtaposition—just as it had been behind *Can't Put It Down*, one of the new books programmes that had emerged under his watch. That programme he compared to 'a Salvation Army Band stationed outside a Public Library with instructions to play cheerful music in order to attract people to go in and read'. 'The idea, as it were, was to make people feel that they were missing "a lovely meal".'[86]

All this could only work, of course, if people were genuinely hungry for unfamiliar intellectual or artistic feasts. Yet by the middle of the decade, there was mounting evidence that many listeners to Radio Four were happier with a more predictable diet. Audience research told the BBC that people were more satisfied with its radio services than with its two television channels, but also that they were far more affronted when let down by radio than by television. In other words, the public's expectation of radio was higher; its abhorrence of something *unexpected* consequently all the more intense. Both Tony Whitby and Clare Lawson Dick had long recognized this conservatism. They knew that very few people listened to Radio Four for long stretches of the day: most tuned in for particular programmes; only some would stay listening to what followed. The audiences for *Weekending* and *Afternoon Theatre*, for example, were very different: the one young, open to scatological language and irreverence, perhaps surprised to find themselves listening to Radio Four at all; the other more elderly, wary of bad language or experimentation, and devoted to the memory of the Home Service. Neither group displayed much desire to explore the schedules, or the dial on their sets, to learn about unfamiliar ideas, opinions, language, or music.[87]

Despite the BBC's adoption of 'generic' radio after *Broadcasting in the Seventies*, with its own attempt at defined and predictable streams of programmes on each network, the purpose of broadcasting and the reaction of the British public was supposed to work differently from this. The BBC had hoped that, once confronted with a choice of several discrete services, most listeners would move between them: listening to Radio Four for topical debate, a little Radio Three when they felt in the mood for classical music, Radio Two when they wished to relax with something lighter. It was an assumption that spoke volumes about BBC Radio's faith in the public's desire to be curious and fully rounded citizens. But it was a faith that appeared to have been ill-rewarded: for it had not taken long to discover that most listeners were emphatically *not* moving between the different BBC networks. In fact, only one listener in every hundred tuned in to all four BBC networks during the course of a week. Nearly half of the population stuck with just one service. This was not even 'channel loyalty', the head of the BBC's Audience Research department had warned: it was simple 'inertia'.[88]

The implications seemed alarming. Radio Four was supposed to be 'mixed', and to offer its listeners a breadth of experiences. But if people really were reluctant to switch between different parts of the dial, was Radio Four mixed *enough*? If Radio Four at its best was almost Proustian in its ability to convey a huge range of voices and ideas describing the world in different and engaging ways, then Radio Four at its worst was, as one audience survey in 1977 put it, more like 'a closed network for closed minds'.[89]

Whatever the good intentions over the past decade or so, certain trends in programming had taken on a momentum of their own. There was now very much less music and very much more news—and many more series loosely related to the news—than had ever been offered on the old Home Service. Questions needed to be asked about what sort of cultural experience Radio Four's listeners were getting with this menu. Were news bulletins focused too narrowly on politics, and paying too little attention to the arts and science or to social affairs? Was 'topicality' being interpreted as meaning anything more complex than what had happened in the last twenty-four hours? Were programme teams falling into routine and predictable approaches to choosing guests and topics?[90] The diffusion of news values across many programmes, the spread of the phone-ins and magazines, the expanding empires of the sequences— *Today, The World at One*, and the rest—all valuing 'relevance' and topicality above everything else, ended up, one critic thought, offering nothing more than endless talk 'related to what at some elephantine level of obviousness we can see going on around us'.[91]

This was a critique that struck at the heart of the BBC's identity as a cultural force in the nation. And it did not go unheeded. The new Controller of Radio Four after 1976 was to prove more than willing to initiate what he called a 'Counter-Reformation': an effort to reinstate Reithian values as he saw them. In so doing, he launched Radio Four into some of the most turbulent and argumentative years in its history.

PART II
COUNTER-REFORMATION:
C. 1976–1983

'All great institutions have their counter-reformations from time to time, and BBC Radio is a very great institution'

Controller of Radio Four, 1976

6

Mac the Knife

'A Reith for the BBC'

Guardian, March 1977

'He is a Monster'

BBC journalist, December 1976

There were five people with a chance of becoming Radio Four's new Controller in 1976. One was Ronald Mason, the Head of Programmes in BBC Northern Ireland, who was keen to leave a troubled Belfast for a London posting. Two others worked in Television: Brian Wenham, the 38-year-old head of Current Affairs, and Monica Sims, the 50-year-old head of Children's Programmes, a former editor of *Woman's Hour* and the candidate tipped as a clear front-runner in the press. A fourth name being mentioned was David Hatch, one of Light Entertainment's young Turks and currently in charge of network radio in Manchester. Several Governors were keen to advance Hatch, but the new Managing Director of Radio, Howard Newby, argued that he needed more experience. Newby urged them instead to appoint a very different person: one of his old Talks Department colleagues, and the regular presenter of *Analysis*, Ian McIntyre. Here, the Governors were told, was a man who worked hard, showed great integrity, and, most important of all, was 'fanatically devoted to radio'. 'Unlike most of his contemporaries', Newby argued, McIntyre thought radio 'really did have an important part to play in the future'. After what McIntyre himself described as a short and straightforward interview in May 1976, he was given the job.[1]

The new Controller had already attracted attention. He had political baggage and the beginnings of a reputation for making uncompromising attacks on what he believed were declining standards in the Corporation. When detractors labelled him a zealot he replied pointedly that the BBC had been founded by one. And he was proud to be able to trace his own line of descent from the Founding Father, having been appointed in 1957 by John Green, the Controller of Talks who had himself been recruited by Reith in the 1930s to help whip Leftish producers into line. Politics, McIntyre agreed, had played some part in his own recruitment, as with Green before him: 'I, like John Green, had been at Cambridge; I, like John Green, had been President of the Union at Cambridge; I, like John Green was a Tory.' After a few years producing the Home Service current affairs series *At Home and Abroad*, and a brief spell at the Independent Television Authority, he acted on his political instincts and joined Scottish Conservative Central Office, before fighting David Steel for a parliamentary seat in the 1966 General Election. It was defeat in that contest that brought him back to the Corporation, though unlike many ex- and future politicians of various hues, it was to Broadcasting House rather than the hothouse of Lime Grove.[2]

The Radio directorate probably struck him as more in tune with his own tastes. The *Observer*'s radio critic Paul Ferris described McIntyre as a man of 'vee-necked pullovers and grammatical sentences'. Words—and their deployment in argument—were certainly important in his life. He required his four children to spend an hour reading for every half-hour they spent watching television. He read voraciously, happily tackling Ibsen in its original Norwegian—the native language of his wife, Leik. He had published a book of his own in 1968, on Israel, and another in 1975 called simply *Words*, based on a series of talks he had given reflecting on the uses of language. In these, McIntyre had attacked the BBC's 'new-style' bulletins for what he felt was their breathless incoherence and their obsession with hurried immediacy. He had not been impressed, either, with the style of Bill Hardcastle and *The World at One*—a programme which, he was not afraid to tell colleagues, had 'got away with murder in terms of quality'. Radio, he reasoned, was, or at least ought to be, *the* medium of language and debate. Yet he smelled in the corridors and offices of Broadcasting House 'an acute loss of nerve' over maintaining the Reithian ethos—and in the very place where he had expected to find it cherished most. There was clearly work to be done. And if there had to be bruising conflicts on the way, McIntyre was unlikely to be the first to flinch: he might have left his party loyalties behind at the door when he had rejoined the BBC, but he showed every sign of retaining the debating skills of a politician, an unshakeable confidence in his own judgement, and what *The Times* called 'nerves of steel'.[3]

MANIFESTOS FOR CHANGE

Once McIntyre was installed, it quickly became clear that very little would escape his forensic attention. 'I spent time going round meeting everybody', he remembers, 'and fairly rapidly began to form a view about how things were and what it would be good to do':

First of all, it seemed to me that the actual standard of performance was in many ways not very good. And this was particularly the case in current affairs broadcasting. Secondly—

and this was a structural thing—numbers of departments, for whatever reason, had been allowed to regard themselves as fiefdoms, as baronies, as 'statelets' within the state.[4]

Departmental pride and shaky programme standards were intimately connected in McIntyre's mind. Drama Department, Light Entertainment, and the huge Current Affairs Group, with its constituent units such as 'Current Affairs Magazine Programmes', 'Special Current Affairs', and the teams responsible for the main sequences—*Today*, *The World at One*, *PM*, *The World This Weekend*, and *The World Tonight*: all these, he thought, now seemed to assume a 'parson's freehold' over the Radio Four schedule. It smacked of complacency. 'When Drama wanted to tell me what they had in mind to do,' McIntyre discovered, 'Martin Esslin, his Assistant Head and perhaps his Script Editor, marched into my office and sat down and put stuff on the table.' The various Current Affairs heads similarly presented McIntyre with a series of programming *faits accomplis*. The new Controller, though, wanted to meet the people who were going to make the programmes, both *before* they made them—to consider how good their idea was—and *after*, in the form of a rigorous post-mortem. What lay behind the various departments' behaviour, he suspected, was not just that they regarded Controllers as little more than glorified schedulers: it was also that they each felt a greater affinity with their own professions in the world outside than they did with the BBC. Drama, for example, saw itself as part of the world of theatre; Current Affairs believed itself, first and foremost, to be in the business of journalism. McIntyre took the view that they were all, first and foremost *broadcasters*, and shared a common goal. 'Everybody across the board had not only a right, but also a duty to have a view about what was going on. Current Affairs people should have a view about Drama; Drama producers should have a view about Current Affairs.'[5]

It was, as he put it, a 'Republican' philosophy, in which criticism—the more honest and well informed the better—would have a cathartic effect on programme standards. Review Board was vital. McIntyre, like his colleague and close confidant George Fischer, felt professionally obliged to use the weekly meeting to manhandle any programme that had not come up to scratch. According to Philip French, McIntyre was 'frighteningly' calm and reasonable on these occasions. But since both McIntyre and Fischer usually ended up winning the argument, producers regularly complained of humiliation and 'ganging up'. McIntyre, on the other hand, was constantly disappointed by the defensiveness shown at Review Board. He saw it as all of a piece with lordly protection by departments of their own long-established programmes: an excuse for avoiding bothersome originality. 'In some areas', he complained to those above him, 'those we describe as producers are no more than programme operatives filling air-space to tired formulae.' Radio, he believed, needed programmes made by people with a clear and original vision of what they wanted to say and how they could say it. In short, it needed producers who behaved like architects.

To his regret, he saw a Radio Four disfigured by the work of mere builders, with programmes thrown together in haste from worn-out blueprints.[6]

McIntyre was in no doubt that current affairs was at the heart of the problem. What he called 'spoken journalism' appeared to be almost everywhere, and he regarded most of it as 'verbal muzak'.[7] With five current affairs sequences every weekday, many producers were 'so busy making their programmes that they were not allowing enough time to sit about and discuss amongst themselves how they were doing'. Worse, 'there was nobody there saying, "sorry, dear that's not good enough, we've got to do better than that, and here are some of the ways in which you might do better"'. As a result the trivial, the derivative, the instant, the merely inadequate, and the frankly incestuous—all were thriving:

There was an awful lot of journalists talking to journalists . . . we were getting onto the air the sort of material, which, in a newspaper office, would simply be chat across the room in the course of preparing the newspaper. It was raw material for next day's paper, but it wasn't the finished article. And I believed we should be broadcasting much more of the finished article, and that it should be much more authoritative in content and much more polished in presentation.[8]

The Controller now wanted standards of writing, presenting, and interviewing to be transformed, and a few more 'sensitive silences' to emerge. Too many programmes struck him as 'slushy and sloppy', awash with unshaped actuality and uninspired narration. 'Great slabs of raw material' was his judgement on one documentary series examining the politics of Africa: where, he asked, was its artistic shape? 'Dentist's waiting room broadcasting' was his cutting verdict on another that looked at religious sects: 'This had not been a real documentary programme', he told Review Board, 'but a collection of recorded material linked together by someone who sounded as if she were reading a script at an audition . . .'. The programme had left him with no sense of enrichment, and no better informed; 'There had been nothing in it', he concluded, 'to justify forty-five minutes of peak time on his network.' In stark contrast, an investigation of the far-right National Front, produced in Manchester by Michael Green and presented by John Eidinow, struck McIntyre as a model of good practice: 'It had clearly been written by a highly literate person who used words properly and economically . . . The programme had also fulfilled another function, that of putting on record opinions held at one particular moment, in the way that *The Times* had once done.' If there could be more programmes like this, he believed, the BBC would demonstrate that 'in radio, at least, Gresham's Law can be stood on its head'.[9]

There was another related problem to be tackled. McIntyre was worried about some of the editorial *values* at work in news and current affairs. 'News', responsible for the bulletins, generally gave McIntyre less cause for concern than 'Current Affairs', responsible for the programmes. News people, as he put it, generally 'did what they were there to do in a fairly straightforward way'. Even so, they had a taste for instant, and somewhat populist stories that would have to be watched, not least because Current Affairs programmes usually reacted to these same stories—reporting events 'under our noses', as McIntyre saw it—rather than doing what he believed they should be doing, namely 'observing trends'.[10]

This was a debate that usually centred on the role of 'human interest' stories. One that had just cropped up was the separation in 1976 of Princess Margaret and Lord Snowdon. The BBC's overall Editor of News and Current Affairs warned staff to avoid 'falling into the baser sorts of Sunday journalism' by reaching for interviews in 'a mindless sort of way'—guidance with which McIntyre no doubt concurred. Down in the Newsroom and the production offices, however, staff were eager to interview Snowdon as soon as possible. Peter Woon, who was in charge of the Newsroom, argued the case for covering events 'which were of great interest to many people'. This, he implied, was 'proper journalism'. 'There are often arguments about whether broadcasting is in competition with newspapers', Woon had once said. 'We have no doubt about it—we are.' This apparent convergence of Fleet Street values and BBC news values created a running sore throughout 1976 over coverage of the capture and trial of several British mercenaries in Angola. When the Conservative leader Margaret Thatcher lunched with BBC Governors in February, she told them she thought the BBC had given excessive coverage to these events. Woon argued again that 'it was the sort of human interest story that made ordinary people take an interest'. Five months later, when events had reached their grisly conclusion in the execution by firing squad of three of the mercenaries, there was anxiety again over broadcasting interviews with relatives. Radio's Head of Current Affairs, Martin Wallace, defended their use. His argument: the public needed to understand 'that it was real people, with real relatives, who got killed'.[11]

To McIntyre's distress, this was just the kind of coverage the new editor of *Today* also liked best. Mike Chaney, who had taken charge earlier in 1976, had previously run Radio One's news programme *Newsbeat* and, before that, worked at the *News of the World*, the *Daily Mirror*, and *The Sun*. He was a big, bluff, 'bear of a man', who set out his own defiantly tabloid stall—the antithesis of everything McIntyre held dear. Chaney wanted shorter news bulletins, fewer scripted sections, such as the review of the morning's papers, and 'a more human-interest orientated approach' throughout. Reporters were told by Chaney to get out and about, to gather vox pops and short features with 'real people's' voices. The new style was encapsulated in September 1977, when, after a young girl had been killed by a 12-year-old boy, *Today* interviewed not just the young girl's parents but those of her attacker too. The story, Chaney argued, was 'of such tragic proportions that one must reveal some of the raw human emotions involved'. McIntyre thought the whole episode was deplorable and the producer on duty should have rejected it as not good enough 'for radio's main current affairs network'. He was supported in his attack by the Controller of Radio Three, Stephen Hearst. Programme-making like this, Hearst suggested, revealed a gulf in the BBC: 'between people reared in a tradition of public service broadcasting and those whose background lay in journalism'.[12]

If Hearst was right—and McIntyre clearly believed he was—it suggested the need for shock therapy. Improving the standard of scriptwriting and presenting would take time, as would any attempt to break defensive attitudes among the programme-making baronies. But a flying start could be made simply by cutting down the sheer amount of regular current affairs, and refusing to broadcast anything that did not meet McIntyre's own minimum standards. It would send the right message—namely that 'if we attempted less the quality would improve'. It would also provide some badly needed elbow-room for the kind of programmes McIntyre wanted to hear more often on Radio Four.[13] It would, in fact, be the first step in a much grander scheme, which he unveiled in typically provocative style at a staff meeting in January 1977. He told the assembled managers, editors, and producers of Broadcasting House about his own personal convictions: how he 'preferred hardbacks to paperbacks, conversation to chat' and would rather 'devote air time to making fun of the inanities of politicians than to offering people advice on problems they did not know they had'. He then went on to remind his audience of the inscription in the foyer of Broadcasting House, which referred to the building as a temple of the arts and muses. 'Some muses, such as drama and entertainment, were already well served,' he told his colleagues, but 'history was less well cared for on Radio Four and music hardly at all.' All this he planned to change. In other words, he announced, there was to be 'a "counter reformation" to the triumph of generic radio in 1970.'[14]

It was not long before McIntyre was awarded the somewhat inevitable soubriquet of 'Mac the Knife' for the unflinching attack on long-held practices and programmes he was about to unleash.[15] Public criticism of his 'counter-reformation' was to prove intensely personal. Yet much of what he proposed, while it certainly reflected his own strongly held convictions, also fitted conveniently with the thinking of other people, both within the Corporation and outside.

In his immediate circle of colleagues, McIntyre could certainly count on both George Fischer and Stephen Hearst to support calls for a tougher line on standards. The biography of Reith that McIntyre went on to write in his retirement was dedicated to Fischer, 'friend and comrade for many years in John Reith's BBC', and Fischer was hand-in-fist with McIntyre throughout this period, constantly reiterating the Controller's complaints about poor standards of writing or insufficient rigour in documentaries and features. Hearst, though more volatile in his tastes, was certainly just as fastidious about radio's need for art, rather than mere industry. He defined the qualities required of a Radio Four presenter thus: not so much a 'news sense', but rather 'a touch of Falstaff, a basic friendliness, a love of language, and a firm, distinctive, and preferably bass, voice'. There were others, such as the Head of Presentation at Radio Four, Jim Black, ready to argue that the task of filling 'endless' series and sequences and the heavy hand of departmental control was stifling creativity among individual producers. In a memo that surely thrilled McIntyre to his core, Black suggested that 'Controllers must control their networks and be judges of quality of output, range of output, tone of the network and the calibre of producers working to it.' Meanwhile, McIntyre's Chief Assistant, Richard Wade, was making common cause with Esslin and Hearst in criticizing the way journalists were being trained as a separate caste within the BBC: why, he asked, should they see only one corner of the BBC when the 'value of cross-fertilisation' was so clear? This was precisely the kind of question posed at some length in an academic study of BBC staff culture that had just been undertaken. After exhaustive interviews with employ-ees, the sociologist Tom Burns had come to the conclusion that there had been a long-term shift away from a devotion to public service ideals and towards an inward-looking ethos of professionalism: BBC journalists, for example, saw themselves as sharing certain values and skills *as journalists* that set them apart from others in the Corporation; they consequently valued the autonomous appraisal of fellow journalists above all other judgements. Even the BBC's Editor of News and Current Affairs acknowledged that some of his own staff 'saw themselves as a kind of "priesthood" '.[16]

Understandably, the public was less concerned with the internal politics of the BBC than with the programmes it broadcast. But there was plenty of evidence in circulation that listeners felt the same disquiet as McIntyre over a surfeit of news and current affairs. When the BBC's journalists went on strike over the Christmas and New Year period in 1975, creating a brief but total absence of news on the air, 84 out of the 107 letters the Corporation received on the matter welcomed the blackout—a phenomenon, the Director of Programmes suggested, on which senior editors might 'like to reflect'. Another uncomfortable statistic they had to confront in 1976 was drawn from the BBC's own audience research. This showed that while there had been almost a doubling of the amount of news and current affairs on BBC Radio since 1970, the amount of time people spent listening to current affairs programmes had dropped by 40 per cent. Consumption of this particular genre, the head of audience research surmised, had 'reached saturation point'. There was also the nagging feeling, as there had been since the late 1960s, that too many news and current affairs programmes were putting people off simply through being so unrelentingly grim. On the face of it, there was a case to be answered. An internal list of subjects tackled by various current affairs programmes on Radio Four in the first months of 1976, for example, included 'dissension within the Labour Party, the problems of the Liberals . . . unemployment . . . inflation and spending cuts . . . hypothermia, abortion, rape, pornography, battered wives, patients' right to die, age of consent, crime levels and immigration'. In the same period *Woman's Hour* had covered 'women alcoholics, social workers, corporal punishment, race relations, crimes against women . . . stillborn children'. And *From the Grass Roots* had dealt with 'censorship, the mentally handicapped and juvenile crime'. Given such a list, it was not altogether surprising to find Malcolm Muggeridge writing in *The Times* of the number of times he had heard the word 'problem' during just one day's listening.[17] There had been rumbles of dissatisfaction, too, from the lay people of the BBC's General Advisory Council.

In February 1976 they had complained of the BBC's 'unremitting effort to excel in the same game as Fleet Street'. Should the choice of what featured in a news programme, one member asked, be based as it was in the press on 'such an ephemeral situation as "what was happening today"'? 'Serious attention' ought to be given to the need for more news 'which was of significance to society', and 'less attention' should be paid in the BBC to 'story journalism'—especially, it was pointed out, because 'this almost invariably meant doom, gloom and misery'.[18]

Their comments clearly drew on a series of articles published in *The Times* the previous September by John Birt and Peter Jay, two London Weekend Television luminaries who had launched a very public assault on the values of broadcast news. Birt and Jay had argued that programmes were guilty of a systematic 'bias against their audience's understanding of the society in which it lives': 'devoting two minutes on successive nights to the latest unemployment figures or the state of the stock market, with no time to put the story in context, gives the viewer no sense of how any of these problems relate to each other', they complained. Although it had been television, not radio, which had been placed under the spotlight, and although both the Director-General Charles Curran and most news staff reacted immediately with snarling hostility, the 'Birt–Jay thesis', as it became known, was widely discussed throughout the BBC over the following months, and seemed to gain currency as it circulated—especially in the Radio directorate. Stephen Hearst, somewhat inevitably, was attracted by what he called 'a significant document'. So, a little more surprisingly, was the Head of Current Affairs Magazine Programmes, Alan Rogers. Despite a previous career in the *Daily Mail*, he told colleagues of the value of Birt and Jay in challenging 'the assumptions brought to the BBC from Fleet Street'. It was, however, the BBC's Governors who were most taken with the philosophy.[19] The Chairman Michael Swann agreed with the BBC's journalists that they needed what he called a powerful built-in philosophy simply in order to get material on the air without too much prevarication; but he also suggested that it 'ought to be challenged from time to time'. Indeed, Swann's own private papers show just how much he was ruminating on the matter at this time. For one meeting of Governors, his own scribbled list of items for discussion included 'Too much NCA'—'NCA' being a reference to News and Current Affairs—as well as 'NCA omissions', 'Loss of credibility by harping on bad', 'could do better if less', 'public bored', 'Experts', 'Background information', and so on. Elsewhere he posed a series of draft questions to his fellow Governors:

Birt, Jay... should we retrieve some of their thoughts, which, I believe, touched, rightly, on our weak spots?

What about journalistic obsessions—talking about things endlessly before they happen... going overboard on matters more fitted for the cheap Press, e.g. the Angolan mercenaries?

Are our values the same as Fleet Street?—answer probably yes—Should they be?—answer probably no.[20]

On the face of it, what Birt and Jay had originally recommended—the continuous blending of reportage and analysis—did not quite match McIntyre's own prescription, which was to put rather more distance between 'News' and 'Current Affairs' than currently existed. But McIntyre's beef was less with the blending as such than with the question of *who* did it. Given his doubts about the quality of Current Affairs, he wanted its encroachment into the territory of News to be curtailed: News staff, on the other hand, might be given the chance to do a bit *more* of the interpretive stuff for themselves. In other words, he wished 'to see News moving some way into what is at present regarded as Current Affairs territory'. This would also force Current Affairs people to rethink their own role. They might, for instance, try to 'revive the tradition of specialisation'— an idea that accorded entirely with Birt and Jay's own suggestion that expert units were needed to ensure journalism was 'knowledgeable and educated'.[21]

Another strand of thinking starting to feed this debate was the work of the Annan Committee into the Future of Broadcasting, set up by the government in 1974. Lord Annan did not publish his report until March 1977, but he had begun taking evidence more than two years before. The very presence of the Committee had prompted open discussion of the philosophy and practices of broadcasting, with BBC staff, outside pressure groups, and various advisory councils all invited to have their say. By the beginning of 1976, hints at the direction Annan was taking had already started to leak out. In February 1975, for example, it was suggested that he would want more 'cross-trailing' between the radio networks, to ensure listeners were exposed to a wider variety of programme genres. A year later, the BBC Chairman thought he detected two other major concerns in the minds of Committee members: one, that the BBC was 'too big and bureaucratic to allow people to be creative', the other that the BBC 'did not take enough notice of what the public thought'. There was, he admitted, 'some truth in both'.[22] When the Annan Report was finally published, the head of Radio Current Affairs noted that the critical references to BBC news and current affairs applied to Television rather than to Radio. And strictly speaking, this was true. Yet there was plenty of thinking in the Report that vindicated McIntyre. 'Radio', Annan announced, 'can provide more than immediate news and music of all kinds.' Yet Radio Four was 'exhibiting symptoms of atrophy'. Much of its programming, he wrote, had become arthritic and timid. The overall format needed disturbing, not least in order to become 'slightly more mixed' and prevent 'the safe but sterile reinforcing' of audience tastes. Annan recognized a tendency to turn 'what should really be a talk into an interview for no particularly good reason', and suggested that producers should work harder to improve scripts. There was certainly little encouragement at any point for going downmarket. 'For many of the intelligentsia', Annan claimed, 'radio not television is their staff of life.' Indeed, with more and more people in Higher Education, there should perhaps be more talks on arts and sciences, politics and society on radio. As for news and current affairs, Annan believed the Birt and Jay assault, and the BBC's reluctance to respond formally to their proposals, had shown a Corporation unwilling to experiment. At the very least, there needed to be 'a more varied news service' on Radio Four:

Some advocates of better and larger news services assumed that most people have an unlimited appetite for news which they will be happy to assuage by cutting other kinds of programmes... What is needed is not more of the same type of information programmes, but more variety in the way such programmes are presented.[23]

If many of Lord Annan's strictures on radio seemed to echo McIntyre's predilections, or those of his close colleague George Fischer, this was not altogether surprising. 'George and I had a couple of sessions with him while he was writing it', McIntyre has since admitted. 'He did a certain amount of freelance nosing about... I think he got the measure of things pretty well.'[24]

Neither McIntyre nor Fischer was popular in Broadcasting House for swimming in this treasonable tide. Most BBC figures preferred to assume a defensive posture in the face of criticism from outside. But when seen alongside all else that was happening—the worrying audience statistics, the complaints of listeners and of some colleagues, the interventions of Birt and Jay, and the messages being delivered to senior Corporation managers by the BBC's Governor's and advisory council members—McIntyre seems much less of an isolated figure at the outset of his project than his critics were to claim. Among an influential minority a consensus in favour of the kind of changes he proposed had emerged. The themes were becoming clearer, too: a trimming of the amount of current affairs, an escape from the news values of the popular end of Fleet Street, an emphasis on careful writing and research rather than immediacy and breathlessness, a renewed attention to programmes of pleasure and escapism—entertainment, music, history, and poetry—and an assault on the power and self-sufficiency of the programme 'baronies'. It was a heavy agenda, and McIntyre was all too aware of the pain it was likely to cause. 'I said to Muggeridge, who was my immediate boss, that I wanted to phase these changes over quite an extended period.' The Director of Programmes' advice, however, was to be decisive. ' "No, no, dear boy: go for the Big Bang! Get it all over and done with, do it all at once!" ' So McIntyre did. 'And within a matter of weeks', he recalls, 'Muggeridge was under his desk... because he had a stream of people bellyaching in his office.'[25]

OCTIMATION

McIntyre's opening move came on 7 October 1976. Having had the chance to listen and to take stock, he sent a memo to the heads of all the main programme-making departments under the misleadingly innocuous title, 'Quality of Output':

I have had much advice, internal and external, about how to freshen/improve/sharpen up/ diversify the network. As I consider this, and think about schedules beyond the first quarter of 1977, I begin to feel the need of a little elbow room—space, that is, to accommodate the best of these new ideas. I have thoughts of my own about how to achieve this, but would welcome yours, too.[26]

So far, so good. But there was a sting in the tail:

Which are your department's weakest programmes? Which would you kill if you were asked to reduce your output by, say, one hour in eight? Would you let me know by the end of October?[27]

Over the next three weeks, the various departments' replies drifted back, most of them containing barely concealed pleas for mercy. The first to respond was the head of Gramophone Programmes. He explained that his staff only produced two programmes for Radio Four—*These You Have Loved* and *Desert Island Discs*. Richard Baker could perhaps be 'rested' from the first show for a while; it might be possible to cut the number of records on *Desert Island Discs* from eight to six. But neither show was open to radical reform. Martin Esslin also refused to offer any easy sacrifices on behalf of Drama. He explained that healthy audiences for Radio Four plays had been built up over the years largely through the regularity with which they appeared in the schedule; the most he could contemplate would be to cut the *Monday Play* from 90 to 60 or 75 minutes from time to time. 'My apologies for seeming unhelpful,' he concluded, 'but I think that the case of drama, which requires long term planning and the careful nurturing of writers, is somewhat different from some other areas of output.' Both David Hatch, in Manchester, and Alan Rogers, the head of Current Affairs Magazine Programmes in London, argued in favour of keeping popular series, such as *A Word in Edgeways*, *Gardeners' Question Time*, and *Jack de Manio Precisely*, but giving them much shorter runs in order to create room for new material. Martin Wallace replied on behalf of Current Affairs by admitting that he saw very little room for radical surgery in the main sequences over which he reigned. He admitted, though, that the Saturday editions of *Today* and *PM Reports* were weak, that the audience for *The World Tonight* was small, and that listening figures for *The World in Focus*, which had recently replaced *Newsdesk* at 7 p.m., were 'erratic'. In an attempt to turn the dialogue to his advantage, Wallace put in a bid for supplying a completely new programme to Radio Four: 'Some two years ago, I suggested to Tony Whitby that there was a gap in our radio output, and that we should have something comparable to *Panorama* to fill the gap between daily journalism and *Analysis*.'[28]

Little of this gave the Controller quite as much movement as he had been looking for. But a few new ideas had emerged, and some of his suspicions about where the axe might fall had been confirmed. On some fronts, therefore, he could move quickly. Just one day after Wallace had written to him, McIntyre declared his intention to end the Saturday edition of *Today*. He planned to fill its slot with a repeat of the previous night's *Weekending*, which was to be lengthened from fifteen to twenty-five minutes. It would, he explained, 'have the valuable effect of increasing the amount of money Light Entertainment can offer their writers'.[29] In the remaining months of 1976 and throughout 1977 there followed a complex merry-go-round of other programme changes. Having decided that there was at least one phone-in too many, McIntyre removed *It's Your Line*—much to the chagrin of Robin Day, who never forgave him for it.[30] *The World This Weekend* was shortened, as was *The World Tonight*—despite McIntyre telling one news-paper that it was, for his money, 'consistently the best' of the daily sequences.[31] Both *The World in Focus* and the Saturday edition of *PM Reports* disappeared completely. Plans for current affairs to cover the government's special Budget in December 1976 were also ditched.

Once the casualties had been identified, some promising gaps started to open up. A few were filled through minor reshuffles: *The Archers*, for instance, moved from just before to just after the 7 p.m. news, occupying the space vacated by *The World in Focus. Kaleidoscope*, under the protective suzerainty of George Fischer, was awarded a Saturday edition for the first time. McIntyre's promise to bring a little music back to Radio Four was redeemed by extending *Desert Island Discs*, and recalling *Choral Evensong*, a programme that had been banished to Radio Three in the face of a vigorous letter-writing campaign during the upheavals of 1970. The Controller even pushed for Radio Four to take over some of the Proms—though without success.[32] Elsewhere, some of McIntyre's 'new projects' started to emerge. The most blatantly Reithian arrival was *Serendipity*, a brief miscellany of music and archive extracts sandwiched between *PM* and *The Six o'Clock News*, which aimed to surprise listeners by defiantly avoiding the events and stories of the day. Another innovation, which had earned the derisive working title of 'Son of *Panorama*' during the early stages of its development, went on air in October 1977 as *File on Four*. Since it was the kind of programme that both McIntyre *and* the Current Affairs people had been looking for—both parties having agreed on the need to fill that neglected 'middle area' somewhere between daily journalism and *Analysis—File on Four* quickly became an accepted part of the schedule.[33] As did the new *Six o'Clock News*, which grew from fifteen minutes to a full half-hour in length. 'All the items had been of substance', George Fischer enthused after the first edition. 'And', he added pointedly, 'there had not been a sloppily written sentence.' McIntyre's own delighted reaction was that he 'could hardly hear for the noise of Current Affairs pulling up their socks'. If they now discovered they had more time on their hands, he told one news-paper, they should perhaps 'read a few more improving books, or take an Open University course'—a tactless remark, no doubt, but one intended to underline his overarching desire to squeeze more effort out of staff he thought had been coasting.[34]

Perhaps the quintessential McIntyre innovation, though, oozing intellectual muscle and a delight in careful scripting, was *Not Now, I'm Listening*. This was a

Sunday lunchtime series conceived by McIntyre as a '*New Yorker* of the Air'. The literary allusion was no accident. The first editions included short stories and poems, as well as scripted talks on opera. All the material was specially commissioned for the programme, and it conveyed everything McIntyre wanted from Radio Four's own weekly journalism: something palpably more reflective and better scripted than the daily variety, and with a more catholic sense of news values than most conventional journalists seemed willing to adopt. He put much of the programme's success down to its producer, Louise Purslow, an American who had previously worked at the New York radio station WABC. She possessed, he said, 'a very, very good sense of what made good radio': she had come up with a programme 'not quite like anything else... it wasn't light entertainment, though it was entertaining; it was political, though not in a hard sense'.[35]

The richness of the brew was as much a result of logistics as it was of aesthetics. Significantly, *Not Now, I'm Listening* had been the handiwork of more than one department: Fischer's Talks and Documentaries had been in charge, but both Light Entertainment and Music had lent their help. In this respect, the programme embodied McIntyre's deliberate attempt to shatter any complacent assumptions over territorial rights. And it is clear that some 'Cinderella' departments gained ground in the reshuffling of responsibilities that was taking place. Coverage of the Budget, once the province of *The World at One* and *PM* team, was handed over to staff on *The Financial World Tonight*. *News Stand*, in which Anthony Howard reviewed the weekly journals, was allocated to Alan Roger's Magazine Programmes team, much to the irritation of the Special Current Affairs Unit, which had been responsible for similar series in the past. Outside Broadcasts, which had recently impressed BBC managers with its coverage of the Queen's 1977 Jubilee walkabouts, took charge of *Going Places*, a new travel magazine programme presented by Barry Norman, and the kind of series that Alan Rogers's team might reasonably have expected to produce. The right to make documentaries for Radio Four's mainstream evening slots was extended to Religious Broadcasting, and rising stars among its producers, such as David Winter, soon achieved success beyond the usual round of the *Daily Service*, *Thought for the Day* and *Sunday*, through one-off features such as *Long Live the First Snowdrop*, a portrait of religious life in Soviet Russia.[36]

But there were bound to be losers too, and the biggest were undoubtedly some of those within the enormous Current Affairs Group. Indeed, easily the most bitter power struggle in McIntyre's first months as Controller concerned the Special Current Affairs Unit, and its plans for covering the results of the American Presidential Election in November 1976. When McIntyre took up his post in September, the unit's plans were already well advanced. There were to be two studio teams, one in London and one in New York, with expert commentary, regular contributions from politicians, and George Scott as the anchorman. Producers envisaged running the programme through most of the election night, or at least 'until we felt the story had run out of steam'. When

McIntyre got hold of these plans he was horrified. Being 'open-ended' sounded rather too much like an invitation to journalistic incontinence as far as he was concerned. He was also suspicious about the mix of punditry on offer. The whole proposal, he thought, was 'a weary sort of repetition of all that had ever been done before'. There was, he told the producers, 'a great deal to be done and to be undone'. In fact, he wanted a brand new proposal offering 'fresh faces and voices'. According to McIntyre, what followed was 'glum silence' followed by long and heated negotiations with Martin Wallace and the head of Special Current Affairs, Bernard Tate. But, he recalled, 'they just wouldn't budge'. The final straw came with his discovery that contracts had already been issued to those featured in the original plans—a 'deviousness' that impressed McIntyre even less than the proposal itself. 'So I said, OK, you're not doing it—I'm giving it to News.'[37]

Over the next three weeks all hell was let loose. McIntyre ordered existing contracts to be cancelled, contributors to be paid off, and for costs to be seized back from the Special Current Affairs Unit. Gerald Priestland and the BBC's Washington Correspondent Angus McDermid were quickly drafted in to fill key presenting roles, while Louise Purslow from George Fischer's Talks and Documentaries team was brought in to help News Division behind the scenes. McIntyre's editorial aims, he told colleagues, were first, to hear more from the United States than from London, and second, 'to keep up a constant flow of news with the "pundits" kept subservient to it'. When the programme was broadcast in its revised form, he was satisfied. It had, he felt, displayed 'economy and clarity'. George Fischer meanwhile, went so far as to tell Review Board that 'his reaction to the results programme had been to feel proud he was working in radio'.[38]

This was not how producers in the Current Affairs Group felt. They were now seething at what they saw as McIntyre's direct interference in their editorial autonomy. Tate, furious at the implied lack of confidence in his staff, wrote to Newby demanding an explanation of where he stood on the matter. At the same time one of Tate's producers wrote urgently to the Director-General in her capacity as the head of the National Union of Journalists' local 'Chapel', telling him about the 'considerable' insecurity among her members:

The Chapel is no longer clear where the line of editorial responsibility lies. In the last few years, certainly, it has been usual for editorial decisions, when necessary, to be referred upwards via the Departmental Head to Editor, News and Current Affairs, Managing Director, Radio, and ultimately, to you. Now, however, it would appear that decisions on editorial aspects of individual current affairs programmes are to be dealt with by Controller, Radio Four.[39]

In fact, the 'line of editorial responsibility' inside the BBC had always been Byzantine. True, programme-makers worked not to Controllers, but to their departmental heads; they in turn were accountable to the Director of Programmes, currently Douglas Muggeridge, and immediately above him the Managing Director of Radio, currently Howard Newby. McIntyre, in other words, had no formal or direct authority over any producer working within the supply departments; he certainly had no direct ability to hire or fire anyone there. Yet it was natural that he would wish to have *some* say in the programmes departments were offering him. 'I took the view that the Controller of Radio Four was in fact the Editor-in-Chief of Radio Four, and that if there were bad programmes it was my fault, and therefore it was my business to procure good programmes.'[40] Since the Controller had the ultimate power of choosing whether to accept or reject any offer, his tastes could not simply be ignored by the supply departments; too many rejected programmes would, in the end, mean decline, redeployment, or redundancy. In the past, the BBC had usually managed this delicate web of rights and duties by a process of mutual flexibility, trial and error, talk and compromise.

But at the end of 1976 there seemed precious little of the spirit of compromise to be found in Broadcasting House. As far as Current Affairs staff were concerned, McIntyre's intervention in the American Presidential Election coverage had directly challenged their own professional judgement. They now recognized that McIntyre meant business. And indeed the Controller was still operating on the assumption that, since Muggeridge and Newby had appointed him, they stood right behind him—had even given formal approval to his plans. 'When you attend Boards people say things like, "What are you going to do with Radio Four?" Now if you're asked that sort of question at an Appointment Board, you take it that if you're appointed you might actually be required to do some of the things you said you were going to do.'[41] There was a sense of unease, but little shock, therefore, when new and unfamiliar draft schedules emerged from the Controller's office in November and December 1976. What they contained hinted at a much more direct assault on Current Affairs to come.

UP TO THE HOUR

Having succeeded magnificently in uniting most Special Current Affairs Unit staff against him within his first three months in office, McIntyre spent much of 1977 picking a fight with producers from *Today*. He had already told Muggeridge that he wanted each of the sequence programmes to be 'rather slimmer'. His barbed comments at Review Board had also already made it plain that *Today* was among the programmes that disappointed him most. What few people realized was quite how radical a change to the programme McIntyre now contemplated. 'Because nobody was prepared to do anything managerially to tone up the quality of the production staff', McIntyre argued, 'it seemed to me that more drastic remedies were called for.'[42]

His strategy was brutal: to cut the programme in half. *Today* would run for just twenty-five minutes from 7.10 a.m., and then again for another thirty-five minutes at 8.10 a.m. Between 7.35 a.m. and the 8 a.m. news bulletin, there was to be a brand new twenty-five-minute programme, called *Up to the Hour*. After a month of pilots, leaks to the Press, and desperate attempts by McIntyre to find enough staff and studio space, *Up to the Hour* made its debut in May 1977. It included the regular 'service' items gathered up from *Today*, such as *Thought for the Day*, weather, *Today's Papers*, and sports news. The announcers who linked all these items were also required to weave in snippets of consumer and entertainment news, comedy sketches, programme trails, and brief pieces of music. One of McIntyre's aims was to make the sequence so completely *un*-newsy that it would throw the main 8 a.m. bulletin into 'sharper relief'.[43]

Staff on *Today* were bewildered and angry. 'It was desperately demoralising', Libby Purves remembers:

We had all this material coming out of our ears, the whole world to report on, stories to tell, and we hungered and thirsted for the *Today* programme to be a proper *Today* programme. It was a kind of physical pain to have to stop for *Up to the Hour* each day with its dreadful bits of old Victor Borge records and junk like that.[44]

Mike Chaney, as the editor of a now dismembered programme, was suitably succinct in his own judgement. 'It was absolute crap, the floor sweepings.' Though not many in Broadcasting House were quite as outspoken as Chaney about the new programme, there were very few prepared to find a good word for it. The editor of *The World Tonight*, Alistair Osborne, described *Up to the Hour* as being like 'the Pearl and Dean period at the cinema, during which one bought ice-cream while waiting for the real programme to start'. Martin Wallace's verdict: 'amateurish in both conception and execution . . . awful'. For the moment, senior managers hedged their bets. Newby tentatively admitted to finding the switch from *Today* to *Up to the Hour* 'disconcerting'; Muggeridge thought a final verdict on *Up to the Hour* 'would have to wait'.[45]

But for how long? Through the summer and autumn of 1977 there was no sign of derision subsiding. True, Radio Four listeners were turning out to be fairly muted on the matter. After four weeks, there had been some 225 letters and phone calls of complaint to the BBC, and only 16 appreciations. This was the kind of response that Review Board could dismiss as surprisingly small, and was easily outnumbered by the number of people calling to get a recording of *Up to the Hour's* signature tune. The national newspapers, on the other hand, were full of woe. Radio Four was now a regular feature of the letters pages. One listener told the *Guardian* of how, 'since all the timings changed on the *Today* programme my whole getting up ritual has gone completely out of sync', adding that '*Up to the Hour* simply has the effect of making me go right back to sleep anyway.' Among the professional critics, Gillian Reynolds described it as 'a peculiar piece of cookery': '*Today* has become slabs of plain cake and *Up to the Hour* all currants.' 'A chaotic hotchpotch' was another judgement. The *Evening Standard* pushed the knife in further by hinting that editors in Broadcasting House had even started listening instead to *Today's* direct rival in London, the LBC morning show *AM*, and were saying 'surprisingly complimentary things' about it. By December a nadir was reached when the Radio Four announcer, Peter Donaldson, revealed to the listening public his own disillusion with the programme. After running through a trail for what was on the other three radio networks, he concluded by saying this: 'But if you're listening to Radio Four—I'm afraid you're stuck with *Up to the Hour*.' 'It was a brave thing to do, mutiny on the air', Chaney thought. 'If McIntyre had had his way he would have been hung by the bollocks outside Broadcasting House.'[46]

The Controller, though, was rather too busy fighting on a second, and ultimately more threatening, front. The tide of adverse comment over his new morning schedule was beginning to weaken the resolve of those above him in the BBC's chain of command. One member of the Management Board had been taken aback during a recording of *Any Questions?* in June. He reported to his colleagues that during the warm-up session beforehand, 'the 350 people present had expressed strong support for one of their number who had criticised the new early morning pattern'. He confessed to having been 'quite surprised by the strength of the feelings expressed'. Newby, meanwhile, was admitting that, 'for his own part, he would like to go back to the old pattern'. The opinion of Ian Trethowan, no longer in charge of BBC Radio, but about to take over from Charles Curran as Director-General, was clearly going to be important. True to form, it was for him largely a matter of political calculation. Only a fortnight earlier he had told the Governors that 'Mr McIntyre might have caught the public mood more accurately than the critics'. Since then, however, the litany of professional criticism and internal bickering had retuned his antennae. Trethowan now warned Newby that the morning programme was the 'most important sequence' on Radio Four:

It had a disproportionate effect on the more informed public, particularly Members of Parliament, who listened to Radio 4 but had little time for watching Television. The programmes at that time of day were an important part of the BBC's journalism.[47]

As if to prove the point, the outgoing Director-General, Charles Curran, received a letter of complaint within the week from an MP condemning the new 'less informative' format. 'A number of my constituents', the MP warned, 'have stated their concern.' Curran reassured him by revealing that audiences, both for *Up to the Hour* and the 7 a.m. and 8 a.m. news bulletins, were apparently 'rather higher than formerly'.[48]

If this was correct, it was good news for McIntyre. But, as always, audience figures were open to interpretation. And in deploying them at this sensitive stage Curran had stumbled unwittingly into a raging dispute between McIntyre and the Current Affairs Group, both parties equally keen to grasp hard evidence that might support their cases. McIntyre had claimed at the beginning of June that the earliest figures to hand suggested there had been a jump of 250,000 in the Radio Four audience at that time of day, and he wrote to *Radio Times*, the *Sunday Express*, and the *New Statesman* to say so. If there had been an increase, Martin Wallace shot back, it was 'due to a long-term trend, which had been established before the new schedule was introduced'. Articles in the *Guardian* and *The Times* soon followed, which cast similar doubts on McIntyre's interpretation. Given the way tempers were flaring, the official line from the BBC's own audience research staff was judiciously neutral: 'there was a high degree of inertia about the radio audience at this time of day and it was unlikely to increase markedly, or decrease, in the short-term'.[49]

Audience figures would eventually count in any decision over the future of the most important part of Radio Four's schedule. And, as Trethowan had now made clear, it would be a question of who listened as well as how many listened. But what mattered just as much to people such as Newby and Muggeridge, the Director-General and the Governors, was the terrible publicity surrounding the whole affair. Bad reviews from professional critics were one thing; a steady stream of internal memos, anonymous briefings, and inflammatory statements making their way into newspapers quite another. By the autumn of 1977, Radio Four had been plagued by leaks for nearly a year. These second-hand accounts had often been inaccurate and their effect inflammatory. When McIntyre's plans for *Today* had reached the Press as soon as they were committed to BBC notepaper back in November 1976, Muggeridge had been forced into reassuring Current Affairs Group staff and their union representatives that 'talk of a massive re-shuffle and a major "carve-up" was nonsense'.[50] On Tuesday 7 December, he and Newby met all the sequence programme editors to discuss McIntyre's plans. The meeting broke up by 6.30 p.m. so that the editors could pass on what had been said to their producers. By 9.30 p.m. the same evening the Press Association had put out a report on the matter on the basis of an obvious—though slightly garbled—leak. Muggeridge was beside himself. 'If every proposal was to be passed on to the press in this way', he told Review Board the following day, 'it would make frank discussion impossible.' Despite his warning, the Sunday papers were full of more lurid reports and off-the-record grumbles. A meeting already scheduled for the following Monday as part of the formal consultation process was labelled in the *Sunday Times* as 'a protest delegation of staff', while the *Observer* wrote of McIntyre 'sending shock waves' through Current Affairs. McIntyre, meanwhile, had decided to join the briefing frenzy himself: 'if they spoke nonsense to the newspapers . . . I was going to respond'. By the end of 1976, positions had hardened. McIntyre remained unrepentant, the Current Affairs staff truculent, and BBC management increasingly nervous about a dispute that showed every signs of spiralling out of control. In the meantime, newspapers sensed a good running story and, crucially, a steady supply of information. 'If members of Broadcasting House staff continue to ring up in such numbers to denounce McIntyre', the *Evening Standard*'s Londoner's Diary boasted just before Christmas, 'we shall have a hot line installed.'[51]

Over the following months, numerous embarrassing vignettes of life in Broadcasting House were revealed to the public. In April, *The Times*'s diarist gossiped about four bottles of champagne seen in a lift on their way to the *Today* studio.

They were, it turned out, destined for consumption by the programme team during its final Saturday edition. McIntyre was incensed at the way the drinking had been described on air, and the apparent refusal of the team to trail the new programme that would replace it. 'Disgraceful', he thundered: 'it would have done the BBC no good at all.' Worse was to come in July when the *Sunday Times* delighted in telling its readers about McIntyre having been pointedly not invited to a wake for the *World in Focus*. 'It was, by all accounts, an emotional event attended by some of the dead programme's most distinguished correspondents', the article reported. 'Black match books were distributed bearing the inscription "Don't Blame Me—I worked for *World in Focus*".' A more serious accusation contained in the same report was that Broadcasting House was now 'ridden with witch-hunting'. '"Threats of the sack are liberally scattered about, aimed at anyone who talks to newspapers".' It was, one senior producer recalled, a 'truly horrible time'.[52]

Talk of 'witch-hunting' alluded to the activities of Bob Huntley, a former head of the Bomb Squad. Huntley was now employed by the BBC and bore the splendidly Orwellian title of 'The Investigator'. He had been called upon in May to investigate a stream of leaks to the *Guardian* and the *Evening Standard*. This time around, they had involved the minutes of Review Board, which had always remained highly confidential. Passing these to journalists would have been a sackable offence. Throughout the first half of 1977, as the flow of leaks continued, accusation and counter-accusation flew back and forth inside Broadcasting House between managers and various Current Affairs staff under suspicion. At first, the finger was pointed at staff on *The World at One*; later, it came to rest on producers in the Magazine Programmes unit, then people at *Today*. At least one programme presenter was also suspected. Finally, it was suggested that Review Board had become so porous that The Investigator should be called upon to track down the culprit. 'What was the point of having such an official if one did not make use of him when necessary?' asked McIntyre. In any case, he added, he had information he was prepared to hand over. 'So', McIntyre recalls, 'Bob Huntley came in . . . He chatted about this and that, and we drank some Scotch. He then went away on his travels, and he tramped the corridors and he spoke to people.' Over the next few weeks, several people were questioned and reminded of their obligation to cooperate fully with his enquiries. The Managing Director of Radio appeared to regard the whole process with as much distaste as did those being investigated. 'Because we do not know who is responsible', Newby confessed, 'suspicion falls on innocent people. The damage wreaked is considerable.'[53] Huntley eventually named the most likely suspects, but he had insufficient evidence to lay any formal charges of misconduct. His efforts also failed to have a deterrent effect, since a fresh wave of leaks began even while he was in the course of his investigations. The heat engendered by months of ill-feeling would not be easily dissipated.

SECOND THOUGHTS FROM ABOVE

McIntyre showed every sign of persevering with the fight. The managers above him, however, did not. Both Muggeridge and Newby had had to endure the almost constant complaints of Current Affairs staff since November 1976, and had tried to force a series of compromises between them and the Controller. Neither man was temperamentally suited to the task. Muggeridge, McIntyre reckoned, 'immediately lost his nerve, and was all over the place'. Newby, an experienced producer and a former Controller of the Third, hugely respected for his grasp of programme values and courteous to a fault, was in McIntyre's opinion hopelessly weak as a manager: 'he hated confrontation'.[54] Unsurprisingly, both men's backing for McIntyre now faltered. Newby, who had been McIntyre's strongest advocate at the time of his appointment, was upset most by the Controller's continuing impact on staff relations:

He knew his own mind. He was no respecter of fools. And unfortunately, in Radio Four, he antagonised particularly the Current Affairs staff and spoke about them disparagingly, not only to their faces but also to the Press, so that there were remarks about Current Affairs producers not commanding the confidence of the network Controller. And delegations of producers waited upon me. I was asked by one of them, 'Do you have confidence in me?' and I said 'Yes, of course', and they said 'Well, why don't you put McIntyre in order?' This was a very difficult thing to do. However, naturally, I wrote the most hostile annual report on Ian McIntyre that I had written about anyone.[55]

McIntyre's probationary period as Controller was due to expire in September 1977, and the BBC Governors now debated whether they should, exceptionally, extend it further. The problem, Trethowan told them, 'was one of personal inflexibility in the face of criticism.'[56] One of the Governors, Mark Bonham-Carter, had admitted to similar doubts in a letter to the Chairman—also sent to Trethowan, who was now Director-General Designate:

I find Ian McIntyre impressive when he describes what he is trying to achieve, and broadly speaking I feel sympathy for his aims. But I also understand some of the hostility which he arouses because of his somewhat priggish and didactic style. Nor does he seem to me to have achieved the aims which he set himself and this is where management comes in. It may be too early to judge but at some point we must judge and that moment will come fairly soon.[57]

One reason for the added urgency in judging McIntyre's future in September 1977 was that those running BBC Radio were turning their minds to a significant event due in fifteen months' time: the transfer of Radio Four from medium wave to the 1500m long wave frequency then occupied by Radio Two. Since the switch would make 'Basic' Radio Four available throughout the whole of the United Kingdom for the first time, they knew it would be a suitable moment for the network to relaunch itself as a unified 'Radio Four UK' and draw attention to its strengths during all the attendant publicity. Yet, given the reaction to *Up to the Hour* and the low morale within Current Affairs, there was less and less confidence that Radio Four was in a fit state to cope. Muggeridge, for one, was increasingly wobbly, and wrote to McIntyre to say so in no uncertain terms:

I am not happy about the new morning changes and I am positively alarmed at the prospect of entering this new phase of R4 broadcasting with the present format. It is true that, despite the continuing trickle of complaints, the public response has been muted. Audience figures also continue to show little change. However, all one's professional instincts cry out against the amateurishness of *Up to the Hour*, with its ragbag of disparate items . . . However, it is not the execution which I believe is so much at fault as the concept. The morning proceeds by fits and starts. There is no flow, no feeling of urgency, no stamp of authority and no sense of overall identity. I am sorry to be so critical. There is no doubt changes were needed, but I fear we have gone in the wrong direction.[58]

A month later Newby weighed in with his own warning. 'I find myself defending the programme on many fronts', he told McIntyre, before adding that at a Board of Management meeting 'the discussion came very near a requirement that I should intervene to alter it . . . Neighbours whom I respect have gone over to LBC because of their dislike of the programme and DG has had the same experience.'[59]

With criticism like this flying about it seemed an unfortunate moment in McIntyre's battle for hearts and minds to find another phase of his Counter-Reformation being unleashed. But October 1977 marked another tranche of new programmes—and the dislodging of two of Radio Four's most cherished long-term fixtures from their traditional Sunday slots. Alistair Cooke's *Letter from America* was shifted from morning to lunchtime, and *The Archers Omnibus* from morning to evening. Radio Four listeners complained in droves. But the Controller's real problem was that on this occasion powerful opinion was also mobilized against him from the start. Sunday mornings, as one BBC manager pointed out, were times when 'MPs, contributors, BBC Governors, and other influential people listened to radio'.[60] Changes then attracted attention.

In shifting *Letter from America*, McIntyre had tried to protect himself by warning Alistair Cooke personally in advance. 'He said it was fine', McIntyre recalls: 'he was interested in the money, basically.' But when Cooke began to receive letters addressed directly to him from disgruntled listeners he went, as McIntyre put it, 'to various chums in the hierarchy—he was always careful to have one or two'. Within the month, McIntyre was paraded before Trethowan, who had just taken over as Director-General, and told in no uncertain terms to think again. 'He simply took me by the arm', McIntyre claimed—'Whips' Office stuff really.' As for *The Archers*, the most intriguing protest came in the form of an abusive note and a kipper nailed to the door of McIntyre's son's room at his Cambridge college. More deadly were the protests that issued from the BBC's gubernatorial ranks. Lady Serota complained that the new time slot had 'up-ended her life, and she could not get used to it'. The change, Trethowan agreed, was somewhat 'perverse'. By November 1977 he was telling Governors that 'when there was a really fundamental movement of hostility to changes one had to change back', and suggested more audience research to measure popular reaction. To which another Governor, Lord Greenhill, replied that 'the number of heads counted mattered less than the identity of their owners'. By this stage Newby had promised a review. Within three months a volte-face had been announced and the displaced programmes were restored. The Governors' comments, Trethowan told them, 'had played a crucial part in bringing these changes'.[61]

1978: BATTLE-LINES DRAWN

By the end of 1977, the *Evening Standard*, which had played a key part in keeping up the flow of attacks on McIntyre over the previous thirteen months, was reporting that events were coming to a head. A sweepstake about McIntyre's future was apparently running at Broadcasting House and Trethowan was now less guarded in his criticism. That there was evidently a fresh wave of leaks only made matters worse. 'Could senior members of Radio go on allowing one of their colleagues to continue to be traduced in this way?' George Fischer asked at one of the Review Boards. Bringing in the Investigator, Stephen Hearst said, had been a 'repugnant step, endangering the whole basis of the frank and friendly relationship between colleagues on which the BBC depended'; but, he added pointedly, 'he was surprised that Current Affairs Group had not so far publicly dissociated itself from what was happening'. That comment, Martin Wallace protested, amounted to a smear on his staff, and he would be discussing the matter with the Managing Director.[62] By now he was just one of many in Broadcasting House who could hardly bear to deal with McIntyre directly; McIntyre, for his part, despaired of 'sly' editors going behind his back to Newby and Muggeridge, or even his own Chief Assistant, Richard Wade; they, in turn, were tired of what they felt was his unwillingness to compromise. Even those who expressed solidarity with McIntyre's editorial ambitions—and there were many—despaired of his *modus operandi*. Professional relationships among those working at the heart of BBC Radio appeared irreparable.

But this was not just about the clash of personality or competition between rival egos. Behind the war of words there was a genuine struggle over competing visions of what Radio Four should be. It was a struggle that seemed to be becoming more and more focused on the central but troubled relationship between the network as a whole and News and Current Affairs in particular. In 1978, it also became ever more sharply expressed on both sides. It was as if McIntyre's assault on the values of Current Affairs now provoked staff there, in turn, to assert just as vociferously the case for more, rather than less, current affairs on his network. There was, for example, a campaign being waged to clear space on Radio Four for regular slices of parliamentary broadcasting, in the wake of the House of Commons' decision to allow live relays of its proceedings.[63] McIntyre resisted. A decision to broadcast Prime Minister's questions regularly twice a week, he suggested, would have 'profound editorial implications' for the network. 'Our afternoon plays attract some of our biggest daytime audiences. There would have to be compelling arguments for disrupting that pattern.'[64]

What complicated the matter, as ever, was a tangle over editorial power. The inadequacy of the BBC's chains of editorial control, with news and current affairs staff who jealously guarded their own lines of editorial accountability facing a Controller determined to act as 'Editor-in-Chief' for his network, had been made all too apparent during the past year or so. This, if nothing else, was about to change. The Annan Report, with its criticism of the BBC's journalism, had pushed the BBC into creating a new post, that of 'Director of News and Current Affairs'. The Corporation wanted to pull together editorial control of News and of Current Affairs across both Radio and Television, and place it in the hands of one individual with heightened status among senior managers. Newspapers were quick to suggest that half of Radio Four's programmes would henceforth fall under the new Director's jurisdiction—a clear blow, they implied, for McIntyre. Since journalists had *always* had a direct line of editorial control that bypassed the Controller, this was misleading. The Controller, formally at least, still had just the same power to influence editorial values indirectly by continuing to exercise his right to select some programmes over others. The new appointment did, however, represent another stage in the steady advance of News and Current Affairs as *the* power within the Corporation. It also appeared to blur the dividing lines between News, on one hand, and Current Affairs on the other. McIntyre's ambition of putting more distance between News and Current Affairs looked as if it was being rapidly overtaken by a process beyond his control. And it was a process that threatened to leave unanswered the more fundamental question implicit in everything he had been doing: whether in fact Current Affairs in the BBC was truly capable of distinguishing itself from News by being analytical and searching, or whether, without the purgative effect of his objective editorial intervention, it was likely to continue its bad habit, as he saw it, of rehashing yesterday's news.[65]

Much now depended on those individuals involved in the new set-up. There were four key figures with whom McIntyre would have to contend. The new Director of News and Current Affairs was Richard ('Dick') Francis, the 43-year-old Controller of BBC Northern Ireland, and a former editor in BBC Television Current Affairs. His experience of studio directing programmes on the Apollo space missions had given him a taste for the spectacular coverage of live news events. It had also left him with an indelible penchant for NASA 'speak': saying 'negative' instead of 'no', 'affirmative' instead of 'yes', or 'eyeball that for me' when sticking a piece of paper under other people's noses. Those who worked with him sensed an inner shyness lurking behind his burly exterior and his public displays of enthusiasm. But whatever his psychological complexities, here was someone convinced there was nothing happening in the world that the BBC should not cover—and assertive enough to push through any reforms to which he had set his mind.[66] He was hardly likely to accept a Radio Four with *less* room for journalism.

Neither would the man serving immediately under Francis, the 'Editor, News and Current Affairs, Radio'. This new post had gone to Peter Woon, the former Editor of the Radio Newsroom, and someone whose editorial values were well known as being at odds with McIntyre's. The third man in the equation was Douglas Muggeridge, whose exasperation with McIntyre was also now obvious, and who switched from being Director of Programmes to the new post of 'Deputy Managing Director of Radio'. As such, he was certainly gaining, rather than losing, influence. He no longer served under Howard Newby, who was retiring from the post of Managing Director. Newby's successor—and the fourth leading man in McIntyre's professional life—was an entirely new figure in BBC Radio, Aubrey Singer.

It was Singer who now became the catalyst in the denouement to McIntyre's regime. He had been a television man through and through, the Controller of BBC 2 and before that Television's head of Outside Broadcasts, Features, and Science Programmes. For McIntyre, who had been appointed Controller largely because, in Newby's words, he 'really believed in radio, he had no thoughts about television', Singer's career history was worrying enough. But there was a question of temperament, too. To the understated culture of Broadcasting House, Singer gave every impression of being large, noisy, and impetuous. McIntyre's first chance to see his new Managing Director close up was during a train journey with him on an official BBC visit to China. 'I was locked in a sleeper with Aubrey for nineteen hours, during which time he (a) smoked cigars, (b) wrote his diary, (c) played Tosca...and (d) talked endlessly and loudly.' Singer's extrovert behaviour spoke of a man who, as Huw Wheldon once said, 'liked to kick things into being'. One of his first leg swings, even before he had formally taken up the post, was to remove McIntyre from his own newly decorated office. ' "I like this, I'll have it",' McIntyre recalls him saying as soon as he had walked in. 'And by God he did...I was pitched out into temporary accommodation.' Singer also asked McIntyre to consider quitting the Controllership and returning to presenting *Analysis*—a manoeuvre, McIntyre suggests, that was only quashed by the intervention of Robert Runcie, then the Bishop of St Albans and a leading member of the BBC's Central Religious Advisory Committee, who spoke to the Chairman on the Controller's behalf.[67]

After making his irritation with McIntyre all too apparent, Singer was faced with sorting out the future of Current Affairs on Radio Four. *Up to the Hour* would have to be abandoned: Muggeridge and Newby had already made that clear. Even McIntyre admitted that it was proving harder and harder to find staff willing to produce it. But the BBC never liked to be seen to be going backwards, so there could be no simple restitution of the old pattern. With the launch of Radio Four as a nationwide long wave service to be considered, the opportunity for a much more radical rethink presented itself. Mike Chaney had, in any case, been elbowed out of *Today* in the first months of 1978 and taken a post in one of the BBC's local radio stations. That meant, at the very least, a new editor, perhaps a completely new vision for breakfast time, maybe even an overhaul for all the network's sequence programmes.

McIntyre had already offered his own thoughts on the matter. *Up to the Hour*, he believed, had had its purgative effect. 'I think the News, standing out in sharper relief from the one-legged clog-dancers, has acquired much greater authority', he reported. Yet within Current Affairs there remained a small rump, 'like the Bourbons' who had 'learned nothing and forgotten nothing'. Quite apart from disbanding the Current Affairs Group, which 'appears to have no editorial identity, offers me little editorial advice, suggests few initiatives', and 'makes practically no programme proposals', he suggested completely separate editorial teams for each of the sequences, with whom he could deal directly. Only *The World Tonight* would stay much as before. In order for the *Six o'Clock News* to stand out, *PM* should be replaced by something altogether softer and less topical, perhaps with a focus on music or entertainment. Any underused Current Affairs staff could be redeployed, perhaps to George Fischer's Talks and Documentaries department, to Outside Broadcasts, or to Magazine Programmes. *The World at One* needed a fresh team, and probably one based in News. As for *Today*, that should be replaced altogether with a more upmarket programme aimed at an audience 'that extends in newspaper terms from the *Times* to the *Express* but stops short of the *Sun* or the *Mirror*'; it should also offer listeners more discussion of books, the theatre and foreign news; characteristically, he added that 'there must be a strong insistence on quality, both in speech and writing'.[68]

This was provocative stuff. But so too, in their very different ways, were the proposals arriving in Singer's office from other parts of Broadcasting House. Quite apart from Mike Chaney's parting shot—a call for a twenty-four-hour rolling news network in place of Radio Four on 1500m long wave—and Peter Woon's push for regular dollops of parliamentary coverage, there was another Woon plan to double the length of *The World at One*, and yet another proposal to replace *The World Tonight* with a live two-hour nightly 'event', encompassing news, arts, parliamentary reports, and sport—though leaving no room for *Book at Bedtime*. This appealed to both Singer and Francis—especially Singer, who was quite prepared to shunt aside a series like *Kaleidoscope* if it made room for at least one main listening event each evening, and who told Review Board that the spine of sequence programmes should remain *primus inter pares* on Radio Four.[69]

When the new schedules were finally announced in the middle of 1978, however, they proved more modest than any of these proposals had foreseen. *Today* would return after all, though with a few changes: co-presentation from Manchester, which had been introduced in 1976 partly as a nod to greater regional coverage and partly to secure the services of Brian Redhead, would be abandoned. After an audacious rearguard campaign by David Hatch to get the entire *Today* operation moved to Manchester, it was decided that it would henceforth come entirely from London. Redhead was also to head south, and John Timpson, back from two years in television, would join him—alongside Libby Purves, who became the third presenter after a failed attempt by Singer to detach Sue MacGregor from *Woman's Hour*. The other sequences survived too, with *The World at One* gaining an extra ten minutes. It was a compromise with which Current Affairs staff would probably find more satisfaction than McIntyre, though he had got his way by achieving the collapse of the Current Affairs Group as a department in its own right.[70]

Differences of opinion over live parliamentary broadcasting remained—and proved to be the Controller's final undoing. After more than fifty years of campaigning by the BBC and a temporary experiment in 1975, permanent relays from the Commons had begun on Monday 3 April 1978. For Trethowan it represented the culmination of a long-cherished ambition, and he for one was adamant that no opportunity should be missed to provide the British listening public with an opportunity to hear democracy at work. Woon, too, declared that parliamentary coverage 'had introduced into broadcast journalism a whole new element of vast importance to the whole output'. Prime Minister's Questions, both men were sure, would be an attractive and important part of Radio Four's afternoon schedules twice a week, while other important debates could be broadcast when circumstances demanded it. Listeners, however, had other ideas. Within the first thirty-six hours of Radio Four's coverage, the BBC received 343 phone calls and letters of complaint; by the end of May they had received 2,799—compared with only thirty-one letters of appreciation. If the letters published in newspapers or the comments made to MPs in their constituency surgeries were any indication, many people, far from enthusiastically reconnecting with parliamentary democracy were appalled at the boorish and posturing behaviour in the House that had just been vividly revealed to them for the first time. Others confessed to finding the proceedings incomprehensible, or simply boring: evidence that journalists in the BBC had been so caught up in a political world they knew so well themselves, that the need to explain—let alone *sell*—the rituals of Parliament to a lay audience had passed them by. But the single most popular complaint from listeners was that they were being denied their usual afternoon programmes. To make room for Parliament, *Woman's Hour*, *Afternoon Theatre*, and *Listen with Mother* had all been shunted to VHF, sometimes at short notice— and this at a time when some 84 per cent of the Radio Four audience still listened on medium wave. Naturally, drama producers were outraged. 'Was parliamentary live coverage so important that all other considerations, including what the audience preferred, should be sacrificed to it?' their Assistant Head asked.[71]

McIntyre's objections were more philosophical. He sensed in much of the live coverage too many of those political 'inanities' which he had consistently sought to avoid. When Review Board came round to discussing coverage of that year's Budget, McIntyre waited patiently until various current affairs editors had finished their praise before launching a wide-ranging rebuke that seemed to convey all his anxieties and hopes from the past two years—as the minutes of the meeting record:

The experience had raised in his mind questions about the whole nature and value of parliamentary broadcasting. Much of the material from Parliament so far had proved very intractable, and during this particular afternoon he had felt he was witnessing a skilled potter offering a lump of raw clay to his customer, instead of a properly fashioned artefact. CR4 [McIntyre] went on to say that much had been made of 'furthering the democratic purpose' by broadcasting from Parliament, but the BBC's Charter contained no such requirement. The BBC's business was making programmes, not relaying the source material for them, and making programmes was a highly skilled artificial business. As for the immediacy of broadcasting from Parliament, he was all for immediacy when it enriched the final result, as had happened in the case of *Today in Parliament*. But there was a difference between immediacy and incontinence. There might be a case, if the BBC had sufficient channels, for having a Network providing raw materials alone, so that one turned on the tap and knew precisely what would flow from it, but that situation did not exist at present... Meanwhile, he regarded many relays from Parliament as 'non-broadcasting' if not 'anti-broadcasting'.[72]

This was a damning indictment of something personally associated with the Director-General, and everyone at Review Board knew that Trethowan, who witnessed the exchange, would not be pleased. As soon as they had dispersed, McIntyre recalls Singer cornering him in the corridor. 'Aubrey said, "Do you often commit professional suicide at Review Board?"'[73] Less than four months later McIntyre was gone, pushed across to be the Controller of Radio Three in the hope of leaving Radio Four in calmer waters.

THE McINTYRE LEGACY

The newspapers quickly decided that it was McIntyre who had lost the epic battle with Current Affairs. He had done so, one suggested, on the day that Peter Woon had been appointed as overall Editor of News and Current Affairs, since it was then that McIntyre lost a direct say in the current affairs sequences.[74] Not only did such an assessment overestimate McIntyre's previous control over the BBC's journalism: it overestimated his reach over *any* part of the programme-making machine. Staff in the production departments viewed Radio Four as theirs as much as McIntyre's. And in many respects they were right. The Controller's position has been likened to that of the captain of an immense ocean-going tanker: unable to change direction rapidly—and certainly unable to change direction without the cooperation of the crew. There would always be a limit, therefore, to how much any one Controller could achieve. If McIntyre had made tactical errors, it was probably in fighting on too many fronts at once and in drawing too much attention to his plans.[75] There was also the question of his provocative personality. It was this that helped entrench positions and frighten a nervous management.

But had McIntyre quietly won the war? The brouhaha he created meant Radio Four had been in the news for the first time in years. And there were plenty of commentators who had come round to his way of thinking. He had tapped into a widely felt suspicion that there was plenty of verbal wallpaper to be stripped from the schedules, that *Today* and *The World at One* had lost their edge, that there was room for more variety and surprise for the listener—in short, that *something* had needed to be done to shake Radio Four out of the sclerosis that had beset it since 1975 and that current affairs would have to be the focus of change. *Up to the Hour*, aesthetically speaking, had been McIntyre's biggest mistake. Perhaps, one reviewer speculated, the torrent of criticism against him was simply because the newspaper journalists who wrote the stories only actually listened to the radio over breakfast—and therefore judged McIntyre by the one programme which committed the sin of banality he otherwise sought to avoid. Professional critics, on the other hand, were paid to listen to radio all day, and their verdicts were correspondingly kinder. Arch-traditionalists, such as John Woodforde in the *Sunday Telegraph*, naturally warmed to McIntyre's embrace of what they took to be old-fashioned Home Service values. Others more suspicious, such as David Wade in *The Times*, concluded that the Good Old Days of Radio could not be recreated unless there was 'some kind of renaissance, a quickening of interest' among the ranks of producers; but even here, he acknowledged, McIntyre's fierce criticism and his willingness to shatter preconceptions might have prompted the beginnings of just such a process. At least, Paul Ferris reminded his readers in the *Observer*, he had tried to 'prop up a decent bit of talking and writing'.[76]

Through the smoke of battle, the outline of some promising new programmes could also be discerned. *Going Places* was regarded as a lively addition; the new half-hour *Six o'Clock News* looked like staying; so too did *File on Four*. Listeners would take their time in coming to regard new programmes with the same affection as the old, and the satisfaction many of them felt in the Controller's squeeze on current affairs evaporated as a result of his other tamperings with the schedule. Yet McIntyre was right to point out that the public reaction was much more averse to the frequent live coverage of Parliament, which he had consistently opposed, than it had ever been to his shunting around of *Letter from America* or *The Archers*. Some of his battles were lost more as a result of machinations within Broadcasting House than through a popular outcry.

Even in Broadcasting House, there were producers who had reason to cheer his period in office. Those in Outside Broadcasts and Religious Programmes undoubtedly felt a little better off in 1978 than they had in 1975, and a little more entitled to swim in the mainstream of Radio Four; so too did those in

Wales, Northern Ireland, and Scotland, who saw their coffers swell modestly. At least one producer from Light Entertainment—a department that had itself benefited from new slots and extra money from repeats—thanked him openly for letting staff 'try out new ideas'; the same line was to be heard from some of those in George Fischer's Talks and Documentaries team. Indeed, McIntyre's assault on the grander departments—the 'baronies'—seemed to represent a subtle shift in the relationship between Controller, Producer, and Department within BBC Radio. In the marketplace of ideas, departments and their heads now had a little less right to assume ownership in perpetuity over certain parts of the Radio Four schedule; producers, conversely, had a little more freedom to sell programmes to the Controller directly—in other words to speak for themselves. There were some who professed themselves too intimidated by McIntyre to take advantage of such freedom. Others admitted that if it 'wasn't comfortable' it was certainly 'stimulating' to be around.[77]

This was a subtle organizational shift that echoed changes outside the BBC. There had been growing public debate in Britain through the mid-1970s over the role of big government and of powerful trade unions—and, in particular, the unions' adherence to the 'closed shop' and 'restrictive practices'. It spoke of a rightward shift in the political and intellectual mood. The 'bad habits' of organized labour were being linked to the country's economic problems; the Labour movement and the progressive Left as a whole appeared to be collapsing from what David Marquand called 'intellectual anaemia'; new ideas all seemed to be coming from the Right, fuelled by the prolific outpourings of the Conservative Philosophy Group, the Centre for Policy Studies, the Institute for Economic Affairs, and the stream of 'Black Papers' criticizing declining standards in education and culture. Margaret Thatcher, in charge of the Conservative Party since 1975, was asserting the merits of economic individualism in replacing old ideas of collectivism. She also contrasted her own strong convictions with the implied weakness of consensus, which was to her no more than a process of avoiding the very issues that had to be solved.[78]

In such a context, Ian McIntyre should perhaps be seen as the first Thatcherite at the BBC as much as the last of the Reithians. His approach to his term of office at Radio Four certainly seems to have embodied as much of the new spirit as the old. Quite apart from his evident impatience with the unions, he had consistently seen the departments as riddled with restrictive practices, displaying professional loyalties not to the BBC, or even to broadcasting, but to their own closed trades. He had been convinced they were lacking in ideas or entrepreneurial spirit—or rather, that the departmental apparatus was stifling whatever initiative individual producers might be capable of showing if only they were liberated to do so. His uncompromising performances at Review Board and the provocative language of his statements to colleagues and the press had not *just* been a matter of temperament, either: they had been an expression of his distaste for consensus—what he described as the habit of people at the BBC to 'sit on their hands'.[79] He had always operated with a different philosophy: the purgative effect of speaking one's mind. It was not an approach that had won him many friends. It tended to divide staff—between those he labelled 'Bourbons', and those both he and George Fischer, had they been so inclined, might have labelled 'One of Us'.

None of this taking sides was what the consensual BBC was used to. In the middle of 1978, the Managing Director of Radio, Aubrey Singer, and above him the Director-General, Ian Trethowan, inevitably looked for a successor to McIntyre who would be more emollient. Peter Woon was tipped as being in the running; so too was Cliff Morgan, the head of Television Outside Broadcasts, and McIntyre's Chief Assistant, Richard Wade. But it was one of the candidates who had been overlooked last time around who got the job. On 21 September it was announced that Monica Sims, who had been in charge of BBC Children's Television for the past eleven years, would be the new Controller.

Sims, who had worked with both Aubrey Singer and Dick Francis during her television career, was also an experienced radio hand. After an early career in adult education and regional theatre, she had joined the BBC as a producer for *Woman's Hour* in 1953. Within two years she had moved across to BBC Television, producing various consumer, travel, drama, and topical discussion programmes, before returning to Broadcasting House as the Editor of *Woman's Hour* in 1964. It was a past which suggested that, like her predecessor, she would respect the tradition of Radio Four as a network of very varied speech: a tradition in which news and current affairs would play an important—but not the only—part. The Counter-Reformation, it seemed, would endure.

Yet nothing was ever that simple at the BBC. For a start, McIntyre's bruising regime had provoked, rather than pacified News and Current Affairs: there were now plenty of staff ready, when the time seemed right, to hit back against the network's 'rich mix' and argue the case not just for more news but for an *all*-news service in its place. Moreover, in Aubrey Singer there was an excitable Managing Director unlikely to leave BBC Radio as he found it. There was no guarantee that he would be a reliable ally in the new Controller's cause. To complicate matters further Sims was busy writing up new BBC-wide guidelines on the portrayal of violence when she was offered the Controllership, which meant she was not able to take up her post until December. By then plans for changing the whole shape of BBC Radio in the 1980s had started to form under Singer's watch. Some of the plans contemplated a future without Radio Four. Before Sims came back to Broadcasting House, she knew she would be faced with having to boost the morale of staff and rebuild an atmosphere of calm. What only became clear after she arrived was that she would have to 'fight like a tigress', as one newspaper put it, to ensure the network survived at all in a form that she, or most listeners, would recognize.

7

Theatres of the Air

'To tell the story... it is best to tell the story of some of the minds behind it.'
The Hitchhiker's Guide to the Galaxy, Radio Four, 1978

Ian McIntyre's run-ins with Current Affairs dominated public discussion of Radio Four between 1976 and 1978—as would Monica Sims's struggles to help it survive in the face of even more radical plans unveiled over the next four years. Yet behind the politicking the essential work of broadcasting went on, and a different layer of historical change was at work. This moved more slowly and less sensationally, and took place not in the Controller's office or the Boardroom but in the studios and offices of ordinary producers where the 'supply' departments ruled. Many of these departments were much older than Radio Four. They were places with inherited traditions and habits, populated by some powerful and well-respected practitioners of their respective crafts. For these men and women, making programmes was rarely a simple matter of filling up the hours with unchanging formulae: traditions there may have been, but aesthetics and techniques constantly evolved. Sometimes new technology opened up the possibility of new styles. Sometimes what was happening in other media provided inspiration. Often there was talk of the *art* of radio as well as the craft of radio, and much talk, too, of the need to prove that the 'invisible' medium was every bit as cutting-edge or as relevant or as influential as that great rival, television.

It was talk that spoke of nervousness as much as of artistic conviction. And nowhere could this be seen more intensely than in the two departments of Drama and Light Entertainment. W. H. Auden had declared in the 1960s that radio drama was 'a dying art'.[1] This was a persistent diagnosis, and was said just as frequently of light entertainment. *Broadcasting in the Seventies*, with its message that radio's future lay in providing streams of information and music had implied that genres like drama and comedy, which seemed to require of an audience that it was paying reasonable attention, would ultimately thrive better on television.

By the start of the 1970s their survival on radio was viewed widely as an act of pity or inertia or *folie de grandeur*.

Yet the darkest predictions did not come to pass. Both Drama and Light Entertainment were to have a good decade. Indeed, they were, if anything, to enhance their reputation as cultural reservoirs, not just for the BBC but also for British broadcasting more generally. The thirty or so producers in Drama, along with the small team working on *The Archers*, effectively constituted the only pool of practitioners of their craft in Britain, and remained the largest concentration in the English-speaking world; the ten or so producers in Light Entertainment had much the same monopoly position in their particular field. Though both worked in the shadow of television, both cost a lot less. Indeed, the average radio play cost about a tenth of the average television play. With price differentials like this, it was much less painful for Broadcasting House to write off the occasional failure. It consequently had more freedom to take risks and seek untested writers or performers. It was, in this sense at least, capable of becoming a laboratory of ideas for the rest of the BBC.[2]

Practicalities always intruded, however. For example: *where* exactly should Radio Drama or Light Entertainment look for talent? And *how* successful could they be at shaping the talents they found? The answers to such questions depended in some measure on the personalities and predilections of those running the two departments. In Drama, there was Martin Esslin, fiercely intellectual and interested in the theatre of ideas, though somewhat less interested in the mechanics of directing actors; then, from 1977, Ronald Mason, a more stolid and less innovative figure, but a pragmatic man with a good understanding of British regional (and especially Northern Irish) theatre.[3] In Light Entertainment there was Con Mahoney, a survivor from the pre-*Goons* era now easing his way into retirement; and, from 1978, David Hatch, the coming man from the *Python* generation. These were all strong characters in their different ways, each capable of setting the tone of the departments they managed and the overall style of the programmes being commissioned.

But leadership was only ever one factor. There were plenty of other strong-minded producers around nurturing their own passions—and much of the day-to-day decision-making would be delegated to them. The highly subjective question of what exactly constituted good drama or good comedy was therefore argued over endlessly—without a consensus necessarily being reached in every case. Nor could programmes ever be fully forged without some consideration of what the Radio Four audience was known to like best, or what current BBC policy dictated, or what was happening elsewhere in theatre or television or literature: as always, judging the mood of the times was vital. Moreover, behind every consideration there was, eternally, the question of money, since although drama and comedy were cheaper in radio than in television they were certainly not cheap by radio's own standards. The creative freedom of both departments was therefore always heavily proscribed by the need to watch costs.[4]

To tell the story of Drama and Light Entertainment in the 1970s and early 1980s, then, is to tell a story of how in broadcasting 'Art' would be compromised in all sorts of ways by the 'Crafts' of production. And it is to tell a story of how, despite the anxiety of purists, the kind of programmes that emerged were sometimes all the better for it: more accessible, better adapted to the medium, and very often better adapted to the age in which they were made.

NO LAUGHING MATTER: COMEDY IN CRISIS

At the start of 1976, comedy on BBC Television was judged to be on the 'crest of a wave'.[5] The schedules were replete with highly popular shows: *The Two Ronnies, Mike Yarwood, Dave Allen, Fawlty Towers, The Good Life, Are You Being Served? Porridge, The Fall and Rise of Reginald Perrin, The Liver Birds, The Goodies, Citizen Smith*. This was a rich haul by any standard. But from the perspective of Broadcasting House it was most discomforting. Light entertainment on Radio Four appeared, by contrast, to be in a state of crisis. Siren voices from Fleet Street and inside Broadcasting House were regularly describing long-running shows as 'jaded', 'predictable', or worse: *Twenty Questions*, which was supposed to have been rescued from senility by the introduction of a new team in 1975, merely offered 'one middle aged man being replaced by another'; *Top of the Form*, described by Ian McIntyre as sounding like 'two prefects going down into the country to bring education to the underprivileged' was 'wearing thin'; *Does the Team Think?*, a compendium of jokes devised in the 1950s by Jimmy Edwards, was 'totally irrelevant to today and objectionable in its constant double-entendres'. Radio Four's few remaining stand-up comedians and variety acts fared no better under the critical gaze. Harry Worth, for example, had enjoyed great success in the past, but was now judged to be 'a terrible bore... making the same joke far too long'. The era of programmes woven around star-turns seemed to be fading, but no obvious alternative had yet come into focus. Even the survival of long-running series like *The Men from the Ministry*, which had been around ever since 1962, merely suggested the ability to create totally fresh work had faltered. Of those new shows that had been launched in the early 1970s, most, apart from *Weekending*, had been dashed on the rocks of public indifference.[6] The fate of a series such as *Home to Roost* was all too typical. This cosy situation comedy in the Light Programme tradition, starring Deryck Guyler as a man coping with retirement, had started out well enough in 1974, with Tony Whitby hoping it might turn out to be a solid attraction for a mainstream audience. 'Very warm, human and real', was Review Board's initial appraisal. Its storylines, however, had quickly run out of steam; audience figures had remained static. It only survived for two series—which was one whole series longer than many other experiments at the time.[7]

How, some asked, could Radio Four appeal to a generation of listeners now 'reared on a tradition of sharper comedy such as *Fawlty Towers*'?[8] The question struck managers as urgently in need of an answer. For a start, the BBC had a strategic interest in light entertainment programmes. Being popular, they were clearly a means by which it could reach the majority of British people. They therefore helped justify the universality of the licence fee. And, as one 1972 policy statement made clear, there were wider cultural considerations:

If the BBC were ever for any reason to stop broadcasting them there would be many people who would no longer turn to it with the same eagerness, the same expectation of being made to laugh or of being pleased. Eventually, no doubt, a good number of them would lose the habit of watching and listening to the BBC. So, inevitably, the audience for more serious programmes would be diminished—and not only diminished but changed in its composition. Moreover, the absence of a light entertainment element in the output could also have an impoverishing effect on the serious programmes themselves. A national broadcasting organisation needs to be able to talk to its audience in a language they understand. It cannot afford to be cut off from the way large numbers of people are feeling, thinking, and talking. Insulation from any substantial element in the nation's life would soon show itself in impaired confidence and an unsure touch. Indeed, it is not too much to say that a BBC shorn of its function to amuse and entertain would be like a man deprived of the use of one of his faculties.[9]

For Radio Four Controllers all this translated into a series of tactical calculations. When a popular show attracted sizeable audiences, the following programme often benefited from the so-called 'inheritance factor': listeners staying tuned through curiosity or inertia. *Weekending* was a notable example of what could be achieved, having gradually lifted Radio Four's audience figures on Friday evenings. The lesson was clear. As Clare Lawson Dick had put it: 'if radio could find a new *Take It From Here* or *Hancock's Half Hour* the word would spread to listeners quickly and audiences would increase'.[10] Better still, when a formula struck gold it had the potential to become a cult attraction, and cults often meant *young* listeners. Audiences would, as the broadcasters' jargon put it, be 'refreshed'.[11] For Ian McIntyre there was one further incentive for infusing comedy with new life: it could be another stick with which to beat the Current Affairs empire—a way of reminding journalists that their territorial rights over the schedule were never absolute. With all these considerations in mind, Light Entertainment was under enormous pressure by 1977 to find new formats that would take off.

This was easier said than done, of course. Developing fresh comedy for an audience described with some justice as 'rather cynical' was difficult at the best of times.[12] And in the short term, supply could not keep up with the level of demand being created. Some of the new programmes that subsequently filled the schedule under McIntyre's watch were greeted by critics as unmitigated disasters. *Radio Burps*, a comedy revue just after the *Six o'Clock News*, was savaged at Review Board for being 'extremely obvious, very unfunny and rather distasteful'. *The Spam Fritter Man*, which appeared for the briefest of moments in 1978, was judged 'appalling' for its 'ancient racialist jokes' and registered an all-time low appreciation index of 28 before being quietly buried. *Hinge and Bracket* and *Reg Ackroyd's Silly Scandals* were two innovations that escaped the most bilious attacks. But in reeking of what one critic called 'palm courts and tea dances' they only served to suggest a stubborn desire on Radio Four to look backwards—a charge given added credence by repeats in 1977 of old editions of *Round the Horne* and the even more ancient *Take It From Here*. None of this, *Television Today* suggested, gave any sign of Light Entertainment 'finding the right recipe for the 1970s'.[13] McIntyre's position had been that new hits would be found through producing 'more and better' comedies.[14] But more was not yet meaning better: there were too many failures and not enough hits. The question, as always, was how to turn this around.

Most thought was applied to finding first-class writers. Light Entertainment had a distinguished roll call of people who had trained with them in the past, but who now did most of their work for television: Frank Muir and Dennis Norden, Ray Galton and Alan Simpson, John Esmonde and Bob Larby, David Renwick and Andrew Marshall. The list went on. Money was a large part of the problem, since Radio offered as little as £200–300 for one whole thirty-minute comedy script—about a fifth of the going rate awarded for the same work at BBC Television and a tenth of that at ITV. Galton and Simpson, who had given radio *Hancock's Half Hour*, now commanded £2,300 per episode for BBC 1's *Steptoe and Son*, with a guaranteed repeat and the possibility of an American spin-off. It was little wonder that successful writers were being sucked away from radio faster than they could be found. One obvious solution—perhaps the only one—was to target new writers who had not yet established themselves. It was here that a younger generation of producers could start to make a difference. Experienced hands like Con Mahoney had imbibed deeply the old showbiz principle, 'If it works, leave it alone.'[15] But many of these 'chaps with cravats', as one young Turk labelled them, were retiring, to be replaced by clever young graduates of whom it was said '*Monty Python* had a place in their hearts rather like the one occupied by *The Goon Show* for those growing up in the fifties.'[16]

The most important of these was David Hatch who came back to London from Manchester, where he had been editor of network radio, to replace Mahoney as Head of Light Entertainment in February 1978. In so doing, he took a rather static, traditional department, and, as Barry Took put it, 'shook it warmly by the throat'. 'Out popped some excellent new programmes and, more to the point, a new generation of writers, producers and performers.'[17] Among the new names to watch were John Lloyd, another Cambridge Footlights man who had been snapped up as a producer in 1974, Griff Rhys-Jones, who was in turn recruited by Lloyd after appearing in a successful Cambridge revue, Geoffrey Perkins, who had been spotted writing and directing the Oxford revues of 1974 and 1975, and Simon Brett, who had co-produced *Weekending* with Hatch back in 1970.[18] Armed with such well-connected, youthful talent inside its own office walls, and a succession of new subsidy schemes offering money and guarantees of employment, Light Entertainment was soon imbued with magnetic properties. By the end of 1978, there were nine new writers working for Hatch and his team. By the end of 1979, a competition for novice writers had secured another thirty-five. Over the next few years, those who benefited directly from BBC contracts for relatively unknown but promising writers included Guy Jenkin, Rory McGrath, Rob Grant, Doug Naylor, and Jimmy Mulville.[19]

The combination of producers and writers of this calibre proved remarkably fertile. Griff Rhys-Jones and Jimmy Mulville both took turns at producing *Weekending*, while Guy Jenkin quickly established himself as the leading script-writer: between them, they ensured that, with a few peaks and troughs, *Weekending* retained its reputation as the most successful of the department's ongoing programmes. Geoffrey Perkins gently refreshed *I'm Sorry I Haven't a Clue* in similar fashion. It had been created in 1972 by Graeme Garden as 'the antidote to panel games', and had its settled team of panellists in Tim Brooke-Taylor, Barry Cryer, and Willie Rushton, with Humphrey Lyttelton as its enduring Chairman. It was Perkins, however, who introduced the deliberately incomprehensible 'Mornington Crescent' with great success. In 1977, John Lloyd helped launch *The News Quiz*, wisely resisting the suggestion of News staff that panellists should consist of journalists giving 'knowledgeable' answers to questions. He stuck firmly to the principle that being amusing about one's ignorance was what mattered—and, fortunately for the series, it was a skill in which Richard Ingrams and John Wells seemed to excel. There were nagging worries over the lack of women panellists—as there were for *Just a Minute*, which had its own regular inner circle of Derek Nimmo, Peter Jones, and Kenneth Williams. 'Women who could talk for just a minute were hard to find,' one Light Entertainment producer declared, somewhat recklessly, at one point. Whether provoked into action by this remark or not, as many as eight new performers were soon tried in the space of just one series, with Joan Bakewell and Miriam Margoyles among them.[20]

Putting crowd-pleasing programmes on a firmer footing was only half the task, however. Attracting outrage was important too. After all, comedy was a genre that thrived when skirting the boundaries of taste: complaints were a measure of its good health. Even the Managing Director of Radio agreed that by its very nature some comedy 'strayed over to the wrong side from time to time'; he for one 'would not want to inhibit' programmes that did so. *Weekending* had done the job successfully in the early 1970s, but showed dangerous signs of mellowing. It was certainly attracting fewer complaints. Hatch thought this might be because listeners had finally accepted that it treated almost *everything* in an irreverent way. It was obvious, nonetheless, that it would benefit—not least from more publicity—if it attracted a little more flak. 'Perhaps', Hatch speculated in 1978, 'a good libel suit was needed.' The programme came close to causing offence the following year when it carried an 'obituary' for the Liberal politician Jeremy Thorpe, and again in 1980 for a sketch about the abortive American attempt to free its hostages in Tehran—one letter-writer to the BBC requesting that the programme team be 'flogged for their effrontery'. It even faced a genuine libel action from Derek Jameson, after he was described as 'the archetypal East End boy made bad . . . who still believes that "erudite" is a glue'. If a 'cult' was going to be found for a new generation of listeners, more knockabout stuff like this was needed. Almost by definition, it would involve causing offence—and not just to particular individuals. 'Comedy programmes tended to divide the Radio Four audience into old and young,' David Hatch told his colleagues in 1980, 'and the old audience always wrote in to complain about the programmes aimed at the young.'[21]

One new programme that fitted this description nicely was *The Burkiss Way*, which ran for six series between 1976 and 1980. Barry Took described it as an irreverent, surreal romp through the conscious and unconscious mind of the Seventies and Eighties, 'written as if Sigmund Freud and A. J. P. Taylor had joined forces with John Cleese'. A foretaste of what was involved had emerged in Radio Three's *The Half Open University*, a 1975 parody of the BBC's Open University broadcasts, written by Andrew Marshall, David Renwick, and John Mason, and produced by Simon Brett. This was then reshaped for Radio Four by Brett—and later by John Lloyd and David Hatch—to become a weekly 'corres-pondence column of the air' led by the fictional Professor Burkiss, and with a cast including Nigel Rees, Fred Harris, Chris Emmett, Denise Coffey, and Jo Ken-dall. Each episode was presented as if it were a lesson: *Pass Examinations The Burkiss Way, Gain Spiritual Fulfilment The Burkiss Way*, and so on. Two consecu-tive episodes in the fifth series were called *Repeat Yourself The Burkiss Way*. It was ostensibly a sketch show, but like *The Goons*, it played with form as much as content: there were countless false endings, fake continuity announcements, and 'technical problems' deliberately disrupting the flow of sketches. Amid the confusion could be found some regular characters and even the odd catchphrase. Chris Emmett's memorable Eric Pode of Croydon was one of them—'Gruntfut-tock without the charm', as one description put it. Took thought the seedy and revolting Pode easily rated with the best of Kenneth Williams's monsters.[22]

The Burkiss Way almost failed to make it beyond the first series. One of Light Entertainment's own producers, Bobby Jaye, wondered whether the programme was aiming for satire or heavy irony and declared it undistinguished. Even Hatch feared it might turn out to be a striking failure. As for Con Mahoney—he had simply wanted more laughs: too many sketches were distasteful; the writers were very talented and spirited, but some of their material 'besides being very clever, tended to be cruel'. The outgoing Managing Director of Radio, Howard Newby, was inclined to agree. There was, he thought, 'a deplorable amount of schoolboy vulgarity' in some editions. Others wondered whether the studio audience made matters worse: vulgarity got the loudest laughs, and seemed to encourage the programme team to respond in kind. Ian McIntyre, on the other hand, was a supporter, as was the Director of Programmes, the incoming

Managing Director, Aubrey Singer, and the Controller of Radio Three, Stephen Hearst—who even thought it 'as good as *Round the Horne*'. They were uncomfortable with its vulgarity, but prepared to agree with Hatch that 'there was a risk of destroying the programme team if control was too oppressive'. Their encouragement, alongside Hatch's protection, was an impressive example of the BBC's willingness to support a show that divided opinion internally as well as externally. A script that walked a tightrope in matters of taste and sometimes fell down on the job, it calculated, was probably worthwhile if a programme reached the much sought-after younger audience.[23]

And for the modest price of some thirteen or so complaints from listeners each week, *The Burkiss Way* had indeed won for Radio Four an audience that was, McIntyre noted admiringly, 'large, young and keen'—as the testimony of one comedy aficionado, Matt Coward, reveals:

I rarely missed a recording of *Burkiss* . . . and not only because the tickets were free. As a live show, it was quite an experience. Its very young, un-Radio 4 studio audience packed the place out, with the overspill sitting on the floor and even on the stage. Many fans would dress up for the occasion, some wearing 'I do it the Burkiss Way' T-shirts—and this wasn't BBC merchandising, people had the shirts made themselves.[24]

The Burkiss Way ended in 1980 much as it had begun, with the last-minute excision of a sketch mocking the Queen Mother's eightieth birthday celebrations and its replacement with six minutes of music. By then it had achieved much that Light Entertainment had been striving for over the past half-decade. David Hatch was confident enough to describe the series as 'almost a "Monty Python" of the radio'.[25] It had not just captured a young audience, but exhibited many other features of the true cult: an audience that grew by word of mouth rather than official publicity, a language of its own that could be shared among fans, and a preparedness to exclude through provocation and obscurantism those who simply 'did not get it'.

Many of these characteristics—and others besides—applied to the most famous programme of all to emerge from Light Entertainment in the late 1970s: *The Hitchhiker's Guide to the Galaxy*. Its date of birth is traditionally given as 4 February 1977. It was then that Simon Brett met the writer Douglas Adams over lunch in a West End club to discuss the possibility of a comedy science-fiction serial. Adams was someone who had struggled to make a full-time living from comic writing since graduating from Cambridge in 1974. He enjoyed a brief, fruitless writing partnership with the ex-Python Graham Chapman, and had tried, unsuccessfully, to provide *Weekending* with the snappy material its particular format demanded. As one of his biographers points out, he could not take topical politics seriously enough to find them ridiculous, for 'his perceptions had already expanded to the point where he found man's place in the universe absurd'. Evolutionary biology, gadgetry, and the works of J. S. Bach, Procul Harum, P. G. Wodehouse, and Charles Dickens—these were just some of his fascinations, and they seemed to feed what friends saw as his immense and unpredictable sense of curiosity at the human condition.[26]

The kind of expansive and surreal comedy that emerged from a mind like this suited a programme such as *The Burkiss Way*, and Adams had indeed contributed to the series. But Brett, who was producing *Burkiss* at the time, recognized that Adams was doomed to be a talent without a niche unless he could find a format of his own. There were others in Light Entertainment ready to champion his cause, too: John Lloyd, who had shared a flat with him in London, and John Simmonds, who admired his handful of sketches for radio. When Adams raised the possibility of a comic science fiction during the February lunch meeting, Brett recognized that here might be the vehicle the writer needed, and seized upon it. Within three weeks, Brett was starting work on a pilot, which was recorded three months later, in June 1977. Brett recalls playing the recording to Con Mahoney, then in his last months before retiring: 'Total silence. Not a single smile muscle twitched. At the end of it my boss turned to me and asked, "Simon, is it funny?" I said, "Yes, I promise you it's funny". And he said—full marks to him for doing so—"In that case we'll back it all the way". And they did.' It was, however, only after sending the script to David Hatch for a second opinion—which turned out to be equally enthusiastic—that Mahoney wrote the cheque.[27] By the end of August 1977, the series was approved and, soon after, Hatch offered Adams the job of a producer in the department he was now taking over.

The moment was propitious, for science fiction had suddenly come back into vogue after a long period in the wilderness, condemned in the BBC as 'very fifties' and lacking popular appeal. Until recently, people such as the Director of Programmes, Douglas Muggeridge, had declared a fierce loathing for it. Even the popularity of *Dr Who* on television—with some fourteen million watching each week—seemed only to have confirmed science fiction's status as an essentially juvenile genre. By the middle of 1977, however, its potential appeal to a mainstream audience had been demonstrated by the huge cinematic success of *Star Wars*. Some in Broadcasting House were soon suggesting 'a strong serial' to build a similar following on radio. Ronald Mason, in Drama, was certainly keen to get involved. Ian McIntyre, however, told colleagues that more interesting results might be achieved if studio managers experienced in special effects were to team up, not with Drama, but with Light Entertainment.[28]

The will to make a science-fiction comedy had taken root; the precise means of translating Adams's idea into a finished programme had yet to be formulated. Throughout 1978 much inventiveness and patience was called for. Assembling a cast was the easiest part: many, such as Simon Jones (who played Arthur Dent) and Geoffrey McGivern (who played Ford Prefect), were old colleagues from the Footlights. For the voice of 'The Book', Adams and Brett sought a matter-of-fact 'Peter Jonesy sound', and, after contemplating Michael Palin, struck on the obvious candidate: Peter Jones himself, a man already familiar to Radio Four listeners for his frequent appearances on *Just a Minute*. Other members of the cast included Mark Wing-Davey, Stephen Moore, David Tate, and Richard Vernon. Providing dialogue was trickier. Adams had a history of missed deadlines. His writing pace was legendarily slow—a result of paralysing perfectionism and self-doubt, rather than laziness, but inconvenient nonetheless for those working to a tight schedule. Matters were made worse by his being offered the job of script editor on *Dr Who* at the same time as having to complete *Hitchhiker's*. Geoffrey Perkins, who had by now taken over as producer from Simon Brett, chivvied Adams along as best he could, and John Lloyd was drawn into writing large chunks of the later episodes. David Hatch subsequently confessed to how 'difficult and demanding' it had been for Adams to complete the scripts, and of how much help he had needed from Perkins.[29] This was something of an understatement. During the actual recording of one episode, Adams was seen in the studio frantically typing out dialogue: it ended with several minutes of eerie wind only because there was no time to include what had originally been planned.

The *sound* of the series was a crucial consideration for Adams. He was clear that he wanted it to sound like a rock album. 'Listening to radio comedy at the time', he wrote, 'we still hadn't progressed much beyond Door Slam A, Door Slam B, Footsteps on a Gravel Path and the odd Comic Boing.' For *Hitchhiker's* he wanted voices and effects and music to be 'so seamlessly orchestrated as to create a coherent picture of a whole other world'.[30] The idea of this seamless mix was not new, of course, and it was exactly the sort of stuff at which the BBC's own Radiophonic Workshop excelled. Yet it was much more time consuming than the quick turn-around of most Light Entertainment shows, which involved recording in front of an audience and removing a few out-takes. For *Hitchhiker's*, the Radiophonic Workshop was asked to supply, among other effects, 'the sound of an office building flying through space in the grip of seven powerful tractor beams', and treatment to make actors' voices sound 'slimy and robotic'. As it turned out, the simplest solutions were sometimes the best. Limping robots were created by the simple expedient of getting someone to walk around with one foot in a wastepaper basket.[31]

There was no studio audience for *Hitchhiker's*, since it took nearly a week per episode to record and post-produce, with much time spent recording scenes out of order, and sometimes with only half the actors in any given scene actually visible on stage. As Perkins recalled, the style of radio performance thus invented had to be given a name all of its own—'cupboard acting':

All the various robots, computers, Vogons and so on had their voice treatments added after the recordings, so it was necessary to separate them from the other actors, and this we did by putting them in cupboards . . . Sometimes when three or four aliens were taking part in a scene you could look out of the control box and there would be nobody on stage at all. They'd all be in various cupboards dotted around the studio. Sometimes the actors played more than one part, sometimes as many as five parts. This of course was so that they could show off their versatility. It was also so that we could manage to bring the show in somewhere in the region of the budget.[32]

The first episode was broadcast at 10.30 p.m. on Wednesday 8 March 1978. One of Adams's biographers has claimed that the BBC were unsure what they had on their hands.[33] But initial reactions were, in fact, almost entirely positive. It was, according to one Drama producer, 'very funny, enjoyable and stylish . . . one of the most imaginative and original series on any network for a very long time'; Ian McIntyre's Chief Assistant, Richard Wade, thought it 'splendid'—both he and his children had been gripped; even the arch sci-fi sceptic Douglas Muggeridge declared it 'a real break-through in radio light entertainment'.[34] As John Lloyd recalled, *Hitchhiker's* 'never had to struggle at all . . . everyone, from the first day, thought it was great'.[35] There was also approbation of a more public kind in the form of two positive newspaper reviews during the first week. The *Observer* went so far as to say that *Hitchhiker's* 'just might be the most original radio comedy for years'. Initial audience figures were negligible, as was to be expected for any programme transmitted late in the evening. But, just as with *The Burkiss Way*, word of mouth took over. By the time the fourth episode was being broadcast, Light Entertainment was receiving some twenty to thirty fan-letters a day, and several enquiries from publishers and record companies trying to buy the rights. Soon after the series had finished in April, the incoming Managing Director of Radio, Aubrey Singer, was urging McIntyre to 'make sure this talent is not lost to us too soon', and contemplating future co-production with National Public Radio in the United States. Events, however, were moving too quickly for Broadcasting House to take full control. By the time Light Entertainment cajoled a second Radio Four series out of Adams for the beginning of 1980, *Hitchhiker's* had become a television adaptation, a best-selling novel, a stage play, an LP, even a commemorative towel. There were also countless clubs and conventions for its fans around the world. It had, in short, become 'the special property of a generation'.[36]

John Lloyd has suggested that *Hitchhiker's Guide to the Galaxy* was so success-ful because it caught the spirit of the moment: 'with hitchhiking and galaxies you have this curious mixture of post-hippie sensibilities and being interested in high tech, digital technology and all that stuff'. This no doubt helped its international success among the young when it had become a book. The success of the original radio series is harder to explain. In one sense, its impact has been exaggerated: audiences never reached the 'millions' that fans of the series believed. BBC figures showed it was nearer half a million each week. What *Hitchhiker's* did do, however, was to change public perceptions of Radio Four. Several listeners have written of the series introducing them to the network: 'ironing in the kitchen and twiddling the dial to find something to listen to', finding it and 'leaving the dial where it was'. They have also written of personal epiphanies: 'When I first encountered *Hitchhiker's Guide the Galaxy* I was still at school . . . and being told I was due for a life of factory work; Douglas so inspired me that

I refused to believe I was as stupid as I was told, and now I'm a PhD student in computer science.' Or even simply: 'I discovered the meaning of life.'

Most of these testimonies came from young listeners, and the richly textured comic-book style of production was no doubt important in attracting a generation uninspired by Radio Four's usual tone. So too, in all probability, was the casting and direction: the cool savoir faire of Peter Jones provided a much-needed narrative thread running through the noise and confusion all around. And there was the writing itself. It was not just witty, but erudite—and in a conversational way. Under the cover of some good jokes, Adams had managed to sneak in plenty of interesting philosophical ideas about life, time, and existence. Here was a series that was devoured by young science-fiction fans *and* subject to serious-minded review on Radio Three. It appealed to both 'lowbrow' and 'highbrow' tastes, without merely splitting the difference awkwardly between the two. As Geoffrey Perkins put it: 'The intellectuals compared it to Swift, and the fourteen year-olds enjoyed hearing depressed robots clanking around.'[37]

For a Light Entertainment department that had seemed distinctly lacklustre only two years earlier, this was no mean achievement. It provided vivid confirmation of what insiders called the 'buzz' created during David Hatch's term in charge. Radio had once again become a pleasurable and supportive spot for young comic writers and comedians to begin their careers. It had also fostered what Barry Took defined as 'a new mood' in comedy itself—a change of direction, new voices, different jokes. There were fewer star-acts of the old variety type, and a new generation of surrealists, into topicality and parody, and nurtured by bright and ambitious producers who had adhered to John Cleese's Three Laws of Comedy for the post-*Goons* era: 'No Puns, No Puns, and No Puns'. Some of their programmes had even achieved the status of cults. For Radio Four, anxious to leaven the mix of seriousness and do-goodery elsewhere on its schedule, anxious to renew its ageing audience, anxious simply to be talked about, this was manna from heaven.

RADIO DRAMA AND 'SOUND CINEMA'

Could Radio Drama pull off the same trick? The problems it faced certainly appeared similar to those confronting Light Entertainment: the need to grab critical and public attention; the need to persuade sceptics of the genre's aesthetic value in a television age; above all, the need to ensure it was enriched by a constantly renewed pool of writers and performers.

As in Light Entertainment, past glory weighed heavily on contemporary expectations and fears. In the 1950s and 1960s there had been a long and impressive list of playwrights who had done some of their earliest—and, some argued, their best—work in radio. John Arden, Giles Cooper, Robert Bolt, Bill

Naughton, John Mortimer, Harold Pinter, Tom Stoppard, Joe Orton: they had all received BBC Radio's institutional kiss of life at crucial moments in their careers. Stoppard, for example, had been making his living from freelance journalism in Bristol when two Radio Drama producers, John Tydeman and Richard Imison, accepted his script for *The Dissolution of Dominic Boot* at the end of 1963. Its broadcast won him the attention of drama critics, and provided just enough money for him to remain in London to pursue his real ambition of writing for the stage.[38] Orton's professional breakthrough had also come at the end of 1963, when *The Ruffian on the Stair* was accepted as a radio play. Its broadcast in 1964 came after a decade of literary failure, but within a few months *Entertaining Mr Sloane* was being staged to great acclaim. It was his radio producer—Tydeman again—who had introduced him to Peggy Ramsey, the theatrical agent.[39] A magnanimous gesture. And proof that the Radio Drama department Esslin had inherited from Val Gielgud, though bitterly divided between conservatives and radicals, was a going concern: staffed by at least a few producers alert to talent and on the lookout for novelty. But it also told a story of writers discovered and nurtured by Radio, then lost to the worlds of television, theatre, and film.

Sometimes, as with comedy, this was a matter of economics. In the early 1970s, established dramatists could expect to receive about £600 for a radio play—about a third of what they would receive for similar work in television. Beginners would earn something nearer £400—roughly a quarter the television rate. Writing an original script for radio was, in short, something that demanded a labour completely at odds with its likely reward. Worse, in an ephemeral medium it was an effort akin to shouting into a deep hole. Writers lived by being noticed; but radio left hardly a trace. Fewer and fewer weekly magazines bothered to review radio's programmes. 'All the novelty, the action, the notice, and the riches', as *The Times*' critic David Wade put it, 'were with television.' Few members of Radio Drama were surprised when talent haemorrhaged away as quickly as it arrived.[40]

Under these conditions, one obvious response was to create a greater sense of occasion for ordinary listeners and critics through offering rather more spectacular productions. And one natural means of achieving this was through the manipulation of sound into weird and wonderful new forms, just as was done in *Hitchhiker's Guide to the Galaxy*.

Inspiration for making radio drama less literary and more cinematic arrived from a number of sources. First, from producers in continental Europe, where there was in the early 1970s something of a 'new wave' in feature-making that stressed the artistic potential of manipulated sound. In West Germany, which had its own rich tradition of radio drama and documentary, practitioners argued, for instance, that television's dominance now 'liberated' radio from the need to tell stories: it could 'concentrate more on the purely auditory aspects of its art'. An international infrastructure of competitions, conferences, and professional exchanges ensured that some of this philosophy was infiltrated into the British radio drama tradition through individuals such as Michael Mason, Hallam Tennyson, and Richard Imison, who were among those travelling back and forth across the English Channel and warning colleagues in Broadcasting House that the BBC would fall behind its continental partners unless it embraced the more exciting techniques they were developing.[41]

A second source of inspiration lay in domestic television, where for the past decade young directors employed by the BBC such as Ken Loach, Stephen Frears, and Roland Joffe had started to dispense with detailed scripts and dialogue, and were taking their increasingly mobile cameras out and about, or working for longer hours in their editing suites in order to construct more striking visual sequences—who were, in short, trying to make television drama less 'writerly' and more influenced by the creativity of the director.[42]

A third source lay within Radio Drama itself: for even under Val Gielgud the department had had its own avant-gardist subculture—nurtured since the 1950s through individuals such as Donald McWhinnie, aided and abetted by a post-1964 infusion of Features producers such as Douglas Cleverdon, and carried into the 1970s by staff congregating in ginger groups such as the so-called 'Creative Radio Committee', the 'Features Workshop' and the long-established 'Rothwell Group'.

Through these initiatives something approaching an *auteur* tradition of 'sound cinema' was forced into being, largely by experimenting with the tactile qualities of new technology. One crucible was the Radiophonic Workshop, which had been established in 1958 specifically in the hope of emulating continental pioneers of *musique concrète* and their ability to distort sound with disorientating results. The Workshop had been used since then to provide countless passing effects—the 'high hum of pure agony', for example, that was required of Giles Cooper's 1958 play *Under the Loofah Tree*, and the sound of Major Bloodnok's stomach for *The Goons*.[43] More recently, Michael Mason had used its armoury of multitrack recorders and synthesizers to create the trademark wash of sounds in his epic features *A Bayeux Tapestry* (1966), *Rus* (1968), and, of course, *The Long March of Everyman* (1971–2). In these, and in later features such as his portrait of Beethoven, *The Marriage of Freedom and Fate* (1974), or his mosaic of maritime sounds wrapped in Sibelius for *The British Seafarer* (1980), Mason was not just testing the BBC's technical resources to the limit: he was hoping to offer listeners a *sensational* experience, in the literal meaning of the term—an experience where sound was important as words, and where narration could be dispensed with altogether.[44]

Mainstream dramatists, being rather respectful of written language, were more circumspect. But even they now dabbled in radiophonics more frequently than hitherto, especially when it came to creating the futuristic aural landscapes demanded of science fiction. It was used to striking effect, for example, in *August 2026*, a 1977 play based on a Ray Bradbury story about an all-electronic home continuing its robotic rituals despite the nuclear annihilation of the family which once owned it—a production, incidentally, which marked the vocoder's British radio debut.

Something embraced in the 1970s with even more evangelical fervour than radiophony was stereophony and its various offshoots. Stereo had been around for decades and the aesthetic potential of having two loudspeakers, each with its own soundtrack, was explored fully in a book published as far back as 1959. *Stereo and Hi-Fi as a Pastime* claimed the technology broke through 'the former limitation of a performance that had to be heard as though squeezed through an 8 to 15 inch hole in the wall' and gave instead 'the effect of the wall between yourself and the concert platform being taken completely away'. It achieved what the book called 'something very near to actuality', first by creating a wide 'stage' of sound, secondly by allowing voices and sounds to 'move' across this stage, and thirdly by allowing listeners to hear clearly two voices speaking at the same time.[45] The dramatic possibilities were tested in a series of experiments on BBC Radio in 1960 and a regular service began hesitantly in 1966. Critical reaction was generally encouraging. When the *Guardian*'s reviewer listened to one of the new-fangled plays in a basement studio of Broadcasting House she was deeply impressed: 'One would at moments have sworn... that the actors themselves were concealed and moving physically about behind the grey silk curtain we all sat facing.'[46]

Over the next ten years, more and more of Radio Four's plays were made in stereo. By the late 1970s it was commonplace. So commonplace, indeed, that its novelty had started to pall. Consequently there were attempts to make radio's sound stage even more realistic by creating 'quadraphony', which doubled the number of speakers to four. The aesthetic appeal of this lay in being able to place listeners in the centre of a 360-degree performing area: they would be sitting, quite literally, in the thick of the action. It was tried for several Proms concerts on Radio Three and a pop concert on Radio One before being tested on a *Saturday Night Theatre* play in 1976 and *The Archers* in 1977. Its high-point came with Ian Cotterell's two-hour production of *Alice in Wonderland* for Radio Four later that year, which was not just recorded in quadraphonic, but also boasted a script by John Wells and an opulent musical score by Carl Davis. By this stage, the BBC was broadcasting about one 'quad' programme a week. This was, however, a rate that gradually declined thereafter. Without a system of encoders and decoders— and the precise system to be adopted was itself a matter of dispute—there was no such thing as a domestic radio set able to receive four bands of information simultaneously, nor were there the wavelengths available to accommodate them.[47] The technology foundered. As did the 'Kunstkopf', an extraordinary German invention that emerged amid much curiosity in 1973. This consisted of a 'dummy' head carefully moulded in order to reproduce the same acoustics as those of a real human head. This was then fitted with two microphones in exactly the same position as the eardrums, and actors were required to move around it while recording their dialogue. When the result was listened to on headphones witnesses testified to 'an amazing increase in depth and definition over ordinary mono or stereo'. Martin Esslin was fascinated, and arranged for the BBC to experiment with it from 1974. Its alien appearance, however, was matched by an unworldly price-tag. This put it well beyond the BBC's reach as a standard tool of the drama studio, and it failed to take root.[48]

The Kunstkopf experiments, like the deployment of stereo or quadraphony, were, in any case, less important for the daily functioning of Radio Drama than for the stir they created in the public arena. When Radio Four launched *Hi-Fi Theatre* in 1978, for instance, the series self-consciously placed the technical quality of a programme centre stage in the hope that superior sound quality would build a sense of occasion: continuity announcers asked listeners to tell their friends about each broadcast and to listen to the plays as though they were attending a real theatre. To make sure the series started with a bang, it launched with a new stereo production of an old classic, Dylan Thomas's *Under Milk Wood*. The new version offended Richard Burton for the innovation of sharing narration between a male and female voice. But it garnered praise at Review Board as a 'marvellous and sensitive production' with excellent sound quality. As with many of the programmes that followed, there was plenty of press coverage.[49]

This technological approach evidently had glamour—a glamour that neatly challenged the derogatory labelling of the medium as 'steam radio'. But not everyone was convinced that Radio Drama had taken the right aesthetic turn by embracing sound cinema so enthusiastically. John Tydeman, one of the leading lights of the Rothwell Group and a keen supporter of experimentation in general, warned that the indiscriminate use of radiophonics risked 'rapidly reproducing an auditory cliché'. Electronic sounds, he argued, created the broad effects of horror or comedy easily enough, but being artificial they rarely invoked tenderness, passion, or soul: they tended, in effect, to dehumanize—a fatal blow to the dramatic appeal of most work. The problem was that many a producer had rather too much of the child about him: 'He must be persuaded not to play with the toys too much of the time.'[50] In the meantime, dark mutterings at Review Board reflected a feeling that producers were overindulging in technique. It was as though good ideas—good *stories*—were being smothered with unwarranted gimmickry. Was it really necessary, for example, for *Hi-Fi Theatre's* 1979 production of *Under the Volcano* to offer what Monica Sims called 'vomiting in high-fidelity'? She, for one, thought not, and turned it off promptly.[51]

Behind the growing suspicion that producers were getting carried away with technique lurked an even more damaging thought: that stereo and high-fidelity undermined the whole imaginative core of radio drama by bringing back the 'proscenium arch'. Producers started telling Review Board of how, when listening to epic productions, they had had the sensation of being in a cinema with their backs to the screen—what one called 'a physical rather than an imaginative experience'.[52] This was disturbing. The particular potency of radio drama was that it worked through a series of symbolic sounds. This allowed—indeed, *required*—the listener to use his or her mental powers of visualization to complete a scene. In so doing it let the action take place within the listener's head, as it were. The 'blindness' of the medium was therefore its greatest asset: it was what forged a unique inwardness and granted to a listener the pleasure of participation. Stereo, by way of contrast, seemed to represent a fumbling attempt to compete with television on unfavourable terms: it invited the listener to be a blind spectator following the movements of actors 'out there', on a stage that was not—and never would be—seen. This thought, now voiced inside Broadcasting House, was soon taken up forcefully by the writer Jonathan Raban, who began with a lament for the new, stereophonic treatment of *Under Milk Wood*:

Much of the language sounded arch and stilted when placed in the context of a 'real' Welsh village constructed with faultless naturalism by the studio technicians. The dream stopped short of the listener's head and took place instead on his carpet ... The play is no longer a code to be deciphered as one deciphers print; it has turned into something like an unrolling tapestry of sound pictures, before which the listener remains a detached, and often puzzled, spectator.[53]

Raban's critique was part of a wide-ranging assault on the whole appeal of 'pure radio'. He feared a future of technically dazzling but arid pieces of what he called 'aural mimesis', where 'medium enthusiasts' turned radio into something obsessively *about* sound: 'a series of ever more ingenious experiments with what is really only the typography of radio, not its deep structure'. The cause, he thought, was clear enough: 'the need which afflicts radio people—the desire to be *sui generis*'. It was as though radio producers—always invisible, their work taken for granted—wanted to be artists, doing something quite different from—but certainly of equal value to—that being celebrated in television, cinema, the theatre, or literature.[54]

In truth, radio was emphatically *not* a spectacular medium, nor, in Radio Four's case, was it one where the audience tolerated anything that smacked of pretentiousness. It was a medium that demanded self-effacement from producers—one where listeners had no desire to notice his or her work, but wished instead to focus on the play and the players. In this, their tastes were straightforward—and the default position of Radio Drama often cynically calculating. As one producer put it, 'You can't go wrong if there's an animal or a mother in the story.'[55]

This exaggerated—but not by much. All the evidence suggested the bulk of Radio Four's audience wanted good plain storytelling, uncluttered by sound effects, with unambiguous endings, and fully respectful of the Aristotelian Unities of time and place and character. These predilections could not be ignored. Nor, indeed, did Radio Drama wish to ignore them; at least not entirely. It was, after all, a central part of the BBC's thinking that the reassuring presence of simple, entertaining, and traditional plays on Radio Four was precisely what made possible—that is, what made *permissible*—'the production of avant-garde and other demanding drama elsewhere'. In any case there was still much to play for. If public taste dictated that the centre of gravity in Radio Drama's repertoire had to be in the middle part of the spectrum, then so be it: the 'middle', as always, was territory so loosely defined that it could be stretched and renovated in ways that might satisfy Radio Drama's evident desire to achieve something of cultural significance—and in ways that even suspicious listeners might tolerate. It was here, in the mainstream of dramatic production and well away from the experiments in 'sound cinema' that the most long-lasting developments in radio drama could be found.

IMPROVING THE 'MIDDLE GROUND'

It would have been easy to keep things much as they were: for if good plain stories and unambiguous endings were what Radio Four listeners wanted, producers already knew how to give satisfaction. In the mainstream slots of *Afternoon Theatre*, *Midweek Theatre*, and *Saturday Night Theatre*, there were predictable winners. Daphne du Maurier, for example, invariably went down well, as did Dorothy L. Sayers, P. G. Wodehouse, or any mildly gothic thriller or murder mystery. The enduring popularity of *Lord Peter Wimsey*, *Man in Black*-style revivals, and several series of *What Ho Jeeves!*—all rewarded with decent audience 'appreciation' figures—was proof enough of that. Entertaining dramas woven around favourite performers, or anything that evoked the flavour of the old Home Service and its era, were also popular. Hence series such as *The Small Intricate Life of Gerald C. Potter*, comic monologues from 1976 designed as a vehicle for Ian Carmichael and described at Review Board as 'reminiscent of an old volume of *Punch*': a series judged to be 'wafer thin but crisp—just right for Radio Four'.[56] Hence, too, the extraordinary success of what might be called nostalgic juvenilia: adaptations of *Alice in Wonderland*, *Wind in the Willows*, *Winnie the Pooh*, and the like. As for *Just William*, Richmal Crompton's deft satire of southern English bourgeois life, filled with gentle self-mockery: that captured the requisite qualities perfectly.[57]

The most enduring marriage of popularity and understated good taste, however, was to be found in Radio Four's adaptation of the literary 'classics'. Radio Drama was supremely well practised at this particular craft. From its earliest pre-television days, the Corporation had committed itself to dramatizing the canon. Charles Dickens had been a favourite of the National Programme in the 1920s and 1930s, as had Anthony Trollope and Jane Austen. Countless productions since then had helped to establish the classic serial as one of the quintessential genres of BBC Radio. Producing the canon was the perfect Reithian enterprise: it introduced an audience to literature almost everyone agreed was 'good', and, provided that it was well acted, the commitment to quality also reflected well on its producers. Radio Four did it well; it thus did well by it.[58]

Certainly, there was no sign of its commitment to classics waning in the 1970s and early 1980s. Indeed, if anything, there was more of it then than ever. One reason for this was that older, out-of-copyright stories were always going to be cheaper than new ones: an important consideration in any inflationary period. Another reason was that television was setting a brisk tempo. Especially after the introduction of colour, period dramas were seen as an opportunity for viewers to wallow in glorious costumes, locations, and landscapes, as well as in solid storylines. The succession of hugely popular productions that followed 1967's *The Forsyte Saga* onto British television screens—*War and Peace* (BBC, 1972), *Emma* (BBC, 1973), *Upstairs, Downstairs* (Granada, 1970–5), *Poldark* (BBC, 1975–7), *The Duchess of Duke Street* (BBC, 1976–7), *I, Claudius* (BBC, 1976), *Testament of Youth* (BBC, 1979)—all these had whetted appetites that Radio Four could readily exploit. Throughout this period, the network was teeming with dramatizations and readings of Trollope, Austen, Hugh Walpole, George Eliot, C. P. Snow, Henry James, Anthony Powell, and Thomas Hardy. Trollope had special appeal, one actor declaring that he offered 'the right stuff': 'not too heavy, not too light; prose that is neither pretentious nor stale'. But it was Dickens who reigned supreme. Between 1974 and 1984, serializations of *The Pickwick Papers*, *Bleak House*, *Martin Chuzzlewit*, *Little Dorrit*, and *Our Mutual Friend* were all broadcast on Radio Four. Their regular producer, Jane Morgan, became an acknowledged expert in adapting Dickens and conjuring fine performances out of the teeming cast his stories demanded.[59]

Historians of British television and film have suggested it was no coincidence that in the 1970s, amid political fractiousness and gloom over the country's economic decline, there was a demand for dramas set in the past, and in particular the Edwardian era, an elegiac period drenched (in the imagination at least) with peace, tranquillity, harmony, stability, and national greatness—in short, a time of better days. Nor, they have added, was it mere coincidence that at the start of the 1980s films such as *Chariots of Fire* and television series such as Granada's *Brideshead Revisited* offered viewers golden days of a wealthy elite and backdrops of sumptuous country houses and exotic locations. They symbolized a shift in the national mood 'from liberalism to conservatism'; they embodied the 'values and iconography of the Thatcher Revolution'; they tapped into a heritage explosion, where history became 'the perfect package holiday' away from the present day.[60]

If so, there is no doubt the same analysis could be applied to Radio Four. But here there was a penalty to be faced. The prevalence of traditional dramas on its schedules already gave Radio Four an uncomfortably nostalgic feel: too many classic serials seemed only to reinforce this impression by suggesting, once again, that here was a network stuck in the past, nervous of portraying the contemporary world in all its ugly reality.

Clearly, one way of redressing this imbalance would have been for Radio Four to find room in its repertoire for a few radical living playwrights addressing contemporary themes. But its record in this area was not good. Indeed, it seemed to be falling further and further behind what was happening elsewhere in British drama. The stage, for example—liberated since 1968 from the Lord Chamberlain's archaic powers of censorship—was rampant with the exploration of politics and sexuality. Those on the Left who were strongly influenced by the counter-cultures of the late 1960s had seized their chance to attack conventions and shock audiences. Edward Bond, David Hare, Howard Brenton, David Edgar, Howard Barker, John McGrath, Trevor Griffiths: these were the names to reckon with in the 1970s. And they talked of a 'theatre of change', a theatre which 'interprets the world . . . does not merely mirror it', a theatre which dramatized extremities of personal behaviour as a metaphor for the violence and iniquities of imperialism and class power. British television would have been hard-pressed to broadcast all of the work in this ideological tradition, but some of it was making its way to the small screen. Under the banner of *Play for Today*, writers such as Edgar, Hare, and Griffiths, as well as Jim Allen, Alan Bleasdale, Mike Leigh, and Dennis Potter, all contributed work that put contemporary Britain under the microscope. As indeed Griffiths thought they had a duty to do. 'I simply cannot understand socialist playwrights who do not devote most of their time to television,' he argued, 'it's just thunderingly exciting to be able to talk to large numbers of people in the working-class.'[61]

Even if these radical playwrights could be persuaded to work in Broadcasting House, rather than Television Centre or the Royal Court—and some in Radio Drama were trying hard to persuade them to do just that—their overtly political dramas would have found a somewhat frosty reception at Radio Four. For a start, there was a problem of balance. Ian McIntyre, for instance, thought he smelled too much ideology and not enough art as it was. He harboured dark suspicions that just as current affairs staff were too close to Fleet Street, drama producers were, as he put it, 'holding the door open uncritically' to 'chums in the theatre'. The result? 'Some of what they served up was ill-disguised political propaganda, and I wasn't particularly interested in having it on the air.'[62] For their part, Drama producers despaired of the debates they had with McIntyre: 'terribly adversarial', they recalled, 'asking us to justify every play, as if it was politics'. Monica Sims was altogether more placatory, but, as one drama producer pointed out, her outlook was certainly 'more Kensington than Hackney': not every proposal was welcome. Direct refusals from either of these two Controllers were extremely rare, but there was undoubtedly a climate of squeamishness over radical voices. A few made themselves heard on Radio Three, but on Radio Four, as John Tydeman complained in 1978, 'Writers such as Brenton, Hare, Edgar, Poliakoff, Gooch do not get an airing.' 'Politically the reasons are understandable', he told his managers; 'artistically they are a loss.'[63]

Then there was the problem of taste. This was not just a matter of listeners' omnipresent sensitivities over bad language. It also concerned their aversion to almost anything unusual, or confrontational, or foreign. Plays from Northern

Ireland were always problematic, if only because so many of them addressed the Troubles. A large minority of listeners were suspicious of the politics, turned off by the violence, or simply hated the accent. But prejudices went wider than that. The British listening public, Martin Esslin claimed, generally disliked 'earnestness, obscurity, and display of learning' and were impatient with anything 'couched in odd, alien or unacceptable forms'. Worse, 'Contrary to popular myth, thirty per cent of the British had no sense of humour at all.' At its best, Esslin concluded, this emotional and intellectual constipation induced in the national literature a powerful form of understatement, 'a poetry not so much of images and metaphors as unexpressed content'. At its worst, it fostered a debilitating literal-mindedness. This was a gross generalization, of course. But all too often, there were just enough Radio Four listeners to confirm the stereotype rather too accurately for comfort. Why else would there have been so many complaints of 'anti-Semitism' in a 1973 *Afternoon Theatre*, which, its producers agreed, had been 'absolutely clear' in offering a savage satire *against* fascism? Or complaints that a spoof thriller for *Saturday Night Theatre* in 1975 was 'melodramatic'? Or, indeed, countless complaints that plays which BBC insiders described as 'light, witty and amusing' were actually 'incomprehensible' and 'offensive'? No wonder Esslin advised Radio Four against even trying to broadcast Ivan Klima's *The Jury*. It was not just foreign, but featured a beheaded corpse. 'There were some Radio Four listeners who wrote to complain if a character in a play was allowed to break a leg.' A play of this kind, he predicted, 'would provoke a formidable volume of correspondence.'[64]

These political and aesthetic sensitivities were worrying enough to anyone keen to stretch the boundaries of mainstream drama on Radio Four. But matters were made worse by the unnerving feeling in professional circles that even if a fiercely contemporary play *did* get on air it stood a fair chance of being performed to what one critic called 'utility' standard.[65] The problem, it seemed, was that by the end of the 1960s television had changed public expectations of what constituted decent acting. Soap operas, kitchen-sink dramas, 'documentary'-style police series: all had accustomed British audiences to more *naturalistic* performances on their screens. In comparison, much of what was heard on radio felt stilted, even *hammy*. To some extent it had always been thus, as it was the theatre that had shaped styles of radio acting since the 1920s. Actors frequently found it difficult to adjust the declamatory style suited to filling a large auditorium to the intimacy of speaking through a studio microphone to individuals listening in their own homes. An exaggerated respect for clear enunciation compounded the error, as did scriptwriters' dogged pursuit of clear and polished dialogue. As a result the BBC producer Lance Sieveking could complain in 1934 of 'an annoying similarity among members of The Profession, in spite of the fact that there are plenty of differences among ordinary people'. Overacting, it was feared, had become embedded as *the* conventional style ever since. In 1976, for example, Stephen Hearst complained of one play that sounded to him like nothing other than 'two actors confronting a microphone'. 'Though', he added acidly, 'it had been no worse in this respect than much acting heard on Radio Four.' Others at Review Board murmured assent, regretting that television performances seemed so much more convincing if only because actors on screen did not have to talk all the time. On radio it was harder to convey the silences of real life, simply because silence brought everything to a halt; harder, too, to convey the imperfect, overlapping, half-caught and half-inaudible speech of everyday conversation, without listeners—even those listening in stereo—being disorientated.[66]

The challenge, though, was inescapable. If television's penchant for grit and authenticity had broken old habits, it seemed essential for radio to follow suit. As Ronald Mason pointed out, an audience that watched television 'wants the same standards of social realism from its radio'. There was consequently more and more talk in Broadcasting House of the need to shake off what was called disparagingly the 'Rep voice'. This referred to the thirty or so actors of the BBC's own Drama Repertory Company, each issued with contracts guaranteeing a succession of roles for up to eighteen months, and whose voices sometimes struck attentive listeners as somewhat ubiquitous, or similar, or both. But the problem was not only with the Rep; and sometimes not really with the Rep at all, since there were many highly competent actors among them. They were merely the put-upon symbols of a more general failure in radio drama: a failure to fully shake off the conventions of non-realism which had prevailed in the 1940s and 1950s.[67]

When a reputation for over-theatrical acting was placed alongside all the cosy children's favourites, the stock-in-trade thrillers and the pleasant amusements of Wodehouse, it was easy to characterize Radio Four drama as overwhelmingly derivative and unadventurous. Critics concluded that too many plays had woven about them an aura of cloying, suburban, predictability. Even the classic serials, they thought, carried a strong odour of aesthetic compromise. As Val Arnold-Forster argued in the *Guardian*, they not only had to satisfy the original creator's intentions and please those who already knew the work well; they were also required to 'attract and please those who either do not know the original or who have found the original uninteresting'. The usual result, she feared, was something betwixt and between, rather than anything with a strong identity of its own. In short, it was the embodiment of classic middlebrow taste: stripped of the power to shock, stripped of anything too avant-garde, safe, sturdy, mildly improving.[68] Faced with a sensitive audience, and trapped in old habits, it looked, indeed, as if Radio Four was playing safe, offering too many plays that, in seeking to avoid offence, ended up saying very little at all. The archetypal afternoon drama, David Wade complained, was merely workmanlike. 'It will never quite have received the kiss of life.' 'Something "not quite right" about the dialogue, the story line, or the characterisation, severally or all at once, tells you that this is a photofit play, not a genuine likeness.'[69]

What was Radio Drama to do about these criticisms? Its experiments in sound cinema had at least created the impression of a medium fully *au fait* with modern techniques; but they would only ever constitute a small avant-garde of work in the margins. It might be possible, with effort, to attract more big-name writers to the medium so that a few plays of stature could add glitter to the schedules; but that would only involve higher fees, and, in any case, it would not necessarily strengthen bread-and-butter work in the middle range. It might be possible, through a combination of better writing and casting and directing, to achieve a greater realism in radio acting; but how could older styles be expunged and newer ones introduced without the sudden lurches in style that always disturbed listeners? Room for manoeuvre was limited. The only solution was to attempt piecemeal progress on several fronts, inching forward through trial and error.

The way this was achieved—and the kind of problems thrown up on the way—can be seen in the progress of one series in particular in the late 1970s and early 1980s: *The Archers*. As it happened, this fell outside the direct control of the Radio Drama department in London. But the questions of writing quality, of subject matter, of casting, even of political ideology—these were all ones with which it had to grapple, and which hung ominously over popular drama elsewhere on Radio Four. Indeed, *The Archers* crystallized a key tension at the heart of all drama in the 'middle ground': the need to balance a desire for authenticity in plot, in character, and in dialogue, with the requirement to supply regular doses of excitement and fantasy. There was a new urgency to this old problem by the end of 1976, for it was then that Review Board posed the one question that always haunted cast and production team: 'Has *The Archers* a future?'[70]

The problem, it seemed, was that in retreating from the heightened melodrama that had briefly taken hold in the early 1970s, the series had only become more credible at the cost of becoming rather dull. 'Trivial and boring' was one listener's description in 1974; 'it isn't interesting and it isn't worth hearing' was another's. Even one of its own scriptwriters thought it 'all a bit dreary'. To Jock Gallagher, still in overall charge at Pebble Mill, these were the 'Dog Days'.[71] Having already tried and failed with the obvious solution, namely to make the action more sensational, it was clear that subtler strategies would have to be pursued.

One thing *The Archers* had going for it was an audience with an average age somewhat lower than usual for Radio Four. This suggested that, at the very least, there was room to refresh the series by bringing younger characters to the fore. Circumstances were favourable. Gwen Berryman, who played Doris Archer, was in her seventies, suffering from arthritis, and finding it ever harder to attend recording sessions. It was decided that she and 'Dan' would disappear for a while, to assess audience reaction to their absence. Younger characters—Tony Archer, Sid and Polly Perks, Shula, Elizabeth, Kenton, and David—now started to be heard instead. The transition was deliberately gradual. While the producer Tony

Shryane talked of reflecting topical events 'more rapidly', the overriding remit for the serial remained one of providing a space on the schedule for 'cosiness'. 'Listening to *The Archers* was rather like going to church,' Ian McIntyre decided. 'Discussing whether it should be changed was like proposing to move Westminster Abbey; one had to accept it as and where it was.' He for one 'had no wish to hear the characters discussing current affairs . . . any more than he had to hearing his vicar hold forth on the Annan Committee'.[72] As ever, the challenge was to provide an element of escapism, yet be close enough to reality to be dramatically convincing.

This, in turn, was linked to the question of how *The Archers* reflected country life. Gallagher insisted it was 'typical of "deepest England"'.[73] But whither deepest England? Not everyone who listened was a farmer, or even a country-dweller. Audience research in 1971 had revealed that out of a sample of nearly 2,000 listeners, only twenty lived on farms. The majority, it turned out, lived in towns or cities. Very often *The Archers* offered what *The Times* called 'a whiff of unpolluted air to people who don't know a pig from a potato and for whom spring is three daffodils in a window box'.[74] Even in the countryside, farming was becoming less and less central to everyday life. In the forty years up to 1971, for example, the percentage of the male working population in Norfolk involved in agriculture in some way had fallen from 44 to 13 per cent; a third of its workers living in rural areas had white-collar jobs; by the start of the 1980s, growing numbers would be second-home owners. Those who stuck with farming found themselves in a world of pesticides, selective breeding, mechanization, job insecurity, and European subsidies.[75] Given all this, the expressed desire of listeners to hear something up-to-date with country life seemed to require a distinctly complex and unromantic dramatic setting. On the other hand, there were plenty of critics ready to chastise it for paying *too much* attention to 'country-club owners', 'antique dealers', and 'a grey variety of Birmingham business people'—or for *any* sign that it was betraying its original purpose of being a 'farming *Dick Barton*'. In the circumstances, Shryane had had no immediate alternative but to pursue a resolutely middle course between what he called 'fantasy' and 'realism'—blending the output of a writing team working in the cause of 'pure entertainment' with the suggestions of an Agricultural Story Editor equipped with elaborate research notes on farming practice so as to ensure that storylines never strayed too far from 'genuine country activities'.[76]

Longer term, more radical steps were needed. The key moment came in 1978, when Shryane retired and Bill Smethurst, the youngest member of the writing team, took charge. 'I noted in my diary', the actor Norman Painting wrote, 'that at the first writers' meeting with Bill in the chair there was a more "creative" atmosphere than I'd felt for some years.'[77]

Under the new regime, the pool of writers was steadily expanded from four to eight. The first woman scriptwriter, Tessa Diamond, had already joined in 1976. Here was someone, in Smethurst's opinion, who had 'invested Brookfield family scenes with colour and warmth in a way that a succession of dour, tweedy male writers had never done before'. In Norman Painting's judgement her scenes were 'totally credible, human and amusing'. Now Diamond was joined by several other women, including Helen Leadbeater, a left-wing lawyer's clerk from Islington, Mary Cutler, a Birmingham schoolteacher, and—for a year or two— the novelist Susan Hill. This notably metropolitan group was balanced by three men—Alan Bower, Tim Rose-Price, and James Robson—all claiming rural roots. Between them, they made more and more of the fictional youngsters. Diamond had already developed Shula, who was turning into a sexually active, 18-year-old, Thatcherite reactionary; Susan Hill took a particular interest in Pat Archer—a strong woman married to a weak if amiable man—as did a later scriptwriter, Margaret Phelan, who succeeded in further sharpening Pat's radical outlook. The changes started to be noticed. By 1980, Julie Burchill felt moved to write about how *The Archers* was changing what 'women are allowed to hear': no longer were the women of Ambridge stuck with 'the gallons of greengage jam old-guard male scriptwriters kept them occupied with for over twenty years'; they were 'into post-natal depression and alcoholism on the way to self-discovery'. Meanwhile, the Grundys, who had not impinged greatly on Ambridge life hitherto, moved centre stage with their various schemes to scratch a living from the land. When the time came to finally kill off Doris Archer in 1980, the *Sunday Times* thought her passing would be 'comparable with Trollope's killing off of Mrs Proudie, and much more regrettable'.[78] But actually there was little impact on the serial itself: it was now teeming nicely with a vividly realized assembly of new lead characters.

Smethurst decided that one means of drawing attention to this progress was to court controversy. When first appointed, he had announced that *The Archers* was going to be 'more aggressively reactionary'. 'If it has attitudes', he told his writers, 'they must be the attitudes of rural England.' Ideally, a scriptwriter 'should be able to reflect rural society, from a pub darts match to a hunt ball, with perception and sympathy'. 'If he's an officer in the Yeomanry, rides to hounds, and runs the tombola every year at the Conservative Garden Fete,' he added, 'then so much the better.'[79]

This was the kind of provocative talk that alarmed managers in Broadcasting House, and caused instant offence among some on the Left. How blood sports were featured was a recurring irritant; agricultural workers' unions had long had a beef with the serial for neglecting issues of poor working conditions or portraying employees as servile; now, with talk of a General Election in either 1978 or 1979, more political balance was being demanded of the programme all round. In September 1978 an official of the Association of Broadcasting Staff who was also a prospective Labour candidate, Tony Banks, wrote to the BBC to complain about the serial's politics; the *Evening Standard* and *Daily Telegraph* gleefully joined in the fray; by the end of the year, even the Bishop of Truro was agitating over the impact on family values of Christine Archer being married in St Stephen's Church to George Barford—a divorcee.[80]

The only thing Smethurst desired more than a good political row was the presence of wit. He wanted to establish the serial as a social comedy, offering satire of a very gentle hue, counterpoised by elements of tragedy, romance, and the observation of manners. 'We should aim, in our grander moments, to write in the traditions of Jane Austen...Laurie Lee and H. E. Bates', Smethurst told his team in 1978. 'I don't think this is setting our sights too high.'[81] It was, indeed, ambitious. But since the drama unfolded in a minor key, with incident as important as plot, it seemed to work. 'What I really like about *The Archers*', Val Arnold-Forster wrote in the *Guardian* in November 1982, 'is that it deals with day-to-day work and day-to-day friendships.' Most soap operas were about times of crisis and the intense relationships between lovers, between parents and children, between rivals in love and war. *The Archers* was about routine jobs and steady untraumatic friendships: 'Considerably more believable than those absurd adulteries that are the basis of too many radio plays.'[82]

By now, most of those attending Review Board complimented the series more often than they criticized it. Scripts, directing and acting, it was agreed, were all 'very good', sometimes 'better than ever'. Even some of the political resentments and cultural sneering that had clung to it were beginning to dissipate. Sociologists of the media noticed that there was beginning to be a certain intellectual cachet in listening. Contrived devices, unlovable characters: they had a certain postmodern ironic appeal. Devotees found they could ally themselves with characters of their choice, since expressing a preference declared one's real-life affinities. 'Grundyism', especially, became a token of anti-Thatcherism. *Marxism Today* threw in its lot with the stoical, socially minded Clarrie Grundy, who, it argued, had 'real depth of character'; the Labour politician Neil Kinnock followed the serial avidly on the basis that it was really the story of 'The Grundys and Their Oppressors'; the Radio One presenter John Peel became another prominent Grundy man. 'Grundy supporters', Smethurst noted, 'tend to be young and inclined to revolution.' Naturally, they loathed Shula—or 'Shul-ugh', as one fan group soon labelled her—and demanded of the scriptwriters that they made her life a misery. In time, a plethora of supporters' clubs emerged, both official and unofficial. Word reached the BBC of one set up by students at the University of East Anglia. Another, 'The Archers Anarchists', started as a splinter group from the 'Eddie Grundy Appreciation Society', which also spawned several 'discussion groups' that were to emerge in the 1990s. None of these groups boasted royal patronage, but the Queen was thought to listen to the Sunday omnibus. In 1984, her sister Princess Margaret let it be known that she wanted desperately to have a walk-on part, and a scene was duly recorded in Kensington Palace. Newspaper commentators seized on it as *the* deciding moment. It was, they judged, the point at which *The Archers*, once the very epitome of radio dowdiness, had become 'fashionable and upmarket, like Sainsburys or a Volkswagen Beetle'.[83]

The success of *The Archers* merely demonstrated a more general lesson for radio dramatists back in Broadcasting House: that writing, acting, and publicity were all intimately linked in the collective effort to throw off deep-rooted and unhelpful stereotypes of their work. *The Archers'* fashionable status was a culmination, rather than a beginning: part of a process that had been going on for six or seven years, and part of a process already under way throughout Radio Four's range of popular drama.

The presence of star performers, and the kind of publicity that came with them, was always one important aspect of the broader battle. This was seen most vividly in the season of Shakespeare and Marlow plays timed for the Queen's Silver Jubilee in 1977 and gathered together under the title *Vivat Rex*. An untypically large wave of advance publicity declared it to be 'the most ambitious drama project ever mounted' on BBC Radio. When it was announced that Richard Burton would have a starring role as the storyteller, there were photographs in the *Guardian*, *Daily Mail*, and *London Evening Standard*. The rest of the cast was also deliberately eye-catching. Among them: Peggy Ashcroft, Michael Redgrave, Robert Hardy, Paul Scofield, Diana Rigg, Billie Whitelaw, Derek Jacobi, John Hurt. Quality acting was mirrored by sumptuous production values: twenty-six episodes, with original music, and dialogue directed by Martin Jenkins and Gerry Jones, two producers with a distinguished track-record in Shakespearean theatre.[84] Four years later, there was a similar fanfare of publicity for Radio Four's new serialization of *The Lord of the Rings*, adapted by Brian Sibley and Michael Bakewell, directed by Jane Morgan, and starring Ian Holm as Frodo, John Le Mesurier as Bilbo Baggins, Bill Nighy as Sam Gamgee, and Michael Hordern as Gandalf. Again, there were twenty-six episodes, original music—and plenty of coverage in the press. Like *Vivat Rex*, this was a production on the epic scale. But equally satisfying for many inside Broadcasting House was that *The Lord of the Rings* played it straight. It was sumptuous but not flash, and satisfied the Tolkien aficionados as well as those new to the work. Crucially, the calibre of the acting had spoken for itself. As one senior editor suggested, the impact of their performances 'would raise the morale of the whole directorate'.[85] And, indeed, it was now, in the early 1980s, that critics wrote more insistently of acting on Radio Four being 'infinitely' better than ever before, and about a self-confidence having returned to Radio Drama.[86]

Yet, no matter how good *The Lord of the Rings* had been, or how much it raised morale, there could not really be a decisive moment when it came to improving standards of performance. They had been rising for some time anyway, in the theatre as well as on radio, as the acting profession responded instinctively to new benchmarks set by television. Not all of the impetus came from outside influences, however. Some of the credit must also be attributed to work conducted within BBC Radio during the course of the preceding few years. In production techniques and in casting, in particular, much had been achieved quietly behind the scenes. One important factor, for example, was the adoption of new recording techniques that could capture performances with the same kind of vivid, high-fidelity naturalism that colour was bringing to television. This had started modestly enough in the studios, where producers began experimenting with real props and costumes: a curious move for an invisible medium, but, apparently, a productive one, for when period dresses were worn in a 1974 production of *Anna Karenina*, producers expressed themselves thrilled with the 'authentic' ambience thereby created, complete with the sound of cast members swishing past the microphone just so.[87] Within a few years, it became even more fashionable to take actors right out of the 'clinical atmosphere' of the studio and record their performances entirely on location. It was hoped this would not only provide more accurate ambient sound; it might also encourage a cast to be less 'stagey'. Martin Esslin had heard the technique being used to good effect in France and Germany in 1971, but it was only tried in earnest by the BBC five or so years later.[88] In 1977, for example, *The Archers* left the familiar surroundings of Pebble Mill and moved to the small Midlands village of Ashton-under-Hill to record a whole week's episode on location. The actor Norman Painting joined his fellow cast members in clambering into real cars and playing a real piano in a real pub crowded to the ceiling: 'it seemed more like filming than radio', he thought.[89] The technique's greatest enthusiasts, however, were the London-based producers, Richard Wortley and Jane Morgan. Wortley produced Peter Everett's *The Cookham Resurrection*, a kaleidoscopic portrait of the painter Stanley Spencer formed from a montage of authentic location acoustics. And in 1980, Morgan produced a *Saturday Night Theatre* drama about football supporters off to the European Championships in Italy that was improvised and recorded by a cast and crew joining the real fans on their journey.

This outdoor activity rarely turned out to be straightforward. For a start, there was always more editing to be done afterwards to remove unwanted noises like passing cars and overhead planes. *The Cookham Resurrection*, for instance, had to be recorded in Hertfordshire, not in the real Cookham-on-Thames, which was under a busy flight-path. And at one stage Morgan's *Saturday Night Theatre* cast had been surrounded by hooligans and tear gas. She reported afterwards that in the circumstances her actors had not had the courage to get as close to the real fans as she had hoped, which was why, despite all the trouble she and her engineer had gone to, the final recording had a somewhat 'detached' feeling.[90] In the circumstances, much of this 'radio verité' was gently derided within Broadcasting House as a waste of time, or plain pretentious. But it was at least tolerated. And in the process something useful was given room to mature. Actors really *did* seem to forget the microphone once they were put in real settings: a situation was created where 'one seemed to be eavesdropping on a real conversation'. Stephen Hearst, who had been especially critical of existing conventions, thought it created acting 'far more convincing than in much radio drama in the past'.[91] Even Norman Painting, whose experience of location recording for *The Archers* was only fleeting, acknowledged that it produced 'a greater feeling of immediacy'.[92] Since this was precisely the quality being sought, the technique was used, though selectively and *sotto voce*, in series like *Sherlock Holmes*, *The Monday Play*, *Afternoon Theatre*, and *The Classic Serial*. What had once been a laboratory experiment had, by the early 1980s infused Radio Four drama as a whole with an extra touch of naturalism. If critics subsequently talked less about the technology or the directorial style involved, and started casually praising the quality of the drama instead, that was all to the good. As the outgoing Assistant Head of Radio Drama, Hallam Tennyson, concluded in 1978, the first flush of enthusiasm for these new techniques had already passed: henceforth stereo, high-fidelity, and effects were 'firmly at the service of plays rather than vice versa'.[93]

When it came to the actors themselves, much steady progress was made within the studio by directors such as Martin Jenkins constantly invoking his famous dictum for the radio medium: 'half the volume, twice the intensity'. But it was the casting that took place beforehand that proved of vital significance. One change was to widen the range of voices on air. The Repertory Company, for instance, was gradually used a little less, their ranks thinned out, and their contracts shortened. Actors were drawn from a larger reservoir of talent: a process that accelerated as the appeal of radio work became more apparent. One attraction was simply the chance to repay a medium that had offered early breaks. Alan Ayckbourn claimed that regular commissions by Alfred Bradley had at one stage been the only thing that kept his young company in Scarborough going. Even in the late 1970s established actors such as Robert Powell, Billie Whitelaw, and Michael Caine were still returning to radio as a direct result of Bradley's efforts.[94]

Like many in the profession they found radio to be convenient. Most ninety-minute plays involved no more than three or four days in the studio; half-hour plays could sometimes be recorded in just a single day. There was little hanging about, and no need to learn lines in advance. Better still, daytime recording sessions were compatible with night-time performances on stage: there was the possibility of holding down two jobs at once. Indeed there could be lots of doubling up, since actors in radio could play innumerable parts at once and they could play parts for which nature had not physically designed them: there was no tyranny of beauty or youth in the invisible medium. Nor was there much pretension, for the atmosphere in most studios was famously unstuffy. When Clive Swift came to Broadcasting House to perform in a Trollope serial he noticed writers, producers, and actors all talking on equal terms. 'I like this easy flow,' he confessed, 'much of the work has a touch of democracy about it.'[95]

The key to everything, though, was writing, for no performance would impress without a decent story or decent dialogue. The biggest task of all, therefore, was for Radio Drama to ensure a steady supply of good scripts. One major step on the road to recovery in this area was to start guaranteeing a repeat for almost every play, so that writers could automatically be offered about twice the previous fee. Another scheme, initiated in 1971, involved the BBC working with overseas broadcasting organizations to jointly commission plays from major dramatists.

In this way, a writer could be offered fees from several broadcasting organizations at once, and the total income thus raised could equate roughly with the sorts of money at the disposal of television. The arrangement funded Terence Rattigan's *Cause Célèbre*, for example, broadcast as a *Monday Play* on Radio Four in 1975. In 1982 Radio Four also splashed out on its own by commissioning plays from John Mortimer, Alan Plater, and Tom Stoppard.[96] Showcases like these were expensive, but they improved the status of radio drama as a whole. They offered proof that it was still a perfectly respectable—sometimes even a modestly lucrative—forum for serious writers. And by the start of the 1980s Radio Four had built up a roll-call of dramatists that compared reasonably well to any from an earlier age: David Edgar, John Arden, Harold Pinter, Tom McGrath, a host of European titans in translation. Most were broadcast as the *Monday Play*, which had always been the most prestigious of the drama slots but was undoubtedly becoming more demanding and more catholic in its range as the 1970s progressed. In so doing, it provided a large and growing audience for the kind of work that just a few years before would only have reached far fewer ears on Radio Three.[97]

The raising of radio's status at the 'upper end' of the dramatic spectrum made it easier for producers to improve the quality of writing elsewhere. A sort of artistic trickle-down effect could be observed, so that, gradually, what the Drama department liked to call 'stronger meat' featured a little more freely on the daytime menu. By 1980, for instance, there were plays such as *The Devils* being broadcast in the afternoon. Monica Sims disliked this particular story intensely, but she agreed with Ronald Mason on one thing: her Radio Four audience must 'be disturbed from time to time'.[98] Apart from recognizing one of drama's inherent purposes—namely, to elicit an emotional response to uncomfortable truths—there was evidently the hope inside Broadcasting House that some form of virtuous spiral could be created: that as daytime listeners became slowly acclimatized to quite muscular material, even more adventurous writing could, in turn, be commissioned. As Richard Imison explained in a memo to the Director-General in 1980:

A listener who had not experienced *Afternoon Theatre* since the 1950s would, I think, be startled by what is now heard there since the evolution of afternoon plays has been considerable in recent years. The vast majority of the regular audience to afternoon plays is not startled; within the context of their regular listening, they have been well-prepared for what they now hear. It is very striking that despite enormous audiences to this slot... the number of complaints about the range of dramatic experience is miniscule... The evidence, therefore, that the public is ready broadly to accept that the range of dramatic material presented may legitimately go beyond their own personal likes and dislikes, is very strong.[99]

And, indeed, the range *was* widening; quality *was* improving. Afternoon listeners had begun to hear the work of accomplished authors whose work might once have been confined to the evenings, or to Radio Three, or perhaps not have appeared on radio at all.

There were, for instance, new plays from Fay Weldon, some of whose radio scripts were later turned into successful novels, and from Susan Hill, already an accomplished novelist, who contributed not just to *The Archers* but to *Afternoon Theatre* regularly from the mid-1970s, and brought to the medium that much-sought-after combination of a distinctive yet utterly comprehensible style. Other writers who showed remarkable loyalty to Radio Four over the years included Tom Mallin, William Trevor, Alan Plater, Rose Tremain, and Jonathan Raban. In each case, authors who could easily have concentrated exclusively on more lucrative pursuits were willing to argue that radio's creative freedom outweighed its modest remuneration and its relative lack of exposure. This creative freedom was not just a question of radio's ability to conjure up for next to no cost any number of scenes and characters that would bankrupt a television special effects department—though that was undoubtedly attractive. It was also, as it was for many actors, a tribute to radio's ways of working. Writers built a relationship with their producers; they were invited to attend recordings; they were encouraged to talk to the cast. 'Most get value out of the studio', one producer claimed: 'protecting their work on the one hand, learning on the other.' This was a long-standing tradition. Tom Stoppard, for instance, believed it was working in radio with John Tydeman that had forced him to tighten his structure and focus his characters. As for Susan Hill, she preferred radio to television because it offered 'the nearest thing stylistically to a novel'. It valued the original words of a writer, whereas the television play, with its complex process of production, disrupted them.[100]

Even *listening* to radio established a bond. Hill claimed it was her childhood experience of avidly devouring plays on the radio in the late 1940s and 1950s that prepared her for the role of dramatist. 'I slipped into the medium as into an old glove', she wrote. It 'seemed to have moulded itself long ago to the shape of my own hand'.[101] Radio's intrinsic diversity, Jonathan Raban thought, was the key to this special relationship, since it was 'a corridor through which the whole world passes':

Radio is by turns gossipy, authoritative, preachy, natural, artificial, confidential, loudly public, and not infrequently wordless...For the dramatist trying to think about the medium in which he has to work it makes bewildering listening, this concatenation of noises and voices. He can at least take from it the consolation that, if radio provides no obvious context, there is almost no imaginable form of writing that will sound obviously out of place on it...much as I admire the radio work of Beckett, Cooper, Pinter and Stoppard, I suspect that I have more to learn as a dramatist from listening to *Start the Week*, *Checkpoint*, *The World at One*, *The Living World*, *Tuesday Call* and all sorts of bits and pieces having nothing to do with official drama.[102]

Here is a hint of Radio Four's real purchase on writing talent: the ability to find it among its very own listeners—sometimes famous, more often unknown—and then nurture it organically. For, despite all the publicity and fuss over high-profile playwrights 'coming back' to radio, it was the proportion of plays written by authors *new* to the medium that rose fastest through the 1970s. Some were recruited from regional and fringe theatres, or through writing competitions; many more through the vast quantities of unsolicited scripts arriving at BBC offices. In Leeds, Alfred Bradley read some 600 unsolicited scripts a year. In London, Richard Imison presided over a team that collectively ploughed through another 10,000. Inevitably, only a small proportion were deemed suitable, but such was the scale of the operation that Radio Four could still fill many of its slots through the uncommissioned work of 'semi-professionals'. In the mid-1970s, for example, *Afternoon Theatre* carried plays by, among others, a probation officer, a gardener at Kew, a Dorset farmer, an Uxbridge factory worker, and several teachers. By 1978, one in four of the *Afternoon Theatres* was a 'first play'. Overall, Radio Drama calculated that each year it was discovering some seventy or eighty new playwrights. Some debuts were, as it delicately put it, 'not quite up to the usual professional standards'. But a less-than-perfect first story or play was deemed worthwhile whenever a writer merited 'encouragement'. This was the kind of patronage that helped secure for BBC Radio the status of being the largest single commissioner of dramatic work in Britain—and, some claimed, the world.[103] If nothing else, the Drama department could claim that if it ever ceased to exist, a very large number of writers would never get their careers off the ground, and would consequently be lost to the national culture.

In writing, as in acting, then, much had been achieved by the early 1980s. There was some pride in Broadcasting House at the steady reduction in the number of adaptations from novels and the stage, and a corresponding increase in the proportion of original plays written for radio. There was also much satisfaction at the regular appearance on Radio Four of 'outstanding' plays of the kind only heard on the Third Programme before 1970. John Arden, so long marginalized from the British stage, had been 'rehabilitated' by radio, so they said, after his 1978 production of *Pearl*; and it was Radio Four, not Radio Three, that provided his platform.[104]

It may have been true, as older critics kept saying, that there were now fewer peaks of achievement compared with the late 1950s or early 1960s. And it was certainly true that much of Radio Four's output was still ordinary. But many plays were also decently accomplished. The middle-to-upper-middle range, in *Afternoon Theatre* especially, had been stiffened by a combination of tighter direction, more realistic acting, and fewer stock characters in scripts. There was a decent flow of work from seasoned professionals like Peter Tegel, Tom Mallin, Elizabeth Troop, Jennifer Phillips, and Frederick Bradnum, and from talented newcomers like Carolyn Sally Jones, Jehane Markham, and Paula McKay—all keen listeners-turned-contributors. Even the most popular drama of all, *The Archers*, had been renovated by an injection of new talent, so that characters and plots were more subtle and knowing than ever.

A great deal of Radio Four's middlebrow fare was despised by the commentators of high culture, as it always had been; but some of its long-standing reputation for suburban predictability and old-fashioned delivery had been dispelled—just as audiences, by and large, had been increased. In this way, Radio Four had introduced many thousands of listeners to the idea that 'serious' literature or drama was at least approachable. Even the sheer scale of its patronage seemed to make Radio Four a force to be reckoned with, for in 1979 the *Financial Times* was arguing that British drama's centre of gravity had shifted *back* to radio and theatre to such an extent that television, by contrast, was being steadily impoverished. 'If only', many in Broadcasting House might have been tempted to say. But, on the whole, they had good reason to be satisfied. As David Wade concluded the following year, 'the general standard of drama on Radio Four is considerably higher than it was when I first began professional listening in the sixties'.[105] Few who had listened as widely or as closely as Wade now argued with that judgement.

IMAGINATION AND PUBLIC SERVICE

Neither Drama nor Light Entertainment entirely shook off the problems that had dogged them since the 1960s.

For a start, there was still no guarantee that *all* the beneficiaries of their patronage would return the favour through a lifetime's loyalty. In Light Entertainment, for instance, the swell of talent in 1977 and 1978 was followed by an ebbing away two or three years later. By then the *Weekending* formula of topical satire was appearing to sharper effect on BBC 2 in *Not the Nine o'Clock News*. The television series had also sucked into its orbit two of radio's brightest comedy producers, John Lloyd and Griff Rhys-Jones.[106] Meanwhile, Simon Brett had joined London Weekend Television, where Andrew Marshall and David Renwick were also helping to create the political satire *Whoops Apocalypse!* The creation of Channel Four in 1982, and the patronage it bestowed on a new generation of 'alternative' stand-up comedians, was another blow, as performers and writers became less dependent on Radio Four as their nursery slope. In short, television had become the laboratory of British comedy once more. And in the meantime *Weekending* was in danger of becoming what Brett called 'an alternative *Down Your Way*'.[107] The man who replaced David Hatch as Radio's Head of Light Entertainment in 1981, Bobby Jaye—an adaptable survivor from the old guard—was clearly faced with some more talent-hunting of his own over the next few years.

Then there were the internal battles to be fought, chiefly against those at the BBC who still regarded the presence of drama or comedy on Radio Four as a strange historical accident standing in the way of the proper business of broadcasting—namely journalism. The start of permanent parliamentary broadcasting in April 1978 was one of the bloodiest fronts in these skirmishes, since it required a number of scheduled plays being shunted to VHF (which most listeners avoided) so that medium wave (which most listener actually used) could carry live relays from the Commons. The editor of *Afternoon Theatre* was aghast at the effect on his ratings: an instant slip from a hard-earned high-water mark of roughly 1.5 million listeners achieved only a few months before, to a troubling 800,000 and falling.[108] Yet for as long as Radio Four was committed to Parliamentary coverage, it looked as if one or other of the two parties would have to give ground: either live political coverage *or* drama would have to move; the only alternative was for some messy compromise to be found that allowed both genres to coexist on the same wavelength. Even that would probably only work if programmes were live and flexible in length—easy enough for news, almost impossible for drama. The inherent tensions in Radio Four's 'rich mix' looked as if they were reaching a critical point: a final resolution would be needed one way or another in the near future.

Drama, in particular, needed to marshall its arguments for survival very carefully. Most in the BBC recognized Light Entertainment's claims for a stake in Radio Four, on the simple grounds that a relentless diet of news would be unbearable without a few laughs. Drama, however, was not always in the business of light relief; some of it could be thoroughly depressing. Indeed, it still struck some (especially some in News and Current Affairs) as nothing but minority fodder for bedridden pensioners. If this attitude could not be shaken, original drama would remain vulnerable in any plan of rationalization that might emerge in the future.

To all these doubters, advocates of drama had two powerful ripostes. First, they had the evidence to show that radio drama was a more popular genre than many supposed: the ratings were generally good. Second, they were able to argue with conviction that it contributed in its own way to the public understanding of contemporary debates—that, in short, it was broadly *relevant*, and that Radio Four was its proper home. In both cases, the aesthetic developments of recent years combined neatly with age-old arguments about the nature of public service broadcasting.

On the question of popularity, the scale of Drama's activity was important. Martin Esslin calculated that a play would have to be performed in a packed thousand-seat West End theatre for five years in order to match the audience for one *Saturday Night Theatre* on Radio Four. And *Saturday Night Theatre* was just one strand out of many. At any given point in the 1970s, each of the department's producers would be involved in about six or seven plays in various stages of completion: an output, on average, of twenty plays a year each, not including various serials or readings. This added up to 600 or more plays annually by the late 1970s: almost half as many again as were being produced in the glory days of the 1950s. Three-quarters of these were now on Radio Four, where drama in all its forms accounted for about forty-four hours a week of output. In one year,

Radio Four broadcast very nearly as many hours of drama as BBC 1, BBC 2, *and* ITV combined; it provided five times as many new productions as the National Theatre in London.[109] The BBC's first head of Drama had once said that the Corporation, acting as a gigantic theatre substitute for those who did not—or could not—attend in person, provided Britain with a 'National Theatre of the Air'. It was a phrase that evidently still held true.

Crucially, quantity could be presented as a *cause*—as much as a symbol—of success. For all his intellectual fascination with the esoteric theatre of ideas, Esslin proved himself thoroughly Reithian, just as his predecessor Val Gielgud had done, in his willingness to bring a large mainstream audience to the genre. Ubiquity was part of the strategy. If radio drama required an extra degree of concentration and commitment from listeners, Esslin had reasoned, then listeners needed 'an absolutely regular diet of drama so that they shall always be familiar with it'. The Radio Four audience had never asked for a play every afternoon of the week. But since 1970 it had been given one. And in time it had come to expect one. Beyond that, the policy had been established of catering for 'varying levels of understanding or artistic absorbability' by dividing output into different theatrical repertoires, so that listeners could, as Esslin put it, 'find drama where and as they want it'.

There was thus little unity to Radio Four's drama: it was more like a loose and diverse confederation. *The Monday Play*, for example, was aimed at what was called the 'committed' listener who turned on 'with the specific intention of listening to the play'. Its selection of fairly challenging contemporary work and classic dramas—Shakespeare, Dostoevsky, Conrad, and Shaw, say—would attract about 200,000 listeners, and another 350,000 for its Sunday afternoon repeat. At the other end of the spectrum was *Saturday Night Theatre*, the U-film of radio drama, with an audience of 300,000 plus, and another 500,000 or so for its Monday afternoon repeat. Its aim was to offer plays 'higher in entertainment value than in intellectual stimulus'. Straddling the very broad dramatic middle ground was *Afternoon Theatre*, its typical audience described by its editor as 'the more intelligent housebound', a category that added up to an audience each day of between 750,000 and a million people, most of whom were assumed to be doing something else while listening. Hence, afternoon plays had to be 'humanly involving' and have a 'compelling narrative structure'.[110]

If, as critics suspected, some of these definitions were tilted in favour of mainstream tastes, then so be it. Making demanding productions that pushed at the limits of experimentation would have satisfied some. But it carried the danger that only the cognoscenti would ever listen: radio drama, in the truly popular sense, would cease to exist. And where was the public service in that? A central tenet of Reithian philosophy held that the BBC could only be a cultural *force* if its programmes reached a respectable proportion of the British people. 'Ultimately it is the members of the audience whom we serve', wrote one leading light of Radio Drama. 'The absence of an audience is terrible. It is a failure.' As

Esslin argued, Drama therefore 'still had a duty to give the maximum number of listeners what they wanted' even while 'catering for specialized groups or levels'.[111] Whatever his frustration with Radio Four listeners' narrowness of taste, he knew they were indispensable: less highbrow than those for Radio Three, but more numerous—and not beyond redemption. After all, the different repertoires of Radio Four's drama were never *quite* as rigidly defined in practice as they were in theory. There was some interchange of plays between Radio Three and Radio Four; Stoppard now contributed to both networks, as did Pinter— who, by 1979, even cropped up on a Saturday afternoon. Indeed, both Pinter and Stoppard embodied the kind of serious-yet-approachable drama that defined Radio Four's growing ambition: they drew from Esslin's beloved tradition of Absurdism, and dabbled in the incomprehensible nature of the universe, but they also incorporated more accessible dramatic architecture: in Pinter's case, an identifiable dash of British kitchen-sink realism; in Stoppard's, an appealing comic idiom.[112]

The steady improvement in quality of Radio Four's middle ground reflected, therefore, a twofold desire: to connect with existing public taste—and then to push it a little further. It was, in other words, an inclination within Broadcasting House to 'do to the listener rather better than he would be done by'.[113] Gently rising audience figures showed this was more than misplaced idealism: provided it was done with discretion, it worked.

Radio Drama's second line of defence was to demonstrate the contribution it now routinely made to the public understanding of topical debates. 'A radio play was a piece of fiction and nothing else', Esslin once claimed; but, he added, the best of it was 'in part, journalism'.[114] This loose talk troubled some in the profession. Don Haworth, a distinguished television documentarist who also wrote for radio, worried about a service so orientated towards news that it forced drama to be 'an extension, a next-door department'. This, David Wade thought, was why Radio Four's plays were overly infused with a 'socio-political' BBC ethos, namely that 'if only we apply ourselves hard enough, then all our problems will be, if not solved, then at least substantially alleviated'.[115] Others believed, on the contrary, that it was precisely the adjacency of drama with news that constituted Radio Four's greatest contribution to public culture. In the *Guardian*, for example, Val Arnold-Forster dissected the range of programmes unfolding during one week in December 1982. There was *The Monday Play* about a pair of Belfast sweethearts meeting in a pub just before a bomb explodes, weaving the threads of an Irish tragedy—the violence on both sides, the accidental shooting, the purposeful destruction, the anti-Irish feeling, the flight from the gunmen, the destruction of young love. There was also a more distant vision of Ireland in the classic serial, *The Kellys and the O'Kellys*, and a more contemporary vision in *File on Four*'s forensic examination of American support for the IRA. Taken together, all these programmes provided a 'chain of perceptions' helping the listener to understand the tangled troubles of Northern Ireland. This was drama not as escape, but as a means of looking at life 'from another point of view'. Fact and fiction were not mutually exclusive. And the implications were obvious. As Monica Sims explained to doubting colleagues: 'It is possible to enjoy plays *and* to be interested in the news.' Indeed, she went on, since 'Radio Four appeals to the "all round" cultured human being', it had a *duty* to 'engage emotions' and 'fire imaginations' as well as to feed minds with information and opinions.[116]

So, despite the absence from Radio Four of the big names in political theatre, there was politics around if one opened one's ears. If it was less striking than work on the British stage, this was partly because it increasingly adopted the characteristic idiom of understatement, and partly because most of it was about the politics of everyday experience. Personal relationships, particularly those involving women, were at the heart of it. And the emphasis was on subtlety: what one producer called 'sharp observation tempered with compassion and humour'. Fay Weldon, for instance, was valued by producers for her ability to depict 'with superb irony the position of women in society and the nature of marriage generally'. Jennifer Phillips was relished for commenting stylishly on the sex war and motherhood. Susan Hill, less overtly political, was recognized for using Gothic spine-chillers to explore both her characters' inner fears *and* their hopes— proving it was possible to 'do "isolation", without toppling over into "lonely-hearts" sentimentality'. Even Anthony Trollope fitted the bill indirectly, with one interpretation of his success with the Radio Four audience lying in his fictional combination of feckless men and feisty women.[117]

Radio Four drama did not so much retreat from politics, then, as domesticate it. With hundreds of plays being broadcast every year, many were bound to slip below the going notions of average. The best among them, though, blended the extraordinary with the quotidian and had an ear for the agony and laughter of 'ordinary' lives. If they featured heroic deeds, they were often as not the deeds of the meek. They rarely sought to change the world in epic ways, as the most radical playwrights of the 1970s had wished to do. But they recognized the central concerns of their audience. As the Oxford sociologist A. H. Halsey observed in a state-of-the-nation essay in 1982, 'most of our consciousness is with more mundane, more immediate, more personal matters':

We do not think much about death or eternity or the fate of nations. We are concerned mostly about our physical well-being today, about how we are getting on with a spouse, a son, the neighbours, the boss at work, etc. In fact we attach much more importance to our meals, our sexual life, our reputations, our football team, the beer in the local pub, or even where we shall go on holiday than to the great collective abstractions like liberty, equality and fraternity which describe our political ideas and debates.[118]

By the early 1980s, leading dramatists, too, were coming round to this way of thinking. Stage plays such as David Edgar's *Maydays* (1983) and David Hare's *A Map of the World* (1983) expressed a thoroughgoing disillusion with radicalism's progress, or rather the lack of it. They, like others, wondered whether all their consciousness-raising had been wasted, and whether the mainstream should perhaps have been penetrated more—and with more subtlety. Some, such as Christopher Hampton in his *Tales from Hollywood* (1983), argued explicitly for a drama of individuals and their personal dilemmas in place of grand political gestures.[119]

Perhaps Radio Four drama should have been these playwrights' natural home all along. Over the past two decades it had felt the full impact of television, reeled under it, tried to emulate it, steadied itself, and begun the slow climb back.[120] Having dabbled with the spectacular and the sensational, it had settled for more prosaic qualities attuned to the coming age: understated naturalism, politics of the most personal kind, and, above all, a drama of words and memories and recollections, where listeners might enter the mind of a character and examine the inner workings of human consciousness. As a genre intrinsically suited to the 'interior monologue' radio drama was no longer trapped in the past, it was ahead of the game. And the lessons it learned could not be contained: for just as drama had become a little more like journalism, so journalism, in turn, was destined to become a little more like drama.

8

Close-Up and Personal

'Weeping in public: it's not considered good form at all, is it, in this country?'
Claire Rayner, *In the Psychiatrist's Chair*

THE 'ME' DECADE

One summer day in 1979, the nineteen-stone broadcaster Tom Vernon decided to pedal his bicycle all the way from Muswell Hill in London through France to the shores of the Mediterranean. Motivating him, he said, was the feeling that he had 'given up being in touch with the world outside':

A radio broadcaster is among the most detached of all. He lives under fluorescent tubes in a windowless studio, and handles words and ideas on little pieces of magnetic tape. The temptation is strong to become more and more a processor of substitute reality, and not very different from a transistor in his tape machine. I wondered: 'Is there still a world out there you can touch?'[1]

Evidently there was, for he returned with plenty of fresh magnetic tape with which he constructed a vivid and intimate portrait of France and her people, viewed through the eyes of a quizzical Englishman. So successful was his programme, *Fat Man on a Bicycle*, that several sequels (not to mention several popular books-of-the-series) appeared at regular intervals over the next few years.

Vernon's programmes were hardly revolutionary in tone. Affectionate portraits of people and places were a staple of the newspaper feature-writers, and the BBC itself had been broadcasting them regularly since the 1930s. But Vernon's approach was a little different, and somehow more appealing to the democratic temper of the age. A series such as *Down Your Way*, as one critic pointed out, had 'rural people doing their party piece, exhibiting their ethnicity and authenticity for the delectation of us alienated urban folk in the listening audience'; Vernon, it was said, showed 'genuine interest in and respect' for the people he met.[2] His style was humorous, gentle, and idiosyncratic in a way that seemed perfectly natural to most Radio Four listeners.

But in its unassuming way, *Fat Man* showed quite explicitly how thin the wall between fact and fiction could sometimes be. There was no dishonesty involved. It represented a fruitful collision of two separate but interrelated trends in broadcasting over the past decade: the desire to escape the confines of the studio or production office in order to get out and about, and the desire to provide explorations of human life that were altogether more intimate and more personal than what had gone before.

The first of these two trends, the interest in recording on location, had, as we know, been tested by dramatists. But it was adopted more systematically—and pushed into new territory—by radio's feature-makers. Ever since the 1950s, they had persistently sought a style freed from script and studio, and the prevalence of portable recorders had allowed them room for manoeuvre. History, too, was on their side. As one radio producer explained, the social turmoil of 1968 had been a 'phenomenon of the *exterior*'. As such, the challenge had been clear: 'to meet this world, not simply make it come to radio'.[3] The challenge was also to move beyond the merely descriptive and to find Art in this meeting-place. One true believer in this possibility had been the Scottish radio producer John Gray, who, back in 1966, had advocated using microphones as 'the sound equivalent of a camera' for impressionistic effect.[4] By the mid-1970s, an improvement in recording technology had made the capture of authentic ambient sounds much easier to undertake, and it was verisimilitude, rather than impressionism, which had become *the* aesthetic imperative. The Kunstkopf may have failed to take root, but a simpler, cheaper, and more portable version was found in the form of 'binaural' stereo recording, which used a pair of microphones in roughly the same position as human ears but without the paraphernalia of a moulded dummy. This appealed to technically adventurous features-producers who wanted to be able to move freely while recording outside, and was soon being tried, among other places, in the BBC's natural history unit in Bristol, as a means of capturing, at point-blank range, the evocative sounds of British wildlife. Binaural was also demonstrated to striking effect in 1977 on *Oil Rig*, a portrait 'in sounds and voices' of life on board a rig in the North Sea.[5]

These productions represented the most polished examples of a more general trend: for radio to become richer in actuality and ambience and lighter on conventional interviewing and narration. It was, in effect, an ethos of objectivity through vicinity—as if the closer radio got to the source of sound, the more authentic (and the less didactic) was the medium's relationship with the listener.

The second trend, namely a desire to infuse programmes with more humanity and intimacy, added a vital refinement to this kind of 'close-up' radio. For all its virtuoso recreation of life among a tangle of noisy machinery and cranes, *Oil Rig* had struck some inside Broadcasting House as curiously unengaging, simply because it lacked an identifiable human dimension, and more specifically, a leading 'character' to draw the listener into its world.

The kind of thing that might be achieved by focusing on people, rather than place, had been demonstrated on television in 1974. Once a week between April and June that year fifteen million viewers had been gripped by BBC 1's 'fly-on-the-wall' series, *The Family*, a portrait of the Wilkinses of Reading—an 'ordinary family in an ordinary town'. The novelty had been in filming them in unflinching close-up. But the popular appeal had undoubtedly been in the family's extraordinary willingness to carry on their normal, slightly messy lives entirely under the public gaze. The problems of housing, racism, and poverty caught on film were familiar themes in almost any current affairs documentary of the time. Yet in *The Family*, there had been no need for officials or academics or politicians or lobbyists to explain them: it had all been acted out for real by the Wilkinses themselves—shown, as it were, rather than merely described secondhand. And it had been *emotionally* involving. *The Family* had been social history and soap opera at the same time. Or, as its director, Paul Watson, put it, 'Hitchcock's *Rear Window* domestic-style'.[6]

This was pioneering stuff as far as British television was concerned. But its blending of verité camerawork and human-scale drama advertised a wider shift in journalistic styles. It had echoes of what, in America, had already come to be called 'the New Journalism'. Its leading proponent, Tom Wolfe, attacked what he saw as the prevailing journalistic ethos, in which 'the bigger the story—i.e. the more it had to do with the matters of power or catastrophe—the better'. The neutral 'pale beige' tones of established newspaper columnists and broadcasters he saw as symbolic of their detachment from the grubby realities of the world and their refusal to acknowledge that reporting could have a dramatic dimension. Writers, he suggested, could make journalism more absorbing by breaking all the rules of objectivity and detachment. They could supply 'novelistic' details of scenes and whole slabs of dialogue, use the historic present tense to add a sense of immediacy, go 'off camera' to record goings-on away from the main event. 'Rather than just come on as the broadcaster describing the big parade', Wolfe explained, 'I would shift as quickly as possible into the eye sockets, as it were, of the people in the story.' 'It seemed all-important to be there', he went on, 'to get the dialogue, the gestures, the facial expressions, the details of the environment.' 'The idea was to give the full objective description, plus something that readers had always had to go to novels and short stories for: namely, the subjective or emotional life of the characters.' His models were Dickens, Thackeray, and Balzac—novelists whose social autopsies of character showed that it was the minute details of behaviour and of possessions that revealed peoples' status and thoughts.[7]

Naturally, none of this washed with those running News in Broadcasting House. For them, strict adherence to objectivity and detachment was supposed to be everything. But there was a vast area of topical programme-making in radio, adjacent to News, for which a more personal, intimate, style of reportage opened up rich possibilities. Among producers lurking inside the Drama department, for example, there were people such as Piers Plowright and John Theocharis, both worrying away at the blurred boundary between drama and documentary. In 1978, they declared that 'the new age of radio features' had arrived, and promptly proceeded to spend the following years replacing the abstract mélanges of *Oil Rig* with a whole succession of more intimate location recordings where people's voices, people's stories, and the little things in people's lives all predominated.[8] In so doing, they forged a kind of 'miniaturist' style, where the Proustian power of a symbolic fragment of sound or a passing remark allowed the listener to enter what Wolfe called 'the character's mind'. People like George Fischer had long been calling for more testimony 'from the horse's mouth'. And now, like television and much printed journalism, radio was discovering that it could be more easily done than first thought: for no matter how little 'ordinary' people knew of high politics or great literature, each and every one of them was undoubtedly the leading expert of his or her *own* life.

'Experience'—which meant the experience of 'real' people, rather than experts—was now firmly recognized as one of the magic ingredients that made almost any programme engaging. More than that, it brought what Monica Sims called 'an understanding of the human predicament'.[9] And it was precisely this empathy, *combined* with a novelist's powers of description, which made Tom Vernon's *Fat Man on a Bicycle* closer to the spirit of New Journalism than many earlier experiments in pure radio verité. 'Though I make radio programmes with my ears,' Vernon explained, 'I start thinking about the world with my eyes.' The result: a series of vignettes about the individuals he met—'because I did my best not to meet the other sort of person'—and about 'their values and their quirks'. Vernon captured human life through its incidental details and on its own turf. But he added his own subjective experience to the mix—not in the form of an omniscient 'Voice-of-God' style of narration, but as the fallible participant-observer. 'I can still tell the truth', he declared, 'but only as it comes—which is in little bits and nuances, particularities and half-truths, all as vague as a cloud of midges.' He told listeners that his mission was simply to say this: 'Here are some of those flies in summer amber: perhaps they will make a pattern.'[10]

This was a style of reportage pursued in grittier vein by Ray Gosling in his portraits of various corners of British life throughout the 1970s, 1980s, and early 1990s. In a succession of series such as *Who Owns Britain*, *Next Door's Doorstep*, and *The Heavy Side of Town*, he displayed the inquisitive approach of the loner, a style that one radio critic described astutely as 'oblique and discursive'.[11] A common concern was with the way people lived their lives in communities struggling to come to terms with industrial decline. He was interested in the same sorts of things as sociologists but was apt to dismiss academic outsiders as 'poverty-mongers': their stories were so riveting he agreed; but 'we were the rivets'.[12] There were certainly traces in Gosling's work of his early apprenticeship to Charles Parker. But unlike Parker, who sculpted his real-life characters into shape slowly and meticulously in the edit-suite, Gosling's interventions came at first acquaintance: he was always palpably *there*, a Wolfe in sheep's clothing one might say, in the thick of the action, mixing with the people he interviewed, getting people untrained in broadcasting to speak to him in remarkably unguarded ways. It was very much first-person and present-tense. And such was his facility with the vernacular that Stephen Hearst pronounced him a Henry Mayhew for the twentieth century. 'What he says', Hearst reckoned, 'will be worth hearing in a hundred years time.'[13]

The intimacy both Gosling and Vernon supplied was only made possible, of course, through people's willingness to talk candidly in the first place. In this respect, people were behaving in ways that had scarcely seemed possible only a decade or so earlier. Clearly, something was changing. Tom Wolfe, again, thought he had the measure of things. In another of his commentaries on the age, he wrote in 1976 of living through 'The Me Decade'. The dream, he said, was now 'changing one's personality—remaking, re-modelling, elevating, and polishing one's very self...and observing, studying, and doting on it'—the natural result, he reckoned, not just of the personal and sexual liberations of the 1960s and new psychological theories but of the thirty-year post-War boom, which had given large numbers of ordinary people surplus income and surplus time—income and time that could be spent on realizing their potential as human beings.[14]

Academic writers lent credence to this vision. In his 1974 study of 'Post-Industrial' society, Daniel Bell wrote of how, in a period that had overcome scarcity in goods, the focus of people's concern would inevitably shift to matters of lifestyle and self-fulfilment. Liberation was less about releasing the human subject from socially enforced bondage and more about dispelling *self-imposed* illusions. Hence, 'We find sociology giving way to psychology, political collect-ivities yielding to the person.'[15] It was, so the New York psychoanalyst Christo-pher Lasch concluded in 1978, all symptomatic of a 'culture of narcissism'—made worse as the decade progressed by a loss of faith in the ability of politicians to tackle fundamental social and economic problems: 'Having no hope of improving their lives in any of the ways that matter', he argued, 'people have convinced themselves that what matters is psychic improvement: getting in touch with their feelings, eating health food, taking lessons in ballet or belly-dancing, immersing themselves in the wisdom of the East, jogging, learning how to "relate", overcoming their "fear of pleasure" '.[16]

It all sounded splendidly un-British. But even in the United Kingdom, behaviour was changing on similar, if not quite identical, lines. Social surveys since the late 1950s had commented on a marked shift from 'work' to 'consump-tion' as the core value of cultural life for most working people. By the 1960s, a majority of male workers saw home rather than place of work as their main site of companionship and sociability, a tendency that had accelerated as suburban housing developments put more and more distance between the two locations.[17] 'I spend therefore I am' was to become the motto of the next three decades.

Shopping gradually became a leisure activity in itself; food tastes diversified; the number of people holidaying overseas rose dramatically; as the proportion of public housing declined and home ownership became a main focus of aspiration, DIY entrenched its position—alongside watching television—as the main leisure pursuit of British men; more men were also willing to buy toiletries and cosmetics, and the range on offer to both sexes proliferated from the 1960s.[18] Clearly, a popular yearning for some level of self-fulfilment was spreading well beyond the United States.

And the BBC had started to notice. Back in 1970, the current affairs editor Steven Bonarjee had written to Tony Whitby, arguing that 'what people actually do with their own time is broadly more interesting to them than their working lives and preoccupations'. Yet, he went on, 'except in the rather special spheres of motoring, gardening and one or two fashionable hobbies there is curiously little about what we actually like doing reflected in Radio or Television.'[19] Strictly speaking, this was a questionable claim, since even in 1962, BBC Television had broadcast *Choice*, in which Richard Dimbleby presented the results of tests conducted by *Which?* and *Shopper's Guide*.[20] And *Woman's Hour* had been a feature of British radio so long that its coverage of consumer affairs—fashion tips and recipes, discussions of the Budget, choice in childbirth, and so on—was clearly being taken for granted.[21] Yet two decades later, no one would have doubted that a change had taken place. The BBC as a whole was increasingly absorbed with how people spent their lives, and what that meant for the sort of programmes they should provide. In the mid-1970s and again in the mid-1980s it produced vast surveys called 'The People's Activities and Use of Time' and 'Daily Life', which described in minute detail the British population's daily habits—getting up, eating, reading, travelling to and from work, going to the cinema, watching television, going to bed—and how all these activities changed according to class, age, sex, and geography.[22]

In the decade that separated these two surveys there was a steady proliferation of programmes embracing consumer interests and leisure pursuits. *You and Yours*, *Parents and Children*, and *Motoring and the Motorist* had all been running for some while. Over the following years they were joined by an impressive list of other series dedicated to all the various ways of spending money and time: in 1973, by *Tuesday Call*, which provided advice on gardening, do-it-yourself, and cookery as well as debate on topical controversies; in 1977, by *Going Places* and *Money Box*; in 1978, by *Parent Power*; in 1979, by the short-lived *Help Yourself*, and the more enduring *Breakaway* and *The Food Programme*. In the meantime, *Kaleidoscope* was being described not as a forum for criticism but as a 'consumer's guide' to the Arts, *Talking about Antiques* was being scrutinized to see if it might widen its focus to encompass a general trend for collecting, and there was talk of new gardening programmes to supplement *Gardener's Question Time*.[23]

But the 'cult of the "individual" ' was supposed to be about more than *things*, or outward appearances. It was also supposed to be about *feelings*. And what on earth could radio broadcasters do to convey those? Tom Wolfe had made it clear that 'to get inside' a person, 'you had to ask him about his thoughts and emotions, along with everything else'.[24] From an American perspective this seemed easy. Having witnessed what had happened at a mass therapy session in one Californian hotel, Wolfe had no doubt that *anyone* given permission to speak about themselves would cooperate wholeheartedly:

They took their fingers right off the old repress button and told the whole room. My husband! My wife! My homosexuality! My inability to communicate, my self-hatred, self-destructiveness, craven fears, puling weaknesses, primordial horrors, premature ejaculation, impotence, frigidity, rigidity, subservience, laziness, alcoholism, major vices, minor vices, grim habits, twisted psyches, tortured souls . . .

And so the list went on, right the way down to the fundamental agonies of haemorrhoids.[25]

By way of contrast, the British—or perhaps more accurately, the English—had long thought of themselves, and been seen by others, as 'an emotionally constipated people'.[26] In July 1970, the producer of Radio Four's *The Time of My Life*—a series manifestly designed to convey the 'real person' behind the personality—moaned about how one (not entirely untypical) guest 'was very good at talking about practical matters, but became inarticulate when asked about her own thoughts and feelings'.[27] And the letters and phone calls pouring in to the BBC complaining about too much sex in afternoon plays, explicit talk, and dreary news, suggested that a vocal part of the Radio Four audience would be just as reluctant to *hear* about people's problems as it would be to supply them.

On the other hand, the BBC could not ignore the therapeutic sensibility of the age. If lots of people now interpreted self-improvement less as a matter of reading the right books or speaking the right way—in short, of emulating standards set by *others*—and more a matter of learning how to be at ease with *oneself*, should not the BBC be there to eavesdrop, perhaps even to help in their project? The answer in both cases was a tentative yes. Tony Whitby had announced even before taking up his post as Controller of Radio Four that he was after 'programmes about people's human situation and emotions as opposed to their political and purely social problems'.[28] The decision to proceed into this new territory had been taken. What remained to be worked out was how on earth therapy could be offered in public without the airwaves being filled with a torrent of dark secrets, self-indulgence, and exhibitionism—characteristics that seemed not just uncomfortable to witness, but somewhat ill-becoming for a public service broadcaster. They were the kinds of questions that would only be resolved by more than a decade of experimentation and dispute.

KNOW THYSELF: COUNSELLING BRITAIN

The first attempt to put the nation on the therapist's couch emerged in 1971, in the form of a Sunday evening discussion programme, *If You Think You've Got Problems*. The series started tentatively, gradually established a reputation for good sense among many in the psychiatric profession, frequently repulsed others both inside and outside the BBC, and ended in recriminations and protests after Ian McIntyre stepped in to cancel a controversial edition in 1977.

The programme's format was simple enough. Letters received from listeners would be sorted, and each week two or three correspondents would be selected to come to the studio and describe their particular problems. Each case would be discussed in turn by a panel, some of whom, in the producers' words, were 'experts' and some of whom provided a 'general commonsense approach to life'. There would also be a 'participating Chairman', though in the early planning stages it was not known who this might be.[29] At Tom Wolfe's Californian therapy session, the role was fulfilled by 'a cocky little bastard... all very casual and spontaneous—after about two hours of trying on different outfits in front of the mirror, *that* kind of casual and spontaneous'.[30] In Broadcasting House, the role belonged to the altogether more self-effacing Jean Metcalfe. She was an inspired choice: well regarded for presenting *Forces Favourites*, *Two-Way Family Favourites*, and *Woman's Hour* years before; tactful; able to draw out the most reluctant of interviewees; and with a deep voice that somehow suggested patient understanding. 'It was up to me to make them feel... that there was someone on their side. Like a schoolteacher, in a way, encouraging them to do themselves justice. But not so well that their flaws and frailties did not show.' It was, she admitted, a way of channelling her own fascination with family life productively 'before I turned into a lonely old net curtain twitcher'.[31]

As to the kind of problems she would have to discuss in her new role, in comparison with what was evidently going on in California, the initial plans for *If You Think You've Got Problems* seemed to provide a rather timid shopping list: husbands or wives who were habitually late for appointments, interfering neighbours, rows over sharing childcare at home, and disputes within families over debts. Whitby urged the producers to show less restraint. 'Let's get away whenever we can from middle-class problems', he told them. And, he added pointedly, 'try to avoid' the danger of 'a marked preference for "nice" problems as opposed to "nasty" ones'.[32]

The hint was taken. Over the next few years the producers expressed a determination to 'weed out the boring and the mundane' as much as possible, while keeping a 'fair balance' between the remaining themes. During the first 238 programmes problems between parents and their children and between husbands and wives were featured more than any other subject, though there were also a large number of items about relationships between unmarried couples, and nearly twice as many discussions about what were called 'psycho-sexual problems' than there were about bereavement. One programme featured older men who felt 'threatened' by accusations of sexual assault made against them by young children. Another offered advice to the working mother of a 13-year-old boy on how to deal with him being alone in the house with his 14-year-old girlfriend. 'I would be extremely surprised if the idea of intercourse had not occurred to him', one panellist told the mother, before suggesting that she should 'open up a discussion about birth control'.[33]

This was all heady stuff. And eye-opening even for those closely involved. 'When the programme got into its stride', Jean Metcalfe later admitted, 'I was shattered to discover I was as worldly as a sex manual written by Brownies':

Two-Way Family Favourites was never like this. Excessive handwashing was symbolic of guilt about sex. A widow's nightmares full of furry animals demonstrated guilt about sex. Even pumping iron could relieve guilt about sex. There was a lot of guilt and sex about which, on Radio 4 in the 1970s was, to say the least, unusual. Before long I was using naughty words like 'orgasm' with scarcely a blush. More problems had their basis in sexual hang-ups it appeared than anything else, but there were many others, which had to do with unmourned death, hidden grief, fear of dying and unexpressed anger...The problems laid out in listeners' letters almost invariably concealed another more complicated one underneath. Downtrodden wives turned out to be secretly dominating people using manipulation to get their own way; truanting children employed school refusal as blackmail for attention; workaholic husbands made the office their excuse for ducking boring homes and demanding wives; 'problem children' were often the whipping boys for difficulties which the rest of the family would not accept as their own. We met agoraphobics by telephone, alcoholics before opening time...and a transvestite who came to the studio as 'Alice' in demure old-fashioned 1950s clothes then went home to become 'David' again and a father to his children.[34]

It did not take long for voices to be raised against the programme. The Editor of the Radio Newsroom loathed it from the start. 'Nasty, scrappy and dirty' was how he described it. 'It smacked of some of the worst features of women's magazines and made one wonder about the real motives behind the programme.' George Fischer worried, too, that it encouraged 'self-display' and an unhealthy interest among listeners—what another head of department labelled 'ecouteurism'. Was it right, Martin Esslin asked, to have a girl discussing on the programme whether or not she should have an abortion, or to hear a woman condemning her in-laws before an audience of around a million? Even the Editor of *Woman's Hour*, a programme that had long made a virtue of discussing controversial problems, thought it 'valueless and distasteful'. Meanwhile, sixteen listeners wrote or phoned in to complain about an edition that discussed a man's sexual interest in young girls. And Mary Whitehouse was roused to write to the BBC Chairman when she heard of the panel's advice to discuss birth control with under-age teenagers.[35]

Some, however, thought *Problems* not nearly permissive enough. When one programme in 1973 discussed homosexuality in a way that both Richard Imison and Howard Newby described as 'moving, remarkable, and amply justified', it prompted a more hostile response within the new Gay Liberation movement. Two of its campaigners took offence at the advice given to a 16-year-old boy who had asked the panel whether he was likely to become homosexual since he was solely attracted to his own sex. 'Don't commit yourself, don't give yourself a label, be open to a variety of experience', the boy had been told on air. 'One needs to translate', the campaigners riposted in a pamphlet published the following year: what the panellist *really* meant was, 'Don't be too eager to say that you are sick; find a girl soon and it may yet be possible to smother your homosexual feelings.' Here, they argued, 'permissive chatter' veiled an underlying disparagement. It was a reminder that even a liberal organization such as the BBC could perpetuate notions of guilt and inferiority. Why else, they wondered, would the programme have insisted that a gay man remain anonymous, except 'presumably to induce the sense of shame and secrecy felt proper to such occasions'?[36]

Homosexuality turned out to be the programme's undoing four years later. An edition that had been pre-recorded for transmission in January 1977 featured four lesbians who had all 'come out'. As Jean Metcalfe explained in her opening to the programme, they were assembled in the studio not so much to *be* advised as to advise others on how they had overcome their own doubts and difficulties. What followed over the next forty-five minutes was an insight into their lives, their upbringing, their relationships, their views on motherhood, feminism, and equality. If the panel of experts took a line it was to extol the benefits of permanence in any relationship, but the overall tone was understanding—and the running theme *about* understanding.[37] Ian McIntyre, however, pricked up his ears when he got wind of it. 'I didn't normally listen to programmes before transmission, but it sounded a little bit unusual, I thought I'd like to listen to it, which I did, and formed the conclusion that it was actually a sort of party political broadcast ... they weren't actually issuing enrolment forms, but jolly nearly.'[38] One radio critic later suggested the content had simply scared McIntyre 'to the depths of his Scottish soul'. 'He talked to me about it for an hour. He kept asking me whether I would let my children hear that kind of programme.'[39] McIntyre's stated belief at the time was that since the participants had neither written in seeking help nor thought they had a problem, the edition had not conformed to the programme's own brief. 'It was not the purpose of *If You Think You've Got Problems*', he told colleagues, 'to provide a group of lesbians with the opportunity to make converts to their particular sexual deviation.'[40]

With just three days to go before transmission, he ordered the programme to be pulled from the schedules, and, rubbing salt into the wound, suggested P. G. Wodehouse as a suitable replacement. 'I walked out through the front door of the building that evening, straight into a damn great picket of people with banners saying, "Hang McIntyre" or "Up with Lesbians", or whatever ... I thought it was very funny to be walking through a demonstration anonymously. Quite a lot of people—thirty or forty: rent-a-crowd had quickly got on the job.'[41]

People were seething inside Broadcasting House, too. Current Affairs Magazine Programmes—known in the BBC by the unfortunate acronym 'CAMP'—was the department responsible for making the programme, and its head, Alan Rogers, immediately wrote in protest to the Director of Programmes. Rogers pointed out that some 275 people had already phoned the BBC to complain of the cancellation. 'The truth is', he went on, '*Problems* has a mature and sympathetic audience': its regular listeners understood the programme's reputation for dealing with subjects sensitively and responsibly. 'One of the reasons that I was pleased with the lesbian programme when I heard it was that it conveyed a genuinely contemporary attitude to an old problem and surely that is something we should do on Radio Four.'[42] The argument now turned on questions of motivation and of morality. McIntyre, with the backing of BBC Radio's Head of Religious Programmes, Michael Mayne, believed the programme should have acknowledged that 'many, perhaps most' Radio Four listeners believed homosexuality was wrong. It therefore exhibited 'moral imbecility' in failing to press its guests on this point.[43] Rogers's retort was that lesbianism, in itself, presented no moral dilemma at all and that professional counsellors would, in any case, shrink from moralising. The aim, he claimed, had been to offer counselling via *success* stories—a perfectly legitimate technique. It had tried to 'inform the general listener, to give him some insight . . . and to offer the succour of shared experience to listeners with a similar problem'.[44] BBC Managers now attempted to adjudicate between the two sides in a manner of sorts. The Director of Programmes, Douglas Muggeridge, ruled that 'lesbianism is clearly a subject which can—and should—be tackled', that there was 'nothing overtly offensive' in *Problems*' treatment of it, but that it had been naive in avoiding the moral issues involved. It should probably have been broadcast, he concluded, but subject to changes in its presentation.[45]

The series never quite recovered. One of the regular panellists, Wendy Greengross had her own dark suspicions about the future. 'Mark my words', she told Metcalfe, 'they'll bring it back for one more season to save face, but that will be the last.' And it was. Audiences had in any case been dipping a little since 1976, and some in BBC Radio had begun wondering if the programme was running out of steam. There was a last straw, and it came when one edition took a sudden and unexpected turn: a man worrying about his financial competence was revealed as the owner of a private centre promoting group sex. Producers had always warned that counselling sessions were unpredictable, given the propensity for people's stated problems to eventually reveal other, more difficult ones lurking beneath. In this case the surprise was particularly alarming and the effect proved terminal.[46]

If You Think You've Got Problems disappeared in 1978, but not without trace. The BBC's case for intruding upon private experiences in the public interest had been established, and patterns of 'best practice' discovered. Through much of its seven-year existence, BBC Governors and Managers had worried most about the series' effect on those taking part. Would they be harmed? Perhaps by being exploited for the entertainment of the wider audience, or being exposed to ridicule from those who knew them back home, or through receiving faulty advice? The programme's producers had worked out some answers. They had, for example, written to each guest three months or so after their appearance, asking them how useful or otherwise their experience had been. The vast majority replied that it had indeed been helpful—perhaps not in removing the problem, but in enabling them to deal with it better.[47] One of the regular panellists also told of how carefully each participant was handled on the day: taken for a coffee and a chat with Metcalfe and the producer at eleven o'clock in the morning, given the chance to see the programme being prepared and the right to request that any part of their interview be edited out. The counselling session on air was all too brief, but producers strove to provide guests with a day-long experience, creating an informal atmosphere and dispelling the inevitable nerves.[48]

It was, Tony Whitby had once made clear, a 'necessary condition' of the series that none of its participants be harmed.[49] Even so, he and his producers did not see this as their main defence. The whole point of the exercise was the help it gave to the audience at large. 'It was all very well', Whitby pointed out, 'for people who were fortunate enough to live in a cosy middle-class world with telephones and easy access to professionally qualified advisers, but there were millions who had no-one to go to with their problems.' In this respect the programme compensated for 'deficiencies in the social services'. It helped reassure people in difficulties that they were not alone. More than that, its supporters suggested, it provided the British public with a model for the 'rational analysis of problems', an 'education in human relations', a kind of ' "teach-in", exposing listeners to worthwhile thinking about society'. If the programme had its own technique it was to suggest the curative power, as one panellist put it, which 'lies in the exchange of warmth and understanding'.[50] The programme was important not just for *what* it discussed, but also for *how* it did so: it helped teach Britons that it was both possible—and desirable—to talk.

Or so the rhetoric went. Whether or not *Problems* actually made any difference in this larger sense is impossible to calibrate. But during its lifetime more and more listeners were certainly writing in—discussing their reactions to what they had heard, seeking more information, sometimes describing their own problems simply in order to keep company with those who had appeared on air. As one member of the audience put it: 'I just happened to be listening and felt the urge to write.' When members of the audience were invited to write in with *their own* advice—to become the experts rather than the subjects for a change—some 300 responded. In most other weeks, nearly a hundred letters were received by the programme team. At the beginning, very few men took part. Over time, however, they supplied a growing proportion of the correspondence: they, too, were gradually finding it easier to talk about their feelings, and admit to emotional difficulties. Often, listeners who had contacted the programme were put in touch with guests who had appeared: informal networks and support groups took on a life of their own.[51] The Current Affairs Magazine Programmes department, which already faced large postbags arriving every day for *Woman's Hour*, *You and Yours*, and *In Touch*, could not always cope with the new burdens being placed on it. Letters could not just be ignored: to do so would imply that the care and support being offered on air was merely pretence, a cynical device of programme-making. Alan Rogers reminded staff that 'we have an obligation to respond even to unsolicited mail because of the expectation our style of programming arouses in the listener'.[52]

Some people, at least, evidently looked upon the BBC as an organization there to help them, to be on their side and make them feel better about themselves. The approach to listeners was a sign, too, of the BBC embedding into its own production processes what was starting to be called 'interaction'. The phrase was used by a panellist on *Problems* in describing how guests, listeners, panellists, and producers were all 'learning' from each other, becoming more skilled in 'dealing with inter-personal relations', creating 'an ongoing experiment in a new way of sharing'.[53] The whole arrangement proved attractive enough for BBC 1 to offer its own version of the format in 1973, in the form of *Let's Talk It Over*. It was on at exactly the same time as *Problems*—6.15 p.m. on Sundays—and it also used Wendy Greengross as one of its panellists.[54] It was a rather unhelpful clash in the schedules. But the imitation was flattering, and it undoubtedly symbolized one thing: that emotional honesty was more than a passing fad.

Naturally, not every programme could become unbuttoned overnight. There were traditions to be upheld, expectations of decorum to be fulfilled. Take, for example, one of Radio Four's most enduring series, *Desert Island Discs*. Here was a programme dedicated to revealing personality and life history, but patently reluctant to pry. Roy Plomley first used the simple format of asking celebrity guests which eight records they would take with them to a desert island in January 1942. And he had occupied the presenter's chair ever since. On each occasion he was courteous to a fault and unbending in his routine. Castaways would be treated to lunch at the Garrick (women would have to be taken to the Lansdowne), steered around the BBC's immense Gramophone Library, then submitted to the gentlest of inquisitions in one of Broadcasting House's basement studios. 'The idea is copyrighted by Roy Plomley', the BBC's Head of Gramophone Programmes reminded colleagues, and 'he is always very loathe to introduce changes. It took many weeks, for example, for me to be able to banish "Ladies and Gentlemen" from his opening sentence.'[55]

The Plomley style can be sensed in just the briefest of extracts from one edition in 1978. At precisely the moment *If You Think You've Got Problems* was being wound up, he welcomed to *Desert Island Discs* the Conservative leader and putative Prime Minister, Margaret Thatcher. This was an act of politeness in itself. Unlike most guests, she had not been invited: Mrs Thatcher, the producer subsequently admitted, 'had asked to appear'.[56] Characteristically, Plomley's starting point was to talk about her childhood:

PLOMLEY. You were born in Grantham, in Lincolnshire. That's quite a small town, isn't it?
THATCHER. Yes, a small town, and very much a community. I loved living in a town where everyone knew everyone else.
PLOMLEY. And you lived in a flat above your father's grocer's shop—right on the Great North Road.
THATCHER. Between the Great North Road and the Great North Railway. The lorries used to rumble past at night, and if we went for a weekend in the country with friends, I used to stay awake—it was too quiet.
PLOMLEY. You weren't an only child, were you?
THATCHER. No, fortunately; I have an elder sister, for which I am eternally grateful. When you've got problems, there's nothing like close relatives.
PLOMLEY. Your forebears had been craftsmen and tradesmen: one was an organ maker.
THATCHER. Great Uncle John! As a great treat, we used to go and stay with him at weekends sometimes...

Later, Plomley moved on to asking which subjects interested her at school, where she went for holidays, about her hobbies at Oxford, her first meeting with her husband Denis. 'I was very impressed by Mrs Thatcher', Plomley later admitted, 'Come to that, I still am.'[57] He had no wish to focus on controversy. And it has to be admitted that in his own calm way he did much to reveal something of the ways this particular politician's outlook had been shaped by background and upbringing: a taste for self-reliance, a small-town mien, even a hint of insomnia—all tantalizingly suggested within three minutes. But Plomley's critics within the BBC tended to despair at his reluctance to follow up interesting statements, or to raise topical issues, or even to change the relentlessly chronological running order of his questions. On some occasions the Plomley approach almost brought the programme grinding to a halt. When Princess Margaret was the guest in January 1981—a 'considerable coup' according to BBC insiders—she turned out to be almost monosyllabic. Perhaps, Monica Sims thought, she felt 'she had to weigh every word'. Or, a current affairs producer suggested, Plomley had simply been too obsequious. Wherever responsibility lay, one BBC Governor decided that the result had been 'terrible'.[58]

Within Broadcasting House, the obvious desire to refresh *Desert Island Discs* throughout the late 1970s and early 1980s was tempered not just by Plomley's continued ownership, but also by the recognition that audience ratings remained very good. Most regular listeners liked it just as it was. The feelings many devotees had towards *Desert Island Discs* in this period (and since) were recorded for posterity by Mass-Observation. Among the several hundred entries on the programme, there is a remarkable unanimity of opinion: 'I feel certain it will be kept within bounds'; 'biographical without going into private aspects'; 'the participants are subjects but are not victims'; 'it is always "clean", and produced with impeccable good taste'; 'I have to confess to having listened to *Desert Island Discs* all my life without ever thinking that it was intrusive'; 'I do not feel like a voyeur'.[59] In a changing world, the unchanging formula of *Desert Island Discs* was part of its appeal, particularly for older listeners. And Radio Four Controllers knew it. In the short term the most they could do was to 'rest' it every now and then—though never for *very* long without newspapers speculating that 'resting' was really a euphemism for dropping it permanently.[60]

More dramatic change became possible when Plomley died in May 1985. The new chairman, Michael Parkinson, was soon reckoned by Review Board to be 'getting more out of his subjects than Roy Plomley had done' and attracting 'a more interesting selection of guests'. He added a little more 'showbiz' and publicity value, too. Though all this was not without cost. Some producers felt he was too obtrusive, and not nearly interested enough in the music. Suspicions were even voiced of a Yorkshire bias in the choice of castaways: it was noted with some concern by the BBC's Board of Management in February 1986 that 'all the guests who had so far appeared on the programme under Michael Parkinson's chairmanship had indeed been born in Yorkshire'. One judicious—and diplo-matic—conclusion being drawn inside Broadcasting House was that, 'those who liked him had liked him very much, and those who had not were vociferous in their objections to his radio manner'.[61]

There was less disagreement, however, about the series becoming more search-ing after March 1988, when Sue Lawley took over from Parkinson—an appoint-ment that coincided with the programme's transfer from the Gramophone Department to Magazine Programmes, and the introduction of a researcher to ensure the new presenter sharpened the line of questioning. Not for Lawley the obsequies of a pre-programme luncheon in Covent Garden or Mayfair. 'I dislike talking to an interviewee in advance', she admitted. 'I worry that it will spoil the spontaneity of our exchange.' Fully aware of the alarm that might be prompted by her background in journalism, she stated publicly that *Desert Island Discs* would remain 'a conversation', and 'not a programme of penetrating interviews or sensational revelations'.[62] But it was to be conversation of a more bracing kind. Thus, during Lawley's first few series, we heard Stephen Fry recounting the prison experiences of his youth, being '90 per cent gay' at Cambridge, of how, now being celibate, he reserved 'the right not to go to bed with people of either sex', and of his choice of a suicide pill as luxury item. We also witnessed the Labour leader Neil Kinnock being asked about his dislike of school and about the death of his parents, what he felt about accusations of ruthlessness, or of being a bit of a 'windbag', whether his wife Glenys was cleverer than him—and being reminded that what she remembered of their first meeting at Cardiff University was 'a loud, ginger person'. There was no sign that Kinnock objected to these questions or felt particularly uncomfortable with answering them. Lawley's style—probing but patently consensual, drawing a distinction between being revealing and being intrusive—undoubtedly played its part. So too did the castaway's willingness to enter fully into the spirit of the programme—a spirit which undoubtedly now required guests to give of themselves a little more fully. *Desert Island Discs*, Lawley explained, 'is properly impressed by power, wealth and ambition, but it knows that the world is made up of more than that'.[63] Hence politicians appearing on the programme—and there were undoubtedly more of them at the end of the 1980s than there had been at the end of the 1970s—knew that their politics was up for discussion. And so, too, was their private life. Indeed, it was readily assumed that a castaway's political convictions could barely be comprehended *without* knowing a little of the emotional and psychological dimensions that may have shaped them.

The logical conclusion to all this emotional honesty was to dispense with any circumlocution or pretence and offer Radio Four listeners the real thing. In 1982, a new format promised to do just that. It was developed by Michael Ember, who had come to Britain from Hungary in 1956 to study psychology and criminology before joining the BBC. Since 1970, he had produced *Start the Week*, *Midweek*, and *Stop the Week*, where, among the regular guests was Anthony Clare, a practising psychiatrist at the Maudsley and St Bartholomew's hospitals in London. Clare's first book, *Psychiatry in Dissent*, had earned him some media attention and a column in *The Spectator*.[64] Ember recognized him as the ideal presenter for *In the Psychiatrist's Chair*. This was a series that would dispense entirely with the biographical details of a person's public life and focus unrelentingly on the private experiences that had shaped his or her behaviour. The prospect of being submitted to a sustained investigation by a trained psychiatrist before a national audience was not universally appealing. Tom Stoppard declined the invitation, telling Ember that 'this must be the least attractive proposition I have received for a long time'.[65] But others succumbed to curiosity. 'In a world of increasing complexity', Clare reasoned, 'almost the only thing any of us can still claim to have substantial competence about and knowledge of is ourselves. We should not be too surprised that given half a chance to talk about ourselves so many of us readily grab it.'[66] The first guest in the first series was the actress Glenda Jackson. The attention of a psychiatrist, she admitted, was very seductive.[67]

Over the next few years *In the Psychiatrist's Chair* provided Radio Four listeners with the chance to hear some astonishingly frank interviews. There was, for example, Sir Michael Tippett providing a moving account of his homosexuality, the novelist Susan Hill detailing the impact on her mental and physical state of a succession of miscarriages, the Conservative minister Edwina Currie describing matter-of-factly the break-up of her relationship with her father, and the tennis-player Arthur Ashe speaking of being haunted with matters of mortality after his mother's death when he was only 6. 'If, or should I say when, you meet your mother what would you say?' Clare asked him at the end of their encounter. 'I don't think I would say anything', Ashe replied, 'I'd probably just let her hold me for a while, for a very long time.'[68]

None of this was exactly like real therapy, of course. Like Lawley in *Desert Island Discs*, Clare did not want to destroy spontaneity by meeting his guests before each recording of *In the Psychiatrist's Chair*. And there would be no follow-up sessions afterwards, either. Even so, many of Clare's guests *sounded* like patients, sometimes like patients in need of real therapy. Most were revealed to be far more complex and troubled than the press cuttings might have suggested. In July 1988, for example, the agony aunt Claire Rayner broke down when Anthony Clare kept pressing her on the effect of her own childhood traumas—what Rayner described elusively as 'mud' she preferred to leave at the bottom of her pond. She had always been suspicious of the talking cure, believing that we all already know 'the pressures that moulded us and made us what we are'. She accepted the invitation, she explained, because she was flattered and because she had been fond of Clare. 'He thought I had accepted because I wanted to talk about painful past experiences, but I flatly refused to do so and stuck by my refusal, even though he reduced me to a jelly for starters and finally to tears.'[69]

Most of her distress was cut from the recording, but enough of it was heard in the programme to prompt heavy criticism of Clare for his persistence. In his defence, he argued that Rayner *knew* he would ask those questions, because he had interviewed her in a typically robust way six years earlier for a similar television programme that was never shown. 'I believed that if she did not want to talk about what still distressed her she would turn down the invitation. The fact that she promptly accepted convinced me that she was prepared to talk.' Given her occupation, which was to purvey advice, reassurance, and sympathy to the thousands who sought it from her, Clare reasoned that it was quite legitimate to discover whether she really was the composed, controlled superwoman she occasionally personified. 'Is the childhood mud related to the adult caring?' he had wondered.[70]

Rayner's self-described 'bloody-mindedness' and Clare's equally matched persistence were almost the rules rather than the exception: the programme was marked by a series of abrasive jousts. Jimmy Savile, for instance, telephoned the producer Michael Ember the day before his appearance to say how much he was looking forward to 'doing down the shrink', and proved strikingly elusive when on Clare's couch.[71] Similarly, Ken Dodd used a stream of words, and rapid changes of pace, topic, and mood, when asked persistently about his bachelor status and attitudes to family life.[72] Indeed it was a feature of the technique at the heart of the programme that the very subject a guest felt most uncomfortable discussing was precisely the one that a psychiatrist would consequently find most interesting, and which would therefore be insisted upon as a matter of debate. 'Perhaps', Clare admitted, 'the individual sitting down in the psychiatrist's chair or lying on the analyst's couch can be compared with a crime to be solved, a case to be cracked.'

Certainly, the excitement of the search was common to the work of both detective and psychiatrist. There was the promise, too, of a moment of revelation.[73] As Auden had pointed out in 1963, detective stories indulged the fantasy of being restored to a state of innocence, a 'Garden of Eden', and it was the *unwittingly* revealed details of a person's behaviour that solved crimes—and hence explained irrationality away.[74] Perhaps, then, *In the Psychiatrist's Chair* appealed to the Radio Four audience because the notion of the psychiatrist as a kind of Sherlock Holmes was simply too rich in dramatic potential to be resisted by a listenership fond of murder mysteries.

Of course, not everyone succumbed to its charms. One of those listeners surveyed by Mass-Observation who had been so delighted with *Desert Island Discs* felt that, in comparison, *In the Psychiatrist's Chair* was all 'a bit creepy'. 'I feel rather embarrassed . . . as if I'm eavesdropping', another wrote. For many listeners, however, there was an overriding attraction: as one put it, 'It enabled one to see beyond the public persona . . . and to see that such people have their insecurities and tragedies too.'[75] This was precisely what Clare himself saw as the programme's real purpose. He believed it was a dangerous fantasy to believe that society was divided between 'healthy, integrated, mature' people on the one hand and 'broken, impaired and disintegrated' people on the other. Even the most successful, competent, and efficient people were not without their muddy pools—though they might find ways of limiting the damage. He was convinced, for example, that Claire Rayner, far from being damaged by her exposure, was revealed 'as a more rounded, more sympathetic, less bossy and authoritarian figure'.[76] The powerful message at the heart of *In the Psychiatrist's Chair* appeared to be this: that we are what we are—fallibility and all—and that even if we are moulded by our past, we do not have to be imprisoned by it.

To a public service broadcaster such as the BBC, this kind of message was important. It gave to a programme, which could so easily have appeared self-indulgent and voyeuristic, a tangibly *social* dimension. As one Radio Four listener pointed out, it posed 'the ultimate question': 'How would *I* cope?'[77] Here was a sign of empathy from an audience famed for its scepticism. Theodore Zeldin, in one of his essays on human intimacy, described such empathy as a sort of 'emotional adhesive'. While he believed compassion has usually been constrained whenever 'a cynical or despairing view of humanity' prevailed, he also recognized that it has flowered whenever people are able to discover the individuality within others. 'Interest in psychology', he added, 'has given additional meaning to the old injunction, "Forgive them, for they know not what they do".' If, as Zeldin argues, the last few decades of the twentieth century witnessed compassion as 'a rising star', it is at least arguable that in their modest way programmes such as *If You Think You've Got Problems*, *In the Psychiatrist's Chair*, and at times even *Desert Island Discs*, had their part to play, simply by opening up to public scrutiny the interior life of the British mind.[78]

CONSUMERS AND CAMPAIGNERS

On the face of it, any programme that treated the Radio Four listener as a consumer rather than a citizen would sit uncomfortably with this rising arc compassion. Was not 'consumption' all about satisfying one's own desire not that of others? And were not affluent Radio Four listeners among the biggest consumers of all? Unemployment was rising dramatically during the late 1970s and 1980s, but so too was the average disposable income of those who remained in work. Popular shareholding, private pension funds, lower taxes, easier credit, the growth in the managerial and white-collar sectors of the economy—all spoke of an expanding middle class, commercially minded, willing to incur debt, and out to protect their own (or their family's) interests in the competitive market-place of goods and services.[79] For those wanting to learn how to put their surplus income to best use, there were programmes such as *Money Box* or *Breakaway* or *The Food Programme*.

Yet such programmes did not dispense entirely with a social, even a paternal-istic, dimension. For in most of Radio Four's consumer programmes the task was not so much to *indulge* the appetites of consumers as to *refine* it: to clarify rights, to explain choices, to warn against pitfalls, in short to make us *better* consumers.

Sometimes, this took the traditional BBC form of nudging listeners towards trying something unfamiliar and improving—a new recipe, a new diet, a new book, a new holiday destination. Thus, to give one small example, when *Tuesday Call* chose to focus on the subject of herbs in March 1977, its main aim, apparently, had been to enlighten 'the ordinary woman whose knowledge was restricted to using mint'—a kind of Reithian course in culinary herbalism, as it were.[80] Sometimes, programmes adopted a rather different kind of paternal-ism—one of unequivocally taking the side of the consumer rather than the producer. Hence, while the old Radio Four programme *Parents and Children* had featured countless interviews with teachers and educationalists, its successor, *Parent Power*, was avowedly 'designed to encourage parents to know their rights' and made much more use of parents and schoolchildren. *Money Box*, too, was about deliberately representing the point of view of the 'small investor'; *Break-away* about sticking up for the holidaymaker; another new series in 1977, *Does He Take Sugar?*, about siding with the disabled.[81] In each case, the very public harrying of private companies or public utilities wherever they failed to deliver on promises made, was both a symbol of the growing culture of consumer rights and a way of showing people how to exert these rights even more.

The ultimate example of this campaigning form of consumer broadcasting was *Checkpoint*, which ran from 1973 until 1985. The programme evolved from a series of investigative reports on *The World at One* by a young New Zealander, Roger Cook.[82] The first programme, which accused opticians of overpricing spectacles on the basis of their monopoly, set the pattern. Cook used his portable recorder to go out and about, enticing stories of betrayal from ordinary victims and confronting those who had apparently cheated on them. Indeed, the fly-on-the-wall recordings of Cook 'door-stepping' villains reluctant to respond to the evidence carefully amassed against them—scenes that ended with Cook having a chamber pot emptied over his head on one memorable occasion, and being under physical attack on at least sixteen others—became a signature theme of the series. As in all the best dramas, *Checkpoint* offered listeners the enjoyment of witnessing a moment of come-uppance as justice was dispensed.

Partisanship was the essence of its style—indeed, its very purpose. For a start, witnesses were 'coached', on the grounds that they were likely to be less experienced speakers than, say, company chairmen who had been media trained. During editing, the victims' recorded testimony was left with as few interruptions as possible from the interviewer, in order to 'make it more "their" programme'.[83] Regular contact with the audience was also a feature. 'Our moral stance', one producer explained, 'is controlled by the indignation of the listener.' The process of making each programme always started with the postbag. In the mid-1970s, some 400 letters arrived each week, all of which were read, and about 40 per cent of which would offer potential stories. '*Checkpoint* may be the closest thing to redress that our complainants ever get', Cook once claimed. But there was a broader goal, too. The production team made a working assumption that ten letters of complaint about one particular individual or organization represented about a thousand other people who had suffered similar problems: it would hint at a story that it was in the *public interest* to tell. Just as *If You Think You've Got Problems* used individual case histories of emotional trauma not so much for the benefit of the person concerned as to offer advice to the broader listening public, *Checkpoint* was in the business of illustrating 'how a *system* fails to provide redress', as Cook put it.[84] The programme offered a series of parables—'a way of teaching how people are caught in traps or unpleasant situations of various kinds . . . to bring out the reasons why the problems have arisen and warn the public at large of the dangers'. *Checkpoint* even offered the Radio Four audience an overarching lesson in human behaviour. It suggested that anybody, no matter how important or rich, might be fallible, just as anybody, however sophisticated or intelligent, could be tricked into misfortune.[85]

Campaigning journalism was new territory for the BBC, and it was clearly nervous. Those on the receiving end were rarely willing to go down without a fight. The opticians' trade organization responded to the first programme by writing to the Director-General to complain bitterly of imbalance, causing months of internal anguish, with memos, clarifications, and legal defences being prepared. Receiving threatening writs became a normal part of life at the *Checkpoint* office. Indeed, for the producers, it was almost a matter of pride—proof that the programme had hit home. Managers and Governors were naturally more circumspect. They worried deeply about any allegation that threatened the Corporation's reputation for impartiality, and imposed tighter editorial supervision over Cook whenever he seemed to be heading towards stories they considered 'indefensible' in courts of law. 'I really don't believe they understood what *Checkpoint* was all about', he recalled. 'They seemed to think that it should offer advice and "point fingers gently".'[86]

Yet if wariness was the predominant response of senior BBC figures in 1973, there was also, in the last resort, a willingness to keep the programme going—and on terms that were largely of its own making. New ground rules were brokered which established the programme's right to make explicit accusations of wrong-doing provided that certain precautions had been taken first. The usual expect-ation of the accused, fostered no doubt by their misunderstanding of the BBC's line on neutrality, was that they should be given some 'right of reply', perhaps in a subsequent programme. Yet the BBC, though striving for neutrality in matters of opinion, had always maintained that it could never be neutral between right and wrong and had a formal commitment to telling the truth as it found it. 'Impar-tiality', the BBC pointed out in 1982, 'implies the consideration of a full range of views, and honestly applied, may result in an unbalanced picture because the truth is itself unbalanced.' 'In exposing abuses against consumers', it added, 'a programme like *Checkpoint* is not balanced—but it *is* impartial and factual.'[87]

To defend this position the programme's reporters had to prove themselves beyond reproach. New practices were therefore developed to make them 'fire-proof'. Producers kept an unedited master tape of recorded interviews, including the habitual opening statement by Cook explaining clearly that a recording was being made; they always invited accused individuals to provide a statement before resorting to doorstepping; defendants' arguments were transmitted in the same order in which they had been recorded; scripts and interviews were placed before one of the BBC's in-house lawyers prior to transmission. None of this prevented accused individuals from taking offence, of course. As one of the BBC's lawyers told Cook, 'The question isn't whether you'll get a writ, but how many and when.' Crucially, though, the default position of the legal team was now 'to make a programme broadcastable whenever possible, not to stop it outright'. In fact, in the first ten years of *Checkpoint*'s existence there were only three successful challenges against it, two being settled out of court and one going no further than the Broadcasting Complaints Commission. By this stage, the Office of Fair Trading had even decided to make its files available to the programme's researchers—a unique privilege at the time.[88]

Checkpoint was not always beyond suspicion. The *Sunday Telegraph* thought it 'anti-City', and in 1975, partly in response to a feeling among some senior editors that there might be some truth in these charges, the BBC's Chairman, Michael Swann, pressed forcefully for the programme to broaden its targets away from 'particular trading organisations' and encompass the service industries and government bureaucracy. Five years later, concern was expressed at Review Board that the series sometimes failed to distinguish between evil and mere ineptitude.[89]

Yet, overall, the programme was an obvious success, garnering headlines, attracting younger listeners, sometimes forcing a change in the law, providing gripping radio—in short, making an impact that no Controller could ignore. And it marked a genuinely significant stage in the British consumer movement, which had roots going back well before the creation of the Consumer's Association in 1956, but which still lacked bite at the start of the 1970s. People had been told of their rights but were aware that many were being ignored. 'We needed to take things a stage further and have a go at people and organisations who were screwing them': that was how the Head of Current Affairs Magazine Programmes, Alan Rogers recalled the mood of the moment. *Checkpoint*, he believed led the field in developing 'the fight of the small man against bureaucracy and big business'. 'There were other investigative programmes over the years', he added, 'but no one has done it with such a regular strike rate and at such a level of cleanness.'[90] With this sort of reputation *Checkpoint* convinced the higher echelons of the BBC that, so long as exacting standards of forensic investigation were being observed, sides could be taken and powerful lobbies offended without damaging the reputation of the Corporation. Indeed, it even suggested there might be some credit in being seen to represent the interests of 'ordinary' people in their battles against the powerful.[91]

RIGHTS OF REPLY

Exerting one's rights as a consumer and a citizen—or, to put it another way, *complaining*—became something of a cultural phenomenon in its own right by the start of the 1980s. Quite apart from *Checkpoint* and its various spin-offs and imitators, there was a wave of books published with titles such as *How to Complain*, *The Innocent Consumer*, *Consumers: Know Your Rights*, and *The Consumer Jungle*. Almost every newspaper ran a consumer advice column. A plethora of rival magazines offered advice on buying hi-fi, food, financial services, cameras, and various white goods. By 1985, there were twenty-five titles devoted solely to choosing cars. As Matthew Hilton has shown, almost all implicitly suggested that 'market imperfections could be rectified through the empowerment of individuals alone'.[92]

For a large organization such as the BBC, a 'producer' of services with consumers of its own in the form of listeners and viewers, there could only be one honest response to all this: to allow the licence-fee-paying public to complain, too, if they felt the Corporation was purveying shoddy goods to them. In short, it had to provide a forum where listeners and viewers could find redress and come to believe that they had some power to influence programmes—to rid the Corporation, so to speak, of its own 'market imperfections'.

People had been complaining about what had been on Radio Four for years, writing to the Director-General or sometimes their MP, writing to Broadcasting House, phoning the Duty Office, even getting in contact with individual programme departments, producers, or presenters. These complaints were compiled by the Corporation's Programme Correspondence Section, and a weekly summary circulated to some 200 people and discussed in forums such as the Review Boards.[93] This allowed senior BBC staff to measure audience reaction, to sense when a programme had created a special thrill or caused particular offence, and to guide producers accordingly. There was also the panoply of advisory councils—and the Board of Governors itself—charged with representing the 'public interest' during the BBC's own deliberations. But apart from those listeners' letters read out on air during, say, *Woman's Hour*, *You and Yours*, and *PM*, or any published in *Radio Times*, all such communication with the public—and any discussion prompted by it—was treated as an internal affair to be acted upon at the Corporation's discretion. Routine contact with the audience remained largely invisible to the world at large. This had one major drawback for the BBC: it meant it received little credit for its efforts. The clamour for accountability now suggested it was in Radio Four's own interests to demonstrate as quickly and as publicly as possible that it, at least, was not indifferent to its customers' opinions and feelings. Accountability, it was realized, must not only operate but it had to be *seen* to operate.

In this spirit, there was a proliferation in the number of leaflets explaining how to contact the Corporation and pursue complaints, each bearing titles such as *It's Your BBC*, *You and the BBC*, and *It's One BBC—And It's Yours*. The first of a new series of public meetings was also held in Truro in 1976. The Annan Report and the government's 1978 White Paper on Broadcasting pressed the BBC to do more, and by the end of 1984 the BBC had organized another 111 meetings around the country, each involving a Governor and a panel of senior Radio staff answering questions.[94] Monica Sims also instituted her own series of roadshows, with Radio Four 'weeks' in Scotland, Yorkshire, the South West, and so on, between 1979 and 1983. Each week on tour involved regular programmes being transported out of London to broadcast special regional editions, and the chance for members of the public to see programmes being made or to speak to some of those involved behind the scenes.

The simplest way for Radio Four to publicize its willingness to listen, however, was to use its own airwaves as a forum for debate. At the end of the 1960s, *Listening Post* had provided a limited opportunity to discuss programmes, and the occasional *It's Your Line* was devoted to listeners' worries about radio output. But the first explicit attempt at a regular space for complaint came with *Disgusted, Tunbridge Wells*, which ran on Sunday mornings for ten months starting in February 1978. Ian McIntyre was keen on the new programme simply because he hoped that fierce criticism might have a tonic effect on complacent producers. And sure enough, by May 1978 he was declaring that *Disgusted, Tunbridge Wells* was indeed 'going like a bomb'.[95] It was certainly creating shock waves in Broadcasting House. In July 1978, David Hatch was roughed up on the programme while trying gamely to defend one of his department's less successful comedies, *The Spam Fritter Man*. The presenter, Derek Robinson, made a virtue of arguing with relish on behalf of those listeners who had complained—and did so with some wit. But over the next few months there were dark mutterings of producers' morale being affected: *Disgusted* had something of 'a Watergate syndrome'; Robinson betrayed too much 'crusading egomania'. He was 'not the Archangel Gabriel, but the paid presenter of a BBC programme', Aubrey Singer remarked pointedly. Within two months the programme was axed. Newspapers reported that it was disappearing because it had been too critical of BBC management—a view described by one BBC press officer as 'well informed'. Its replacement programme, *Feedback*, was launched in April 1979, with Tom Vernon as one of the regular presenters. Some within Broadcasting House thought it 'no more than a pale shadow' of its predecessor, though over the next few years it proved itself to have easily enough bite to cause a proper degree of anxiety within Broadcasting House.[96]

Many of the complaints on *Feedback*, just like those on *Disgusted, Tunbridge Wells*, or those delivered by phone to the Duty Office in Broadcasting House, were construed on the basis that the BBC could easily and quickly 'put its house in order'. But this misunderstood the BBC's structure and ethos. Programme-makers did not usually spend their days responding to orders from above, changed at a moment's notice. If creativity was not to be stifled, producers had to be allowed a fair degree of initiative. Their programmes were subject to critical but *retrospective* review. The number of complaints arriving at the Corporation also had to be weighed against the findings of the BBC's own formal audience research. This gathered the opinions of far larger numbers of listeners—and had been doing so every day since the 1930s. It almost always discovered that the passive majority of the general public were usually content with the very same programmes that the majority of complainants had condemned. Those bothering to complain were untypical. But vocal. By default, the dominant flavour of programmes such as *Disgusted, Tunbridge Wells*, was, so *The Times* thought, 'as sour as an old and dried up lemon': listeners constantly grizzled about musical jingles, sex, bad language, morbid themes, reception problems, scheduling, regional accents, and so on, though less often about what programmes said or signified. The trouble, it concluded, was not just that any programme built around complaint was by its nature likely to exaggerate dissent, but that most listeners were simply 'not well-enough informed' to pass judgement.[97]

Most in the BBC believed this too, but they could hardly come out and say it. What they could—and did—say, though, was this: that while they recognized public accountability to be important, 'the BBC must, ultimately, take editorial responsibility' for how it made its programmes. It would not judge only what the public wanted, nor only what it needed, but 'what the public needs *and* wants'.

Staff knew they would have to teach listeners to moderate their expectations, to understand the BBC's nature, to be a little more sympathetic to its predicament. Hence even *Feedback* was described internally as being 'as much to inform the audience about broadcasting matters as to provide an opportunity for airing criticism'.[98] As for responding directly to public suggestions, Ian McIntyre, who was happy enough for producers to be put on their guard by *Disgusted, Tunbridge Wells*, was equally adamant that 'he had no intention of accepting "scheduling by referendum"'.[99]

In the end, the effects of public pressure on Radio Four, as with pressure on the rest of the BBC, were gradual, indirect, and highly filtered. This was no doubt an example of a wider resistance among the British Establishment to submitting to the popular will, what the historian Jeremy Black described as 'a paternalism born of a conviction that the state knew best'. Even in the early 1980s, Black suggests, hostility to populism was 'strongly ingrained in administrative culture'.[100]

It is difficult to know how else a quintessentially liberal organization such as the BBC might have behaved. It had long agonized over the question of whether to lead or to follow in matters of morality, manners, taste, and opinion. And it had gradually settled, especially since the days of Hugh Carleton-Greene, for the strategy of doing a bit of both. To have 'scheduled by referendum', as McIntyre put it, would have been to abandon an ethos of 'uplift' that, while barely uttered publicly, was still assumed internally to exist. A programme such as *Checkpoint* did not just represent the British citizen-consumer, but offered lessons in how to be *better* citizen-consumers. Phone-ins offering recipes were not just informational, they offered lessons in how to be more adventurous cooks. Programmes such as *If You Think You've Got Problems* and *In the Psychiatrist's Chair* offered lessons in how to be better talkers and better listeners. Indeed, they took it as axiomatic that it was 'good to talk': that many problems could be solved if only we could learn to communicate better, that better communication was about a willingness to talk honestly and openly and, in turn, about listening tolerantly without passing judgement—a classically liberal sentiment that focused more on the virtues of rational debate and consensus than on the virtues of argument and passionate conflict.[101] The new mood for consumer rights, for individualism, for personal storytelling, for talking straight: all this was absorbed by the BBC and offered back to the British public in ways that accorded with its older traditions of public service, of moral guidance, and improvement.

But things could not stand still entirely. This was not quite the same old BBC. Between the mid-1970s and the mid-1980s, Radio Four, like other parts of the Corporation, took a further step along the road to a less elite and more demotic style of broadcasting. If ordinary people's *opinions* were still treated warily, their *experiences* and their *feelings* were now central to the broadcasting mission. As the BBC's Assistant Director-General put it, producers were now simply 'less inclined to take pundits at face value'. 'Ordinary' people—'real' people—were in favour. Programmes were after authenticity—one of the new buzz words of the time, along with consumerism, intimacy, frankness, and interaction—and found it in 'the individual with direct experience of the subject'.[102] It was not just programmes like *Checkpoint*—overtly on the side of the consumer—or programmes like *If You Think You've Got Problems*—overtly interested in the feelings of ordinary people—that reflected this. It emerged in all sorts of other, more subtle ways. Analysts in the new discipline of media discourse noticed the habit of presenters or reporters increasingly to adopt more 'inclusive' styles of delivery: talking more conversationally, using 'you' (rather than 'one') as the indefinite pronoun of choice, talking to 'us' about 'them' in a way that made broadcasters sound as if they were more part of 'our' world than 'theirs'.[103] Tom Vernon and Ray Gosling were undoubtedly among the most striking progenitors of the new style, but it spread far and wide, evolving—sometimes elegantly, sometimes less so—into the modified Received Pronunciation 'commonsense' tone of the network. Indeed, so pervasive was the trend that, in time, one newspaper columnist was driven to bemoan the 'banal knowingness' that had, to his ears at least, become the house style of Radio Four.[104] Listeners, it seemed, could invariably detect false bonhomie: if the label of authenticity was to be retained, it had to be rationed and used with care.

Indeed, Radio Four listeners were starting to get all sorts of ideas in their heads. Giving them the status of 'consumers' and encouraging them to complain was probably asking for trouble. A formidably articulate lobbying group was beginning to form, and the kind of venom with which it might be capable of acting could be glimpsed in a programme such as *Disgusted, Tunbridge Wells*. It somehow encapsulated the anger that simmered beneath the surface of middle-class gentility. Listening to it, one heard a member of the audience who had written in on a dainty notelet decorated with lilies of the valley asking for the Head of Radio Drama to walk under a fast-moving bus. 'If anybody has reason to be disgusted, it isn't Tunbridge Wells at all,' wrote David Wade in *The Times*, 'it's the BBC with its listeners.'[105]

But listeners had to be listened to. And that constituted a new force for conservatism. Gillian Reynolds now wondered whether *any* change to Radio Four, no matter how well intentioned, was possible: its listeners were so 'accustomed to consumerism, and constructive complaint, and lobbying' that the network was now their prisoner.[106] In the longer term, this was to be a cause of considerable anxiety for those Radio Four's Controllers inclined to bring even modest change to the schedules. In the short term, Monica Sims was going to be grateful for the strength of this emerging lobby. If it frustrated reform from within, it also provided a formidable bulwark against more dangerous attacks on the network from outside—as events between 1978 and 1983 were to show.

9

Under Siege

*'When I went to Radio Four I had no idea it might have been under threat—
and there's no doubt about it, it was under threat...I felt under siege.'*

Monica Sims, Controller

BUCKLING AT THE KNEES

November 1978 should have been a moment of triumph for Radio Four, because
an exciting rebirth was under way. Across Britain, Boy Scouts called on thousands
of homes, marched the occupants towards their radio sets, retuned each dial, and
placed a diamond-shaped sticker on the spot marked 1500 metres long wave.
Letters landing on doormats were franked with slogans bearing the same magic
number. By the end of the month, twenty-two million stickers and several
million printed leaflets were in circulation throughout the United Kingdom,
all featuring the names of various radio networks and lots of numbers representing different wavelengths. Nearly half a million pounds had been spent and
12,000 phone calls answered by a special unit in the BBC.

The cause of all the excitement was, on the surface at least, somewhat mundane.
Following the latest international agreement on the allocation of wavelengths, the
BBC had reshuffled its pack of national networks. Radio Four was switching from
the family of medium wave transmitters it had inherited from the Home Service to
the single 1500 metres long wave transmitter previously occupied by Radio Two.
The change was now due to come into force. On the morning of 23 November,
after BBC engineers spent five hours switching over a total of 109 transmitters, a
new signature tune from Fritz Spiegl burst onto the air, and the era of Radio Four
Long Wave began.[1]

The BBC was nervous—and understandably so. Moving its stations to a
different place on the dial was fraught with danger. Pushbutton radios with
'preset' tuning were still exotic rarities: listeners trying to follow their favourite
station might find themselves lost on the dial. The thought of it brought the BBC
out in a collective cold sweat. But, for Radio Four at least, the anxiety was worth
it: 1500 metres long wave was the one radio frequency that reached the whole
country. It was why the Shipping Forecast had always been carried on it, and why

it would now remain there, to leave the embrace of Radio Two and become part of the furniture on Radio Four. In turn, Radio Four was to be 'Radio Four UK' in deed as well as name. In Scotland, those who had previously been able to hear only those Radio Four programmes that were carried on Radio Scotland now had a choice: Radio Scotland on VHF or Radio Four UK on long wave. The same applied to listeners in Wales and Northern Ireland. Of course, if nationalist sentiments were to be allayed—and in 1978 they were at something of a high-water mark—it was beholden on Radio Four to try harder than ever to be truly British in flavour and content. The new opening signature tune was one imme-diate signal of good intentions, providing as it did a judicious medley of *Londonderry Air, Annie Laurie, Men of Harlech, Scotland the Brave,* the *Trumpet Voluntary,* and *Rule Britannia.*[2] Over the next few years creating a less English-hued range of programmes across the whole schedule would be crucial to the station's credibility in the 'National Regions'. In the meantime there was much to cheer. Across most of the country, the long wave signal was undoubtedly more robust than the old medium wave one. And for schedulers, long harried by the demands of the various Regions to have fixed points in the Radio Four schedule for their opt-outs, the new sense of unity was liberating. Suddenly, the Controller really did seem to be in control, and the timetable of programmes could begin to loosen up a little.

Yet for a good many listeners the daily practicalities of hearing Radio Four now seemed no better, and sometimes worse than ever. In Edinburgh and Oxford reception on long wave proved to be dreadful; in north London there was interference from the commercial news station LBC; and across large parts of inner London, the signal was disrupted by a deadly combination of transmis-sions from the Soviet Union and the electromagnetic properties of high steel-framed buildings. The Barbican was one particular black spot, as, apparently, was Buckingham Palace, since one unspecified member of the Royal Family complained to the BBC's Managing Director of Radio, Aubrey Singer, about Radio Four's sudden inaudibility. The BBC's own Director of Engineering observed that Radio Two listeners in London had put up with this interference on long wave for years; Radio Four listeners, he now realized, were 'more critical' altogether.[3]

Most local technical glitches like this could be ironed out. More intractable structural problems remained. Not the least of these was the constant need for Radio Four listeners everywhere to keep fiddling with their sets. Since April 1978, anyone seeking refuge from live parliamentary broadcasting on weekday after-noons had to retune to VHF if they wished to catch the afternoon play. A good thing too, many BBC planners thought: if listeners wanted to benefit from the full range of services on offer they simply *had to* get used to switching around, and anything that might force them to experience the superior sound of VHF—something they had irrationally resisted for so long—was to be welcomed.[4] But the practicalities did not make this easy. For those living in parts of Scotland,

Wales, and Northern Ireland beyond the reach of an English VHF transmitter—
and that meant most of the population—there was little option but to miss the
afternoon play and listen instead to Prime Minister's Question Time, since their
own VHF frequencies were now assigned to the new national regional services, all
of which were busy shedding their Radio Four 'filling' programmes as fast as they
could. Radio Scotland, for one, had celebrated its *decree absolute* from Radio Four
'Basic' by cutting the amount of London programming from about 60 per cent to
nearer 10 per cent. Nearly 1,400 people in Scotland were so irritated by this state
of affairs that they signed a petition in February 1979 demanding that either
Radio Scotland be 'improved'—that is, carry more 'serious' material of the kind
once supplied by Radio Four—or that Radio Four itself be made available north
of the border on medium wave or VHF.[5] In the meantime, listeners in England
driven to VHF during weekday afternoons were having to switch back to long
wave at other times of the week if they wished to avoid Open University or Schools
and find, say, *From Our Own Correspondent* or *Morning Story*; some listeners in
London were even having to use medium wave during parts of the day.[6]

In short, to stand any chance of hearing the full range of programmes on Radio
Four listeners needed not just bottomless reserves of patience but also a three-
band radio—that is, a set with long wave, medium wave, *and* VHF. This was
asking too much. In 1978, between two and three million people owned radios
without VHF; others who had recently bought Japanese cars or invested in
fashionable hi-fi systems found they had VHF and medium wave but not long
wave.[7] Even those who had VHF *and* the will to retune constantly were discovering that reception was not all it had been cracked up to be by BBC
engineers: beautifully clear on a good day, but crackly and temperamental on
most others. The sorry truth was that the BBC's VHF system had been designed
in the early 1950s on the false assumption that radio would be heard on mains-
powered sets using decent rooftop aerials. It was not really robust enough for
small portable transistors—which was what most people had.[8]

This was a mess based, quite simply, on a shortage of slots on the dial—and
specifically, the failure—or unwillingness—of successive governments to secure
a workable allocation of VHF slots for the BBC during international negotiations. The Managing Director of Radio, Aubrey Singer, oversaw what were, in
effect, six different radio services: Radios One through to Four; the national
regional stations in Scotland, Wales, and Northern Ireland together with the
chain of local radio stations in England (a 'fifth' service); and the miscellany of
Schools, Open University, and live parliamentary programmes (which effectively
constituted a nascent 'sixth' service). These six were being squeezed into just three-
and-a-half slots on the dial: Radio One and Two sharing a VHF frequency,
educational programmes and parliamentary coverage being carried on Radio
Four, and the local radio chain as yet half-formed. In the circumstances, the
weight of conflicting demands placed upon Radio Four, in particular, seemed
likely to end with it buckling at the knees. 'Can we compete with the national

regions, broadcast Parliament, maintain our drama output, meet our obligations to schools, push out the frontiers in the creative documentary field and continue as the main news and current affairs channel all at the same time?' Ian McIntyre asked Singer at the end of his tenure as Controller.[9]

Singer thought not. And, having realized the extent of the audience's difficulties with reception, he now made it his task to look for a solution. Room for manoeuvre was strictly limited, however. Take, for example, Schools and Open University programmes. One way of clearing the logjam would have been to move them onto a separate VHF frequency of their own. This depended, however, on the government granting the BBC an additional frequency, and until that happened there was only one other option in sight: putting programmes out overnight and encouraging teachers or students to tape them. There were several experiments along these lines in 1979, all of which showed it could work. But the Open University was suspicious, and the technology of 'time-shift' recording was in its infancy.[10] This was, in other words, a mid-term option at best. Clearly, Radio Four would have to accommodate educational programmes on its schedule for some time to come.

As for news and current affairs, which accounted for just over half of Radio Four's output, there was little desire among radio managers to provide listeners with any less, and considerable pressure from the BBC's journalists to provide listeners with a whole lot more. Parliamentary broadcasting was just one leg of this campaign, with constant requests from politics junkies among the BBC's journalists for longer and more frequent coverage of Commons debates, open-ended reportage of Budget speeches, live relays of crucial votes and election counts, and so on. As long as the Director-General was Ian Trethowan, the main architect of parliamentary broadcasting on the BBC, these bids could hardly be rejected out of hand by the Controller of Radio Four, no matter how vocal were the complaints of Drama producers seeing their afternoon plays shunted aside. The second leg of this push for more live journalism was the oft-expressed desire for more 'flexibility' across the whole schedule so that any newsworthy event could be covered as it happened. In this respect, the growing success of the commercial news station in London, LBC, was an added incentive for the BBC to do more. LBC had been boasting of its ability to cover Prime Minister's Questions twice a week without any disruption to its regular programmes. It was also broadcasting around the clock, as were at least six other commercial stations across the country by 1978.[11] People such as Peter Woon, Radio's Editor of News and Current Affairs, argued vociferously that there was both a demand for—and a duty on the BBC to provide—extensive coverage of 'public affairs', and that it was Radio Four's daytime schedules that should respond accordingly. The outgoing editor of *Today*, Mike Chaney—with whom McIntyre had clashed so often—also told Singer that for Radio Four to carry on doing 'different things at different times of the day' was to invite failure. 'We could get big audiences at all times', he wrote, 'But we can do this only if we make it an instinctive reaction to turn to radio for "the latest".' In short, 'We need an all-live, all-hours rolling network, available to update all ages and all classes all the time, 24 hours a day, 365 days a year. And that service should be on 1500m.'[12]

These words articulated the journalists' collective goal. They could do without the nonsense of hi-fi and stereo on VHF. They accepted that Radio One and Two were popular just as they were, and that Radio Three had some inviolable claim to cultural greatness. What they prized most was the long wave slot Radio Four now occupied, since only it had the national reach they were after. Some things—to be blunt, just two things: news and current affairs—were so important that they had to be available to everyone. Radio Four, the thinking went, was a news and current affairs network waiting to happen. Only the irritating anachronism of what Chaney called 'minority fodder'—drama, readings, light entertainment, religious programmes, arts coverage, poetry, and the like—stood, inexplicably, in the way. This kind of stuff would have to be redistributed to other networks or quietly done away with altogether.[13]

Until then, some sort of rough-and-ready accommodation with existing structures appeared necessary. Simply offering more and more 'splitting', with a choice of Parliament on long wave and drama on VHF, was the least desirable option, since there was little sign of the audience being reconciled to it. The only sensible strategy, therefore, was to create a little more flexibility within the existing schedule. Thus, getting rid of Jack de Manio's chat show, *Jack de Manio Precisely*, and giving *Afternoon Theatre* a slightly later start time, allowed Commons debates to be covered more extensively by delaying, rather than displacing, programmes.[14] But again, the unanswered question was this: if *Afternoon Theatre* could be shunted to a later time for Parliament, why not for other even more newsworthy occasions as they arose?

The kernel of what might be possible was beginning to take shape. The 'sequence' programmes—*Today*, *The World at One*, *PM*, and *The World To-night*—were all being reviewed throughout 1978 to see if they could be recast in longer, 'rolling' formats, with fewer 'fixed' points and more opportunity for uninterrupted live reportage for anything from a vote in the commons to an evening football result.[15] Singer joined both Ian McIntyre and Monica Sims in resisting such large-scale change. Two hours of *The World Tonight*? The Managing Director was at one with the Governors: 'There could be too much of a good thing.'[16] For now at least, the plans were to be scaled back considerably. Yet, by November 1978 the underlying momentum to push matters to a logical conclusion already seemed unstoppable. And it was a momentum that came from two directions at once. Peter Woon, for instance, was busy urging Singer to contemplate turning Radio Four long wave into 'the prime national information channel' and exiling its non-news programmes onto a VHF 'Radio England'.[17] He stood at the spearhead of a long column of News and Current Affairs staff fighting for some form of all-news service. Alongside them, but only in loose alliance, another army also hove into view: the ranks of the BBC's local radio managers. These men and women were pushing to expand their own empire, were dismissive of Radio Four's metropolitan air, and were acutely jealous of its resources. As the manoeuvrings of the next four years were to show, the two groups were not always after the same thing. But both proceeded—and drew strength—from a common starting point: the apparently infallible conclusion to be drawn from audience research that Radio Four was in terminal decline. It was this that made Radio Four particularly vulnerable to their attacks.

The evidence at their disposal certainly seemed compelling. Here was the BBC's most expensive radio network, costing some £15 million a year—compared with £13 million for Radio Three, £12 million for Radio Two, £10 million for the national regional services, and £7 million apiece for Radio One and the chain of local radio stations. Each hour of output on Radio Four took about £2,275 to make—slightly more expensive than Radio Three and twenty-five times the figure for local radio.[18] Yet what was Radio Four doing with all this money? Losing audiences, as it had been for years. Between 1971 and 1978 its share of the national radio audience had declined steadily from 19 per cent— almost one in five listeners—to 13 per cent—nearer one in eight.[19]

There were two lessons being drawn from all this. First, that if such rates of attrition were accurate, the audience for Radio Four would be gone completely in little more than a decade. Second, that Radio Four's apparent decline was in inverse proportion to the success of local radio, where ratings were edging steadily upward. From this point, things could surely only get worse. After a freeze under Heath's Conservative government, the number of local stations was due to expand further—indeed, there were plans for as many as sixty in the fullness of time. They were seen as the BBC's most important source of new listeners over the decade to come.[20]

None of this was lost on Aubrey Singer. In common with other senior BBC managers, he knew that local radio brought political and cultural benefits to the Corporation. Quite apart from putting it in touch with grassroots community life, there was another tactical consideration: that, as Singer put it, 'the three hundred or so MPs who gained an outlet through it at constituency level were also potential friends of the BBC'.[21] Now he was convinced, too, that if the BBC had any hope of defending its share of the total radio audience, local radio needed nurturing and its half-realized chain needed completing as quickly as possible. Radio Three and Radio Four were important, of course, but their right to exist as minority channels depended on the blood spilled in the bigger struggle for the popular audience. The universal licence fee that paid for quality could only be justified if the BBC served a clear majority of the licence-fee-paying public. And it would be local radio, along with Radios One and Two that would be in the front line of this battle for ratings—a battle that Singer, as a Television man, would relish.

There would have to be some changes in the way things were done in Broadcasting House. From the middle of 1978, ratings suddenly played a bigger part in Review Board discussions; from that point, too, there were to be local station managers at every Board, and their programmes were to be discussed regularly; staff on the national networks, it was suggested, might profit from visiting local stations; they might even contemplate working attachments there.[22] In short, local radio was being given a voice at the centre of deliberations in Radio, and its importance in the collective mind of BBC management was being brought home vividly to producers who had tended to overlook it—and in some cases, actively resent it—for the past ten years. Quite apart from anything else, this was something of a culture shock. At the very first new-style Review Board at which network staff were confronted with local radio programmes—in this case, a programme on the Midlands folk revival—one Controller expressed himself appalled at the 'ghastly' accents and 'council house English' to which he had been subjected. This was, the manager from Birmingham explained patiently, how people talked where he lived.[23]

The local radio people now turning up at Review Board also presented a more immediate strategic challenge to Radio Four. They made it quite plain they were getting by on very limited resources and that getting decent programmes out was always a struggle. Some in Broadcasting House worried deeply about what was being done in the Corporation's name when effort was spread so thinly. Local radio, in other words, appeared to have the opposite problem to Radio Four. It was, as one phrase put it, 'a library with more shelves than books', whereas Radio Four, with all the conflicting demands being placed on it, was 'a library with more books than shelves'.[24] Might some redistribution of resources between the two make sense?

At the end of 1978, this was an idea growing in currency just as much as the idea pursued by senior journalists of trying to find space among the BBC's various frequencies for an all-news channel. A pincer movement was advancing on Radio Four. And Singer, who dearly wished to see Radio sorted into neater 'packages', was not averse to responding with the big gesture. He was keen to make his mark, and the Radio directorate over which he had charge was now subject to closer scrutiny from the Governors than ever before, thanks to the strictures of the Annan Report in 1977 and the subsequent government White Paper of 1978, both of which had demanded more accountability. Over the next few years Singer supplied the various new Gubernatorial committees with the fruits of a bewildering array of investigations, consultancy reports, and working parties, all charged by him with reshaping BBC Radio. In the course of this labour, some radical schemes emerged, only to sink again without trace. Singer also changed his own mind on more than one occasion. This added to a mood of uncertainty. But some themes remained in focus throughout: the troubled relationship between local radio and network radio, the ambitions of News and Current Affairs, the need for 'flexibility' in the schedules, the amount of money to pay for it all. And almost none of it boded well for Radio Four itself.

A 'LOCAL HOME SERVICE'

Events started to move quickly. Within Singer's small team of planners was Michael Starks, a man just recruited from the commercial broadcasters' regulator the Independent Broadcasting Authority. Here was someone business-minded and with no vested interest in any part of the Radio empire: someone, in other words, able to challenge programme-makers' sensitivities and BBC traditions.

Starks first made his presence felt between October 1978 and February 1979, by drawing up several drafts of a scheme, unofficially labelled 'Radio in the Eighties', designed to tackle the various pressures on BBC Radio through a programme of expansion. This contemplated a tailor-made 'sustaining' service to provide local stations with three hours of 'American-style "rolling news" ', produced and distributed from London, in order to create a proper 'fifth' BBC service. It also asked the government to grant a sixth frequency dedicated to educational programmes, and called for large-scale capital investment, first on transmitters, so that there could be a separate VHF frequency for each of the BBC's services, and secondly on tackling an accumulation of decrepit studios. The need for capital investment seemed especially urgent, since the number of break-downs was beginning to overwhelm engineers: 25,000 failures a year in 1978 and rising. More and more plant was now defined as 'worn out'—so much of it, in fact, that three-quarters of BBC Radio's capital fund had to be spent on replacement rather than improvement. The real costs of previous economies were starting to show. And a radical solution was now proposed: to cut future losses by moving out of Broadcasting House and into a brand new purpose-built Radio complex across the road in Langham Place.[25] It would not be cheap, but it might, so to speak, be worth it.

Starks's plan was ambitious. But it found no place for the all-news network the journalists had been after. So in order to accommodate the desire for more 'public affairs' broadcasting he went on to suggest that Radio Four should be defined as a network of 'topical speech'. There would still be drama, comedy, and so on; but the expectation of topicality being the dominant flavour—what the document called the 'key' to the network—was made explicit. This was loaded phraseology. Since Radio Four had to be topical, Starks pointed out, it 'ought ideally to be the most flexible of our services'. For a network with so many fixed-length programmes in its schedule, many of which were distinctly *un*topical, this did not sound like the status quo. Indeed, when one of the BBC's General Advisory Council members greeted the plan by saying that 'topical speech should *always* have priority over entertainment, because Radio Four was essentially a flexible service of news and current affairs', the dangers ahead were starting to crystallize.[26]

The BBC's Governors and senior managers thought highly of the plan. However: money. The Starks scheme was expensive—relying on something like an 8 per cent growth in total radio spending. This was optimistic, to say the least. Though the BBC had been hoping for an increase in the licence fee to £30 in the autumn of 1978, Callaghan's Labour government was in its dying days, and its ability to deliver was questionable. Negotiations dragged. When the new fee was eventually announced, it came to an ungenerous £25, and would last for just one year. The BBC's initial response was to be sanguine. Since the Corporation had just kept within its budget, underspending by 0.1 per cent that financial year, Radio's 'mildly expansionist' plans 'would probably go ahead', Singer thought— provided, that was, the Corporation could borrow to its limit, inflation was kept under control, pay settlements would keep within national guidelines, and any future government would hand over a new VHF frequency. This, too, was all rather optimistic. For once the Press was nearer to the mark by declaring the licence-fee settlement to be just enough for the BBC 'to bleed very slowly to death'.[27] Certainly, the expectation of government generosity in the future was soon proved entirely misplaced. After Conservative victory in the May 1979 General Election, there was a government ideologically committed to the commercial sector, and, in Margaret Thatcher, a Prime Minister who instinctively regarded a public sector organization such as the BBC as ripe for cutting down to size. To get things going, the 1979 licence-fee settlement was set at a level no more generous than Labour's a year before. Its impact, however, was more damaging, since by the end of the year the government had succeeded in driving inflation up to nearly 20 per cent and was standing back as mouth-watering pay settlements were awarded to staff in commercial television—setting new benchmarks for the broadcasting industry as a whole. Costs for the BBC were spiralling upwards, while its income remained fixed. And it was no good the Radio directorate calling on Television colleagues to bail it out, for the new government was also busy unleashing a wave of deregulation that would usher in all sorts of competition—a fourth commercial television channel, direct satellite broadcasting, cable, breakfast TV. Senior Corporation executives made it very clear to their Radio staff that in such an unfriendly environment BBC Television would need all the money it could get if it stood any chance of protecting its own audience share.[28]

The net effect of all this was to accept, as the Director-General put it, that 'what the BBC wanted to do and what it might be able to afford to do were two very different things'.[29] Instead of expansion there now had to be cuts. By the spring of 1980, Radio had to look for savings of about £4 million—some 5 per cent of its total budget. Orchestras that had survived the culls of 1969 were now threatened with disbandment; Radio Two's drama serial *Waggoner's Walk* was axed; Radio Three was shut down early each evening. For now, although there was some talk of *The Archers* being scrapped too, there were no seismic changes to Radio Four's output. But penny-pinching started to leak through to programmes in irritating ways. Why, Review Board demanded, were the letters on *Woman's Hour* being read out so unevenly these days? Because, the answer came, they now had to be recited by producers rather than the usual paid actors. Why had the cast employed in the dramatized reconstruction scenes of a documentary been over-acting? Because each actor was now required to read many more parts than before—something that forced them to exaggerate character differences rather too much. Why were so few programmes being offered from Wales and Scot-land? Because producer posts in the national regions had gone unfilled.[30]

The biggest effect of the cuts, however, was hidden from audiences. It was to encourage a hasty retreat from all mention inside Broadcasting House of ambi-tious schemes for the future of Radio. The era of steady expansion within the BBC—one that stretched back, with only minor interruptions, to the 1960s—was giving way definitively to one of retrenchment or, at best, a 'solid state' existence. Review Boards, committee meetings, and executive away-days organ-ized by the BBC throughout 1979 and 1980 were now full of chatter about the need to create 'an orderly retreat' or 'concentration' or 'patrolling a smaller waterfront' or needing to 'shed the monopoly attitude of doing everything'. In Radio, the talk was about a future not of six networks but of four, and perhaps if things got really bad, just three. For, as Singer pointed out, 'unless the BBC produced a meaningful rationalization, someone else might do so'. And if this meant one of the existing national networks had to be sacrificed at some point, so be it. 'The status quo', he warned, 'could not be maintained for ever.'[31]

Broadcasting House was soon awash with proposals and counter-proposals from interested parties. Ian McIntyre, from his new eyrie at Radio Three, made a call to start from first principles and focus on what the BBC did best. He would dispense with local radio, and, if push came to shove he would advocate, too, that Radio Four might have to be split apart—its entertainment combining with a little light music to create a 'Channel 1', its higher-brow material combined with classical music to create a cultural 'Channel 2', and its news and current affairs—'very broadly defined'—forming the basis of an informative 'Channel 3'.[32] Radical thinking like this appealed to both Singer and Starks. But they needed a model with local radio in it. Their suggestion was to push faster and harder than ever to complete the chain of local stations. They reasoned that if the BBC could manage to get more than 90 per cent of England covered in this way it would, in effect, have created for itself a new national VHF network—piecemeal and *de facto* rather than strictly *de jure*, but technically quite capable of relaying programmes hitherto carried on Radios One through to Four. With this possibility in mind it was but one small step to reasoning that one of the national networks could *combine* with local radio—first of all acting as a form of sustaining service and, in the fullness of time, surrendering its old national frequency in the service of strengthening the BBC's local tier.[33]

The question various network Controllers, consultants, and managers now tried to answer was *which* national network should be sacrificed in this way? Neither Radio One nor Radio Three were right for such a forced marriage: one obviously too brash, the other obviously too upmarket. That left Radio Two and

Radio Four as the natural candidates. And it seemed as if there was little to choose between them, for between the middle of 1979 and the middle of 1980, first one network, then the other, was scrutinized closely. And it was by no means clear which of the two would ultimately survive.

To begin with, Radio Two looked the more vulnerable. It was the network most local stations already chose to fill their evening schedules, it played broadly similar music, it had broadly similar listeners: middle-aged (or older) and predominantly working class. All that was needed in the short term was to order local stations to cut their own hours of output in order to save money and make room for a bigger, better sustaining service from London.[34] There might even be room to go further: to make local radio a kind of 'opt-out' of Radio Two. There would have to be some indication that a fresh start was being made, rather than a takeover. At this stage, the planned hybrid network was therefore given the working title of 'Town and Country Radio'.[35] The idea was floated by Stephen Hearst, the former Controller of Radio Three who now held the grand title of Controller, Future Policy, and was charged with conjuring such visions—a task for which he also earned the unofficial moniker among colleagues of 'Deep Thought'. For Hearst, the advantages of this scheme were twofold: local radio would be elevated from parochialism, and the remaining national networks would be left largely intact. Radio Four, at least, was left untouched by the plan, as he felt it should be. As indeed the Controller of Radio Four, Monica Sims, and her Chief Assistant, Richard Wade, felt it should be too. They knew that the 'Town and Country' scheme was the best hope of directing attention away from their own network, and both spoke well of its virtues.

But the battle was not yet won. Their Managing Director's ability to change direction and take everyone by surprise was legendary, and he now lived up to his reputation. At the end of June 1979, less than three weeks after welcoming the Hearst plan, Singer wrote to Sims with a warning. 'We are examining all the options on this proposal', he told her, before adding ominously that 'Apart from Radio Two being a sustaining service, Radio Four is also one of the options.'[36]

What seemed to have changed his thinking was the latest detailed audience research reaching his desk that summer. It appeared to confirm several trends that severely weakened Radio Four's case for immunity. Radio Four's decline in ratings had continued. Radio Two's, in the meantime, appeared to have been reversed. Indeed, it was now proving to be as much of a success story as local radio. And to merge two audience-winners suddenly seemed counter-productive. Researchers concluded that BBC Radio as a whole had been competing against itself by concentrating rather too much on services to the middle classes and the middle-aged, and failing to provide enough choice for the working classes and the young. There was a regional dimension, too, with Radio Four's share of the audience generally getting smaller the further away from London one went: a third of the station's listeners were Londoners, and, compared with the national spread of population, it had more than its fair share in the whole of the South; in the North-East of England, however, it had barely half the audience it should have had, and in Scotland less than half.[37] Something about this did not feel right. 'There is no special public service merit in failing to devise programming of appeal to certain areas of the country and certain sections of the population', Michael Starks wrote in September 1979: 'they all pay the licence fee.' 'Accordingly', he concluded, 'in framing options for the future, regard needs to be paid to these listening-pattern figures.'[38] There could be no clearer indication of the stress now being placed on ratings at the heart of corporate thinking. And the message was clear. If BBC Radio was going to protect its audience share as a whole, its appeal to younger and more working-class listeners was the crucial test—and it was a test that Radio Four was evidently failing.

The front-runner in BBC Radio's Austerity Derby now became a plan to merge local radio not with Radio Two, but with Radio Four. Instead of 'Town and Country Radio' there would be a 'Local Home Service'.[39] The potential gains were obvious: Radio Four would get more grassroots appeal, while local radio would become a little more polished. The scheduling implications, however, were nasty. Not every programme on Radio Four would blend easily with the kind of fare put out on local radio. There would have to be the kind of process McIntyre had suggested, namely an unpacking of Radio Four's constituent elements and a more general reshuffling of programmes across the networks as a whole. But done gradually. 'Listening habits are in general fairly conservative', the new plan stated. 'Evolutionary change is to be preferred to a sudden reshaping.'[40]

Thus saved from instant death, Radio Four became more vulnerable than ever to attack by stealth. Those who had wanted an all-news network, or a culture network, or some other parcelling out of Radio Four's properties now saw their chance to push matters in the appropriate direction and speed up the evolutionary process. The Controller of Local Radio argued for a sustaining service taking programmes 'from a variety of networks' and leaving what remained to be gathered up and shared out as best as possible. The Controller of Radio One wanted Radio One to remain much as it was, and for Radios Three and Four to merge. Ian McIntyre thought local radio should go, and perhaps Radio One as well. The Head of Audience Research wanted any pattern that made the average BBC audience younger and more 'downmarket'. Whatever happened, Singer argued, he wanted to see '(a) streamed classical music and (b) an all-news network'.[41]

Most plans had one feature in common: they eviscerated Radio Four. Those who envisaged the creation of a 'public information' channel contemplated Radio Four's programmes being sent off in three directions: typically, highbrow cultural programmes, *The Monday Play*, say, or book readings, might go to a revised Radio Three; more popular programmes, such as *The Archers*, quizzes, comedy series, and *Woman's Hour*, might become part of the 'mixed' service of local opt-outs on Radio Two; news and current affairs would be left to form the backbone of a rolling news or 'public information' channel. Nominally, Radio Four would survive, though it would be more live, more 'topical', more focused on news. It would be 'freed', as one document put it, from the 'extensive obligations' and 'conflicting commitments' of having to provide so much drama, light entertainment, talks, documentaries, religion, and the like.[42]

Once the full extent of these scheduling implications had become clear, some in Broadcasting House baulked at the plan. In an increasingly farcical search for a solution, another internal 'Green Paper' circulating towards the end of 1979 talked once more of Radio Two providing the bulk of 'sustaining' programmes for local radio's 'federal' service. But by now, too much had been said that could not be unsaid. The idea of Radio Four becoming more flexible, of it having 'substantially less' drama to make way for more live news, of it having *some* kind of programme-sharing arrangement with other parts of the BBC Radio system: all these retained their currency value.[43] Singer, in particular, remained unconvinced that Radio Two should risk being diluted. 'Aubrey was very easily swayed by some of the arguments,' Monica Sims recalls, 'particularly if they would save money, and particularly if they made a neater kind of schedule of output.' He fretted away. The choice between merging local radio with Radio Two or Radio Four, Singer told Governors in the spring of 1980, was still 'finely balanced', the way ahead 'by no means clear'.[44]

'OPTION FOUR' AND THE FALKLANDS WAR

By the middle of 1980, then, discussions had fought themselves to a standstill. But with a steadily deteriorating financial outlook for the BBC, it soon looked more likely than ever that one of the two networks was going to have to be 'fused' with local radio. In the circumstances, it seemed sensible to know which one it was to be sooner rather than later, if only to make the journey towards merger as organized as possible. A 'Radio Network Working Party' was therefore created, under the chairmanship of Stephen Hearst, and with Michael Starks as its Secretary. Among its other members were the Editor of News and Current Affairs, Peter Woon, the Head of Audience Research, Peter Meneer, the Controller of Local Radio, Michael Barton, and the Controllers of both Radio Four and Radio Two, Monica Sims and Charles McLelland. All were charged with coming up with as many options as they could identify, ranging from something like the status quo to ideas in the realm of the unthinkable— provided of course that any scheme allowed for the necessary capital investment *and* somehow saved money. They spent until January 1981 taking evidence from witnesses, writing drafts, and arguing among themselves. By the time their Report was published and made known to the outside world one month later,

Stephen Hearst admitted with some feeling that every phrase in the document had been 'a Passchendaele'.[45]

The trenches across Broadcasting House were certainly cut along familiar lines. Those fighting on behalf of local radio bombarded the Working Party with statistics pointing to the value for money they represented and to the virtues of a future without Radio Four.[46] Peter Meneer deployed the heavy artillery of his Audience Research department to suggest that each class or age group in Britain should be provided with no more and no less than two services—a pattern which would produce a pop channel, a music and entertainment channel, a classical music and culture channel, and a 'local radio federal network', but, again, no Radio Four.[47] Peter Woon and his successor, John Wilson, meanwhile, stood at the head of several long supply-lines bringing regular dispatches about missed opportunities in the battle for news coverage: too little time being allocated for coverage of the revolutionary budgets of the Conservative Chancellor of the Exchequer, Geoffrey Howe; too little on the release of the American hostages in Iran in January 1981; an unwillingness to interrupt a Radio Four play when President Reagan was shot; and so on.[48] Perhaps the most bizarre news event to be invoked in the cause, however, emerged in May 1980, during the unfolding drama—shown live on television and reported live on the commercial radio station LBC—of SAS soldiers storming the Iranian Embassy in London, where several people were being held hostage. At one stage the gunmen had demanded that a message be broadcast on the BBC, and this was eventually done during a Radio Two news bulletin. The gunmen missed the broadcast, however, because they had been tuned instead to Radio Four on 1500 metres long wave. The BBC's immediate reaction to this confusion was to go into a corporate spasm over the lives that might have been lost. Once that moment had passed many journalists drew what seemed to them the obvious lesson, namely that there should have been extensive live reporting of the whole affair on Radio Four all along. And Singer concurred. The lack of continuous coverage, he believed, had been regrettable.[49]

What threw BBC Radio's inadequacy in news coverage into particularly stark relief was the example being set by overseas broadcasters. During the course of 1980 and 1981, several foreign reconnoitres were undertaken—Singer heading west to America, intrigued by the success of rolling news formats; Starks heading east to France, reporting on *Inter*, a popular mix of news, music, and speech which he described as 'Radio Two and Radio Four combined'; other studies were made of radio in Canada and Sweden and West Germany. Such foreign excursions were tactically useful for BBC managers, since they allowed them to lay siege to shibboleths back home. Take, for example, the sweeping prescription offered by one news editor whose imaginative powers journeyed even further east than Paris. 'The following', he wrote, 'is the view I would submit if posted here from Tokyo to bring British radio into line with the new look in cars, TV sets, micro-chips, etc':

Radio Three and Four: Combined, with the best from both. All programmes with zero or near-zero ratings to be eliminated . . . The basis of the network would be a thread of rolling news, not vicarage tea party chatter or grave pronouncements. All sequences would standardise . . . Editors would not be free to run separate qualities, but would follow the direction of a central network Editor whose status would depend on constancy of output from dawn till midnight . . . *Kaleidoscope* is supposed to be opening windows on the world of art and entertainment to the listening millions, so why is its material not split up and included in Sequences rolling throughout the day? . . . Current Affairs Magazine Department contains masses of material which—removed altogether from its separate cubby-hole—could enrich and enliven the rolling Sequences . . . There would be <u>no</u> editorial freedom for separate editors to depart from the central personality and purpose of the network.[50]

Pressure for some form of all-news service was clearly building. The only questions now appeared to be precisely when and precisely how a breakthrough of any sort could be achieved.

One major obstacle to be overcome by those campaigning for a news takeover was Stephen Hearst. Throughout the Working Party's life, he was inclined to be somewhat suspicious of the news and current affairs lobby. Here was a man instinctively drawn more to programmes lovingly crafted over time than to the live, interview-based 'rolling' style now in vogue on current affairs programmes such as *Today*. This made him naturally averse to talk of a 'public affairs' network if it came at the expense of either Radio Three or Radio Four. And his convictions were strengthened by what he saw as the defensive behaviour of many of his journalist colleagues. He was, he told Review Board, "reminded by the responses of senior editors to criticism of the British Army in Egypt at the end of the last century": their motto when under attack had been "Form up in a square and shoot outwards!" '[51]

Nevertheless, it was difficult to argue with live ammunition. Months—indeed years—of being caught in the crossfire took its toll. Hearst must have known, too, that he had been appointed by Singer to do his master's bidding. The final report of his Working Party therefore had to be a clever concoction which acknowledged the pressure for change. When presented to Governors in February 1981, it started by making clear the need for capital investment: new transmitters, the completion of a reduced 38-station chain of local radio stations, a reaffirmed commitment to new headquarters in central London, and so on. Some of this could be paid for by streamlining production, cutting some technical staff, general economies. Beyond that, there were eleven options put forward for combining local, regional, and network radio services in a variety of money-saving ways. Some were close to maintaining the status quo; others suggested a different range of services on air at different times of the day; yet more involved merging Radio Four or Radio Two with local radio, and creating a rolling news service; a few showed how various options could be combined and possible compromises created. The permutations, though not quite endless, were certainly bewildering.[52]

All now depended on the response of the BBC's senior managers and Governors. But as always there was the reaction of the Press to be reckoned with. And after that, the listeners. *The Economist* got hold of the first leak and quickly focused on 'Option Four', which threatened 'a draconian killing off of Radio Four altogether'. When the published report percolated through Fleet Street the following week, coverage focused on the 'dismemberment' of Radio Four, prompting Singer and Hearst to fight a rearguard action, writing to newspapers and going on the BBC's own airwaves to reassure listeners that they were not proposing to 'do away' with Radio Four at all. Everyone, they complained, was paying too much attention to Option Four. True, its plan to carve Radio Four into an all-news 'public affairs' service and a 'Local Home Service' had been explained in more detail than any other scheme, but only because it was both radical and complicated. This had, unfortunately, given it undue prominence. In the meantime, Singer put it about that any moves to get a 'save Radio Four' lobby going were to be deplored. 'There was no threat to Radio Four, and it was most regrettable that anyone should encourage the public to think that there was.'[53]

Was he right? It was certainly true that no firm decisions had yet been taken. As promised, Singer treated the Working Party Report merely as a basis for further discussion—discussion which appeared to reach a more reassuring conclusion than many once feared when, in July, the Governors declared in favour of keeping existing network structures.[54] Even so, any assurances that Radio Four was 'safe' were usually modified quietly with the addition of three significant words: 'at the moment'. Things could change. In the company of the BBC's Governors, Singer described Option Four as 'very interesting'—something, indeed, that would 'repay further consideration' even if there had to be 'some cutting back' of drama and a battle with the actors' union, Equity. The Governors, for their part, were broadly happy to contemplate the measures necessary to put something like Option Four into effect. All these plays currently on Radio Four, the Vice-Chairman said, they were very good, but did anyone actually *listen* to them nowadays?[55]

The most dangerous agitation, however, probably came from the Director of News and Current Affairs, Dick Francis. He clearly felt an opportunity was being lost as a result of Hearst having left matters so open-ended. 'The Report fails to grasp the editorial nettle—the place of News and Current Affairs in network radio', he complained to Singer. 'The BBC has no national outlet carrying breaking news, relaying press conferences and live news events, quite apart from Parliamentary broadcasting, in the manner of LBC ... We can't afford not to be on the air on the occasions when it's all happening.' His conclusion was blunt: 'I don't think we can much longer avoid this central issue.'[56] This turned out to be highly prescient, since in January 1982, Dick Francis took over from Singer as the Managing Director of Radio, and was suddenly in a position to make good his thwarted plan.

External circumstances now played into Francis's hands. Within three months of his appointment, Argentine forces invaded the Falkland Islands, and a British

Task Force was dispatched to the South Atlantic in order to repulse them. The Falklands War rumbled on for nearly eighty days. Between invasion on 2 April 1982 and surrender on 14 June 1982, Francis was in possession of an ongoing news story of the kind he had been waiting for, replete with location reports from the field of conflict, political debate at home in special sittings of Parliament, and regular press conferences fronted by the lugubrious Ian McDonald at the Ministry of Defence. It was also a story in which Radio stood a good chance of beating Television in the speed and quality of coverage.

Until British forces had physically landed on Falkland Islands soil, getting television pictures back to Britain from the South Atlantic was tortuous. The BBC was not allowed to use the Royal navy's own satellite system, so footage had to be taken by boat to Ascension Island before being transmitted on to London. The average length of time between filming and final broadcast was seventeen days, but it could sometimes take much longer, especially with Ministry of Defence censorship in operation at either end of the chain. Three weeks elapsed before British viewers could see even a still picture of the capture of South Georgia. As Robert Harris observed, this was one day longer than it had taken *The Times* to provide its readers with a graphic description of the Charge of the Light Brigade in 1854.[57] Radio's man in the field, Robert Fox, faced the same machinery of Ministry censorship as his Television colleague Brian Hanrahan, but his technological requirements were altogether more modest; the speed with which he could provide dispatches correspondingly faster. As *The Times*'s television critic pointed out, the effects were striking. 'Brian Hanrahan's voice coupled with his motionless picture on BBC 1 could in no way compete with the sound of Robert Fox squelching ashore on Radio Four...suddenly, magically, we were there too.'[58]

The Falklands War was, then, a radio war. And ordinary listeners seemed to confirm that the medium appeared to come back into its own—in the workplace as well as in the home and car—as the conflict progressed. 'Someone has brought a radio in and news bulletins are listened to eagerly', one man recorded in his diary at the end of April. 'Tea break discussions are devoted exclusively to the crisis with opinions on whether we ought to use force becoming divided.'[59]

Within Broadcasting House, Monica Sims and her Chief Assistant, Richard Wade, pored over the Radio Four schedules daily—shifting some programmes, cancelling others, squeezing extra news coverage into the countless gaps thus created. By the end of the War in June, the published schedules had been altered something like 300 times.[60] For Dick Francis, this was not quite enough. Indeed, as far as he was concerned, the fact that scheduled programmes had had to be sacrificed to make way for coverage only magnified the basic problem at hand— namely the absence of a network capable of responding easily, naturally, *flexibly*, to 'unpredictable or extended news'. He raised the recurring complaint, that no matter how hard Radio Four tried, its 'conflicting editorial roles' remained: the protection of 'creative' radio—by which he meant crafted, imaginative, 'built' programmes of fixed length—invariably meant the blockage of 'live' radio. This would no longer do. Large investments had been made in gathering news, he told BBC Governors: it would be criminally wasteful not to put more of it on air. Live radio needed 'liberating'.[61]

This became the manifesto cry behind a new 'White Paper' that Francis now championed along with the Editor of News and Current Affairs, John Wilson, and which was subsequently debated widely—and with much heat—in Broadcasting House and throughout Fleet Street between June 1982 and the following spring. 'BBC Radio for the Nineties', as the Paper was eventually called, was in many respects a natural evolution from the debates of 1980 and 1981. It recognized that there was no immediate prospect of the government giving the BBC an extra frequency for a separate news service or educational channel, and nor would there be the money to pay for it. This time, however, there would be no wholesale mergers. Instead, individual programmes were to be shuffled around to ensure that at least one network—and that meant Radio Four— would be flexible enough to accommodate live news as and when it was needed. Indeed, the philosophy was now quite explicit, the shift in balance decisive. Radio Four, the document said, would be '*based* on news and current affairs', and would broadcast 'built' programmes only insofar as they were 'commensurate with the need for flexibility'. Radio Four, in short, would have a 'simplified editorial brief ': it would move towards being 'an informational channel'.[62]

Within Francis's team of planners, Michael Starks had already done some thinking on what exactly this might involve. Networks, he had suggested, might coordinate the start and end times of their programmes, so that, for example, Radio Four's afternoon play could be shifted to Radio Three at short notice should the need arise to relay a parliamentary debate. Perhaps some comedy series and panel games could go to either Radio One or Radio Two and some dramas and book readings to Radio Three, leaving more breathing space for looser, longer, live sequences on Radio Four.[63] These were schemes circulated in private, and they showed no inhibition. The more public pages of 'Radio for the Nineties' were less explicit. But it was clear to anyone skilled in BBC Kremlinology that drama, once again, was most vulnerable. The formal position was that the question of whether 'all of it' or only 'some' of it would leave Radio Four would 'need to be determined' at some point in the future. Informally, there was much talk inside Broadcasting House of up to 60 per cent of Drama department's work being permanently lost.[64]

The inevitable tensions within Radio were heightened after October 1982 when details of the White Paper were leaked. The *Daily Telegraph*, reporting that 'Radio Four would be restricted to news, information and consumer affairs programmes except at weekends', added that there was 'much anxiety among heads of department' in Broadcasting House. The *Sun* called the plans 'grotesque', and laid into 'those very superior people the nabobs of the BBC' for threatening what it called 'the housewives' favourite'. Warming to the same theme, the *Daily Mail* told its readers that 'the housewives' favourites *Morning Story* and *Afternoon Theatre* are threatened, while perennials such as *Gardeners' Question Time* and *The Archers* could be farmed out to the backwaters of BBC local radio'. The most persistent agitator was Geoffrey Cannon in the *Sunday Times*. Under the headline 'Barricades Go up at Radio 4', he wrote that the Drama department was 'preparing an Alamo-type defence against the news and current affairs hordes', and posed this question: 'Do you, readers of the *Sunday Times*, want Radio Four to become more streamed, more news and current affairs oriented, or stay a mixed channel?'[65] Once again, a Managing Director of Radio was forced into repeating that 'People have got the wrong end of the stick.' Privately, the BBC's Assistant Director-General, and the man in overall command of its journalists, Alan Protheroe, was fuming. He had found *Radio for the Nineties* 'excellent and refined'. In attacking it, the Press was exhibiting British journalism at its worse—hysterical and inaccurate, some of it even malevolent.[66]

Malevolent or not, it was Press coverage that created the climate in which, on 21 October 1982, the BBC Governors met—after weaving their way through some forty or so protesting actors and writers—to consider whether to approve or reject the latest plan. Francis told the Board that as well as a 'small, but vociferous' lobby wanting Radio Four left unchanged, there was a 'quieter, but perhaps more significant group' wanting an all-news network. What he wanted most was to square the circle by creating more flexibility within the existing pattern. Some of the Governors agreed that here, at last, might be a workable compromise. There were plenty of defenders of the status quo, too. But since, strictly speaking, there was no plan to actually abolish the network, it was deemed safe to agree that a final 'White Paper' be prepared on the basis of Francis's plans—provided, the Director-General added, that it stressed the BBC would 'continue to encourage creative radio and in particular drama'.[67]

Events were now drawing to a temporary close. Several newspapers interpreted the Governors' statement that Radio Four would not be abolished as a victory for the 'No Change' lobby. The *Daily Mail* wrote of Governors having 'backed away' from the proposals, and the *Guardian*'s news pages reported that Radio Four's future was henceforward assured. Other observers, wisely, refused to drop their guard. On the *Guardian*'s inside pages, Val Arnold-Forster called Francis a 'top-class obfuscator'. He was, after all, still going around talking about Radio Four being overburdened. What on earth could that mean, except that drama, comedy, and the like were still in his sights? The conclusion was obvious: 'The pot still simmers.'[68]

In truth, what Francis and his senior managers had done was to learn the publicity advantage of stressing continuity and of downplaying change. Throughout the tail end of 1982 and the first months of 1983, Francis repeated his mantra that there was to be no all-news channel, that change would be 'by evolution, not by blueprint', that contrary to the alarmist cries of dramatists and writers the full range of programmes currently being broadcast by BBC Radio would continue—if not on Radio Four then certainly *somewhere*.[69]

Change, however, there was certainly going to be. Francis's right-hand man, Michael Starks, was already working on schemes for implementing the new philosophy of in-built flexibility on Radio Four. 'We need to manage change, forcing the pace a little', he told Francis. His suggestion: to contemplate what was called 'block-scheduling'. This involved whole stretches of the schedule—two or three hours at a time—where programmes previously regarded as separate entities became free-floating, moveable features in a loosely structured live format. Francis had recently witnessed it working well on the Canadian Broadcasting Corporation's three-hour amalgam of news, documentaries, and features, *Sunday Morning*.[70] There seemed no obvious reason why something similar could not work on Radio Four. With its interchangeable ingredients it provided familiar landmarks *and* flexibility at one and the same time. It was, in short, the 'magazine' programme writ large. Not so much 'rolling news', but something in which news could intrude if required—a more amorphous, less generic 'rollercoaster' of speech. It sounded like the future. And, as Chapter 11 will show, it was soon to be part of the fractious present.

DEFENDING THE RICH MIX

For now, though, there was a victory of sorts to be celebrated by all those who had fought to preserve Radio Four's mixed character. Over the past four years or so there had been a very real sense that Radio Four might disappear, or be ejected from its new home on long wave, or stripped of programmes that had long been at the heart of its schedule. Under Aubrey Singer, the local radio lobby had been given its head and ratings had been deployed to show Radio Four in a poor light—as hopelessly middle class, unfashionably metropolitan, and in steady overall decline. Under Singer's successor, Dick Francis, the main danger—from a powerful news and current affairs division wanting to stretch its wings—had remained. As had the hopeless financial outlook, which placed the question of savings high on any checklist of considerations in BBC planning. In the face of all this, Radio Four's survival was remarkable. It had even managed to remain substantially the same network it had been half a decade earlier. Its essential character—its 'rich mix'—was still there.

How had this come to pass? One answer is that it was the result of the sheer bloody-mindedness of the Controller, Monica Sims, and her deputy, Richard Wade. They spent much of their waking hours during these four years replying to proposals, attending meetings and working parties, and talking to producers, managers, audience researchers, engineers, accountants, Governors, and journalists, all the while extolling the virtues of the rich mix, rebuffing the most harmful schemes, pointing out the dangers of change. It was a dogged battle for hearts and minds. And it was fought on many fronts.

For a start, there was the audience research to dispute. Sims and Wade were convinced Radio Four's overall decline in the ratings had been exaggerated. True, Radio Four had been losing its share of the audience over the past ten years, but since 1978 the haemorrhage had slowed almost to a standstill: the annual loss of listeners was now to be measured in thousands rather than millions.[71] Furthermore, even this modest decline could be misleading. The so-called 'daily survey' upon which the ratings were based involved opinion-polling in the street. It did not take fully into account the growing number of people listening to the radio in their cars, nor did it adequately represent those who were housebound. These were two big constituencies for Radio Four.[72] Another oversight involved local radio. In the early 1970s, it had been common practice for the BBC's local stations to relay some of Radio Four's news bulletins and *The World at One*. Anyone listening to these was counted as a Radio Four listener. By 1978, however, this statistical anomaly had been removed: they now appeared, quite reasonably, under the column of their local station's ratings. This had the effect of artificially inflating Radio Four's audience figures in the early part of the decade, and exaggerating decline in the latter part.[73]

Corrected figures were vital to Sims and Wade in combating the image of decline. But there was another tactical advantage in establishing healthier ratings: it made Radio Four more cost-effective. Local station managers pointed to Radio Four's heavy cost *per hour*, which made it the most expensive network. Sims countered with her own statistics on cost *per listener*. In 1980, Radio Four spent £14 million of the licence fee on five million listeners; local radio spent £8.5 million on two million listeners. By this measure, Radio Four was costing each of its listeners £2.80 for the year, while local radio was costing nearly £4.30; the national regions were four times as expensive, Radio Three nearly seven times.[74] Radio Four looked cheap at the price.

The distinctive social composition of the Radio Four audience—middle-aged, middle class, Home Counties—was harder to dispute. But even here there was room for argument. In 1982, the average age of the Radio Four listener was somewhere around 53—stuck resolutely where it had been in 1967. This suggested the network had failed to attract many younger listeners. Yet the fact that the average age had not gone *up* as the core audience inexorably grew older was significant. Younger listeners were joining at roughly the same rate that older ones were dying. There appeared to be a natural pattern in operation. Many people, particularly women in their twenties and thirties, were evidently starting to listen to Radio Four when they found themselves at home bringing up young children and in need of stimulating adult company. As a result, Radio Four—to use the broadcaster's own jargon—was 'refreshing' its audience quite satisfactorily.[75]

As for the regional bias, there was no doubt that Radio Four was listened to far less in the North and West of England, in Scotland, Wales, and Northern Ireland than it was in the South-East. Some of this, perhaps, was simply because of problems over VHF reception. Some, no doubt, was a genuine reflection of the station being seen as metropolitan and aloof. A lot could be put down to the geographical concentration of the middle classes, who formed such a large part of the Radio Four audience. If they clustered in the South-East of England, so too would the Radio Four audience. Class, then, was the base factor. And it was indisputable that the middle classes in particular had a special relationship with Radio Four. Though, once again, statistics needed careful treatment. Take the BBC's own figures from 1980. They calculated that out of every hundred Radio Four listeners fourteen were 'upper middle class', compared with only six in the population at large; another forty were 'lower middle class', compared with twenty-four in the population at large. In other words, while somewhere between a quarter and a third of Britons were categorized as middle class, just over half of the Radio Four audience was counted as such. Sims nevertheless used to get furious with the criticism that her audience was overwhelmingly middle class and elderly. The network clearly attracted the middle classes *disproportionately*. But the largest single category of listeners—forty-six out of every hundred—was still officially 'working class'.[76] This was—or should have been—salutary. Averages always concealed heterogeneity. The typical listener to *The Hitchhiker's Guide to the Galaxy* was 31 years old and 'more upmarket' than even the typical Radio Three listener; the typical devotee of the *Morning Service* was 62 and almost as 'downmarket' as the typical Radio Two listener.[77] As one head of department inside Broadcasting House pointed out, in circumstances like this it was misleading of any of his colleagues to speak of the 'typical' Radio Four listener. 'What is true', he reminded them, 'is that half our audience are working class and half middle class, and that half are under fifty and half are over fifty.'[78] Not everyone heard him. Stereotypes were too useful, myths too hard to dispel.

There was, in any case, a virtue in embracing the station's audience for what it was—indeed, for presenting it as a mark of distinction. Thus, when Michael Starks talked of Radio Four's need to attract a wider cross-section of the audience, Richard Wade turned the telescope around. If Radio Four's audience *was* middle-aged, 'higher class', and 'better educated than the norm', he told Starks, was that not just because that was exactly what 'any literate speech network will attract'?[79] And if this *was* a minority, was it not a broad one? 'There is still a large number of people in Britain who read books and magazines, discuss ideas, and travel beyond the intellectual boundaries of tabloid life', he suggested.[80]

The BBC's own statistics were clear on the overall picture: the more middle class and educated one was, the more one listened to speech radio.[81] The sensible thing to do seemed to be to build on this, rather than to deny it. 'It would be foolish to run after new audiences', Sims suggested: they simply 'might not have the social and educational background' to cope.[82] Radio Four was for clever folk—not intellectuals (they had Radio Three), but ordinary, intelligent people, able to concentrate, and infused with the spirit of curiosity and modest self-improvement. This, indeed, struck one of the BBC's Governors, the poet Roy Fuller, as Radio Four's very essence. Whenever he contributed to one of its programmes, he said, he was invariably surprised by how many old acquaintances would hear him. The network was evidently 'a gathering point for the still numerous mentally alert, un-academic and non-phoney people I have known about, and taken hope from, all my life'. These were—note the strong whiff of nostalgia—'the amateur singers, actors and etchers of my provincial youth; the aspirers in the armed forces to a better quality of post-war life; and, more recently, those who have striven to hold on to values in a shallow and amoral society'.[83]

This undoubtedly yearned for a Golden Age. Yet Sims and Wade were convinced they could see something similar when looking to the imminent future. There would soon be breakfast TV, satellite TV, cable TV, a fourth terrestrial channel; more information services such as Ceefax and Prestel; by Christmas 1982, home computers and video recorders were readily available in British high-street shops. Wade, who had come to Radio Four after a career on the television science programme *Tomorrow's World*, was very clear about the profound implications of it all. In this competitive and fragmented ecology, rival television channels would be fighting for the attentions of the mass audience. If so, there could be a bigger role than ever for BBC radio to be a fully fledged refuge—*the* place where a minority desire for 'surprise, educating and broadening' could be satisfied.[84] You could see it starting to happen: BBC 1 and ITV were already 'moving towards Lowest Common Denominator' programming. Sims referred to 'TV candy floss such as *Wonder Woman*'; Wade's chosen *bête noir* was *It's a Knockout*. In the face of this stuff, intelligent people were obviously being driven to radio—and liking what they heard. In an age of free markets and burgeoning choice, Radio Four, in fact, had nothing to fear. As Sims saw it, 'the shop that continues to sell hand-crafted goods or high-quality food still satisfies customers of all ages who prefer them to mass-produced imitations'.[85] The issue was quality, not quantity. The overall *number* of people watching television was growing all the time, but as far as it was possible to measure these things, *satisfaction* with the medium was on a downward trend at the end of the 1970s. The public view of radio appeared to be heading in the other direction.[86] In short, Radio Four was—and might become even more—the *antidote* to television. It needed to accept its fate as a minority affair, and revel in it. In the age of mass-appeal television, it was no bad thing to be left holding the torch for Culture and Quality; the BBC had built its reputation upon these, after all.

But what of news and current affairs, the 'topical speech' and 'public affairs' of which so many schemes spoke when planning the future of Radio Four? Was this not an essential element in the Reithian principles of 'surprise, educating and broadening'? Well, yes. Neither Sims nor Wade wanted to lose the 'spine' of *Today, The World at One, PM, The World Tonight, File on Four*, and the various bulletins, and news-related programmes that ran throughout the day. They were, they all agreed, part of what gave the network its character, and they guaranteed that people would turn to it for information—particularly at times of crisis.

Whether such programmes were 'broadening' the listeners' minds as much as the Controller and her assistant hoped was quite another matter. There seemed to be too much Westminster politics for a start—not just the new live coverage of Parliament, but too much of a Westminster 'agenda' to everything else.[87] Journalists' definition of what constituted 'current affairs' also appeared uncompromisingly narrow. In various 'reviews of the year' put out by Current Affairs, there often appeared to be what Wade called 'a solid wodge' on economics and politics, but noticeably less on technology, science, religion, or the arts. Editors commonly replied that such matters were left out 'on the grounds of space'. But it was, of course, all a matter of priorities, and what did or did not count as current affairs was an old debate. Which is another way of saying that attitudes were not shifting. Back in 1970, Tony Whitby had been disappointed there had been no 'idiosyncrasy' or 'pop' in the review of the year, on the grounds that both had obviously been 'part of the "scene"'. Twelve months later, there had been similar disquiet at Review Board over neglect of 'society and morality', and a feeling that the review 'simply gave any listener who kept up with the news information with which he was already familiar'. But a little more familiarity was exactly what some journalists now thought Radio Four needed, and not just in news programmes but across the board. One senior editor, for example, expressed irritation with *Stop the Week* because he simply did not want to hear 'references to books he had not read or plays he had not seen'.[88] This was hardly in the spirit of 'surprise, educating and broadening', and it was an attitude that explained exactly why both Sims and Wade were aghast at any definition of their network that placed 'topical speech' before anything else. Topicality, as Ian McIntyre and George Fischer had argued before, was no simple matter. In the hands of the hard news men it too easily became a diminished thing.

The listeners' opinions on this were important, for all parties wanted to show popular support for the positions they had staked out. Journalists pointed to unequivocal evidence that it was their programmes that attracted the best ratings. Radio Four's share of the national audience peaked at 7 a.m., 1 p.m., 6 p.m., and 10 p.m.—the main news times through the day.[89] 'Everybody switches on for the news,' Sims acknowledged. She did exactly the same herself. But this did not mean that the more news Radio Four provided, the more listeners it would get. People switched on at these particular times partly because they were only able to do so then: they coincided with mealtimes or breaks in the working day. If people switched off afterwards it was not because they did not want to carry on listening but because they had to get on with other things. In any case, there were already plenty of other listeners who avoided the news and switched Radio Four on for *The Archers*, *Afternoon Theatre*, the *Daily Service*, or *Desert Island Discs*. By being in possession of the choicest slots, news and current affairs seemed to have a good enough deal already, Sims thought. It was churlish of them to complain.[90] As for the possibility of any *more* news outside these times, listeners had made it clear enough to her what their views were. Ever since the changes wrought by *Broadcasting in the Seventies*, each major news story covered on Radio Four was followed by a flurry of letters and phone calls from members of the audience objecting to excessive treatment. There had been more than 1,500 letters of complaint within a month of the start of live parliamentary broadcasting in April 1978—compared with 21 offering praise.[91] The release of the American hostages in Iran in January 1981, which the BBC's own journalists thought had been covered rather scantily, prompted thirty-six phone calls inside a week from listeners disgruntled at what they saw as the large amount of attention given.[92] This was four or five times the number of complaints that might be expected in any given week about bad language on an afternoon play.

The Falklands War distilled such complaints and added some new ones all of its own. Grumbling at the BBC from the dedicated band of habitual anti-news complainers was inevitable, of course. But their voices were not entirely unrepresentative, since there was evidence of a wider mood of irritation with news coverage among ordinary listeners. One such wrote in his diary of the sense of time-filling on air during the early days of the campaign, 'the way in which we are all waiting with bated breath for our fleet to assemble in the battle zone whilst the media do their best to maintain the tension with their regular reports from the fleet at sea'. 'Many commentators talked rubbish', thought another: 'so much time and money was spent making maps and models for "schoolboys" to play games on TV and radio.' For many, a keen sense of fatigue gradually set in. 'It's been going on for too long... it's been reheated and we're having it for every meal.' Another complained of 'becoming tired of the constant stream of news and extended bulletins' which 'attempted to squeeze every last drop of information out of those directly involved in the affair...' All this talk, all this worry, all this speculation. It struck one contemporary diarist as absurdly unreal. 'The sun is shining, people are pruning their roses and going to work as normal knowing that even if we became involved in a serious full-scale war it cannot affect life on mainland Britain whilst the conflict takes place in deepest winter on the other side of the world.' Life on mainland Britain, however, was not all a bed of roses. Indeed, that was part of the beef. 'The Falkland issue has blacked out all news of local or national matters', one writer complained. In the midst of a biting deflationary recession, so much, it seemed, was being left unsaid about unemployment, housing, environmental pollution, the health service. As for the victory parade after the fighting was over, that did not go down at all well: 'staged to restore the Tory government image and to divert attention from unemployment', 'bread-and-circuses', 'a little frivolity to take people's mind off the economic slump'.[93] In true McLuhanite fashion, medium and message were being identified as one and the same.

The prospect of more news, then, was never going to be terribly appealing to many regular Radio Four listeners. And when Dick Francis unveiled 'Radio for the Nineties' towards the end of 1982, he reaped the whirlwind. More than 2,000 letters poured into the BBC expressing outrage, sadness, distress, or incredulity at what was planned—or thought to be planned. 'I physically shuddered when I heard they are going to tamper with Radio Four', wrote a Mrs Phillips from Oxford. 'Why do the media insist on beating us round the head with news?' asked Mrs Preston in Cornwall. 'So many people that I speak to about Radio Four like it a great deal, BUT they all say there is far too much news already—the thought of any more appals them as it does me', said a Mr Lowe from Reading. These three letters, like all the rest, tell a tale of passionate attachment to the status quo. And if there was one recurring theme it was the pleasure to be found in variety. Letter after letter praised the 'well-balanced output of current-affairs, magazine programmes, stories, music and drama', the 'wonderful mixture', the 'serendipity of the network', its suitability for people—'everyone we know'—who wanted to be 'informed *and* entertained' in roughly equal measure. 'Radio Four's variety is the spice of life', one correspondent concluded, 'so please don't try to squeeze Radio Four into a strict category just to satisfy a bureaucratic urge for tidiness.'[94]

Inside Broadcasting House, the Radio Four Controller and her Chief Assistant knew that many stories circulating in Fleet Street were exaggerated. But they were prepared to ride the tiger of outraged opinion and harness it to their cause. Yes, they admitted, there was no formal plan to replace Radio Four. But the practical *effect* of 'Radio for the Nineties' would be the extinction of everything it stood for, and this amounted to the same thing. If the network was going to have to be 'flexible', Wade argued, it should in all honesty be called the Information Channel or Radio Six 'to distinguish it from Radio Four as we know it'. As soon as the emphasis was put on the need to present news 'as it happens' pre-recorded programmes of fixed length would always be regarded as boulders in the stream. 'Drama, Light Entertainment, music, features, readings, arts programmes, religion, general magazines and most "built" programmes would have to go', he explained. 'You cannot be flexible *and* have built programmes. It might be nice to think that's possible but anyone who has scheduled a network knows it simply wouldn't work. You can't have this cake and eat it.'[95]

Those were the practical objections. Sims, who had digested all the letters from listeners, put the philosophical one. What Francis and Starks and Singer and Woon and Wilson and all the rest had seen as 'the conflict' between Radio Four's different roles, she suggested, was not a conflict at all. It was precisely the *combination* of these roles—and in a delicate equilibrium—that was the heart of the network's achievement. 'In spite of *Broadcasting in the Seventies*, Radio Four has continued in listeners' minds to be the descendent of the old Home Service', she told Francis. It was a heritage that had shaped her, too. 'I took it for granted that Radio Four would be, like the old Home Service, a reliable source of information, but I also wanted it to be an inspiration.' The mixture was all. For variety and range was what provided its listeners with mental stimulus: 'Surprise, through different perspectives on life through satire, poetry, storytelling, songs . . . argument, defining ideas, contact with opinion formers, writers, scientists, historians, philosophers . . . and imaginative stimulus through works of art, music, drama, literature . . . ' Undiluted news, she warned, tended to offer listeners the clash of predictable views, but 'in a mixture, you get a different collection of people—people who are not geared to the political and current affairs agenda, but who are more like our forebears, in an oral tradition, when there was far more argument and conversation and exchange of ideas about faith, belief, philosophy'.[96] This was not just a passive affair for listeners. It transformed them. Radio Four was heard by 'the "all-round" cultured human being' *and* helped create that being. It 'took risks', 'it broadened the span of interests'. In short, 'it showed us that the world is wider than we'd thought'.[97]

There were countless other arguments deployed in Radio Four's defence: that it set standards of technical and editorial quality that were a yardstick for the whole of British broadcasting; that popular programmes were as important as the demanding ones, since many heard the latter by accident if they had stayed tuned after hearing the former; that well-written stories and plays provided a balance to 'the proliferation of news-speak and hastily written topical reporting'; that if drama was to be shifted to Radio Three, then it would languish unheard by all but the dedicated few; that without comedy on Radio Four, a cultural reservoir of talent that fed the whole of the BBC—Television included—would be destroyed.[98] All these points were raised by Sims and Wade *ad infinitum*. They circulated widely along the corridors of Broadcasting House and through the pages of newspapers. And they did their work well, for they exposed the Francis plan, like its predecessors, to the charge of cultural vandalism.

But the one all-encompassing idea that drew these various arguments together was that the 'rich mix' was somehow the quintessence of the Reithian ideal—and that to dismantle it would be a betrayal of the founding mission of the BBC. This, more than anything, had the capacity to supercharge the whole debate, since what was done to Radio Four would now be seen by the Press and the public as a measure of other deeper, grander issues at the BBC: the Corporation's respect for its own heritage, its commitment to public service values, its responsiveness to its own consumers, its loyalty to British values. As always, Radio Four stood for something more than itself.

Naturally, what *precisely* it stood for varied. Richard Wade, like Tony Whitby before him, thought of it as a library—clearly labelled but sufficiently well stocked to contain surprises. Ian McIntyre spoke of a stately home, held in trust for future generations. But the most common metaphor of all was horticultural. Radio Four, Clare Lawson Dick had once explained, was 'like a garden'. There were new plants to be put in, and old ones to be removed. Tending it was not a single event, but a whole way of life. Lawson Dick, indeed, described her job as 'a constant weeding out of tired or out-of-date programmes'. Whitby, too, had talked of the changes he wrought in the early 1970s not as a wholesale ripping up of plants, but as 'weeding here a little, weeding there a little'. And Monica Sims described her patronage of talented producers and presenters at the end of the decade as 'nurturing the seeds'. Controllers, it was said, 'planted' ideas and let programmes 'take root', they allowed talent to 'bloom' and new series to 'bear fruit'—provided, naturally, that 'the soil' was right, and the prevailing climate suitably 'temperate'. Once established, long-running programmes might become 'perennials'—again, provided they were not 'transplanted' too often and were allowed a 'sunny spot' in which to thrive. In its most ancient sense, broadcasting was, after all, a process of casting seed. And it was the parable of the sower that Martin Esslin employed in 1976: 'broadcasting', he told colleagues, 'meant scattering widely'—and an assumption 'that some of the seed would take root and grow'. In broadcasting, just as in gardening, quality emerged not from rapid change and zealous assaults, but from a steady, organic growth nurtured with patient care. 'It was extraordinary', the Editor of *Woman's Hour* once pointed out, 'how good gardeners were always good broadcasters.'[99]

   Gardening, of course, was an activity rich in meanings of its own. For a start, it had long seemed an intensely English sort of thing to do. After all, England itself had often been viewed in national mythology as a kind of garden.[100] The metaphor embodied the temperance of its climate, the understated commitment to steady, pragmatic progress in matters of the constitution, of culture, or, indeed, of cultivation. The garden, too, meant home, a place of security to which one could retreat from the afflictions of the city, the office, or the factory. And if England was a garden, it was a garden of a particular type, a kind of domesticated wilderness. For nearly 300 years, native landscape-gardening books had extolled the virtues of pleasing irregularity. Batty Langley's *New Principles of Gardening* offered thirty-seven rules of good design, almost wholly concerned with rejecting geometry and creating what Loudon later called the 'gardenesque'. For twentieth-century practitioners, the most influential voice was that of Gertrude Jekyll, whose turbulent, colourful, prolific gardens had fruit and vegetables and hardy annuals all mixed up and paths meandering through foxgloves and snapdragons. The kind of impact she had could be seen in the garden of the painter and amateur gardener, Paul Nash. Here weeds and the odd dead tree were tolerated so that the garden might 'merge imperceptibly with the wildwood' and tidiness could never 'get near suburbanness, the ultimate damned state'. One writer less well known publicly but who happened to be both a gardener *and* a broadcaster, was Archie Gordon, George Fischer's predecessor and a vigorous critic of *Gardener's Question Time* in the early 1970s for what he saw as its failure to do justice to 'the greatest of the English arts'. While working for the Council for the Protection of Rural England in 1939 he had written a paean to the country cottage and its garden. Like Langley, Loudon, Jekyll, and Nash before him, he wove together the metaphors of time, climate, design, and nationality with ease. Anyone trying to create the cottage idyll from scratch, he warned, would be faced with something horribly new and threadbare. If we wished to achieve that 'comfortable and benign mellowness which in time enhances all

1. Gerald Mansell, Chief of the Home Service then Controller of Radio Four, 1965–9. (Copyright © BBC)

2. William Hardcastle, the presenter of *The World at One*, 1965–75. (Copyright © BBC)

3. Tony Whitby, the Controller of Radio Four, 1969–75. (Photograph courtesy of Joy Whitby and *Radio Times*)

4. Robin Day (right) and his producer Walter Wallich, preparing an edition of *It's Your Line*, 1975. (Copyright © BBC)

5. Gerald Priestland and Jacky Gillot getting ready to present *Newsdesk*, 1971. (Copyright © BBC)

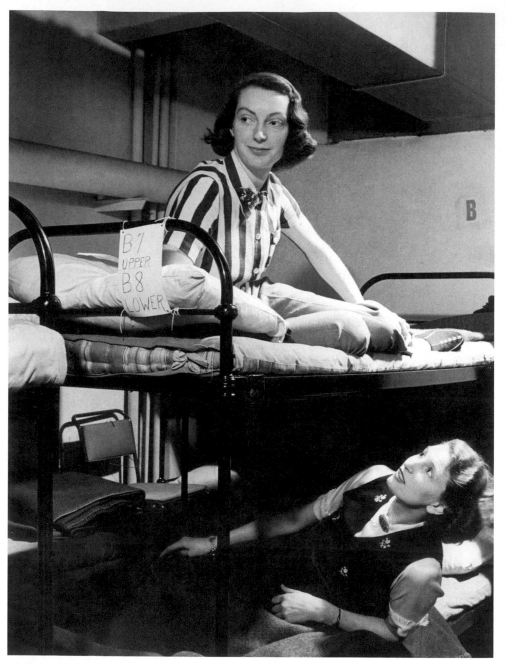

6. Clare Lawson Dick, the Controller of Radio Four, 1975–6, shown in the top bunk of her sleeping quarters in Broadcasting House, 1941. In the lower bunk is one of her colleagues, Margot Osborn. (Copyright © BBC)

7. Three *Today* presenters of 1974: Robert Robinson and John Timpson (foreground), and Des Lynam (background). (Copyright © BBC)

8. Sue MacGregor presenting *Woman's Hour* in 1973. (Copyright © BBC)

9. Ian McIntyre, the Controller of Radio Four, 1976–8. (Copyright © BBC)

10. *The Hitchhiker's Guide to the Galaxy* is put together in the studio, 1978. At the back: Lisa Braun and Colin Duff. At the mixing desk, from left: Douglas Adams, Anne Ling, and Alick Hale-Munro. Leaning: Geoffrey Perkins. (Copyright © BBC)

11. Cast members from *The Archers* on location in 1980. Seated: Norman Painting as Phil Archer and Judy Bennett as Shula. Standing, from left: Graham Roberts as George Barford, Brian Hewlett as Neil Carter, Trevor Harrison as Eddie Grundy, Charles Collingwood as Brian Aldridge, and Bob Arnold as Tom Forrest. (Copyright © BBC)

12. Michael Hordern (Gandalf), John Le Mesurier (Bilbo), and Ian Holm (Frodo), reading their scripts for *Lord of the Rings*, 1981. (Copyright © BBC)

13. Roy Plomley and the Conservative leader, Margaret Thatcher, discuss *Desert Island Discs*, 1978. (Copyright © BBC)

14. Roger Cook in the *Checkpoint* office, chasing a story in 1983. (Copyright © BBC)

15. Monica Sims, the Controller of Radio Four, 1978–83. (Copyright © BBC)

16. Nicholas Barnes as Nigel (later Adrian) Mole, in January 1982. (Copyright © BBC)

17. David Hatch, the Controller of Radio Four, 1983–6, pictured (standing on the right), rehearsing *I'm Sorry I'll Read That Again* in 1968. Others, from left: Bill Oddie, John Cleese, Tim Brooke-Taylor, Jo Kendall, and Graeme Garden. (Copyright © BBC)

18. Brian Redhead, photographed in Manchester in 1976, scans the papers ready for *Today*. (Copyright © BBC)

19. The *Rollercoaster* presenters in 1984. From left: David Davies, Patti Coldwell, Richard Baker, and Peter Adamson. (Copyright © BBC)

20. The cast of *Citizens*, 1987. From left: Beverley Hills, Russell Boulter, Kate Duchene (holding Sally Street), James MacPherson, and Seeta Indrani. (Copyright © Press Association)

21. Michael Green, the Controller of Radio Four, 1986–96. (Copyright © BBC)

22. Gerry Anderson, the presenter of *Anderson Country*, 1994. (Copyright © BBC)

23. Prunella Scales, Joan Sanderson, and Gerry Cowper: the three stars of *After Henry*, 1985–9. (Copyright © BBC)

24. John Humphrys in the *Today* office, Broadcasting House, on the occasion of the last edition made in the building before the move to White City in 1998. (Copyright © BBC)

English art', then 'we must learn to appreciate the value of waiting for maturity'. No foreign influence could improve matters, for the English cottage and its garden demonstrated the virtues of 'gorgeous insularity'. He favoured things that were 'almost a natural growth out of the soil on which they stood . . . built entirely of local materials . . . part of the local scene, and not an imposition upon it'. The native model moulds itself 'informally but with manners, into an existing pattern'. And this was its strength. 'It vaunteth not itself, is not puffed up (nor easily blown down).'[101]

The 'English garden', then, was one with little paths meandering up to personal points of view, symbolic of English liberties, and stuffed with plants and ornaments that had blended together slowly, just like the constitution. As opposed to the continental version, all dominating designs, straight lines, central axes, radiating lines of surveillance—equally symbolic of, say, French despotism. It was a caricature of course, but a persistent one. As Robert Colls has shown in precisely this context, 'identity draws on history and myth, both as forms of truth'.[102]

A hundred and fifty years later, and in the carpeted, urban sanctum of Broadcasting House, something of the same spirit held sway. For if England and Radio Four were gardens both, it seemed to make sense to think, in turn, of Radio Four standing somehow for England. 'I have always believed', Clare Lawson Dick once confessed, 'that the Home Service and later Radio Four should appeal not only to the intellect but also to the emotions—all of them— and that it should also call up race memories.'[103] Race memories? It is a phrase that speaks of something deep, inherent, native, perhaps hidden by the accretions of modern life and all its diversity, but ultimately the bedrock of a national character that still survived. Which is why, perhaps, the BBC's Governor for Wales, when presented with Francis's plans for changing Radio Four in 1982, declared that Radio Four needed preserving much as it was, because 'if he wanted to touch certain strands of Englishry it was to Radio Four that he turned'. People, he thought, felt that both the world of broadcasting and the world at large were changing too rapidly, that identities were becoming confused, and that Radio Four stood out as a place of consistency and reassurance. Yes, another Governor agreed, when she was travelling and away from home, she, too, regarded Radio Four 'as a comfort'.[104] It offered familiarity but also, in its profusion and its meander, the opportunity to chance upon something surprising in the schedule. It was rather as if one had turned a corner in one's cottage garden and found a plant unexpectedly in bloom.

What on earth would happen if Radio Four were to be more single-minded, more focused on news? Recall the language. 'All programmes with zero or near-zero ratings to be eliminated . . . all sequences would be standardised . . . Editors would follow the direction of a central network editor.' The rhetoric conjured up a vision of the Radio equivalent of Versailles, or perhaps—this was the start of the 1980s after all—one of those new-fangled 'make-over' gardens that ripped up beds and lawns to impose a geometry of decking and terraces. The vision of the future was not always French: the view was sometimes 'from Tokyo', Montreal, New York, or even Shepherd's Bush. But it was certainly alien. Radio Four, like the cottage gardens of old England, was a natural growth built of native material, too deeply ensconced to be treated this way: perhaps English, perhaps British (the matter was usually blurred), but certainly *something* to do with the nation—or at least with the decent, upright folk who were the backbone of its body politic. 'Radio Four occupied a special position in national life', one of the Governors, Sir John Johnston, asserted in 1982. Partly it was because 'of its descent from the old Home Service, partly it was because 'of the importance of the audience it addressed'. But mostly it was because it was 'the one service' which provided a variety of ways with which the nation could view itself:

Radio Four was the Broad Church of Radio. Not only BBC Radio, but the country itself would be diminished if it were to undergo radical change . . . If you lopped off a leg here and an arm there you would inevitably end up by stopping the heart . . . There was a need for a national kaleidoscope. The BBC would be inflicting a grievous wound on itself if it changed Radio Four in the way proposed. It would be seen to be acting out of competitive, corporate interests, rather than in the national interest.[105]

There were going to be lots more argument over the coming years about whether this was a 'national kaleidoscope' rich and varied enough to show all the colours of Britain. Radio Four still looked too much like the home of the blue-rinsed and purple-faced. There they were, one newspaper said: 'Mrs Cosy-sides, knitting to the accompaniment of *Woman's Hour* and poised to seize the blue Biro and Basildon Bond every time she hears the word "abortion" pass Sue Macgregor's lips . . . The Lt Col (Rtd.) in the Old Rectory in the shires, sounding off about left-wing bias in the *PM* programme.'[106]

But, as with all that was written about gardens and national identity, truth was again mixed with mythology. Many of the letters of support reaching Monica Sims were from deepest England. But many, too, were from young mothers with children in Scotland and Wales, from drivers and mechanics, from actors, writers, painters, and fashion-designers in the sophisticated heart of the capital, from people in Scandinavia, the Netherlands, and France who had overheard and stayed tuned, from people who had travelled and seen and heard the world but liked most what they knew best back home. 'If Radio Four is for the "middle class", why do I, working-class, choose it for my listening?' asked one woman in a letter from Scotland. Because, she answered herself, its programmes 'surely represent the tastes of a certain level of intelligence, which is not confined to any one class'.[107] 'Intelligence' could be as loaded a term as class, of course, since there was always the question of whether it was innate, acquired—or indeed bought. But there were other, better, words in circulation. 'Curiosity' was one of them. 'On this one network you can quite simply find more than any other',

David Wade suggested in *The Times*: 'it takes in idle chat and domesticity at one end of the spectrum, thoughtful, penetrating programmes at the other.' Because of that, Radio Four offered 'very nearly the only place' where there was 'something of that essential, catholic curiosity about human beings'.[108]

And what about maturity as a defining appeal? 'Radio Four is for grown-ups', Valerie Groves argued in the *Evening Standard*. 'Essentially, like all good things, it has stayed put, knowing that listeners will come home again, as it were, to the Home Service.' 'In my teens and twenties you would never have caught me listening to *Gardeners' Question Time* ... But gardening is something you grow into. Sooner or later we all come to the question of mulch around the roses.'[109]

This was conservatism, but of a multifaceted kind. Indeed, with a Conservative government intent on radical change to Britain—unleashing market forces, erasing 'sickly' industries and collectivist institutions, multiplying television channels and commercial radio stations in the name of choice, and unabashed at the social dislocation and lowest-common-denominator entertainment that came along with it all—the appeal of a radio service that seemed committed to organic evolution and infused with a spirit of mild improvement now spread evenly across the political spectrum. Radio Four, Groves concluded, was 'a stronghold of intelligence and amusement and awareness in an increasingly unintelligible and humourless world':

We've been amputated from our own past and our own familiar favourite things once too often. We have watched with a hopeless shrug as buildings were bulldozed and institutions revamped. I want to rely on Radio Four to remain, Stopping and Starting and Middling the Week, panels and chats and dramas and documentaries and all.[110]

A large part of Radio Four's seductive appeal was its delicate balance of variousness *and* certainty. Like all the best gardens, it provided familiarity and surprise, continuity and change, light and shade. It was why Governors and newspapers and listeners felt moved to thwart the boldest designs of the news and local radio lobbies between 1978 and 1983. To have uprooted even some of the plants in the garden was to have risked upsetting the overall effect.

In the end, Radio Four's rich mix was its strength. It best reflected the Reithian soul of the BBC, and therefore rallied influential people and ordinary affronted listeners to its defence. It was also, of course, its weakness. In the consumer world of the late 1980s and 1990s, a clear-cut image was to be the *sine qua non* of competing in the marketplace. The BBC was going to be changing—having to show itself more responsive to its 'customers', having to divest itself of some of the trappings of paternalism, needing to reflect the entrepreneurial, delayered, hard-edged, efficient, populist, and individualist climate of the times. How would Radio Four's very particular brand of serendipity and other-worldliness survive all that?

PART III
LISTENER POWER:
C.1983–1997

'The Old World in which the BBC's traditional role and services were developed has passed into history'

BBC, 1992

10

Years Zero

'A great deal of ill-will was brewing'

Sue MacGregor, *Today* presenter

THE IMPACT OF THATCHERISM

In June 1983, with the wind of a Falklands War victory in her sails, Margaret Thatcher achieved a second decisive election victory. Henceforward, the climate within which the BBC operated became a potent brew of political, economic, and personal hostility. For broadcasters, her first government had been less intrusive than they might have expected. Macroeconomic policy had loomed largest in the Prime Minister's concerns. There had also been the restraining influence at the Home Office of William Whitelaw, a man of the One Nation establishment quite at ease with the BBC–ITV duopoly. But now, quite apart from being given four more years to pursue her unique brand of economic liberalism and social authoritarianism, Mrs Thatcher had the opportunity to pick some new fights. She had an increased Commons majority, an Opposition in disarray, fewer 'wets' in the Cabinet to restrain her, and a strengthened conviction that whenever she stood her ground and followed her instincts she would invariably triumph against the odds. It was the moment to make good on the philosophy she had articulated in 1981. 'Economics are the method,' she had said then; 'the object is to change the heart and soul.'[1]

One obvious target for her corrective force was the 'liberal establishment': the Church, the universities and schools, the Civil Service, the NHS. They were not just symbols of the Corporate State, or of inefficiency and restricted practices: they were the ideological heartlands of Consensus, riddled with attitudes that were at best woolly, and at worst socialist. They were structurally—perhaps pathologically—unable to embrace the new era of privatization, free markets, consumer sovereignty, and choice. The BBC, which had so offended Thatcherite opinion over its coverage of the Falklands War, seemed to embody the liberal establishment at its most dangerous. It was also influential, and it appeared truculent. From 1983, it was inevitable that the Prime Minister would have it in her sights. The disaffection, though, was to be mutual. And for several years it seemed destined to be self-reinforcing.

Mrs Thatcher's own view of the Corporation had always been highly coloured. She thought it stuffed full of leftists, unpatriotic, and—having grown fat on the licence fee (which she pointedly refused to call anything other than a 'compulsory levy')—emblematic of the bloated, inefficient, complacent, public sector strongholds that claimed to act for 'some common good' in the hope of protecting themselves from the correcting force of competition.[2] But she was not alone in her instincts. Her minister Norman Tebbit undoubtedly best summed up the visceral loathing of the average Tory backbencher when he memorably described the BBC as that 'insufferable, smug, sanctimonious, naïve, guilt-ridden, wet, pink orthodoxy of that sunset home of third-rate minds of that third-rate decade, the Sixties'.[3] Fortified in this view, he and many other senior Conservatives were prepared to put the boot in as the opportunity arose. Sweeping government denunciations of the BBC's bias in its news coverage became routine throughout the decade, and were ably supported by a hostile Press whipping up public feeling. One cheerleader was the London *Evening Standard*, which wrote of the BBC's 'remorseless mediocrity', of it being 'lost for a cause'. Another was the *Daily Mail*, which labelled the Corporation 'Biased, Bankrupt, Corrupt'. But the most consistent hostility came from the house magazines of Rupert Murdoch, a man with ambitious plans to expand his media empire and who clearly resented the BBC's continued dominance in the marketplace. In 1985, *The Times* ran leading articles on three consecutive days, each calling for the break-up and selling of the BBC; the *Sun*, meanwhile, shamelessly accused it of being 'boring' one day, and 'sleazy' the next. Tales of profligacy, arrogance, and breaches of decorum abounded. Northern Ireland was a recurring flashpoint, with critics choosing to interpret exposure of a controversial viewpoint as endorsement. But there was a rich and varied succession of causes célèbres: interviews with paramilitaries in *Real Lives*, a *Panorama* on 'Maggie's Militant Tendency' which suggested there had been far-Right infiltration of the Conservative Party, 'unpatriotic' and 'factually inaccurate' television plays such as *The Monocled Mutineer* and *Tumbledown*, Kate Adie's reporting of the Tripoli bombings. Through most of this, the BBC's Assistant Director-General, Alan Protheroe, did his best to act as a 'flak-catcher general', rebutting the most outlandish claims at every turn.[4] But the flow of unhelpful rows was unrelenting. Each conspired to suggest to ill-disposed minds that the BBC was, at the very least, editorially out of control, and, at worst, treasonable or morally bankrupt.

This populist cheerleading on editorial matters—what has been called Thatcherism in its Maoist phase—was only one wing of the Conservative attack. The other was more strategic and less immediately visible to the public in its effects: to steadily weaken the BBC's competitive position in the broadcasting marketplace. The Corporation was vulnerable at the best of times, through its reliance on the government to set the level of the licence fee. But worse threatened. Among the Prime Minister's loyal lieutenants were those, such as her policy adviser Brian

Griffiths and ministers like Nigel Lawson, Nicholas Ridley, and David Young, who consistently urged an end to the licence fee altogether as a precursor to a heavily scaled-back Corporation in which whole radio networks and television channels might be auctioned off. Even those ministers inclined to be more supportive were putting it about that the licence fee could no longer 'be regarded as immortal'.[5]

Getting rid of it was easier said than done, however. The government-appointed Peacock Committee of 1986, led by a Scottish economist of impeccable free-market credentials, failed to deliver the recommendation ministers had been hoping for, namely that the BBC be required to take advertising. Even so, the size and shape of the Corporation had been raised as an issue, and that could not go away. Other levers of control were to be manipulated. The licence fee was pegged to the retail price index, which at a time of steeply rising production costs inevitably necessitated real-term cuts within the BBC. The government also moved to deregulate the broadcasting industry and hugely expand the commercial sector. Beyond legislating for cable and satellite television, quality thresholds were removed for commercial operators, new licences were made available, and the BBC was required to source at least a quarter of its television programmes from the fledgling 'independent' sector and to supplement its licence fee from programme sales abroad. As the number of operators expanded, the BBC's share of the audience inevitably declined. By 1993, BBC 1's share of viewing had slipped to just under 29 per cent of the national audience, its lowest point for eight years. With such a showing, its traditional claim to be the 'national instrument' of broadcasting looked increasingly threadbare—to the point, indeed, where the imposition of a universal licence fee on people patently *not* watching BBC programmes began, conveniently, to seem rather unjust.[6]

The BBC's response to all this was to duck and weave in every way it could. But it was in no position to present a united front. Its own Board of Governors was now being filled by people whom the Prime Minister could rely on to represent her views—most notably the former *Times* editor and Conservative parliamentary candidate William Rees-Mogg, a man who was said to loath the BBC 'and everyone in it', as Vice-Chairman, and the ebullient former Grenadier Guardsman and head of Times Newspapers, Marmaduke Hussey, as Chairman from 1986. Though Hussey knew little about broadcasting, and absolutely nothing about the BBC, his job, as Norman Tebbit put it, was to 'get in there and sort the place out'. The new Chairman obligingly declared the Corporation to be 'a sick place where no-one has a grip', and presented himself as a man on a perpetual mission to uncover fresh examples of its incompetence or wickedness. To help him he had as his willing partner the former Labour minister, Joel Barnett, identified firmly with the right wing of his party, who had by now succeeded Rees-Mogg as Vice-Chairman. The Board of Governors, meanwhile, was described variously as 'an unfortunate combination of low calibre and high prejudice' and 'ranging from the steely through bombastic to cranky'.[7]

This was not just deeply demoralizing to staff. It also marked a significant shift in power inside the Corporation, with Governors intervening more widely than before in major policy decisions and day-to-day management. Formally, the Governors had always had enormous power, but the tradition had been to use it sparingly. Now, they were more unabashed and set a series of danger-ous precedents. They insisted on viewing *Real Lives* before transmission, and demanded its withdrawal; they put pressure on the BBC's Board of Management to settle a libel action against the 'Maggie's Militant Tendency' edition of *Panorama*; above all, they began to exercise in full their right to hire and fire Directors-General. Between them they engineered, in turn: the summary dis-missal in January 1987 of Alasdair Milne, a man they suspected of being temperamentally unable to introduce the internal changes needed after Peacock; his replacement by the Corporation's leading accountant, Michael Checkland; and the appointment of John Birt—first, in 1987, as Deputy Director-General in charge of news and current affairs and then as Checkland's successor from 1992.

THE BIRT REVOLUTION ARRIVES

Checkland's ascension in 1987 was greeted with some dismay by many BBC staff. Here, they thought, was a money man rather than a programme-maker, someone happy to describe the BBC as a 'billion pound business'. And the message seemed clear: henceforward balancing the books would be a priority. As it turned out, Checkland surprised many by his ability to look beyond bean-counting. He had, after all, served the BBC for more than twenty years: he was decent, loyal, modest, cleverer than most allowed, and he cared passionately about pro-grammes. Most important of all, he had the knack of being able conjure up badly needed pots of money at short notice from reserves prudently set aside in an obscure corner of his accounting system. He thus proved to be thoroughly adept at making savings while generally minimizing any disruption to output or working practices. Under him, the BBC quietly but effectively tightened its belt without too many howls of pain from inside.[8]

Quiet efficiency, however, only went to suggest how little was being done to introduce the radical economies that would satisfy the government, or indeed the Governors. It was John Birt's arrival in 1987 that marked a real watershed in this respect. Here was someone who had never worked for the BBC—who had, indeed, been rejected by it when he had applied in his youth to be a trainee. Since then he had experienced a meteoric rise through the ranks of commercial television, first at Granada and later at London Weekend Television, where he had been responsible for the austere and serious current affairs programme *Weekend World* and the distinctly more populist entertainment of *Blind Date*.

He cut an unfamiliar figure on his arrival at Broadcasting House. One Corporation old-timer had pointed out that 'a traditional BBC man is basically a Civil Servant with a secret spangled tutu worn under his suit'. Checkland's choice of outerwear was reckoned to be from Marks & Spencer. Birt, famously, wore Armani. Even more famously, for those at the Corporation with longer memories, he had been an arch-critic of the BBC's own standards of journalism—the author with Peter Jay of the 'Bias against Understanding' *Times* articles of 1975. Even as Deputy Director-General, then, he was someone highly unlikely to be content with catching flak: he looked like a man with an ambition to make his mark.[9]

Birt knew full well his status as an outsider. He was, as he later put it, 'as welcome as a Protestant made Pope'. And his first pronouncements did little to dispel any distrust, for they made clear his disdain for what he had found. There were good programmes being made, he admitted, but the Corporation was a 'bureaucratic monolith' riddled with waste and with no proper budgets; staff and facilities had 'accreted for years, relentlessly expanding without challenge'; it was culturally resistant to change, cut off from the wider, brisker, more entrepreneurial world of Eighties Britain—more civil service, Church, or public school common room, still, than 'Covent Garden or Soho'; and it had 'no governing brain' to guide its responses to government policy—or, indeed, to direct its journalism, which had consequently become lightweight rather than enquiring, and sometimes downright sloppy. At one editorial session he attended, a producer asked him which BBC current affairs programmes he liked. 'To be honest', he replied, 'there's nothing I like.' What he wanted, it appeared, was more specialist journalism, more analysis, more focus on stories of historical significance, more scripting and planning in advance. The truth of a news story, he implied, could be arrived at intellectually through proper research, not necessarily through the rather more random and risky tradition of journalists digging around and following their noses. Above all, good journalism—indeed, good broadcasting—was best achieved through a proper system of managerial control. If the structures were correct, he seemed to believe, the right sort of programmes would follow. There would, for example, be full-scale reorganizations of departments—not the least of which was the merger of news and current affairs across Radio and Television—as well as new posts and job titles, new working parties, new editorial guidelines, new ways of brokering deals, new mechanisms for commissioning programmes, new mission statements, new rigour about editorial standards. In short, a new way of working.[10]

Much of this 'Birtist' rhetoric rewrote history. It certainly overlooked the BBC's very real experience of cutbacks and staff purges at the time of *Broadcasting in the Seventies*, or again in 1975 and 1980—not to mention the creation of new structures of financial control after 1969, or the elaborate mechanism of programme review which had ensured editorial policy was disseminated throughout the Corporation. But the Director-General's claim to represent a break with the past was an important part of his project. How else might a sceptical government be convinced that the BBC was truly reforming itself? How else might a stay of execution be won, unless the BBC visibly adopted for itself the culture of markets, choice, and efficiency? Birt was no Pol Pot, as one of his chief detractors had claimed, but he certainly promised the BBC its own Year Zero.

On the face of it, little of this appeared to have much to do with Radio Four. Indeed, Birt showed little immediate interest in BBC Radio as a whole. Not long after he had arrived in 1987, he admitted that he had not been listening very much on the grounds that he was too busy fighting a television ratings war. It was difficult at this stage to judge whether his professed ignorance would amount to a future for Radio of benign neglect or one of subjugation, but the signs were, on balance, promising. If he had a gut instinct, it was that the radio networks were 'in altogether better shape' than BBC Television. Radio's journalism 'needed refreshing' but it had not 'lost its way' as he thought television journalism had done. Radio Four, in particular, was 'a treasure trove of intelligent news, information and wit'.[11] The changes made by Ian McIntyre at the time of the Annan Report—tightening scripts, encouraging more analytical current affairs, attempting to widen the range of reportage—had evidently paid dividends. McIntyre's successor, Monica Sims, had continued the emphasis on quality and rigour, trying to shift the focus away from Westminster a little, but certainly offering no encouragement to slacken standards. The Peacock Committee had also provided a clean bill of health, having fixed on Radios One and Two as the obvious candidates for privatization, should the government be so inclined: Radios Four and Three were deemed to be self-evidently broadcasting in the public service. Even a Board of Governors packed with Tories presented little danger, since, as members of the opinion-forming class Radio Four was in any case likely to be their first choice of listening. Governors might express an opinion on various programmes—particularly what they had overheard on the *Today* programme every morning—but they were unlikely to bring the network crashing to the ground. Radio Four appeared to provide a model of what worked well in the BBC and of where the Corporation was distinguishing itself from the commercial sector in matters of quality. It had, so they assumed, a 'guaranteed place in the sun'.[12]

Even so, the wider context of change and turbulence mattered, for the network could not exist in glorious isolation. Any rows with the government over bias, for instance, were bound to suck in Radio Four, if only because it remained the BBC's main outlet for news and current affairs, and because its breakfast programme seemed to be influencing the British news agenda more than ever before. As Margaret Thatcher's Press Secretary, Bernard Ingham, once admitted: 'Most damage to Government–BBC relations was done between 6.30am and 9am by my former *Guardian* colleague, Brian Redhead.' Birt's suzerainty over the BBC's journalism from 1987 seemed to draw some of the sting out of the government's attacks: most ministers now believed that something was being done at last to sort out the rank and file. But the price paid internally seemed to be an overpowering editorial supervision exercised by Birt and his deputies, and this applied to all those programmes on the Radio Four schedule that came under the purview of the new and mighty News and Current Affairs Directorate. Staff on the main sequences—*Today, The World at One, PM, The World Tonight, The World This Weekend*—as well as the main current affairs programmes—*Analysis, File on Four,* and so on—were now subject to exactly the same strictures and guidelines as their colleagues in Television. And they showed themselves just as bemused—or exasperated—by the new fashion for micro-managing working practices. One much-ridiculed example was the issuing to every producer and presenter of a long memo entitled 'Interviewing on the BBC'. It was, as Sue MacGregor said, 'a strange guide to send to experienced broadcasters'. So too was a brochure doing the rounds a few years later that informed journalists, among other things, of the times when bulletins were broadcast. As one producer told the *Daily Telegraph*: 'If I ever forget what time my own programme is transmitted this will be very useful. Other than that it is a complete waste of time and money.'13

In a climate like this, it was hardly surprising that George Fischer's old Talks and Documentaries department tried desperately to halt its incorporation into Birt's new directorate—and that staff in radio's Current Affairs Magazine Programmes lopped the first two words off their departmental name so that they, too, might escape News and Current Affairs. By and large, resistance was futile. The new directorate was now the centre of gravity within the BBC and even those producers on the margins of journalism found themselves caught in its orbit.

The political and financial necessity for savings by the BBC also had its impact on Radio. Indeed, in many ways Radio was hit hardest by cuts in resources: being such a cheap medium, the amounts of money involved were smaller and there was less fat to be trimmed. The overall prognosis was not good. While the Peacock Committee sat in 1985 and 1986, and the diminishing returns of the licence fee took inexorable effect, economies had to be found right across the Corporation. One internal working party, with the ominous-sounding epithet 'Black Spot', dug up £32 million of potential savings in the spring of 1985, mostly in behind-the-scenes facilities.14 This could not be the end of it, however, since the need was not just to make cuts but also to make sure that they were noticed: they had to shout loudly of a BBC embracing efficiency day in day out. Hence a further round of cuts, this time worth around £75 million in current expenditure and more still in capital spending, was unveiled in 1991, through a report called 'Funding the Future'. On Radio Four, successive economies meant reducing the number of handcrafted feature programmes on air during the daytime, and replacing them with more repeats. Plans to extend the number of VHF transmitters in Scotland, Wales, and Northern Ireland were also curtailed, thereby prolonging the inability of listeners there to hear Radio Four on anything other than long wave. The need for savings also lay behind a large cut in the number of drama serials, a reduction in technical support available to producers in the studios, the ending of contracts for actors in the Radio Drama Repertory Company and for singers in the *Daily Service*. Perhaps most dramatically it lay behind the ditching, at the Board of Governors' instigation, of Dick Francis's grand plan to create a new Norman Foster-designed radio building in the West End, first, in favour of a much smaller affair next to Television Centre in White City, and then, five years later in 1990, the sudden abandonment of even that diminished fall-back.

Behind the ad hoc measures, there was usually some strategic thinking at work, and most of it threatened to change the way Radio Four operated in one way or another. There was briefly talk of the network taking sponsorship, rather in the manner of National Public Radio in the United States, or perhaps being available by subscription. Other, less shocking ideas took a firmer hold. Brian Wenham, who had taken over from Francis as Managing Director in 1986, saw one long-term task as 'tilting' resources further away from the evenings and towards the daytime, when radio audiences were largest. This 'Dark Hours' policy, as it was labelled, would mean fewer networks during the evenings—Radio Four, for instance, combining with the regional services in Wales, Scotland, and Northern Ireland after 7 p.m. Efficiency could also be trumpeted by moving production effort out of London to regional centres like Manchester and Bristol, where, so it seemed, some studios were habitually underused. There was even talk, well before John Birt's arrival in 1987, of radio producers working alongside television colleagues, in areas such as sport, light entertainment, drama, and news and current affairs.[15]

Sharing staff, office space, and raw programme material between Television and Radio would obviously save overheads and tighten editorial control. But it struck a blow at the sense of pride and independence in Broadcasting House. 'Bi-medialism', as it came to be known in the fully fledged form that John Birt introduced, raised the disturbing prospect of radio being constantly subordinated to the demands of the larger medium. Most of those who worked in news and current affairs instinctively inhabited a collective identity as journalists: bi-medialism held few terrors for them. But for others in Broadcasting House who believed radio to be a medium in its own right, it prompted deep and enduring gloom.

PRODUCER CHOICE, PRODUCER VOICES

The sense of pessimism among radio staff reached one of its many peaks in 1993, when a main plank of Birt's reforms fell into place: the introduction of an 'internal market' under the rubric of 'Producer Choice'. One of its architects was Michael Starks, who had been so instrumental in plans for changing the structure of the radio networks between 1978 and 1983. What Birt now called Starks's 'take-no-prisoners' quality produced a scheme in which the fashionable concept of market testing was introduced throughout the Corporation—on April Fools' Day.[16]

Put simply, Producer Choice involved a nominal share of the BBC's over-heads—the cost of studios, catering, administration, transport, and so on—being charged to each individual programme team or department, so that the true cost of the facilities producers had supposedly been taking for granted would be brought home to them. Long and ill-disciplined studio sessions, unnecessary trips, flashy new equipment, more actors than were strictly necessary: all these inefficiencies would be squeezed out of the system as producers faced what Birt called 'the full blast of market pressure'. Since producers could now choose to look outside the BBC for facilities rather than be stuck with using in-house support staff, while these same support staff were denied the freedom to tout for any compensatory business of their own, Producer Choice was also designed to rid the Corporation of 'excess capacity'. In this respect, it was stunningly effective: more than 10,000 employees were made redundant or 'transferred out' by the end of the decade. And where they were 'transferred out' *to* was the 'independent sector'. Since 1992—as part of a deal to stave off yet another government plan to privatize Radios One and Two—the BBC had imposed on itself a pre-emptive ruling that henceforward Radio would source up to 10 per cent of its programmes from private production companies. The fact that a private production sector barely existed in radio, as it did in television, was beside the point. A full-blown one would be created. Staff could leave the BBC, set up their own companies, and then win contracts with their old employer to make the sort of programmes they had done before—but, it was assumed, at lower cost.[17]

With its market rhetoric—'sleepy old departments . . . transformed into business units', the BBC transformed from a command economy into a 'trading institution'—Producer Choice was guaranteed to appeal to a Conservative government, which, though no longer ideologically opposed to the BBC, still extolled the virtues of 'value for money' and, of course, 'choice' itself. It was also hoped that the fledgling independent sector would gradually inject a new style of programmes into the staid old Corporation, making it less monolithic in tone. Certainly, it implied a wholly new organizational structure, since the meaningful distinction between 'Radio' and 'Television' was now less important than the one between 'purchaser' and 'provider'—a situation that, by 1996, produced the logical outcome of forcing on the BBC a complete division between production and commissioning. From November that year, it was decreed, no one in Broadcasting House any longer worked for 'Radio' as such. Controllers running the four networks now joined those running BBC 1 and BBC 2 in constituting 'BBC Broadcast'—the purchasing side of the Corporation. Meanwhile, on the 'supply' side of this trading relationship were the vast majority of producers—whether from radio or television. They now worked in a gigantic division called 'BBC Production', and within that, were assigned to one of eighteen bi-media units such as 'BBC Drama', 'BBC Entertainment', 'BBC Topical Features', and so on. The idea: to 'make programmes more efficiently', share ideas and reduce duplication of effort.[18]

Whatever the rhetoric, the reality was unedifying. A Controller of Radio Four was in charge of relatively small amounts of money, compared with, say, the Controller of BBC 1 or BBC 2. But the number of separate programmes he or she needed to commission in order to fill the schedule over the course of a year was much greater: 'thousands of one-dollar shows', compared with television's handful of 'one-thousand-dollar shows', as one Controller put it. Yet Producer Choice demanded that the cost of every aspect of each individual programme production now had to be identified. Each act of commissioning therefore generated a mountain of paperwork that seemed disproportionate to the problem. Indeed, one producer who decided to work out the cost of ordering a new lightbulb for his office calculated that it amounted to £42 worth of total bureaucratic effort. In a medium as cheap and simple to produce as radio the large number of transactions being generated seemed Kafkaesque. Producers complained of having to spend time on budgets and paperwork at the expense of thinking about their programmes—being 'bogged down in a mire of bumf' as one put it. What made matters worse was that so much of this bureaucracy seemed to destroy economies of scale. In the old system, for example, producers needing a particular piece of music would borrow a recording stored at the BBC's central Gramophone Library. Now that the library was obliged to make an internal charge of £8 for each separate loan, producers realized that it was marginally cheaper for them to buy their own copy of the record from a high-street shop. Each business unit 'saved' a notional amount of money, of course, but the BBC as a whole was spending considerably more. The danger was that producers would decide it was better to hold back—abandon the trip to the record shop, or spurn the advice of the BBC Pronunciation Unit, or neglect to get a bundle of newspaper cuttings, and save the £10 or so that would have cost. But with fewer transactions taking place, internal resource departments found they had to charge even more for their services to survive, thus becoming steadily less cost-effective. There was a real risk that internal trading charges were becoming locked into an upward spiral of their own making.[19]

Senior editors in Broadcasting House, while welcoming some degree of transparency in costs, were determined to protect radio from the worst effects of this absurd imposition. Controllers and the old heads of departments gradually introduced block deals for studios and resources. This was clearly against the spirit of the internal market, but it reduced to a much more manageable level the number of individual transactions and ensured a minimal level of job security. Even so, much that was frustrating, not to say demoralizing, remained. The creation of BBC Production in 1996 left all but one of the eighteen new bi-media units headed by television people. Radio producers, now in huge departments overwhelmingly devoted to television, felt abandoned by the networks they served; those running the radio networks, in turn, had no power to nurture production talent; each department devoted more and more time to working up proposals in order to survive—knowing that 90 per cent would be rejected and that any accepted would be at someone else's expense. The whole process of commissioning had now been formalized. Controllers complained that schedules were 'locked down' in advance, making it more difficult for a supposedly fleet-footed medium to respond intuitively to events or ideas as they arose. Production staff grumbled that they faced months of uncertainty and the constant need to woo layers of commissioning editors with proposals 'honed more finely than any actual programme'. Creativity and trust and cooperation: all, it seemed, were being squeezed as much as costs. A sclerotic effect appeared to be creeping through the entire system. And there seemed little prospect of relief. The *Midweek* presenter, Libby Purves, tentatively asked the Director-General when things were going to settle down. His answer? 'Never!'[20]

With talk of permanent revolution, the cumulative effect on morale was predictable. As one observer put it, a 'widespread cynicism, both angry and bemused, swept through the Corporation'. Some of this was simply a collective unease over job security. Some of it, however, expressed a real fear that an 'old BBC' was about to be lost forever. Libby Purves tried to capture the ethos of this dying regime when she recalled 'the ghastly 1990s' in her memoirs. Once upon a time, she wrote, the Corporation was stuffed full of 'Oswalds', a type she named after the elaborately dysfunctional, anorakish figure played by Timothy Spall in Stephen Poliakoff's celebrated drama about a threatened photograph library, *Shooting the Past*. 'An Oswald', Purves went on to explain, 'is someone who holds the soul of an institution in his hands; who cares passionately about the detail and the tradition and the wonder of what he deals with.' Such 'donnish, otherworldly figures' had not been highly paid, she said, but they had been tolerated, protected even. Now, like the Picts, 'they were driven out or driven underground'. If complex, serious, witty, erudite programmes still got made—and they did—it was in spite of the new structures, not because of them.

It has to be said that not everyone thought of the *ancien régime* as an unalloyed fount of creativity. Even in Broadcasting House, many managers welcomed what they saw as a more business-like approach to Corporation life. One of Libby Purves's producers at the time, Chris Paling, also painted an ambivalent picture in his satirical novel, *The Silent Sentry*, which he chose to set in Broadcasting House during exactly this period. In one comic scene, a group of seen-it-all-before producers gather at a weekly departmental meeting to sell reheated ideas to their editor, the cynical narrator explaining the verbal shorthand in use as programme ingredients are lobbed back and forth:

A 'follow-up' was a story the producer discovered had been done by another producer the week before—but with different guests. An 'exploration' of a subject was one in which the two or three guests all knew and felt exactly the same about the item in question: they would then have a 'discursive' discussion which was shorthand for meandering, consensual, and usually boring. A 'polemic' or 'polarised' discussion was one in which two people shouted at each other for about six or seven minutes (the format, of course, much favoured by news producers). A 'character' interview was usually a mentally deficient person with a regional accent. A 'human interest' interview... was one in which the interviewee was a victim of something—a rare disease, child abuse, alien abduction, a cult, the police or criminal fraternity, HIV, CJD, racism, sexism (most isms, in fact) or, occasionally, their own success.[21]

And so the list goes on. Elsewhere in Paling's novel we discover members of BBC staff 'jobbing' it, content to while away their working hours doing just enough to keep 'the quality sufficiently even to avoid attention: positive or negative'.

And yet, even here, there is an elegiac tone that echoes Poliakoff's. 'Real art', one of Paling's old hands explains, 'has to be allowed to ferment among the inertia of creative inactivity.' Unfortunately, he adds, 'creative inactivity cannot be costed. And in this brave new world of "efficiencies" and "choice" and "transparency", it *don't* fit.' Our hero, the slightly overweight and lethargic producer Maurice Reid, sees that he and his colleagues are 'a dying profession': 'I just want to cry all the time', he tells his doctor, before revealing the depths of his sadness, his anxiety, his feeling of 'valuelessness'. 'Change. Revolution. The arrival of the market economy', his doctor explains. 'It's no different, I imagine, from what's happened to those of us in the Health Service... Like alcohol, food, and, ah, sex, change is good in moderation. One can have too much of it.' Reid's editor, meanwhile, a man in his mid-fifties itching deep down to retire early and leave the country, survives the many purges only to be sucked into the lower reaches of management and face a future of endless hours in meetings: 'liaison meetings, strategy meetings, meetings with resources, meetings with editors, meetings with controllers, watching dull people in ill-fitting suits writing dull things on whiteboards, projecting inane statements onto screens... patronising me with gobbets of American management speak...' He stays, it seems, because despite everything, here in the BBC 'those who complained about the system most vociferously were those who loved it the most wholeheartedly'. For such people, 'it was impossible to say how the Corporation worked: it just did'. Yet when they looked all about, this unspoken understanding was being reduced by focus groups, management gurus, and alien processes, into mission statements, Venn diagrams, and spreadsheets. Commercialism and managerialism had taken hold of the collective consciousness. 'The fabric was crumbling.'[22]

In these fictional images drawn from personal experience, as in so much else that staff were saying to each other or to their contacts in the Press at the time, creativity was being defined as less a matter of managerial structure (*pace* John Birt) and more as the fruit born organically from the collective effort of ordinary staff who were sustained by an underlying, if sometimes grudging, loyalty to the BBC. Producer Choice seemed to reflect a disdain for nurturing such people's long-term careers as creative people—even if it allowed them to survive as business managers. Guarantees of future work evaporated, as contracts shortened and staff turnover rocketed. Continuity of experience was being lost, and so too, it was feared, was the ethos of working as part of a team, working in some tangible way for the public service, working by instinct as much as by preconceived format, and working to maintain quality at all costs.

It was exactly this lurking sense of betrayal that motivated one of Radio Four's most respected voices, the BBC's Delhi Correspondent Mark Tully, to speak out against the Birtist Revolution in a very public industry forum in 1993. Since the Corporation depended so much on 'individual human talent', he told the audience, it needed to retain 'some flexibility, perhaps even an element of chaos, to allow for experimenters and eccentrics'. What he claimed to see instead was a place where bureaucracy, and worse, *fear*, was rampant. His words constituted an act of open dissent, and within days a halo had been painted onto his photograph in the foyer of Broadcasting House. Administrators quickly removed it, and John Birt responded by complaining of 'old BBC soldiers sniping with their muskets'. The mood was set, and the military metaphors for what was happening inside the BBC proved irresistible. As one of the Corporation's distinguished drama directors put it at the time, it seemed 'like the Americans in Vietnam, trying to win a war by exterminating a culture'.[23]

THE COMPETITION FOR AUDIENCES

In the meantime, deregulation of broadcasting had proceeded apace. Quite apart from the prospect of more television channels broadcasting throughout the day and eating into radio's remaining peak times, there was the proliferation of commercial radio to worry about in the competition for audiences. In the circumstances, Radio Four's share of the audience could surely only diminish—very gently, admittedly, though nonetheless relentlessly: from about nine million tuning in each week in 1986, for example, to nearer eight million by 1989. As it happened, this fall was not nearly as marked as it was for Radio One or Radio Three for much of this period: Radio Four was probably doing as well as could be expected.[24] But the prospect of three *national* commercial radio stations did not bode well since it soon became clear that one of them was destined to supply news and speech. In 1986 and 1987 there was open talk among policy-makers of this new speech channel being seen as a direct competitor to Radio Four, even talk of Radio Four being kicked off its VHF slot to make way for it.[25] When the station did finally open in February 1995, as 'Talk Radio', it had to make do with a medium wave slot; it was also quickly apparent that this newcomer was sufficiently downmarket and under-resourced to offer no real threat. Indeed, by this stage, Radio Four's audience figures were stable, even gently rising. Yet, as happened in 1973, the BBC had by then spent several years worrying ceaselessly about what sort of competition *might* be in prospect and how it ought to respond in order to meet it. If it was going to have to change, the Corporation always preferred to do so *before* a commercial rival arrived, not after. And the direction of change required for a network like Radio Four seemed clear. If it was to prevent its overall ratings from falling further, and to provide a more balanced spread of social classes in its audience, it would have to reach beyond its heartlands of the middle class and middle-aged.

This was a familiar cry, of course, and even those well disposed to the network had always exhibited spasms of guilt—or frustration—over its 'excluding' tone. Radio's head of Religious Programmes, Colin Semper had praised the rich mix but worried over whether it 'did enough to attract and hold younger listeners'. His colleague, the head of Music Programmes, Ernest Warburton, had complained that there were 'still too many ladies with condescending home counties attitudes and accents' for his taste. And soon enough John Birt was joining in: yes, Radio Four was in good shape, but 'it is skewed far too much in its concerns and its appeal towards the southern middle classes', he announced in 1993. He made clear that its appeal would have to be 'broadened'.26

This did not tell managers in Broadcasting House anything they did not already know. Controllers of Radio Four were only too aware that their audience ratings would steadily decline as their audience aged, unless new listeners were constantly recruited. Most Controllers had been keen to widen the social mix, and generational appeal of their network. Most also recognized that programmes of minority appeal needed to be balanced by a scattering of popular ones in order to achieve a minimum level of ratings—indeed, in order to remain part of the mainstream of national consciousness and avoid drifting slowly into the margins of British broadcasting. Their difficulty, as always, was *how* exactly to go about broadening the station's appeal without offending those who already listened. This, indeed, was the biggest—and most perplexing—question that Controllers had to confront, day after day, in the decade to come.

Throughout the late 1980s and 1990s, a whole series of detailed audience research reports on this topic were conducted, and the results were full of foreboding. One showed that the only thing both 'established' listeners and 'potential' listeners agreed on was that it was middle class and 'mature' in tone. The two groups diverged on whether this counted for it or against it. Established listeners thought the image alluring. They liked the fact Radio Four was 'well presented', interesting, and that it sometimes surprised them. If the station was a person, they said, it would be 'a reliable, modestly successful, well-informed, interesting, humorous professional man', somewhat conservative but not dull, 'laid-back, well-educated, middle-of-the-road...not short of money but not polluted with it'—in short, 'how we all want to be, eventually'. They talked of a 'Radio Four voice' that was familiar, professional. They worried about bias, 'bad' language, too much news, and too many 'heavy' and confusing plays. But

generally they liked it as it was, and their one recurring message to the Controller
was simple enough—'please don't mess it around'.[27]

Potential listeners, on the other hand—those who had tried it occasionally but
needed more persuading to stay—saw Radio Four, if it were a person, as a 'plump
antique dealer'. They thought programmes were too long and therefore too
difficult to 'join' or 'leave'. They wanted a little *less* speech and a little *more*
music. And what—they asked—about a serial that was a little jollier than *The
Archers*, 'as light as *Neighbours* or *Eastenders*'? Or changing the title of *Woman's
Hour* for male listeners so that they could talk to their friends about what they
had heard without getting 'funny looks' in the pub?[28]

There was little if any overlap here: clearly almost any move to entice potential
listeners risked great offence to those already devoted. Indeed, to the ultra-
loyalists, Radio Four, despite being a collection of disparate programmes, had
become an organic whole. It had a tone, an attitude, a style that was somehow
recognizably its own. And it had woven itself so effectively into their lives that its
transformation was now unthinkable. One couple had told Monica Sims of how
Radio Four was 'the finest companion anyone can wish for... we rejoice in your
fellowship seven days a week'. Others had written about it keeping them 'sane', of
it being their 'lifeline', of it being 'not merely for amusement, information or
pleasure' but of being 'as vital' to them as food and warmth.[29] It was, in short, the
kind of thing worth *fighting* for.

And here was another watershed in 1983. The rumbling campaign to 'save'
Radio Four from the worst of Aubrey Singer's and Dick Francis's plans over the
previous five years had hinted at what might be provoked by any clumsy act of
force majeure. The listeners had shown themselves to be highly educated, opinion
forming and well connected. They had not at that stage been very organized. But
the times were now in favour of popular complaint mutating into popular action.
This was the year when 100,000 CND supporters linked arms at Greenham
Common; when, in the field of broadcasting, do-it-yourself expression revealed
itself in the sudden eruption of urban 'pirate' radio stations, the founding of the
Community Radio Association, and the craze for Citizen's Band. Sociologists had
been talking of the 'revolt of the Middle Classes' since the mid-1970s,
when ratepayers had grumbled, anti-airport campaigners had leafleted, even
private armies had been mustered. They believed that nothing quite as organized
as the French Poujadistes would ever materialize in Britain, so strong was the
reluctance of the native middle classes to acknowledge anything like a coherent
class consciousness. But now, they wrote, 'this could be changing': the will to
form networks of support was emerging, slowly, haltingly.[30] And the Radio Four
listeners were not immune. Among the 2,000 or so letters of protest that arrived
at Broadcasting House during the furore over *Radio for the Nineties* was one from
Jocelyn Hay in Kent. She wrote not to complain, but to warn. An association had
just been formed, she told Sims at the beginning of March. It would represent
'The Voice of the Listener', and press statements and campaign literature would

follow.[31] In November the organization was formally launched. From that point on any deliberations over Radio Four had to contend with an organized lobby, growing in number, well versed in the art of dealing with sympathetic journalists, demanding representation, and passionately committed to defending the status quo.

So the strength of feeling among long-standing Radio Four listeners was more audible than ever. Their predilection for familiarity was no secret: the audience data spoke for itself. 'If the BBC wanted a quiet life', John Birt acknowledged, it would 'never change a thing on the network.' But, of course he, for one, was *not* after the quiet life. The BBC was changing, and so too would Radio Four. Moreover, his task was to make the change as public as possible. Controllers, by contrast, preferred stealth, but they, too, saw the virtue in forcing the pace a little. As their audience researchers had told them, 'the conservative demands of established listeners need not rule out some *subtle grooming* of Radio Four's image or content to make it seem more desirable'.[32]

Here, though, was the nub of the problem. In the overwrought climate of the 1980s and 1990s, with a government constantly breathing down the neck of the BBC, with competitive pressures intensifying the battle for audiences, with a Director-General busying himself with the politically necessary work of talking up his own reforms and talking down those of the past two decades, with production staff suspicious and resentful, with listeners increasingly agitated over their right to have a say—with all this going on, even 'subtle grooming' looked like a Trojan horse for more horrifying alterations to come. *Any* tampering with Radio Four was therefore going to be bitterly contested. And, as events were to prove, the fear of change could so easily get out of hand.

The network had already shown itself best suited to organic evolution, trying to become a little less formal ever since the mid-1960s. It would continue to do so both during and after Birt's tenure at the Corporation. As Lawson Dick had said, weeding and planting was a continuous process. But if the upheavals at Radio Four throughout this period were less dramatic than some feared, they were also going to be bolder than many wished. For there was undoubtedly a gathering urgency to changes in the schedule as the 1980s progressed. Indeed, they sometimes proceeded in such fits and starts that the impression was created of panic inside Broadcasting House—what looked like a 'twitchy populism', a loss of confidence in the value of Radio Four's traditions by those who should have been its guardians. Certainly, the outrage of loyal listeners gathered momentum too, as they became more organized and more convinced they were being betrayed.

The determination of those running Radio Four to find new, more socially mixed, and preferably younger listeners, gradually became the issue that seemed to unite all other complaints. What it all added up to was *popularization*. And for several years, whatever managers did to give the station the grooming they felt it deserved—whether it was simply to provide more entertainment, or to exude more 'warmth', or to sharpen news coverage, or to modernize religious programmes, or to boost audience ratings at certain times of the day—it was interpreted as playing a part, possibly sinister, in this larger plan. In one way or another, it lurked behind almost all the arguments about what listeners and broadcasters really cared about most—the programmes themselves.

11

Provocations

'*Radio Four needs to toughen up . . . Let the Radio Four listeners howl. Their unique ability to squawk does not entitle them to a fossilised image of their own past.*'

Sunday Telegraph, 31 May 1987

Programmes on Radio Four were lightning rods. Anxiety over the BBC's internal upheavals, over the search for an acceptable mean between 'popularity' and 'distinctiveness', over the need to find new listeners without losing old ones: all this would find public expression in the reaction to individual programmes. For those on the outside they were the most sensible way of judging the health of the BBC. New programmes, or any changes to existing ones, were the ultimate measure of the Corporation's ability to move with the times—and to do so by absorbing the best features of the age rather than the worst. Even in the 1980s and 1990s, most of the Radio Four schedule remained as it had been for years. So continuity was the dominant theme. But new Controllers would always have new ideas, and in the decade-and-a-half after 1983 Radio Four was in the hands of two men who clearly wished to accelerate the rate of change wherever they could. In fact, there was to be innovation in every corner of the schedule. Most of it was modest; some of it, however, was radical.

This chapter surveys the most celebrated examples—and focuses on the strident resentments they provoked. So here, instead of one all-encompassing storyline there are several: the events that surrounded *Rollercoaster* in 1984 and *Citizens* in 1987, the various attempts to woo younger listeners in the early 1990s through new comedy and new presenters, rows over language, the role of *Today* and *Thought for the Day* in the mornings, the rescheduling of *Woman's Hour* in 1991, the failure of *Anderson Country* in 1994. It is a parade of programmes that tries to look at Radio Four from several different perspectives. But there is a unifying theme of sorts, for in every case the rows these individual programmes provoked revealed a Radio Four that continued to be a surrogate for all sorts of wider, deeper disgruntlements among its audience. In the late 1960s and early 1970s, a lot of anxiety had become focused on questions of permissiveness and of political bias. In the 1980s and 1990s, these two issues retained their power to offend, and were joined by other, newer, concerns—over mediocrity, blandness, superficiality, folksiness, rudeness, aggressiveness, political correctness. Some of these would later be grouped together and labelled 'dumbing down'. Some, perversely, sounded more like a process of 'toughening up'.

Could *all* this possibly be happening simultaneously? The contradictions were noticed: commentators wondered whether Radio Four was undergoing some sort of identity crisis. What emerges in retrospect, however, is the story of another stage in Radio Four's evolutionary journey from an age of Paternalism to an age of Pluralism.

ROLLERCOASTER

The appointment of David Hatch as the new Controller of Radio Four in 1983 captured some of these tensions perfectly. Here was a popularizer *and* loyalist rolled up in one. When he was told he had got the job he was on a tour of radio stations in the USA, gathering tips on the dark art of scheduling, formats, personality-led shows, American glitz—all the vital ingredients of streamlined, pop radio. He was then the Controller of Radio Two: someone who knew a thing or two about popular tastes and the public demand for friendly presenters. He had brought Kenny Everett back to the BBC, brightened up the Jimmy Young programme, added more sport to his network, making it all 'less middle-aged, less dusty at the edges' in the judgement of one radio critic. He was fiercely loyal to his closest colleagues, capable of being impatient, brisk in manner, convivial, a showman as much as a manager, and above all witty: someone who promised to bring a sense of fun and irreverence to his new job. Yet Radio Four was also in his blood. For two years before joining Radio Two in 1980 he had been a hugely influential Head of Light Entertainment, for four years before that the head of network radio in Manchester, and, even further back, the Cambridge Circus performer and pioneering producer of *I'm Sorry I'll Read That Again* and *Weekending*. His parents had been Home Service listeners, and while growing up he had absorbed the notion that here indeed was the citadel of BBC values. He talked of Radio Four as 'the soul of the BBC', 'the last bastion' of the Reithian mission to inform, educate, and entertain. To be its Controller was like inheriting a long-established country estate that had to be handed on intact. 'I love it and will cherish it', he said not long after he had taken up the post. Even if he were a madman with an axe, he suggested, there was no way he could destroy it: 'There are too many people watching every move I make.'[1]

Yet move he did. For a start, he decided that the way things were done would have to become a little sharper and more businesslike. His immediate predecessor, Monica Sims, had been strikingly down to earth in her routines: eating sandwiches at her desk at lunchtime, hurrying around the building with carrier bags rather than executive briefcases, often a few minutes late for wherever she was going. She had impressed many staff with her abilities: able to throw parties with 'not a single administrator in sight', to spot (then groom) individual talent, to quietly—almost surreptitiously—coax a raft of new programmes onto the air, above all to defend the network's core values.[2] What Hatch wanted was to draw attention to the network and to do what he had once done to the Light Entertainment department, namely to create a 'buzz'. 'Radio Four is one of the best kept secrets from the British public,' he announced, 'and I want to change that . . . I want them to know what we have done, are doing, and will do, very loudly.'[3]

His first message to the fourteen departmental heads supplying Radio Four was one of reassurance, and it was delivered in his characteristically disarming style. He would be dropping in, he said, and floating all kinds of ideas, 'digging up' every root he could find. But producers should be told that as yet he had 'no set opinions' about anything:

If they hear rumours flying about the place they can rest assured that it's merely chatter. I don't want to get wind of campaigns that I am for this or against that. I am simply going to listen, prompt discussion, and then go away and have a good think. So the message please is they will be consulted and their views taken into account, and in return I don't expect to 'hear of wars and rumours of wars'—Matthew, Chapter 24 v6. The chapter then goes on in Verse 28 to talk of 'wheresoever the carcase is there will the eagles be gathered together' so stop at Verse 6, thank you.[4]

Hatch then told the departmental heads that he was looking to them for 'revolutionary *and* reactionary tendencies'. But it did not take long for the Controller's own preference to be revealed. Almost the first thing he did was to recite to his colleagues the full day's schedule from ten years before, to demonstrate how very little on Radio Four had changed: *Today, Start the Week, Daily Service, Morning Story, You and Yours, Desert Island Discs, Woman's Hour, Afternoon Theatre, PM, Six o'Clock News, Just a Minute, The Archers, The Monday Play, The World Tonight, Book at Bedtime, Kaleidoscope, Closedown.* 'It's somewhat daunting to think that all those programmes are still there,' he told them, 'and where will the new programmes come from or be placed if something doesn't move?'[5]

There had been *some* changes, of course. Indeed, under Ian McIntyre it was widely thought there had been too many. Even under Monica Sims, whose guiding principle had been gradualism, *Listen with Mother* had been abandoned as a lost cause, new series such as *In the Psychiatrist's Chair* had emerged, and *Analysis* and *File on Four* had been given daytime repeats (for women stuck at home, Sims said, 'who wanted some things with a bit of meat to them').[6] There had, however, been no major innovation to disturb the essential tone of the network. Sims had been seen as keen on civilizing values, good stories, and programmes with charm. Radio Four, she had told her superiors, was 'bound to change', but only 'imperceptibly' so.[7] After five years of this, Hatch was eager to move things on. Indeed, he felt it was now vital to do so, if there was to be any hope of reversing the long-term decline in ratings. 'Numbers are not unimportant, even on a cultural channel', he reasoned. Radio Four cost £9 million more than any other radio network each year, and it needed to repay this by enticing enough people to listen. How much was enough? 'A smidgeon more than not enough.' How could they be enticed? By offering 'more joy and delight'. Radio Four, he thought, was too relentlessly serious for its own good: not just telling of the world's disasters and problems through its news service, but raining down upon its listeners a succession of programmes that told them they had brought the wrong insurance, might have cancer, might have a drink problem, and so on, ad nauseam:

Perhaps one reason we are losing audiences, albeit slowly, is that in the wee small hours, as they recall all that they have heard, our listeners conclude that they are failures as providers, fathers, neighbours, sons and lovers, and that there's nothing that they can contribute to help the sick, the disabled, the poor and the inadequate, and they shoot themselves in despair. Radio Four is a theatrical expression of the whole of life but there are two masks in this theatre and one bears a smile; we must bring pleasure as well as tragedy.[8]

Once again, it was a horticultural metaphor that revealed what Hatch had in mind. Radio Four, he said, was a wonderful piece of old English countryside, 'with great oaks, fields of King Edwards and ripe corn, new saplings and surprising colours'. He would not dream of putting a motorway through such arcadian delight. But he thought it needed 'a path or two so that the uninitiated can see the view and learn of its pleasures'. 'The odd tree must come down, the bottom meadow needs ploughing and resowing and perhaps we need to shoot the odd rabbit.'[9]

A concrete scheme soon emerged. In scheduling terms, the 'bottom meadow' was the middle of the weekday morning. Several million listeners deserted the network after each edition of *Today*, and there was usually a three-hour gap before some of them drifted back. Controllers called it the 'mid-morning dip'—something that few other networks seemed to suffer to such an extent—and it was at its worst on Thursdays.[10] The 'rabbits' to be shot were *Desert Island Discs*, *Down Your Way*, and *Gardeners' Question Time*. They were not going to be killed outright, but 'rested' for a few weeks. As any Controller knew, only by taking away the old would there be any room for the new. And in this case the newcomer was *Rollercoaster*, which arrived on 5 April 1984.

Rollercoaster's novelty—and, it seemed, its problem—was that it was not really a programme at all. Every Thursday morning, instead of separate 'built' programmes following *Today* in stately procession until *You and Yours* at midday, listeners would get three hours of Richard Baker acting as a guiding host. He would preside—warmly, smoothly, pervasively—over a pot-pourri of programme fragments: news, chat, topical phone-ins, traffic reports, features. There were a few familiar land-marks—an abbreviated *Daily Service*, a *Morning Story* read by the former *Coronation Street* actor Peter Adamson, Laurie Taylor offering a guide to modern manners, a satirical radio strip-cartoon called *Able Seagull Herring*, a running computer game, and ad hoc link-ups with local radio stations around the country. Programme boundaries were blurred: they would not necessarily start at rigidly fixed times, and Baker would introduce them as seamlessly as possible.

For producers, it had the flexibility of the live magazine format: without the roadblocks of a fixed schedule, the running order could be stretched, squeezed or reshuffled, and the interwoven chat could be fluid enough to respond to the events of the day. For listeners trying to do other things about the house, it had the advantage of being more easily digestible, less demanding in its timetable. For a Controller concerned with ratings, it had the advantage of removing clearly identifiable programme junctions, which were always an unwelcome opportunity for listeners to reach for the off-button. Its looser, more informal style might also attract a newer, younger audience altogether.

The newspaper critics, on the other hand, sensed the first trumpet blast of the approaching barbarian hordes. The *Guardian* launched a broadside at Hatch well before *Rollercoaster* was born, declaring in a leading article that 'People who talk in terms of "seamless packaging" are almost always up to no good.' 'On behalf of the cultural establishment', it added, 'we warn Mr Hatch: we are not to be bought in this way.' As far back as August 1983, the paper had started referring to plans for a 'three-hour American-type programme'. And the unfavourable impression of something alien to Radio Four—perhaps a transatlantic offering, certainly something with the whiff of Radio Two or local radio about it—had stuck ever since. Now that *Rollercoaster* had arrived, it was generally agreed that it lived down to its reputation. Baker embodied the uncontroversial; the title was suspiciously whizzbang; some of the content too frothy. Indeed, the entire project seemed a waste of effort, since speech radio—unlike music radio—could never *really* be listened to in the background and would therefore always be switched off when people drifted to work, regardless of the precise form it took. What really discomfited the critics, however, was that this new programme, designed apparently to cause minimal offence and provide no noticeable breaks, flew in the face of the Radio Four ethos. Its listeners liked to think of themselves as *discriminating*. They wanted to switch on when they chose and switch *off* when they chose—an option *Rollercoaster* seemed to take away.[11]

The programme was given six months to prove itself. But during that time everyone seemed to be breathing furiously down the Controller's neck. Quite apart from the steady stream of ridicule from the Press, the programme faced regular scrutiny at the Board of Governors and in the BBC's General Advisory Council. The Director-General, Alasdair Milne, and the Assistant Director-General, Alan

Protheroe, were both jumpy—Milne because he worried over the Governors' proprietary interest in the network, Protheroe because, as he told Hatch, he was at that 'dangerous age' when one felt that 'part of Radio Four's charm is its predictability'. Fellow editors also offered distinctly mixed reviews. Some thought the overall content nicely eclectic and that it 'generated a feeling of companionship', others that it was 'predictable' and the overall presentation 'somewhat bland'. Even the programme's producers confessed to not always being clear what the programme was trying to do. In the face of all this, Hatch admitted that he felt 'very exposed' and needed all the friends he could get.[12]

It was therefore either brave or foolhardy—but certainly in character—that he chose to throw himself upon the mercy of the listeners themselves by inviting them to write in. Out of 1,167 letters eventually received, only 176 were positive. The other 991 arrived swinging mean expletives and plenty of vicious assaults on the Controller's mental state: 'What's on your mind, if you will forgive the overstatement?' 'If brains were dynamite, you couldn't blow your nose.' 'Go back to Radio 2—you're someone who will always revert to tripe.' 'Hate mail on Radio 2 was gentle and polite,' Hatch recalled: 'they simply asked for a change of mind about whatever.' The Radio Four audience, he had discovered, insisted on 'instant reversal, copy to 10 Downing Street, Chairman of the Governors, the DG—and all my friends think so, too'. Despite this, he professed to be enjoying all the fuss. He even went on the offensive. His crime, he suggested, had been the equivalent of having served claret with fish: detractors were 'intellectual hooligans'.[13]

What no doubt stiffened his resolve was the hard evidence of a ratings success on his hands. By December, Hatch was able to tell the Board that audiences were up by nearly a third on the previous year's figures. Those listening to *Rollercoaster* were also staying tuned for longer than most Radio Four listeners. And, after a shaky start, levels of appreciation—the so-called 'RI' indices—were averaging a respectable figure somewhere between 76 and 80. Best of all, there were more under-45-year-olds and fewer over-65-year-olds listening to Radio Four on Thursdays than on any other day of the week. *Rollercoaster* was attracting new listeners, and, overall, they were younger and more socially mixed than was typical for the network. This fulfilled almost every ambition the Controller had for it, and soon enough there was confidential talk of it becoming a fixture, even of there being two editions a week.[14]

Unfortunately, audience research had also revealed that the much sought-after patronage of these slightly younger, more working-class listeners was won at the cost of alienating a significant part of the 'core' middle-class audience. Nearly half of these thought *Rollercoaster* was not up to usual Radio Four standards, over a third of them found it trivial, and most of them were now listening for *less* time than before. This represented a notable backlash among traditionalists, and could not be set aside. The question of *Rollercoaster*'s future was therefore finely balanced. The consensus among senior managers was that the experiment ought to be allowed to continue. Hatch thought much of the initial criticism had been prompted by the title itself, and that any permanent programme would have to find a new name. But there were other considerations, not least the financial implications of keeping it going. And since the licence-fee settlement that autumn had again been ungenerous, the prospect of enough money being available was worsening all the time. By May 1985 financial expediency had quietly buried it for good. 'It's a pity', Hatch declared, 'because *Rollercoaster* proved an audience winner, but it required more staff and it required more money, and both those things are unobtainable now.'[15]

Throughout its existence, David Hatch had faced sustained and heated personal attacks for *Rollercoaster*'s offence against Radio Four's traditions. Yet the programme was merely the most recent manifestation of a longer-term struggle to shake up the whole tone and style of the network by changing the way it was presented on air. The specific idea of a three-hour 'rolling' sequence for the mid-morning had been mooted in June 1982—fully one year before Hatch took charge of the network—when Dick Francis was seeking the extra flexibility he had wanted during the Falklands War; planning for a new 'live daily morning talk show' had been going on within the Current Affairs Magazine Programmes unit earlier still. In fact, the idea of a looser style of scheduling on Radio Four had been circulating around Broadcasting House since 1978.[16] As had the idea of a looser style of presentation—not so much within programmes as *between* programmes. A transformed art of continuity, it was thought, could 'pull together' the disparate programmes with their hugely different styles and brow-levels, and help create an attractive 'warmth' that was felt to be missing—in short, give Radio Four a stronger overall identity, and one in closer sympathy with the informality of the age. The Presentation Editor on Radio Four, Jim Black, had talked of announcers being transformed into 'network presenters'.[17] Monica Sims's deputy, Richard Wade, had even developed a scheme in 1981 to turn them into 'hosts', charged with providing a little casual banter—and, indeed, there were off-air pilots that summer, with Barry Took and Barbara Myers among the freelance talent deployed at the microphone in place of the regular continuity announcers.[18]

Rollercoaster, then, did not arrive on Radio Four as the unbidden and aberrant monstrosity some thought. It was rooted firmly in a long and continuing effort within Broadcasting House to 'loosen' the schedule and project a friendlier face. Its real mistake had been to appear too big and too sudden a change for a network used to evolution through tiny, incremental steps. It had also appeared at a particularly troubling time for the BBC. In 1984 and early 1985, the Corporation faced extraordinarily hostile coverage in the press. Most of it involved accusations of profligacy or editorial transgressions on television. But the overall impression—as sections of the press had hoped—was of a Corporation constantly stumbling in its attempts at providing licence fee payers with both quality and value for money. *Rollercoaster* seemed to fit the larger pattern. It affected only one weekday morning on the Radio Four schedule—a tiny part of the overall mix. But in the prevailing climate of distrust, it was all too easy to imagine it as the beginning of a larger executive plan to hurtle pell-mell towards a ratings-driven future *even* on Radio Four. If *Rollercoaster* were to be successful, many wondered, what then? Would the format spread like Ground Elder through the rest of the Radio Four garden?

Hatch had recognized the dangers. His original conception had been to run *Rollercoaster* on *only* one wavelength. The call for more flexibility could not be answered, he felt, except by forcing a full-scale split in the network, creating a choice for listeners between two different Radio Fours: one of 'built' programmes on VHF and one of live, loosely linked programmes, capable of being interrupted for news, on long wave. It was not to be. Because managers were under enormous pressure to save money and *reduce* the number of BBC services, and because there was still the problem of Radio Four VHF being almost impossible to receive in parts of the country, the plan for a split was vetoed. Without this, the Controller knew even before his experiment began that its chances of succeeding were not high. 'I'm not particularly optimistic that it will prove popular on its own', he warned privately.[19]

In ratings terms, this pessimism turned out to be misplaced. But Hatch was pragmatic enough to realize that decent audience figures were not enough to compensate for all the howls of pain and anger. Nor did he want to repeat McIntyre's experience and get bogged down in a long campaign he could obviously not win.

Hatch's consolation was to see that other programmes in the same 'looser' spirit might be possible in the future. One, appearing briefly in the summer months of 1985, was *Pirate Radio 4*, a live three-hour magazine for children and teenagers that spread across Thursday mornings, and, like *Rollercoaster*, was a carapace for shorter programmes hidden within: new episodes of *Doctor Who*, readings, studio guests, outside broadcasts. As it happened, the critics were generally unimpressed. 'Local radio at its worst,' one wrote: 'banal, uncouth, noisy and mindless.' But the seeds had been sown for a new way of production that would reappear in the not-too-distant future: the bringing together of people from several different departments to create free-wheeling programmes refusing to fit neatly into any predetermined genre. Hatch claimed on the eve of his departure as Controller that 'little that any broadcaster does lasts beyond the midnight pips'. But it was to become clear over the next few years that even the most unloved programmes were able to have many descendants, as well as many ancestors.[20]

CITIZENS AND CELEBRITIES: TALKING TO A YOUNGER GENERATION

When David Hatch was elevated to the role of Director of Programmes for BBC Radio in July 1986, he was replaced by Michael Green, the head of network radio in Manchester, who had been a producer of *Analysis* and the founding editor of

File on Four. Before the new Controller had even finished his first press conference, he was in no doubt about what lay in store. Everyone, but everyone, he noticed, seemed to have a view about the schedules. 'I had not recognised the extent to which Radio Four is an institution as much as a BBC channel', he confided to a colleague. He also soon discovered that as an institution Radio Four was not fully his to lead: a listener had dispatched a welcoming letter telling him bluntly that, 'You are simply the custodian of *our* network.'[21]

But even temporary custodians like to beat the bounds of their parish, and Green was no exception. After his transfer south he cast an eye over the schedule. What struck him most about Radio Four was that 'the light and shade of the network was very much in favour of the shade'. 'Extended listening', he concluded, 'would encourage you to slit your wrists.'[22] Coming from a man schooled in BBC current affairs of the most serious kind, this seemed a curious reaction. But Green was someone who also enjoyed the pleasures of life— travelling to France (he had studied languages at Oxford), walking canals, visiting the cinema—and he firmly believed that entertainment was as important a part of the mix on Radio Four as were education and information. If his documentary-making past made its presence felt, it was to be in the cool and calculated way that he identified problems and prepared the way for possible solutions.

A careful perusal of the listening figures soon revealed the network's weak points. There was the enduring problem of the mid-morning dip that *Roller-coaster* had tried to address. The mid-afternoon schedule looked just as fragile. The comedy was a bit hit-and-miss. There were too many single plays that disappeared into the ether without making an impact—and, more to the point, that came and went without encouraging in the audience the habit of listening regularly. Indeed, Radio Four listeners as a whole seemed to be among the most 'promiscuous' on the dial: fewer than one in six of them now listened *only* to Radio Four; the rest also tuned regularly to Radio Two, or Classic FM, or local radio; one in five of them were regular Radio One listeners.[23] Clearly, loyalty was a scarce resource. Especially, Green felt, in the case of people in their twenties and thirties, for whom there were more and more distractions in the newly deregulated, ever-expanding field of entertainment. Securing the attention of this generation would be a major prize. And the signs were that it *could* be done. Since its launch in October 1986, the *Independent* newspaper had managed to build an upmarket circle of readers, of whom fully half were under 35 years old. As things stood, just 12 per cent of Radio Four's listeners were in this age group.[24] The Controller looked about and saw a large cohort of people who had gone to university, who were reading broadsheet papers, who were interested in the cinema and the theatre and contemporary affairs—an intelligent, and inevitably mainly middle-class crowd, but one for whom Radio Four probably sounded, as one unkind critic put it at the time, like the voice of 'an England composed entirely of lifeboatmen, bell-ringers, corn-dolly braiders and retired tea ladies whose grandfathers had their dressings changed by Florence

Nightingale'.[25] A brutal parody, perhaps. But perception was as important as reality in the battle for hearts and minds. As the BBC's own audience research showed, those who had never yet listened to Radio Four only knew it by its reputation—and that was very much as the aural equivalent, as one respondent put it, of 'a square in a brown suit'. When asked what might draw them to Radio Four, these much sought-after people told BBC researchers that it would be 'a younger image', 'more publicity', 'modern "faces" known from TV or other radio networks'.[26]

This was all food for thought. And with such findings in mind, Green formulated a two-pronged movement to 'gently refresh' the network in a way that would draw in this new generation. First, he would try to 'toughen up' its tone: make it sharper, brisker, grittier, more rigorous, and more controversial, so that lively debate could rage and, occasionally, sparks might fly. Secondly, he would offer more lightness and fun: bring in fresh voices, add glamour, take risks.[27] The bulk of the schedule would remain undisturbed in the middle of these two poles of change. But the desired long-term effect was clear: there would be a wider range and richer texture than ever before. Woven into the large, warm blanket of the reassuring and familiar on Radio Four, there would be the unmistakable thread of a contemporary, and sometimes dissonant, world.

Green's first move was one of his boldest. In the autumn of 1986 he turned for help to his colleagues in the Drama Department. Could it be, he asked, that the mid-morning dip might be propped up, a modern tone introduced, younger listeners secured, and the loyalty of the audience 'locked in', all through the creation of a popular serial? The prospect was enticing. There had been plenty of talk for years inside Broadcasting House about whether the network could find a way to balance *The Archers* with something a little more urban, more working class, grittier—in short, the radio equivalent of *Coronation Street*. Green, true to his northern roots, was an aficionado of the Granada series himself. But his need was for something less class bound and a little younger.[28]

After months of deliberation, what the Controller unveiled in October 1987 turned out to be closer in feel to BBC 1's *EastEnders* or Channel Four's *Brookside*: a twice-weekly series, *Citizens*, featuring characters—almost all in their early twenties—who shared a flat in the fictional Limerick Road, London SW21. Here resided Alex, her lodgers—Julia, Michael, Anita, and Hugh, all old friends from university—and a sitting tenant, Ernest. Together they had the social and ethnic spectrum of 1980s Britain wrapped up. Alex was a single mother who worked at a local arts centre; Julia and Michael were Irish Catholic twins from Liverpool, the one in management, the other unemployed; Anita was a hospital doctor from a Hindu family in Birmingham; Hugh was a working-class merchant banker from Scotland. The influence of *EastEnders* was obvious—not least in the plan to broadcast it twice a week in half-hour episodes. But the two producers in day-to-day charge of operations, Marilyn Imrie and Anthony Quinn, wanted to create a serial that would also stand on its own merits. They had spent six months researching ideas: working with estate agents to find the right kind of house, looking at all the ways in which the action might be able to roam around the country, finding people on whom their main characters could be based, trying to ensure the serial would be 'real' as well as funny.[29]

Unfortunately, *Citizens* quickly gained a reputation for unrelenting drabness. It was, the reviewers suggested, more soap box than soap opera: 'radio drama's answer to watching paint dry'.[30] Characters seemed to spend most of their time bickering with one another, there were too few cliffhangers, too many meandering storylines, too many issues. It was, in other words, *too* true to life. 'At the end of each episode of *The Archers* you're left wondering what's going to happen to Jack or Shula', Green pointed out. No one seemed to care very much about the fate of Alex and her friends.[31]

Throughout 1988 and 1989 there followed endless discussions between the Controller and the production team over how to sharpen scripts and characters. After another year, and the drafting-in of a new editor, Clive Brill, someone who had the advantage of having worked for *The Archers* and Radio One, there was further effort at making it more entertaining and 'less angst-ridden'. But since it had been launched precisely in order to lift Radio Four's sagging mid-morning audiences, its success could only really be judged by a cool-headed look at the ratings. In this respect, it lagged well behind *The Archers*, with about 350,000, rather than 950,000, listeners for each episode. This was no worse than figures for other programmes in the mid-morning slot, but the ratings were clearly becalmed when they needed to have risen. The only good news was the higher proportion of working-class listeners among its audience. This allowed the network to shift its 'demographics' a little in the right direction. Yet, as with *Rollercoaster*, even this achievement seemed to have come about through the desertion of previously loyal middle-class listeners: a demographic shift by default.[32]

By 1991, after more than three-and-a-half years of waiting, Green's patience ran out and he decided that this particular experiment would have to be brought to an end. Perhaps if *Citizens* had run every day, in thirteen-minute episodes like *The Archers*, it might have stood a better chance of seeping into the national consciousness. But that would have doubled its costs. Neither the money nor the effort seemed quite worth it for a series so resolutely refusing to please.[33] Its technical qualities, however, *had* been admired in Broadcasting House, and something of its style therefore survived. In 1994, for example, the creator of Channel Four's *Brookside*, Phil Redmond, a leading advocate of location recording, realistic settings, younger characters, and sharper dialogue, provided Radio Four listeners with *Doctors*, a six-part hospital drama that represented another attempt at a new serial format and had a clear echo of *Citizens'* gritty texture. This was also the era of the so-called 'Brookside-ization' of *The Archers*—a label coined by the critics not just because the serial's new editor Vanessa Whitburn was a graduate of Redmond's television drama, but because Ambridge was featuring younger characters and 'issues' as never before.[34] *Citizens* had failed to establish a foothold, but, like *Rollercoaster*, it had not really disappeared without leaving a footprint.

The critics had suggested a great deal had been riding on *Citizens* because it was emblematic of Radio Four's 'new, young, vital, contemporary, thrusting, aware, not-just-for-fogies image'.[35] And so it was. But it was just one manoeuvre in a much wider campaign. And elsewhere on the field of battle there were more encouraging signs of success.

Green's determination to 'toughen up' some of the network's speech had taken a decisive step forward in 1987, for example, with the departure of Richard Baker from *Start the Week*. There had been concern for some time that the series was failing to rise above the mundane, despite the bad-taste jokes of its regular contributor Kenneth Robinson. Baker's immediate replacement, Russell Harty, brought to the programme his barbed and unpredictable wit, and after his untimely death in 1988, Melvyn Bragg brought to it a new reputation for gravitas and an ability to provoke what the producer called 'a slight rub' among the heavyweights gathered in the studio. The transformation was remarkable. The first ever edition back in 1970 had featured a cookery slot and a discussion on pigeons; twenty-six years later it was featuring a three-way conversation between Arthur Miller, Gore Vidal, and Amos Oz. Bragg's irritation with guests who failed to serve up intellectual red meat was evident, and a steady stream of listeners grumbled at what they saw as his habitual rudeness. Professional critics, on the other hand, adored Bragg's 'rampaging' manner and the promise of blazing arguments between intellectuals. Green had always talked of the programme as a potential flagship for the network. Now he rated it as a 'must-listen-to' programme. And not just because of the rows: ratings, too, were steady or rising. By 1996, with a figure of between 1 and 1.5 million listeners each week, it was overtaking the more middlebrow *Midweek*. Some of its listeners were even starting to ring Broadcasting House for advice on background reading on the scientific, literary, or philosophical questions under discussion. In short, *Start the Week* was demonstrating that even at nine o'clock in the morning there was a demand for serious debate—a demand that Radio Four might actually be helping to create.[36]

Presenting a more *youthful* face to the world was altogether trickier, since it involved a high-wire balancing act in matters of taste. The millions of older listeners were too valuable an inheritance to throw away by confronting them all the time with youth in full cry. Indeed, many of them had tuned to Radio Four precisely to escape from all their noise and brashness. If some manageable coexistence was to be achieved, there obviously needed to be some careful scheduling and a few compromises.

In fact, even under Green, there ended up being very few programmes that explicitly addressed—or spoke on behalf of—teenagers or young adults. Two notable exceptions to the rule were *The Radio Four Generation*, which charted the attitudes of a group reaching voting age at the time of the 1987 General Election, and a Young Playwrights Festival that ran for two weeks in 1988. The Festival was particularly unusual in that it handed over all Radio Four's regular drama slots to writers under 30, and among the scripts chosen was early work by Benjamin Zephaniah, as well as *Static*, the broadcasting debut of the novelist Jeanette Winterson. The series' editor Jeremy Mortimer had promised his writers that each play would be broadcast 'as written', imperfections, stylistic excesses, rough language and all. And there was certainly an unfamiliar rawness to some of the subject matter: the Edinburgh drugs scene, a Friday night in the lonely life of an unemployed man, a Rastafarian wanting to join the police.[37]

Generally, however, it was in the field of comedy that youthful irreverence could be heard at its most insistent. Green spent a great deal of time during his early years as Controller creating slots for late-evening shows, where the boundaries of taste could be nudged forwards well away from the prying ears of regular daytime listeners. One man in Light Entertainment who helped him considerably in this task was Jonathan James-Moore, a Falstaffian figure of unkempt red hair and beard who had been filling Douglas Adams's old post since 1978. As a producer, and then as head of department, James-Moore championed alternative comedy, and invested considerable effort in making sure his own talent-spotters were at the Edinburgh Festival Fringe and various stand-up events throughout Britain during the late 1980s and early 1990s. With its corporate ear thus closer to the ground, Radio Light Entertainment gradually caught up once more with television as the place where new performers and new formats were likely to be heard first. *The Cabaret Upstairs*, which brought the Comedy Store compère Clive Anderson to radio, *The Million Pound Radio Show*, which featured the talents, among others, of Andy Hamilton, Nick Revell, and Harry Enfield, *Saturday Night Fry* (1988), with the eponymous Stephen Fry, *The Masterson Inheritance* (1993–5), with improvisation from Josie Lawrence, Paul Merton, and Caroline Quentin, and *Whose Line is it Anyway?*, another improvisational format bringing together performers from several of the preceding series: these were just a few of the shows that established minor cult followings in the post-*Hitchhiker's* era, and which provided identifiable times of the day when younger listeners could find something to their taste on a network they generally spurned.[38]

Comedy aside, the affluent and well-educated baby-boomers in their twenties and thirties were generally seen by the Controller as people looking for programmes that were 'smart' or 'sophisticated'. These, of course, were elusive qualities, since one person's sophistication was another person's pretentiousness, and yet another's banality. A model of sorts already existed in the form of the chat-show *Loose Ends*. Some critics had shuddered at its self-congratulatory tone ever since it had been launched in 1985. But the brittle repartee that flowed between Ned Sherrin and his regular acolytes (which included Robert Elms, Craig Charles, Carol Thatcher, Victoria Mather, Emma Freud, Victor Lewis-Smith, and Stephen Fry) exuded a metropolitan chic that evidently had a certain appeal, for the ratings were good and the 'RI' index of appreciation reached a more-than-respectable figure of 80. It had an audience profile slightly younger than the Radio Four average.[39] The question, then, was this: was it the sort of trick that could be deployed elsewhere?

The issue was tested in a whole series of programmes that blurred commerce and culture and threw in a dash of metropolitan style for good measure. One such was *Consuming Passions*, a weekly magazine launched in 1988 that aimed to report on the worlds of design and style in the name of 'upmarket consumerism'. Two others in roughly the same mould were the media magazine *Mediumwave*, which displaced the trio of *News Stand*, *Stop Press*, and *The Radio Programme* in 1993, and a Sunday-morning programme devoted to food and drink called *Cut the Mustard*. *Mediumwave* was perhaps most emblematic of Green's underlying aims, in that it promised a 'rather younger and sharper' style. But it was also judged by the critics to range far too widely—and thus succumb rather too easily to a superficial kind of 'lifestyle' journalism. Similar charges were levelled at *Consuming Passions* (which, according to one acerbic review, allowed 'people to talk to each other for an hour about the cut of their trousers') and *Cut the Mustard* (described as a 'bewildering succession of lightweight items'). Indeed, for a while in 1993 there seemed to be no end to the number of disposable 'lifestyle' programmes getting on air. There was, for instance, *The Locker Room*, a vague stab at a *Woman's Hour* for men, which featured, among other items, a report on the agonies of men being intimidated in expensive designer boutiques, and which drew the barbed comment from one reviewer that it was full of nothing but 'pony-tailed, emasculated New Men' gabbling on about 'getting in touch with their emotions'. In this kind of critical climate, even those programmes that went out of their way to retain a judicious Radio Four balance of the serious and the entertaining were viewed suspiciously. Hence the pioneering Valentine's Day magazine show for gay men and lesbians, *Sunday Outing*, which included reports on the 'pink economy', the plight of black lesbians and gays in South Africa, and on gay and lesbian funerals, side by side with travel reports for 'hiking dykes', vaudeville from Blackpool, and a quiz slot called 'Queeries'—all loathed by many of Radio Four's diehards and damned by the *Sunday Telegraph* as too 'silly' by half.[40]

Green's problem was that when a few too many programmes of roughly the same hue arrived at roughly the same time, the professional critics would detect a larger pattern unfolding. And in this case what they saw was a Radio Four succumbing to some of the worst features of the Consumer Age: superficiality, disposability, an unhealthy interest in conspicuous consumption, and, in its desperate desire to please everyone in the free market for goods and ideas, an unwillingness to distinguish between the good, the bad, and the irrelevant. Radio Four, they suggested, was merely swapping a 'Home Counties bungalow image' for a 'Sloanie wine-bar-and-style' image, and betraying a 'slow but unmistakeable loss of substance and weight'.[41]

In this climate, *anything* the Controller did looked like a grab for easy popularity. Under Green, the departure of Radio Four's most venerated talent became a new running sore. Thus, when Brian Johnston left *Down Your Way* in 1987, there was outrage at some of those who succeeded him: celebrities such as the *EastEnders* actor Tom Watt, the weatherman Ian McCaskill, the astrologer Russell Grant. Worse still was the arrival that same year of Noel Edmonds from Radio One, whose Monday morning series, *Awayday*, succeeded in attracting nothing but undiluted venom from listeners and critics alike.[42] Soon, Robin Day was leaving *The World at One*, John Timpson was leaving *Any Questions?*, and *Private Eye* was quoting 'one very senior radio executive' preparing to dispense with the woman who had presented *Pick of the Week* since 1974: 'who the bloody hell wants to see the world through Margaret Howard's chintz curtains?' The answer, of course, was that very many Radio Four stalwarts did, since in her crisp, well-enunciated delivery they saw the very essence of what Radio Four was supposed to sound like. Which was precisely what made her an obstacle in the way of a younger, fresher style. The predicted expulsion came in November 1990 when Green gave her six months' notice of his intention to try a rota of new people in the *Pick of Week* chair. When her time was up the following May, Howard signed off her last programme with an item about female orgasms. 'So much for coming,' she quipped, 'I'm going.' But she did not go quietly. 'I don't want to be drummed out of Radio Four', she told the *Daily Mail* in a bitter tell-all: she was being forced out because the Controller 'wants black people, he wants youngsters, he wants to widen the range . . . the way things are going in radio they want trivia and personality'.[43]

Many of the new arrivals belied this somewhat bleak assessment. James Naughtie, Nick Ross, Sue Lawley, Jonathan Dimbleby: they were hardly light-weights, and their presence was a useful counterbalance to the likes of Noel Edmonds and Russell Grant, neither of whom, it is worth noting, were retained for long. Similarly, when Stefan Buczacki and his fellow *Gardeners' Question Time* panellists left Radio Four for Classic FM, having failed to secure guarantees of future employment from the independent production company taking over the series in 1994, their replacements—among them, Eric Robson, Geoff Hamilton, Pippa Greenwood, Bob Flowerdew—could hardly be accused of lacking in expertise.[44] But suspicions remained, especially over the number of personalities being imported from television. These, the critics suggested, were people used to being stars in their own right who did not necessarily have the self-effacement, or the natural gift for painting a scene in words alone, that the invisible medium required. In hiring them Radio Four was 'in danger of sounding less like itself and more like everything else'. It was Radio Four's *resistance* to fashion and showbiz that attracted listeners for life—provided, of course, they had reached 'the age of discretion'. As the *Daily Telegraph* pointed out, the twenty-five-to-thirty-fives for whom many programmes now seemed tailor-made were exactly the same people buying into the retro-styling of the Filofax and adopting *The*

Archers as a fashion accessory: if there was one thing they liked about Radio Four it was probably the Young Fogey image the network seemed intent on discarding.[45]

This was a powerful argument in favour of Radio Four aiming decisively for what *The Listener* called 'its natural constituency among the thinking classes and decision-makers', for it to remain 'true to itself'—waiting for new listeners to come to *it*, abandoning all efforts to go to *them*.[46] But in the circumstances of the time, doing this—and nothing else—would have been politically impossible. It was not just that the Controller was instinctively in favour of modernization. It was also that those above him in the BBC were quite clear that networks like his *had* to widen their appeal beyond their 'natural constituency'. If some of the programme changes that followed from this sometimes looked like a failure to distinguish clearly between the good, the bad, and the indifferent, it has to be remembered that paternalism was out of fashion: in the culture of the market-place, the customer's choice was supposed to be sovereign. If people genuinely wanted Noel Edmonds or Russell Grant on Radio Four, who on earth were the professional critics or the panjandrums of the BBC to disagree?

This, at least, was how one half of the rhetoric went. But there was still a strong notion within the BBC—and certainly among many of the programme-makers serving Radio Four—that Reith had been right when he said that people might not actually know what they wanted until they had heard it. There was evidence, too, that while much of the rest of the broadcasting industry was free to pursue an all-out ratings battle, Radio Four had a solid and vociferous constituency of listeners for whom enduring 'values' still mattered above all else. When 'Quality' and 'Popularity' came together, as it seemed to do in a programme like *Start the Week*, the Controller could breathe a sigh of relief. But for much of the time, he was navigating across treacherous terrain. Twenty years before, the great debate had been whether the BBC should lead or follow public taste. Yet public taste was now a fractured, complex, segmented thing, with ever more subtle distinctions between age groups, income groups, regions, and sexes. A Radio Four required to 'widen' its appeal was therefore a Radio Four destined to go on dividing opinion. Listeners would be offended. They might learn to be tolerant. Or they could simply get used to the fact that no longer would every programme they heard on Radio Four be exclusively for them.

LANGUAGE AND LITERATURE

There was one simple test of the limits of tolerance, for every now and then anxieties over the vulgarization of Radio Four—or indeed vulgarization in the world at large—were crystallized around the fundamental matter of language on air. And the sharpest rows of all were almost always provoked by *bad* language.

The enduring tension lay between descriptive and prescriptive postures, though the BBC had worked its way towards something of a compromise during the 1970s by refusing to ban certain taboo words outright but insisting on upwards referral through the editorial chain of command—while simultaneously encouraging a climate of sensitivity among producers. The rough-and-ready rule on swearing was expressed informally by one of Aubrey Singer's characteristic edicts: 'If these words sometimes come up naturally in the heat of the moment, fine. But I will not have people sitting down and *typing them out*.'[47]

Naturally, this was the kind of ruling that left plenty of room for transgression in the broader matter of 'rudeness'. And Michael Green's plan to leaven his schedules with more youth and informality, and with sharper, more entertaining exchanges, undoubtedly created the impression that private linguistic standards were leaking into the public domain rather more frequently than hitherto. Melvyn Bragg's abrasive style on *Start the Week*, for example, brought a stream of complaints about his being 'overbearing'. *Midweek* and *Loose Ends* were also collared regularly, one columnist complaining in 1989 of how they 'now seem to allow participants to throw around "Gods" and "bitches" as if at a private party'.[48] Many programme-makers remained surprised by the offence caused when plain language was deployed in even the most appropriate of circumstances. Sue MacGregor, for instance, was appalled to discover that merely saying the word 'vagina' during a discussion of a pioneering hysterectomy technique on *Today* should be the cause of agonized editorial discussion behind the scenes.[49] Yet offended people undoubtedly were—or at least a significant minority of those motivated to complain. 'Things have been said which suggest that Radio Four is not what it was', Mary Whitehouse announced in 1986.[50] Over the next two years sympathetic voices in the press started to urge the new Broadcasting Standards Council to turn its attentions away from the output of Television Centre and towards what was happening in Broadcasting House.

The real problem, as ever, was one of wildly contrasting expectations. As the BBC's Head of Religious Broadcasting, Colin Morris, put it in 1986, 'the plurality of opinions within the nation multiplies apace, the cultural flow moving strongly towards diversities of taste rather than unanimity'. Morris had been charged with trying to pin down some guiding principles over sex, language, and violence—the first attempt by the BBC to provide a coherent pronouncement on these matters since 1973. But even he almost admitted defeat. The norm, he agreed, was set by the producer's conscience, and it would become obvious that anyone who persistently overstepped the boundaries of public taste was in the wrong job. He thought expletives fairly harmless, though suggested a watch be kept on their frequency of use lest 'word pollution spreads like a blight through the land'. But hard-and-fast rules were as elusive as ever: deciding by fiat was 'like trying to paint a white line on a swirl of fog'.[51]

Drama, once again, forced the issue. Writers generally believed that, twenty years on from the abolition of theatre censorship, plays really should have been able to reflect what they called the 'language of today'. Yet awareness of public sensitivity had taught producers the virtues of self-restraint. 'The desired dramatic effect', the Head of Radio Drama pointed out, 'can often be better achieved by a small number of well-placed, well-chosen expletives than by a Pelion upon Ossa pile-up.' The main defence mechanism against public attack, however, had come with careful scheduling: harder-edged material for the Royal Court crowd in the *Monday Play*, safer stuff for the Chichester Rep folk in the afternoons. Unfortunately, there was a deadly design fault in the system. Since most evening plays were now being given an automatic repeat in an afternoon slot in order to boost writers' fees, there was always the risk of strong dialogue being put before those listeners least expecting it. As one critic argued, language deemed unremarkable at night arrived 'crashing like bricks through the windscreen' when heard in the afternoon.[52]

The problem came to a head in 1988 when Michael Green cancelled the scheduled afternoon repeats of two evening plays, Ken Blakeson's *Excess Baggage*, which had painted a raw portrait of life among army wives, and Frederick Harrison's *The Cassandra Generation*, a play about the Falklands War that included a descriptive sex scene. Green professed himself an admirer of Blakeson's writing, and thought *Excess Baggage* a 'fine' drama that was simply too violent in its language for afternoon listening. The previous Controller, David Hatch, who was now Managing Director of Radio, backed him up. 'Forty-odd "shits" in one of the husband and wife scenes in *Excess Baggage* and a barrage of verbal violence in *The Cassandra Generation*' was Hatch's succinct summary of the problem. Many in the Drama department, however, were outraged when they heard of the cancellation. Quite apart from what they interpreted as stifling self-censorship, they professed uncertainty over what was to be done in the future. Would all plays now have to be suitable for afternoon listening? Couldn't audiences be told to grow thicker skins? Might there be ways of accommodating tougher material through better signposting? Could Radio Four learn from film or television, by 'classifying' different dramas into the equivalent of a PG or 18 rating, or by providing the aural equivalent of Channel Four's then infamous red triangle?[53]

In June 1988, Green and Tydeman hastily organized a one-day seminar in Broadcasting House to chew over the issue. The writer of *Excess Baggage* spoke at the meeting, and admitted to having been taken aback by the cancellation. 'To omit the word "fuck" or "fucking" from any play about the army is to be a liar', he complained. 'If these plays are censored', he went on, 'writers will start to censor themselves, and you'll get weak-kneed drama.' The debate, however, extended far beyond the treatment of the two plays in question. In the fashionable spirit of glasnost, dramatists, psychiatrists, theologians, journalists, and listener representatives were all in attendance, along with members of BBC staff, to scrutinize the whole issue of language. The case against any overarching new code of conduct was put by producers such as Peter Atkin, from Light

Entertainment, and Jeremy Mortimer, Richard Imison, Clive Brill, Martin Jenkins, and Penny Gold from Drama, who generally argued that listeners did not have the right *never* to be offended and that edging all difficult material to late-night slots would amount to 'suffocating the very material that we want to promote'. How could listeners have their experience broadened or their sensibilities changed, the argument went, if they never chanced upon potentially shocking or offensive material? One of the writers for *Weekending* suggested that he, in any case, felt constrained enough already. Younger listeners probably wanted to hear the likes of Alexei Sayle, Gerry Sadowitz, or Billy Connolly, he thought, and 'it would be nice' to have their maniacal rage on air 'just for occasional use'.[54]

The argument for more caution was advanced most forcefully by Jocelyn Hay, from the Voice of the Listener group. She told BBC producers that broadcasting helped establish norms of behaviour: 'Our language is a living, organic thing and you hold its future health in your hands.' Her members, she said, were concerned most about 'lavatorial humour' on early-evening comedies and the 'sheer stupidity' of repeating evening plays in the afternoons. Rabbi Jonathan Sacks, who pointed out that he for one could not recall any instance of blasphemy on Radio Four, also told the meeting that he regarded *all* language as holy: the challenge in the public domain was therefore to 'retain a sense of the sacredness and, hence, of the necessary restraints of the spoken word'.[55]

The idea of the seminar was to air the issues rather than impose firm rulings. Yet one person's freedom of expression was always someone else's filth. True to form, the *Daily Mail* berated the whole affair as 'a fudged compromise that pleased no-one' since it had produced no guarantee that bad language would be banned outright.[56] Producers and playwrights, on the other hand, continued to mutter about a climate of censorship taking an ever-tighter grip. Green replied by pointing out that if he had really wanted to be censorious he would hardly have allowed either of the plays in question to be broadcast in the first place. Indeed, he said, if he followed what most listeners told him they wanted, he would scarcely be allowing any contemporary drama at all. As for the Managing Director, David Hatch, he was as incensed by what he saw as staff paranoia as by journalistic misrepresentation of the event. The general policy, he insisted, had not been changed—either by the seminar itself or by the treatment given to the two plays that had prompted it. 'In radio broadcasting', he maintained, 'in *certain* contexts, *perhaps* at *certain* times of day, *maybe* on *specific* networks, a degree of offensive language is *possibly* justifiable.' The italics were his, and they underlined his wish to reaffirm caution as the starting point for any debate on the matter. There were, however, a few new lessons to be drawn. First, that producers seriously underestimated the offence caused specifically by blasphemy, and that all departments therefore needed to 'tighten up in that area immediately'. Secondly, that if Radio Four wanted to retain the principle that serious drama should be allowed an airing before the larger audiences of daytime, each and every play needed to be 'stripped of *unnecessary* offence'. Thirdly, that more on-air warnings about imminent bad language needed to be provided. And finally, that there would no longer be automatic repeats for every evening play: they would henceforward be judged on a case-by-case basis.[57]

Having thus brought Radio Four's daytime drama under tighter supervision, the question now was what might be permissible in the late-night margins of its schedule. David Hatch had been clear after the seminar that he did not want on-air warnings to become an excuse for abandoning all restraint. Green also made clear that he had no plans, as he put it, to 'let language rip'. But as Controller he remained committed to finding more room for what he called 'tougher' material.

One obvious space to be exploited was *Book at Bedtime*. By 1990, it had been pushed from the 9.45 p.m. slot Green had inherited to the later time of 10.45 p.m. This extra hour made it harder to argue that children were likely to be listening, and a more adventurous repertoire of readings suddenly became possible. With the long-serving editor of the series, Maurice Leitch, now retired, a new editor, David Benedictus, made a conscious decision to mark the occasion by offering listeners *Lady Chatterley's Lover*, which ran abridged— but unexpurgated—over fifteen episodes at the beginning of 1990. A similar version of James Joyce's *Ulysses* followed. In both cases Green was confident of defending his position on the grounds that these books had long ago reached the status of literary classics. As for *Lady Chatterley*, the courts had cleared it. 'Who are we', he asked, 'to argue and fiddle about with it' after that? The experiment clearly paid dividends, since the number of complaints from the public after it was broadcast was encouragingly small: just twenty-one.[58] This represented a firm signal that more change in this direction was possible, and over the next few years, under Benedictus's editorship and with Green's blessing, late-evening listeners became steadily habituated to more grit in the book readings on offer.

There was, nevertheless, plenty of contemporary fiction in the high-street bookshops containing the sort of language that went well beyond what had ever been heard on Radio Four. For a *Book at Bedtime* keen on adapting more contemporary publications alongside the classics this was a problem. Neither Angela Carter's *Nights at the Circus* nor James Kelman's *How Late it Was, How Late*—two very different, but equally well-regarded novels of the time—went down terribly well, even cut to the bone. The solution proposed at the beginning of 1995 was to create a completely new slot even later in the day: *The Late Book*, which ran after the midnight news, and which, controversially, entailed a minor rescheduling of the *Shipping Forecast*. For its efforts, the new series quickly gained the popular epithet awarded earlier to *Lady Chatterley*—'Bonk at Bedtime'. Many of the *enfants terrible* of literary fiction in the mid-1990s were among its beneficiaries. Martin Amis (*The Information*), Armistead Maupin (*Maybe the Moon*), Jay McInery (*Bright Lights, Big City*), and Julian Barnes (*Metroland*) constituted the first wave of chosen authors; Margaret Attwood, J. G. Ballard, Salman Rushdie, and Don De Lillo followed. As if to offer reassurance to the traditional Radio Four audience, the licence accorded to *The Late Book* was balanced by *Book at Bedtime* returning to a somewhat tamer choice of material. A new editor now talked of sending his listeners off to bed 'with a smile'. The afternoon *Short Story*, the *Woman's Hour* serial, and parliamentary recess readings, meanwhile, continued their tradition of ensuring that genre literature—such as romance, crime, or children's favourites—was just as much a part of regular output as the classical canon and the cutting-edge. Indeed, one obvious sop to traditionalist sentiment came with a 1995 season 'to celebrate romance' with the novels of Georgette Heyer and Barbara Cartland.[59]

Such patronage, with Barbara Cartland at one end of the spectrum and Angela Carter at the other, was easily interpreted by the BBC's critics as yet another example of the Corporation's cultural centre of gravity swinging awkwardly from one extreme to another, a sign of a chronically confused organization. But the underlying philosophy was clear enough: to offer a sufficiently wide range to be able to claim with confidence that most licence payers would find something to please them. And, in the area of Radio Four readings at least, it is possible to see a centre of gravity moving tentatively more upmarket—or, perhaps more accurately, moving towards the more challenging and the more contemporary. It was, after all, not *The Late Book*, but the mainstream *Short Story*, which in 1995 provided its half a million or so listeners with Susan Sontag's account of directing *Waiting for Godot* in Sarajevo. Her book was involving, upsetting, intellectually stimulating, and as topical as could be. But by the mid-1990s it was no longer exceptional. In questions of taste, subject matter, and language, a willingness to push the boundaries a little in the matter of readings had helped Radio Four to sound more eclectic, sharper, and a little less nostalgic, than even just a decade before.

DUELLING AT DAWN: *TODAY* IN THE EIGHTIES AND NINETIES

When it came to controversy of a more overtly political kind, the most hotly contested programmes on Radio Four were to be found at breakfast time. In the late 1960s and the 1970s it was *The World at One* that had reigned supreme as the chief target of disgruntled politicians—especially when Bill Hardcastle and Robin Day had been in the chair. During the 1980s the mantle passed decisively to *Today*, where, more than anyone else, it was Brian Redhead who came to assume the role of the politician's—especially the Tory politician's—chief irritant. *Today* enjoyed Radio Four's largest audiences of the day: some 2.5 million tuning in between 7.30 and 8 o'clock each morning, some six million or so over the course of a week—figures that seemed to grow steadily well into the 1990s, and thus became ever more important to Radio Four's ratings more generally. It also became required listening for politicians, journalists, and other 'opinion-formers', largely through a virtuous cycle of cause and effect. Here was the one programme that succeeded, day after day, in having 'big hitters' among the government and the opposition as its guests, thus signalling to others with a role in running the country that here was the one programme on which they, too, should appear, and which, at the very least, should never be missed when getting ready for work.

Today's mutation into an organ of the British constitution had proceeded by incremental stages.[60] When Ken Goudie, a veteran of the Radio Newsroom, took editorial control in 1978 after the ill-fated experiment of *Up to the Hour*, the programme was streamlined by the removal of *Prayer for the Day* (which henceforth preceded the programme) and the insertion of more news summaries and headlines. The next editor, Julian Holland, brought experience of working for both the *Daily Mail* and *The World at One*. His main aim was to ensure a succession of serious and high-profile interviewees, and from 1981, when he took over, the programme gradually became heavier in tone and more overtly political. Holland wanted *Today* to be written about and noticed. Every set-piece interview was expected to create what the programme team called a 'news line': something that would be quoted in forthcoming news bulletins, or the *Evening Standard*, or the next day's papers—or preferably all three. His successor from 1986, Jenny Abramsky, had also worked at *The World at One* before editing *PM*. She was described by one regular presenter as 'someone who stood no nonsense, used her charm sparingly, and was in a hurry to get things done'. And what Abramsky wanted to get done was to turn *Today* into a programme that 'took everything forward' rather than spending its time reflecting on what had already happened. 'Our job', as she put it, 'was to set the agenda.' After only eighteen months, Abramsky was succeeded, in turn, by Phil Harding and, in 1993, by Roger Mosey—both political journalists to their fingertips. It was their era that saw the programme hiring its very own publicity officer and the programme team devoting itself at nine each morning to phoning the national paper's news desks with quotes from interviews that they might have missed. The impact of the programme on the day's news was monitored obsessively. Harding would watch BBC Television's *Nine o'Clock News* every night, and, as one of his producers recalled, if he saw on it any stories which had not been on *Today* that morning, he always wanted to know why. Mosey, yet another graduate of *The World at One*, adored the cut and thrust of politics. He wanted *Today* to reflect the minutiae of its daily unfolding, and he ensured that every twist and turn of British party politics was conducted in front of his listeners.

There were changes in presentation, too, and it was these that most struck the listeners as a measure of the programme's evolving style. Sue MacGregor had joined the programme part-time in September 1984, becoming its first regular female presenter since Libby Purves had left in 1981. She remained for nearly two decades, adding a quintessential Radio Four flavour to proceedings. As one reviewer put it, hers was the voice 'one would like to hear on the loudspeakers shepherding you to higher ground if ever the Thames Barrier broke down'.

Something of the same calming tone was evident in Peter Hobday, who had joined *Today* three years before MacGregor, but who was removed unceremoniously in 1996. Press speculation centred on the idea that he was too middle class, or too old; BBC managers implied he was too much the 'third man' in an era that demanded a high public profile for their flagship current affairs programme. Certainly there were colleagues, then and since, with more muscular track-records: John Humphrys, an experienced reporter who had worked his way up from local newspapers to presenting the *Nine o'Clock* News on BBC 1, and who combined a scepticism towards power and privilege with palpable machismo; Anna Ford, familiar as a newsreader on both ITN and BBC 1, a member of the original TV-AM breakfast team, and a person with deeply held political views unafraid to occasionally speak her mind; and, from 1994, James Naughtie, who had presented *The World at One*, been a Chief Political Correspondent for the *Guardian*, and was a man with a legendary depth of knowledge on politics. Measured against such apparently predatory creatures, Hobday came to believe that as 'a fat, middle-aged hack' he simply no longer fitted 'the lean, mean interview machine' that *Today* had become. 'When people say my interviewing wasn't as "sharp" as it could be, perhaps what they mean is that it wasn't invasive and I didn't feel the need to scream and shout.' Neither, as it happened, did his old colleague John Timpson, who had been in the presenter's chair off and on since the end of the de Manio era, but who had also left at the end of 1986 muttering that as the programme had become tougher and more political it 'wasn't the fun it used to be'.

For much of his time on *Today*, Timpson had presented alongside Brian Redhead—thereby forging a professional pairing that came to embody the programme's sound for a generation of listeners. Redhead-and-Timpson. They seemed to balance each other out and spark each other off: the one an irritant the other emollient; one speaking for the North the other for the South; one Town one Country; one Left one Right. They were, as one listener put it, a 'perfect and unbeatable duo'. Timpson exuded a taste for old-fashioned, rather courtly whimsy and an implicit respect for the Establishment. Redhead, a bad-tempered sprite behind the scenes, was cocksure, bumptious, clever, quick. He was also proud of his journalistic pedigree as the Northern Editor of the *Guardian* and Editor of the *Manchester Evening News*, and spoke, as a fellow presenter put it, 'for the clever, chippy classes'. His on-air style mellowed a little with time—a process some detected as early as 1982, when his teenage son was killed in a road accident and he was drawn towards a more deeply felt Christian belief, and which others associate with the diabetes and chronic hip pain that debilitated him later on. But he never softened enough to resist taunting those in power through a succession of quips and one-liners. And since it was just one party that remained in power, it was always the same party that remained the chief recipient of his attentions. Of the Boat Race he once told listeners, 'There was a time when such an important occasion divided the nation—now we leave that to the Tory party.'

His jovial references to endless repairs and traffic delays on the M6 could somehow be made to sound like merciless ridicule of government transport policy. Even his asides on the motorway's out-of-order emergency telephones were all too easily interpreted in Downing Street as coded attacks on the privatization of British Telecom.

Number Ten's interest in the programme mattered, for it allowed the entire Tory party to focus their general loathing of the BBC onto one programme and one person in particular. Mrs Thatcher's press secretary Bernard Ingham claimed that, apart from a daily glance at the front page of the *Evening Standard* or any press digests placed before her, most of the Prime Minister's knowledge of what was going on in the world was 'imbibed from the BBC's *Today* programme'— except, he added, 'when she cut herself off from its mischief'.[61] Others have suggested it was Mrs Thatcher's husband Denis who did most of the listening, and that the Prime Minister's irritation with its iniquities was prompted by his ready-filtered interpretations of what had gone on. Ingham's version appears, in fact, to have been closer to the truth, at least for the earliest part of her premiership. A BBC memo providing an account of a lunchtime conversation between a senior Broadcasting House manager and Mrs Thatcher's chief press officer in September 1979 confirmed that she listened to the World Service from 6 a.m., and then 'always switches to *Today* at approx. 6.30am and listens through to 8.45 am every day'. He then added, as Ingham implied, that her whole approach to the day was 'conditioned by what she hears on the *Today* programme'.[62]

Whatever change took place in her listening habits later on, *Today* always rankled. But it could not be ignored, simply because it was a trough from which the British media drank profusely. National newspapers invariably discussed its contents at their morning editorial conferences; the programme's interest in any given story would help create what journalists called 'critical mass', the point at which it became impossible for other journalists to pass by; ambitious politicians, especially those keen to catch the Prime Minister's attention, sought the imprimatur of an appearance. In short, no one in the opinion-forming class could afford to miss it. Even if there was occasionally a rather ritualized flavour to the daily jousting between Brian Redhead or John Humphrys and whichever government minister was on at the time, it was undeniable that *Today* was becoming a cockpit of national debate. Redhead talked of it being the programme in which one could 'drop a word in the ear of the nation', Humphrys of it being a place where politicians would always be held publicly to account. By the end of the 1980s, with deepening divisions among Conservatives over economic policy, Europe, and the leadership, it sometimes seemed that all the programme had to do was invite an MP or minister on air for three minutes and the British public would be witness to a ruling party eviscerating itself in public.

Unsurprisingly, a general air of tetchiness prevailed in relations between *Today* and the government. One of the most uncomfortable clashes came in March

1987, when Redhead was interviewing the Chancellor of the Exchequer, Nigel Lawson, on the morning after his Budget. When the Chancellor suggested that unemployment figures were falling as a result of government policies, Redhead put it to him that many new jobs were not 'real': they were low-paid and part-time, merely the result of special measures such as 'job clubs'. At that point, producers in the studio's control room recalled seeing a moment of 'controlled anger' unfold before them as Lawson made his reply:

LAWSON.   Well, you've been a supporter of the Labour Party all your life, Brian, so I expect you to say something like that. But you really shouldn't sneer at these job clubs, which are giving real hope to the long-term unemployed, getting them out of their depressed state of mind many of them are in and they are going to get real jobs.

REDHEAD.   Do you think we should have a one-minute silence now in this interview, one for you to apologise for daring to suggest that you know how I vote, and secondly perhaps in memory of monetarism, which you've now discarded?[63]

There were countless encounters of this kind: Lawson calling *Today* an 'opposition programme' in 1985; Peter Lilley repeating the allegation that Redhead was a Labour party supporter during another bad-tempered bout in 1991; Brian Mawhinney accusing presenters of asking 'smeary' questions during an interview with Sue MacGregor in 1996. And so on.

Some of this was clumsy anxiety over *Today*'s influence; some part of a much wider campaign of hostility waged against the BBC; some, as the Tory's Deputy Chairman, Jeffrey Archer admitted, was simply playing to the gallery. It was all too easy, he explained, to stir up the party faithful whenever they were feeling down by saying in a speech something like, 'Did you hear the *Today* programme last week, what a bunch of leftie communists.' He did not believe it for a moment, he confessed, but he knew it was enough to get his own audience cheering and shouting and screaming. Conservative commentators in the press were more than happy to fan the flames. Hence, when the Party's one-man 'Media Monitoring Unit' claimed in 1990 that a sample of the programme's output had shown a systematic bias against the government, the Tory peer Woodrow Wyatt used his column in *The Times* to demand to know how each member of the *Today* team voted. Not surprisingly, he was refused this information. If the BBC *had* indeed decided to inquire on his behalf, it would have concluded that as far as was known or suspected Brian Redhead had voted Tory on at least one recent occasion (as a mark of personal support, he had hinted, for his local MP, Nicholas Winterton), while John Timpson was thought to lean towards the Liberals and Sue MacGregor had voted for all three main parties. Meanwhile, in Frances Halewood the programme had a deputy editor who was later to work for Conservative Central Office, and among its producers were at least two future Tory MPs. This was hardly a band of revolutionaries. And there was an agreed defence. Governments, they explained, simply *did* more than

Oppositions: in a programme as political as *Today*, Ministers were going to face more scrutiny whether they liked it or not.

In any case, by the end of 1990 some of the heat was dissipating. Unlike his predecessor, the new Prime Minister, John Major, did not see much point in listening to *Today* when he got up. If the programme continued to show his government slowly unravelling on air he was also less inclined to see in this an ideological act of opposition from the BBC as a whole.[64] Some of his lieutenants remained edgy, especially as the 1997 election approached, and the Downing Street and Conservative Party press machines did their best to dictate who appeared on the programme on behalf of the government. Producers, however, found them less than proficient in their efforts—'nice Sloanes, helpful, but definitely amateurs', according to one. Indeed, it was the Labour Party, sensing the chance to govern for the first time in nearly two decades and guided by Peter Mandelson, which now laid siege to the programme with terrifying efficiency. The aim, one Labour MP later explained, was to ensure that during the 1997 campaign, 'in nine cases out of ten' a policy initiative was launched on *Today*. Day in, day out, there would be lengthy battles over the phone: over who would appear, when in the running order, what they would talk about, and who would be interviewing them. Mandelson and one of his deputies, Tim Allan, also wrote regularly to senior BBC managers complaining about individual producers or editors. It is hard to find specific evidence of such interventions having a direct bearing on the programme's editorial decisions during the campaign. But one member of the production team recalls a cumulative effect taking hold: producers, faced day after day with the prospect of querulous phone calls from party headquarters, occasionally succumbing to some sort of compromise deal.[65] Mandelson's masterly coordination of Labour appearances on *Today* also allowed the party to stay 'on message' at the crucial stage of every twenty-four-hour 'news cycle'. It all put *Today*'s staff under almost unbearable pressure. Yet it was a back-handed tribute to them—an acknowledgement that, even towards the end of the 1990s, theirs was a programme that still counted more than any other in the corridors of power.

Not everyone was convinced that this pre-eminence—or the manner in which it had been achieved over the years—was altogether healthy, either for democracy or for the art of broadcasting. Take, for example, the programme's pattern of interviewing. John Humphrys' persistent style had its fans, not the least of whom was John Humphrys himself, arguing that in the absence of public meetings or proper parliamentary reporting in the daily papers, it is largely in broadcasting that 'the real probing of what politicians are up to has to happen'.[66] But there were critics too. Robin Day, who had been regularly ticked off by listeners for his allegedly bad-tempered performances on *The World at One*, told one newspaper in 1993 of how he felt that 'one or two' *Today* presenters interrupted too much.[67] There was a steady supply of Radio Four listeners who agreed, and who generally saw it as yet one more example of the BBC's chronic impertinence. Since many complainants seemed to object only when it was someone being mauled with whom they sympathized politically, their case was rather weak. But there was another more damaging objection to these gladiatorial combats, and it was one raised by *Today's* own presenter, Sue MacGregor. After she had left the programme she admitted to being uncomfortable with the element of 'theatre' involved in many interviews. 'A sort of relentless ferocity sometimes works', she suggested. But not always, and perhaps only with diminishing returns.[68] Politicians responded by training themselves to be more adept at blocking probes, or avoiding firm commitments that might be quoted back at them. Some learned to give as good as they got. The alleged result: a diminution in the quality of political debate. The Conservative minister Virginia Bottomley believed that politicians, through no fault of their own, now risked appearing 'less emollient and reasonable' than before. Labour's Robin Cook talked of feeling more and more like a participant in a fight. 'It has got to the point', he claimed in 1996, 'where it is no longer possible for the politician to communicate either what is a legitimate political point or what is actually the news story that got him the invitation on to the programme in the first place.' As one radio critic put it, too many *Today* interviews ended up as three-minute pantomimes.[69] Worse, they risked reducing debate to a template of binary conflict. A working party of the BBC's General Advisory Council had warned as much in 1985. 'Could the emphasis be placed on deeper political and social questions rather than on party political attitudes?' it had asked, for most issues were 'grey rather than black and white'.[70]

Many politicians, of course, were often only too willing to sharpen differences of opinion for themselves, and it was in the nature of daily journalism to reflect this. But there was another question to be posed. Was *Today* leaving enough room in its running order for journalism beyond Westminster? The programme could point to a succession of extraordinary reportage across a wide range of subject matter and places: forensic investigations into the child abuse scandals of the 1980s, vivid outside broadcasts from the scene of the Brighton bombing in 1984, the Lockerbie air crash in 1988, from all over eastern Europe and the Soviet Union as Communist regimes collapsed between 1989 and 1991, from the refugee camps of Kurdish Iraq in 1991.[71] But there was also a recurring complaint that on most days the programme's agenda was hopelessly narrow. The Trades Union Congress grumbled about the lack of coverage given to bread-and-butter work issues; those working in the Arts grumbled about the neglect of cultural news; the *Guardian* grumbled about the routine exclusion of dissident views beyond the three main parties.[72] There was exasperation, too, at *Today's* predilection for trying to anticipate the day's events. 'If only they waited 24 hours they'd know', one critic pointed out. The programme, she argued, was turning into a self-devouring animal, speckling its news bulletins with stories prefaced by the words 'speaking on this programme'.[73]

Some of these criticisms carried the implicit accusation that *Today* smacked a little too much of self-importance. And there were certainly those in Broadcasting House who detected an air of tribal separatism lurking in the programme's fourth-floor offices. 'There was a definite *Today* type', Libby Purves recalled: the sort of person who preferred to work through the night when there were no managers about.[74] It spoke of a certain buccaneering spirit, slightly at odds with the 'civil service' culture that was assumed to reign in other parts of the building. Given the large audiences the programme won for Radio Four every weekday morning, a large measure of pride was certainly well earned. Despite everything—perhaps precisely *because* of all the bare-knuckle political coverage—*Today* added to what Humphrys called 'the gaiety of the nation' as much as to the democratic life of the nation.[75] Its listenership and its profile made it the one programme the network could not do without. But there was some irony in this too. For such was *Today*'s mass appeal that a large share of its listeners listened to no other programme on Radio Four. For them, it *was* Radio Four. Those responsible for all the other programmes on the schedule—the discussion programmes, magazines, quizzes, comedies, dramas, and readings that followed—could be forgiven for looking on in envy, wondering how the millions of *Today* listeners could be persuaded from switching off in droves at 9 a.m., or be enticed into coming back later in the day, or even to see that Radio Four as a whole offered more light and shade, more depth, more humour, more tragedy, more *poetry*, than was often on show in the political jousts transmitted each morning from studio 4A.

BREAKFAST PULPIT: *THOUGHT FOR THE DAY*

One programme embedded within *Today*, but over which its journalists had no editorial control whatsoever, was *Thought for the Day*, an interloper from BBC Radio's Religious Programmes department, which had evolved in 1970 from the old *Ten to Eight* and the Home Service's *Lift up Your Hearts*. Officially, it stood as a slot where speakers were asked to 'reflect on the events of the day from the perspective of religious faith'.[76] Religious Broadcasting had always been clear that it was not intended to become a wayside pulpit. And most of its contributors duly obliged. 'My general approach', the Bishop of Oxford, Richard Harries, once revealed, was 'to give people a bit of poetry and some hidden theology', but never, he added, any moral exhortation. And herein lay *Thought for the Day*'s enduring difficulty. For religious absolutists the Bishop's approach spoke of soggy liberalism or weak-kneed relativism. For rationalists and hard-headed journalists it was the kind of thinking that ended in too many trite 'life-is-like-a-sardine tin' analogies. For many programme-makers—not least the staff of *Today*, perennially frustrated by its intrusion in their flow of news just as the morning audience was hitting a peak—*Thought for the Day* was an irritating anachronism. As Martin Esslin once said, it was as if a show at the Palladium were interrupted for a homily.[77]

The situation, however, was dynamic. In line with what was happening elsewhere on Radio Four, *Thought for the Day* was being encouraged over time to adopt a sharper tone and a more relevant, wider-reaching appeal. Indeed, the man in charge of religious programmes in Radio right from the outset in 1970, John Lang, declared that his producers were explicitly charged with responding to 'changing times'. In an area of broadcasting which many traditionalists regarded as hallowed ground, the recurring problem was *how* exactly this might be done. There was, for instance, the difficulty of what Lang's successor Michael Mayne called 'the great divide'—a fundamental distinction between those who believed Christianity impinged on every area of life, 'including man's relationship to man', and those who would limit it to a narrower area, namely 'man's relationship to God'. Mayne was clear that he, for one, supported the wider interpretation. And since he reflected majority opinion in his department, a great many religious programmes in this period were intended, as he put it, 'to explore the moral factors of current political questions'.[78] *Thought for the Day* would not proselytize, but it would also not be afraid to provoke. As Mayne's own successor Colin Semper put it in 1979, it was better for it to be noticed than for it to be so bland that it 'did not mean anything to anybody'. There was, after all, 'no purpose in expounding theology without indicating its practical application': issues such as homosexuality, abortion, poverty, and race would be fair game.[79] In religious broadcasting as elsewhere the trend was away from grand abstractions and towards the concrete and the personal.

This created sharper programmes, but spelled political trouble. 'The great divide' in Christian thinking was uncomfortably close to the secular rift between progressives and conservatives, between Left and Right. Hence the steady stream of complaints from listeners whenever radical speakers such as Lord Soper or Paul Oestreicher were heard, and the much more muted response when conservative contributors such as Edward Norman had their turn. The matter was regularly discussed inside BBC Radio, where staff from the Religious Programmes department regularly made the case for greater topicality, and where people such as George Fischer and Ian McIntyre just as readily made the case for sticking to 'things spiritual'. How nice it was, Fischer told colleagues when Edward Norman had appeared, *not* to hear 'for once' about Vietnam or about how to share the national wealth.[80]

Every now and then differences of opinion would spin out of control. The first occasion came back in 1971, when Colin Morris, then a Methodist minister in London freshly returned from living in Zaire, provided a devastating critique of the Heath government's draft Immigration Bill, which proposed denying entry to anyone without a father or grandfather born in Britain. Morris, in skittish mood, had pointed out that under the Bill's terms the patron saints David, Andrew, and

George, having their roots in France, Palestine, and Libya rather than within Britain, would most definitely have been excluded. As, indeed, would Jesus. The government, he concluded, should think again. 'I heard it while sitting on my bed', one producer recalled, 'and knew trouble was in store.' Later that same morning the entire Religious Broadcasting department was called to a meeting to air the various arguments for and against the broadcast. Some spoke in favour of the piece as a brilliant example of Christian polemic; others said they would have tried to tone it down. Either way, it was too late to avoid a public row. People had already phoned the BBC to complain; more had got in touch with Conservative Central Office. The government made their inevitable protests, and when Morris was unceremoniously dropped for a few months more than seventy Opposition MPs signed a motion deploring the BBC's reaction.[81]

A similar row erupted in October 1979, when the Labour MP Tony Benn was phoned up the day before the first of three contributions he had recorded for *Thought for the Day* was due to be transmitted, only to be told it was being postponed for the duration of the party conference season. After appealing to the Controller of Radio Four and being told that the Director-General himself had been party to discussions, Benn contacted the Press Association to advertise his disgust and arranged for the *Morning Star* to publish the scripts. The real reason for the postponement remained a matter of confidentiality within the BBC: the Conservative MP Rhodes Boyson, who was scheduled to speak on *Thought for the Day* after Benn, had apparently found it difficult writing his scripts and had looked as though he might not be able to deliver in time. With Boyson's contribution likely to fail, the Labour MP's own efforts would have created an imbalance at a politically sensitive moment. Benn's recordings were broadcast three weeks later, though not before he had seized the chance to castigate the Corporation loudly for political censorship. Inevitably, the row also stimulated another bout of scrutiny from the Conservative press, which—equally inevitably—took a rather different line. The *Daily Telegraph* renewed its complaint that religion at the BBC was generally 'being forsaken in favour of sociology or politics'.[82]

The root of the problem had been identified by the BBC's head of religious programmes as early as 1971. 'Difficulties of this kind never arose during periods when the church was dormant,' he claimed, 'yet when the church awoke to its public responsibilities it was capable of acting in a highly biased way.'[83] In the early 1970s apartheid and immigration had been among the issues upon which almost every articulate Christian seemed to agree. By the mid-1980s attention had turned to Britain's inner cities, racked as they were by growing unemployment, rising levels of disorder, and a widening divide between rich and poor. As historians of the post-war Church have demonstrated, the Church of England was wedded morally to the notion of social consensus and therefore slipped 'almost inadvertently' into articulating the anxieties of a society in turmoil in a way that the official Labour opposition had sometimes conspicuously failed to do.[84] The Church of England's *Faith in the City* report of 1985, which urged more social intervention by government (and the Church) to prevent the spread of material and spiritual malaise in urban areas—and thus denounced by Norman Tebbit as 'pure Marxist theology'—was one iconic statement of this latest political engagement. The barbed comments of the Bishop of Durham, David Jenkins, were another. His enthronement sermon the year before came in the middle of the bitterly contested miners' strike, when he was angered by the idea that those running the mines and the country were together bent on total victory. An unwillingness to compromise, he told his congregation, was 'outrageously self-righteous, deeply inhuman and damnably dangerous'. 'This Government' behaved as if it were 'indifferent to poverty and powerlessness'.[85]

Margaret Thatcher, it seemed, could provoke the ire of the clerics like no other. And, as the incoming head of religious programmes, David Winter, pointed out, countless numbers of speakers on *Thought for the Day* during the 1980s pleaded with their producers for the opportunity to attack her with the weapons at their disposal: theology, morality, and compassion.[86] Jim Thompson and Tom Butler were both inner-city bishops who appeared regularly on air, and as Butler later explained, 'We felt we had a duty to describe what we saw'—even if, as Thompson suspected, it prompted the Prime Minister to veto their appointment to higher rank. Even Richard Harries, who had offered Thatcher qualified support at the time of the Falklands War, could not fully disguise his distaste with the government's social policies.[87]

Producers were required to remain neutral on such matters, but they too were men and women of the Church and it was impossible for them to inoculate themselves entirely against the oppositional mood. Among their number were several pillars of the Establishment: a future chaplain to the Queen (John Lang) and a future Dean of Westminster Abbey (Michael Mayne). Others had more humble origins and were of a more radical mien: people such as John Newbury, who had worked as a Methodist minister on Merseyside, and Colin Morris, who, despite his transgression in 1971, had since returned for a spell as the BBC's overall Head of Religious Broadcasting. All aspired to combine the wisdom of Solomon and the patience of Job. But very few could agree with the Prime Minister that there was no such thing as society. Their centre of gravity, as with the Church at large, was to be found a degree or two to the left of centre.

The situation had to be managed carefully. As the 1987 General Election approached, and the BBC sought to fend off Conservative accusations of bias, extra vigilance was demanded of producers. 'I don't want some lefty bishop on *Thought for the Day* queering our pitch', the Managing Director, David Hatch told one meeting. David Winter was therefore charged with ensuring his producers would hold the line:

I called a departmental meeting and came as near as I temperamentally could to reading the riot act. Every speaker, each sermon, all our stories and features were to be scrupulously overhauled. Fine tooth-combs should scrape through every script. Our broadcasters, even (or perhaps especially) bishops and other turbulent priests, were to be warned as to their future conduct.[88]

Perversely, the one programme that came near to catastrophe was usually among the most anodyne: *Prayer for the Day*. One edition was scrapped when a speaker chosen for the closing stages of the election campaign was found to have punctuated his talk on the church at Thyatira and its troublesome Jezebel with the divine (but highly pertinent) message, 'The time has come to get rid of this terrible woman.'[89]

This degree of censorship was unsustainable beyond election times, if only because no one in Broadcasting House wanted a prime spot on *Today* to be anything less than rigorously topical. Normal service demanded more incisiveness, not less. One way of achieving this was simply to cut its allotted duration— and this was done in incremental stages, first from five minutes to four-and-a-half, and then again, when Jenny Abramsky was in charge of *Today*, to just two minutes and fifty seconds. In this leaner form, there were plenty of opportunities for creating an explosive effect with the occasional well-crafted literary hand-grenade. In an uncanny echo of Tony Benn's difficulties in 1979, Canon Eric James used a talk in 1990 to defend the actions of the poll tax protestors, and planned to speak approvingly of 'the spiritual value of revolt' for a contribution coinciding with the opening day of the Labour Party conference. When the producer required the script to be changed, Canon James felt obliged to resign, telling the *Church Times* of the continual censorship he had endured. Several years later, another regular contributor, Canon Philip Crowe, reported similar experiences, claiming that Conservative ministers had twice asked the Director-General for him to be removed.[90] Curiously, there was no such censorship applied to Anne Atkins in October 1996, when she stated that 'homophobia is reprehensible' before proceeding to denounce the Church of England for its tolerance towards homosexuals. The Church suggested that in this case a little censorship might have been a good thing. But at least one producer on *Today* was delighted with her performance: 'It provoked controversy and did what the rest of *Today*'s journalism always seeks to do by setting a story running in the newspapers.'[91] His preference would have been to get rid of *Thought for the Day* altogether: a more controversial version was the next best thing.

Concision and controversy were two devices for attracting attention. Another was to widen *Thought for the Day*'s appeal ecumenically. One turning point came in 1996, when it emerged that as many as seven regulars were to be 'rested'. The outgoing names were George Austin, Philip Crowe, Leslie Griffiths, Richard Harries, Oliver McTernan, Donald English, and John Newbury. Those incoming included Anne Atkins and the Catholic commentator Christina Odone. 'Some people had become a little complacent or just tedious', the producer, David Coomes, explained: 'we had to bring in some new blood.' But this was blood-letting of a rather humiliating kind, not just because it felt like real intellectual weight was being lost, but because of the way the whole process had been handled. Richard Harries, otherwise sympathetic to the need for new voices, was stung at receiving a standard letter and no proper explanation for the move. Others in the Church grumbled at what they saw as the BBC's declining commitment to traditional Christianity: it had not gone unnoticed that all those severed from the programme were male, white, ordained Christian ministers.[92]

At a time when the country's religious profile was changing fast, opening up *Thought for the Day* to other faiths self-evidently made sense. But it was also a delicate matter, since for most of its history BBC religion had remained essentially the Church of England at the microphone. Any change had to be by evolution if traditional sensibilities were to be respected. Yet the need for *something* to be done was clear enough—and had been for some time. As early as August 1970, the head of religious programmes in BBC Radio had warned speakers on *Thought for the Day* that they could no longer assume the mass of their audience was necessarily Christian.[93] One indicator of change was declining church attendance among Anglicans; another, the steady growth in the number of British people who were Muslim, Hindu, or Sikh. In 1975, for instance, there were at least 400,000 practising Muslims in the country—a figure that was to rise to nearly 1 million by 1993.[94] The religious policy of the BBC changed in subtle but decisive ways to reflect these trends: the stated principle from the mid-1970s was 'to reflect the worship, thought and action of the principle religious traditions represented in Britain'.[95]

Given the need to nurture a new generation of speakers, not all of whom had English as their first language, putting principles into practice was slow work. Jewish speakers had made the first inroads many years before and continued to be represented by the likes of Hugo Gryn and Jonathan Sacks. In time, they were joined by Indarjit Singh, the editor of the *Sikh Messenger*, and the first regular Muslim speaker, Umar Hegedus, who was recruited in 1992. After the cull of 1996, the overall pool of thirty contributors included one Muslim, a Sikh, a Hindu, two orthodox Jews and a reform Jew, as well as representatives of most branches of Christianity. Some faiths remained more elusive. There had been a handful of Buddhist talks as early as 1975, but twenty years later, the producer of *Thought for the Day* was struggling to find any adherents who could supply the 'hard nosed' scripts required: 'the way they think about things tends to be rather soft and gentle', he complained.[96] More elusive still were humanists or atheists. They had been campaigning for access to the slot for as long as it had existed, but, in one of the BBC's most crass acts of censorship, they seemed to be the only group for whom the new ecumenical spirit still did not apply. Their case had been examined formally by the BBC's Head of Religious Broadcasting, Ernest Rea in 1994, when even the *Church Times* was arguing that 'Believers have no monopoly of the illumination needed on dark mornings.' Rea, however, decided a monopoly should be retained for the foreseeable future: 'Allowing atheists to present it would turn it into an exercise in God-bashing.'[97]

If there was no humanism as such on *Thought for the Day*, it was still the presence of a 'human touch' that most effectively endeared it to many Radio Four listeners. All the BBC surveys showed there was among them only a core of committed Christians who were after unadulterated preaching: a larger group of listeners found it sanctimonious; most found it just plain dull. But it was no more unpopular than the *Today* programme's sports or business news, and four out of five listeners in 1994 said they were content for it to remain.[98] For this vaguely contented majority, *Thought for the Day* generally exuded a tone that accorded well enough with their own attitude to religion: loosely spiritual rather than narrowly dogmatic, generally muted, and mercifully to the point—a kind of 'belief without belonging'.[99]

In the hands of someone like Rabbi Lionel Blue, it was also shot through with warmth and personality. 'If you want to cry, why not?' he told listeners one typical Monday morning. 'Tears don't run down your cheek for nothing, and somewhere on the way you must have got hurt':

Love yourself with something. I love myself with a 1/4 lb of whole nut chocolate for depression, and a 1/2 lb bar for anxieties. Now treat yourself to some milk of human kindness: you can provide your own. Beat one raw egg, 3/4 pint of chilled milk, a few drops of vanilla, 3 tablespoons of sugar and a grating of nutmeg. You have to stop crying, or your tears will make the milk salty.[100]

As always Blue teetered near the edge of banality but redeemed himself through snappy writing and self-deprecation. Over the years, Radio Four listeners heard about his mental breakdown, his homosexuality, his rift with his mother, his youthful dalliance with Christianity and Marxism, his difficulty in believing in an external God. His thinly disguised psychotherapy managed to convey a sense of a vulnerable, rather damaged soul trying to reach out. He offered ambiguity and confusion, and an endless supply of jokes on the way people cope with problems they cannot solve. This had an appeal all of its own— one that more than matched the dogmatic certainties of those other speakers who so delighted the encircling journalists on *Today*.[101] Devotees of *Thought for the Day* did not necessarily see it as such, but it was a triumph of sorts for secularism. Or rather, for a religion sufficiently inclusive and benign—or perhaps just sufficiently opaque—to be palatable to that silent, uncommitted majority listening at home and busy getting ready for work.

AFTERNOON SHIFTS: *WOMAN'S HOUR* AND *ANDERSON COUNTRY*

By the start of the 1990s, one unresolved problem for Radio Four—what to do about the alarming 'mid-morning dip' in audiences—was joined by a fresh one: how to deal with the forthcoming launch of a national commercial station and the BBC's own new national radio network, Radio Five, which had been designed to accommodate schools programmes, children's programmes, and sport. The dial was clearly becoming a more competitive place. It seemed a good moment for the Controller to take stock of Radio Four's strengths and to shore up the weakest points in its defences.

The failure of *Rollercoaster* to establish itself had left Green with a mid-morning schedule that still seemed to lack character. *The Daily Service*, various ad hoc features, the odd story, bits and pieces: each programme had its devotees, but none was a big hitter in the ratings, and collectively, Green felt, they offered 'no great consistency'.[102] The audience at home was assumed to be busy—able to do little more than dip in and out of listening. What Radio Four offered was mostly 'built' programmes that seemed to demand rather too much continuous attention.

What better, then, than to install in their place one of the network's strongest magazine programmes, *Woman's Hour*? It could be plucked from its traditional post-lunchtime slot to create a 'central attraction' each morning. It would, as Green put it, be going 'into the Maginot line', rather than being held in reserve. It was a strong 'brand', so its half-a-million or so regular daily listeners would probably move with it. The programme might also find a whole new audience. Already, about one in five of its listeners were men, and audience research told Green that even more of them would be available to listen in the mornings. The move might even be an excuse for rejuvenating the programme's style, freshening its content, quickening its pace. Indeed, perhaps the name itself could change. The existing title undoubtedly made sense back in 1946, when the programme was unashamedly designed to appeal to housewives, and to entice women war-workers back into the home. But with more women going out to work and more men listening, with a new time slot and a refreshed style, with all the progress that had been made in sex equality, how sensible would it be to keep calling it *Woman's Hour* in the decade to come?[103]

The arguments were strong, and Green made his move. From September 1991, he announced, there would be a new time slot and, perhaps, a new title. A modest proposal for changing the schedule had formed into something more radical.

Green believed his plans were a vote of confidence in the programme. But to those making *Woman's Hour*, it felt like a death sentence. A move to the morning was bad enough; losing the name hurt more. *Woman's Hour* had always been distinctively *for* women—and in more ways than one. Right from the start, there had been plenty of domesticity of the traditional kind, of course: cookery, childcare, tips on how to make do and mend. But the programme had also established a reputation for breaking many broadcasting taboos. It operated, so to speak, under cover of daytime, when few senior BBC managers bothered to listen. In 1948, no other programme on the BBC would have discussed the menopause, as *Woman's Hour* did—causing, it has to be said, one senior Corporation figure to come out in a cold sweat over all the talk of hot flushes, and thus prompting a flurry of anxious memos.[104] Under its editors from the mid-1960s onwards—Monica Sims, Mollie Lee, and Wyn Knowles—the boundaries were slowly extended, and, as the programme moved from becoming less scripted and rehearsed to becoming more live and spontaneous, so too was the amount of topical discussion. By the 1970s, its presenter Sue MacGregor recalls, it was presiding over 'gynaecological talks... regular discussions on abortion, the pill, homosexuality, piles and incontinence... divorce, single parenthood, physical and mental handicap'. 'Anything could be considered', she concluded, 'as long as it was well done, interesting and relevant.' By including more political topics, *Woman's Hour* also supplied what one reviewer called 'a horizon beyond the ironing board'. Women's liberation, equal pay, equal opportunities, Barbara Castle, Germaine Greer, Fay Weldon: they had all put in an appearance.[105] They were, it has to be noted, greeted with polite acknowledgement rather than wholesale approval, since Editors were usually at pains to remind their producers that most listeners were 'home bodies' alienated by too much talk of all-women communes or workplace revolutionaries. Indeed, to identify fully with the feminist movement would have alienated many of the producers themselves. Few, yet, were of the Greer generation, and many shared a conviction that refusing to bow to fashion or ideology helped preserve *Woman's Hour* as a programme for all women regardless of their position on sexual politics. Hence the epithets it attracted: a 'clever mixture of Women's Institute and Women's Lib', or, more prosaically, a 'unique mixture of jam, Jerusalem and genital warts'.[106]

Michael Green's plans for the programme came at a point in the programme's history when this equilibrium was being disturbed from within. The appointment of Sandra Chalmers as editor in 1982 had been one straw in the wind. Here was a single mother with two teenagers, sympathetic to the needs of producers who were also mothers, and eager to establish a chattier, friendlier tone with listeners. When she was replaced four years later by Clare Selerie, with Sally Feldman becoming her deputy on the same day, and Jenni Murray joining soon after as a regular presenter, the average age of the *Woman's Hour* team dropped a further ten years almost overnight. It was now a programme led by a triumvirate in their thirties with a collective determination to speak their mind and grab attention. Behind the scenes, they were busy nurturing a proto-feminist working environment, creating flexible shift patterns and job-sharing schemes unheard of elsewhere in Broadcasting House. On air, Jenni Murray was sounding warm, angry, upset, sympathetic, always somehow *on the listener's side*. There was a subtle but noticeable shift in sexual frankness, typified by Emma Thompson's guest appearance, in which she famously asserted that men faked orgasms too. The three women denied they had any plan to turn the programme into a mouthpiece for feminism. But with a whole raft of other general interest magazines on Radio Four they were acutely aware that *Woman's Hour* had to work harder to distinguish itself in a crowded marketplace.[107] The obvious response was to give voice more consistently than ever to the collective experience of women and display the virtues of autonomous women's journalism.

Green thus saw the potential to open up the programme to more men just as its production team were busy driving it in a more distinctive direction, deliberately choosing women speakers for even the most general topics, concentrating on women writers in the serial, featuring men only when they had something to say about, or to, women. It was hardly surprising, then, that when he unveiled his plans to the producers at the end of November 1990, they were distraught. Sally Feldman, who was acting editor at the time, promptly made a call to arms. 'I don't want your tears,' she told her staff, 'I want your anger.'[108] She got it, too. And over the next year, it echoed throughout Broadcasting House and Fleet Street.

The press immediately saw another delicious opportunity to attack the BBC, for as Ian Hislop, the editor of *Private Eye*, put it at the time, 'We love it when the grey suits fuck up.'[109] The timing of the announcement had been unfortunate, coming only days after Margaret Thatcher's resignation as Prime Minister and John Major's subsequent elevation. *The Times* could not resist forging a connection. 'First John Major selects no woman for his cabinet,' it complained, 'Then, far worse, *Woman's Hour*, star in the galaxy of public service broadcasting in Britain, is to be summarily dispatched.' No matter how hard the BBC press officers invoked the mantra 'Not axed, moved,' the opportunities for causing mischief at the BBC's expense were too tempting. *Woman's Hour* was as much of an institution as Radio Four, and it served to embody in miniature the network's ability to be a touchstone of wider anxieties. Fiddling with *Woman's Hour*, *The Times* fulminated, was yet another instance of 'the BBC's periodic failures of nerve':

The changes must be reversed: perhaps by a mass switch-off on the part of disgusted licence payers, followed by a march to Broadcasting House and if necessary a ritual burning of the Radio Times. BBC planners will have to learn that there are programmes which are bigger than they, programmes of which they are mere custodians. *Woman's Hour* is one such. It must remain sacrosanct.[110]

The Controller was soon besieged from all directions. On one side, he faced a sustained mutiny from the *Women's Hour* team itself, who were busy making badges bearing the legend 'I'm a Woman's Hour Man' and sending them out to any male listener who had written in to support them. The producer responsible for the daily serial, Pat McLoughlin, crept unseen into the Council Chamber of Broadcasting House late one evening, and pinned some of the badges onto all the portraits of past Directors-General, much to the delight of journalists attending a BBC party there the following day.[111] In the House of Commons there was a motion 'deploring' the plans. BBC 1's *Nine o'Clock News* was covering the story. And letters from the listening public were starting to pour in expressing anger and disgust—some 2,000 or so by January 1991. 'It was a very violent reaction', the

Controller admitted. 'My name was mud around town, I couldn't go to any gathering of women without being generally beaten up.'[112] Green had already been in post for nearly five years and was inured to a good kicking every few months. Even so, this was noisome stuff and he knew when it was wise to retreat. At the end of January 1991, the *Woman's Hour* team showed him some of their own market research, which suggested the programme's title was as powerful a brand as, say, British Airways or Marks & Spencer. Green relented. Although the move to the morning would have to go ahead the name could remain. It was, he admitted, a 'useful handle' to guide listeners to the new slot.[113]

The task now was to devise a new morning style for *Woman's Hour*: one that was faster paced, sufficiently appealing to the new listeners Green wanted to attract, especially any men—but which remained overwhelmingly familiar to devotees. The editor, Sally Feldman, talked of maintaining a 'Twin Peaks' approach: covering areas of special interest to women and looking at the world from a female perspective. She also promised a leavening of short, snappy items, a few more time-checks, more live material, more informality, more 'audience interaction'. Celebrity guests were lined up for the first few weeks: Katherine Hepburn, Glenn Close, the Duchess of York. Taking a cue from their earlier campaigning badges, the programme team also created a series of trails that were sprinkled liberally across the Radio Four schedule. Many featured testimonials from some of *Woman's Hour*'s most loyal male listeners—Alan Bennett, Tony Benn, Peregrine Worsthorne, John Harvey-Jones. The England football captain, Gary Lineker, added one too, boasting that he had 'scored on *Woman's Hour*'.[114]

When, at last, the first edition went out in its new slot, on 16 September 1991, there were the inevitable laments. 'Poor Jenni Murray', the actor Judy Cornwell told the *Daily Mail*, she sounded as if she had 'been put on a running machine . . . The programme has lost its sense of being a lovely haven of tranquillity.' The audience figures, however, told Green a more encouraging story. There were indeed more men listening—up from about a quarter of the audience just before the change to a third immediately after. The total audience had risen too, from 500,000 to 700,000 each day. 'The programme team were magnificent', Green recalled. 'They weren't pleased with me one jot, but after a bit they quite relished the challenge of showing me what they were made of, and the programme leapt forward.' Those making the programme also felt they had been rehabilitated without making too many concessions. Women's issues and women's perspectives had not been abandoned: the campaign of trails seemed to have done enough in themselves to convince more men that they were welcome to listen. If anything was different, it was probably the pugnacious self-consciousness with which the producers had trailed and publicized the 'new' *Woman's Hour*.[115] The campaign was a potent symbol, both of the enduring fear of change, and of the kind of marketing effort that might just be able to allay it.

Woman's Hour's move had taken place with no long-term damage to the programme itself, and it had brought some badly needed lift to Radio Four's mid-morning audience figures. But it did nothing to help Radio Four's mid-afternoon ratings, which had an alarming dip all of their own. Perhaps, the Controller wondered, listeners were simply sated with Radio Four's style of speech by 3 p.m., and thus easily seduced by music elsewhere on the dial. Whatever the precise cause, Green decided that what was needed was something deliberately different from the usual fare: something that would cross the traditional boundaries of the various radio genres, embracing features, conversation, and debate; something that would be loose, and hence have what was called 'listener dippability', as well as being unpredictable and entertaining—the kind of thing that could probably only be held together by an 'engaging' character. The presenter's role would obviously be crucial, but there was a conscious decision to avoid what Green called 'the usual suspects'. The choice fell, instead, on Gerry Anderson, a Northern Irish broadcaster with several years' local radio experience who had also recently provided Radio Four with *Stroke City*, a series of colourful talks about living in Derry. They were well written, witty, and the audience had loved them. Choosing Anderson was a risk, as was the experimental format; but it was a calculated one. There was little reason to suppose that public reaction to the new series would be quite as vicious as it turned out to be.[116]

Within a month of its debut in March 1994, *Anderson Country* was being written about in the newspapers as 'the most reviled radio programme for years'. The critics were merciless. A 'concoction of disconnected features, voices and phone-calls, loosely strung together by Anderson's astonishing flow of clichés, puns and fatuities' was one early judgement. 'A bizarre mix of saloon bar folksiness and supposedly heavyweight issues' was another. Radio Four's own *Feedback* programme was deluged with complaints—most expressed in an unprecedented tone of contempt. Listeners, its presenter said, had never written with such unanimity, with a feeling that they were offended by a programme simply because it was so utterly not what they expected to hear on Radio Four. Some correspondents made clear that it was Anderson's accent that grated. They were at least being consistent in their prejudice, since Northern Irish accents had always attracted particular opprobrium from a section of the Radio Four audience. The more general charge, however, was of banality. The presenter, they believed, was trying too hard to exhibit his laid-back personality. Too many interviews seemed to feature non-entities talking about non-issues. Anderson was an advocate of allowing ordinary people a voice on the airwaves, even if they had little of national importance to say and lacked the experience to say it with polish. 'At least they were saying what they *felt*', he would explain. Regular Radio Four listeners, on the other hand, pointed out that they were used to hearing people with something to say, and who could say it well. They also argued that the programme had a central structural defect—that since one never knew quite what was going to be on each afternoon, one had no pressing reason to listen at all.[117]

Anderson Country was, Michael Green has since admitted, 'more in intensive care' than any other programme he had ever been involved in. Throughout the spring and summer months of 1994, the Controller worked with Sharon Banoff, the programme's producer, to see if something approaching full health could be achieved. Gradually, more serious topics were included and Anderson was given more direction in the studio. The first audience figures were starting to be encouraging too—just as they had been with *Rollercoaster* a decade before. Indeed, during *Anderson Country*'s first three months, the number of people listening to Radio Four between 3 p.m. and 4 p.m. on weekday afternoons rose by 20,000 overall. The proportion listening in Scotland and the North of England also went up, which offered tangible proof of the network widening its appeal in just the way the Director-General had wanted.[118]

'The worst is over', Gerry Anderson declared in May. This was misplaced optimism. The volume and intensity of public complaint remained. By August, there had been 1,500 complaints to the BBC; by the following January, *Feedback* had another 16,000 on file. The Managing Director of Radio, Liz Forgan, was forced to concede that the criticism was unprecedented. 'I have never in all my life as a broadcaster seen such a violent, continuous and unmerciful onslaught on a programme', she told the *Guardian* at the beginning of 1995. It was, she added, 'a million miles' from the worst programme ever made. But it was clear to many in Broadcasting House that the programme had been badly misconceived, with no clear editorial mission, and thus no discernible identity or *raison d'être*. As for Anderson, even Green admitted that he had been miscast: obviously ill at ease with the more serious material being put before him, reluctant to be briefed by his producers, and with an increasingly diffident manner on air that betrayed his own unhappiness. Green therefore accepted that *Anderson Country* was beyond redemption in its current form and that Anderson was 'not going to make it in this role'. On 17 January 1995, he left the programme 'by mutual agreement'—a senior editor having been dispatched from Broadcasting House to his Derry home to talk to him face to face. Daire Brehan from *You and Yours* and Laurie Taylor were drafted in to share the presenting role, and the programme was renamed *Afternoon Shift*.[119]

Both new men showed, in their very different ways, that they were fully at ease talking about any subject that came along. But *Afternoon Shift* never quite escaped the stigma that had attached to its immediate progenitor, and only survived three more years. It did, however, leave something of a long-term legacy, as *Rollercoaster* had done before, by establishing a more discursive style of programme on Radio Four. This emerged in the shape of *Offspring* (1995–7) and, even later, *Home Truths* (1998–2006). These, too, were hybrids woven in a looser style, with no clear prescription as to subject matter save the broad remit to chew over the foibles of family life. As *Radio Times* promised, the ground to be covered ranged 'From pets and parenthood to puberty and piano teachers'.[120] If these series worked better than their 1994 predecessor (and not everyone agreed that they did) it was mainly because in John Peel they were to find a presenter who managed with some panache the handbrake turns in tone and pace this bastardized format demanded.

IDENTITY CRISIS?

In retrospect, Green regarded *Anderson Country* as the biggest mistake of his ten-year Controllership. It had proved too bold a stroke, both aesthetically and logistically, and for this Green blamed himself. 'You were asking a production team to do the most difficult thing: you were telling them that here was five hours of time a week, and they could do with it what they want . . . If it had been done once or maybe twice a week, and with a different broadcaster at the helm, it would have found its feet, I think.'[121] Yet *Anderson Country* suffered not just as a result of its own shortcomings—which were many—but also because hostility towards it gelled together all the complaints that long-standing Radio Four listeners had been accumulating over recent years. The 'tarting up' of *The Archers*, the axing of *The Radio Programme* to make way for *Mediumwave*, getting rid of Margaret Howard, moving *Woman's Hour*: the list seemed endless. Indeed that was precisely the problem. Change worried the regular listeners, and too many changes in quick succession tended to induce panic. Press comment encouraged them to join the dots. *Anderson Country*, they learned, was merely the latest and most egregious example of John Birt's injunction to 'broaden the base', part of a gradual process of Radio Four being 'dragged downmarket', part of the creation of a 'chattified continuum'. Sometimes, objections were a surrogate of distress being felt in Middle England. As one of the more kindly reviews of *Anderson Country* put it, 'The Government looks corrupt and incompetent, the country can't win at cricket, and now some Londonderry airhead is blocking up the afternoons on Radio Four.'[122] With mood music like this playing in the background, the slightest miscalculation among programme-makers or Controllers was going to be repaid with exaggerated contempt.

Even so, there was a genuine sense of loss over what appeared to be happening on air, for the 'core' Radio Four audience looked upon the network as theirs. They believed that with every change being made, ownership was slipping further from their grasp. And, in truth, this was precisely what the Controllers intended. The devotees, they knew, were only a small part of the audience: other people had to be catered for too. The tricky part of the equation was how to appeal to a broader spread of taste. As Ian McIntyre had warned as far back as 1978, there was always the danger that 'if we try to please too many people we could end up by pleasing very few'.[123] Michael Green had been clear that he, for one, was interested in pursuing the educated, curious, broadsheet-reading, theatre-going, cinema-going, thirty-somethings. But even they were far from a homogeneous group. The more audience research that was now done, the more the subtle differences in people's taste and lifestyle seemed to multiply, both within and between the generations.

Consumerism and politics were here intertwined, and they made it next to impossible for the BBC to speak with one voice. As David Watt wrote in *The Times* in February 1985, Thatcherism 'helped to create a polarised political climate in which Reithian aspirations find it hard to survive':

The problem is really much deeper than political ideology. National consciousness is at present dissolved to the point where no single organisation can possibly 'represent' it. Where there is no centre of cultural gravity, high-mindedness can indeed be labelled 'pomposity'. The protection of standards with which one disagrees becomes 'pretentiousness', and the conscious attempt to spread them 'flagrant bias'. Any sign of self-confidence or independence is 'dangerous self-assurance'.[124]

Conversely, he might have added, attempts at popularity can be labelled 'mediocrity', accessibility becomes 'dumbing down', and any sign of giving people what they want becomes 'an identity crisis'. Balancing popularity with quality was the BBC's eternal burden, of course. There was nothing new there. But with British culture diversifying all the time, the 'centre of cultural gravity' seemed to have evaporated. Add to this a government laying siege to the very ethos of public service broadcasting and the stresses and strains of the ongoing Birtist Revolution, and the Corporation's attempt to do the right thing sometimes ended up looking like what one retired manager called 'a rat in a trap chewing itself to death'.[125]

The extraordinary thing is that Radio Four actually seemed to find a way through this hideous tangle of competing pressures. In part this was a personal achievement of the Controllers. Both David Hatch and Michael Green had enough charm to persuade other colleagues to take risks—and the good grace to admit to their errors when an experiment failed. Hatch carried many people in Broadcasting House with him by creating that intangible thing, a 'buzz'. Green, it was reckoned, worked by stealth and careful forewarning of change. Which was why, when John Birt had so publicly called on Radio Four to broaden its appeal, Green was so cross. 'I could have killed him', he later admitted; 'I was heading in that direction anyway... It was the sort of remark that the press love.'[126] He was engaged in 'gentle refreshment', and most of the time this involved no more change than had always taken place gradually over time, perhaps quickening in pace a little every now and then as new producers arrived. The press might have written of the 'Brookeside-ization' of *The Archers*, but only because they had a handy new label for something rather older: Ambridge had been changing in fits and starts since 1967. Radical and sudden change to the network as a whole was structurally impossible, in any case. Programmes were made by a whole range of departments in Broadcasting House and beyond: production talent was diffused, and no Controller had direct command over it all. Radio Four belonged to the producers as well as the audience, and even in the age of Producer Choice no overhaul could be achieved except through some rough-and-ready consensus between managers and the shop-floor. The extraordinary tensions of Ian McIntyre's tenure had already shown that.

The real measure of success, however, was in the way the Radio Four schedule was being reinvented as a deliberately more eclectic thing. Despite what many feared, Green did not try to make the network *as a whole* younger. His tactic had been to identify 'entry points' where new listeners could be drawn in; the remaining three-quarters or more of the output remained exactly as it had always been. The balance was delicate. At the same time as new, sharper comedy was being tried out in the late evenings, John Gielgud was being led into the studio to read *The Bible* in the morning—an experiment that led later to *This Sceptr'd Isle*, another archetypal programme in the Home Service tradition. Few other parts of the British media seemed able to encompass this range. There was little overlap in tastes or attitudes between, say, the *Daily Mail* and the *Guardian*. But Radio Four was listened to by the readers of both, and sometimes sounded a little like both. Occasionally, the separate cultures collided, and the result could be ludicrous and pleasing in equal measure. As Libby Purves pointed out, where else in the early 1990s but in a programme like Radio Four's *Midweek* could one find a former Chancellor of the Exchequer in conversation with the head of the London School of Striptease?[127] Most of the time there was a clearer demarcation of styles. And within the mix were enough heavyweight documentary series, gritty and contemporary book readings, sharp debates, edgy plays and comedy shows to prove that a commitment to serious journalism and serious culture had survived.

Some in the BBC had started to call such delicately balanced programming 'neo-Reithian': a constantly fluctuating, regulated balance between paternalism and pluralism.[128] It was the old debate, between 'leading or following', but recast for a different age—one where the question that now had to be asked was this: follow *who* exactly? The question could not be answered passively. Controllers of Radio Four knew that sometimes only by unveiling some experiments would they—and their listeners—discover what it was that they did or did not like. Indeed, they might well have heard ringing in their ears those famous lines from Kipling:

> Our England is a garden, and such gardens are not made
> By singing 'Oh how beautiful!' and sitting in the shade.[129]

12

A Long Wave Goodbye?

'What do we want?'
'Radio 4!'
'Where do we want it?'
'Long Wave!'
'And what do we say?'
'Please!'

Slogans at a listeners' protest march, 1993

GATHERING STORMS

In the early hours of Friday 16 October 1987 a severe storm swept across a great swathe of southern England, the worst to hit the region in more than 200 years. Wind speeds reached 140 km an hour, ripping whole roofs off houses, tearing down power cables, hurling telegraph poles, bricks, tiles, cars, motorbikes, and vans along streets. By daybreak, nineteen people had been killed, fifteen million trees uprooted, and nearly £1 billion worth of damage inflicted on property. For a while, the full impact of the storm remained hidden. 'Most of us had a fair night's sleep', one writer recalled. 'Some did not realise that anything really out of the way had happened until they stepped outdoors, and found the landscape transformed.'[1]

One reason why it was hard to get much information about the night's events, or what the day would bring for those trying to get to work or to school, was that transmitters had been damaged, power and phone lines disrupted, and many road and rail routes made impassable. Broadcasters were therefore struggling to get their programmes on air. Breakfast Television found the odds too heavily stacked against it, and gave up; so, too, did many regional television services. In Broadcasting House the telephone system was playing up and the building running on emergency generators. For BBC employees and general public alike information was sketchy. But radio could get by with fewer staff and less technology than television. Scripts were therefore written and tapes edited by candlelight; makeshift lines of communication were lashed up. And *Today* went on air at 6.30 a.m. as scheduled. For the next two-and-a-half hours it reported as best it could on the various devastations wrought by the storm. Indeed, for a while, it was one of the few sources of information available to the national audience.²

At 9 a.m., however, *Today* wound up, as it always did, and Radio Four carried on with the rest of the day's programmes as planned. The woman in charge of news and current affairs in BBC Radio, Jenny Abramsky, was immensely frustrated at the flow of coverage being cut off in this manner, since there seemed so much more to report. John Birt, newly installed as Deputy Director-General, felt the same way, and decided to leave his third-floor office in Broadcasting House, walk up one flight of stairs, and confront the Controller of Radio Four, Michael Green. As Green recalls:

He came to my office at about 11 am, and said, 'Why are we not continuing with the hurricane coverage?' And I said, 'well, there's nothing to say John: it's happened, we're cleaning up, and it's the job now for local radio to get on with it. It doesn't affect anywhere north of Watford . . . furthermore the newsroom hasn't offered me anything else, because they can't reach the scene'. And John thought it shocking. And he then went down to the Newsroom and shouted at them, asking why they weren't offering more stuff.³

BBC journalists had been dreaming of a rolling news channel since the early 1970s. But, as far as the Deputy Director-General was concerned, the need for 'continuing, comprehensive coverage' had just been proven beyond doubt. The perceived inadequacy of Radio's response that October morning became an article of faith among many staff working in news and current affairs. Abramsky and Birt differed in one key respect: she had worked in Radio for years, and valued its traditions and its diversity; he, on the other hand, was an outsider with few inhibitions about tearing up existing arrangements. Both, however, committed themselves from that moment to pursuing vigorously the idea of a rolling news service on BBC Radio. A sharp and unexpected turn in the British weather had kick-started the process of changing the journalists' dream into reality.

Green knew straight away that Radio Four was especially vulnerable. Only a year before, the prospect of his network having to make room for a news service had seemed remote. The Managing Director of Radio, Brian Wenham, had declared in 1986 that if there was to be a 'flexible network for "breaking news" ', it made sense for it to be Radio Two, not Radio Four.⁴ His statement seemed to draw a line under years of scheming, and in the summer of 1987 one newspaper was confident enough to announce there were 'no more threats of a rolling all-day news service'.⁵ By the time of the October storms, however, everything had changed. Wenham was gone, Birt had arrived, and the first fruit of his work, the mighty News and Current Affairs directorate, was in place. Having wrenched all relevant programmes from the Radio and Television directorates, this new beast now had control over the entire range of BBC journalism. Radio's incoming Managing Director, David Hatch, had written to Michael Checkland to place on record his 'heartfelt objection' to this systematic filleting of his domain. But now, like Michael Green, he had to accept defeat and live with the consequences, namely that news and current affairs staff working *on* radio were no longer working *for* Radio: they were, so to speak, a law unto themselves.[6]

From their new position of autonomy, the BBC's journalists could afford to be a little more detached about the fate of Radio Four. As far as some were concerned, it was essentially a news channel anyway—or at least it would be, were it not still encumbered with the baroque adornments of drama, readings, quizzes, and the rest. It certainly made no sense that it still had two whole frequencies to itself—one on FM, one on long wave—while other BBC networks were being restricted to just one in order to make room for commercial radio at the government's behest. News and Current Affairs was also expanding fast: it had access to more and more satellite technology and lightweight recording equipment, more and more foreign correspondents in new bases such as Warsaw, Beijing, and Tokyo, and more and more reporters at home in specialist units devoted to social affairs, education, economics, the arts.[7] The raw material of news was being produced in bulk, and BBC journalism was better placed than ever before to cover events, wherever and whenever they happened. What it lacked was an adequate means of distribution, since with no network of its own the time available to actually broadcast this abundant material remained utterly finite. Radio Four looked like the main roadblock. And it seemed sensible to move it aside.

Against this rising pressure for more news, Green's first line of defence was to find as much space for it as he could within the existing schedule. He had already reinstated the Saturday edition of *Today*; now the midnight news bulletin was extended to a full thirty minutes and more editions of *File on Four* and *Analysis* were unveiled. Green also made clear that his long wave frequency would readily make way for the extended live coverage of events: up to six hours a week, should there be major news stories, important parliamentary debates, or state occasions. Green calculated that, taken together, these concessions were just enough to appease News and Current Affairs without causing undue disturbance to his regular listeners. The room for manoeuvre was narrow. Even this very limited use of long wave as an 'events' channel, first announced just a week or so after the October storm, had prompted a wave of letters to newspapers denouncing the BBC for 'proposing to take away Radio Four'. Over a thousand signatures had also been gathered from EEC and NATO employees in Brussels expressing equal alarm.[8] When Birt pressed Green for more and more of Radio Four's airtime, Green's response was quite naturally shaped by his awareness of acute public sensitivity. 'I was saying go gently with this, because we may have some blood on our hands, and the listeners will go berserk.'[9]

The issue lapsed for a while—not least because Birt had other battles to fight. But with each big news story over the next three years—IRA bombings, Piper Alpha, Lockerbie, Tiananmen Square, the collapse of Communist regimes in eastern Europe and of Margaret Thatcher's premiership in Britain, the freeing of the Beirut hostages—there was a frisson of frustration from News and Current

Affairs. In almost every case, Radio Four distinguished itself by its extensive reportage and analysis. Indeed, in 1989 Birt himself praised the 'astonishing array', the 'tone of reason and dispassion', it was supplying in all its regular outlets. But, as Abramsky complained, what Radio Four did not offer—because it could not—was *continuous* coverage. And it was continuous coverage that she and her fellow journalists craved most. Sky TV had been supplying it since 1989. A little-known outfit in America, CNN, had been doing it for years. It was the modern, fashionable, democratic, and efficient thing to do. And the BBC should be doing it too.[10]

By the start of the 1990s, then, it looked as if all it would take to tip the argument decisively News and Current Affairs' way was just one more big news story. Then, in August 1990, the Iraqi leader Saddam Hussain invaded Kuwait. Over the next five months international diplomacy tried—and failed—to persuade him to leave. The United States responded by moving hundreds of thousands of troops to the Gulf, building a coalition of allies, and preparing an all-out assault to drive him out. Desert Shield was about to become Desert Storm. It was another sharp turn in the weather. And it looked like the best opportunity yet for the BBC's journalists to make good the missed chances of the 'hurricane' three years before.

SCUD-FM

The Gulf War began at 9.50 p.m., London time, on Wednesday 16 January 1991, with a fusillade of cruise missiles launched from Coalition warships. By midnight they had reached their targets, and US and British warplanes were approaching Baghdad to unload a further wave of devastation. Aerial bombing continued for another five weeks or so, followed in the early hours of 24 February by a ground assault that overwhelmed Iraqi forces and lasted just four days before the US called a halt to operations.[11]

Desert Storm was covered by more than 1,400 journalists from around the world, and the BBC had spent unprecedented sums ensuring it was well represented among them. By the outbreak of hostilities it had Kate Adie and Stephen Sackur embedded with the British First Armoured Division, other reporters onboard some of the twenty-six Royal Navy ships in the Gulf, or billeted at operational headquarters in Riyadh and Dhahran. Overseas bureaux in Jordan, Israel, the Soviet Union, and the United States had also been reinforced with extra staff. And in Baghdad itself two other BBC correspondents, Bob Simpson and his namesake John, had disobeyed an order to return home and remained hunkered down in the Al-Rashid Hotel, morphine tablets in their pockets, determined to make as much use as they could of a satellite phone smuggled in a few days before the start of hostilities.[12]

There was, then, an impressive array of newsgathering talent in the field. But the crucial decision for those running the BBC was how to put all this to best use on the air. One week before the air assault began Jenny Abramsky had persuaded Michael Green to allow News and Current Affairs to take over Radio Four's FM frequency should war break out. Abramsky's position was clear: as a public service broadcaster the BBC had a democratic duty to keep licence-fee payers in general, and the families and friends of service personnel in particular, informed as to the progress of the war; this could not be done effectively if coverage was confined to the usual built schedule of Radio Four. Michael Green was less certain about the best course to take. He was a journalist by background and instinctively in favour of extra news coverage for such a momentous event; he also knew there was a public appetite for more news at moments of crisis. But splitting the network would irritate some regular listeners, and any news service offered in Radio Four's name had to be done in what he called 'a decent journalistic way'. Most worrying of all, a news service for the Gulf War could be a Trojan horse: once established it might never disappear.[13]

As the first bombs landed in Baghdad on the night of 16 January, a hastily improvised compromise unfolded back in Broadcasting House. The Radio Four midnight news was allowed to stay on air an extra four hours—though it had to make do with just the one regular newsreader and there were no spare correspondents anywhere in the building who could help out. By daybreak enough staff had been drafted in to provide extended news coverage, and such was the expected level of interest that it was allowed at first to run on both long wave and FM, displacing most regular Radio Four programmes. By Saturday, however, an agreed split had taken effect: news coverage continued on FM, while normal service resumed on long wave. From then until 6 p.m., Saturday 2 March, when the terms of a ceasefire were being finalized at the United Nations, what was officially called 'Radio Four News FM' was on the air seventeen hours a day, seven days a week. Continuous news at the BBC had been born.[14]

Very soon, there were other names in circulation for this new creature, not all of them complimentary. Some correspondents in the field adapted Saddam Hussain's rhetoric and referred to the news service as 'Mother of all Battles Radio'; many more called it 'Scud-FM', which, given the discovery that Iraq's once-feared Scud missiles were turning out to be misguided duds, was not as neutral a title as it first sounded. Most of the producers and reporters drafted in from normal Radio Four news programmes, however, simply referred to it as 'Rolling Bollocks', an inauspicious title conveying two measures of disillusion to every half measure of affection.

One problem with the service was that after the first onslaught of air strikes was over and the threat of Israeli retaliation for Iraq's Scud-missile attacks had abated, there was little news to report. There were daily briefings from military headquarters in Saudi Arabia, of course. Given the bravura performance of those on stage—people such as General Norman Schwarzkopf or Group Captain Niall

Irving, with their talk of smart-bombs and a succession of irresistible superlatives ('the biggest raid in history')—these set-piece events offered a rich supply of information to be chewed over, not to mention a regular dose of showmanship. Elsewhere, hard information arrived slowly. In Baghdad, Bob Simpson was facing nightly bombing raids, the interference of Iraqi minders, and the frustrations and dangers of moving about in a malfunctioning city: like his colleague, John Simpson, he was only able to file reports fitfully. Those attached to ground forces found that with so much of the war being fought in the air, there was often little to relay but a sense of expectation. Even when the land offensive began the Pentagon imposed an immediate and all-embracing news blackout across the allied lines for 48 hours. Journalists had already been required to sign up to 'Ground Rules for War Correspondents' drawn up by the Ministry of Defence, which obliged them to stay with their military escorts and subjected all their scripts to 'review' by officers. As one disappointed reporter put it, 'Much witnessing was left undone.'[15]

The effect of all this on Radio Four News FM was to leave hours of airtime to be filled by a mixture of analysis, commentary, and speculation. Sue MacGregor was on the rota of presenters and recalled the air of improvisation that prevailed. 'On one of my first mornings on duty I was slipped a piece of paper. On it were written the names of two experts and the succinct rubric: "Discussion on water supplies in the Middle East. Keep going for twenty minutes".' 'I did my best', she added, 'but I fear it may not have made entirely compelling listening.'[16]

Something of what listeners thought of this endless, sometimes meandering coverage, is revealed in contemporary diaries kept by Mass-Observation. Many entries simply relay natural abhorrence at the violence being unleashed; others grumble that news was probably being censored; yet more rail against the BBC for the sheer amount of coverage, and its cumulative effect. They tell the story of grim fascination being overtaken by weariness, even frustration:

Thursday 17 January: 'I watched television from 12.10 a.m. to 1am until I felt so tired I went upstairs and then listened to Radio 4 until I fell asleep . . . woke in the morning with a dull feeling of gloom and dread and a huge headache . . . The Brian Redhead Today programme stayed on until 10am and The World at One took over. I couldn't listen to more . . . More news did come in—great waves of it. So much so, that saturation coverage was reached by about 11.30am with me. Endless interviews with "experts" and military men rapidly bored me . . .'

Thursday 24 January: 'The 5pm Radio 4 programme PM resembles an enormous war game. You can almost see the grid somewhere in the studio as the participants and experts throw dice to move their pieces'.

Monday 28 January: 'The eternal "news" churns out' . . . 'The BBC has run amok and has commandeered Radio 4 on FM, leaving the grotty old Long Wave for the normal programmes. I don't listen, but my husband does, all the time, so I catch nauseating snippets as I go down to his room to attend to him . . .'

Tuesday 29 January: 'The bombardment of news, speculation and "video pictures" has continued here at home—and once again I have closed my mind for most of each day...'

Wednesday 30 January: 'Such a plethora of news and views—you don't remember things. The most odd thing is the way the Gulf War distorts the "news" altogether. Apparently white people are rioting in South Africa concerning Black Rule—now imminent... Also Linda Chalker has succeeded in getting both sides in the Ethiopian War to meet for talks in London. Again, this is hardly reported. Even the Poll Tax has sunk almost without trace.'

Tuesday 12 February: Today I tuned in to Radio 4 about 11am to hear Brian Redhead of Today interviewing ad nauseam about the Gulf War. Has this been normal daily fare on FM? I understand it has. I don't understand the purpose of this media coverage. It obviously whips up <u>some</u> people but must surely turn an awful lot of others completely off. The endless discussions over tiny pieces of propaganda given out by various sources, sound like children's arguments over "rules" in the playground. Meanwhile, we grind to a halt from an inch or 2 of snow and people freeze to death on the streets for want of shelter...'[17]

The BBC's own audience research found rather less evidence of public revulsion, but confirmed the impression of unease. Regular Radio Four listeners worried most over what they saw as the surfeit of opinion and dearth of facts on News FM. As one member of the audience put it, '<u>News</u>, yes, we want <u>News</u>. Endless speculation and discussion by journalists and "expert" civilians, no I do <u>not</u> want and consider it an unhelpful waste of time.' Among a sample of some 500 listeners, 'the number of complaints about excessive coverage is striking', the researchers concluded, adding that '"Armchair generals" and other "pundits" were especially disliked.'[18]

There were voices raised in News FM's defence. The charge that it provided nothing but endless speculation, some commentators argued, was overplayed. Despite the heavy restrictions enforced on reporters in the field, technology had advanced since the Falklands War, when journalists had been entirely dependent on the military for all telephone contact with London. This time around, correspondents could travel with their own satellite communications: whatever restrictions applied, there was at least the possibility of occasionally hearing broadcasts coming direct from the battlefield. And indeed, moments of vivid first-hand journalism pushed their way onto the air. Alan Little's grisly recounting of the carnage at Amiriyah in Baghdad, where coalition planes had incinerated a civilian shelter, was one. Another was Stephen Sackur's report on the apocalyptic scenes of the Basra road, where a column of Iraqis fleeing Kuwait had been burnt beyond recognition by an onslaught of cluster-bombs dropped from above—'saloon cars, tanks, military vehicles sitting nose-to-tail in a stalled procession' as far as the low grey clouds allowed him to see. And when Bob Simpson succeeded, despite everything, in sending his reports from Baghdad, they were, as John Simpson put it, 'conspicuously more rounded and descriptive than the "Holy Cow!" offerings of CNN'. These dispatches were generally measured in tone, and sometimes brutally frank about the real meaning of 'collateral damage'. As such, they offered a powerful rebuke to the most articulate critic of Gulf War journalism, the *Independent*'s Robert Fisk, who believed that 'journalists covered the war, supported it, became part of it'. They also won over the *Daily Telegraph*'s critic Gillian Reynolds. 'I have never heard an American all-news station which even aims at the depth of background, at the range of reference, which is going out on Radio Four News FM', she wrote. It benefited from the BBC's ranks of correspondents, its banks of information, its power to attract big-hitting interviewees and experts, creating a service that was 'instant, informed, urgent without being hysterical'. 'It can't show you missiles disappearing into airshafts', she admitted. But it offered something better: 'describing with sober tact the reality of what is going on'. 'There is no mistaking the tune,' she concluded: 'the voices of Brian Redhead, Nick Clarke, Robin Lustig and the rest are saying this is serious, this is war, and this is radio doing a historic job of reporting it.'[19]

Whatever the grumbles, over a million people were listening regularly to Radio Four News FM by the end of February. Over two-thirds of Radio Four's usual listeners had tried it. The number sticking with the regular output on long wave was also holding. Most listeners, it seemed, had found it easy enough to retune their dials to find *The Archers*, while a whole new audience appeared to have been found for the FM service. Better still, the newcomers were younger and a touch more working class than usual for Radio Four—even the proportion of listeners from Scotland, the North, and Wales, was higher.[20] Politically speaking, the FM service had extended Radio Four's audience profile in all the right directions. Choice, it seemed, had triumphed. Raw, 'unmediated' news, it seemed, had worked.

Whether there was a taste for this kind of rolling news service during peace-time conditions was altogether less clear. When BBC researchers asked focus groups of Radio Four listeners whether they would like a permanent news service, most were inclined to concentrate their praise on existing programmes, such as *Today*, and *The World at One*, and were overwhelmingly negative about the idea of a 'rolling' service. Non-Radio Four listeners were even less interested in the idea, unless it was going to offer music too. But no matter. Commentators on the Right, enamoured of consumer sovereignty and always suspicious of the BBC's editorial values, were quick to seize on the lessons of the war for the Corporation. In *The Times*, Janet Daley wrote of 'the right of the ordinary citizen to have information made available to him as quickly as to anyone else'—the 'anyone else' being those busybodies at the BBC who insisted on hearing the news first before deciding 'what one ought to be told'. The BBC, despite itself, had somehow stumbled into finally giving the public what it actually wanted, so her reasoning went—though, naturally, only by abandoning its usual outdated paternalist nonsense. Being the sluggish bureaucracy it was, it would probably return to its old ways. But it ought not to. The era of 'pre-digested' news was over, Daley concluded, and the BBC needed to wake up to the future.[21]

In fact, by the time News FM ceased operations the idea of a permanent news network had already taken a firm hold in the minds of those running News and Current Affairs at the BBC. Indeed, Birt had been hoping from the outset that News FM might simply be able to carry on forever, ceasefire or not. This tactic of creating a permanent rolling news service by stealth had been thwarted when David Hatch persuaded the Director-General Michael Checkland to rule that News FM could last only as long as the war itself. Hatch, like Michael Green, had actually wanted Checkland to close the service down just one week into the conflict, when the air campaign had settled into a familiar routine and time-filling on air seemed to be at its height. That it had been allowed to continue at all was an ominous sign that the News and Current Affairs Directorate now had as much, if not more, influence within the BBC than the Radio Directorate. Momentum was on the side of Birt and on the side of the journalists. 'In terms of a future all-news service, there are no plans', Abramsky told the press in the immediate aftermath of war. Yet, she added pointedly, 'the debate will not go away'.[22]

With the makeshift Gulf War service at an end, the BBC had an opportunity to think through what a permanent version might be like. The Corporation's whole pattern of programmes was in the process of being reviewed anyway, in order to present as businesslike a face as possible to the government in the run-up to negotiations over renewing the Royal Charter, due to expire in 1996. Over the following twelve months or so, a plethora of internal 'task forces', strategy groups, committees, and working parties were convened, and talk of a rolling news service was now folded into many of their discussions. Only a long and tortuous handover of power at the top of the BBC, from Michael Checkland to his heir-apparent John Birt, delayed a final decision. But the direction in which events were moving was clear enough. Newspaper headlines started predicting confidently that News FM was 'set for a comeback' and that an all-news radio service would be launched 'before the election' in 1992. Soon, even a dubious David Hatch conceded that a news service was 'going to happen'.[23] It was no longer a question of *if*, merely a matter of *when*. And, more problematically, *how*.

THE WAR OF BROADCASTING HOUSE

Hatch had suggested that Broadcasting House would debate any plans for a permanent news service 'calmly and sensibly'. This turned out to be overoptimistic, since there was already considerable hostility between the News and Current Affairs stronghold on the third floor and the Radio directorate's headquarters on the fourth. One had a news network as its key objective; the other had as its main goal the stopping of it. There were doubters and apostates on either side, of course. But the barricades were going up fast, and the risk, as ever, was of positions becoming deeply entrenched.[24]

To begin with, programmes were at the root of the dispute. John Birt had always been taken with the idea that a news network should seize from Radio Four established news programmes such as *Today*, *The World at One*, *PM*, and *The World Tonight*. In the absence of *Today*, Birt reasoned, Radio Four might contemplate having, say, comedy in the mornings. The prospect appalled Green. He knew that losing *Today*—or indeed any of the sequences—would devastate Radio Four's ratings and probably prove fatal. After more than two decades of defending the 'rich mix' of Radio Four against *too much* news, there was now the possibility of it being taken away completely and handed over to a rival channel. 'It sort of explained my resistance to this, and my anxiety about it', Green later admitted.[25]

The obvious compromise seemed to be that proposed in November 1991 by a committee chaired by the Controller of BBC Scotland, John McCormick, and including senior television executives such as Michael Jackson and Janet Street-Porter. Their task had been to examine the BBC's role as an 'information provider'. They concluded that a twenty-four-hour radio news network must indeed be provided—but that it should *share* the main news sequence programmes with Radio Four.[26] This meant Radio Four would keep hold of its biggest ratings successes; it also raised a whole new set of difficulties to be overcome. Some of these had already been identified by a second task force, chaired by the editor of *The World Tonight*, Margaret Budy. Together with a group of producers, she had looked in some detail at exactly what difficulties sharing programmes might create. Would all or some of the 'sequences' be shared? If so, which ones? Would these carefully structured programmes have to change in order to be compatible with a live news network? What about weekly programmes such as *Analysis* and *File on Four*: were they to be shared too? And if so, how could they continue to run for up to forty-five minutes when they were on a live network supposedly devoted to breaking news? Might they become shorter, run in instalments, even become more like live magazines? If that sort of thing happened, would it not change the nature of Radio Four itself?[27]

There were no easy answers to any of these questions, for sharing programmes between networks had always been immensely complex, as those who had managed the intricate series of opt-ins and opt-outs between 'Basic' Radio Four and the Regions in the late 1960s and early 1970s could have testified. Trying to marry 'live' programmes with 'built' ones was a thankless task purely on the practical level. Even worse, however, it raised serious philosophical questions as to the essential purpose of BBC journalism. Janet Daley might rail against the BBC's tradition of 'pre-digesting' the news and urge more live coverage, but there were others speaking up for the virtues of editorial polish. One such was Sheena McDonald, who pointed out that in broadcast journalism less was usually more. A continuous live news network would not only erode the editorial skills of selecting information and communicating it in a considered fashion: it would also 'sensationalise minor events to fill the time; over-rely on speculation and opinion for the same reason; absorb the energies of good people and the revenues of licence payers in its insatiable maw'. Another experienced correspondent, the BBC's own Charles Wheeler, warned that rolling news would force journalists to spend more and more time on air—and consequently less and less doing the essential work of conducting their own investigations. It was, he thought, the BBC's 'worst idea yet'.[28]

The McCormick task force had made one other recommendation, and it was the one that proved in the end to be the most controversial of all: that the twenty-four-hour news service should find its home on Radio Four's long wave frequency.

The choice of long wave, as opposed to the FM frequency occupied during the Gulf War, was, on the face of it, perfectly rational. BBC Radio had been trying hard to get the public to embrace FM since the late 1960s. During the brouhaha over live coverage of Parliament in 1975 and 1978, radio drama producers had stressed that it was FM, with its high-fidelity stereo sound, which made the best of their productions; long wave was low fidelity and old hat, much more suitable for any extended news coverage. Journalists concurred: stereo had little relevance for the bread-and-butter speech they traded in, and the universal reach of long wave seemed a valuable means of disseminating 'national' debates. By 1991, the slow push to make Radio Four's FM frequency its *main* outlet, and the long wave frequency its *secondary* outlet, was reaching a critical stage. An on-air advertising campaign featured Carter, a character from Peter Tinniswood's *Uncle Mort* stories, encouraging listeners to switch to FM: 'you can get it in stereo and the signal's as sharp as buggery', he kept telling them in his inimitable northern fashion. Meanwhile, there was to be a little more 'splitting', with the *Daily Service* and John Gielgud's Bible readings on long wave and *Woman's Hour* on FM in its new morning slot. This represented a new element of choice for Radio Four listeners. Green did not regard long wave as superfluous: it provided some badly needed room for manoeuvre in scheduling his portfolio of regular Radio Four programmes. Yet there was no doubt that these changes conspired to mark it down, implicitly, as less than central to Radio Four's future—and up for grabs as far as News and Current Affairs was concerned. It was long wave, not FM, which was used in August 1991 to provide a small-scale and temporary revival of the Gulf War service during the Soviet coup against Mikhail Gorbachev. It was long wave, the London *Evening Standard* now declared unhelpfully, which was 'the disposable wavelength'.[29]

The vulnerability of Radio Four's second frequency was confirmed the following spring when one of John Birt's favoured managerial tricks was deployed, and outside consultants were brought in to advise on the matter. McKinsey & Company, who had helped pave the way for *Broadcasting in the Seventies* back in 1969, now returned at the invitation of the News and Current Affairs directorate to examine the likely impact of the loss of long wave on Radio Four. Green recalled the key moment when their findings were unveiled:

They made their presentation to John [Birt], and David Hatch, and me, and their conclusion was that there were only going to be about 16,000 listeners deprived of Radio Four if longwave was taken away and they had to rely on FM only. I remember saying, 'well, you're wrong'... And, of course, the McKinsey proposition was accepted... I was overruled... They [the Governors] accepted the McKinsey research and John's proposition—that there was a risk, but an entirely manageable risk, there would be some fallout, but easily managed.[30]

Green knew that he and his senior colleagues in the Radio directorate had now lost the argument internally. There was nevertheless considerable shock when on 14 July 1992 the Director-General Michael Checkland suddenly announced at a speech in Birmingham that a twenty-four-hour news network would indeed be launched—by January 1994 at the latest, and on Radio Four's long wave. Sky News, CNN, and Radio Four's own Gulf War service, he said, had changed everything. There was now 'an increasing demand for live, on-the-spot coverage of unfolding events', and the BBC needed to satisfy that demand in order to retain its place as 'the leading provider of news and information'. The only concession to anxieties over reception was Checkland's announcement that the BBC would speed up its programme of building more FM transmitters; the only concession to anxieties over programme content was his promise that the new service would avoid cheap phone-ins to fill airtime. In all other respects, the worst fears of those running Radio were confirmed. News and Current Affairs was going to seize airtime, resources, and money—most likely, at their expense. Journalists would leave Broadcasting House altogether, and run the new service alongside their television counterparts at a £30 million complex next to Television Centre in White City. The ongoing costs of the new network would be £9 million a year, a sum to be met from existing resources through 'efficiencies and economies'.[31]

One newspaper columnist wrote that it was as if the BBC had 'taken a knife to its own heart'. As for the Controller of Radio Four, it was a moment when he seriously considered resigning. He now faced a future travelling up and down the country to ascend public platforms and defend a decision that was not his own. 'Whoever sits in the Radio Four chair gets blamed for everything', he said.[32] And indeed, the next eighteen months were to be the most uncomfortable of his professional life. Yet events did not quite unfold as he expected. The BBC was about to experience one of the most extraordinary displays of listener power in its history—a campaign that would end in an equally extraordinary volte-face by the Corporation, and save long wave for Radio Four after all.

THE SAVE RADIO FOUR LONG WAVE CAMPAIGN

Michael Checkland's announcement had come just as the holiday season was beginning. By the end of September, however, the impact of the change had sunk in and a backlash was gaining momentum. At first, the protestations were spontaneous and uncoordinated. Among the earliest to grumble were expatriates and foreign Anglophiles in western Europe, who were entirely dependent on long wave for hearing Radio Four. One estimate put their number at about 500,000. Among the most dedicated of them were diplomatic staff and their families, but since 1992 also happened to be the year of the Single Market in Europe, these were joined by the fast-expanding ranks of British business people venturing abroad. Letters now started arriving at Broadcasting House from Paris, Normandy, Brittany, Lille, from people working at NATO and EEC headquarters and the British School in Brussels, from the Netherlands, from Ireland. They wrote, as they had in 1987, of Radio Four being their 'lifeline to Britain'. 'It is not just the news and views I value,' one British resident in Paris explained, 'it is the tone of voice, the flavour and what could loosely be termed the culture.'[33]

What really took senior BBC executives by surprise was that so many people living *within* British shores seemed to echo this attachment to long wave, even though most of them had recourse to FM. An eternal truth of radio reception was reiterated. Long wave might have been fuzzy and unfashionably mono, but its signal was as solid as granite. FM, by comparison, was as shifting sand tossed about in the electromagnetic swell. As Brenda Maddox pointed out in the *Daily Telegraph*, it was next to useless in her car, it was completely useless in her house in Wales, it was useless, in fact, whenever her radio was near computers, or passing motorbikes, or among mountains and valleys. In a repeat of the events of November 1978, a stream of similar complaints now flowed toward the BBC from all corners of the country. There were great swathes of Devon, Gloucestershire, and Cornwall where listeners claimed that FM reception was at best temperamental and at worst non-existent; the foothills of the Marlborough Downs were another blackspot; Birmingham was hit-and-miss; the Channel Islands touch-and-go. The most widespread difficulties in receiving FM, however, were felt, as before, in Scotland. And it was here, bizarrely, that organized revolt of a very English kind now began. Among the occasional residents of Drumnadrochit, a village at the head of Urquhart Bay on Loch Ness, was a 29-year-old maths teacher from Winchester called Nick Mackinnon. He had been listening to Radio Four ever since his first day as an undergraduate in Oxford, when he came across *The Archers* while tuning the Binatone clock-radio in his college room. Nowadays what he liked more than anything else was Radio Four's plays, short stories, comedies, and panel games. Whenever he went on his regular rock-climbing trips to Scotland, he would tune to long wave so that he could hear these favourites. That they might now be lost to a news network so incensed Mackinnon that he wrote to Radio Four's *Feedback* programme, not just to express his own rage but to call on other listeners to join him in a campaign to 'Save Radio Four Long Wave'. 'My own instinct was that it was completely stupid, and I had time to do something about it, because I was in plaster after a rock-climbing accident in Skye.' His call for direct action, broadcast on Friday 25 September, and repeated on *Feedback*'s Sunday edition two days later, galvanized

Radio Four loyalists. It also prompted a flurry of newspaper attention, which fanned the flames of revolt further still. Journalists spotted in Mackinnon 'a perfect young hero for the chattering classes': respectable, yes, but young, bright and articulate, rather than blimpish; someone who clearly threatened to put the BBC on the run.[34]

The opening salvo of Mackinnon's campaign was to invite those who shared his anger to contact him forthwith. Within three days he had received 400 letters. Five days, and several incendiary newspaper interviews later, he had received 1,000. Within a fortnight, the number was 6,000 and rising. Soon, the Post Office was delivering one whole sack of new letters to his home every day. Concealed in this mountain of Basildon Bond were countless pleas for direct action. 'Feelings are so strong', Mackinnon warned one newspaper, 'I wouldn't be surprised if you had old ladies throwing themselves under Michael Checkland's car.' His own preference was for less spectacular but nonetheless distinctly militant tactics. He appeared on BBC 1 tearing up his television licence, and suggested other listeners might do likewise; he suggested that the BBC Chairman, Marmaduke Hussey, should resign; that there should be a march on Broadcasting House, or picket lines across its entrance, even occupation. 'I was making this stuff up as I went along', MacKinnon later confessed. But to the outside world, the organizational fervour was striking. It certainly reinvigorated the European campaign. More than 200 people turned up to the British School in Brussels for the first meeting of 'North Europe Save Radio Four'; coordinators sprang up for groups of expatriates in various parts of France, Ireland, Germany, Luxembourg, and the Netherlands, and they, in turn, initiated further mass rallies; newsletters such as *The British European* kept the disparate groups informed; testimonials from prominent foreigners were collated, with Jacques Delors, the European Commission President, telling people of how he started each day by listening to *Farming Today*, and the US Ambassador to Belgium speaking of Radio Four as a diplomat for British culture and values.[35]

By the second week of October, protest groups from Winchester to Brussels were giddy with the oxygen of publicity and evidence of rising popular support. The *Daily Telegraph*, ever sensitive to the feelings of Middle England and Expatriate Britain, now threw its weight behind the campaign. Its chief radio critic, Gillian Reynolds, had been a prominent fan of Radio Four's Gulf War service and had even called on the BBC to find a permanent home for a news service. But she was disturbed at the unresolved question of whether it would rob Radio Four of its essential news programmes, and felt that losing long wave was too high a price to pay for twenty-four-hour news. She asked the Director-General to think again, and then asked her own readers to vote in a 'Radio Referendum'. When the results were published they reflected the collective opinion of more than 12,000 *Telegraph* readers. Eighty-eight per cent of them claimed to listen to Radio Four mainly on long wave; 94 per cent of them said they did not want an all-news network on BBC Radio; of those who *did* want an all-news network, most wanted it on FM. These responses were what professional audience researchers called 'self-selecting' and hence not entirely typical, even of *Daily Telegraph* readers. Yet when Gallup carried out a more representative poll for the same newspaper at the turn of the year, the results, though less extreme, conveyed much the same message: 60 per cent against a news network.[36] On the scales of public opinion, Quantity weighed heavily against change.

And so, very soon, did Quality. One of the first among a fast expanding cast of the famous to endorse the long wave campaign was the former Labour leader Neil Kinnock; over the following months, he was joined by a small handful of businessmen, including Lord Weidenfeld, Rocco Forte, and Mohammed Al-Fayed, and by a more numerous collection of actors, theatre directors, writers, publishers, and musicians—among them Prunella Scales, Simon Callow, Robert Lindsay, Maggie Smith, Edward Fox, Tom Conti, Emma Thompson, Peter Brook, John Gielgud, Georg Solti, Anita Brookner, Alan Ayckbourn, David Bailey, Spike Milligan, Dirk Bogarde, Carmen Callil, Jeremy Isaacs, and Nicholas Serota.[37] In publicity terms the *coup de grâce* came with the news in October 1992 that Prince Charles himself had intervened on the campaign's behalf by writing to the BBC Chairman Marmaduke Hussey to demand an explanation for the Corporation's plans. Indeed, by this stage it was getting hard to find *anyone* willing to support the news network publicly—aside from Janet Daley in *The Times*, who, despite her own campaign for the BBC to respond to the needs of 'the ordinary citizen', now called the long wave protests an 'eminently silly crusade'.[38]

Inside Broadcasting House, opinion was as sharply divided as ever. On one side, there were the original advocates of the BBC's News and Current Affairs directorate, not least Jenny Abramsky and the head of the directorate, Tony Hall. Far from being swayed by the groundswell of opposition, both were now convinced that Radio Four's coverage of 'Black Wednesday' on 16 September 1992 had decisively proven their case. Throughout the morning sterling had crashed in value on the world's markets forcing drastic interest rate rises and billions of pounds to be spent by the Bank of England in a failed attempt to hold the currency above the floor of the European Exchange Rate mechanism. Between the end of *Today* and the start of *The World at One*, however, Radio Four's fixed schedule had only left room for its usual hourly news summaries and one news flash at 11.15 a.m.—a pattern repeated through the afternoon and evening as the government's economic policy dramatically fell apart in its hands. Abramsky and Hall's reading of events was clear: here was the day when the global power of market speculation had been revealed, the day when the government's reputation for economic competence was destroyed, the day, perhaps, when the Conservatives had lost the next election—and BBC coverage had been tardy and sporadic. As far as they were concerned a twenty-four-hour news network could not come soon enough.[39] Facing them, however, was a large fifth column of unnamed programme-makers and presenters giving tacit support to the Save Radio Four Long Wave campaign. Indeed, as one newspaper reported with only a touch of hyperbole, if everyone inside Broadcasting House who agreed with the campaign were to join in, 'there would hardly be anyone left to put out the lights'. There was no doubt that the Managing Director of Radio and the Controller of Radio Four were also both buoyed by the gathering momentum of public protest—and its continued coverage on Radio Four's own *Feedback* programme. Though he could hardly say so at the time, Michael Green has since admitted that both he and David Hatch were 'absolutely delighted' by Mackinnon's campaign. 'It was', he said, 'a wonderful moment of listener power.' Both men had been overruled by the Governors and felt let down by their own Board of Management.[40] The combination of listener protests, negative press coverage, and criticism in high places gave them succour in dark times. It also stirred their first real hopes that there might be a change of heart from the top.

The BBC's initial response to the furore had not been impressive. First, came three weeks of official silence, and then, when public statements did start to emerge, there was little sign of flexibility. Listeners abroad, the Corporation said, had no right to complain since they were not licence-fee payers; 98 per cent of those who *did* pay a licence fee could pick up FM if they tried; and in any case the twenty-four-hour channel would not be some endlessly speculative and repetitive American-style 'rolling news' machine, but something more sophisticated—a 'current affairs and events network' of 'richness and originality', properly crafted in the traditional BBC manner. The tone was defensive and served only to rile critical opinion further. An *Observer* editorial complained of a BBC 'which has lost touch with its most loyal supporters'. Another in the *Independent* accused the BBC of 'arrogance'. It seemed to treat enemies and friends with equal ineptitude, perhaps because it did not always recognize which were which.[41]

Yet some chinks were already appearing in the corporate armour. Prince Charles's intervention had come just as the long wave campaigners were planning a march from Speaker's Corner to Broadcasting House. By an uncanny coincidence, Mackinnon was suddenly invited to meet BBC apparatchiks at Television Centre. Two days later, the Board of Governors met in Leeds. There they confirmed once again that the news network would indeed be launched as planned by April 1994, and that it would indeed be on Radio Four's long wave. But one member of the Board, the Oxford historian John Roberts, had managed to raise the issue of poor FM reception on the campaigners' behalf, and persuaded his fellow Governors to offer a concession: Radio Four, they agreed, would remain on long wave *until* FM transmission was satisfactory. It was a terribly vague promise. After all, what counted as 'satisfactory' was already heartily disputed. The *Guardian* even called the Board's statement 'deliberately misleading'. But it was enough to call off the protest march. And for MacKinnon, who had been told of the decision personally in a phone call from one of the Governors, it was enough to express cautious optimism that a corner had been turned.[42]

Certainly, it was the first sign that BBC Governors, who up till now had ridden roughshod over Radio directorate, were beginning to wobble in their unqualified support for John Birt's favoured News and Current Affairs empire. Part of their embarrassment was that the BBC had only recently committed itself to a policy of being more open and responsive to public opinion. With the government's Green Paper on the future of the BBC imminent, they recognized that a greater taste for accountability needed to be on show, and quickly. The alternative was a glaringly contradictory message to licence-fee holders at the most politically sensitive of moments. As Michael Green pointed out, 'You couldn't on the one hand say, you are our stakeholders, and on the other hand say well, we don't care what you say.'[43] A second factor in the Governor's weakening resolve was simply that the Save Radio Four Long Wave campaign was getting to them. The kind of people most agitated—diplomats, the cultural glitterati, the 'chattering classes' at large—were precisely the same people Governors regularly found themselves sitting next to at dinner or in the boardroom. Hussey himself complained that it was the BBC's misfortune that he, as Chairman, seemed to know the 'ten per cent' of the population for whom FM would never do, and found them to be 'intelligent, articulate and angry'. If the Governors rapidly 'lost their bottle', as Green put it succinctly, it was, in part, because they were now regularly 'getting their heads banged' by everyone about them.[44]

Feeling the pain was one thing. Finding a way to stop it quite another. There seemed no obvious middle course between an audience that would not be appeased if long wave were turned over to news, and an incoming Director-General who would not be appeased if a continuous news service did not arrive within eighteen months. As even Birt himself recognized when he took over from Michael Checkland in January 1993, the BBC was in 'a hole we had dug for ourselves'.[45] And prevarication was only fuelling suspicion. The Save Radio Four Long Wave campaign, only momentarily mollified by the Governors' assurances of October, was soon back in the headlines. With an exhausted MacKinnon back at work, it had a new leader, Rachel Mawhood, and another lease of life. It talked of suing the BBC, or trying to paralyse it with a fax inundation; it even planned another march on Broadcasting House in April—one that would go ahead this time, regardless of what the BBC said.

Just as the campaign was regaining momentum, however, the BBC found someone who promised to find a way out of its difficulties. One of Birt's first appointments when he became Director-General was to hire as his new Managing Director of Radio Liz Forgan, the head of programmes at Channel Four. Radio staff in Broadcasting House were taken aback. Birt had persuaded Forgan to take the job after a series of secret discussions at her London flat, so her appointment had come out of the blue. She also had no professional experience in radio whatsoever. Her arrival seemed to be yet another sign that television principles and television power would be imposed on Broadcasting House during the Birt regime. To the sceptics' surprise, however, she quickly established a rapport with

most staff in the directorate. She told them of how she had been born listening to
Radio Four, of how she had come to the BBC 'because I love the way BBC Radio
is, not because I hate it and want to destroy it'. She also staked a claim to being
open to ideas by telling producers that her office door would be ajar and that
anyone passing should feel free to call in and talk. She was variously described as
intellectually rigorous, committed, enthusiastic, jolly, principled, liberal, tough-
minded. She was, the Chairman concluded, someone to 'light up the Board of
Management like a Christmas tree'. She also had one thing in common with
the man who had given John Birt such a headache over the past year, Nick
MacKinnon: she had a holiday home in Scotland. Like MacKinnon, therefore,
she knew from experience that Radio Four really was only available on long wave
in some parts of the country. As a result, she had a natural sympathy with the
campaigners' complaint over the inadequacy of Radio Four's FM signal. Personal
inclination aligned nicely with her professional independence from the Broadcasting House old guard. As an outsider she could look at the whole family of BBC
Radio networks and frequencies with a fresh pair of eyes. As a Birt and Hussey
booking, any decision she took was unlikely to be interpreted by either man as
defending vested interests. The window of opportunity was hers for the taking.[46]

In February 1993, Forgan made her move by going back to the drawing board.
The editor of *Today*, Phil Harding, was put in charge of a new committee looking
afresh at BBC Radio's use of frequencies. He sent a small army of researchers out
to interview a representative sample of listeners about their reception experiences;
engineers were told to visit homes in London, Manchester, and the Midlands. It
did not take long for them to discover that McKinseys appeared to have
drastically underestimated the number of people who would be disenfranchised
through the loss of long wave: the real figure was likely to be in the region of 1.5
million listeners. Green and Hatch had been right all along. Within a month,
Harding was briefing journalists that the news network might not be on long
wave after all: Radio Four's FM frequency might be seized instead.[47] Then
Forgan struck upon a more radical option altogether—inspired, she said, by
hearing the commentary of a football match, which was simultaneously 'expert'
and 'demotic'.[48] Jenny Abramsky recalled the moment:

It was on a Friday in May in 1993 and she came down from the fourth floor in
Broadcasting House to the third to have a private word with me. If she were to axe
Radio Five, did I think it possible to combine our News proposition with the sport on
Radio Five? Could it work? If I thought it could, she would suggest it to the Board. She
wanted an answer on the Monday morning when the Board of Management were due to
meet to discuss the Long Wave News Service.[49]

The idea of using Radio Five's medium wave frequency to combine news and
sport was not entirely novel. Gillian Reynolds had suggested it as the best way to keep
a rolling news service going immediately after the Gulf War in February 1991.[50]
Combining news and sport seemed to offer a good match. Live broadcasting suited

them both, for a start. And while news tended to garner a disproportionate number of middle-class listeners, sport was classless or, if anything, a little more working class in its appeal: the resulting audience mix could be very attractive. As it stood, Radio Five was exposed. In an age that favoured clearly defined radio formats, it was even more of an anomaly than Radio Four. It had inherited sport from Radio Two, as well as Schools, Continuing Education, Open University, and children's programmes from Radio Three and Radio Four, and a miscellany of output from the World Service. Its children's programmes were admired, and its coverage of major sports events (for which the BBC had lost television rights to ITV and Sky) was recognized as strategically valuable. But its ratings overall were low, its tone resolutely inconsistent, its character, frankly, inaudible. In truth, it had been born out of expediency—a warehouse for storing all the material that had fallen out of the other networks. In its three years of existence, it had never quite shaken off the epithet circulating in Broadcasting House: it was, so the cruellest voices said, a 'Radio Dustbin'.[51] It must have seemed to Forgan that Middle England was unlikely to march in *its* defence as they had for Radio Four.

In any case, Abramsky was now sufficiently taken with Forgan's proposal to spend the weekend working out possible schedules. On the Monday morning she was able to show her a draft schedule for the new service. 'Yes, it could work very well', she announced.[52] Phil Harding's committee was now asked to concentrate its gaze on Radio Five's medium wave frequency and on the detail of how news and sport might be combined. There was as yet no public announcement over the latest plan. Even the BBC's own Sports department was kept in the dark. But as several hundred Save Radio Four Long Wave protestors dutifully assembled on 3 April 1993 for their big set-piece event—a march from Hyde Park to Broadcasting House—the *Daily Telegraph* was reporting that the campaign was suddenly being listened to with a new sense of respect at the BBC, that there was now 'a remarkable absence of paranoia and mistrust' between the two sides. One obstacle to be negotiated *within* Broadcasting House was Birt's unease at the turn of events. He had always had a distinctly upmarket news and current affairs channel in mind and remained unconvinced a combination of news and sport would work. Forgan now appealed directly to the Chairman, telling him of Birt's doubts. 'It's a brilliant idea', Hussey replied. 'I'll back that and the governors will back me. Go ahead.' With that imperious promise, the die was cast. In June word leaked out that the closure of Radio Five was now the BBC's 'preferred option'. There were the seeds of a campaign to save the network—lobbying from the Society of Authors, a Commons motion signed by 200 MPs—but they never took root before the axe fell. On Monday 11 October 1993 the plan for a rolling news and sports service on medium wave, to be called Radio Five Live, was formally accepted by the BBC's Board of Governors. Long wave, it seemed, was safe at last. 'An orchestrated lobby by thousands of indignant individuals has salvaged a pillar of middle-to-high-brow values', an editorial in the *Telegraph* declared. Alan Ayckbourn called it 'a victory for civilization'. The Controller of

Radio Four, who, like his Managing Director, had been required to adopt a position of neutrality in public, could at last express his huge sense of relief. 'We couldn't believe our luck', he admitted. 'We huddled together and went off for a drink.'[53]

'PEOPLE LIKE US'

Rolling news arrived at the BBC the following April, but as far as the Radio Four loyalists were concerned, it was safely out of sight and out of mind. What they cared about most was their own network, and it had survived. Indeed, it had not just retained its cherished long wave frequency: it had also kept hold of the established news programmes that formed the spine of its schedule. Given the air of defeat that had hung over the Radio directorate a year or so before, this was an extraordinary achievement. Popular intervention, executed in an organized fashion and with a canny eye for publicity, had been decisive. When Marmaduke Hussey looked back at the events of 1992 and 1993, he expressed surprise at the open revolt he had witnessed. 'A protest march by Radio 4 listeners! Who'd have thought it', he wrote in his memoirs.[54]

But the omens had been there for some time. Listeners—or at least the most vocal among them—had always claimed strong proprietary rights over the network. At the end of the 1960s and the start of the 1970s they had shown they were more likely than any other section of the BBC audience to complain about what they saw as a breach in standards, moral, aesthetic, or political. They had kept up the pressure ever since. Most complaints were spontaneous acts by individual listeners; sometimes they were prompted by newspaper reports, accurate or otherwise. But it was only in 1983, with the creation of 'The Voice of the Listener' that disorganized protest started turning into organized campaigning. Even then, the revolution in listener power had been incomplete, for 'The Voice of the Listener' was concerned with coolly representing listeners' opinions on a broad range of broadcasting policy: it sought to work *with* the BBC rather than *against* it.[55] The Save Radio Four Long Wave campaign was different. It was built around a single issue and had limited goals; it was also antagonistic, even insurrectionary in its approach. And it arrived at a propitious moment. Hussey himself had been swept to power at the BBC by a political climate that professed to put 'consumers' before 'producers' and popular sentiment before Establishment (especially *liberal* Establishment) opinion. Even after Margaret Thatcher's demise in 1990, there was the Citizen's Charter. When John Major launched it in July 1991, he declared that using consumer rights as a means of making public servants more accountable was to be 'the central theme for public life in the 1990s'.[56] The BBC could not be seen to buck the trend. It, too, embraced transparency and accountability with a new fervour in the early 1990s. Or, at least, that was the claim. When it appeared, as it did in 1992, to be imposing something on listeners by diktat the contradiction was all too obvious. It was only a matter of time before mild-mannered grumbling in the Radio Four heartlands turned to guerrilla warfare of a peculiarly British middle-class kind.

Single-issue campaigners they may have been, but Radio Four loyalists drew their strength from a feeling that more was at stake than the future of Radio Four. In parts of the Yorkshire Dales, the poor quality of Radio Four reception on FM was treated as just one more example of official indifference to rural life, along with post office closures and the cutting of bus services. To the expatriate actor Dirk Bogarde writing from his French retreat, losing Radio Four long wave had threatened to amputate 'yet another healthy flourishing limb of our dying reputation and honour abroad'. Radio Four, he believed, offered foreigners a glimpse of true, *deep* Britain: cultured, civilized, idiosyncratic, humorous, with points of view 'most sensibly and calmly argued' and voiced through 'the elegance and perfection of our spoken word'. 'God knows', he added, 'there is precious little else left now that is fit for export.' The true Britain of Radio Four was being overlaid with another newer version, one that was 'brutal', eroded by the 'gangrenous' decay of 'standards and qualities'. The theme was of decline. And it was no less strong among grassroots activists. 'You can see it all about us, a certain way of life being undermined', Nick MacKinnon had once said: 'the museums charging for entrance and feeling that they have to be viable in the market place; the disappearance of the O-level; the end of formal history teaching; the weakening of the armed forces; the crumbling of the monarchy.' It was time for ordinary people—those whom MacKinnon called 'people like us'—to take a stand.[57] This was Middle England par excellence. It was conservative in instinct, often Tory in its politics, but it was falling out of love with Thatcherism's unanticipated effects. It was starting to draw on deeper traditions of provincial dissent. And it was on the move.

Newspaper reporters were apt to see in all this an Ealing comedy that had come to life. Several hundred Long Wave campaigners marching from Hyde Park to Broadcasting House in April 1993 made perfect copy. Here they were: a column of polite individuals, holding balloons, marshalled by stewards eccentrically attired in pistachio green berets. No one shouted. Everyone spoke Standard English and 'within statutory decibel levels'. These people even thanked photographers and the police for their help—a striking contrast with the poll tax protestors who had unleashed their fury in central London exactly three years before. The imagery, in other words, was of a quaint and toothless affair. But this was misleading. The campaign as a whole had not just been effective in achieving its limited goals: it had also been a revelatory experience for many of its participants. Not only had it shown them what could be done through being organized. It had also introduced the Radio Four audience to *itself* in a remarkable way. Radio audiences were supposed to be rather fragmentary things, consisting of scattered individuals listening in the privacy of their own homes or their own cars. If these individuals felt a sense of 'community' as listeners to a particular station, it was one that generally had to be *imagined* into being through reading the letters pages of the press, having conversations with friends, relatives, and neighbours, or through hearing like-minded souls on pro-grammes like *Feedback*. But in 1992 and 1993, at the height of the Save Long Wave campaign, Radio Four listeners were everywhere: quoted and photographed in the papers, speaking on the radio, appearing on television, getting together in meetings and marches. In short, they were revealed—en masse and individually—as never before. And they got to *know* one another as never before. As always, the more attention that was paid to them, and that they paid to each other, the more the stereotypes melted away. Middle England was here, for sure, but it was a broad middle with a few radical fringes: altogether a reasonably heterogeneous bunch. Significantly though, this heterogeneous bunch had cohered. As one true believer, Lynn Truss, explained, it was collective protest that made 'this sense of community real': 'The idea that other listeners, in other kitchens, in other baths, in other traffic jams, are yelling the same thing is a comforting notion.'[58] Whatever their differ-ences, listeners were discovering that believing in the importance of Radio Four to the fabric of the nation was neither idiosyncratic nor futile. They had experienced a sense of congregation around a common cause, and they knew they could draw strength from each other. They were unlikely to look back.

STINGS IN THE TAIL

One local difficulty had been resolved, but larger battles over the way in which the BBC ran its affairs had further to run. That was the problem with single-issue campaigns: they could deal with symptoms, but often remained powerless to tackle the underlying causes of change. Indeed, they were often entirely oblivious to the way in which the relentless march of deregulation, marketization, and managerialism threatened to undermine the very services they valued most. On the surface, the BBC was a less febrile place in the mid-1990s than it had been in the mid-1980s. But underneath there were nagging worries about whether the Corporation's capacity to think clearly and be creative was fatally damaged. In the same month that long wave was finally 'saved', the internal market of Producer Choice began. Over the following years, the experiment of bi-media working in news and current affairs was pushed to its logical conclusions; new internal structures and efficiency drives were introduced; new people arrived, old hands departed. The Birtist Revolution, in other words, was incomplete. And as the later stages were revealed, its consequences sometimes unfolded in unpredictable ways.

For a start, resources—and specifically, space on the dial—remained strictly limited. The celebratory mood of the long wave campaigners was therefore cut short almost immediately by an unforeseen by-product of the closure of the old

Radio Five. BBC schedulers now realized that ball-by-ball commentary of cricket test matches was homeless again. It used to be on Radio Three's medium wave frequency until that had been taken from the BBC; more recently, it had been surviving on Radio Five. The new Radio Five Live was less hospitable. A *news*-and-sports network could hardly cover test matches for hours at a time without compromising its ability to cover breaking stories. Cricket would have to go elsewhere. In the spring of 1994, the inevitable happened and *Test Match Special* occupied Radio Four's long wave. Here was a programme with a distinguished history and a body of devotees ready to enjoy what *The Listener* described as its 'nonchalant professionalism, easy-going courtesy, boyish fun... unashamedly fixated in an innocent past, a world of pop, tuck and practical jokes'.[59] But to those listeners less enamoured with cricket, losing Radio Four's regular output seemed a high price for giving it houseroom. They now had to do what they had always wanted to avoid, namely seek refuge in fiddly, unreliable FM. It was a slap in the face for the Save Radio Four Long Wave campaign. And it was not long before its supporters emerged from hibernation. A new stream of letters appeared in the various broadsheets, from listeners outraged at this latest, and unantici-pated, betrayal. Rachel Mawhood revealed that the campaign itself had mutated into 'Radio Four Watch', which promised to be a permanent channel of com-plaint. 'It is a truth universally acknowledged', the *Telegraph* reminded the BBC, 'that those brought up on Radio Four do not lack for eloquence.' Corporation managers were not free yet to escape the intense gaze of public scrutiny.

There were new fissures opening up inside Broadcasting House too. One was the professional rivalry between established news programmes on Radio Four and the upstarts on Five Live. When the new network was about to be launched a policy of 'News Priority' was declared. Its main provision was that BBC corres-pondents were obliged to offer any breaking news to Five Live first and other networks second. Staff on programmes such as *Today* were appalled; some even threatened to sabotage the network's launch. The squabble became focused on plans being drawn up for covering the South African elections in April 1994. It was eventually agreed that John Humphrys could go there to present a special edition of *Today*, but similar requests by *The World Tonight* and *PM*, which had both broadcast special editions from overseas in the recent past, were turned down. In sharp contrast, Radio Five Live would be using several correspondents and its own team of producers in situ.[60] Journalists on Radio Four drew the obvious conclusions. The new network was sucking resources away from Radio Four's existing news programmes, basking, or so it seemed, in its status as the favoured child of management. There were now persistent grumbles about Five Live's encroachments—and not just in news. The network soon offered a range of programmes occupying the outer fringes of current affairs—magazines, for ex-ample, on health, travel, computers, and fishing. This was Radio Four's turf, and long-serving producers knew it. Their complaints echoed old battles between the various 'baronies' of the BBC. But they also told of a new and uncomfortable truth: Radio Four had finally lost its monopoly as a nationwide all-speech radio station. Whether this was an opportunity or a threat was, as yet, unclear. At a stroke, the new network reached the very audience groups—younger, non-southern, a little more working class—that Radio Four had apparently been pursuing for itself over recent years.

Did this represent a defeat for the evolutionary approach of Radio Four—damning it for ever to be what the *Guardian* called a 'low-reach niche station for southern ABs'? Or was it an opportunity—a chance for Radio Four to retire from the fight and concentrate on what it seemed to do best, namely to 'super-serve' its traditional, disproportionately middle-class audience? The kind of programme changes Michael Green made throughout the mid-1990s suggested he wanted the 'gradual refreshment' of Radio Four to continue—and with it a precarious balance between enticing new listeners and keeping traditionalists happy, a kind of broadcasting Third Way. Yet the presence of Radio Five Live undoubtedly gave him less room to manoeuvre. The news-and-sport network offered a breezy, matey, down-to-earth, *accessible* style all of its own. Radio Four was in danger of suddenly sounding rather stiff by comparison. It made no sense, of course, for Radio Four to copy the new station: BBC policy was for networks to complement each other rather than compete. Yet here, now, was an alternative model of what speech radio *could* sound like. And its presence exposed Radio Four to a running rebuke: if Five Live could manage to 'reach out' so easily why could other networks not do the same? Losing its monopoly, it seemed, revived all the old uncertainties—and sharpened all the old debates—over Radio Four's essential identity.

Identity, though, was a thing shaped by many forces. And the status of News and Current Affairs remained a complicating factor. The directorate had been thwarted in its original plan to take over long wave, but it had won its own network in the end. It also retained control over a sizeable chunk of Radio Four's own output. Nick MacKinnon, for one, was unsure whether his Save Radio Four Long Wave campaign had really tasted victory at all. As far as he could see, 'the whole sad affair' had simply reinforced the journalists' collective grip over Broadcasting House. He now talked of a 'cabal' ensconced since Birt's arrival and complained that while there were thousands of job losses elsewhere in the BBC, News and Current Affairs still seemed to be expanding fast. It certainly seemed to be tightening its grip, steadily extending the reach of its editorial writ as time went on.

One danger was that of a creeping uniformity to the BBC's journalism feeding back into Radio Four. In 1997, for example, Birt unveiled a plan to replace the individual editors of the network's main sequence programmes with a tier of five 'executive editors' who would decide on a shared agenda for the whole day's output. The *Today* producer Tim Luckhurst called the plan 'frankly demented'. Sue MacGregor thought it 'absurd'. Her fellow presenters, Robin Lustig from *The World Tonight*, James Cox from *The World This Weekend*, and Nick Clarke from *The World at One*, were sufficiently perturbed to write a joint letter to the Director-General. 'It is beyond us to understand', they told him, 'how a single commissioning team across all the programmes could possibly provide the richness and variety of material that the programmes generate at present.' *Today*, *The World at One*, and the rest of the sequences, all had separate histories of their own, and each represented a subtly different version of broadcast journalism. Some were more domestic in focus, others more international; some offered reportage, others the drama of set-piece studio interviews; some were reactive, others analytical. They rarely led on the same story, and each programme was 'handcrafted' by staff used to working in their own teams. If there was a culture in common it was probably something akin to eighteenth-century nonconformism. 'News', Jeremy Paxman reminded Birt at the time, 'is not a sausage machine.' But with rolling news, a stronger corporate editorial brand, and the omnipresent talk of efficiency, the danger was always one of standardization.

Although the Director-General's latest scheme was quietly dropped, there remained the sense that a tipping point was being reached in the industrialization of news. Some producers had suspected all along that 'rolling news' had been an attempt by a generation of neo-Thatcherite managers to squeeze more work out of existing staff. In the end, the natural evolution of bi-medialism seemed to amount to the same thing. It had begun as a means of establishing editorial unity between the Television and Radio wings of BBC journalism. But efficiency now demanded a new stage in the relationship: sharing a physical space. Thus, within a year, all News and Current Affairs staff in Radio were required to leave Broadcasting House and head west to work alongside their television colleagues in a bleak and unlovely new building at White City, known in BBC jargon as 'Stage Six'. When she eventually got there, Sue MacGregor looked about her new surroundings and despaired. 'The *Today* office was now a series of islands in the middle of a vast sea dominated by computer consoles. Breakfast Television was to one side; to the other, *The World at One*. Clusters of researchers and planners filled the spare spaces.' She, like her producers, was anxious about whether busy opinion-forming interviewees, used to the convenience of visiting a studio in Portland Place, would be willing to travel to West London at the crack of dawn for a *Today* appearance. But there was personal disillusionment too, for the mass evacuation seemed to offer final confirmation that a new ethos had triumphed. Liz Forgan called Stage Six a 'journalism factory'. Here, the Managing Director concluded, was a physical symbol of corporate purpose, and the corporate purpose was efficiency at all costs: 'practical arguments about the needs of programmes and programme-makers were secondary'. Forgan despaired at what she saw as the bogus economics of the move, tried to stop it by appealing to the Governors, and after failing by just one vote to get Birt's relocation reversed, she promptly resigned.[61]

Hussey was immensely frustrated, for he thought highly of Forgan. And she was the second senior Radio manager to be lost in this way. David Hatch, who had been acting as special adviser to John Birt since Forgan's arrival, had also departed unhappily. He had been upset at the fate of the original Radio Five, which was largely his creation, and he was particularly dismayed by the sudden loss of children's programmes. He told friends that he accepted 'the transient nature of all management decisions and of life itself '. But, he added mournfully, 'everything one builds, one's successors tear down'.[62] His departure, like Forgan's, represented the loss to the BBC of an astute and committed champion of radio. He had been a hugely influential force in comedy; he had cheered up staff after the traumas of McIntyre's regime; he had taught Brian Wenham that Radio, far from being a millstone around the Corporation's neck (a common enough sentiment in Television directorate) could still be a central part of its public service mission; he had even offered Birt what the Director-General called 'wise, canny, candid counsel'—a factor, no doubt, in slowly educating yet another television man to the ways of the older medium. Allowing both Forgan *and* Hatch to escape, Hussey decided, was 'careless' of John Birt—a comment that spoke of growing disenchantment between the Chairman and his Director-General.[63]

The 'journalism factory' was a reality, however. In Broadcasting House, offices were left empty and miles of wires trailed around the faded Art Deco corridors. Someone said that it was as if the heart had been torn out of the building. And it certainly was a strange end to the long battle to establish a proper working relationship between Radio Four and BBC journalism. For most of the past thirty years, those running the network had been quite content with a mix of programmes in which news and current affairs formed the central 'spine'. They were even prepared to treat news as being *primus inter pares*. What they had never wanted was for news to either take over the network entirely *or* desert it completely. One path would have destroyed the 'rich mix'; the other would have fatally compromised its role at the heart of national political debate. Both threats had arisen, first between 1978 and 1982, and now, more recently, between 1990 and 1993. In each case they had been seen off, and the rich mix had survived. Indeed, in 1997 Radio Four's schedule retained almost exactly the same proportion of news and current affairs as it had done ever since 1973—namely, a little over half. Even more significantly, there was now a definitive end to years of pressure on Radio Four to blend its complex schedule of 'built' programmes with enough flexibility to break news or cover events live when the need arose. It had always seemed an impossible task for one network to accommodate both styles of broadcasting, and now the task had been abandoned in favour of a clean division of labour: Radio Five Live would do the flexible stuff; Radio Four's complex mosaic of fixed points and hand-crafted programmes could remain. Within the mosaic, drama would leaven news, and topicality would infuse drama.

What happened on air, however, was only part of the story. For behind the scenes the 'rich mix' looked vulnerable. With the journalism factory of Stage Six in full production, it was rare—indeed, now next to impossible—for producers of plays, or quizzes, or comedies, or magazines, or religious programmes to bump into staff from any of Radio Four's news or current affairs programmes in the course of a day's work. Casual conversation, and the intangible exchange of perspectives that went with it, was supposed to have been part of the culture of the place. It was true that this had been more the stuff of wishful thinking than of reality for much of the time. Departmental separatism had always thrived; Review Board meetings had always been witness to territorial feuds; many shoulders had remained resolutely unrubbed. Yet there had always been the hope at least that something of what Ian McIntyre called a Republic of Ideas would hold forth. It was part, indeed, of the alchemical process. Now Sue MacGregor spoke of a new era of 'semi-detached broadcasting'.[64] Listeners had always been encouraged by Radio Four's rich mix to cross boundaries, to sample different genres—in short, to experience the Reithian delights of information, education, and entertainment in close and infectious proximity to one another. Yet, in a world of efficiency, of restructuring, of professionalism, of market trading, of endless measuring and costing, the BBC, perversely, seemed to be further away than ever from reaching this unquantifiable, though priceless, aim of broadening horizons among its own people.

13

Pleasures

*'Radio Four: more like a necessity, but certainly a great pleasure, especially the
quite unexpected little aural treat.'*

A listener, Mass-Observation, 1993

So much campaigning, so many years of complaining. Sometimes it was easy to
forget that for most listeners, most of the time, the pleasures to be gained from
Radio Four outweighed all the irritations. They did, after all, *stick* with it.
Sometimes they expressed their utter devotion to it. Even for producers who
could see nothing but bureaucracy, penny-pinching, and job losses all around
them at the BBC, Radio Four still offered a place where good programmes
survived and new ones might be conjured up from time to time. So after
describing all the provocations and the rows, there is a need to redress the
balance. This chapter, then, tries to turn its back on the failures and the dissent.
It tries instead to capture a sense of what *worked* and what *pleased*.

Pleasure, of course, was no easy thing to define, let alone to guarantee. Everyone
attached to Radio Four would always have their own personal hit parade of
programmes. There was also an inherent tension between what producers wanted
and what listeners wanted. Those who made programmes valued creativity, by
which they meant the opportunity to offer something unfamiliar, or something up
to date in subject matter and style, perhaps something even a little challenging or
unsettling. Listeners, on the other hand, were strongly attached to familiarity. They
had their favourite programmes, and chief among them were the network's work-
horses, *The Archers, Today, The News Quiz, In the Psychiatrist's Chair*, and so on. Yet
producers and listeners, both, would sometimes surprise themselves by finding
common ground in unexpected places. The slow but relentless turnover of programmes would sometimes throw up the unanticipated hit. Radio Four's schedule
was a thing of complexity, where pleasures could be found in the interstices and
darkest corners, as well as in the well-lit heartlands. Indeed, it was often in the realm
of the unexpected and the unasked-for that pleasure bloomed most intensely. There

were few clear formulae for success, not least because listeners were suspicious of anything made to order. It was also the case that what touched a nerve in the audience could do so in quite unexpected ways. For as we shall see, the qualities required for pleasurable listening always had an irreducible element of the intangible and inexplicable.

PARODIES AND DRAMEDIES

One of the striking features of Radio Four's comedy renaissance during the late 1980s and early 1990s was the number of series willing to bite the hand that fed them and take direct aim at the station itself. For parody, it seemed, was all the rage again. Three striking examples of the genre in this new wave were *On the Hour*, which ran for two series in 1991 and 1992, *Knowing Me, Knowing You*, which ran for just six programmes between 1992 and 1993, and *People Like Us*, which had three series from 1995 until 1997. All three programmes went on to achieve success on television, and all brought public attention to a new generation of comic talent that had been incubated somewhere along the fertile axis running between the Edinburgh Festival Fringe and Broadcasting House.

On the Hour was perhaps the most celebrated of the three, not least because it launched so many memorable characters and was, the critics agreed, bitingly funny. One chronicler of radio comedy has gone so far as to call it 'easily the most effective satire ever broadcast'.[1] Certainly it hit its targets, which happened to be the conventions of contemporary radio journalism as it saw them: endless aural clichés, self-aggrandizing presenters, a barely concealed obsession with the topical and the sensational, above all the assumption that news was as important to life as the air that we breathe and that, consequently, all else should make way for it. *On the Hour* offered listeners a version of the broadcast news magazine with its innate absurdities amplified tenfold. Its anchorman, played by Chris Morris, was the presiding genius, trampling on the sensibilities of witless interviewees and fellow broadcasters alike. He would veer between the monotone delivery of a BBC newsreader and the crazed exhortations of a demagogue, spewing out sober-voiced headlines interspersed with a clamorous sales patter blending self-importance with machismo:

'I'm Christopher Morris—for it is I'

'Doctor Fact is knocking at the door. Someone—please—*let the man in!*'

'*On The Hour*: modern, yet palatable news presentation!'

'*On the Hour*: maximum use of the BBC's news resources!'

Around Morris's rampages flowed a stream of information gobbets, inconsequential but full of self-importance: vox-pops in which people in the street would say whatever they thought the interviewer wanted them to say; the painfully matey Jimmy Tinker from the Consumer Unit with his *Your Things*

slot ('Good morning—and of course "good" is what it's all about on *Your Things!*');
Peter O'Hanrahahanrahan, the location reporter whose interchanges with the
domineering Morris became increasingly contrived; and Monsignor Trebe-Lopez's
religious homilies, with contemporary vignettes from his own dysfunctional life
and miniature parables blended in thirty seconds flat.

Aside from Morris, the writer-performers behind these characters included
Rebecca Front, Doon Mackichan, Patrick Marber, David Schneider, and the producer, Armando Iannucci.[2] Iannucci, who had been cutting his teeth on *Weekending*,
was to become something of a British comedy impresario over the following
years. Indeed, all the performers and most of the writers would have lucrative
careers ahead of them. *On the Hour*'s most immediate 'hit' character, however,
was provided by the remaining cast member, Steve Coogan, whose adopted
persona was Alan Partridge, a half-witted sports reporter forever mangling
metaphors and overindulging in the details of groin injuries. Unlike Morris's
anchorman, who was a monster, Partridge gave us pathos. His dogged determination to report on pointless fixtures on the margins of the sporting calendar,
combined with the unwitting revelations of the inadequacies in his own life,
meant that, despite everything, we felt for him.

Naturally, sympathy cannot be overindulged in the world of satire. Hence, when
the *On the Hour* team put Partridge centre stage in *Knowing Me, Knowing You*, our
patience was tested to the limit. A man already out of his depth in the narrow
confines of sports reporting could be heard drowning in ineptitude when holding
together an entire show of his own. There were, for example, the horribly contrived
openings:

Music: 'Knowing Me, Knowing You'

ALAN. Ah-haa! *(Applause)* Ah-haa. No, please, shh.
  Welcome to *Knowing Me, Knowing You.*
  Knowing me, Alan Partridge, knowing you, the audience, here in the studio, or
    you, the listener at home, in the car, or somewhere else, but with a radio...[3]

Then there was the tactless interviewing style, which unfailingly provoked the
most patient of guests. Thus, the 'greatest living novelist' reduced to arguing over
whether Sherlock Holmes was fictional or real, a minor Royal reminded of her
son's drug habit, and the freed hostage asked how he passed his two years chained
to a radiator in a cell:

ALAN. Whilst you were there, there must have been some funny incidents. Something
    funny must have happened.
CHRIS. Well no, not re—I mean you've got to imagine the situation—you're in the cell
    basically for twenty-four hours a day.
ALAN. I know—
CHRIS. There's no exercise—
ALAN. I know it was depressing, I just don't want to dwell on that. I really don't want to—
    it's—

CHRIS. I really can't—you know, it wasn't that sort—

ALAN. I'm not asking for that, look, I'm just saying will you do something amusing? Can you tell us an amusing story? C'mon!

CHRIS. Well. After about six months in prison, I found, scuttering across the floor, a little beetle, and I called it Hope. And after about six months, I fell asleep and the matchbox was open and Hope escaped, but—in a way I wasn't sad because Hope had escaped and I felt that pre-figured in a way my own escape, which indeed it did, because I escaped twelve months later—

ALAN. Hmm. You're absolutely sure that's the funniest thing? Listen, if you can remember anything, please, this is very important—

CHRIS. Well, I can't guarantee—

ALAN. If you can remember anything funny in the rest of the interview just cut straight in with it.

CHRIS. OK. Right. Fine—

ALAN. *(Whispers)* D'you know—and if you want—you can make something up, it doesn't really matter—in fact—if you want to get one of the researchers to get *Frank Muir's Book of Anecdotes*, just dress it up, change the location, it doesn't matter, and, I just want you to get the audience on your side—because I have to say, at the moment, you're coming across as a bit of a sour-puss . . . [4]

And so it went, from bad to worse.

This was parody with an acute ear for the kind of embarrassment only ever a hair's breadth away in any public examination of private lives—a forum where the values of entertainment, information, and education were often in contradictory motion.

Celebrity chat-shows, like daily news programmes, were relatively soft targets, of course. But even documentaries, which were supposed to be altogether less formulaic affairs, fell victim to the new wave of parody. The essentially unreal nature of the 'fly-on-the-wall' technique was laid bare to comic effect in *People Like Us*, a spoof documentary series written by John Morton and starring Chris Langham as the supremely inept reporter, Roy Mallard. Again, the humour lay in imitating beautifully the conventions of the genre, then twisting them into grotesque new forms. Thus, in his day-in-the-life portraits of a farmer, head teacher, vicar, doctor, solicitor, estate agent, hotel manager, and the like, Mallard naively hoped to stay unnoticed in the background, merely lobbing the odd question at those he recorded *en passant*. Instead, he ended up changing irreparably the behaviour of those he sought to portray, sometimes with tragic results. As for his ability to narrate scenes unfolding before him on our behalf, his lack of fluency surpassed even Partridge's. Everything was brought to a crashing halt as he hurled out a non sequitur a minute ('set back from the road is *Hillside*, which, as its name suggests, is a house'), or lost himself utterly in an overextended metaphor:

The world of hotel life is a microcosm of the world of life outside, in the world of the . . . of the world. Except for the fact that it's not at sea, a hotel like . . . and it's not a ship . . . a hotel like The Georgian is very like a ship at sea. The hotel guests are the passengers, and the staff are the crew, who . . . crew together, below the surface, to create a safe haven, an island of . . . a floating island, but stabilised, of . . . ship-shaped . . . calmness, in the middle of a stormy sea of shifting . . . current . . . tidings.[5]

Mallard's tragedy was that he attempted profundity but rarely transcended inanity. And, as with Partridge, we began to feel a little sorry for the man. He always failed in even the most basic of missions—to acquire a cup of coffee from his hosts, say, or to convince those he met that he had a wife. We could not see him, but it was obvious he was no catch. In short, he was the antithesis of the journalist as all-action hero. That, in any case, was how we British probably liked our journalists best: it was supposed to be in our nature to side with the underdog. As J. B. Priestley pointed out in his celebrated 1928 essay on *English Humour*, 'knowing more or less what we want and what we like but never knowing exactly why, it is perhaps easier for us English to achieve that balance of sympathy and antipathy necessary for the full appreciation of the ludicrous'.[6]

Were we to do to these three series what they did to their own source material, and strip them down to their basics, we would find, naturally enough, that their essence was hardly novel. Parody drew on ancient traditions of imitation and inversion that stretched back to the Greece of Aristophanes, taking in *Don Quixote*, nineteenth-century novels, and music hall burlesques along the way.[7] More to the point there was nothing new about *radio* poking fun at *radio*. *Band Waggon* and *ITMA* had done it to great effect in the 1930s and 1940s; *The Goons* had done much the same throughout the 1950s.[8] More recently, *Radio Active* had been laughing mercilessly at the amateurishness prevalent in some corners of broadcasting with its presentation of 'Britain's first national local radio station'. The same mid-1980s period had even seen a very specific parody of Roger Cook's *Checkpoint* programme, in the form of *Delve Special*, a series written by Tony Sarchet and starring Stephen Fry as the physically put-upon investigative reporter David Lander. *On the Hour*, *Knowing Me, Knowing You*, and *People Like Us* can be seen as standing firmly in an established comedy tradition. To some extent, like their predecessors, they were a parade of in-jokes that indulged their targets as much as they savaged them. Yet, in the 1990s, there was a deadly seriousness at the heart of it all that struck the critics as reaching new levels of ferocity. These programmes were meant to hurt. Parody had always contained a critical dimension, of course. Priestley wrote of it as a kind of *trial* by the 'ordeal of laughter'—a purgative that hoped to leave good art uninjured and kill bad art stone dead.[9]

The precise choice of target, however, changed according to the circumstances of the time. And in the early 1990s, when journalism seemed to be reaching a triumphal new stage in its long ascendancy within the BBC, it was inevitably news, and news values that seemed to merit parody the most. *On the Hour* arrived at an exquisite moment: just after the Gulf War, when plans were being laid for rolling news on Radio Four's long wave. If radio succumbed to such machinations, the programme seemed to be saying, this is what you might get. The conventions of rolling news were there in embryonic form on Radio Four's news sequences. Suspicious minds could see a whole culture already in thrall to a journalistic style—one that traded in bombastic delivery, clichéd aural short-hand, bite-sized attention spans, and an increasing fascination with celebrity. The target, then, was not *just* news as such, but rather a broadcasting ethos apparently inclined to put its faith in the kind of here-today-gone-tomorrow superficiality it typified. That a man so lacking in talent as Alan Partridge could be given his own chat-show on prime-time national radio—this was satire in itself: it suggested, for one thing, that the judgement of commissioning editors at the BBC was questionable; but it also suggested that we, as listeners, might end up with radio this awful if we didn't stop colluding with it and start demanding something better. If all this sounded like a bitter pill to swallow, good writing and good performances always sweetened the taste. Skilfully delivered, the Radio Four audience could usually find pleasure in an in-joke. After all, the cleverer the humour, the cleverer those who got it could feel.

For many listeners, though, it was mockery of a gentler kind that offered the greatest pleasure. What *they* liked best about the Radio Four schedule were not its fierce satires but rather the wittily observed comedies of manners that also flourished during the 1980s and 1990s. Series such as *After Henry, No Commitments*, and *King Street Junior*, or any number of those by writers such as Peter Tinniswood, Sue Limb, and Sue Townsend, which mixed laughter and compassion in the grey area between comedy and drama, the realm of so-called 'dramedy': these were the programmes that succeeded in touching a popular nerve, as the number of successful spin-offs in publishing and television went on to prove. The range of style and subject matter was eclectic, but most turned the spotlight away from broadcasting and towards the lives of ordinary—if distinctly middle-class—people. In short, they brought the Radio Four listeners the pleasure of self-recognition.

Among the most celebrated examples of the genre was Sue Townsend's tale of adolescent growing pains, *The Secret Diary of Adrian Mole, Aged 13¾*. This had begun life on New Year's Day in 1982 when it was broadcast on Radio Four as a one-off play. The production was overheard by the publishers Methuen, who immediately issued Townsend with a contract. By the time her book came out the following September, *Mole* had run again on Radio Four as a *Morning Reading*, prompting a flurry of public interest. The initial print-run of 7,000 copies sold out quickly—a first step in making Townsend the best-selling British author of the 1980s. History had repeated itself, for the man who spotted the potential of Townsend's script was John Tydeman—the same producer who had kick-started the career of another Leicester resident, Joe Orton, back in 1963. It was Tydeman who now suggested to Townsend that her hero's name should be Adrian—not Nigel, as originally planned—and that he should be 13¾ years old, not 14¾.[10] Thus reconfigured, the lineaments of both plot and character were established in Mole's very first diary entry:

Thursday January 1ˢᵗ
Bank Holiday in England, Ireland, Scotland and Wales
These are my New Year's resolutions:

1. I will help the blind across the road.
2. I will hang my trousers up.
3. I will put the sleeves back on my records.
4. I will not start smoking.
5. I will stop squeezing my spots.
6. I will be kind to the dog.
7. I will help the poor and ignorant.
8. After hearing the disgusting noises from downstairs last night, I have also vowed never to drink alcohol.

My father got the dog drunk on cherry brandy at the party last night. If the RSPCA hear about it he could get done. Eight days have gone by since Christmas Day but my mother still hasn't worn the green lurex apron I bought her for Christmas! She will get bathcubes next year.
Just my luck, I've got a spot on my chin for the first day of the New Year![11]

Here was distilled the combination of self-righteousness and naivety that any parent of an adolescent would recognize. And what followed was not just the unfolding drama of Mole's own life—his endless battle against spots, his unrequited love for Pandora, his misplaced attempts at creative writing and political activism: we also experienced the drama in the lives of adults around him—his parents and their neighbours. We got, in other words, a comedy straight from the heartlands of the Radio Four audience: British suburbia. It was a tale of class friction, infidelity, and petty betrayals, as well as of innocence. And the fact that it reached us solely through Mole's own witless version of events doubled its appeal: *we* knew that his mother was having an affair with Mr Lucas next door, but *he*, bless him, did not. The trick was in the writing, but fortuitous casting had its part, too. Nicholas Barnes, who played Mole, was exactly 13¾ years old when he entered the recording studio for the first time. As Tydeman recalls, 'he didn't understand most of the jokes, which was why he sounded so brilliant'.[12]

Barnes, Mole, Townsend, Tydeman: for the next decade actor, character, writer, and producer joined forces behind the scenes. Mole, needless to say, was a keen listener ('Saturday... stayed in bed until five-thirty... listened to Radio Four play about domestic unhappiness'). Townsend wrote letters to Tydeman on his behalf, begging for the chance to have his creative work aired on the BBC. Tydeman ran with the joke and replied as if they were real, letting down the tyro dramatist as gently as professional honesty permitted. Townsend then included Tydeman's rejection letters in subsequent scripts: 'we went a little barmy and thought of him as a real person'. Indeed, being realistic seemed to be an important part of the whole project, for this was writing that wanted to capture the zeitgeist of Britain in the 1980s and 1990s. Mole lived through the Falklands War, the miners' strike, privatization, the rise of the cappuccino bar—most of the Thatcher era, as well as 'the Major Years'. Thus there was some hard politics woven into the script: Townsend, no fan of the Tory governments, would have a dig at the impact of their policies: Mole's own father being made redundant, the struggle to pay bills, family break-ups. And there were cultural jibes, too: 'At the age of 13¾, I thought it was sufficient to just have a life', Mole tells us at one point. 'I honestly didn't know then that you can't just have a life—you have to have a *lifestyle*.' None of this, though, was terribly didactic, and even when Mole got on his own soapbox we forgave him. Self-righteous and naïve he may have been, but he *cared*—for dogs, for the awkward pensioner Bert Baxter, for the state of the world. To John Tydeman, then, Mole's popularity was entirely explicable, and in the end quite conventional: 'although he is, I think, probably what we would call a nerd, he is one of the sweetest people you are ever likely to meet. He doesn't know it, but he is kindness incarnate.'[13]

Strife leavened by kindness—and settings the audience could recognize: it all represented something of a running theme in the profusion of Radio Four dramedies on offer. The foibles of middle-class life—ranging from young urban professionals through all layers of suburbia to the faded gentry of old England—were on display. Each programme, however, gave the genre its own twist. *King Street Junior*, for instance, centred on the working lives of teachers at a multi-racial inner-city primary school, and drew on the absurdities of trying to cope with large class sizes, poor facilities, interfering politicians, and an array of harassed colleagues. Through ten series between 1985 and 1998, it retained an air of pithy accuracy.[14] Peter Tinniswood's work—his *Uncle Mort* series of North Country ramblings, cricketing stories in *Tales from the Long Room*, and *Winston*, the portrait of a poacher and the middle-class family with whom he was involved—offered rather more fantastical characters, though, again, created humour from the minor incidents of everyday life. Sue Limb's comic creations ranged more widely in time and space, but series such as *Little Blighty on the Down*—a parochial microcosm of Thatcherite Britain—*The Wordsmiths of Gorsemere*—her spoof on the Lakeland poets—and *Up the Garden Path*—about the life and loves of the schoolteacher Izzy—all had in common the pricking of bourgeois pretensions (whether petit or grand) and an obvious affection for even the most infuriating of characters.

The archetypal Radio Four dramedy of the era, however, was probably *After Henry*, written by Simon Brett and produced by Peter Atkin, and lasting four series between 1985 and 1989. *After Henry* offered intergenerational conflict between three women living on different floors of the same house: the newly widowed Sarah (played by Prunella Scales), her mother Eleanor (Joan Sanderson)—domineering, cunning, gossipy—and her teenage daughter Clare (Gerry Cowper)—truculently demanding independence but in need of support. Through constantly shifting allegiances they searched for a way to cope with each other as best they could. Russell, the gay owner of a second-hand bookshop was one external source of sympathy and wisdom. But it was Sarah herself, aged 42, and the kind of woman who would almost certainly have listened to Radio Four, who was in the middle of it all—chronologically, physically, and figuratively. Hers was the point of view that we heard most—and hers was the point of view that many listeners undoubtedly empathized with most. It was, in any case, 'the best comedy anywhere on the air' according to one critic at the time—'a little gem' the *Listener* judged.[15]

BBC Television's then head of comedy complained that *After Henry* was 'middle-aged and middle-class' and 'the most serious thing that happened is they ran out of ice for the gin and tonics'.[16] He promptly turned down the chance to adapt the series—just as he spurned Brett's subsequent series, *No Commitments* (about three grown-up sisters), and Sue Limb's *Up the Garden Path*. All three series found a place on commercial television quickly enough. And when Thames Television snapped up the rights to *After Henry* it basked in a very healthy audience of some fourteen million. The experience taught the BBC an important lesson. Its Television entertainment wing had always been sceptical of Radio Four's middle-class flavour: now it recognized the work being produced in Broadcasting House might, after all, possess an appeal beyond the middle-class heartlands—perhaps, too, that those heartlands were themselves expanding. The end of the 1980s was therefore something of a turning point in relations between the Radio and Television Light Entertainment departments. When the rights to Radio Four's improvisation series *Whose Line Is It Anyway?* were lost to Channel Four in 1989, John Birt decided that formats developed by Radio had been overlooked once too often and tighter linkage between the two parts of the Corporation was enforced.[17] New deals were struck, money flowed both ways, talent and resources began to be shared—a rapprochement that paved the way for the television transfers of the 1990s and beyond: not just *On the Hour* (which became *The Day Today*), Alan Partridge, and *People Like Us*, but, later, a second new-wave of Radio Four comedy, including *Goodness Gracious Me*, *The League of Gentlemen*, *Dead Ringers*, and *Little Britain*.

In any case, though BBC Television in all its twitchy populism could not always see it, the world of ice and gin-and-tonics was only ever a matter of plot and setting. What resonated in *After Henry*, as with all the other Radio Four dramedies of the era, was the drama that lay beneath—the conflict between generations and within families, between work and leisure, between ideals and pragmatism, between different cultures and classes. The appeal was not quite universal, but it was certainly more broadly based and more contemporary in tone than many of its sceptics allowed. One way or another, most series had the kernel of truth. Peter Tinniswood was an established radio dramatist and successful novelist, but his background was also in journalism, and this gave him an ear for authentic language and the minor details of daily existence. Similarly, Jim

Eldridge brought to his *King Street Junior* scripts a supply teacher's experience. His stories of 'making do' amid a clash of values would have made sense to a great many harassed public sector workers at the time. More, they offered what one critic called a fine balance of 'fun, compassion and social conscience'. This delicate mix surely got to the heart of the appeal of almost all the parodies and dramedies of the time. For although the great British middle class that constituted the epicentre of the Radio Four audience was often socially conservative and suspicious of change, it was equally capable of being open-minded, mildly self-improving, sceptical of those in positions of power and influence, and charitable to those with imperfections. As Gillian Reynolds pointed out, 'Sound, sensible people with kind hearts and an intelligent interest in what is going on in the world listen to Radio Four, and, by and large, the network does handsomely by them.'[18]

REDEEMING FEATURES

There was, then, a melancholic undercurrent to some of Radio Four's entertainment. But it was in its documentaries and features that true darkness was more often to be found. Sometimes, indeed, the network seemed to be drowning in misery, such was its determination to show the world as it was—injustices and suffering and all. Every Controller had worried over this, from Tony Whitby complaining in 1973 about the sheer number of 'sad and depressing programmes about contemporary life', through to Michael Green declaring in frustration that 'if I hear another gloomy documentary I'll scream'. For those wanting more sweetness and light it must have felt like a quarter of a century of editorial guidance had made no impact whatsoever: whether for reasons of compassion or simple dramatic interest, producers still thrived on unhappy tales. The quintessential Radio Four documentary, one satirical wag suggested in 1995, remained the mythical 'Beryl's Story'—the portrait of a victim of child abuse who 'grew up in care, was pregnant at 15, on drugs at 16, on the game at 17, in jail at 18, went blind at 19, became paralysed from the neck down at 20 and was given six months to live'.[19]

Curiously, though, listeners were not always repelled. Indeed, one or two documentaries came along that created a minor sensation—proving that there were pleasures to be found *even* in tales of woe. These documentaries also gave Controllers hope that something in BBC culture might have been shifting after all: that, by finding new and more subtle ways to depict suffering and how it might be faced, producers were finding ways to avoid inducing weary indifference or revulsion. What some in Broadcasting House labelled 'do-goodery'—quintessential 1970s programme-making which sounded dangerously like social work, or which exuded a faintly hectoring tone—was giving way a little more to programmes in which listeners were being drawn in emotionally by the classic devices of storytelling: a reliance on character, plot, suspense, disruption, and, very often, redemption.[20]

One outstanding example of a documentary that used these tricks and which succeeded in moving listeners at home was *A Lone Voice*, broadcast in March 1988.[21] This told the story of Glyn Worsnip. Or, to be more precise, it had Glyn Worsnip telling us his own story. Worsnip had become well known to the British public through presenting *That's Life* and *Nationwide* on BBC 1 in the 1970s and early 1980s. He had also been working on Radio Four, presenting the occasional *Pick of the Week* or *Stop Press*. In 1987, however, a few complaints started to trickle into Broadcasting House about his delivery on air. Listeners claimed that his speech was not as fluent as it ought to be, not as fluent as it *used* to be. Worsnip had noticed it too, and so had close colleagues—his producer, Emily Buchanan, the head of Special Current Affairs Programmes, Anne Sloman, and the deputy head of Current Affairs Magazine Programmes, Caroline Millington. What no one knew, until Worsnip went to the National Hospital for Nervous Diseases in August, was that he had cerebella ataxia, a degenerative brain disease that was gradually and inexorably destroying his powers of movement—and his powers of speech. When he talked to Millington about what to do, they both decided it might be possible to 'come out' on air. A new documentary series called *Soundtrack* was being planned for the following spring, and one of its producers, Sharon Banoff, realized that Worsnip's plans could fit with hers. She presented Worsnip with one condition: that if he wanted to do a straightforward factual documentary about cerebella ataxia then she was not interested—she was, he recalled, after 'a personal story'.[22]

The deal was done. And what emerged after several weeks of clandestine production work at Banoff's London flat was an 'audio diary', which revealed to an unsuspecting audience the full, ghastly truth of Worsnip's condition. In the space of twenty-five minutes, he told, for example, of falling over on escalators and of the minor traumas of a restaurant meal with friends, where his body would shake and his voice begin to slur: 'There were the usual witty remarks about "one too many", but the sad fact was that even then two was one too many, and perhaps even one. A glass of wine would make me incapable, but not drunk.' There were also his nightly confessionals, where he identified the first symptoms of a body losing control; the visits to doctors, where we heard steadily more pessimistic prognoses; even the painful preparations for one of his regular Radio Four programmes, complete with the innumerable stumbles that had to be edited out of the final tape. When Worsnip listened to the finished programme for the first time at home he broke down completely. He recognized it for what it was: a journey of discovery running in one direction only—to a future of growing incapacity, increasing isolation, and, almost certainly, an early death.

In preparing *A Lone Voice*, Banoff clearly had to walk what Worsnip called 'the delicate tightrope between personal exploitation and professional exigency'. By his reckoning she 'did it beautifully'. The listeners must have thought so too, for within weeks the BBC was forced to employ extra secretarial help to deal with a flood of correspondence. Most people wrote directly to Worsnip. Many told him they too were suffering with cerebella ataxia; others had completely different disabilities and wanted to tell their stories; several were old school and university friends he had not seen or spoken to in thirty years; most were strangers who simply expressed their solidarity. 'I was never so popular as when I was ill', Worsnip concluded.[23]

In one respect, the programme only went to prove that tragedy makes for the best drama. Or perhaps it went to prove, as the literary critic John Carey has suggested, that reportage provides the contemporary age with something akin to a religious experience: a way to appreciate one's own continued existence by witnessing at second hand the inflictions visited upon others. Or perhaps it offered the same indirect pleasures that were seen in Lee Hall's 1998 radio play *Spoonface Steinberg*, which centred on the audio diary of a young girl dying from cancer, interleaved with echoes of the Holocaust: a chance to bathe in a sense of compassion and understanding.[24] Whatever the reason, *A Lone Voice* gripped. And it was certainly not a genre unto itself, for the sheer number of other programmes about death, or decline, or loss, or loneliness, or foreboding, or suffering on Radio Four during this period was striking. Some, such as *Pain—a Way of Life*, which focused on cancer, or *Never the Same Again*, which looked at the way lives could be turned upside down by sudden events, tackled suffering head on and simply talked, unflinchingly, to the people directly affected. Others were more elliptical in their approach. *Friday Lives*, for example, featured people telling their own unusual tales—drifting alone in the Pacific Ocean for days, say, or donating a kidney to a close relative—while *End of a Line* centred on those such as lighthouse keepers and freshwater pearl fishermen whose work would die with them. In these, and other programmes like them, a sense of loss or danger was rarely far away, and the act of personal storytelling was an essential part of the format.

Such features also fitted the fashion for putting individuals or families centre stage. The grand themes of human existence were being explored, but through the testimony of ordinary people—or rather, as one Radio Four Controller put it, through featuring 'extraordinary people who don't happen to be famous'.[25] There was a consequent fascination with everyday objects, minor incidents, and overlooked byways. Thus, for example, Ian McMillan's visits to an allotment, a seaside caravan park, and a roadside café to pay tribute to the ability of mundane places to evoke extraordinary memories—good or bad—in his 1990 series *Hearing Voices, Seeing Things*, and Phil Smith's 1991 *Family Fortunes*, exploring the life of a Northern working-class family across three generations. It was not hard to hear other programmes in similar vein: on the pleasure and solace to be found in visits to the supermarket or in buying shoes, on a couple with their own pagan temple, on a family living underground, on the rituals of being fitted for a suit, on the wistful qualities of churchyards. And so on. The list was long and telling: a powerful testament to the growing assumption that culture really was something that we *all* had, that it was, as Raymond Williams had told us it was, a *way of life* and not just a matter of the best that has been said and done, as Matthew Arnold had once argued. Inevitably, critics raised the question of value, intimating that quality was being diluted through oversupply, or through a pervasive, institutionalized style in which the notion that significance lay in the minutiae of life had run amok. One reviewer worried that feature-makers on Radio Four were 'hooked on quaintness'; another complained that too many programmes were now like a 'radio version of a *Readers' Digest* feature', where 'you get a little history, a few facts, some self-styled expert comment and a lot of light-hearted froth about subjects—traffic jams, bathrooms, maybe rollerblading—that you have absolutely no desire to know anything about'.[26]

To such a critique one could argue, as when the ice ran out in *After Henry*, that in the finest novels of Jane Austen a whole life pivots on the simple question of whether one person asks another to dance. But the BBC could also respond to its critics by pointing to the work of a small band of producers obviously committed to the radio feature as something of an art form—people who created a corpus of work which rose above the mean and which was recognizably *theirs*. There was, for example, Peter Everett, who offered listeners an evening at a Leeds Working Men's Club in *The Ballad of Belle Isle* (1980) and a rich evocation of teenage life across the decades in *You'll Never Be Sixteen Again* (1985–6). Or Piers Plowright, a 'realist-magician' whose *Setting Sail*, weaving together intimate reflections on approaching death, bore all the signatures of his oeuvre: closely observed portraits gently lobbed in the listeners' direction in the hope of starting a few ripples of emotion and thought. Or Matt Thompson, whose preferred style was to seek psychological insight through quirky behavioural experiments, as in *Touching the Elephant* (1997), which re-enacted the ancient Indian tale of a group of blind people handling different parts of an elephant and contemplating what kind of creature it was.[27]

All these programmes showed there was some room on the schedule for work that was idiosyncratic and richly allusive. Significantly, though, it was work that succeeded in being creative without falling for the rather self-conscious manner that BBC features had so often adopted in the past. What seemed to have changed decisively was the attitude to the human voice and to the layering of sound. Everett, for example, was obviously just as fascinated as Charles Parker had once been by the unaffected honesty and musicality to be found in the voices of working people. But in *The Ballad of Belle Isle* working-class life somehow felt less straitjacketed than it had been in Parker's earlier Ballads, largely because Everett's interviewees were by and large left to speak for themselves. It was also art of a rather different hue from that which had been attempted in the features revivals of the late 1960s and early 1970s, when producers such as Michael

Mason had blended speech and music and actuality in epic proportion and widescreen style. With Everett, Plowright, Thompson, and others the temptation to add layer upon layer of sound was often eschewed for programmes 'as transparent as a glass of tap water'.[28] Many radio producers naturally continued to hanker after the kind of recognition their contemporaries in other media enjoyed. Thus *Soundtrack* borrowed the same sales pitch as Mason had deployed in claiming to offer 'films for radio'. But if this was cinema, it was a cinema of character and plot rather than of special effects. And it was the relative seclusion of Radio Four rather than the glare of BBC 1 that Glyn Worsnip had consciously chosen for his coming out. It was, he reckoned, simply 'more intimate... less self-indulgent'.[29]

This stylistic tilt towards understatement and intimacy was neither entirely novel nor wholly exclusive. It echoed, for example, the work of long-forgotten producers such as Denis Mitchell, who had shown back in the 1950s how a 'minimalist' approach could extract more meaning by seeming to say less. And although it was uninterested in the forensic analysis of facts or the clash of opinions—both meat and drink to journalists—it was an aesthetic that had also borrowed some of the raw, 'realist' texture of news and current affairs. Through the blending of the mildly experimental and the vaguely familiar, however, radio features had redeemed themselves. Once, they had been marginal and somewhat awkward participants in the Radio Four schedule—revered certainly, and demanding of critical attention, but slightly ostentatious and set apart from the mainstream by their very different tone and style, not to say expensive to make in staff effort and studio time. Now, possessed of a social conscience but wearing their politics and their art much more lightly, they fitted the general warp and weft of Radio Four better than ever—and came relatively cheap. They survived into the 1990s, when so many had predicted their demise, because they had accommodated themselves not just to the more democratic temper of the age but also to the realities of radio's status—namely as an everyday affair more suited to the pleasures of storytelling and of intimacy than to those of spectacle. Naturally, there was always a risk: that in swapping the institutional isolation they experienced immediately after the abolition of the Features Department in 1964 for the centralized editorial control they experienced in the 1980s and 1990s, a certain mass-produced sameness would emerge. And it was true that very little that was genuinely outré reached listeners' ears. Most features sat quite comfortably alongside the news sequences, comedies, and dramas of Radio Four. In one sense they had become more 'invisible', more mainstream, than ever before. Yet they still offered a tone and texture a *touch* different from the norm: moments in the schedule generally free of hard topicality and imbued instead with a more impressionistic style. Piers Plowright talked of their appeal to listeners seeking something richer in flavour than the 'children's food' elsewhere on radio and television; his fellow feature-maker John Theocharis said they were essential in an age 'when our ears are constantly attacked by trash and meaningless noise'.[30] They certainly helped in making Radio Four the rich mix that it still claimed to be, since many listeners—and most producers inside Broadcasting House—now recognized that without them, the schedule would have been a blander, straighter, more arid terrain altogether.

REVERIES

For those wanting even more relief from the 'trash and meaningless noise' of contemporary life, there was one corner of the Radio Four schedule that seemed to surpass all others in the pleasures it gave. This was the fifteen minutes or so set aside each day for that poetic marriage of the functional and the sublime, the *Shipping Forecast*. Here was a programme with an identity and a history all of its own, for it emerged originally not from the BBC but a government agency, the Meteorological Office, and it belonged officially not to any one radio network but to long wave, which alone among frequencies could be heard across the entirety of the British Isles. Yet once it had been transferred from Radio Two in 1978, it did not take long for the *Shipping Forecast* to feel as if it had been on Radio Four forever. Within it was distilled the essence of the network's own intangible but deep appeal. It roused the same subliminal notions of home and family and national identity. It was mysterious, yet familiar. Above all, perhaps, it showed the enduring attraction of the unadorned human voice. By the 1990s, indeed, it was barely possible to imagine it anywhere else *but* on Radio Four. And it was barely possible to imagine Radio Four without it.

It was longevity that lodged the *Shipping Forecast* in our collective unconsciousness. A daily weather report for British waters had been broadcast on the BBC since the 1920s—and, whatever its reputation for being immutable, this was long enough for it to have been reinvented several times over. When it started appearing regularly, for example, there were just thirteen sea areas, not the present thirty-one. It was only with a dramatic expansion in shipping traffic around the British Isles after the Second World War that it became more detailed. Individual names also came and went: Heligoland became German Bight in 1955; North and South Utsire were added in 1984; Finisterre was to make way for Fitzroy in 2002.[31] There were subtle shifts, too, in the style of its delivery on air. The BBC experimented in 1967 with making its opening words 'much simpler and more informal' so that they were in tune with a contemporary taste for the bright and breezy. Indeed, there were signs that in this new age of streamlined radio, an over-anxious BBC would have liked to see the *Shipping Forecast* disappear altogether. Official thinking appeared to be that if it survived it was only out of a public service obligation to those at sea, and, as one senior Radio manager remarked confidentially, in a broadcasting service for the general public it was 'an unwelcome intrusion'.[32] Listeners could sometimes sense this lack of commitment. Every now and then they aired dark suspicions that reading was speeding up: sailors placed in peril by a race against the clock. Indeed, when fifteen lives were actually lost as a freak storm hit the Fastnet yacht race in 1979, some alleged that it was BBC Radio's failure to provide adequate forecasts that was largely to blame for the tragedy.[33]

In truth, both the BBC and its critics had got it wrong. Advances in technology were gradually making it easier for vessels around the British coast to receive their weather information automatically: a *Shipping Forecast* over the airwaves was becoming *less* important for sailors by the last decade of the century. Members of the landlocked general public, on the other hand, felt more and more as if *they* could not do without one. Hence, when Michael Green announced in 1995 that the midnight edition was to move by a mere twelve minutes, there was a rash of leading articles in the newspapers, angry parliamentary debate, and a shot across the bow from veterans of the Save Radio Four Long Wave campaign aghast at a BBC that had, they said, 'totally lost sight of the concept of public service broadcasting'. Moving the *Shipping Forecast*, so it seemed, was little short of treasonable. Getting rid of it was unthinkable. It had been around for so long that past innovations had been forgiven—or, more likely, forgotten. 'It's always there,' the travel writer Charlie Connelly claimed, 'always has been, always will be.'[34] Green happily assured his critics that it would survive as long as the regular Radio Four listeners wanted it. As a source of hard information, he acknowledged, it was largely redundant. Its value now was as an icon, a metaphor, a soothing, intangible, but somehow *necessary* pleasure.

At the heart of its appeal has always been the aesthetic quality of the language itself, unfolding as it does in a mesmerizing incantation at once familiar and mystifying. Every six hours, as night follows day, gale warnings followed in orderly succession by the general synopsis and thirty-one area forecasts: a clockwise circumnavigation of the British Isles from Viking and North Utsire to the Faroes and South East Iceland. It spans 3,500 kilometres from north to south, 1,400 kilometres from west to east in a mere 350 or so carefully chosen, solemnly recited words, shorn of all unnecessary repetition. We are left with the mere bullet points of wind speed, visibility, and prevailing conditions:

Southeast backing easterly 4 or 5, increasing 6 in the south. Mainly fair. Moderate or good.

It is the language of the sea and of meteorological science—alien to most of us, a precise meaning always just out of reach. Poets have an ear for this kind of thing, and consequently are among those most easily caught in its spell. Seamus Heaney wrote in his *Glanmore Sonnet VII* of its 'strong gale-warning voice', of

Dogger, Rockall, Malin, Irish Sea:
Green, swift upsurges, North Atlantic flux[35]

For Carol Ann Duffy, the *Shipping Forecast*'s power lay in it being like a sudden utterance carried through the air, unbidden but somehow consoling:

> Darkness outside. Inside, the radio's prayer—
> Rockall. Malin. Dogger. Finisterre.[36]

It is the names themselves and the manner in which they are recited that beguiles. The poet Sean Street hears in it a kind of litany: 'the singing of sounds—this minimal chanting', conjuring 'weather's unlistening geography'.[37] The act of imagining is given a helping hand by those charged with bringing the *Shipping Forecast* onto the airwaves. They recognize that it is *their* words and *their* voices that help to burnish the raw data into blank verse. It is, for instance, in the unromantic and landlocked surroundings of the Meteorological Office in Bracknell that each script is first assembled. 'When I'm writing it', one of the forecasters there explains, 'I do try to imagine I'm taking a trawler out of Peterhead or on a ferry in the Solent.' Further along the chain there is the studio in Broadcasting House, where a Radio Four announcer will consider its delivery on air. 'If it was strictly for the people who need it, the people on the ships, you'd read it in the same manner all the time', one of them explains. The task, however, is aesthetic, rather than functional. 'Without exception everybody who reads it loves reading it', the announcer suggests. 'It's not just a question of reading a list of words, you really have to let it flow through you.' And this flow has a diurnal rhythm. The midday forecast, coming straight after a news bulletin, is dealt with briskly, the mood described thus: 'Here it is, watch out, here comes the weather.' After midnight it is different. 'I think about everybody going to bed . . . I read it much more gently than the daytime broadcasts, and it's lovely, a time when the forecast is at its most poetic.'[38]

Radio and poetry, Sean Street points out, have a lot in common. In the right hands both 'supply clues without telling us how to interpret'.[39] For each of us, then, the precise aesthetic effect of listening to the *Shipping Forecast* will be different. But among writers and artists who have tried to articulate its intangible qualities on our behalf, the recurring theme is its power to evoke feelings of belonging, order, and security—and in a way that connects the epic with the quotidian.

Take, to start with, the epic connotations. Here, a sense of nationhood, of belonging to an island community, is contained within. David Chandler, for example, sees in the forecast a 'landscape of the imagination' with a romantic version of the British Isles at its centre. 'For those of us safely ashore, its messages from "out there", its warnings from a dangerous peripheral world of extremes and uncertainty are reassuring.' Indeed, the more volatile the world out there is, he suggests, the more that 'home' and 'nation' are reinforced as places of safety, order, even divine protection.[40] This sense of belonging runs deep. The archaeologist Barry Cunliffe has written of the power of the sea to define the culture and mindset of the Atlantic peoples of western Europe over the past nine millennia or more. Its constant ability to support life—and, just as decisively, to take it away—has left us in awe of it. We who face the ocean inherit a 'unifying bond' that sets us apart from dwellers of the continental interior: it is our shared and 'timeless human experience'.[41] Cunliffe's perspective is international and historical. Chandler writes of Britain and of the present day. But if it is a present in which Britons have lost intimate knowledge of the ocean, it is also one in which we crave relief from our busy, technological, image-saturated lives, and where the residual feelings that Cunliffe so eloquently portrays can still be stirred by the forecast's simple litany. 'In those brief moments when its alien language of the sea interrupts the day', Chandler concludes, it 'offers to complete the enveloping circle and rekindle a picture of Britain glowing with a sense of unity.' It casts a metaphorical net around us, creating in our minds a geographical space 'free from current political conflict, complexity and social tensions'. Outside all is raging, but inside there is peace. And implicit too, in the ebb and flow of tides and storms, is the possibility of a return to calmer conditions, of a happy ending.[42]

As for the forecast's quotidian appeal, we need look no further than the cumulative evidence of its part in the private rituals of hearth and bedroom, of getting up and going to bed. Charlie Connelly, for instance, recalls that all through his childhood he had been wrapped in its 'soothing, *homely* aspect'. Hearing it then meant quite simply that 'everything was alright'. Hearing it now, as an adult, is 'cosily reassuring', provided, that is, one is inside:

There's definitely something comforting about the fact that although some salty sea dog in a draughty wheelhouse somewhere will be buttoning his sou'wester even tighter at the news there are warnings of gales in Rockall, Malin and Bailey, you can turn up the heating and see if there's a nice film on the telly.[43]

For James Fenton, pleasure is given in daily doses at dawn by the contrast its 'cool, non-invasive poetry' offers to the relentless 'get-on-with-it' flow of most breakfast radio, the *Today* programme included. The morning forecast never feels the need to explain itself, never cracks jokes, and always retains its mystery. Above all, it 'proceeds at its stately pace and one has time to adjust' to the hours of wakefulness.[44]

For many listeners, however, it is the very last edition of the day, at forty-eight minutes past midnight, which brings the greatest reward. Then they can enjoy the 'promise' of a gale at sea with 'the bed-clothes pulled high and the radio turned low'.[45] It is the time of darkness and of sleep—a time when, for the greater part of humankind, we have been afforded what one historian has called 'a sanctuary from ordinary existence'. In pre-industrial Europe the customary name for nightfall was 'shutting-in'—'a time to bar doors and bolt shutters once watchdogs had been loosed abroad'. There would be nocturnal anxieties, of course, but also the knowledge that sleep was restorative. And so minds would have to be set at rest by the recital of charms or the conducting of prayers, while soporific medicines abounded—laudanum for the better-off, leaves of nightshade, bags of aniseed or rags with camomile, bread and vinegar wrapped around the feet of more humble folk.[46] Nowadays, we have the radio, and the nightly *Shipping Forecast*, preceded as it is with *Sailing By*. For a few, the dreamy cadence of the music is enough in itself to induce sleep, as if by Pavlovian reflex. For those who make it to the forecast proper, there is the pleasure of hearing the longest and most unhurried script of the day, since of all four bulletins it alone includes sea area Trafalgar and it alone escapes the tyranny of the clock—the need to finish in time for a programme to follow. Its pace, therefore, is even more leisurely than at dawn, and the opportunity this time is for listeners to adjust to the hours of rest. Soothing, reassuring, enclosing, life affirming: these are the qualities that make the *Shipping Forecast* more even than a 'landscape of the imagination' or a moment of poetry, or even an unbidden prayer. In these hours of darkness it is revealed as nothing less than the sleeping-draught of the age.

CONTINUITIES

That something as simple as the *Shipping Forecast* can be so rich in meaning shows why most radical experiments in Radio Four's presentation since 1967 came to naught. Continuity announcers becoming 'hosts', more and more jingles, a smattering of theme tunes: all this had been tried each time BBC managers were seized by the conviction that Radio Four had to brighten up its act and proclaim an 'Identity' if it was to survive competition. Behind their anxiety was a belief that bare speech and functional language was simply old hat—a 'turn-off'. But by the 1990s, even Fritz Spiegl, the man responsible for any number of Radio Four's most celebrated (or reviled) musical interludes, was having second thoughts about all this dressing up. Despite the panic, no competing station on the dial had begun to sound anything like Radio Four. Instead, 'junk radio', as Spiegl called it, had simply 'lapsed into breathless, ill-stressed disco-babble'. Now all Radio Four had to do to remain distinct was to hold steady and play it straight. As far as he was concerned the pips of the Greenwich Time Signal were enough to tell us that News was imminent. They marked time with a stark simplicity, and had the virtue of having done so for as long as, well, time immemorial. The novelist Jenny Diski recalls first hearing the pips consciously at nine o'clock in the morning on 13 July 1955, when they signalled the moment Ruth Ellis was hanged. Ever since, they seemed to 'ring out the story of passion, tragedy and mortality every hour and on the hour'.[47]

Once again, less was more. And satisfaction—or if not satisfaction then *meaning*—could be found in the most elemental of ingredients: a straightforward time-check, the simple words 'This is Radio Four', Big Ben, the pips—any of these were enough for listeners to locate themselves in time and space. In Radio

Four's tapestry of programmes, there was little need for enforced jollity, or banter or showmanship, because listeners so evidently felt at home with simple acoustic icons and continuity announcers calmly stitching the various programme threads together with the smallest inflection in their voices. Hence there were thousands in thrall to Charlotte Green—an announcer once judged to be 'a ceremonial presence, like the old-style Royal Family' who retained her 'mystery and her dignity'. This was flattering stuff, but what such a description missed was a more subtle ingredient in each continuity announcement: as one enraptured listener put it when writing of Peter Jefferson, what we invariably heard was 'decorum and authority, *laced with a warming trace of friendliness*'. Announcers such as Green and Jefferson, along with the likes of Peter Donaldson, Laurie Macmillan, and Brian Perkins were all judged as having what the professional critics called a 'natural' tone, delicately poised between the extremes of 'old-fashioned pomposity' at one end and 'trying to show off' at the other. Their reading was unobtrusive, but possessed of an 'occasional flash of real wit'; it betrayed assurance, intelligence, and 'an admirable readiness to understand and serve their material'. It was, then, not so much their dignity as their *unassuming* presence that appealed most. As Libby Purves pointed out, they had 'the humility to act as human signposts . . . yet the humanity to indicate by the slightest twitch of their voice that they too have been moved, or amused or surprised by the programme they are signing off '.[48]

For Purves, these qualities were vital because they embodied 'the very best of Radio Four and hence the soul of the BBC'. For, in the end, 'continuity' too was a concept rich in meanings of its own. It was about the linking together of Radio Four's disparate parade of programmes through the day. It was also about the network's enduring links with its own past. And it was the combination of these meanings that allowed Radio Four to offer its listeners what Tony Whitby had so memorably called 'the tide of the familiar bringing in the unfamiliar'.[49] Continuity announcers quite literally provided the continuity that held the network together. Any awkward clashes between new programmes and old, between the traditional and the experimental, between the serious and the frivolous, the uplifting and the downbeat, between the highbrow and the lowbrow—all these were smoothed over and wrapped around. Perhaps this 'unifying' job was getting a little easier anyway. For despite all the howls of discomfort behind the scenes at Broadcasting House, with producers railing against the structural upheavals of the Birt era, and despite the periodic flashes of insurrection from members of the listening public over *Rollercoaster* or bad language or the move of *Woman's Hour* or the appearance on air of Gerry Anderson or the plans for rolling news or the countless other transgressions inflicted upon them, this was a network that by and large gave the impression of becoming steadily more at ease with itself, more at ease with its audience, even more at ease with its own contradictions and idiosyncrasies. The fierce parodies of *On the Hour* showed a network confident enough to laugh at its own clichés. They were like twisted love-letters to an old friend—a warning of the monster Radio Four could become if it let down its guard. Dramedies such as *After Henry* showed a network happy to indulge its audience with stories of the middle-aged and middle-classed. Features and documentaries swapped a taste for the epic with a taste for the intimate and the everyday and eased themselves into the fabric of the place. The *Shipping Forecast* remained on air for no reason other than it was still wanted by many thousands of people who had no logical purpose in listening to it—other than the most basic purpose of all, of course, which was to make life a little bit richer in some intangible way. Across all the genres, new programmes contained traditional elements, while traditional programmes were gently refreshed; there were plenty of sad tales, but most contained redemption and compassion; almost every programme strived to be topical, but in series like *The Secret Diary of Adrian Mole* and in countless features and documentaries, issues were raised in muted rather than hectoring tones; almost every programme had storytelling at its heart; most strove for a matter-of-fact tone. In short, the excesses of theorizing or overt intellectualizing, of showmanship or over-familiarity were all generally, *blissfully*, absent. There was the occasional sharp edge or surprise or affront, but enough of what was heard on air had the aura of the decent, the sensible, the mildly uplifting, the pleasantly amusing, the gently poetic.

If this seems a modest achievement, then we must recall the essence of what radio was—and still is—about. The painter Tom Phillips, whose twin preoccupations were the everyday and the esoteric, once described radio—and specifically Radio Four—as an 'undercoat' of sound that supported his art. It was unobtrusively in the background, and always had been since he had listened to the Home Service during the War. Its invisibility belied the way it would 'employ and free' his mind. Behind every shape and stripe of colour on the canvas, he said, lay 'traces of my radio days—a lifetime's cricket, a thousand plays'. For him, radio was a 'sightless Odeon' where voices 'aloof but warm' materialized 'imperceptibly'. They did not force him to attend to them so much as quietly ingratiated themselves into his mind.[50] It was, then, precisely its background status, so feared in the 1950s and 1960s with the rise of television, that redeemed radio for many—and not just radio as a stream of music or news, but radio as a stream of stories, of ideas, of individual voices, and of metaphors. Hence, Jenny Diski's perceptive argument that while broadcasters desperately wanted radio to belong to 'the sharp end of the media', it was not really part of the media at all. 'Radio isn't like TV or newspapers, which burst in on us from the world outside,' she suggested, 'it's more like running water or electricity, just there, part of everyday life, always has been, unthinkable that it shouldn't be.' For her, there was 'indescribable security' in knowing exactly what was going to trickle past her mind's ear over the course of a few hours. Radio Four was master of the art, providing a regular tidal flow of the reassuring and the familiar with the occasional undercurrent of the esoteric and the surprising. It 'does its best to keep you in touch with the present', she concluded, 'but the pill is so well sugared with the traditional, you don't get a bitter taste in your mouth at all.'[51]

No wonder, then, that among the British public, ardent listeners have willingly ranked listening to Radio Four alongside sunshine, gardening, walking, chocolate, puddings, reading, the sea, Sunday lie-ins, breakfast, long warm evenings sitting outside drinking wine, children, grandchildren, solitude.[52] In the mid-1990s, surveys told us, these were the tokens of an ordinary life well lived. And Radio Four seemed comfortably at home among them.

Are these pleasures—or the common qualities they convey—explicable? Not entirely, for to probe too deeply would be to reduce Radio Four's success to a precise formula, when it clearly thrives on a largely *indefinable* resonance with the private lives and personal memories of many listeners. Indeed to explain fully would be, as Priestley once wrote of the English mentality, to destroy the very qualities that lie at its core. As with the English landscape, he wrote, there was in this mind 'a haze, rubbing away the hard edges of ideas, softening and blending the hues of passion':

Reason is there but it is not all-conquering and triumphant, setting up its pyramids and obelisks or marking out long straight roads down which the battalions of thoughts must march. The country does not show a face like a glaring map; nothing is as clearly marked out, and no boundaries can be discovered; the solid earth is there but sunlight and mist have given it vague enchantment.

As for the future, that was another matter altogether. For there were dangers to be faced whichever path was taken away from this middle terrain, this blend of smoothed edges and softened passions:

Let the sunlight disappear, and everything is grey and very soon seems heavy and sodden. Let the mist be completely banished and the land lies naked and quivering in the sunlight, and there is an end to this enchantment.[53]

Epilogue: 1997 and Since

In October 1997, Radio Four broadcast a rather curious programme imagining its own sorry demise in the mid-twenty-first century. *The Death of Radio* provided a nightmarish phantasmagoria in which the BBC had been taken over by Bill Gates, the *Shipping Forecast* had been sold to a pornographer for an 'erotic' makeover complete with French accents and heavy breathing, and Peter Donaldson turned out to be a computer facsimile—the real announcer having been terminated years before when a focus group declared his voice 'unfriendly'. Inane jingles barked messages like 'Radio Four: it's sorted! Are you?' To which the answer was evidently yes, since broadcasters could supply drugs that reduced a listener's curiosity, while a neat household device blocked any programme that might personally offend so that nothing could be heard that might 'override your own personal agenda'.[1]

This was satire that came from the heart. One of its producers, Matt Thompson, had just left Broadcasting House to join the new breed of independent companies. He *had* to leave, he said, before his love for the medium died. Power, he explained, was becoming concentrated increasingly in the hands of commissioning editors mesmerized by audience research and ever more risk averse. Computers allowed them to handle data in all sorts of ways; sometimes it even allowed them to pronounce on the most desirable narrative shape for a programme, which meant, in practice, proscribing anything too allusive and open-ended; satellite technology, mobile phones, and the Internet were conspiring to create a pervasive taste for immediacy in place of reflection. It was, he thought, all part of a culture suspicious of intuition, and one trickling down from above through John Birt's 'Newtonian' attempt to control a world that was essentially uncertain—an uncertainty which was, for Thompson at least, precisely its joy. 'Once I was sitting in my office at the BBC looking out of the window and a manager came in and said "what are you doing?" When I said thinking he was shocked. Thinking was latterly considered subversive.'[2]

As in the 1960s, so in the final years of the twentieth century and the first years of the twenty-first: a powerful rhetoric of decline attached itself to the broadcasting industry.

Quite apart from Thompson's satire there have been the dire warnings of the American sociologist, Richard Sennett. His main focus has been the large corporation, such as Wal-Mart or IBM. But he has worked in Britain long enough to reach a considered view of recent changes inside public sector bodies such as the BBC. Here, as elsewhere, he sees a new business model relentlessly orientated to the short term, where 'institutional beauty' consists in demonstrating 'signs of internal change and flexibility'. An employee's accumulated experience is less important than an ability to keep jumping from project to project; computerization applies rules swiftly and unambiguously. With less room to make interpretative decisions of their own, staff face the 'spectre of uselessness'. He notes, as does the social anthropologist Georgina Born, the tendency for 'quick-strike' consultants to view deep knowledge as a barrier to swift change, and the concomitant tendency of long-serving staff to find themselves 'cast adrift' in their own institutions—or, as with Thompson and others, to find themselves leaving altogether.[3]

Everything has changed, Sennett implies; and mostly for the worse. But there is a second rhetorical tradition: one that seemingly contradicts this interpretation entirely, and which attaches specifically to Radio Four. This says that *nothing* has changed over the years and the network remains untouched by nearly four decades of social upheaval in British life. Hence: it still sounds 'as if Jimmy Porter had never spoken'. Or: the schedule is still heaving with 'dead wood'— programmes handcrafted for '*Daily Express* curtain-twitchers' and delivered in a 'fusspot, busy-body tone'. Or again: on *Midweek* 'there's *always* a single-handed yachtswoman'. Some—including those at the top of the BBC—indulge in a variant of this theme, which says, in effect, that the BBC *has* changed yet Radio Four represents a shamefully unreconstructed corner of this sleek new Corporation. Thus John Birt's successor as Director-General, Greg Dyke, repeating in his recent autobiography the by-now familiar (indeed inevitable) statement: that in an increasingly demotic and outward-looking BBC, Radio Four still 'disproportionately' serves the southern middle classes.[4]

These are serious critiques. Many other voices from within the Corporation concur that much has indeed been lost—and yet more remains to be done. But the history of Radio Four between 1967 and 1997 traced here—and much that has happened in the ten years since—appears, to me at least, to point to a different, more promising conclusion: that a great deal *has* changed; and, if we take the long view, it has generally been change for the *better*.

This is not to deny the existence of huge trauma behind the scenes at Broadcasting House, some of it destructive. Sennett is surely right to claim that whatever other benefits can be claimed to accrue from commercialization and globalization and managerialism, 'a better quality of institutional life is not among them'.[5] Nor, is it to deny the presence of programmes that are banal, or inelegant, or cloying, or dull, or which fail in any number of other ways identified regularly by the professional critics and dedicated listeners. Rather, it is to claim that, *despite* all this, many self-evidently good programmes do get made—perhaps more than were made in 1967 or before—and that, *despite* all this, Radio Four has succeeded in remaining part of the national consciousness.

Indeed, I would argue that it has been *change*—though change of a strictly organic kind—that has helped to ensure its survival on such positive terms.

First of all, it is clear that some of the crises facing Radio Four have been acute, rather than chronic. Looking back from the perspective of 2006, it is striking, for example, how the cries of pain from Broadcasting House were collectively at their loudest in the 1990s, and diminished thereafter. For Radio Four especially it was the three years between 1996 and 2000 that represented a high-water mark of anxiety. This, of course, was when Birt's corporate restructuring had just pulled the journalistic guts out of Radio's centre of operations, and when both Liz Forgan and Michael Green had left, both in some despair at the directorate's apparently diminished status. It was also the period of James Boyle's Controllership.

In itself, this was traumatic. Boyle, a quiet and cultivated man, had arrived with the unfortunate epithet of 'MacBirt', earned for the rigour with which he had pursued reform in his previous fiefdom, Radio Scotland. Once installed in London, and with the full support of his Director, Matthew Bannister, and his Director-General, John Birt, he unveiled a similarly radical re-engineering of Radio Four. From April 1998, a new schedule did away with series such as *Afternoon Shift*, *Mediumwave*, *Kaleidoscope*, *Weekending*, and *Breakaway*, launched new series such as *Home Truths* and *Broadcasting House*, permanently extended *Today* until 9 a.m., introduced an extra weekly episode of *The Archers*, and restricted *Yesterday in Parliament* to long wave. Boyle thus disturbed at least four constituencies simultaneously: producers who worried at losing commissions, MPs who lost public exposure, newspaper critics who smelt a classic case of 'dumbing down', and those listeners who hated any change, let alone change on this scale. The outburst was certainly loud and sustained, with newspapers and phone-ins once again deluged with furious complaint. It also became politically charged for the BBC when the Speaker of the Commons, Betty Boothroyd, began coordinating a parliamentary campaign of opposition that culminated in a government minister accusing Radio Four of contributing to a lowering of national standards of literacy and more than one MP asking for Boyle's resignation.[6]

In fact, the Controller's schedule was based on impeccable reasoning: he had proceeded after spending a year travelling around the country talking to listeners and on the basis of an avalanche of data, every programme having been analysed and listening habits having been mapped in microscopic detail. All the evidence told him that some series were clearly better than others at winning audiences, that it made sense for programmes to begin and end at times that were easy for listeners to predict, that new series and new presenters might attract new listeners. For the critics, of course, such rigorous logic was precisely the problem: it spoke of a Radio Four suddenly in thrall, like the rest of broadcasting, to ratings or computer-driven commissioning, more interested in form than in content, neglectful of intuition or serendipity—a view apparently confirmed when the first new batch of lunchtime quiz-shows and early-evening comedies commissioned in 1998 were badly received in the press. By autumn, even the BBC's Chairman, Christopher Bland, and the Director-General John Birt, had admitted to 'disappointment', and several of the new series were ditched. In 1999, delicate negotiations also produced a concession to MPs through the reappearance on FM of a cut-down version of *Yesterday in Parliament*. By now, the BBC acknowledged officially that too much had been done too quickly: the new schedule had not just offended Radio Four's diehards; it had also led to some hastily produced programmes appearing on air. When Boyle left in 2000, Birt praised him publicly for having been both bold and brave; privately, and with the benefit of hindsight, he thought he should probably have done more to hold him back.[7]

In the longer term, some of Boyle's changes appeared to bed in remarkably well. The darkest rumours of a Radio Four awash with 'youth-orientated' programmes and 'docu-soaps' proved exaggerated: an extra £1 million had been found for large-scale drama; the parliamentary backlash had been skilfully defused; the commissioning process streamlined; several of the new presenters and new programmes—Mark Lawson at *Front Row,* John Peel at *Home Truths*, Eddie Mair at *Broadcasting House*, Richard Uridge at *Open Country,* for instance— looked like becoming quintessential Radio Four 'fixtures'. And overall, the network seemed, if anything, a little more 'upmarket' than ever. By 2000 it was even winning more industry awards for its programmes than ever. In this respect, Boyle's shock therapy had clear echoes of McIntyre's regime two decades before: painful and unpopular upheaval followed by a more promising legacy. Above all, Boyle could point to good audience ratings, which—after an initial and predictable drop—started to rise persistently from the middle of 1999. His strategy of giving more space on the schedule to the network's two most popular programmes, namely *Today* and *The Archers*, appeared to lift figures across the board. From a brief low-point of some 7.7 million listeners tuning in each week in the autumn of 1998, Radio Four's overall 'reach' rose steadily—boosted, in part, by new ways of audience measurement—to some 9.5 million by the end of 1999.[8]

Crucially, this meant that when Helen Boaden took over as the new Controller in 2000, she inherited a network which had already been through one of its periodic shocks and which already boasted ratings on a strong upward trajectory. Unsurprisingly, neither Boaden nor her eventual successor, Mark Damazer, overturned Boyle's schedule in any significant way.

Boaden, in particular, was in the fortunate position of being able to reap the benefits of relative quietude. She also had the tactical advantage of being a Radio Four 'insider', having served with distinction at *Woman's Hour* and *File on Four*. This she built on astutely, talking from the outset of Radio Four being 'in her bloodstream', of working 'in partnership' with programme-makers and listeners, of 'consolidation' rather than revolution. By the end of her tenure, it was generally agreed that while exuding sheer niceness and an impression of 'masterly inactivity' she had managed to innovate by stealth on several fronts. Just one example, out of many, was her reintroduction of children's programmes: not just the weekly *Go 4 It!*, but a series of epic one-offs that also had proven adult appeal, such as the dramatization of Philip Pullman's *His Dark Materials* trilogy, a timely repeat of the 1981 serialization of *Lord of the Rings* following the release of Peter Jackson's film, and—after much negotiation—the uninterrupted broadcast on Boxing Day 2000 of Stephen Fry's eight-and-a-half hour reading of *Harry Potter and the Philosopher's Stone*. It was Boaden's period of office that also saw the launch of a systematic 'listen again' service on the BBC's website and the digital station 'BBC 7', both of which successfully advertised Radio Four's archive of programmes to a wider, slightly younger, audience.[9]

Similarly, Mark Damazer came to office in 2004 talking not of grand plans but of a commitment to enduring values: Radio Four, he said, would remain 'the home for intelligence, flair and wit'. His curriculum vitae, with a starred-first in history at Cambridge, time at Harvard, and a series of positions at the more cerebral end of British journalism, also appeared to provide copper-bottom guarantees that Radio Four was in the hands of a Controller unlikely to take it downmarket. By the end of 2006, his most audacious move had been to add an early-morning 'News Briefing' through dropping the *UK Theme*, Fritz Spiegl's medley of tunes that had opened the station for three decades. Between January 2006, when the plan was first announced, and April, when it finally took effect, the axing of the *UK Theme* became a classic Radio Four cause célèbre: a campaign, quickly got up with more than 18,000 listeners signing a petition for it to be retained and boosted by the celebrity endorsement of *Newsnight*'s presenter Jeremy Paxman; the Prime Minster, Tony Blair, telling MPs of the 'strong feeling' being aroused by its disappearance; protestors dressed as Britannia stationed outside Broadcasting House. The offence for some had been to replace a piece of harmless musical eccentricity with yet more news—another step in the long march toward 'unending sameness' on air. For others, the expunging of a tune that made them 'feel good about life and the country' was yet more dastardly political correctness.[10] It was certainly a strong reminder of the audience's innate conservatism and of their continued ability to mobilize.

Viewed against other crises over the years, it was also a sign of how little Radio Four was now changing in its fundamentals. The *UK Theme* was, after all, right on the fringes of the schedule. That *it*, of all programmes, should be the leading cause of controversy in Damazer's first two years: this showed just how many of the big battles had already been won.

And the mainstream of Radio Four really *had* changed in fundamental ways since the 1960s. At the beginning there had been considerable pessimism over the future of radio, and, in particular, the future of speech radio. Television was triumphant, having already captured the all-important evening audience; radio, it seemed, might only survive as a source of background music and news—and in the battles over *Broadcasting in the Seventies*, and among a considerable body of journalists, there were plenty who conceived the family of BBC networks largely in those restricted terms. For a Home Service burdened with a history of 'Establishment' values and Establishment voices, there were other terrors. The decline of deference, the questioning of the canon, the desire to 'dress down' one's class and one's voice, the apparently waning authority of age and wisdom, the sheer *embarrassment* of being middle-aged and middle-class: none of this seemed to bode well. That something as complex and seemingly anachronistic as Radio Four emerged in 1967 represented an extraordinary act of faith in itself. That it went on to survive—even to thrive—was certainly not pre-ordained. From that point onwards, success depended on both the steady recruitment of new listeners to replace those who were dying off *and* some accommodation with its chief rival, namely television.

In the end, recruiting new listeners could only be done by engaging with the attitudes and outlook of those Britons in their thirties and forties, not just those in their fifties and sixties. To meet them halfway, most programmes became less scripted and more spontaneous; they became brisker, busier, less aloof, more demotic. As a result, the network's median 'voice', though still fundamentally calm and reassuring, gradually became more questioning and irreverent. Nowadays, even the oldest properties—programmes such as *Today*, *The Archers*, and *Desert Island Discs*—are undoubtedly a world apart from their 1967 incarnations. To call them habitually 'rude' or 'sex-obsessed' or 'impertinent', as some newspapers have done, certainly overstates their iconoclastic status. But history suggests that much of Radio Four's content has been revolutionized—and sometimes revolutionized most strikingly where format and title have remained outwardly traditional.

Dealing with television has been trickier, since the battle for critical and public attention has so often been one-sided. Radio Four's early attempts at eye-catching productions, dabbling with stereo and quadraphony and multitrack trickery, met with a distinctly mixed response from listeners. But the ambition was understandable: a desire to establish that the *art* of radio survived, and a wish to create the same sense of occasion that television regularly enjoyed. In the longer term, a more complementary relationship was forged with the dominant medium. One approach was to make Radio Four more amenable to casual listening—classically through the magazine format, which multiplied in the 1970s and 1980s. Another was to recognize Radio Four's potential to *compensate* for television's perceived inadequacies—especially what Richard Wade once called its 'lowest common denominator' tendencies—by offering unapologetically authoritative debate on a regular basis. Indeed, despite the many awkward attempts at popularization that have been charted over preceding chapters, the underlying trend was undoubtedly for Radio Four to become steadily *tougher* over time. Demanding programmes had always been there, of course, but over the past four decades they—or, at least, something of their style—gradually migrated from the once all-important evening schedule to infuse the generality of radio's new heartland: the daytime. One need only mention some of the programmes recently scheduled at 9 a.m. on weekday mornings to gauge instantly what this has meant: *Start the Week*, indisputably more intellectually vigorous than its 1970 forebear; *The Choice* and *The Candidate*, both providing forensic one-to-one interviews on emotionally traumatic terrain; and, perhaps most celebrated of all since its debut in 1998, *In Our Time*, with its uncompromising workouts on the Great Ideas of history. In this respect, Mark Damazer's decision to transmit Daniel Barenboim's 2006 *Reith Lectures*—what would once have been regarded as an evening event for the 'dedicated' listener—at 9 a.m. on Fridays made perfect scheduling sense: it was planted in ground that had been well fertilized for nearly two decades.

Perhaps *the* defining change in Radio Four's character, even more than what Controllers called a 'stiffening' in the standard of debate, has been a *widening* in the range of voices and styles the network encompasses on a daily basis. This, too, has been a consistent thread over the past forty years. When Tony Whitby wanted to enforce a mix of genres in order to fend off accusations that Radio Four was about to become an arid zone of news, he talked of Radio Four as 'three-networks-in-one', of the need for a range of 'textures'. Later, David Hatch talked of wanting Radio Four to provide its listeners with 'pleasure as well as tragedy'. Later still, Michael Green talked of bringing a few more listeners to the network by achieving diversity-within-unity.

This policy of eclecticism swam with the cultural tide. In 1981, the BBC's own Radio Network Working Party, like Annan four years before, declared that radio was no longer the 'mass medium' it had been in the 1930s and 1940s when cultural certainties 'gave coherence' to output: it was 'a mobile attendant to our individual needs and wishes'. 'As a community we are now breathing in several cultures simultaneously', the Working Party pointed out: 'The broadcasting consequences of this state of affairs are immense.'[11] Clearly one immense consequence was this: that culture was less and less able to fulfil its classic, Arnoldian role of reconciliation, and became instead the very medium in which battle was engaged. The only possible response appeared to be official recognition that no single tone of voice, or linguistic register, or mood, or genre, could be assumed to work for everyone.

Diversification was embedded as a fundamental goal. Usually in broadcasting, this was achieved by differentiating output across more channels; on Radio Four diversification took place under one roof. And the long-term effects of this are often underestimated by the casual observer. A truly persistent Radio Four listener of the past decade might, for instance, have caught: a 95-year-old Alistair Cooke delivering *Letter from America*—'poised', 'measured', bland 'in the nicest sense' and 'mildly reactionary'; Linda Smith delivering one of her comic diatribes in what Jeremy Hardy called an unapologetically flat 'suburban working-class, Kentish drone', disdainful of pomposity, angry at hypocrisy, and somehow both 'very Yorkshire' and 'very Jewish'; the Black American film director Melvin Van

Peebles in a series devoted to hip-hop culture; magisterial reflections on the twentieth century in John Tusa's and Michael Ignatieff's *20/20*; performance poets rapping away inside Manchester bus-shelters; evocative, yet resolutely *un*nostalgiac accounts of wartime in Charles Wheeler's *The Evacuation*.[12]

The list is random; perhaps it draws on the untypical. But the immense variation in tone it contains is echoed in even the most regular of programmes. Take just two series that emerged during Boyle's troubled era. The first, *In Our Time*, has been described as 'the most cerebral 45 minutes on British radio'. In the course of just one series, for instance, it has tackled Homer's *Odyssey*, Eighteenth Century Politeness, Agincourt, The Origins of Life, Jean-Paul Sartre, and Pi. In each edition, Melvyn Bragg chairs a sustained discussion between three academic experts. On paper the format is utterly forbidding; it is certainly characterized by a high level of seriousness. As one reviewer points out, where else could a presenter get away with saying 'Can I move on to Burckhardt?' or talk of 'the Renaissance reaction against scholasticism and the Ciceronian reaction against Olympian theology'? In his recent study of British intellectuals, Stefan Collini shows how broadcasting habitually disguises academic debate: in a BBC overwhelmed by 'nervous populism', he says, it is all too rare to find it at all. Yet, in naming *In Our Time* as one of several places where intellectualism *is* allowed to express itself, Collini also acknowledges radio's special potential as a medium for the communication of ideas—though he resists making explicit an obvious conclusion: that the Third Programme tradition that many still mourn has in fact already been reborn—and on the old 'middlebrow' network.[13]

The same could hardly be said of *Home Truths*, which ran for eight years before its presenter, John Peel, was finally deemed irreplaceable in 2006. Here was a programme drawing on very different strands of radio history: the whimsy of *Down Your Way*, perhaps, or the intimacies of *If You Think You've Got Problems*, even (if only elliptically) the warming homeliness of the *Shipping Forecast*. Its brief was to provide 'extraordinary stories from ordinary folk', and its chosen method was to blend tragedy and absurdity. Which meant an item on people with a phobia about buttons could follow a woman speaking of burials. Or a woman devoted to sniffing her pets could rub up against a 9-year-old boy caring for his epileptic mother. At first, the mix was baffling. Over time, the connecting tissue was more obvious: family, eccentricity, age, Britishness. As such the series entirely matched Peel's—and Radio Four's—predilection for a kind of gently self-mocking world-view that would not have felt out of place coming from a provincial newspaper humorist of the 1950s. The appeal was never entirely archaic, however. Like its immediate predecessor, *Offspring*, it was also imbued with Peel's innate ability to transcend the generations in a way that might have appeared unimaginable in 1967. One of the programme's concerns, he explained, was 'the means by which parents establish at least the semblance of some sort of working relationship with their children': 'children', he added, 'whose own happiness and sense of achievement may depend on making this theoretically workable relationship unworkable'. With a presenter so palpably sympathetic, *Home Truths* gradually built up a large and intensely loyal fan base of its own— some 1.5 million listeners, for whom human fallibilities were no less worthy a subject for broadcasting on Radio Four than the human achievements debated in elevated style on *In Our Time*.[14]

The unavoidable corollary of this highly fluid tone to Radio Four has been that very few listeners or critics could bear everything they hear. So while *Home Truths* struck a chord with some, it grated horribly with others. Emails sent to the producers accused it of being 'inconsequential', 'puerile', 'inane'. A majority of newspaper critics declared themselves unmoved—or, rather, moved only to turn off their sets when they heard the opening bars of its theme music. For one reviewer it was nothing more than a 'sick-making bag of suburban spittle'. Similarly, a programme such as *The Moral Maze*, while delighting some with its tough-minded treatment of ethical dilemmas, provoked others to rail at the apparently reductive nature of its adversarial style. As one critic judged, everyone was obliged to shout at each other and no one could say anything interesting before being interrupted. The overall effect? A kind of 'tinnitus'. Even *Start the Week*, which usually garnered favourable reviews all round, provoked the occasional grumble: that—post-Bragg, post-Paxman—the tendency was to steer every discussion, whether on history or art or science, back to politics. As for the debut in 2006 of a Jamaican-British continuity announcer—that caused a steady rumble of complaints on the Radio Four message-boards, suggesting in sometimes intemperate language that the proper 'tone' of the network had been destroyed by his Caribbean inflections.[15]

Perhaps the most serious criticism of all over the past decade was one levelled at *Today*, or at least the kind of journalism it was accused of practising. This emerged from a complex chain of events triggered on 29 May 2003, when one of *Today*'s reporters, Andrew Gilligan claimed during a live interview that the government had ordered a key security dossier to be 'sexed up' by asserting that Saddam Hussein could launch an attack in forty-five minutes—and that the government probably already knew the assertion to be incorrect. If true, Gilligan's charge would be devastating: it suggested, in effect, that the government had deliberately falsified a key reason for going to war in Iraq. And over the next twelve months it unleashed vigorous government protests, the suicide of Gilligan's main source, David Kelly, investigations by two parliamentary select committees, the Hutton Inquiry, the sudden departure of both the BBC's Chairman and its Director-General, and an internal review of the Corporation's entire journalistic ethos. Amid the turbulence, two uncomfortable facts emerged: that Gilligan did not have a full contemporaneous record of his conversations with Kelly, and that *Today*'s own editor had privately expressed concern over his reporter's 'loose use of language'. The Hutton Inquiry eventually ruled that Gilligan's central claim was 'unfounded'.[16] Naturally, most journalists were aghast at this outcome. Whatever slips were made, they insisted, Gilligan had been right in all the essentials: a vital truth about government 'spin' had emerged, and in the face of a Downing Street machine apparently out to 'get' the BBC for its perceived bias in the coverage of Iraq, here was a reporter who had done his duty by being properly sceptical. A very different response came from the *Financial Times* journalist, John Lloyd. For him, the whole furore had been 'an accident waiting to happen'. The BBC had not just supplied 'carelessly done' reportage when it should have been setting a gold standard for accuracy; it had succumbed more widely to the cynical assumption that politicians were born liars and rogues. The kind of jousting practised by *Today* betrayed a journalism 'ravenous for conflict', a kind likely to increase 'the anomie and distrust within civil society'. What the country needed, he argued, was not 'laser-guided' journalism, but a journalism that would 'illuminate our public life rather than degrade it': detailed, subtle, rational, courteous—and 'which admits—indeed insists on—diversity in the causes of events'.[17]

Whichever view was to be believed, the row over Gilligan revealed a vital truth of its own. Finding the right 'voice' in broadcasting was not always a simple question of personal taste: it was recognized as something that determined the health of the whole public realm. This was one reason Hutton proved so traumatic for a public service broadcaster like the BBC. Yet, significantly, little of the fallout reflected badly on Radio Four. Partly, this was because *Today* remained what it had been for some time: an institution-within-an-institution, its status unmoored from that of its parent network and tethered instead to the fissile worlds of high politics and daily journalism. Partly, it was because Radio Four as a whole so obviously came close to providing a virtual matrix of what Lloyd sought: a medium—when heard in the round—that was 'conflicting, contradictory, and rich in layers of meaning'. Within the confines of its journalism, for instance, Radio Four offered series such as *File on Four*, which was committed to a forensic treatment of issues, or *Europhile*, which took the unusual step for the British media of taking continental affairs seriously, or any number of documentaries which looked at the wider world in 'detailed, subtle, rational, courteous' ways. The 2006 series *Uncovering Iran* was a model in this respect, trying to get under the skin of a country increasingly represented elsewhere in dangerously polarized terms. One of its presenters, the BBC's Foreign Affairs Editor, John Simpson, had already looked across the Radio Four schedule in 1998, noting with admiration how much 'good reporting and good writing' had 'broken surface' on the network.[18] And beyond journalism? There was always Radio Four's drama and literature and satire and conversation: all, in their different ways, attempting to throw light on the crooked timber of humanity.

This, of course, was the essence of the 'rich mix' Monica Sims had fought so hard to defend at the beginning of the 1980s. It was, she had said then, all about providing for—and helping to forge—the 'rounded' citizen. But she had not been the only Controller to find this 'cottage garden' model of Radio Four under attack from those who saw more virtue in 'neat packages'. At the end of the

1960s, the BBC's Managing Director of Radio, Ian Trethowan, had wanted Radio Four to be focused almost exclusively on news—something that had to be resisted by both Gerard Mansell and Tony Whitby. Two decades later, David Hatch and Michael Green faced similar battles, though this time from ultra-loyalist listeners, who resented programmes such as *Rollercoaster* or *Citizens* or *Anderson Country* for having diluted what they understood to be the one true, 'authorized' tone of *their* network. The press, meanwhile, chastised Radio Four for not trying hard enough to be accessible, or, perversely, for trying too hard with jingles or phone-ins or celebrity presenters. And consultants and apparatchiks periodically hatched plans for 'pulling together' Radio Four and giving it the clearer 'identity' and 'unity of tone' they felt it deserved in the new, competitive broadcasting age.

Some of this pressure to narrow Radio Four's range, though ill conceived, was well meant: a sign of deep attachment to one particular conception of what worked best. Some of it, as Georgina Born implies in her recent study of the BBC, was more disingenuous. The Corporation's eternal paradox, she reminds us, is that it *has* to be popular in order to justify the universality of the licence fee but that it also *has* to serve minority tastes in order to prove its difference from commercial services. Hence the commitment to mixed programming. Hence, too, it being perpetually criticized *both* for chasing ratings *and* for being unsuccessful in the mass arena. Competitors suggest, somewhat tautologically, that both 'failures' show the Corporation to be undeserving of public money. 'Lowbrow, highbrow; damned if it does and damned if it doesn't,' Born writes in despair: 'the complex functioning of the BBC—its purposefully mixed cultural economy—is travestied in these carping refrains.'[19]

Here we touch upon *the* central theme of Radio Four's history over the past forty years. For, whether we call it a 'rich mix' or a 'rag-bag', what Born calls the BBC's 'purposefully mixed cultural economy' is something that has been retained in its purest form on Radio Four. And consequently, over the years, Radio Four has been accused more than any other part of the BBC of having an unresolved identity crisis—at least by those for whom the lack of a singular identity is a gross offence. That, so far, attempts to give it a narrower, more homogeneous identity have been frustrated, that it still fails to satisfy *anyone* completely: this, surely, is a mark of achievement rather than of failure. Disunity is part of its DNA: symbolic, both of that older Reithian injunction 'to inform, to educate, and to entertain', and, one senses, of a newer—and sometimes hesitant—commitment to cultural diversity.

How has this essential disunity been protected? The first, and rather unfashionable answer is that it has happened in part through what Reith once called the brute force of monopoly. Very rarely did the innovations that allowed Radio Four to evolve and diversify over the years arrive in response to *public* demand. They usually came from Controllers and producers who could risk at least some programmes of appeal to 'fringe' tastes, simply because in a deregulated broadcasting era they found themselves in an unusually privileged position: the kind of radio that Radio Four delivered was just too expensive for a commercial operator to emulate. With no direct competitor, they knew that core listeners simply had nowhere else to go—no matter how loudly they complained. The diehards were consequently in no position to hold Controllers 'hostage'—or, at least, not entirely. Naturally, many of the experiments forged in this monopolistic space failed. But, as the experience of countless comedy producers showed, for every four or five flops there would eventually be a hit. Evolution was often through trial and error. This, it is worth noting, was antithetical to the prevailing business model of reducing risk through being highly predictive. But it was the essence of creativity and craftsmanship. As Richard Sennett observed in his study of the modern corporation, steady improvement in the quality of output has generally come in those places where workers have been free to make mistakes and then go over their work again and again. Something of this freedom has been preserved in Broadcasting House over the past forty years. And it has generally been done without the 'brute force of monopoly' being exercised recklessly. The evidence left by the conduct of everyday business suggests that programming decisions usually arose from a complex mosaic of considerations: the personal instincts of Controllers and producers, yes, but also a sense of how any given programme fitted the Corporation's ethos, a calculation of the political or critical climate, the pragmatic dictates of time and money, the constant weighing of public attitudes. Hence, Radio Four's treatment of language or politics—to take but two examples—was always as much a matter of intense debate within Broadcasting House as it was outside. This endless self-criticism was sometimes stifling, yet since the 1960s it ensured a nuanced response to cultural change. And while the pace of this response could be glacially slow, a degree of flexibility was at least hard-wired into the system.

There was another factor in Radio Four's survival: a profound remoulding of Britain's social demography that slowly worked in its favour. By almost every objective or subjective measure, the proportion of the population broadly regarded as 'middle class' grew significantly from the 1960s. Indeed, if we were to take home ownership as a defining feature of middle-class identity, as some do, we would now reckon on some two-thirds of the nation falling into the category. Even the more cautious indicators of class agree on the general direction of travel: a steady growth in 'professional' jobs since the 1970s; a steady growth in the number of two-income households; a staggering fivefold increase in the number of university students since the mid-1960s; an expanding number of people happy to *define themselves* as middle class. When Radio Four was born in 1967, it had never been so unfashionable to be middle class. Now, by contrast, the middle class has 'never been so secure'.[20] It certainly provides an expanding constituency for Radio Four—especially since in parallel to the expansion and growing self-confidence of the middle class there has been a burgeoning community of the middle-aged.

These fifty-somethings, of course, are the very same teenagers we met back in 1967 in that metaphorical bus rolling past the Home Service diehards, yelling words of rebellion and spattering them with mud. And as they matured into the latest generation of listeners, they brought with them a whiff of the Sixties. Their tastes, Helen Boaden once explained, were 'conditioned by the rock 'n' roll years': when *they* seek reminders of their youth, they look for programmes about the Rolling Stones or the Vietnam War. Even if they vaguely remember the Home Service, nostalgia is for them a less intense emotion than for previous generations. They enjoy greater affluence and better health, for a start. But more significantly, so Controllers such as Boaden reckon, they are more likely to embrace the modern world and to show a greater scepticism towards authority. They are also far more eclectic in their outlooks and lifestyle.[21]

Naturally enough, this does *not* always translate into boundless tolerance: taste remains highly divisive, as reactions to a series such as *Home Truths* proved. The increasing heterogeneity of the middle-aged and middle class can therefore present us with a Radio Four audience that often feels like a set of competing, mutually exclusive subcultures, each clinging to its favourite programmes with something akin to the old Blitz spirit. But it is also possible to see a transcendent sense of curiosity and open-mindedness having taken root. This, after all, is the generation of listeners that could muster no more than a single phone call of complaint in 2003 when the unexpurgated reading of Ian McEwan's novel *Atonement* aired language that would have provoked spluttering outrage thirty years before. Even more spectacularly, it is the generation that voted Karl Marx the greatest philosopher of all time for an *In Our Time* poll: not the mass conversion of Middle England to firm socialist principles, perhaps, and more likely a reflection of the close attendance of Britain's *bien-pensants*; yet Plato (who lagged in fifth place) would have recognized something of his particular philosophy at work: an implicit recognition that the *process* of debate is more important than its product—that 'one can reject a conclusion, but it is much harder to reject a process of imaginative expansion'.[22]

For me, this notion of 'imaginative expansion' probably captures Radio Four's surviving ethos better than any other description so far. And if it sounds rather grandiose, perhaps we should pause briefly, and finally, to reflect on Radio Four's most fundamental achievements over forty years.

First, there is the remarkable fact that, despite sticking with programmes that demand attention while more populist distractions have proliferated all about, its audience figures have remained buoyant. They reached their highest level for over a decade during the 2003 war in Iraq, when some eleven million people listened each week. At about the same point, it even started eating into television's evening ratings, reversing decades of retreat. News coverage remains a cornerstone of Radio Four's appeal, but the number of listeners has been driven upwards through a whole range of programmes. *The Archers'* own audience, for example, has risen steadily from about four million a week in the early 1990s to some five million in 2005; 6.5 million people now listen to some Radio Four drama every week; 4.5 million listen to its comedy shows; three million to *Woman's Hour*. As for *In Our Time*, witheringly dismissed by one journalist as 'like being locked in a university library with several tutors': it managed in 2005 to become British broadcasting's most popular podcast, confirming, as one rather more astute commentator suggested, that debate had become 'the new rock 'n' roll'.[23]

Radio Four is not unique in tapping into a thriving tradition of autodidacticism, as the current popularity of reading groups and public lectures has shown. But in the world of mainstream broadcasting it is a striking anomaly. In America, for example, there is National Public Radio: vaguely familiar in tone, but also marginal, underfunded, a trifle earnest. As for commercial talk radio, Stephen Miller's recent survey of more than 2,000 years of the conversational arts ended with his tuning in to several examples of the genre. What he heard was not true conversation, with its etiquette of restraint, but a slew of 'anger communities' at war: bombasts, hotheads, egomaniacs, and zealots, all out to confirm existing opinions rather than challenge them. At best, Miller concluded, radio—like the iPod or the mobile phone—had become merely a 'conversational avoidance device', protecting us from the real thing.[24]

Might Radio Four make the British context different in a vital way? Significantly, one of the few British voices Miller quotes is a woman who regards the 'real' conversation of dinner parties as nothing but 'egos shouting' and turns to the radio instead. 'I really enjoy other people having conversation for me', she tells him. One suspects she is a Radio Four listener: for her, what is found on the dial really is as 'solid' a conversational experience as anything else in her life.

The highly fluid tone, the adjacency of fact and fiction, the rubbing together of the demotic and the high-flown or the banal and the significant: this mix defines Radio Four—and this mix has a cultural value of its own. All too often, Amartya Sen points out, we live in a world where a diversity of cultures 'pass each other like ships in the night', where complex identities and ideas are neatly packaged and isolated to the detriment of mutual understanding and respect. His solution? 'We have to make sure, above all, that our mind is not halved by a horizon.'[25]

This, then, has become Radio Four's new purpose: not so much to lift us up from 'low' culture to 'high'—for who now can be certain which is which?—but to *widen* our horizons a little as the world of fragmenting tastes and ideologies pulls us further apart. The critic John Carey cautions against asking too much of culture. There is, he says, no definitive proof that it makes us better people. But he also sees its potential when it engages with ideas. For him, personally, this comes through literature. It provides 'a field of comparisons and contrasts, spreading infinitely outwards, so that whatever we read constantly modifies, adapts, questions or abrogates whatever we have read before'. 'Diversity, counter-argument, reappraisal and qualification are its essence': it is what supplies the materials for thought. As for its imaginative power, that comes through the inability of words to be as fixed and definite as pictures: its 'indistinctiveness' leaves the reader with the space to create. Its meanings become as illimitable as humanity itself.[26]

This is an eloquent argument. But much of what Carey says about literature also applies to the medium of radio—or, to be more precise, it applies to Radio Four. After forty years, here is a network whose fluidity still provides us with 'comparisons and contrasts' that resist neat packaging. As long as it goes on broadcasting, it also does so 'infinitely'. For someone such as Libby Purves, who has worked for it and listened to it all her life, its Reithian mix 'doubles the usefulness and value' of each day. For her—and, we must suppose, for countless others—it makes 'the dull physical jobs tolerable' and fits her better for 'the mental ones to come'. In short, she says, it makes her 'more alive'.

There will always be quarrels, estrangements, lingering bad blood. Radio Four is as much a lightning rod for national anxieties today as it was in 1967. But if we still complain it is because it *matters*. Not just because 'it is family', but because, against all the odds, it still promises to enlarge minds as well as pass time pleasurably. It has learned, like the rest of broadcasting, to speak to us in many voices rather than just one. Rather more unusually, it has also held to a rather rational sort of relativism, where the collective value of argument, deliberation, observation, and imagination is still recognized, and where a belief in the public appetite for curiosity remains firm. It began life as an anachronism; in an era of sensationalism and world-weary fatalism it has been remade as a kind of *conscience*. For all its imperfections and irritations, it reaches middle age as the one network broadcasting as a whole cannot do without.

Timeline of Personnel

CONTROLLERS OF THE HOME SERVICE AND RADIO FOUR

Between 1939 and 1945, the Home Service and Forces Programme were run jointly by a Director of Programme Planning, Godfrey Adams. From 1945 the Controllers (sometimes called 'Chiefs') were as follows:

Lindsay Wellington	1945–52
Andrew Stewart	1952–7
Ronald Lewin	1957–64
Gerard Mansell	1965–9
Tony Whitby	1969–75
Clare Lawson Dick	1975–6
Ian McIntyre	1976–8
Monica Sims	1978–83
David Hatch	1983–6
Michael Green	1986–96
James Boyle	1996–2000
Helen Boaden	2000–4
Mark Damazer	2004–

MANAGING DIRECTORS OF RADIO

Lindsay Wellington	1952–63	('Director, Sound Broadcasting')
Frank Gillard	1963–70	('Director, Sound Broadcasting' to 1967)
Ian Trethowan	1970–6	
Howard Newby	1976–8	
Aubrey Singer	1978–82	
Richard 'Dick' Francis	1982–6	
Brian Wenham	1986–7	
David Hatch	1987–93	
Liz Forgan	1993–6	
Michael Green	1996	
Matthew Bannister	1996–8	('Director, Radio')
Jenny Abramsky	1999–	('Director, Radio and Music')

DIRECTORS OF PROGRAMMES, RADIO*

Richard 'Dick' Marriott	1957–69	('Assistant Director, Sound' to 1967)
Gerard Mansell	1969–71	

Howard Newby   1971–5
Douglas Muggeridge   1976–80   ('Deputy Managing Director, Radio')
Charles McLelland   1980–3   ('Deputy Managing Director, Radio')
Monica Sims   1983–6
David Hatch   1986–7
Michael Green   1993–6   ('Deputy Managing Director, Radio')

* At various times this post was redesignated as 'Deputy Managing Director, Radio' ('DMDR'); it also occasionally existed separately alongside the DMDR post.

Timeline of Key Events

1922   First broadcasts by the British Broadcasting Company from Studio 2LO in London.

1927   The British Broadcasting Company becomes the British Broadcasting Corporation.

1939   The Home Service replaces the BBC's pre-war National and Regional Programmes.

1945   Post-war Home Service (with Regional variations) launched. Light Programme also introduced. Third Programme starts the following year.

1957   First edition of *Today*.

1963   Frank Gillard takes over as Director of Sound Broadcasting. The BBC says the Home Service will offer 'tougher, faster and more immediate news'. Val Gielgud retires as Head of Drama; Martin Esslin takes over.

1964   Ending of *For the Young* (formerly *Children's Hour*) announced.
        Plans unveiled for the Home Service to carry more speech to enable the Light Programme to carry more music.
        Closure of Features Department announced.

1965   Gerard Mansell takes over as Controller of Home Service.
        The World at One starts, with William Hardcastle as its first presenter.
        Experiments begin with the use of live telephone interviews on air.

1966   A new 'more informal' style introduced to Home Service announcements.
        Economy measures introduced in studio recording and tape-editing.
        BBC starts permanent stereo broadcasts for a limited range of programmes.
        Plans announced for *The Archers* to be transferred from the Light Programme to the Home Service. Other speech programmes, such as *In Your Garden* have already been switched.

1967   Discussions begin about renaming the various services when a new pop service is launched. The Home Service's new title is confirmed as 'Radio Four' during the summer.
        Stephen Bonarjee begins reorganizing the *Today* programme to make it more topical and to widen appeal.
        Mary Whitehouse accuses *The World at One* of being 'a platform for extreme, secular, humanist views'.
        BBC replaces 'Sound' with the word 'Radio' throughout its internal organization.
        September: *The World This Weekend* begins.

30 September: Home Service becomes Radio Four; Radios One, Two, and Three also start.

November: BBC's first local station, Radio Leicester, goes on air. A Working Party is established to begin a review of radio services and finances that will eventually lead to the *Broadcasting in the Seventies* report.

December: first edition of *Just a Minute*.

1968   News-flash speakers introduced into studios.

Experiments begin with jingles between programmes.

November: agreed to 'accelerate' the phasing-out of remaining references to Radio Four as the Home Service.

1969   Charles Curran takes over as Director-General from Hugh Carleton-Greene.

Ian Trethowan takes over from Frank Gillard as Managing Director of Radio.

New opening music for Radio Four: Handel's Water Music is replaced by Boyce's Second Symphony.

The Critics is dropped. There is speculation that *The Archers* might also end.

July: *Broadcasting in the Seventies* is published, unveiling plans for more streamed radio services, with Radio Four concentrating almost entirely on speech.

More voice reports from correspondents introduced to news bulletins.

December: Tony Whitby becomes Controller, Radio Four; Gerard Mansell becomes Trethowan's deputy, as Director of Programmes.

1970   The Post Office approves plan for a Radio Four phone-in.

BBC staff write a letter to *The Times* protesting at *Broadcasting in the Seventies*, and its impact on cultural programmes.

4 April: a new Radio Four schedule begins, introducing changes wrought by *Broadcasting in the Seventies*. New programmes include *PM*, *The World Tonight*, *Newsdesk*, *From the Grassroots*, *Analysis*, *Start the Week*, and *Weekending*. The number of regional opt-outs is also reduced, with Regions becoming 'network production centres'.

Conservative ministers attack *The World at One* for left-wing bias.

October: new programmes include *It's Your Line* (Radio Four's first phone-in), *You and Yours*, and *Sunday*.

Experimental Christmas holiday children's programme: *The Orange-Coloured Peppermint Humbug Holiday Show*.

1971   Radio-only licence ends.

Start of Open University programmes.

Howard Newby replaces Gerard Mansell as Director of Programmes.

Mary Whitehouse complains about permissiveness in Schools programmes, and objects to a Radio Four documentary, *The Abortion Dilemma*.

Colin Morris criticizes government immigration policy on *Thought for the Day*.

Jack de Manio is dropped from *Today*, to be replaced by Robert Robinson.

If You Think You've Got Problems begins, described by the *Sun* as an 'agony column of the air'.

The Classic Serial is lengthened from thirty minutes to one hour.

Start of *The Long March of Everyman*.

Four-letter words in *Woman's Hour* provoke widespread controversy. Extensive debates begin on language, taste, and decency in programmes.

1972   Large number of complaints about BBC coverage of violence in Northern Ireland.

BBC produces new guidelines for producers on taste and language.

Sound Broadcasting Act legislates for commercial radio to begin.

April: first series of *I'm Sorry I Haven't a Clue*.

Start of the children's programme, *4th Dimension*.

1973   *Kaleidoscope* begins, combining arts and science coverage.

Further reductions in regional opt-outs.

Schools programmes restricted to Radio Four VHF. Medium wave freed for additional programmes, including *Woman's Hour*, which is transferred from Radio Two, as well as more news bulletins and new series such as *Checkpoint* and *Tuesday Call*.

New Fritz Spiegl-composed Radio Four signature tune begins. It is based on a traditional children's skipping song. Some listeners write to complain.

Britain's first commercial radio station, London Broadcasting Company (LBC) begins broadcasting in London.

1974   *Election Call* phone-ins chaired by Robin Day for both General Elections. *Weekending* is cancelled during Election periods.

Women in Media campaigns for more women announcers on Radio Four.

Kaleidoscope drops its science coverage to concentrate on the arts. *Science Now* begins.

Radio's 'Current Affairs and Talks Group' is broken up, with 'Talks and Documentaries' formally hived off to a separate unit under the control of George Fischer. Martin Wallace takes over control of the remaining empire.

BBC Radio starts occasional quadraphonic broadcasts.

Terry Wogan's Radio Four chat-show, *Wogan's World*, is launched.

The Controller of Radio Three, Stephen Hearst, attacks the 'growing insularity and triviality of British journalism'.

Stop the Week with Robert Robinson begins, designed as 'a more modern, smarter *In Town Tonight*'.

Following a tight licence-fee settlement, BBC Radio plans a range of economy measures: *Down Your Way* is to be dropped, and Radios Three and Four have to merge on Saturday afternoons with the loss of *Weekend Woman's Hour* and *Afternoon Theatre*.

1975   February: Tony Whitby dies at the age of 45. Clare Lawson Dick becomes Controller.

Anthony Jay and John Birt present their 'Bias against Understanding' critique of broadcast journalism.

The children's series *4th Dimension* is dropped after consistently low audience figures.

June: month-long experiment in broadcasting Parliament. Protests from listeners over disruption to *Listen with Mother*, *Afternoon Theatre*, and *Woman's Hour*.

Some economy measures in place since January are revoked. *Weekend Woman's Hour* (renamed just *Weekend*) and *Down Your Way* return later in the year; a new Saturday drama series is unveiled.

Growing internal BBC criticism of *Today* for being trivial. In October it is announced that Brian Redhead will join the programme.

November: William Hardcastle dies.

1976 January: Ian Trethowan becomes Managing Director of Television, and is succeeded as Managing Director of Radio by Howard Newby. Douglas Muggeridge replaces Newby as Director of Programmes.

Today starts 'split presentation' from London and Manchester, in order to increase Brian Redhead's appearances and to 'give a significantly wider, non-metropolitan appeal'.

Newsdesk ends, to be replaced by *The World in Focus*.

Detailed discussions begin between the BBC and MPs over making broadcasting of Parliament permanent.

September: Ian McIntyre becomes Controller of Radio Four on Clare Lawson Dick's retirement.

First series of *The Burkiss Way*.

McIntyre cancels existing arrangements for covering the US Presidential Election, provoking a running argument with the Special Current Affairs Unit. McIntyre also announces plans to trim back the daily current affairs 'sequences' in order to concentrate effort and diversify the range of reportage.

1977 Ronald Mason replaces Martin Esslin as Head of Radio Drama.

File on Four, *Profile*, and *Money Box* begin. The *Six o'Clock News* is lengthened.

McIntyre cancels an edition of *If You Think You've Got Problems* about lesbianism. The series ends within twelve months.

Twenty-six-part *Vivat Rex* is broadcast as part of the Queen's Silver Jubilee.

Today is cut in two to make room for the new programme, *Up to the Hour*.

'The Investigator' is asked to track down BBC staff, critical of McIntyre, making leaks to Fleet Street.

The Men from the Ministry ends.

Large number of complaints about *The Archers Omnibus* moving from Sunday mornings to Sunday evenings.

October: Ian Trethowan takes over from Charles Curran as Director-General.

1978   David Hatch becomes Head of Light Entertainment; Michael Green replaces him as Network Editor in Manchester.
Start of *Disgusted, Tunbridge Wells* as a regular slot for listener feedback.
First series of *The Hitchhiker's Guide to the Galaxy* begins.
Start of permanent radio broadcasting from Parliament. Large number of complaints from listeners over loss of *Woman's Hour*, *Afternoon Theatre*, and *Listen with Mother* from medium wave.
Some of McIntyre's programme changes are modified or reversed. *Up to the Hour* ends and *Today* is restored.
John Timpson returns to *Today* after eighteen months in Television, to begin a long-lasting pairing with Brian Redhead.
In Touch begins.
June: Howard Newby retires; Aubrey Singer replaces him as Managing Director, Radio.
Monica Sims is appointed as Controller of Radio Four.
Planning begins for rearranging BBC Radio Services in the 1980s, including making Radio Four more 'topical' and news orientated.
November: Radio Four switches from medium wave to 1500 m long wave, inherits the *Shipping Forecast*, and is relaunched as 'Radio Four UK', with a new theme tune by Fritz Spiegl (a medley including Irish, Scottish, Welsh, and English tunes). A limited number of Radio Four jingles are also introduced.

1979   In Scotland, 1,400 people sign a petition demanding access to Radio Four on VHF.
First editions of *Feedback*, which replaces *Disgusted, Tunbridge Wells*.
The retired announcer Alvar Lidell complains about standards of newsreading on Radio Four; a sharp rise in the number of public complaints follows.
'Three Wise Men' are appointed to report on standards of Spoken English on BBC Radio.
Planning continues within Broadcasting House for rearranging the pattern of networks, including a possible merger of Radio Four and Local Radio.
Radio Four's jingles are dropped.
First radio programmes recorded digitally.

1980   January: second series of *The Hitchhiker's Guide to the Galaxy*.
Cutbacks in BBC Radio announced, following another tight licence-fee settlement.
'Radio Network Working Party' is set up under chairmanship of Stephen Hearst, to look at the future pattern of BBC Radio.

1981   David Hatch becomes Controller, Radio Two; Bobby Jaye takes over as Head of Light Entertainment, Radio.

The Director of News and Current Affairs, Dick Francis, presses for Radio Four to be split, with long wave used for continuous news.

The Radio Network Working Party publishes its report, outlining a series of possible changes to BBC Radio, including turning Radio Four into a 'public affairs' network and its possible merger with local radio. An editorial in *The Sun* declares 'Hands off Radio Four!'

A twenty-six-part dramatization of *Lord of the Rings* is broadcast.

Radio Four pilots the idea of personality 'hosts' in place of continuity announcers.

1982   Alasdair Milne replaces Ian Trethowan as Director-General. Dick Francis takes over from Aubrey Singer as Managing Director, Radio.

First full series of *In the Psychiatrist's Chair* and *The Secret Diary of Adrian Mole, Aged 13¾*.

Radio Four makes a large number of last-minute schedule changes to cover the Falklands War. *The Times*'s TV critic admits that 'radio came back into its own' during the conflict.

Evolution of the BBC's 'Radio for the Nineties' document: Dick Francis declares there will be no 'restructuring' of the networks but 'some realignment of programmes'. He wants Radio Four to do less drama and become more 'flexible' in order to accommodate breaking news. Sims later describes the plans as 'the dismantling of Radio Four'.

Listen with Mother ends after years of poor audience figures.

As 'Radio for the Nineties' is leaked to the press, a campaign begins to 'save' Radio Four, with actors, playwrights, and listeners lobbying BBC Governors and managers.

Plans emerge from the Managing Director's office for Radio Four to switch to 'block scheduling', with the abolition of fixed programme boundaries and the creation of three-hour personality-led sequences shows.

1983   Start of breakfast broadcasting on BBC and ITV, threatening radio's peak-time audiences.

Today introduces—and then drops—its own theme music and jingles.

Monica Sims becomes Director of Programmes, Radio; David Hatch takes over as Controller of Radio Four.

Hatch raises the idea of splitting Radio Four's output, to provide a 'live rollercoaster' on long wave and a service of repeats and schools programmes on VHF. The idea is rejected.

Pilots for a once-a-week *Rollercoaster*; Hatch announces that *Desert Island Discs*, *Gardeners' Question Time*, and *Down Your Way* would be 'rested' for short periods.

Voice of the Listener, planned since 1982, is formally launched as an audience lobby group to protect BBC values on Radio Four.

1984   Planning begins for a 'Radio Five' to accommodate schools, sport, and children's programmes.

Rollercoaster runs for three hours on Thursday mornings, boosting ratings but proving unpopular with critics and a significant proportion of regular Radio Four listeners.

In One Ear begins, 'radio's first live comedy show since the *Goons*'.

The Cable and Broadcasting Act legislates for cable television.

December: BBC Managers and Governors agree to continue the *Rollercoaster* experiment, pending the licence-fee settlement.

1985   A tight licence-fee settlement forces a series of programme cuts, extra repeats, and scaling-back the building of new VHF transmitters. Hatch is appointed to a 'Black Spot' committee charged with finding further economies.

Economies force the relaunch of *Rollercoaster* to be abandoned, cuts in the number of drama serials, and a moratorium on features.

After Henry and *King Street Junior* begin.

Pirate Radio Four adopts the *Rollercoaster* three-hour format in order to attract teenage listeners during the summer holiday period. The series is condemned by one critic as 'banal, uncouth, noisy and mindless'.

November: a BBC discussion paper contemplates a future in which Radio Four has to be funded by sponsorship or subscription.

1986   Michael Parkinson presents *Desert Island Discs*, following the death in 1985 of Roy Plomley, and amid complaints of him featuring 'a Yorkshire mafia' of guests.

John Tydeman becomes Head of Radio Drama.

Radio Four long wave splits from regular output to cover the resignation of Michael Heseltine from the cabinet.

Checkpoint is succeeded by *Face the Facts* (developed with the working title *Gotcha!*).

Report of the government-appointed Peacock Committee. Radio Four is praised, but the BBC as a whole is required to be more commercially minded and begins commissioning independent producers.

The removal of Dick Francis as Managing Director of Radio prompts a reshuffle. Brian Wenham comes from BBC Television to replace Francis; David Hatch is promoted to Director of Programmes, Radio; Michael Green becomes Controller, Radio Four.

Marmaduke Hussey is appointed BBC Chairman.

The Conservative government freezes the licence fee until 1988.

The Saturday edition of *Today* (dropped under McIntyre) returns. The extra edition is funded through cutting back features. John Humphrys joins as presenter.

1987   Governors sack Alasdair Milne; Michael Checkland becomes Director-General. John Birt is later appointed as his Deputy, with special responsibility for News and Current Affairs.

Plans are discussed for Radio Four to merge with Radio Scotland and Radio Wales in the evenings to provide more money for daytime broadcasting.

John Timpson leaves *Any Questions?* Brian Johnston leaves *Down Your Way.* Richard Baker leaves *Start the Week.* Green talks of 'refreshing' Radio Four with presenters more likely to be 'in their forties'. Jonathan Dimbleby becomes the new chairman of *Any Questions?*

Radio and Television News and Current Affairs are merged under one directorate.

The BBC responds to a government Green Paper on broadcasting, by announcing an end to 'simulcasting' the same output on FM and AM, so that spare frequencies can be allocated to commercial stations. This creates pressure for Radio Four to differentiate its long wave and VHF output more strongly. BBC publicity refers to Radio Four long wave as an 'events' network, prompting complaints from listeners in continental Europe worried at missing regular programmes.

The first episode of *Citizens*, a new twice-weekly soap serial.

A Radio Four documentary about the security services, *My Country: Right or Wrong*, is temporarily blocked by a government injunction, despite having been cleared by the D-notice committee.

1988 The *Midnight News* is extended to thirty minutes.

Michael Green blocks an afternoon repeat for two evening plays—*Excess Baggage* and *Cassandra Generation*—prompting a wide-ranging debate about strong language on radio drama. Eventually, the automatic repeat of evening plays is ended.

Drama Department links up with the Los Angeles Classic Theatre group to produce a series of dramas with leading Hollywood actors, including Ed Asner, Richard Dreyfuss, and Stacey Keach.

First editions of *Consuming Passions*, a design and lifestyle show.

The government injunction on the documentary, *My Country: Right or Wrong*, is lifted.

Whose Line Is It Anyway? transfers to Channel Four, eventually prompting a new arrangement between Television Centre and Broadcasting House to ensure the BBC keeps control of Radio Four's comedy formats in the future.

1989 A new editor for *Citizens*, but no sign yet of critical or ratings success.

John Birt praises the 'astonishing array' of Radio Four's coverage of the political upheavals in eastern Europe, the Soviet Union, and China during 1989.

Sky Television launches a rolling news service.

Book at Bedtime shifts to later in the evening, allowing a more adventurous range of material to be scheduled.

A new round of cuts is being planned for BBC Radio.

1990 *Lady Chatterley's Lover* is read unexpurgated on *Book at Bedtime*.

An intense press campaign alleges *Today* is biased against the Conservative government.

Radio Five starts broadcasting.

A *Thought for the Day* talk by Canon Eric James defends the spiritual value of revolt against the poll tax.

Green announces *Citizens* will end and that *Woman's Hour* will move from afternoons to mornings.

1991   A continuous news service, 'Radio Four News FM', is launched to report the Gulf War. It stays on air until early March.

Margaret Howard is dropped as presenter of *Pick of the Week*.

Various feasibility studies examine the possibility of a permanent all-news radio service.

John Birt named as Director-General Designate, in readiness for Checkland's departure.

Morning Story is dropped; the *Daily Service* moves to long wave only, and *Woman's Hour* begins in the morning.

'Stephen Fry's Guide to Radio Four' is distributed to University campuses in a new effort to target student listeners.

1992   April: Radio Four's ratings rise during the General Election campaign, while television's fall.

Leaks suggest the BBC is faced with a new round of cutbacks to tackle a deficit.

Michael Checkland announces firm plans for a continuous news service on Radio Four long wave. BBC also announces that 10 per cent of radio programmes will be made by independent producers within four years.

National commercial radio begins with the launch of Classic FM.

The 'Save Radio Four Long Wave' campaign is launched, linking listeners' groups in Britain and continental Europe.

1993   John Birt becomes Director-General; Liz Forgan is appointed Managing Director of Radio, while David Hatch becomes a special adviser to Birt.

Sunday Outing, Radio Four's first gay and lesbian programme, is broadcast on St Valentine's Day.

Forgan announces a review of plans for an all-news service on long wave.

The BBC's internal market, *Producer's Choice*, begins. 'Save Radio Four Long Wave' campaigners march from Hyde Park to Broadcasting House.

Birt claims that Radio Four is 'skewed far too much' towards the southern middle classes.

News Stand, *Stop Press*, and *The Radio Programme* end, to be replaced with *Mediumwave*.

Plans are announced for *Gardeners' Question Time* and *Feedback* to be produced outside the BBC by independent producers.

October: the BBC announces that Radio Four will not lose its long wave after all, and that Radio Five will be relaunched as a rolling news and sport network.

1994   *Gardeners' Question Time* panellists defect to Classic FM after disagreements with the independent production team taking over responsibility for the programme. Radio Four appoints a new panel and retains the title.
Press rumours circulate that Classic FM is also interested in *Desert Island Discs* and Virgin Radio is interested in securing *In the Psychiatrist's Chair*.
Radio Five Live is launched.
Anderson Country begins and becomes 'the most reviled programme for years'.
Protests begin about Radio Four long wave having to be used for cricket coverage.
The Religious department considers (and rejects) *Thought for the Day* being opened to humanists.

1995   The national commercial station TalkRadio UK begins.
Gerry Anderson stops presenting *Anderson Country*; the programme is renamed *Afternoon Shift*, with Laurie Taylor becoming one of the regular presenters.
This Sceptr'd Isle begins its first run of 200 episodes.
A new series, *The Late Book*—nicknamed 'Bonk at Bedtime'—allows more demanding contemporary novels to be adapted for readings. The *Shipping Forecast* is moved by twelve minutes to accommodate the new series, provoking a row.

1996   BBC Radio staff are split between two new divisions, 'Broadcast' and 'Production'. Preparations begin for News and Current Affairs staff to leave Broadcasting House by 1998.
Liz Forgan resigns as Managing Director, Radio.
Michael Green briefly replaces Forgan, before leaving the BBC. In the new structure, the new post of 'Director' will not be a member of the BBC's executive board. The *Guardian* says, 'In a stroke, radio is being downgraded in the BBC hierarchy.'
James Boyle becomes the new Controller, after press speculation that Melvyn Bragg was 'favourite'. Radio One's Controller, Matthew Bannister, becomes Director of Radio.
Thought for the Day 'rests' several long-standing contributors in a bid to find new voices.
A new round of financial cutbacks begins. *Saturday Night Theatre* is axed.

1997   Boyle says he wants to avoid Radio Four being a 'museum piece', prompting speculation that radical change is planned.
July: Boyle unveils his plans. Several series, including *Afternoon Shift*, *Mediumwave*, *Kaleidoscope*, *Weekending*, and *Breakaway* are to go; *The Archers* is to gain a Sunday episode; there will be new programmes on Saturday and Sunday mornings (*Home Truths* and *Broadcasting House*), and

a new arts programme (*Front Row*). *Today* is extended to 9 a.m., which entails *Yesterday in Parliament* being restricted to long wave; *The Week in Westminster* is also given a less prominent place on the schedule.

December: MPs begin campaigning against the move of *Yesterday in Parliament* and *The Week in Westminster*.

1998   April: Boyle's new schedule takes effect. Protests begin from listeners.

Melvyn Bragg leaves *Start the Week* after being made a Labour peer; Jeremy Paxman takes over. Bragg later begins a new series about the history of ideas, *In Our Time*.

October: MPs continue criticizing changes to parliamentary coverage.

1999   Radio Four audience figures start to rise. Ratings for *The Archers* rise notably. *Yesterday in Parliament* returns in abbreviated form to Radio Four FM, following discussions between MPs and BBC Governors.

The last audience figures for the year show more than nine million listening to Radio Four each week—and people listening for longer.

2000   Boyle retires; Helen Boaden is appointed as Controller. She hints at consolidation rather than radical change.

The Prime Minister's press spokesman Alistair Campbell criticizes reporting on Europe by Andrew Gilligan on *Today*. The programme's editor, Rod Liddle, talks of his desire for more scoops.

First series of *Dead Ringers*.

After lengthy negotiations, Radio Four broadcasts, unabridged, the entire 8½ -hour Stephen Fry reading of *Harry Potter and the Philosopher's Stone* on Boxing Day.

2001   First series of *Little Britain* and *Sunday Format*. *Dead Ringers* continues on Radio Four while also transferring to BBC Television. Radio Four proclaims a 'new emphasis' on comedy.

Regular children's programmes return, with *Go 4 It!* beginning on Sunday evenings.

Audience ratings continue to rise, reaching nearly ten million listeners a week—the highest figures for a decade. A million extra listen to *Today* in the months following the September terrorist attacks in New York.

2002   The 1981 *Lord of the Rings* production is repeated, following the release of a film version, and achieves the highest ratings for a radio drama in ten years. The weekly audience rises above ten million. Figures for *The Archers* reach nearly five million.

Jeremy Paxman leaves *Start the Week*, to be replaced by Andrew Marr.

A new campaign to allow atheists to appear on *Thought for the Day* is rejected after an internal review. The programme promises to be sharper, and to include more Muslims and more women.

Rod Liddle is forced to resign from *Today* after writing an article critical of Countryside Alliance campaigners. Kevin Marsh, from *The World at One*, takes over.

2003   Radio Four dramatizes Philip Pullman's *His Dark Materials* trilogy.
Audiences for *The Archers* overtake those for Channel Four's *Brookside*.
During coverage of the Iraq War, Radio Four's weekly audience reaches
nearly eleven million.
May: on *Today*, Andrew Gilligan accuses the government of having
manipulated an intelligence dossier in order to exaggerate the threat from Iraq.
Downing Street asks the BBC to apologize over Gilligan's report, and accuses
BBC journalism of being 'debased beyond belief'. The BBC rejects
Downing Street's complaints.

2004   January: the Hutton Report, critical of Gilligan's reporting and the BBC's
editorial structures, prompts the resignation of the Chairman, Gavyn Davies,
and the Director-General, Greg Dyke.
An internal review later tightens editorial supervision of 'breaking stories'
and the freelance activities of BBC journalists, introduces a new complaints
procedure, and announces new training initiatives.
March: Alistair Cooke retires from *Letter from America* on medical advice,
and dies just a few weeks later.
Radio Four wins a national 'Station of the Year' award for the second time
running. But audience figures are down slightly, especially for *Today*. Boaden
admits there is 'a sort of weariness' with coverage of Iraq.
Douglas Adams's later sequels to *The Hitchhiker's Guide to the Galaxy* are
dramatized, using many of the cast from the original 1978 series.
Boaden becomes head of BBC News; Mark Damazer takes over as
Controller.
October: John Peel dies suddenly, leaving *Home Truths* without its regular
presenter.

2005   Radio Four faces budget cuts as part of a larger restructuring plan by the
BBC's new Director-General, Mark Thompson.
Karl Marx is voted the greatest philosopher by listeners to *In Our Time*.
Damazer declares that 'dissent must be one of the qualities of Radio Four'
and that 'sex and strong language are not something for Radio Four to be
frightened of'.
December: Andy Kershaw says that debate is 'the new rock 'n' roll'—and
Radio Four should 'get rid of that bloody UK Theme'.

2006   January: Damazer announces the early-morning UK Theme tune is to be
replaced by a 'pacy news briefing'; 18,000 listeners sign an online petition for
the Theme to be saved, and MPs table motions condemning the plan.
April: the UK Theme disappears from the schedules. A CD version is
released by disgruntled campaigners.
Sue Lawley announces she will leave *Desert Island Discs* after eighteen years.

Notes

INTRODUCTION

1. *Today*, 14 May 1988; *Sunday Times*, 15 September 1991.
2. BBC, *Annual Report and Accounts 2005–2006* (London: British Broadcasting Corporation, 2006), 37; *Sunday Telegraph*, 27 August 1989; P. Donovan, *All Our Todays: Forty Years of the Today Programme* (London: Jonathan Cape, 1997), 193.
3. A. Briggs, *The History of Broadcasting in the United Kingdom*, v: *Competition, 1955–1974* (Oxford: Oxford University Press, 1995), 577.
4. Quoted in P. Scannell, 'Public Service Broadcasting: The History of a Concept', in E. Buscombe (ed.), *British Television: A Reader* (Oxford: Oxford University Press, 2000), 47.
5. R. Samuel, 'The Voice of Britain', in A. Light (ed.), *Island Stories: Unravelling Britain. Theatres of Memory*, ii (London: Verso, 1998), 183–4.
6. Quoted in H. Carpenter, *The Envy of the World: 50 Years of the BBC Third Programme and Radio 3* (London: Weidenfeld & Nicolson, 1996), 110.
7. Samuel, 'The Voice of Britain', 176.
8. Quoted in T. Burns, *The BBC: Public Institution and Private World* (London: Macmillan, 1977), 26.
9. Ibid. p. xiii.
10. J. Seaton, 'Writing the History of Broadcasting', in D. Cannadine (ed.), *History and the Media* (London: Macmillan, 2004), 150, 157.
11. Burns, *Public Institution and Private World*, xiii, 45; G. Born, *Uncertain Vision: Birt, Dyke and the Reinvention of the BBC* (London: Vintage, 2005), 31.
12. BBC, *Annual Report and Accounts, 2005–2006* (London: British Broadcasting Corporation, 2006), 35, 143, 106–9, 150.
13. *Guardian*, 27 September 2004.
14. Seaton, 'Writing the History of Broadcasting', 152.
15. Briggs, *History of Broadcasting*, v, Preface, xv.

CHAPTER 1.   SEPTEMBER 1967

1. *Radio Times*, 28 September 1967; *The Archive Hour*, BBC Radio Four, 18 March 2006.
2. *Financial Times*, 28 July 1967. See also Current Affairs Group, Radio, Minutes, 5 September 1967, BBC Written Archives Centre (hereafter 'BBC WAC'), R51/1085/1.
3. *Radio Times*, 28 September 1967; A. Briggs, *The History of Broadcasting in the United Kingdom*, 5 vols. (Oxford: Oxford University Press, 1995), vol. v: *Competition*, 574–5; *Times*, 30 September and 2 October 1967; *Guardian*, 30 September and 2 October 1967; *Listener*, 5 October 1967; *Sunday Times*, 1 October 1967; *Sunday Telegraph*, 1 October 1967.

4. Briggs, *Broadcasting*, v. 564–5, 573. On the internal BBC debate over the nomenclature of each radio service, see BBC WAC: Memos, 9 February 1967, R78/620/21, and 2 August 1967, R51/1085/1.

5. *Observer*, 6 August 1967.

6. The origins of these programmes can be traced in the various volumes of Briggs's *History of Broadcasting*: for *Saturday Night Theatre*, see i. 256, ii. 150, and iii. 529–30; for *Radio Newsreel*, see v. 62; for *The Archers*, see iv. 99; for *Desert Island Discs*, see iv. 52; for the *Daily Service*, see ii. 25, 213–17.

7. For the cultural trends of the 1960s, I have drawn on: A. Marwick, *The Sixties: Cultural Revolution in Britain, France, Italy, and the United States, c.1958–1974* (Oxford: Oxford University Press, 1998); J. Green, *All Dressed up: The Sixties and the Counter-Culture* (London: Pimlico, 1999); R. Hewison, *Culture and Consensus: England, Art and Politics since 1940* (London: Methuen, 1995); D. Sandbrook, *Never Had It So Good: A History of Britain from Suez to the Beatles 1956–63* (London: Little Brown, 2005), and *White Heat: A History of Britain in the Swinging Sixties 1964–70* (London: Little Brown, 2006); R. Stevenson, *The Oxford English Literary History*, xii: *1960–2000* (Oxford: Oxford University Press, 2004). Vivid personal accounts are in: C. Landau, *Growing up in the Sixties* (London: Optima, 1991), D. Nobbs, *I Didn't Get Where I Am Today: An Autobiography* (London: Arrow, 2004), and R. Gosling, *Personal Copy: A Memoir of the Sixties* (London: Faber & Faber, 1980). On the Beatles, see: A. Moore, *The Beatles: Sergeant Pepper's Lonely Hearts Club Band* (Cambridge: Cambridge University Press, 1997); *Listener*, 3 August 1967; Sandbrook, *White Heat*, 410–20.

8. *Spectator*, 22 September 1967.

9. *Sunday Times*, 8 October 1967.

10. *Sunday Times*, 24 September 1967; *Sunday Telegraph*, 24 September and 1 October 1967; *Listener*, 7 September and 5 October 1967; A. Wilson, *No Laughing Matter* (London: Secker & Warburg, 1967). On the wider context of permissiveness in theatre, film, and language, see: D. Hendy, 'Bad Language and BBC Radio Four in the 1960s and 1970s', *Twentieth Century British History*, 17/1 (2006), 74–102; G. Hughes, *Swearing: A Social History of Foul Language, Oaths and Profanity in English* (London: Penguin, 1998), 190–7; D. Shellard and S. Nicholson, with M. Handley (eds.), *The Lord Chamberlain Regrets: A History of British Theatre Censorship* (London: British Library, 2004), 133–77; A. Aldgate, *Censorship and the Permissive Society: British Cinema and Theatre, 1955–1965* (Oxford: Oxford University Press, 1995); J. Weeks, *Sex, Politics and Society: The Regulation of Sexuality since 1800* (London: Longman, 1981); Stevenson, *Literary History*, 301–31.

11. R. McKibbin, *Classes and Cultures: England 1918–1951* (Oxford: Oxford University Press, 1998), 527–36; J. R. Brown, *A Short Guide to Modern British Drama* (London: Heinemann, 1982); H. Carpenter, *That Was Satire That Was* (London: Victor Gollancz, 2000) and *The Angry Young Men: A Literary Comedy of the 1950s* (London: Allen Lane, 2002). See also A. Higson, ' "Britain's Outstanding Contribution to the Film": The Documentary-Realist Tradition', and B. McFarlane, 'A Literary Cinema? British Films and British Novels', both in C. Barr (ed.), *All Our Yesterdays: 90 Years of British Cinema* (London: BFI, 1986).

12. Marwick, *Sixties*, 409–11; P. Clarke, *Hope and Glory: Britain 1900–1990* (London: Penguin, 1996), 283–93; E. Hobsbawm, *The Age of Extremes: The Short Twentieth*

Century 1914–1991 (London: Abacus, 1994), 324–5, 328; M. Young, *The Rise of the Meritocracy 1870–2023: An Essay on Education and Equality* (London: Thames & Hudson, 1958).

13. On the gathering protest movement, see: *Listener*, 14 September 1967; *Sunday Times*, 1 October 1967; *Times*, 2 October 1967; J. Rex and R. Moore, *Race, Conflict and Community: A Study of Sparkbrook* (Oxford: Oxford University Press, 1967).

14. Sandbrook, *Never Had It So Good*, pp. xvi–xxii, and *White Heat*, p. xvii; P. Mandler, 'Two Cultures—One—or Many?' in K. Burk (ed.), *The British Isles since 1945* (Oxford: Oxford University Press, 2003); G. L. Bernstein, *The Myth of Decline: The Rise of Britain since 1945* (London: Pimlico, 2004), 448–57.

15. Clarke, *Hope and Glory*, 293–318; J. Callaghan, 'Industrial Militancy, 1945–79: The Failure of the British Road to Socialism', *Twentieth Century British History*, 15/4 (2004), 388–409.

16. G. Steiner, *Language and Silence: Essays 1958–1966* (London: Faber & Faber, 1967).

17. R. Colls, *Identity of England* (Oxford: Oxford University Press, 2002), 153–4. See also: McKibbin, *Classes and Cultures*, 491.

18. R. Weight, *Patriots: National Identity in Britain, 1940–2000* (London: Pan Books, 2004), 380.

19. T. Judt, *Postwar: A History of Europe since 1945* (London: Heinemann, 2005), 448.

20. M. Arnold, *Culture and Anarchy* (London: Smith, Elder, & Co., 1869); R. Williams, *Culture and Society 1780–1950* (London: Chatto & Windus, 1958). See also Colls, *Identity of England*, 150.

21. R. Williams, *Communications*, rev. edn. (London: Chatto & Windus, 1966); M. McLuhan, *Understanding Media: The Extensions of Man* (London: Sphere Books, 1967) and *The Medium is the Massage* (London: Penguin, 1967); *Listener*, 28 September 1967; *Sunday Times*, 1 October 1967; *Sunday Telegraph*, 1 October 1967; *Radio Times*, 7 September 1967.

22. P. Scannell and D. Cardiff, *A Social History of British Broadcasting*, i: *1922–1939: Serving the Nation* (Oxford: Blackwell, 1991), 3–19, 316; J. Curran, and J. Seaton, *Power without Responsibility: The Press and Broadcasting in Britain*, 5th edn. (London: Routledge, 1997), 112–27; D. L. LeMahieu, *A Culture for Democracy: Mass Communication and the Cultivated Mind in Britain between the Wars* (Oxford: Clarendon Press, 1988), 138–54.

23. On changes at the BBC between 1939 and the 1960s, see in particular: A. Briggs, *A History of Broadcasting in the United Kingdom*, vols. iii, iv, and v (Oxford: Oxford University Press, 1995); Curran and Seaton, *Power without Responsibility*, 128–79; S. Nicholas, *The Echo of War: Home Front Propaganda and the Wartime BBC 1939–45* (Manchester: Manchester University Press, 1996); S. Nicholas, 'The People's Radio: The BBC and its Audience, 1939–1945', in N. Hayes and J. Hill (eds.), *'Millions Like Us? British Culture in the Second World War* (Liverpool: Liverpool University Press, 1999), 62–92; McKibbin, *Classes and* Cultures, 457–76.

24. H. Greene, *The Third Floor Front: A View of Broadcasting in the Sixties* (London: The Bodley Head, 1969), 74–6.

25. Ibid. 13; BBC WAC Oral History Project: Frank Gillard.

26. Greene, *Third Floor*, 13–14, 94; Briggs, *Broadcasting*, v. 323.

27. Briggs, *Broadcasting*, v. 339.

28. Briggs, *Broadcasting*, v. 350–72, 519–30; L. Cooke, *British Television Drama: A History* (London: BFI, 2003), 29–89; Carpenter, *That Was Satire*, 203–82.

29. Greene, *Third Floor*, 134–5.

30. *Radio Times*, 28 September 1967.

31. *Radio Times*, 31 August and 7 September 1967.

32. *Radio Times*, 28 September 1967; Cooke, *Television Drama*, 33, 49–50.

33. Quoted in Sandbrook, *Never Had It So Good*, 355.

34. J. Grist, 'The Century before Yesterday: John Grist's BBC and Other Broadcasting Tales, Volume 2' (unpublished memoir), 49–131; G. Wyndham-Goldie, *Facing the Nation: Television and Politics 1936–1976* (London: Bodley Head, 1977), 187–305; Marriott, 14 September 1967, BBC WAC R34/1599/1.

35. L. Purves, *Radio: A True Love Story* (London: Hodder & Stoughton, 2002), 30.

36. J. Simpson, *Strange Places, Questionable People* (London: Pan, 1999), 17, 21–3, 76–9; W. Wyatt, *The Fun Factory: A Life in the BBC* (London: Aurum Press, 2003), 27–33.

37. Purves, *Radio*, 65; Monica Sims, interview with author, London, 10 February 2003; R. Heppenstall, *Portrait of the Artist as a Professional Man* (London: Peter Owen, 1969), 155–79.

38. Sims, interview; Grist, 'Century', 28–34.

39. Purves, *Radio*, 24–5.

40. *Listener*, 7 September and 19 October 1967; *Spectator*, 22 September 1967.

41. Letter from Evelyn Barish, 5 September 1967, BBC WAC R34/1599/1.

42. *Sunday Telegraph*, 1 October 1967; see also F. Grisewood, *The World Goes By: The Autobiography of Frederick Grisewood* (London: Secker & Warburg, 1952), 124–248.

43. *Daily Mail*, 16 September 1967.

44. A. Crisell, *An Introductory History of British Broadcasting*, 2nd edn. (London: Routledge, 2002), 74–6.

45. BBC WAC Oral History Project: Clare Lawson Dick.

46. This section on the Home Service during the War draws largely on Briggs, *History of Broadcasting*, iii; Nicholas, *Echo of War*, 24–6, 50–3, 133–8; Nicholas, 'The People's Radio'; Curran and Seaton, *Power without Responsibility*, 128–50; M. Doherty, *Nazi Wireless Propaganda: Lord Haw-Haw and British Public Opinion in the Second World War* (Edinburgh: Edinburgh University Press, 2000), 87–125; McKibbin, *Classes and Cultures*, 468–71; P. Scannell, 'The *Brains Trust*: A Historical Study of the Management of Liveness on Radio', in S. Cottle (ed.), *Media Organisation and Production* (London: Sage, 2003), 99–112; F. Worsley, *ITMA 1939–1948* (London: Vox Mundi, 1948).

47. Crisell, *Introductory History*, 76; *Listener*, 10 December 1970; M. Coward, *The Pocket Essential Classic Radio Comedy* (Harpenden: Pocket Essentials, 2003), 26–41; A. Foster and S. Furst, *Radio Comedy, 1938–1968* (Virgin: London, 1996), 144–5; B. Took, *Laughter in the Air: An Informal History of British Radio Comedy* (London: BBC, 1981), 56–67.

48. The 'Green Book' guidelines are reproduced in Took, *Laughter*, 83–92. For *Round the Horne* (which most listeners heard on the Light but which was regularly repeated on the Home) see: Took, *Laughter*, 136–55; B. Took, and M. Feldman, *Round the Horne* (London: Futura, 1975); B. Took, *Round the Horne: The Complete and Utter*

History (London: Boxtree, 1998); Coward, *Classic Radio Comedy*, 56–68; Purves, *Radio*, 2–24.

49. H. Chignell, 'BBC Radio 4's "Analysis", 1970–1983: A Selective History and Case Study of BBC Current Affairs Radio', Ph.D. thesis (Bournemouth, 2004), 42–4. See also Briggs, *Broadcasting*, v. 327.

50. 'I am a child of the BBC Home Service': A. Bennett, *Untold Stories* (London: Faber & Faber, 2005), 416. 'We had a radio, medium wave only, permanently tuned to the Home Service': Gosling, *Personal Copy*, 23. See also Rayner, C., *How Did I Get Here from There?* (London: Virago, 2003); Nobbs, *I Didn't Get*, 29–30; Simpson, *Strange Places*, 21–2; S. Garfield, *Our Hidden Lives: The Everyday Diaries of a Forgotten Britain 1945–1948* (London: Ebury Press, 2004); Monica Sims, interview and personal correspondence; David Hatch, interview with author, London, 5 February 2003.

51. This section draws on: Briggs, *Broadcasting*, iv. 4, 26, 46–77; D. G. Bridson, *Prospero and Ariel: The Rise and Fall of Radio—a Personal Recollection* (London: Victor Gollancz, 1971), 179.

52. Briggs, *Broadcasting*, iv. 58.

53. Ibid., v. 38–47.

54. Ibid. 48.

55. BBC WAC Oral History Project: Lawson Dick.

56. Briggs, *Broadcasting*, v. 30, 220–3; Sandbrook, *Never Had It So Good*, 360–1.

57. BBC WAC Oral History Project: Lawson Dick.

58. Bridson, *Prospero and Ariel*, 225.

59. Briggs, *Broadcasting*, v. 33–4; *Times*, 13 November 1991; BBC WAC Oral History Project: Lawson Dick.

60. Bridson, *Prospero and Ariel*, 227.

61. BBC WAC Oral History Project: Lawson Dick.

62. G. Priestland, *Something Understood: An Autobiography* (London: Andre Deutsch, 1986), 93–5.

63. Bridson, *Prospero and Ariel*, 154, 226–31, 235.

64. Briggs, *Broadcasting*, v. 47.

65. H. Carpenter, *The Envy of the World: Fifty Years of the BBC Third Programme and Radio 3* (London: Weidenfeld & Nicolson, 1996), 73; *Guardian*, 2 October 1967.

66. Philip French, interview with author, London, 12 May 2005.

67. Simpson, *Strange Places*, 84–5. There was fear of young people as well as interest in them, since in 1968 the BBC was also making detailed plans for transferring its radio newsroom to Birmingham in the event of a national emergency similar to that unfolding in France: Caroline Millington, personal communication, 18 July 2006.

68. 'Today audience figures', 4 September 1967, BBC WAC R51/1297/2. For details of Bonarjee's other work in the BBC, see Briggs, *Broadcasting*, v. 156, 224.

69. *Radio Times*, 14 September 1967, 21 September 1967, 28 September 1967.

70. *Listener*, 3 August 1967.

71. 'The BBC's Communications with the Public', General Advisory Council Paper, 11 April 1967, BBC WAC; Mary Whitehouse quoted in Briggs, *Broadcasting*, v. 309.

72. Ibid. 501–2.

73. Heppenstall, *Portrait*, 75.

74. Details of economies can be followed in Current Affairs Group (Radio), Minutes, 25 January, 15 February, 19 April, 13 September 1967, BBC WAC R51/1085/1.
75. Briggs, *Broadcasting*, v. 594–606. On Hill, see also: Grist, 'Century', 118–19, 142–3; BBC WAC Oral History Project: Gillard.
76. Philip French, interview.
77. Greene, *Third Floor Front*, 136.
78. *Guardian*, 2 October 1967.
79. Mandler, 'Two Cultures', 127–8.

CHAPTER 2. RECONSTRUCTION

1. D. G. Bridson, *Prospero and Ariel: The Rise and Fall of Radio—a Personal Recollection* (London: Victor Gollancz, 1971), 331.
2. A. Briggs, *History of Broadcasting in the United Kingdom*, iv: *Sound and Vision 1945–1955* (Oxford: Oxford University Press, 1995), 88–9.
3. BBC WAC Oral History Project: Frank Gillard; Bridson, *Prospero*, 299–300.
4. BBC WAC Oral History Project: F. Gillard; *Evening Standard*, 5 and 8 November 1963; *Times*, 17 January 1964; *Guardian*, 17 January 1964; *Sunday Telegraph*, 19 January 1964; Briggs, *History of Broadcasting*, v. 342–7.
5. D. Cleverdon, *The Growth of Milk Wood* (London: Dent, 1969), 17; K. Whitehead, *The Third Programme: A Literary History* (Oxford: Clarendon Press, 1989), 109–34; J. Thomas, 'A History of the BBC Features Department, 1924–1964', D.Phil. thesis (Oxford, 1993); Bridson, *Prospero*, 254–7, 281, 287, 290–5, 298. *Under Milk Wood* was first broadcast in January 1954 on the Third Programme, with subsequent repeats on the Home Service.
6. *Times*, 7 March 1964.
7. Whitehead, *Third Programme*, 109–34; P. Scannell, and D. Cardiff, *A Social History of British Broadcasting*, i: *1922–1939: Serving the Nation* (Oxford: Blackwell, 1991), 134–52; L. Gilliam (ed.), *BBC Features* (London: Evans, 1950), 204–8; Bridson, *Prospero*, 295–6; H. P. Priessnitz, 'British Radio Drama: A Survey', in P. Lewis (ed.), *Radio Drama* (London: Longman, 1981), 28–47; R. Heppenstall, *Portrait of the Artist as a Professional* (London: Peter Owen, 1969).
8. Heppenstall, *Portrait*, 10–15, 107–12; H. Carpenter, *The Envy of the World: Fifty Years of the BBC Third Programme and Radio 3* (London: Weidenfeld & Nicolson, 1996), 212–14; Bridson, *Prospero*, 293; BBC WAC Oral History Project: Gillard.
9. Heppenstall, *Portrait*, 112–20; Bridson, *Prospero*, 303.
10. *Guardian*, 20 August 1963.
11. BBC WAC Oral History Project: Gillard.
12. *Daily Telegraph*, 8 May 1965; *Guardian*, 23 November 1966; Carpenter, *Envy*, 230–1.
13. *Times*, 7 March 1964.
14. *Financial Times*, 28 August 1965. The idea of 'mixed' programming, as developed in the 1920s, is described in Scannell and Cardiff, *Social History*, 371–5.
15. Gerard Mansell, interview with author, London, June 2001.
16. *Guardian*, 31 May 1969.
17. Mansell, interview; BBC WAC Oral History Project: Clare Lawson Dick; Mansell to Lawson Dick, 23 January 1968, BBC WAC R51/1174/1.

18. BBC WAC Oral History Project: Lawson Dick; *Sunday Telegraph*, 23 May 1965; *Guardian*, 31 May 1969; *Times*, 10 July 1969; Mansell, interview; *Observer*, 29 August 1965.
19. *Daily Telegraph*, 5 March and 20 September 1963.
20. BBC WAC: Mansell to Gillard, 3 March 1967, R51/1045/1; Note by Mansell, 30 August 1967, R51/1078/1.
21. BBC WAC: Current Affairs Group (Radio), 5 September 1967, 13 September 1967, 13 March 1968, R51/1085/1; Radio Planning Committee, 27 March, 31 July, 28 August 1968.
22. See, for example, Radio Planning Committee, 19 June 1968, BBC WAC.
23. BBC WAC Oral History Project: Gillard; Mansell, interview.
24. Mansell, interview.
25. Current Affairs Group (Radio), 17 April 1968, BBC WAC R51/1085/1.
26. Mansell, interview.
27. Mansell: 'News and Current Affairs', 30 August 1967, BBC WAC R51/1078/1.
28. Crawley: 'News and Current Affairs', 5 September 1967, BBC WAC R51/1078/1.
29. Radio Planning Committee, 14 August 1968, BBC WAC.
30. Mansell, interview.
31. *Listener*, 11 February 1963.
32. G. Wyndham Goldie, *Facing the Nation: Television and Politics, 1936–1976* (London: The Bodley Head, 1977), 239–305; B. Pimlott, *Harold Wilson* (London: Harper Collins, 1992), 269; Current Affairs Group (Radio), 7 June 1967, BBC WAC R51/1085/1.
33. Whitley: 'A Shift in the Wind', Board of Management Paper, 12 August 1965, BBC WAC R51/1078/1.
34. John Timpson, a News Reporter in 1959, and later to become one of the *Today* programme presenters, gives a vivid account of the 'midget' recorder in his memoirs: J. Timpson, *Today and Yesterday* (London: George Allen & Unwin, 1976), 38.
35. Briggs, *History of Broadcasting*, v. 579.
36. *Sunday Times*, 29 January 1967; Radio Planning Committee, 31 July 1968, 20 November 1968, 29 October 1969, BBC WAC; *Listener*, 2 November 1965. On changes to *Focus*, see also: Current Affairs Group (Radio), March/April 1968, BBC WAC R51/1085/1; Bridson, *Prospero*, 140, 165, 319.
37. Timpson, *Today*, 83–4; 102; J. Simpson, *Strange Places, Questionable People* (London: Pan, 1999), 90.
38. Mansell, 23 August 1965, BBC WAC R51/1078/1.
39. Mansell, interview; S. MacGregor, *Woman of Today: An Autobiography* (London: Headline, 2002), 120–48.
40. Reports on Programme Correspondence, March 1970, BBC WAC R41/260/4.
41. *Listener*, 14 October 1965; *Times*, 7 June 1967; *Financial Times*, 6 December 1965; *Guardian*, 23 June 1966.
42. MacGregor, *Woman*, 120–48.
43. *Financial Times*, 6 December 1965; *Times*, 11 November 1975.
44. *Listener*, 18 November 1965.
45. *Times*, 29 July 1967; *Radio Times*, 14 September 1967; *Spectator*, 22 September 1967; *Listener*, 28 September 1967.

46. Timpson, *Today*, 74; P. Donovan, *All Our Todays: Forty Years of the Today Programme* (London: Jonathan Cape, 1997), 1–45.
47. BBC WAC: Redhouse, 16 April 1968, R51/1297/1; Bonarjee, 19 April 1968, R51/1297/1; Current Affairs Group (Radio), 24 April, 1 May, 8 May 1968, R51/1085/1; Bonarjee, 26 April 1968, R51/1297/1; Bonarjee, 9 May 1968, R51/1297/1. See also: Briggs, *Broadcasting*, v. 223–4, 330.
48. Brent, 8 July 1968, BBC WAC R51/1297/1. See also Briggs, *Broadcasting*, v. 223–4.
49. Note, 30 August 1967, BBC WAC R51/1085/1; Undated (*c.* June 1967), 'Agreed Draft for Today Anniversary Brochure', BBC WAC R51/1297/2.
50. Current Affairs Group (Radio), 25 June and 5 November 1969, BBC WAC R13/446/1.
51. BBC WAC Oral History Project: Lawson Dick.
52. Current Affairs Group (Radio), 22 November 1967, BBC WAC R51/1085/1.
53. Bridson, *Prospero*, 317–18.
54. Briggs, *Broadcasting*, v. 501–2.
55. BBC WAC: Arts, Science and Documentaries, Meetings, 1 June 1965 and 18 October 1966, R51/1045/1; Current Affairs Group (Radio), 13 September 1967, R51/1085/1; Radio Planning Committee, 10 April 1968.
56. Trethowan, 'Note on Radio Finances', 30 May 1973, Papers of Michael Meredith Swann, Edinburgh University Library, File E49.
57. Briggs, *Broadcasting*, v. 719–809.
58. Ibid. 737.
59. Ibid. 738–47.
60. Mansell, interview; BBC WAC Oral History Project: Ian Trethowan.
61. Briggs, *Broadcasting*, v. 748–66.
62. I. Trethowan, *Split Screen* (London: Hamish Hamilton, 1984), 119–24; BBC WAC Oral History Project: Trethowan.
63. Mansell, interview; Briggs, *Broadcasting*, v. 766–80.
64. Briggs, *Broadcasting*, v. 772.
65. *Times*, 14 February 1970; Bridson, *Prospero*, 333; Trethowan, *Split Screen*, 126.
66. *Times*, 19 January 1970. See also Briggs, *Broadcasting*, v. 783–9. The King's College letter was discussed at Review Board on 28 January 1970. The Head of Religious Broadcasting 'had recently been a guest at King's', the minutes record. He reported that 'a large number of those who had signed the letter had been under the false impression that the new network arrangement would involve substantial cuts in the amount of serious music. Apparently many of them also disagreed with individual points in the letter, but felt bound to support what they regarded as a liberal point of view': BBC WAC.
67. J. Abramsky, *Sound Matters: Soundtrack for the UK—How Did We Get Here?* Lecture, 30 January 2002, Green College, Oxford University.
68. BBC WAC Oral History Project: Gillard.
69. Trethowan, *Split Screen*, 126–7.
70. BBC WAC Oral History Project: Gillard.
71. Mansell, letters to *Guardian*, 3 October and 4 December 1969.
72. Briggs, *Broadcasting*, v. 778–9; letters in *Guardian*, 1, 3, and 7 October 1969.
73. BBC WAC Oral History Project: Lawson Dick.

CHAPTER 3. THREE-IN-ONE

1. Philip French, interview with author, London, 12 May 2005; Michael Mason, interview with author, Farnham, 4 June 2003.
2. Mitchell: 'BBC Goes Generic for the 70s', June/July 1970, BBC WAC R78/1389/1.
3. Mason, interview.
4. J. Grist, *The Century before Yesterday: John Grist's BBC and Other Broadcasting Tales*, ii (unpublished memoir), 90–2; BBC WAC Oral History Project: Clare Lawson Dick; Joy Whitby, interview with author, London, 28 May 2003; A. Briggs, *The History of Broadcasting in the United Kingdom*, v: *Competition, 1955–1974* (Oxford: Oxford University Press, 1995), 800.
5. A. Lesser, *Meet Me by Moonlight: A Play with Music in Three Acts* (London: Evan Brothers, 1958).
6. Briggs, *Broadcasting*, v. 800.
7. Joy Whitby, interview with author, London, 28 May 2003; BBC WAC Oral History Project: Lawson Dick.
8. A. Lesser, *Love by Appointment: A Comedy* (London: Samuel French, 1966); A. Lesser, *The Chicken Girl: A Comedy* (London: Samuel French, 1967); T. Lesser, *The Bedwinner: A Comedy* (London: Samuel French, 1975).
9. Joy Whitby, interview.
10. Briggs, *Broadcasting*, v. 793.
11. Joy Whitby, interview; BBC WAC Oral History Project: Lawson Dick.
12. David Hatch, interview with author, London, 5 February 2003.
13. George Fischer, interview with the author, London, 30 June 2003.
14. Gerard Mansell, interview with the author, London, 2001.
15. *Radio Times*, 12 March 1970.
16. *Sunday Times*, 22 February 1970; *Sunday Telegraph*, 22 March 1970; *Daily Telegraph*, 18 March 1970; *Economist*, 11 April 1970; Whitby, letter to *Guardian*, 23 February 1970; *Guardian*, 21 February 1970.
17. Trethowan, 12 February 1973, BBC WAC R78/1389/1; *Guardian*, 15 February 1973; Whitby, 26 July 1973, BBC WAC R101/314/1; BBC, *BBC Handbook 1973* (London: BBC, 1973), 63; BBC, *BBC Handbook 1974* (London: BBC, 1974), 129.
18. BBC WAC: 'Farming and Gardening Programmes', April 1969, M2/126/9; Mansell letter, 2 March 1970, R51/1135/1; Audience Research Reports, January 1973, R51/1135/1.
19. Miller, 13 April 1971, BBC WAC R51/1135/1.
20. BBC WAC: Review Board, 3 March 1971; Gordon: 'Garden Radio', 5 March 1971, and Gordon, 30 June 1971, R51/1135/1.
21. Mason: 'A History of the British People: Project for a Major Venture in Audio', 9 March 1970, BBC WAC R34/1489/1; *Listener*, 18 November 1971.
22. Briggs, *Broadcasting*, v. 941–3; P. Burke, *What is Cultural History?* (Cambridge: Polity Press, 2004), 6–46; R. Hewison, *Culture and Consensus: England, Art and Politics since 1940* (London: Methuen, 1995), 93–9, 125.
23. *Listener*, 18 November 1971; Mason: 'A History of the British People', 9 March 1970, BBC WAC R34/1489/1.

24. Ibid. For details of *Rus* (1968) and *A Bayeux Tapestry* see BBC WAC R51/1265/1 and R34/1382.
25. *Listener*, 18 November 1971.
26. Mason, interview; Briggs, *Broadcasting*, v. 941–3.
27. *The Long March of Everyman*, Episode 1, Radio Four, 21 November 1971, British Library Sound Archive, BBC T35060.
28. *Listener*, 4 May 1972.
29. Hill, 7 April 1972, BBC WAC R51/1171/1.
30. *Listener*, 11 May 1972; Review Board, 24 November 1971 and 26 January 1972, BBC WAC.
31. *Guardian*, 27 November 1971.
32. *Listener*, 9 December 1971.
33. BBC WAC: Review Board, 13 February 1974; Correspondence and telephone calls for the week ending 30 November 1971, R41/266/7.
34. Review Board, 1 July 1970, 24 November 1971, 26 January 1972, 11 December 1974, BBC WAC.
35. Review Board, 21 January 1970, BBC WAC.
36. Review Board, 20 November 1974 and 15 October 1975, BBC WAC; *Plain Tales from the Raj, Episode 2: 'Lances and Rifles'*, BBC T36194, British Library Sound Archive.
37. H. Chignell, 'BBC Radio 4's "Analysis", 1970–1983: A Selective History and Case Study of BBC Current Affairs Radio', Ph.D. thesis (Bournemouth, 2004).
38. Review Board, 15 April 1970, 13 May 1970, 20 May 1970, 6 December 1972, BBC WAC; Chignell, 'Analysis'; *Guardian*, 25 April 1970.
39. Quoted in Chignell, 'Analysis'.
40. Fischer, interview; Fischer, 27 July 1970, BBC WAC R51/1332/1.
41. Review Board, 10 May 1972, 3 June 1970, 23 June 1971, 12 June 1974, 18 December 1974, BBC WAC; Fischer, interview.
42. Review Board, 19 January 1972, BBC WAC.
43. Joy Whitby, interview; BBC WAC Oral History Project: Lawson Dick.
44. Briggs, *Broadcasting*, v. 634–5.
45. C. Curran, *A Seamless Robe: Broadcasting Philosophy and Practice* (London: Collins, 1979), 105–7.
46. BBC WAC: Ferguson, 31 October 1969, R51/1332/5; Whitby, 27 November 1969, R51/1078/1; Current Affairs Group (Radio), 7 January 1970, R13/446/1.
47. BBC WAC: Whitby, 25 June 1970, R101/314/1; Review Board, 14 October 1970.
48. Review Board, 30 August 1972, BBC WAC.
49. *Guardian*, 2 September 1972; Review Board, 30 August, 6 September, 27 September 1972, BBC WAC; *Daily Telegraph*, 4 September 1972.
50. Review Board, 21 October 1970, BBC WAC; *Radio Times*, 2 September 1971.
51. K. Miller (ed.), *A Second Listener Anthology* (London: BBC 1973), 97–105; Review Board, 16 December 1970, BBC WAC; *Radio Times*, 2 September 1971.
52. Review Board, 8 December 1971, 5 January 1972, 17 January 1973, BBC WAC.
53. BBC WAC: Hutchinson, 1 October 1973, R34/1489/3; Review Board, 19 September 1973, 31 October 1973, 1 May 1974, 18 December 1974.

54. Review Board, 23 February 1972, 2 May 1973, 1 May 1974, 30 October 1974, BBC WAC.
55. Review Board, 23 February 1972, BBC WAC.
56. Programme Correspondence, April 1970, BBC WAC R41/260/4; BBC, *Handbook 1973*, 51–2; *New Society*, 23 April 1970; *Guardian*, 25 April 1970.
57. Programme Correspondence, April and July 1970, BBC WAC R41/260/4.
58. Review Board, 8 April 1970, 13 May 1970, 25 September 1973, BBC WAC.
59. G. Priestland, *Something Understood: An Autobiography* (London: Andre Deutsch, 1986), 239.
60. BBC WAC: Bonarjee: 'Commuter Magazine, 5–6pm', 7 November 1969, R51/1078/1; Review Board, 29 April, 6 May, 13 May, 24 June, 8 July 1970.
61. *New Society*, 23 April 1970; Review Board, 29 April 1970, 6 May 1970, 13 May 1970, 24 June 1970, 8 July 1970, 24 November 1971, 29 March 1972, 2 May 1973, 26 September 1973, 13 August 1975, BBC WAC; *Guardian*, 11 January 1971; *Times*, 16 September 1970.
62. Programme Correspondence, 1970, BBC WAC R41/260/4.
63. Review Board, 1 July 1970, BBC WAC; *Times*, 13 December 1969; *Guardian*, 25 April 1970.
64. Review Board, 29 April 1970 and 14 July 1971, BBC WAC.
65. Whitby, 22 February 1973, BBC WAC R34/1489/3.
66. Review Board, 12 August 1970, 11 October and 18 October 1972, BBC WAC. Review Board members observed that younger listeners 'were connoisseurs of *Monty Python* and of Spike Milligan's television shows and thought the Goon Show was nothing to make a fuss about'.
67. *Daily Telegraph*, 22 November 1971.
68. *Daily Telegraph*, 22 November 1971; Review Board, 19 April 1972, BBC WAC; *Guardian*, 1 September 1972.
69. Review Board, 1 July 1970, 19 July 1972, 13 March 1974, BBC WAC; *Guardian*, 10 December 1982.
70. *Guardian*, 11 January 1971.
71. M. Coward, *The Pocket Essential Classic Radio Comedy* (Harpenden: Pocket Essentials, 2003), 71.
72. Whitby, 27 November 1969 and 6 March 1970, BBC WAC R101/314/1; Hatch, interview; *Daily Telegraph* and *Times*, 18 March 1970.
73. Hatch, interview; Ian McIntyre, interview with the author, Radlett, 27 January 2003. The 'ex-bomber pilots' quote was apparently originally coined by John Peel, and is relayed by Simon Brett in N. Webb, *Wish You Were Here: The Official Biography of Douglas Adams* (London: Headline, 2003), 106–8.
74. BBC WAC: Hatch, 5 November 1971, R19/2269/1; Review Board, 15 April 1970, 26 June 1974; Hatch, interview.
75. BBC WAC: Hatch and Brett, 29 May 1970, R19/2269/1; Review Board, 1 December 1971, 26 June 1974, 20 November 1974.
76. BBC WAC: Review Board, 7 January 1970, 27 October 1971, 20 February 1974, 'Light Entertainment: Television and Radio', General Advisory Council Paper 379, 1972.
77. *Sunday Times*, 29 April 1973.
78. Whitby: 'Overlap in Magazine Programmes', 1 March 1973, BBC WAC R51/1078/1.

79. Whitby, 25 June 1970, BBC WAC R101/314/1; *Financial Times* and *Daily Telegraph*, 16 September 1970; Review Board, 14 October 1970, BBC WAC.

80. Review Board, 1 August 1973, BBC WAC.

81. Philip French, interview with author, London, 12 May 2005; Review Board, 8 March and 19 April 1972, BBC WAC; French: 'New Radio 4 Arts Series', 12 July 1972, BBC WAC R51/1332/4.

82. On magazine formats, see A. Crisell, *Understanding Radio*, 2nd edn. (London: Routledge, 1994), 72–3.

83. BBC WAC: various memos between Whitby and Cohn, 21 November 1969–15 January 1970, R51/1332/2; Bonarjee, 29 December 1969, R51/1078/1; Review Board, 20 May 1970; Hutchinson, 31 July 1973; Whitby, 8 August 1973, R34/1489/3; Briggs, *Broadcasting*, v. 868 ff.

84. M. Hilmes, *Radio Voices: American Broadcasting, 1922–1952* (Minneapolis: University of Minnesota Press, 1997), 149, 274–81; S. Nicholas, *The Echo of War: Home Front Propaganda and the Wartime BBC 1939–45* (Manchester: Manchester University Press, 1996), 70–107, 139.

85. R. Hoggart, *The Uses of Literacy* (London: Penguin, 1958), 194–205.

86. R. Hoggart, *Only Connect: On Culture and Communication. The BBC Reith Lectures 1971* (London: Chatto & Windus, 1972), 87.

87. Review Board, 17 November 1971, BBC WAC.

88. *Times*, 4 September 1971, 1 September 1973.

89. *Observer*, 6 May 1973; *Sunday Times*, 29 April 1973; *Guardian*, 8 September 1973.

90. Moore: 'The Benchmark Papers', 20 October 1969, BBC WAC R51/1332/1.

91. P. Scannell and D. Cardiff, *A Social History of British Broadcasting*, i: *1922–1939: Serving the Nation* (Oxford: Blackwell, 1991), 356–80.

92. R. Carver (ed.), *Ariel at Bay: Reflections on Broadcasting and the Arts—Critics' Forum Festschrift for Philip French* (Manchester: Carcanet, 1990), 15–18, 27–30 French, interview.

93. Miller, 13 August 1973, BBC WAC R34/1489/3.

94. Review Board, 24 January 1973, BBC WAC.

95. Hoggart, *Literacy*, 196.

96. Whitby, 5 June 1974, BBC WAC R34/1439/1; Fischer, interview.

97. Whitby, 5 June 1974, BBC WAC R34/1439/1.

98. BBC WAC: Annual Report 1972–3, R78/1389/1; Miller, 15 August 1973, R34/1489/3.

99. BBC WAC: Whitby, 13 July 1973, R101/314/1; Review Board, 25 August 1971, 18 October 1972; Audience Research Report: 'Today', 1972, 1 May 1972, R9/855/1; *Daily Express*, 18 April 1971; J. Timpson, *Today and Yesterday* (London: George Allen & Unwin, 1976), 106–17.

100. Annual Report 1972–3, BBC WAC R78/1389/1.

101. Whitby, 30 August 1973, BBC WAC R51/1312/8.

CHAPTER 4. POLITICS AND PERMISSIVENESS

1. C. Booker, *The Seventies: The Decade that Changed the Future* (New York: Stein & Day, 1981); E. Hobsbawm, *Age of Extremes: The Short Twentieth Century,*

1914–1991 (London: Abacus, 1994), 283–6; T. Judt, *Postwar: A History of Europe since 1945* (London: Heinemann, 2005), 453–503; K. Kumar, 'Holding the Middle Ground: The BBC, the Public and the Professional Broadcaster', in J. Curran, M. Gurevitch, and J. Woollacott (eds.), *Mass Communication and Society* (London: Edward Arnold, 1977), 231–48; A. Marwick, *The Sixties: Cultural Revolution in Britain, France, Italy, and the United States, c.1958–1974* (Oxford: Oxford University Press, 1998), 758–96, 802; M. Amis, *The War against Cliché: Essays and Reviews 1971–2000* (London: Vintage, 2002), pp. xi–xv; D. Hendy, 'Bad Language and BBC Radio Four in the 1960s and 1970s', *Twentieth Century British History*, 17/1 (2006), 74–102.

2. C. Curran, *A Seamless Robe: Broadcasting Philosophy and Practice* (London: Collins, 1979), 89–143.
3. Ibid. 91.
4. Antony Jay made the comments in a Radio Three programme in the series *The Communicators*, 21 December 1972: a transcript exists in Papers of Michael Meredith Swann, Edinburgh University Library, File E21; *Times*, 14 November 1972.
5. The *Times* poll was quoted in 'Taste and Standards in BBC Programmes', General Advisory Council Paper (GAC 362), 21 March 1972, BBC WAC.
6. *Listener*, 14 December 1972.
7. Programme Correspondence, January–December 1970, BBC WAC R41/260/4; W. Smethurst, *The Archers: The History of Radio's Most Famous Programme* (London: Michael O'Mara, 1997), 129.
8. Briggs, *Broadcasting*, v. 879–81; J. Grist, 'The Century before Yesterday: John Grist's BBC and other Broadcasting Tales', ii (unpublished memoir), 98–9.
9. Briggs, *History of Broadcasting*, v. 892–915.
10. BBC WAC: 'The Broadcasting of News in the United Kingdom', General Advisory Council Paper, 24 January 1974; General Advisory Council, Minutes, 6 February 1974, R6/29/10.
11. S. Hall, 'A World at One with Itself', *New Society*, 403 (18 June 1970), 1056–8; Briggs, *History of Broadcasting*, v. 795–6.
12. Gardner, 22 October 1968, BBC WAC R51/1332/3.
13. Note from Lord Hill, 10 October 1972, Papers of Michael Meredith Swann, Edinburgh University Library, File E18.
14. *The Communicators*, Radio Three, 21 December 1972; Note on a meeting at 10 Downing Street, 16 February 1973, Papers of Michael Meredith Swann, Edinburgh University Library, File E36; *Times*, 23 May 1972.
15. 'News and Current Affairs: The Making of Editorial Decisions', General Advisory Council Paper (GAC 299), 28 June 1968, BBC WAC; 'Principles and Practice in News and Current Affairs', General Advisory Council Paper (GAC 341), 29 March 1971, BBC WAC; Grist, 'Century before Yesterday', 53.
16. Note by the Chairman on a meeting with Harold Wilson, 20 March 1973, Papers of Michael Meredith Swann, Edinburgh University Library, File E37. See also *Daily Telegraph*, 28 June 1971, which reported that 'Mr Wilson's feeling that the Current Affairs Group of BBC Television has a particular dislike of him does not extend to BBC Radio'.
17. Quoted in *Daily Telegraph*, 1 June 1970.

18. BBC WAC: Review Board, 12 January 1972; 'The Task of Broadcasting News', General Advisory Council Paper (GAC 490), 21 January 1976.
19. BBC, *BBC Handbook 1973* (London: BBC, 1972), 47, 63; News and Current Affairs Meeting, 9 February 1973, BBC WAC R3/57/1.
20. Undated letters, *c.* January/February 1973, BBC WAC R51/1117/1; S. MacGregor, *Woman of Today: An Autobiography* (London: Headline, 2002), 113–48.
21. *Guardian*, 19 July 1967; *Daily Telegraph*, 20 August 1971; Review Board, 20 August and 3 September 1969, 8 September 1971, BBC WAC.
22. *Guardian*, 19 July 1967; *Daily Telegraph*, 20 August 1971; Review Board, 20 August and 3 September 1969, 8 September 1971, BBC WAC.
23. BBC WAC: Programme Correspondence, 1970, R41/260/4; Review Board, 7 and 14 July 1971.
24. BBC WAC: Review Board, 14 April 1971, 19 May 1971, 16 June 1971, 7 March 1973, 16 January 1974, 6 February 1974, 4 September 1974; Programme Correspondence, 1970, R41/260/4.
25. Memos, March 1971, BBC WAC R51/1332/7.
26. Memos, 10 July and 4 September 1968, BBC WAC R51/1085/1. See also: *Daily Telegraph*, 23 January 1969; Review Board, 24 February 1971 and 26 April 1972, 21 March 1973, BBC WAC. The relevant statements by both Greene and Haley were contained in 'Principles and Practice in News and Current Affairs', General Advisory Council Paper, 29 March 1971, BBC WAC.
27. BBC WAC: Review Board, 3 January 1973; News and Current Affairs Meeting, 9 February 1973, R3/57/1; letter, 2 July 1971, Chief Assistant, Talks and Current Affairs Group (Radio), 13 July 1971, and letter to complainant, 21 July 1971, R51/1332/2.
28. BBC WAC: Review Board, 7 July 1971, 14 July 1971, 10 July 1974; Draft Letter for the Chairman, 25 March 1971, R51/1099/1; Director-General's News and Current Affairs Meeting, 5 January 1973, R3/57/1.
29. Review Board, 27 February 1974, BBC WAC.
30. Note on a meeting at 10 Downing Street, 16 February 1973, Papers of Michael Meredith Swann, Edinburgh University Library, File E36.
31. H. Chignell, 'BBC Radio 4's "Analysis", 1970–1983: A Selective History and Case Study of BBC Current Affairs Radio', unpublished Ph.D. thesis (Bournemouth, 2004).
32. Ian McIntyre, interview with author, Radlett, 27 January 2003; Review Board, 13 March 1974, BBC WAC.
33. BBC WAC: News and Current Affairs Meeting, 9 February 1973, R3/57/1; Review Board, 13 June, 27 June, 11 July, 10 October 1973.
34. BBC WAC: 'The BBC and the February 1974 General Election', General Advisory Council Paper, 4 July 1974; General Advisory Council, Minutes, 3 April 1974, R6/29/10.
35. Review Board, 29 January 1975, BBC WAC.
36. BBC WAC: 'The BBC and the February 1974 General Election', General Advisory Council Paper, 4 July 1974; Review Board, 20 February 1974, 27 February 1974, 6 March 1974; General Advisory Council, Minutes, 3 April 1974, R6/29/10. See also: *Daily Telegraph*, 10 October 1974.
37. Bonarjee, 9 February 1970, BBC WAC R51/1078/1.
38. Review Board, 6 May 1970, 25 March 1971, 5 May 1971, BBC WAC.

39. BBC WAC: *Woman's Hour*, 29 March 1973, R51/1312/8; Review Board, 16 June 1971. See also: *Radio Times*, 30 June 1973.

40. Review Board, 6 January 1971, 28 March 1973, 5 November 1975, BBC WAC; MacGregor, *Woman of Today*, 156–9.

41. *Daily Telegraph*, 4 September 1972; *Daily Mail*, 4 September 1972; *Times*, 9 July 1973; Correspondence, 25 March–3 May 1974, BBC WAC R34/1439/1; Review Board, 16 June 1971, 20 September 1972, 18 July 1974, 22 October 1975, BBC WAC.

42. *Newsdesk* transcript and correspondence, 10–15 November 1971, BBC WAC R51/1171/1.

43. Kumar, 'Holding the Middle Ground', 231–48.

44. 'Summary of Public Reactions to the BBC', *c.* June 1970, General Advisory Council Paper (GAC 330), BBC WAC.

45. Seminar on the Annan Inquiry, 2 July 1974, BBC WAC R78/521/1; Curran, *Seamless Robe*, 143.

46. G. Hughes, *Swearing: A Social History of Foul Language, Oaths and Profanity in English* (London: Penguin, 1998), 195; Briggs, *History of Broadcasting*, v. 529–30.

47. Curran, *Seamless Robe*, 102.

48. Review Board, 27 August 1975, BBC WAC R3/118/2.

49. O. Shapley, *Broadcasting a Life* (London: Scarlet Press, 1996), 37; P. Scannell and D. Cardiff, *A Social History of British Broadcasting*, i: *1922–1939: Serving the Nation* (Oxford: Blackwell, 1991), 298–9.

50. J. Tydeman, 'Bad Language and Radio Drama: A Personal View', in A. M. Hargrave (ed.), *A Matter of Manners? The Limits of Broadcast Language*, Broadcasting Standards Council Research Monograph Series 3 (London: Broadcasting Standards Council, 1991), 65–9.

51. Ibid. 65.

52. J. Sutherland, *Offensive Literature: Decensorship in Britain, 1960–1982* (London: Junction Books, 1982), 4, 10–31, 79–85.

53. V. Gielgud, *Years of the Locust* (London: Nicholson & Watson, 1947); *Times*, 22 April 1963; Briggs, *History of Broadcasting*, v. 190–2; H. Carpenter, *The Envy of the World: Fifty Years of the BBC Third Programme and Radio 3* (London: Weidenfeld & Nicolson, 1996), 144–5, 150–3, 209–11; BBC WAC Oral History Project: Martin Esslin, Val Gielgud.

54. BBC WAC Oral History Project: Esslin; *Guardian*, 27 February 2002; M. Esslin, *The Theatre of the Absurd*, 3rd edn. (London: Methuen, 2001); *Sunday Times*, 29 September 1963.

55. D. Shellard, and S. Nicholson, with M. Handley (eds.), *The Lord Chamberlain Regrets: A History of British Theatre Censorship* (London: British Library, 2004), 171; Esslin, *Theatre of the Absurd*, 258–9; H. Pinter, *Plays (3)* (London: Faber & Faber, 1997), 165–88; Review Board, 13 March 1968, BBC WAC.

56. Review Board, 7 July 1971 and 7 February 1973, BBC WAC; Note of a Colloquy, 4 November 1971, Papers of Michael Meredith Swann, Edinburgh University Library, File E16; Carpenter, *Envy of the World*, 285–6.

57. Whitby, 6 March 1970, BBC WAC R101/314/1.

58. BBC WAC: Board of Management, 5 June 1972, R78/2640/1; Review Board, 7 June 1972.

59. Notes to Whitby, 25 and 26 June 1970, BBC WAC R34/1470/1.
60. Mason: 'Four-Letter Word in Programme 25 (World War II)', 13 April 1972, and Gordon, 14 April 1972, BBC WAC R51/1171/1.
61. New York Office to Whitby, 30 April 1974, and Telex reply, 3 May 1974, in BBC WAC R34/1491/2.
62. Trethowan wrote to the Director-General on 23 July 1970 to argue in favour of letting the programme go ahead: BBC WAC R101/315/1. See also Review Board, 10 November 1971, BBC WAC, where Whitby recalls 'a precedent in a Radio 4 drama discussion programme when, after due consideration upwards' it had 'been decided to let the word stand'.
63. Review Board, 22 September 1971, BBC WAC.
64. BBC WAC: *Filthy Fryer and the Woman of Maturer Years*, Play Library; Review Board, 14 October 1970.
65. *Listener*, 12 January 1979; N. Painting, *Forever Ambridge: Twenty Five Years of The Archers* (London: Michael Joseph, 1975), 244.
66. *Ambridge in the Decade of Love*, BBC Radio Four, 9 and 16 May 2003; W. Smethurst, *The Archers: The History of Radio's Most Famous Programme* (London: Michael O'Mara, 1997).
67. *Independent*, 9 October 2003; Board of Management, 2 February 1970, BBC WAC R78/2698/1; Gallagher, 11 August 1970: 'The Archers', BBC WAC M9/26/1; Smethurst, *The Archers*, 116–22; Jock Gallagher, interview with author, Bewdley, 16 June 2005.
68. Smethurst, *The Archers*, 131.
69. Review Board, 6, 13, 20, 27 September and 11 October 1972, BBC WAC.
70. BBC WAC: Programme Correspondence, 1970, R41/260/4; Review Board, 22 September 1971; Memo, undated, 1968, R34/1488/1.
71. Review Board, 14 October 1970, BBC WAC.
72. Hughes, *Swearing*, 186–7; E. M. Eppel and M. Eppel, *Adolescents and Morality: A Study of some Moral Values and Dilemmas of Working Adolescents in the Context of a Changing Climate of Opinion* (London: Routledge & Kegan Paul, 1966), 187; Review Board, 10 November 1971, BBC WAC; Note of a Colloquy, 10 February 1972, Papers of Michael Meredith Swann, Edinburgh University Library, File E16.
73. Tydeman, 'Bad Language and Radio Drama', 65–71; Review Board, 27 September 1972, BBC WAC.
74. Review Board, 10 May 1972, BBC WAC. See also comments on *The Monday Play: A Damsel and also a Rough Bird*, Review Board, 22 May 1974, in which the 'Northern context' of the language was discussed.
75. Note by BBC Secretary: 'Language and Programmes', 24 June and 15 September 1971, BBC WAC R101/315/1.
76. BBC WAC: Review Board, 27 August 1980, General Advisory Council, 4 April 1973, R6/29/10; 'Summary of Public Reactions to the BBC', General Advisory Council Paper, March 1973; Review Board, 10 November 1971.
77. H. Tennyson, *The Haunted Mind: An Autobiography* (London: Andre Deutsch, 1984). The three plays concerned were *Now She Laughs, Now She Cries*, *Valmouth*, and *The Litmus Question*: Review Board, 16 April, 23 April, 7 May, 25 June, and 9 July 1975, BBC WAC R3/118/1–2.

78. BBC WAC: Review Board, 17 September 1975, R3/118/3; Letter, 13 September 1975, Muggeridge, 22 September 1975; Letter to Lawson Dick, 26 September 1975, and Lawson Dick, 26 September 1975, R51/1332/6.

79. Review Board, 19 May 1971 and 1 March 1972, BBC WAC; Papers of Michael Meredith Swann, Edinburgh University Library, File E35.

80. Review Board, 27 September 1972, 28 May 1975, BBC WAC.

81. Review Board, 14 October 1970, BBC WAC.

82. Review Board, 26 May 1971, BBC WAC.

83. Attenborough, 28 June 1971, BBC WAC R101/315/1.

84. 'Language and Programmes', 15 September 1971, BBC WAC R101/315/1; Curran to Robert Runcie, 29 October 1973, Papers of Michael Meredith Swann, Edinburgh University Library, File E105.

85. Hughes, *Swearing*, 196–7.

86. Ibid.; Weeks, *Sex, Politics and Society*, 276–9; Memorandum from the National Festival of Light Delegation to the BBC, 1971, General Advisory Council Paper (GAC 368).

87. Notes of Colloquy, 4 November 1971, 10 February 1972, and 20 July 1972, Papers of Michael Meredith Swann, Edinburgh University Library, File E16.

88. BBC WAC: Review Board, 10 and 17 November 1971; 'Bad Language in Woman's Hour': Memo, Trethowan, to Director-General, 16 November 1971, R101/315/1.

89. BBC WAC: Trethowan, 8 May 1972, R101/315/1; Gordon, 14 April 1972, R51/1171/1.

90. Review Board, 22 and 29 September 1971, BBC WAC.

91. *Times*, 7 December 1971; BBC WAC: Review Board, 12 January 1972; 'Language and Programmes', 23 June and 15 September 1971, R101/315/1; 'Taste and Standards in BBC Programmes', 21 March 1972, General Advisory Council Paper (GAC 362); *Times* and *Guardian*, 7 February 1973.

92. Review Board, 28 November 1973, 24 April 1974, 10 July 1974, BBC WAC.

93. Cardy, 10 September 1970, BBC WAC R51/1332/3.

94. Speech, 23 February 1974, Papers of Michael Meredith Swann, Edinburgh University Library, File E128.

95. BBC WAC: Review Board, 12 June 1974, 9 October 1974, 17 September 1975; 'Taste and Standards in BBC Programmes', 21 March 1972, General Advisory Council Paper (GAC 362).

96. Marwick, *The Sixties*, 12–13.

97. H. Perkin, *The Rise of Professional Society: England since 1880* (London: Routledge, 1989), 433.

98. Whitby, 22 October 1974, BBC WAC R51/1147/1.

99. Review Board, 4 September 1974, BBC WAC.

100. Review Board, 27 August 1975, 2 June 1976, BBC WAC.

CHAPTER 5.   CRISES

1. BBC WAC: Ditchley Park Conference, 10–12 January 1975, General Advisory Council Paper (GAC 456); General Advisory Council, Minutes, 5 February 1975, R6/29/11.

2. Bonarjee, 25 May 1971, BBC WAC R51/1332/3.
3. Michael Green, interview with author, London, 13 December 2005; BBC WAC: Lawson Dick, 20 July 1972, R34/1489/3; 'One Day Conference on Radio Strategy', 8 July 1975, R78/521/1; General Advisory Council, Minutes, 7 February 1973, R6/29/10.
4. Philip French, interview with author, London, 12 May 2005.
5. W. H. McDowell, *The History of BBC Broadcasting in Scotland, 1923–1983* (Edinburgh: Edinburgh University Press, 1992); J. Davies, *Broadcasting and the BBC in Wales* (Cardiff: University of Wales Press, 1994), 308–24.
6. J. Gray, 'Broadcasting and Scottish Culture', in D. Daiches (ed.), *A Companion to Scottish Culture* (London: Edward Arnold, 1981), 42; D. Cranston, 'From Portland Stone to the River Foyle: The Decentralising and Democratising of BBC Radio', in M. McLoone (ed.), *Broadcasting in a Divided Community: Seventy Years of the BBC in Northern Ireland* (Belfast: Institute of Irish Studies, 1996), 35–50, and J. Bardon, *Beyond the Studio: A History of BBC Northern Ireland* (Belfast: Blackstaff Press, 2000).
7. Home Service listeners in the North-East of England and in Northern Ireland had to share a frequency for a long period, while large parts of the West Country could only hear broadcasts from Wales: A. Briggs, *The History of Broadcasting in the United Kingdom*, v: *Competition, 1955–1974* (Oxford: Oxford University Press, 1995), 621–76.
8. BBC WAC: 'The Broadcasting Role of the English Regions', General Advisory Council Paper (GAC 381), 12 December 1972; Review Board, 12 August and 16 September 1970.
9. BBC, *BBC Handbook 1974* (London: BBC, 1974), 18, 72; *Guardian*, 17 March 1973; Osborne, 2 December 1974, BBC WAC R51/1297/3; Memo to Whitby, March 1970, BBC WAC R51/1078/1.
10. J. Timpson, *Today and Yesterday* (London: George Allen & Unwin, 1976), 108–9.
11. Mansell, 11 September 1970, BBC WAC R51/1297/1.
12. Jock Gallagher, interview with author, Bewdley, 16 June 2005.
13. *Guardian*, 18 March 2004; BBC WAC: Whitby, 31 October 1974, R34/1489/4; Review Board, 24 June 1970, 11 December 1974, 16 March 1977; BBC, *BBC Handbook 1973* (London: BBC, 1972), 70–1.
14. BBC WAC: Memos, Radio Talks, Bristol, January–February 1976, R51/1332/1; Radio Network Direction Meeting, 20 September 1974, R92/124/1, and 9 April 1976, R92/125/1; Memo to Chief Assistant, 27 April 1976, R34/1470/1; Lawson Dick, 29 April 1976, R34/1470; Lawson Dick, 3 May 1976, R34/1470; Review Board, 24 June 1974, 29 September 1976, 27 July 1977; BBC, *BBC Handbook 1973*, 71; BBC, *BBC Handbook 1974* (London: BBC, 1974), 56; BBC, *BBC Handbook 1975* (London: BBC, 1975), 58; BBC, *BBC Handbook 1976* (London: BBC, 1976), 45, 117.
15. BBC, *Handbook 1973*, 71–2; BBC, *Handbook 1974*, 57; BBC, *Handbook 1975*, 58; BBC, *Handbook 1976*, 46–7; *Times*, 2 June 1973; BBC WAC: Bradley: 'The Regional Drama Producer', 13 August 1978, R92/69/1; Whitby, 22 February 1973, Miller, 9 July 1973, and Whitby, 19 July 1973, R34/1489/3; Gallagher, interview.

16. Charles Parker faced compulsory 'retirement' in 1972. See: Briggs, *History of Broadcasting*, v. 349 f.; P. Long, 'British Radio and the Politics of Culture in Post-war Britain: The Work of Charles Parker', *The Radio Journal: International Studies in Broadcast and Audio Media*, 2/3 (2004), 131–52.

17. Gallagher, interview; BBC, *Handbook 1975*, 57; BBC, *Handbook 1976*, 44–5; BBC WAC: Whitby, 12 March 1974, R34/1488/2; Review Board, 15 April 1970, 10 July and 18 July 1974; Whitby, 30 October 1974, R34/1470/1.

18. Bradley: 'The Regional Drama Producer', 13 August 1978, BBC WAC R92/69/1.

19. Review Board, 27 November 1974, 27 August 1980, BBC WAC.

20. 'One-Day Conference on Radio Strategy', 8 July 1975, BBC WAC R78/521/1. See also N. Morris, 'US Voices on UK Radio', *European Journal of Communication*, 14/1 (1999), 37–59.

21. HMSO, *A Language for Life: Report of the Committee of Inquiry Appointed by the Secretary of State for Education and Science under the Chairmanship of Sir Alan Bullock FBA* (London, 1975); Review Board, 23 May 1973, BBC WAC.

22. Programme Correspondence, January–December 1970, BBC WAC R41/260/4; P. Trudgill, 'The Meanings of Words Should Not Be Allowed to Vary or Change', in L. Bauer and P. Trudgill (eds.), *Language Myths* (London: Penguin, 1998); L. Mugglestone, *'Talking Proper': The Rise of Accent as Social Symbol* (Oxford: Clarendon, 1997); D. Crystal, *The English Language*, 2nd edn. (London: Penguin, 2002), 29; Review Board, 24 October 1979, BBC WAC.

23. 'The Quality of Spoken English on Radio: A Note', 4 October 1979, File E576, Papers of Michael Meredith Swann, Edinburgh University Library, File E576; Review Board, 27 June 1973, 6 February 1974, 28 May 1975, 23 July 1975, 11 August 1976, 4 January 1978, 25 January 1978, BBC WAC.

24. R. Burchfield, *The Spoken Word: A BBC Guide* (London: BBC, 1981), 9; A. L. James, *The Broadcast Word* (London, 1935); BBC, *Broadcast English: Recommendations to Announcers Regarding Certain Words of Doubtful Pronunciation, with an Introduction by A. Lloyd James*, 3rd edn. (London: BBC, 1935, originally 1928), 10–11; B. Storey, *The Way to Good Speech* (London: Nelson, 1937), 12; H. C. Wyld, *A History of Modern Colloquial English* (London: Unwin, 1920), 18. For the background to Burchfield's appointment, see: *Listener*, 5 April 1979 and 3 January 1980; BBC WAC: Review Board, 11 April, 25 April, 16 May, and 20 June 1979; Notes, Managing Director of Radio, 4 October 1979, Papers of Michael Meredith Swann, Edinburgh University Library, File E576; G. Leitner, 'The Social Background of the Language of Radio', in H. Davis and P. Walton (eds.), *Language, Image, Media* (Oxford: Basil Blackwell, 1983).

25. Whitby, 22 February 1973, Miller, 9 July 1973, and Whitby 19 July 1973, BBC WAC R34/1489/3.

26. D. Hendy, 'Speaking to Middle England: Radio Four and its Listeners', in J. Aitchison and D. Lewis (eds.), *New Media Language* (London: Routledge, 2003).

27. Gallagher, interview; Review Board, 15 April 1970, BBC WAC; 'The BBC and the Future: Paper VIII: The BBC's Radio Services', Board of Governors Paper, 21 November 1972, Papers of Michael Meredith Swann, Edinburgh University Library, File E28.

28. Review Board, 15 April 1970, BBC WAC.

29. BBC WAC: Whitby, 9 May and 11 May 1973, R51/1332/4; Review Board, 16 May 1973.
30. Gallagher, interview; Green, interview.
31. Review Board, 6 April 1977, BBC WAC; McDowell, *Broadcasting in Scotland*, 210.
32. BBC, *BBC Handbook 1974*, 54, 127; BBC, *Handbook 1976*, 117.
33. Davies, *BBC in Wales*, 308–47; One-Day Conference, 8 July 1975, BBC WAC R78/521/1.
34. See, for example, Walter Shaw writing in the *Scotsman*, 15 May 1974; Davies, *BBC in Wales*, 345.
35. BBC WAC: One-Day Conference, 8 July 1975, R78/521/1; Whitby, 12 March 1974, R34/1488/2; Review Board, 6 April 1977.
36. P. Clarke, *Hope and Glory: Britain 1900–1990* (London: Penguin, 1996), 332, 344.
37. BBC, *BBC Handbook 1975*, 9, 13–14; BBC, *Handbook 1976*, 9–10; I. Trethowan, *The Development of Radio*, BBC Lunchtime Lectures Ninth Series, Number 4 (London: BBC, 1975); BBC WAC: Review Board, 19 March 1975; General Advisory Council, Minutes, 17 July and 23 October 1974, R6/29/10.
38. BBC, *BBC Handbook 1975*, 95.
39. BBC WAC Oral History Project: Ian Trethowan.
40. Trethowan: 'Note on Radio Finances', 30 May 1973, Papers of Michael Meredith Swann, Edinburgh University Library, File E49; BBC WAC: Whitby, various memos, undated (*c*. September 1971), R34/1489/2; Radio Network Direction Meeting, 14 March 1975, R92/124/1; Review Board, 25 February 1970, 19 March 1975.
41. BBC WAC: 'The Shadow of Napoleon: Report on Production', Mason, April 1970, R51/1332/6; Calculation of Productivity from Current Affairs Magazine Programmes for Radio Four, Third Quarter 1973, 20 June 1973, R51/1078/1; Whitby: 'Developments on R4', 25 June 1973, R101/314/1; George Fischer, interview with author, London, 30 June 2003.
42. BBC WAC: Memo to Whitby, 'Down Your Way', 19 December 1974, and Whitby, 31 December 1974, both R34/1470/1.
43. BBC WAC: Review Board, 15 and 22 January 1975; Radio Network Direction Meeting, 24 January 1975, R92/124/1; H. Carpenter, *The Envy of the World: Fifty Years of the BBC Third Programme and Radio 3* (London: Weidenfeld & Nicolson, 1996), 293–5.
44. BBC WAC: 'Summary of Public Reactions to the BBC', 1975, General Advisory Council Paper (GAC 455); Review Board, 29 January and 19 February 1975.
45. BBC WAC: General Advisory Council, Minutes, 5 February 1975, R6/29/11; Radio Network Direction Meeting, 14 February 1975, R92/124/1.
46. Trethowan, *The Development of Radio*, 6.
47. Ibid. 6–7.
48. 'One BBC', General Advisory Council Paper (GAC 332), 7 October 1970, BBC WAC.
49. E. F. Schumacher, *Small is Beautiful: A Study of Economics as if People Mattered* (London: Blond & Briggs, 1973); K. Kumar, *Utopia and Anti-Utopia in Modern Times* (Oxford: Blackwell, 1987), 405–8; 'Seminar on the Annan Inquiry', 2 July 1974, BBC WAC R78/521/1.

50. The stories were 'alas, true': Board of Management, 19 January 1976, BBC WAC R2/29/1.

51. BBC WAC: Review Board, 14 July, 21 July, 28 July 1976; General Advisory Council, 21 July 1976, BBC WAC R6/29/11.

52. BBC WAC: Board of Management, 19 January 1976, R2/29/1; Trethowan, 10 June 1975, R78/521/1.

53. Joy Whitby, interview with author, London, 28 May, 2003.

54. BBC WAC Oral History Project: Lawson Dick.

55. Address by the Reverend Michael Mayne, Private Papers of Joy Whitby.

56. *Times*, 1 March 1975.

57. *Listener*, 6 March 1975.

58. Letter to Joy Whitby, 24 February 1976, Private papers of Joy Whitby.

59. BBC WAC Oral History Project: Lawson Dick; Review Board, 2 April 1975, BBC WAC; *Guardian, Daily Telegraph*, and *Evening Standard*, 3 April 1975; *Observer*, 6 April 1975; *Listener*, 5 January 1978; *Times*, 17 June 1987; Joy Whitby, interview; Gerard Mansell, interview with author, London, 2001.

60. BBC WAC Oral History Project: Lawson Dick; *Daily Telegraph*, 3 April 1975.

61. Radio Network Direction Meeting, 25 April and 13 June 1975, BBC WAC R92/124/1; *Daily Telegraph*, 24 June 1975; *Evening Standard*, 21 July 1975.

62. Review Board, 3 September 1975, BBC WAC.

63. BBC WAC: Hatch, 11 December 1975, R51/1135/1; Review Board, 9 July 1975, 1 October 1975, 8 October 1975, 15 October 1975, 12 November 1975, 3 March 1976.

64. *Observer*, 4 April 1971; BBC WAC: Hutchinson, 16 January 1973, R101/314/1; Review Board, 11 October 1972.

65. Review Board, 10, 24, and 31 October 1973, 10 April and 1 May 1974, BBC WAC.

66. McDowell, *BBC Broadcasting in Scotland*, 209; Review Board, 15 May 1974, BBC WAC. Street, *Concise History*, 119–22, gives a good account of programmes still being produced on Radio Clyde and other commercial radio stations into the 1980s.

67. BBC WAC: Review Board, 29 November 1972, 14 March 1973; Annual Report, Trethowan, 26 June 1973, R78/1389/1; Board of Management, 11 December 1972, R78/621/1; Editor, Morning Current Affairs Programmes, 22 May 1973, R51/1297/3; BBC, *Handbook 1976*, 48–50.

68. BBC WAC: Miller, 10 January 1972, R34/1489/3; Review Board, 22 September 1971, 3 January 1973, 9 April 1975, 11 February 1976; Memo to Hatch, 7 April 1975, R51/1135/1; Hatch, 11 December 1975, R51/1135/1; *Sunday Telegraph*, 23 April 1972.

69. Review Board, 26 March 1975, BBC WAC.

70. Review Board, 22 March 1972, BBC WAC.

71. See Chapter 7 for a fuller discussion of drama and features during the period *c*.1970–83.

72. Whitby, 1 May 1973, BBC WAC R34/1547/1.

73. Review Board, 6 August 1975, BBC WAC.

74. BBC WAC Oral History Project: Martin Esslin; *The Archive Hour: The Theatre of the Absurd*, BBC Radio Four, 3 May 2003; *Guardian*, 27 February 2002; Obituary,

Stanford Magazine, July/August 2002; D. Snowman, *The Hitler Émigrés: The Cultural Impact on Britain of Refugees from Nazism* (London: Pimlico, 2003).

75. Snowman, *Hitler Émigrés*, 297–8; Ian McIntyre, interview with author, Radlett, 27 January 2003.

76. Snowman, *Hitler Émigrés*, 298 f.; Carpenter, *Envy*, 238; George Fischer, interview with Hugh Chignell, London, 22 September 2000; BBC WAC Oral History Project: Trethowan; G. Priestland, *Something Understood: An Autobiography* (London: Andre Deutsch, 1986), 248; Philip French, personal communication with author, 25 December 2005. T. Fischer, *Under the Frog* (London: Penguin, 1992) provides a fictionalized account of George Fischer's life in Budapest in the period running up to the Soviet invasion of 1956.

77. Carpenter, *Envy*, 279–84; Snowman, *Hitler Émigrés*, 299; *The Archive Hour: The Theatre of the Absurd*, BBC Radio Four, 3 May 2003.

78. N. Annan, *Our Age: The Generation that Made Post-War Britain* (London: Fontana, 1991), 3–19; McIntyre, interview.

79. Gallagher, interview.

80. Annan, *Our Age*, 11–12.

81. Heshel, 18 July 1975, BBC WAC R34/1491/2.

82. Review Board, 13 August 1975, BBC WAC.

83. Review Board, 18 November 1970, 28 April 1971, 7 May 1972, 8 November 1972, 20 December 1972, BBC WAC.

84. Review Board, 18 November 1970, 28 April 1971, 7 May 1972, 8 November 1972, 20 December 1972, 3 January 1973, 14 March 1973, 12 December 1973, 22 May 1974, 20 November 1974, 18 December 1974, 8 January 1975, 13 August 1975, 19 November 1975, 8 November 1978, BBC WAC; Philip French, interview with author, London, 12 May 2005.

85. Review Board, 2 April 1975, 28 March 1973, 26 March 1975, BBC WAC.

86. BBC WAC: Review Board, 19 December 1973, 6 March 1974; Whitby, 6 July 1973, R101/314/1.

87. This sense of the audience existing in 'mutually exclusive auditory niches' is explored in S. Douglas, *Listening In: Radio and the American Imagination, from Amos 'n' Andy and Edward R. Murrow to Wolfman Jack and Howard Stern* (New York: Times, 1999), 256–7.

88. Review Board, 31 March 1971, 14 April 1971, 30 June 1971, 19 January 1972, BBC WAC.

89. *Times*, 3 July 1971; 'Radio Four Study', 3–14 October 1977, BBC WAC Management Registry File B7/2.

90. Fischer: 'Kaleidoscope', 21 May 1973, BBC WAC R51/1332/4.

91. *Times*, 3 July 1971.

CHAPTER 6.   MAC THE KNIFE

1. *Daily Mail*, 29 March 1976; *Evening Standard*, 17 May 1976; Ian McIntyre, interview with author, Radlett, 27 January 2003; BBC WAC Oral History Project: Howard Newby.

2. H. Carpenter, *The Envy of the World: Fifty Years of the BBC Third Programme and Radio 3* (London: Weidenfeld & Nicolson, 1996), 298–9; Ian McIntyre, interview with Hugh Chignell, 26 February 1999, Radlett; *New Society*, 20 October 1977.

3. *Observer*, 1 January 1978; BBC WAC Oral History Project: Newby.

4. McIntyre, interview.

5. McIntyre, 15 November 1976, BBC WAC Records Management Registry File B7-2; McIntyre, interview.

6. Ibid.; Carpenter, *Envy*, 300–2; McIntyre, 22 September 1978, BBC WAC Registry File B7-2; Review Board, 12 October 1977, BBC WAC.

7. McIntyre, 22 September 1978, BBC WAC Registry File B7-2.

8. McIntyre, interview.

9. BBC WAC: Review Board, 11 August, 22 September, 29 September 1976, 25 January 1978, 1 March 1978; Memos on Talks Fees, various, July–September 1976, R51/1332/2; McIntyre to Muggeridge, 15 November 1976, Registry File B7-2; Caroline Millington, interview with author, 3 August 2006.

10. McIntyre, interview.

11. BBC WAC: Review Board, 14 July 1976, 19 January 1977; McIntyre, 22 September 1978, Registry File B7-2; News and Current Affairs Meeting, 20 February 1976 and 2 April 1976, R3/60/1; J. Timpson, *Today and Yesterday* (London: George Allen & Unwin, 1976), 102.

12. BBC WAC: Chaney, 25 February 1976, R51/1297/3; Review Board, 7 April 1976, 5 May 1976, 28 September 1977; P. Donovan, *All Our Todays: Forty Years of Radio 4's 'Today' Programme* (London: Jonathan Cape, 1997), 60–3; L. Purves, *Radio: A True Love Story* (London: Hodder & Stoughton, 2002), 158–60.

13. McIntyre, 15 November 1976, BBC WAC Registry File B7-2.

14. Special Meeting on the Planning of Network Radio, 26 January 1977, BBC WAC R78/1389/1.

15. General Advisory Council Paper (GAC 512), *c.* January 1977, BBC WAC.

16. I. McIntyre, *The Expense of Glory: A Life of John Reith* (London: Harper Collins, 1993); BBC WAC: Review Board, 1 September and 15 September 1976; 'The Sequences—Their Home', 6 April 1978, R92/69/1; T. Burns, *The BBC: Public Institution and Private World* (London: Macmillan, 1977); H. Perkin, *The Rise of Professional Society: England since 1880* (London: Routledge, 1989); J. Bakewell and N. Garnham, *The New Priesthood: British Television Today* (London: Allen Lane, 1970).

17. Review Board, 7 January, 11 February, 26 May, 23 June, 7 July 1976, BBC WAC; Douglas Muggeridge: 'Current Affairs Coverage on Radio', February/March 1976, Papers of Michael Meredith Swann, Edinburgh University Library, File E340.

18. General Advisory Council, Minutes, 4 February 1976, BBC WAC R6/29/11.

19. *Times*, 28 and 30 September 1975; BBC WAC: Review Board, 19 March 1976; Oral History Project: Brian Wenham.

20. 'Future Thinking on the BBC's Problems and Possibilities', August–October 1977, Papers of Michael Meredith Swann, Edinburgh: Swann, File E442.

21. McIntyre to Muggeridge, 15 November 1976, BBC WAC Registry File B7-2.

22. Review Board, 19 February 1975, BBC WAC.

23. Review Board, 23 March 1977, BBC WAC; Cmnd. 6753: *Report of the Committee on the Future of Broadcasting* (Chairman: Lord Annan) (London: HMSO, March 1977), 84–7, 284–6, 330.

24. McIntyre, interview.

25. Ibid. McIntyre's version of events is supported by the minutes of a 'Radio Network Development Meeting' held on 3 December 1976, in which Muggeridge is quoted as follows: 'DPR [Director of Programmes, Radio] said he thought that there would be greater impact on the press and listeners if schedule changes were announced in one package' (BBC WAC R92/125/1).

26. McIntyre, 7 October 1976, BBC WAC Registry File B7-2.

27. Ibid.

28. BBC WAC Registry File B7-2: Head, Gramophone Programmes, 12 October 1976; Head of Drama, 12 October 1976; Network Editor, Radio, Manchester, 19 October 1976; Head of Current Affairs Magazine Programmes, 22 October 1976; Head of Current Affairs Group, 25 October 1976.

29. McIntyre: 'Radio 4: Saturday Mornings', 26 October 1976, BBC WAC Registry File B7-2.

30. McIntyre, interview.

31. *Sunday Times*, 12 December 1976.

32. Radio Network Direction Meeting, 18 March and 23 September 1977, BBC WAC R92/125/1.

33. *Sunday Times*, 17 July 1977; Review Board, 2 November 1977, BBC WAC.

34. Review Board 6 July 1977, BBC WAC; *Sunday Times*, 17 July 1977.

35. Review Board, 5 October 1977; *Guardian*, 18 September 1977; George Fischer, interview with author, London, 30 June 2003; McIntyre, interview.

36. BBC WAC: Radio Network Direction Meeting, 25 February and 4 March 1977, R92/125/1; Review Board, 15 June 1977, 13 July 1977, 1 March 1978; *Guardian*, 2 March 1977.

37. BBC WAC: 'Current Plans for American Election Results Programme', 11 October 1976, R51/1079/1; McIntyre, 13 October 1976, BBC WAC R51/1079/1; McIntyre, interview.

38. BBC WAC: Purslow, 22 October 1976, R51/1079/1; 'Note of Expenditure for US Election Results Programme', 1 November 1976, R51/1079/1; 'US Presidential Election Results Programme', 4 November 1976, R51/1079/1; Review Board, 3 November 1976.

39. Millington, 2 November 1976, BBC WAC Registry File B007-001.

40. McIntyre, interview.

41. Ibid.; Memo to Newby, 14 December 1976, BBC WAC Registry File E2/RD4-2.

42. McIntyre, interview.

43. 'Radio 4 Programme Changes', 22 April 1977, BBC WAC Registry File E2/RD4-2; *Times*, 4 July 1977.

44. Donovan, *All Our Todays*, 65.

45. Ibid.; Review Board, 11 May 1977, BBC WAC.

46. Review Board, 18 May, 1 June, 22 June, 14 December 1977, BBC WAC; *Guardian*, 29 December 1977; *Daily Telegraph*, 18 May 1977; *Evening Standard*, 19 May 1977; *Daily Telegraph*, 13 July 1977; Purves, *Radio*, 173; Donovan, *All Our Todays*, 64–5.

47. 'Programme Matters: Breakfast Time on Radio 4', 20 June 1977, BBC WAC Registry File B007-001.

48. Note to Curran, 24 June 1977, and Curran reply, 15 July 1977, BBC WAC Registry, File B7-2.

49. BBC WAC: Review Board, 1 June, 15 June, 6 July 1977; Memo to Newby, 12 July 1977, R108/51/1; *Guardian*, 7 July 1977; *Times*, 4 July 1977.

50. *Evening Standard*, 23 and 30 November 1976; *Financial Times*, 8 December 1976; Review Board, 24 November 1976, BBC WAC.

51. BBC WAC: Memo, 9 December 1976, Registry, File E2/RD4-2; Review Board, 8 December 1976; Radio Network Development Meeting, 10 December 1976, R92/125/1; *Sunday Times*, 12 December 1976; *Observer*, 12 December 1976; *Evening Standard*, 15 December 1976.

52. BBC WAC: Review Board, 27 April 1977; Board of Governors, 28 April 1977, Registry, File B7-2; *Sunday Times*, 17 July 1977; Caroline Millington, interview.

53. BBC WAC: Board of Management, 10 January 1977, Registry, File B007-001. Details of the internal investigations are contained in R108/51/1 and Review Board, 25 May 1977; McIntyre, interview.

54. McIntyre, interview; *Guardian*, 18 March 1977; Carpenter, *Envy*, 189–92; BBC WAC: Review Board, 23 March 1977; Radio Network Development Meeting, 22 July 1977, R92/125/1; Oral History Project: Martin Esslin.

55. BBC WAC Oral History Project: Howard Newby.

56. Board of Governors, 22 September 1977, BBC WAC Registry, File B7-2.

57. Letter to Swann, 27 August 1977, Papers of Michael Meredith Swann, Edinburgh University Library, File E443.

58. Muggeridge: 'Early Morning on R4', 5 August 1977, BBC WAC Registry File B7-2.

59. Newby, 21 September 1977, BBC WAC Registry File B7-2.

60. *Guardian*, 23 September 1977; Review Board, 5 October 1977 and 11 January 1978, BBC WAC.

61. BBC WAC: Review Board, 11 January 1978; Board of Governors, 20 October 1977, 17 November 1977, and 19 January 1978, and Board of Management, 24 October 1977, Registry, File B7-2; McIntyre, interview.

62. *Evening Standard*, 1 and 6 December 1977; Review Board, 7 December 1977, BBC WAC.

63. See, for example: Memo, 24 February 1978, BBC WAC Registry, File B7-2.

64. McIntyre, 1 March 1978, BBC WAC Registry, File B7-2.

65. *Daily Telegraph*, 21 December 1977; *Guardian*, 21 December and 22 December 1977.

66. Briggs, *Broadcasting*, v. 882, 902, 988–9; J. Grist, 'The Century before Yesterday: John Grist's BBC and Other Broadcasting Tales, Volume 2' (unpublished memoir), 121; McIntyre, interview; *Times*, 27 June and 1 July 1992; *Independent*, 29 June 1992, *Guardian*, 29 June 1992.

67. Briggs, *Broadcasting*, v. 468–9, 966–8; BBC WAC Oral History Project: Newby; Grist, 'The Century before Yesterday', 60; McIntyre, interview.

68. BBC WAC Registry, File B7-2: McIntyre, 19 September 1977; McIntyre, 16 November 1977; McIntyre, 19 April 1978; Memo to McIntyre, 18 April 1978.

69. BBC WAC Registry, File B7-2: Woon, 14 June 1978; Osborne: 'Towards 1500— Some Thoughts on Evening Current Affairs', 17 May 1978; Memo to McIntyre, 22 May 1978. See also Review Board, 12 July 1978.

70. BBC WAC Registry: McIntyre to Woon, 29 June 1978, File B7-2; Hatch to Muggeridge, 12 January 1977, File 10007679; *Daily Telegraph*, 20 June 1978 and 31 July 1978.

71. Review Board, 5 April, 12 April, 19 April, 26 April, 3 May, 17 May, 24 May, and 31 May 1978, BBC WAC; *Daily Telegraph*, 31 March, 17 April, 18 April 1978; *Guardian*, 5 and 7 April 1978.

72. Review Board, 12 April 1978, BBC WAC.

73. McIntyre, interview.

74. *Sunday Telegraph*, 6 August 1978.

75. Richard Wade, interview with author, Oxford, 12 December 2005.

76. *Guardian*, 10 December 1976; *Television Today*, 4 August 1977; *Sunday Telegraph*, 6 August 1978; *Sunday Telegraph*, 30 January 1977; *Times*, 16 July 1977; *Observer*, 10 July 1977.

77. Review Board, 7 September 1977, BBC WAC; Carpenter, *Envy*, 300–1.

78. P. Clarke, *Hope and Glory: Britain 1900–1990* (London: Penguin, 1996), 329–84; R. Hewison, *Culture and Consensus: England, Art and Politics since 1940* (London: Methuen, 1995), 206–9; T. Judt, *Postwar: A History of Europe since 1945* (London: Heinemann, 2005), 535–47; R. Colls, *Identity of England* (Oxford: Oxford University Press, 2002), 146–55; K. Middlemas, *Power, Competition and the State*, ii: *Threats to the Postwar Settlement, Britain 1961–1974* (Basingstoke: Macmillan, 1990), 294, 392; C. Barnett, *The Audit of War: The Illusion and Reality of Britain as a Great Nation* (London: Macmillan, 1986), 241; R. Sennett, *The Culture of the New Capitalism* (New Haven: Yale University Press, 2006), 15–82.

79. McIntyre, interview.

CHAPTER 7.   THEATRES OF THE AIR

1. W. H. Auden, 'Introduction', in L. MacNeice, *Persons from Porlock and Other Plays for Radio* (London: BBC, 1969), 9.

2. J. Tydeman, 'The Producer and Radio Drama—A Personal View', in P. Lewis (ed.), *Radio Drama* (London: Longman, 1981), 18.

3. John Tydeman, interview with author, London, 30 June 2006.

4. Ibid.

5. 'Television Service Annual Plan: Report to the Board', 14 January 1976, Board of Governors' Papers, 1976, BBC WAC R1/112/2.

6. Review Board, 21 March 1973, 26 June 1974, 26 March 1975, 30 April 1975, 13 October 1976, 11 October 1978, 20 February 1980, BBC WAC; *Daily Telegraph*, 17 February 1975; Observer, 10 July 1977; B. Took, *Laughter in the Air: An Informal History of British Radio Comedy* (London: BBC, 1981), 160, 166.

7. BBC WAC: Whitby, 2 July 1973, R34/1470; Report on *Home to Roost*, 1 November 1973, R34/1470; Whitby, 30 October 1974, R34/1470; Review Board, 28 August, 11 September, 25 September 1974, 13 August 1975.

8. Review Board, 2 June 1976, BBC WAC.

9. 'Light Entertainment: Television and Radio': General Advisory Council Paper (GAC 379), *c.* October/November 1972, BBC WAC.

10. Review Board, 2 June 1976, BBC WAC.

11. Review Board discussed on more than one occasion how 'the hard core' of those who enjoyed what was called 'Monty Python kind of humour' were now thought likely to be Radio One listeners. There was speculation that *I'm Sorry I'll Read That Again*, 'might well move there in the future' at Review Board, 23 May 1973 and 2 January 1974, BBC WAC.

12. Review Board, 5 December 1979, BBC WAC.

13. On *Radio Burps* see: Review Board, 11 May 1977, BBC WAC, and *Daily Telegraph*, 18 May 1977. On *The Spam Fritter Man*, see: Review Board, 14 June 1978, 19 July 1978, 16 August 1978, BBC WAC, and P. Donovan, *The Radio Companion* (London: Grafton, 1992), 82. For general criticism, see: *Television Today*, 4 August 1977, 29 September 1977, and *Observer*, 10 July 1977.

14. Review Board, 12 October 1977, BBC WAC.

15. Review Board, 26 June 1974, 13 October 1976, 11 October 1978, BBC WAC.

16. The 'chaps with cravats' description has been attributed to Geoffrey Perkins: N. Webb, *Wish You Were Here: The Official Biography of Douglas Adams* (London: Headline, 2004), 79, 107.

17. Took, *Laughter*, 169.

18. Ibid. 169–77; Webb, *Wish You Were Here*, 69, 87, 95–6; Italia Prize, 1979, BBC WAC R92/59/2; D. Adams, *The Hitchhiker's Guide to the Galaxy: The Original Radio Scripts*, updated edn. (London: Pan, 2003).

19. Review Board, 20 December 1978, 11 April 1979, 21 November 1979, BBC WAC; Took, *Laughter*, 175.

20. *Daily Telegraph*, 28 February 1978; Took, *Laughter*, 169–77; M. Coward, *The Pocket Essential Classic Radio Comedy* (Harpenden: Pocket Essentials, 2003), 72–9; Review Board, 14 September 1977, 5 October 1977, 28 March 1979, 15 August 1979, 12 December 1979, BBC WAC.

21. Review Board, 11 October 1978, 17 October 1979, 23 April 1980, 30 April 1980, 16 July 1980, BBC WAC. For details of the Jameson case, see Donovan, *Radio Companion*, 141–2.

22. Coward, *Radio Comedy*, 73; Took, *Laughter*, 177–80; Webb, *Wish You Were Here*, 107.

23. Review Board, 15 September 1976, 22 December 1976, 5 January 1977, 24 August 1977, 4 January 1978, 11 January 1978, 18 January 1978, 8 February 1978, BBC WAC.

24. Coward, *Radio Comedy*, 73.

25. Ibid. 74; Review Board, 5 November 1980, 19 November 1980, BBC WAC.

26. Webb, *Wish You Were Here*, 88. See also: N. Gaiman, *Don't Panic: Douglas Adams and The Hitchhiker's Guide to the Galaxy* (London: Titan, 2003); M. J. Simpson, *Hitchhiker: A Biography of Douglas Adams* (London: Hodder & Stoughton, 2003).

27. Simon Brett, 'Hitchhiker Memories': www.bbc.co.uk/radio4/hitchhikers, (accessed 27.9.05); Webb, *Wish You Were Here*, 108–9.

28. On science fiction at the BBC, see: D. Briscoe and R. Curtis-Bramwell, *The BBC Radiophonic Workshop: The First 25 Years* (London: BBC, 1983), 146; D. Wade, 'British Radio Drama since 1960', in J. Drakakis (ed.), *British Radio Drama*

(Cambridge: Cambridge University Press, 1981), 241; L. Cooke, *British Television Drama: A History* (London: BFI, 2003), 60–3; Simpson, *Hitchhiker*, 84; Gaiman, *Don't Panic*, 24; Webb, *Wish You Were Here*, 98; Tydeman, 'The Producer and Radio Drama', 18–25; *Television Today*, 29 September 1977; *Times*, 26 May 1973; Review Board, 18 May 1977, 10 January 1979, 21 November 1979, BBC WAC.

29. Review Board, 23 January 1980, BBC WAC.

30. 'Introduction', in Adams, *Scripts*; Webb, *Wish You Were Here*, 169; Gaiman, *Don't Panic*, 33.

31. Briscoe and Curtis-Bramwell, *Radiophonic*, 141–3.

32. Perkins, 'Introduction to the First Edition', in Adams, *Scripts*. For further details of the production process, see Gaiman, *Don't Panic*, 33–5; Webb, *Wish You Were Here*, 129–32, 168–9; Simpson, *Hitchhiker's*, 108–11.

33. Gaiman, *Don't Panic*, 36.

34. Review Board, 22 March 1978, BBC WAC.

35. Quoted in Gaiman, *Don't Panic*, 37.

36. 'Radio Four Programmes', 16 May 1978, BBC WAC Registry File B7-2; Webb, *Wish You Were Here*, 79.

37. Gaiman, *Don't Panic*, 59–60; Review Board, 28 June 1978, BBC WAC; BBC Radio Four Online: www.bbc.co.uk/radio4/hitchhikers (accessed 27.9.05); Took, *Laughter*, 181; Webb, *Wish You Were Here*, 156.

38. I. Nadel, *Double Act: A Life of Tom Stoppard* (London: Methuen, 2002), 88, 124–7, 248. Stoppard also received encouragement from Patrick Dromgoole, a BBC producer based in Bristol.

39. J. Lahr, *Prick up Your Ears: The Biography of Joe Orton* (London: Bloomsbury, 2002), 128, 144.

40. G. Murdock, 'Organising the Imagination: Sociological Perspectives on Radio Drama', in P. Lewis (ed.), *Radio Drama* (London: Longman, 1981); Review Board, 8 July 1970, 4 November 1970, 5 March 1975, BBC WAC; R. Heppenstall, *Portrait of the Artist as a Professional Man* (London: Peter Owen, 1969); Wade, 'British Radio Drama since 1960'; see also H. P. Priessnitz, 'British Radio Drama: A Survey', in P. Lewis (ed.), *Radio Drama* (London: Longman, 1981), 28–9.

41. Meeting of the EBU Radio Programme Committee Meeting of Drama Experts, Basle, 6–7 December 1973, BBC WAC R34/1312/2. See also: V. M. Madsen, 'Radio and the Documentary Imagination: Thirty Years of Experiment, Innovation and Revelation', *The Radio Journal: International Studies in Broadcast and Audio Media*, 3/3 (2006), 189–98; D. Hendy, 'Reality Radio: The Documentary', in A. Crisell (ed.), *More than a Music Box: Radio Cultures and Communities in a Multi-Media World* (London: Berghahn, 2004).

42. Cooke, *Television Drama*, 61–79, 92–5.

43. Briscoe and Curtis-Bramwell, *Radiophonic*, 12, 18–37; M. Chanan, *Repeated Takes: A Short History of Recording and its Effects on Music* (London: Verso, 1995), 140–2. See also M. Shingler, 'Some Recurring Features of European Avant-Garde Radio', *Journal of Radio Studies*, 7/1 (2000), 196–212.

44. Michael Mason left a particularly rich and informative corpus of programme plans during his career at the BBC. This account is drawn from the following in BBC WAC: Note on Michael Mason (undated), R34/1382/1; 'Finnegan's Rus', 7 November 1966,

R51/1265/1; Mason, 15 January 1971, R51/1265/1; Bridson, 12 July 1968, R51/1265/1; Gillard, 1 April 1968, R51/1265/1; 'A History of the British People: Project for a Major Venture in Audio', 9 March 1970, R34/1489/1; Review Board, 16 April 1980; Reid: 'Technical Developments', 6 September 1978, R92/69/1; Michael Mason, interview with author, Farnham, 4 June 2003; *Listener*, 18 November 1971.

45. D. Gardiner, *Stereo and Hi-Fi as a Pastime* (London: Souvenir Press, 1959), 17–18, 92–6, 104. See also B. Winston, *Media, Technology and Society: A History from the Telegraph to the Internet* (London: Routledge, 1998), 134.

46. J. Thomas, 'A History of the BBC Features Department, 1924–1964', unpublished D.Phil. thesis (Oxford, 1993), 314–15, 384; *Guardian*, 2 September 1966.

47. BBC WAC: Reid: 'Technical Developments', 7 September 1978, R92/69/1; Radio Network Direction Meeting, 5 November 1976, R92/125/1; Review Board, 14 December 1977.

48. BBC WAC: European Broadcasting Union Radio Programme Committee Meeting of Drama Experts, Basle, 6–7 December 1973, R34/1312/2; Review Board, 26 June 1974, 10 July 1974; Radio Network Development Meeting, 12 July 1974, R92/124/1.

49. *Guardian*, 24 November 1978; Review Board, 22 November 1978 and 10 January 1979, BBC WAC.

50. Tydeman, 'The Producer', 19–26; Briscoe and Curtis-Bramwell, *Radiophonic*, 41.

51. Review Board, 14 March 1979, BBC WAC.

52. *Guardian*, 2 September 1966; Review Board, 9 February 1977, BBC WAC R3/120/1.

53. J. Raban, 'Icon or Symbol: The Writer and the "Medium"', in P. Lewis (ed.), *Radio Drama* (London: Longman, 1981), 82–3.

54. Ibid. 79–84.

55. The producer was quoted by Philip French: interview with author, London, 12 May 2005. See also Tydeman, 'The Producer', 27.

56. Review Board, 8 May 1974, 29 May 1974, 18 February 1976, 24 March 1976, 3 October 1979, 25 June 1980, 15 October 1980, BBC WAC.

57. R. McKibbin, *Classes and Cultures: England 1918–1951* (Oxford: Oxford University Press, 1998), 502–3.

58. R. Giddings, and K. Selby, *The Classic Serial on Television and Radio* (Basingstoke: Palgrave, 2001), 9–27; Heppenstall, *Portrait*, 26–7.

59. Giddings and Selby, *Classic Serial*, 9–12, 51; C. Swift, 'A Proteus at the Beeb: Acting with BBC Radio Rep', *Theatre Quarterly*, 4/13 (1974), 12; Review Board, 25 February 1976, BBC WAC; Tydeman, interview.

60. Cooke, *Television Drama*, 83–113; Giddings and Selby, *Classic Serial*, 28–57; P. Mandler, 'Two Cultures—One—or Many?', in K. Burk (ed.), *The British Isles since 1945* (Oxford: Oxford University Press, 2003), 146–8.

61. J. Sutherland, *Offensive Literature: Decensorship in Britain, 1960–1982* (London: Junction Books, 1982) 85; R. Stevenson, *The Oxford English Literary History*, xii: *1960–2000: The Last of England?* (Oxford: Oxford University Press, 2004), 299–345; D. Watt, '"The Maker and the Tool": Charles Parker, Documentary Performance, and the Search for a Popular Culture', *New Theatre Quarterly*, 19/1 (2003), 41–66; P. Long, 'British Radio and the Politics of Culture in Post-war

Britain: The Work of Charles Parker', *The Radio Journal: International Studies in Broadcast and Audio Media*, 2/3 (2004), 131–52; Cooke, *Television Drama*, 92–8.

62. Ian McIntyre, interview with author, Radlett, 27 January 2003.

63. Quoted in H. Carpenter, *The Envy of the World: Fifty Years of the BBC Third Programme and Radio 3* (London: Weidenfeld & Nicolson, 1996), 300–1; BBC WAC: Review Board, 14 February 1979; Tydeman to Mason: 'New Writing', undated (*c.* September 1978), R92/69/1.

64. Tydeman, interview; *Guardian*, 22 May 1967; BBC WAC: Review Board, 28 January 1970, 26 April 1972, 14 January 1973, 13 March 1974, 22 May 1974, 20 August 1975; Esslin, 18 January 1971, R34/1312/2.

65. Gillian Reynolds quoted in *Voices in the Air*, BBC Radio 4, British Library Sound Archive, B5555/10.

66. Cooke, *Television Drama*, provides an account of the development of styles since the War. For critical comments on radio acting see: *Spectator*, 1 October 1965; *Daily Telegraph*, 19 June 1974; L. Sieveking, *The Stuff of Radio* (London: Cassell & Co. Ltd.), 86; Review Board, 4 August 1976, 6 July 1977, BBC WAC.

67. Quoted in Wade, 'British Radio Drama since 1960', 229; Review Board, 7 June 1978, BBC WAC.

68. *Guardian*, 20 July 1979. For discussions of 'middlebrow' culture see: D. Cannadine, *Class in Britain* (New Haven: Yale University Press, 1998); J. Carey, *The Intellectuals and the Masses: Pride and Prejudice among the Literary Intelligentsia, 1880–1939* (London: Faber & Faber, 1992); N. Humble, *The Feminine Middlebrow Novel 1920s to 1950s* (Oxford: Oxford University Press, 2001); and D. Hendy, 'Speaking to Middle England: Radio Four and Its Listeners', in J. Aitchison and D. M. Lewis (eds.), *New Media Language* (London: Routledge, 2003).

69. *Guardian*, 5 September 1970; Wade, 'British Radio Drama since 1960', 222.

70. Review Board, 7 January and 10 November 1976, BBC WAC.

71. On *The Archers*, see in particular: N. Painting, *Forever Ambridge: Thirty Years of The Archers*, rev. edn. (London: Michael Joseph, 1980) and W. Smethurst, *The Archers: The History of Radio's Most Famous Programme* (London: Michael O'Mara, 1997). Some useful plot summaries are contained in V. Whitburn, *The Archers: The Official Inside Story* (London: Virgin, 1996) and J. Toye, *The Archers 1968–1986: Looking for Love* (London: BBC, 1999).

72. Review Board, 10 November 1976, BBC WAC; Smethurst, *Archers*, 137–40; Whitburn, *Archers*, 171–2.

73. Review Board, 10 November 1976, BBC WAC.

74. Head of Audience Research, 14 June 1971, BBC WAC R78/2698/1; Painting, *Forever Ambridge*, 198.

75. A. Howkins, *The Death of Rural England: A Social History of the Countryside since 1900* (London: Routledge, 2003), 151–84. See also: J. Burchardt, *Paradise Lost: Rural Idyll and Social Change since 1800* (London: Tauris, 2002) and D. Matless, *Landscape and Englishness* (London: Reaktion, 1998).

76. BBC WAC: Review Board, 30 October 1974, 18 February 1976; 'The Archers and the Agricultural Community', 18 May 1976, R78/2698/1; *Daily Telegraph*, 23 August 1971; Painting, *Forever Ambridge*, 218; Smethurst, *Archers*, 137–8; Whitburn, *Archers*, 115, 138.

77. Painting, *Forever Ambridge*, 268, 274.
78. Review Board, 1 September 1976, BBC WAC; Smethurst, *Archers*, 148, 158; Painting, *Forever Ambridge*, 250, 288; Whitburn, *Archers*, 135–6, 169–71; *New Musical Express*, 1 March 1980; Smethurst, *Archers*, 173.
79. Smethurst, *Archers*, 161.
80. Review Board, 14 January 1976, 18 February 1976, 17 March 1976, 22 December 1976, 23 August 1978, 6 September 1978, 13 September 1978, 8 December 1978, BBC WAC; *Daily Telegraph*, 14 January 1976; Painting, *Forever Ambridge*, 268; Whitburn, *Archers*, 146.
81. Smethurst, *Archers*, 156. See also: Whitburn, *Archers*, 72–114; Painting, *Forever Ambridge*, 268.
82. *Guardian*, 19 November 1982.
83. Review Board, 10 November 1976, 20 September 1978, 11 June 1980, 7 January 1981, BBC WAC; *Times*, 4 November 1980; Smethurst, *Archers*, 190–3, 198, 217; Murdock, 'Organising the Imagination', 158–9; Whitburn, *Archers*, 154.
84. BBC WAC: Radio Network Development Meeting, 28 May 1976, R92/125/1; Review Board, 8 December 1976, 16 February 1977; *Daily Telegraph*, 10 November 1976; *Sunday Telegraph* and *Observer*, 13 February 1977.
85. Review Board, 14 January 1981, 11 March 1981, BBC WAC.
86. Wade, in *Voices in the Air*, BBC Radio Four.
87. Review Board, 20 January 1971, BBC WAC; *Evening News*, 3 June 1974.
88. Cologne meeting on European radio drama, Minutes, 25 January 1971, BBC WAC R34/1312/2; Cooke, *Television Drama*, 68; Rodger, *Radio Drama*, 140.
89. Painting, *Forever Ambridge*, 257.
90. Review Board, 11 February 1976, 6 July 1977, 7 June 1978, 27 June 1979, 4 July 1979, 18 July 1979, 2 July 1980, 23 July 1980, BBC WAC.
91. Review Board, 11 February 1976, 6 July 1977, BBC WAC.
92. Painting, *Forever Ambridge*, 257.
93. Review Board, 4 October 1978, BBC WAC; Tydeman, 'The Producer', 27.
94. Bradley: 'The Regional Drama Producer', 13 August 1978, BBC WAC R92/69/1.
95. Review Board, 20 September 1978, BBC WAC; Tydeman, 'The Producer', 15; Swift, 'Proteus', 5–13.
96. BBC WAC: Review Board, 2 June 1971, 5 and 12 July 1972, 9 January 1974, 24 July 1974, 2 October 1974, 5 November 1974; Imison: 'Drama Department—International Collaboration', 27 September 1978, R92/69/1; *Guardian*, 5 September 1970; *Times* and *Daily Telegraph*, 29 September 1982; Wade, 'Radio Drama', 219–23.
97. BBC WAC: Review Board, 22 November 1978, 23 and 30 May 1979, 23 January 1980, 22 October 1980, 10 December 1980; Acting Script Editor: 'Material on Radio Drama Plans for the General Advisory Council', 23 August 1978, R92/69/1; Memo to Mason, undated (*c.* August 1978), R92/69/1; 'Future of Radio', 11 August 1978, R92/69/1; Wade, 'Radio Drama', 222.
98. Review Board, 23 January 1980, BBC WAC.
99. Imison: 'The Use of Language in Radio Drama, with Special Reference to Radio 3', 31 July 1980, BBC WAC R78/2640/1.

100. *Daily Telegraph*, 30 May 1981; *New Statesman*, 27 August 1982; Nadel, *Tom Stoppard*, 124; Memo to Mason, 23 August 1978, R92/69/1.
101. *Daily Telegraph*, 30 May 1981.
102. Raban, 'Icon or Symbol', 86–9.
103. BBC WAC: 'The Regional Drama Producer', 13 August 1978, R92/69/1; 'BBC Support for the Arts', General Advisory Council Paper (GAC 290), 26 September 1967; 'Future of Radio', 11 August 1978, R92/69/1; 'Material on Radio Drama Plans for the General Advisory Council', 23 August 1978, R92/69/1; 'Afternoon Theatre Policy', 25 August 1978, R92/69/1; 'Parents and Children and Morning Story', Board Report, 16 March 1970, R51/1332/5; Review Board, 4 December 1974, 22 November 1978, 23 May 1979, 30 May 1979, 23 January 1980, 22 October 1980, 10 December 1980; Cologne meeting on European radio drama, Minutes, 25 January 1971, R34/1312/2; *Times*, 30 January 1964, Tydeman, 'The Producer', 16–18; Wade, 'Radio Drama', 220–2.
104. Review Board, 5 July 1978; F. Gray, 'The Nature of Radio Drama', in P. Lewis (ed.), *Radio Drama* (London: Longman, 1981); J. Drakakis, 'Introduction', in J. Drakakis (ed.), *British Radio Drama* (Cambridge: Cambridge University Press, 1981), 18.
105. Review Board, 17 October 1979, BBC WAC; Wade, 'Radio Drama', 222.
106. Review Board, 16 January 1980, BBC WAC; *The Reunion: Not the Nine o'Clock News*, BBC Radio Four, 31 July 2005.
107. Donovan, *Radio Companion*, 283.
108. 'Afternoon Theatre', 11 August 1978, BBC WAC R92/69/1.
109. Review Board, 22 February 1978, BBC WAC; Priessnitz, 'British Radio Drama', 30–3; Murdock, 'Organising the Imagination', 143–4; P. Lewis, 'Radio Drama and English Literature', in P. Lewis (ed.), *Radio Drama* (London: Longman, 1981), 174; Wade, 'Radio Drama', 219.
110. BBC WAC: Minutes of the European Broadcasting Union Radio Programme Committee Meeting of Drama Experts, Basle, 6–7 December 1973, R34/1312/2; Esslin: 'Quality of Output', 12 October 1976, Registry File B7-2; '*Saturday Night Theatre* and *The Monday Play*', undated memo (*c.* August 1978), R92/69/1; 'Future of Radio', 11 August 1978, R92/69/1; 'Afternoon Theatre', 25 August 1978, R92/69/1; *Daily Telegraph*, 22 March 1970.
111. Tydeman, 'The Producer', 13; Minutes of the meeting of the EBU Radio Programme Committee Meeting of Drama Experts, Basle, 6–7 December 1973, BBC WAC R34/1312/2.
112. Stevenson, *Oxford English Literary History*, 348–53.
113. Wade, 'Radio Drama', 222.
114. Minutes of the meeting of the EBU Radio Programme Committee Meeting of Drama Experts, Basle, 6–7 December 1973, BBC WAC R34/1312/2.
115. Wade, 'Radio Drama', 236–7.
116. *Guardian*, 10 December 1982; BBC WAC: 'Afternoon Theatre Policy', 25 August 1978, R92/69/1; Sims, 16 September 1982, R78/2062/1.
117. 'Afternoon Theatre Policy', 25 August 1978, BBC WAC R92/69/1; Priessnitz, 'British Radio Drama', 39–40; D. A. Low, 'Telling the Story: Susan Hill and Dorothy L. Sayers', in J. Drakakis (ed.), *British Radio Drama* (Cambridge: Cambridge University Press, 1981).

118. Quoted in A. Moncrieff, *Messages to the Future: The Story of the BBC Time Capsule* (London: Futura, 1984), 118–21.

119. Stevenson, *Oxford English Literary History*, 325, 359–60; R. Hewison, *Culture and Consensus: England, Art and Politics since 1940* (London: Methuen, 1995), 178.

120. Meeting of the EBU Radio Programme Committee Meeting of Drama Experts, Basle, 6–7 December 1973, BBC WAC R34/1312/2; Wade, 'Radio Drama', 222, 239–44.

CHAPTER 8.   CLOSE-UP AND PERSONAL

1. T. Vernon, *Fat Man on a Bicycle: A Discovery of France by Tom Vernon* (London: Michael Joseph, 1981), 17–18.

2. *New Society*, 22 August 1983.

3. V. M. Madsen, 'Radio and the Documentary Imagination: Thirty Years of Experiment, Innovation and Revelation', *The Radio Journal: International Studies in Broadcast and Audio Media*, 3/3 (2006), 189, 193.

4. Gray, 11 October 1966, BBC WAC R34/1550.

5. D. Jones, *Microphones and Muddy Boots: A Journey into Natural History Broadcasting* (London: David & Charles, 1987), 43, 49–50, 100–3; *Oil Rig*, British Library Sound Archive, P1136–1137BW; BBC WAC: Italia Prize 1977, Oil Rig, R92/57/2; Review Board, 9, 16, and 23 February 1977.

6. *The Reunion*, BBC Radio Four, 16 April 2006; *Radio Times*, 12–18 October 1974, 17–19.

7. T. Wolfe, *The New Journalism* (London: Picador, 1975), 17, 31–5, 47, 60.

8. Plowright, 18 September 1978, BBC WAC R92/69/1; J. Thomas, 'A History of the BBC Features Department, 1924–1964', unpublished D.Phil. thesis (Oxford, 1993), 417–25.

9. Review Board, 18 July 1979, BBC WAC.

10. T. Vernon, *Fat Man on a Roman Road* (London: Michael Joseph, 1983), 9; Vernon, *Bicycle*, 9.

11. P. Donovan, *The Radio Companion* (London: Grafton, 1992), 111.

12. R. Gosling, *Personal Copy: A Memoir of the Sixties* (London: Faber & Faber, 1980), 193.

13. Review Board, 19 December 1973, BBC WAC.

14. T. Wolfe, 'The Me Decade and the Third Great Awakening', in T. Wolfe, *The Purple Decades* (London: Jonathan Cape, 1983), 265–93.

15. D. Bell, *The Coming of Post-Industrial Society: A Venture in Social Forecasting* (London: Heinemann, 1974).

16. C. Lasch, *The Culture of Narcissism: American Life in an Age of Diminishing Expectations* (New York: W. W. Norton & Co., 1978). See also T. Judt, *Postwar: A History of Europe since 1945* (London: Heinemann, 2005), 477–9.

17. J. Harris, 'Tradition and Transformation: Society and Civil Society in Britain, 1945–2001', in K. Burk (ed.), *The British Isles since 1945* (Oxford: Oxford University Press, 2003); M. Hilton, *Consumerism in Twentieth Century Britain: The Search for a Historical Movement* (Cambridge: Cambridge University Press,

2003); R. McKibbin, *Classes and Cultures: England 1918–1951* (Oxford: Oxford University Press, 1998), 196–8.

18. J. Black, *Britain since the Seventies: Politics and Society in the Consumer Age* (London: Reaktion Books, 2004), 11–49.
19. Bonarjee, 9 February 1970, BBC WAC R51/1078/1.
20. Hilton, *Consumerism*, 187.
21. See: W. Knowles and K. Evans (eds.), *The Woman's Hour Book* (London: Sidgwick & Jackson and BBC, 1981); M. Lee (ed.), *Woman's Hour: A Selection* (London: BBC, 1967).
22. 'The People's Activities and Their Use of Time', 1974–5, and 'Daily Life in the 1980s', 1984, BBC WAC.
23. The description of *Kaleidoscope* as a 'consumer's guide' belonged to Martin Esslin. See: Review Board, 12 February 1975 and 16 March 1977, BBC WAC.
24. Wolfe, *New Journalism*, 47.
25. Wolfe, *The Purple Decades*, 266.
26. P. Mandler, 'Two Cultures—One—or Many?' in K. Burk (ed.), *The British Isles since 1945* (Oxford: Oxford University Press, 2003), 137.
27. Review Board, 15 July 1970, BBC WAC.
28. Whitby, 27 November 1969, BBC WAC R51/1078/1.
29. Heshel and Smith: 'Problem Programme Proposal', 26 March 1971, BBC WAC R108/50/1.
30. Wolfe, *The Purple Decades*, 266.
31. C. Michelmore and J. Metcalfe, *Two-Way Story* (London: Hamish Hamilton/Elm Tree Books, 1986), 156–64; *Guardian*, 29 January 2000.
32. BBC WAC: Heshel and Smith, 26 March 1971, R108/50/1; Whitby, 2 July 1971, R108/50/1.
33. BBC WAC: Review Board, 9 February 1972; Heshel, 30 October 1973, R51/1147/1; Transcript, undated, R108/50/1.
34. Michelmore and Metcalfe, *Two-Way Story*, 156–64.
35. Review Board, 24 November 1971, 9 February 1972, 6 December 1972, 7 November 1973, 11 June 1975, BBC WAC.
36. A. Hodges and D. Hutter, *With Downcast Gays* (London: Pomegranate Press, 1974); Review Board, 19 September 1973, BBC WAC.
37. Transcript, 26 January 1977, BBC WAC R108/50/1.
38. Ian McIntyre, interview with author, Radlett, Hertfordshire, 27 January 2003.
39. *Guardian*, 23 March 1977. See also: *Sunday Times*, 17 July 1977; *New Society*, 20 October 1977.
40. Review Board, 2 February 1977, BBC WAC.
41. McIntyre interview.
42. Memo to Muggeridge, 26 January 1977, BBC WAC R108/50/1.
43. BBC WAC: Memo to Muggeridge, 8 February 1977, R108/50/1; Review Board, 2 February 1977.
44. Memo to Muggeridge, 26 January 1977, BBC WAC R108/50/1.
45. BBC WAC: Muggeridge, 3 February 1977, R108/50/1; Board of Governors, 17 February 1977, R92/69/1.

46. Michelmore and Metcalfe, *Two-Way Story*, 156–64; Lawson Dick, 28 July 1976, BBC WAC R34/1470.

47. BBC WAC: 'Preliminary Results of Follow-up Questionnaire', 30 October 1973, R51/1147/1; Heshel, 4 April 1974, R51/1147/1; Newby, 14 October 1974, R51/1147/1; Memo to Newby, 17 October 1974, R51/1147/1; 'Participation in *If You Think You've Got Problems*', 17 October 1974, R51/1147/1; 'Outline Analysis of Letters Received in Second Season', undated (*c.*1972–3), R51/1147/1.

48. 'Radio Counselling', 4 November 1974, BBC WAC R51/1147/1.

49. Review Board, 19 September 1973, BBC WAC.

50. BBC WAC: Review Board, 9 February 1972, 6 December 1972, 1 May 1974; Whitby, 11 April 1974 and 22 October 1974, R51/1147/1.

51. BBC WAC: 'Radio Counselling', 4 November 1974, R51/1147/1; Review Board, 31 January 1973 and 11 July 1973; Heshel, 30 October 1973, R51/1147/1.

52. Memo, 2 October 1974, BBC WAC R51/1332/5.

53. 'Radio Counselling', 4 November 1974, BBC WAC R51/1147/1.

54. BBC WAC R51/1147/1: Memo, 18 May 1973; Memo to Newby, 12 June 1973; Whitby, 14 June 1973.

55. 'Quality of Output', 12 October 1976, BBC WAC Registry, File B7/2.

56. Review Board, 22 February 1978, BBC WAC.

57. R. Plomley, *Plomley's Pick of Desert Island Discs* (London: Weidenfeld & Nicolson, 1982), 187–8.

58. Review Board, 6 September 1978, 21 and 28 January 1981, BBC WAC.

59. Mass-Observation Archive, Sussex (hereafter 'MOA'): Directive 63, Summer 2001 (2) 'Reality TV and Radio' (Women, A–Z). Although the survey was conducted in 2001, I have referred to older respondents who were explicit about having listened to *Desert Island Discs* over many years.

60. Review Board, 8 September 1971, 13 November 1974, 3 September 1975, 17 August 1977, 6 September 1978; *Guardian*, 20 October 1983.

61. Board of Management, 18 November 1985, BBC WAC R78/2809/1.

62. S. Lawley, *Sue Lawley's Desert Island Discs* (London: Mandarin, 1991), 1–3.

63. Ibid.

64. A. Clare, *Psychiatry in Dissent: Controversial Issues in Thought and Practice* (London: Tavistock, 1976). A. Clare and S. Thompson, *Let's Talk about Me: A Critical Examination of the New Psychotherapies* (London: BBC, 1981).

65. *In the Psychiatrist's Chair*, BBC Radio Four Online: www.bbc.co.uk/ (accessed 17.10.05).

66. A. Clare, *In the Psychiatrist's Chair* (London: Mandarin, 1993), 21.

67. *In the Psychiatrist's Chair*, BBC Radio Four Online www.bbc.co.uk/ , (accessed 17.10.05).

68. Clare, *Psychiatrist's Chair*, 1–20.

69. C. Rayner, *How Did I Get Here from There?* (London: Virago, 2003).

70. Clare, *Psychiatrist's Chair*, 217–35.

71. *In the Psychiatrist's Chair*, BBC Radio Four Online www.bbc.co.uk/ , (accessed 17.10.05).

72. Clare, *Psychiatrist's Chair*, 40–1.

73. Ibid. 131–2.

74. W. H. Auden, 'The Guilty Vicarage', in *The Dyer's Hand and Other Essays* (London: Faber & Faber, 1963).
75. MOA: 'Reality TV and Radio'. The survey was conducted in 2001, but I have referred to older respondents who were explicit about having listened to—or chosen not to have listened to—*In the Psychiatrist's Chair* over a long period.
76. Clare, *Psychiatrist's Chair*, 220–1, 93.
77. MOA: 'Reality TV and Radio'.
78. T. Zeldin, *An Intimate History of Humanity* (London: Vintage, 1995), 236–53.
79. Harris, 'Tradition and Transformation', 110–17.
80. Review Board, 16 March 1977, BBC WAC.
81. Review Board,1 October 1977, 19 October 1977, 1 November 1978, BBC WAC.
82. Review Board, 18 July 1973, BBC WAC; J. Wilson, *Roger Cook's Checkpoint* (London: Ariel Books, 1983), 23–5.
83. Wilson, *Checkpoint*, 59.
84. Ibid. 44–50.
85. Ibid. 46.
86. Ibid. 26–30.
87. 'Holding the Balance': General Advisory Council Paper (GAC 637), November 1982, BBC WAC.
88. Wilson, *Checkpoint*, 40, 15–16, 29–31, 143–4; Review Board, 2 July 1975, BBC WAC.
89. BBC WAC: Review Board, 29 August 1973, 28 November 1973, 2 July 1975, 10 May 1978, 18 December 1980; Audience Research Report, *Checkpoint*, 14 December 1973, R51/1332/1; Memo: 'Checkpoint', 24 March 1975, Papers of Michael Meredith Swann, Edinburgh University Library, File E115.
90. Quoted in Wilson, *Checkpoint*, 143.
91. Quoted in Wilson. 146–8.
92. Hilton, *Consumerism*, 250.
93. 'The BBC and Its Audience: Accountability and Response', General Advisory Council Paper (GAC 670), January 1985, BBC WAC.
94. Ibid.
95. Review Board, 17 May 1978, BBC WAC.
96. Review Board, 19 July 1978, 13 September 1978, 11 October 1978, 15 November 1978, 4 April 1979, 25 June 1980, 10 December 1980, 1 April 1981, BBC WAC; *Daily Telegraph*, 10 November 1978.
97. *Times*, 18 March 1978.
98. 'The BBC and Its Audience: Accountability and Response', General Advisory Council Paper, January 1985, BBC WAC.
99. Review Board, 1 March 1978, BBC WAC.
100. Black, *Britain since the Seventies*, 35.
101. D. Cameron, *Good to Talk? Living and Working in a Communication Culture* (London: Sage, 2000).
102. 'Holding the Balance': General Advisory Council Paper, November 1982, BBC WAC.
103. See the analysis of speech on *Medicine Now*, *High Resolution*, and *Today* in N. Fairclough, *Media Discourse* (London: Arnold, 1995).

104. *Sunday Times*, 6 October 1985.
105. *Times*, 18 March 1978.
106. *Broadcast*, 2 September 1983.

CHAPTER 9.   UNDER SIEGE

1. Review Board, 29 November 1978, BBC WAC; *Guardian*, 14 August and 24 November 1978; *Daily Telegraph*, 28 September 1978; *Evening Standard*, 23 November 1978.
2. *Evening Standard*, 23 November 1978; *Times*, 24 November 1978.
3. BBC WAC: Review Board, 29 November, 20 December 1978, 3, 7, and 14 February 1979, 27 June 1979; Radio Programme Policy Committee, 28 June 1979, R1/144/1; *Times*, 30 November 1978; *Daily Telegraph*, 1 December 1979; *Guardian*, 27 February 1979 and 12 November 1979; *Evening Standard*, 27 February 1979 and 10 September 1979; *Sun*, 28 February 1979.
4. Review Board, 28 March 79, BBC WAC.
5. Review Board, 7 February 1979, BBC WAC. See also letters to the editor, *Guardian*, 9 March 1979.
6. Singer referred to the 'enormous volume' of complaints from listeners over the subject of frequencies: Radio Programme Policy Committee, 26 April 1979, BBC WAC R1/144/1. See also: *Guardian*, 14 August 1978; *Evening Standard*, 10 September 1979.
7. *Guardian*, 7 April and 14 August 1978; Review Board, 30 August 1978, BBC WAC.
8. BBC WAC: 'Background Note on Band II VHF', 3 April 1979, R92/70/1; 'The Future of Radio: an Advisory Opinion', 10 May 1979, R92/70/1.
9. McIntyre, 17 April 1978, BBC WAC Registry File B7-2.
10. BBC WAC: Review Board, 21 February 1979; Board of Management, 30 April 1979, R78/1170/1; Radio Programme Policy Committee, 26 April 1979, R1/144/1.
11. BBC WAC: 'Morning Sequence', 24 February 1978, Registry File B7-2; Review Board, 11 January 1978 and 15 February 1978.
12. 'The Future of "News" Broadcasting on Radio', 7 March 1978, BBC WAC Registry File B7-2.
13. Ibid.
14. Review Board, 17 May and 21 June 1978, BBC WAC; *Daily Telegraph*, 17 April 1978; *Guardian*, 9 September 1978.
15. BBC WAC Registry File B7-2: Managing Director of Radio's Management Meeting, 11 April 1978; 'Radio 4 Sequences', 14 June 1978; 'Proposed 5–6pm magazine programme', 18 April 1978; 'Radio Four wavelength changes', 17 May 1978; *Guardian*, 11 April 1978; *Daily Telegraph*, 20 June 1978.
16. BBC WAC: Review Board, 12 July 1978; Radio Programme Policy Committee, 28 June 1979, R1/144/1.
17. Woon, 10 and 17 May 1978, BBC WAC Registry File B7-2.
18. BBC WAC: 'Radio Finances', General Advisory Council Paper, December 1978, R92/69/1; Note by the Secretary, 22 January 1979, R78/1170/1.

19. BBC WAC: 'Radio Four Patronage and Share', 22 October 1982, R92/2/1; 'Audience Research', 10 September 1980, R78/1176/1; Review Board 31 May 1978, 18 October 1978, 25 October 1978, 1 November 1978, BBC WAC.
20. BBC WAC: Review Board, 14 March 1979; 'Radio Development Plans', 31 July 1979, R92/70/1.
21. Review Board, 14 June 1978, BBC WAC.
22. BBC WAC: Review Board, 31 May 1978, 7 June 1978, 14 June 1978, 19 July 1978, 31 January 1979; Radio Programme Policy Committee, 8 February 1979, R78/1170/1.
23. Review Board, 7 June 1978, BBC WAC.
24. 'Radio in the Late Eighties', 12 June 1979, BBC WAC R92/70/1.
25. BBC WAC: 'Draft Paper on Radio Programme Policy', 22 November 1978, R78/1170/1; 'Radio Programme Policy', General Advisory Council Paper (GAC 556), 7 February 1979; 'Radio Programme Policy', revised, 7 December 1978, and 'Summary of Questions for General Advisory Council', 30 November 1978, R78/1170/1; Board of Management, 18 December 1978, R78/1170/1; General Advisory Council, 7 February 1979, R78/1170/1; 'The Future of Radio: An Advisory Opinion', 10 May 1979, R92/70/1; Review Board, 18 October 1978, 22 November 1978, 14 February 1979, 18 April 1979, 28 May 1980; 'Radio Planning Group: Outline of Capital Investment Programme', 21 July 1982, R92/2/1.
26. BBC WAC: 'Draft Paper on Radio Programme Policy', 22 November 1978, R78/1170/1; 'Radio Programme Policy', General Advisory Council Paper, 7 February 1979; General Advisory Council, 7 February 1979, R78/1170/1.
27. Review Board, 27 September 1978, 4 October 1978, 29 November 1978, 6 December 1978, 4 April 1979, BBC WAC; BBC, *BBC Handbook 1980* (London: BBC, 1980), 1–5.
28. BBC WAC: Review Board, 21 March 1979 and 28 November 1979; Board of Management, 23 April 1979, R78/1170/1; Radio Programme Policy Committee, 26 April 1979, R1/144/1; *Guardian* and *Daily Telegraph*, 28 November 1979.
29. Board of Management, 23 April 1979, BBC WAC R78/1170/1.
30. John Tydeman, interview with author, London, 30 June 2006; BBC WAC: Review Board, 19 December 1979, 9 January 1980, 5 March 1980, 19 March 1980, 26 March 1980, 9 July 1980; Radio Programme Policy Committee, 24 January 1980, and note dated 17 January 1980, R78/1170/1; 'The £34 licence: Note by The Secretary', General Advisory Council Paper (GAC 581), 22 January 1980; *Evening Standard*, 24 March 1980.
31. Plans for rationalization can be traced in a long series of meetings and papers throughout 1979 and 1980, most of which are recorded in BBC WAC R92/2/1, R92/70/1, and R78/1170/1, and in Review Board, 31 January 1979, 21 March 1979. See also: 'Radio 1985–1995' and 'Directing the BBC's Journalism', Ditchley Conference, 21–23 March 1980, Papers of Michael Meredith Swann, Edinburgh University Library, Files E662 and E666.
32. BBC WAC: Board of Management, 9 April 1979, R78/1170/1; Managing Director, Radio's Management Meeting, 10 April 1979, R92/70/1; 'Broadcasting in the 90s', 14 May 1979, R92/70/1; 'A Three Channel Radio Service', 13 March 1980, R92/2/1.

33. BBC WAC: 'Radio Programme Policy: Further Study', 4 April 1979, R78/1170/1; Radio Programme Policy Committee, 26 April 1979, R1/144/1.

34. BBC WAC: Board of Management, 4 and 11 June 1979, R78/1170/1; Radio Programme Policy Committee, 28 June 1979, R1/144/1.

35. BBC WAC: Board of Management, 4 and 11 June 1979, R78/1170/1; Singer, 5 June 1979, R78/1170/1; 'The Future of Radio: An Advisory Opinion by the Future Policy Group', 7 June 1979, R78/1170/1; 'Town and Country Radio', 22 June 1979, R92/70/1.

36. 'Town and Country Radio', 22 June 1979, BBC WAC R92/70/1.

37. BBC WAC: Radio Programme Policy Committee, 26 April 1979 and 28 June 1979, R1/144/1; 'Town and Country Radio', 6 July 1979, R92/70/1; 'Radio Listening Patterns',17 July 1979, R92/70/1; Radio Management Meeting, 17 July 1979, R78/1170/1; Memo to Deputy Secretary, 20 July 1979, R78/1170/1; 'Radio's Development Plan: Listening Patterns', 6 September 1979, R78/1170/1; 'Radio's Development Plans: An Alternative Approach', 17 September 1979, R78/1170/1; 'Radio Two and Radio Four Regular Programmes: Regional Analysis', 16 June 1980, R78/1176/1.

38. 'Radio's Development Plans: An Alternative Approach', 17 September 1979, BBC WAC R78/1170/1.

39. BBC WAC: 'The Future of Radio: An Advisory Opinion', 10 May 1979, R92/70/1. Radio Programme Policy Committee, 26 April 1979 and 28 June 1979, R1/144/1.

40. 'Radio's Development Plans: An Alternative Approach', 17 September 1979, BBC WAC R78/1170/1.

41. Ibid.; BBC WAC: Starks, 19 September 1979, R78/1170/1; Singer, 20 September 1979, R78/1170/1; 'Radio Development Plans: A Look at the Options', 25 September 1979, R92/71/1; Manager, Radio Derby, 28 September 1979, R92/71/1; 'Note of a Weekend Conference Held at Lane End Conference Centre, High Wycombe, 28–30 September', 1979, R78/1170/1; Managing Director of Radio's Management Meeting, 2 October 1979, R78/1170/1.

42. Ibid.

43. BBC WAC: 'Radio Programme Policy: A Radio Management "Green Paper"', 26 October 1979, R78/1170/1; Singer, 8 November 1979, R78/1170/1; Radio Programme Policy Committee Paper, 6 December 1979, R78/1170/1; Radio Programme Policy Committee, 20 December 1979 and 24 January 1980, R1/144/1.

44. Monica Sims, interview with author, London, 10 February 2003; BBC WAC: 'Supplementary Note' on Radio Programme Policy, 17 January 1980, R78/1170/1; Radio Programme Policy Committee, 24 January 1980, R1/144/1; 'Radio 1985–1995', 21 February 1980, R78/1170/1; Special Meeting, 26 February 1980, R78/1170/1.

45. BBC WAC: Board of Management, 21 April 1980, R78/856/1; Singer, 1 and 13 May 1980, R78/856/1; 'Terms of Reference', 24 June 1980, R78/856/1; Radio Programme Policy Committee, 19 February 1981, R1/144/1; 'Report of the Radio Network Working Party', 16 January 1981, Private Papers of Monica Sims.

46. See, for example, the submission from the Radio Leicester Local Broadcasting Council, 21 August 1980, BBC WAC R78/1176/1.

47. BBC WAC: Memo to Future Policy Group, 6 June 1980, R78/1176/1; memo to Working Party, 10 June 1980, R78/1176/1.
48. Review Board, 13 June 1979, 21 January and April 1981, BBC WAC.
49. Review Board, 7 and 14 May 1980, BBC WAC.
50. BBC WAC: 'Network Development', 8 July 1980, R78/1176/1; Report on visit to Radio France, 28 July 1980, R78/1176/1.
51. Review Board, 6 August 1980, BBC WAC.
52. Report of the Radio Network Working Party, 16 January 1981, Private Papers of Monica Sims; Radio Programme Policy Committee, 19 February 1981, BBC WAC R1/144/1; *Times*, 28 February 1981.
53. *Economist*, 21 February 1981; *Financial Times*, 26 February 1981; *Sun*, 27 February 1981; *Daily Mail*, 9 March 1981; Review Board, 11 March 1981, 1 April 1981, BBC WAC.
54. *Daily Telegraph*, 9 July 1981 and 31 December 1981.
55. BBC WAC: Review Board, 1 April 1981; Radio Programme Policy Committee, 19 February 1981, R1/144/1.
56. Francis: 'Radio Network Working Party Report', 9 February 1981, BBC WAC R78/1176/1.
57. R. Harris, *Gotcha! The Media, the Government, and the Falklands Crisis* (London: Faber & Faber, 1983), 87. See also A. Milne, *DG: The Memoirs of a British Broadcaster* (London: Hodder & Stoughton, 1988), 86–94.
58. *Times*, 24 May 1982.
59. Mass-Observation Archive (hereafter 'MOA'), Sussex: Directive 5, 1982: The Falkland Islands Crisis 1982: Men, A–Z.
60. Monica Sims, interview; Richard Wade, interview with author, Oxford, 12 December 2005.
61. BBC WAC: 'White Paper', 27 October 1982, R78/2062/1; 'Radio: The Terrain Ahead', 15 April 1982, R78/2062/1; 'The Leeds Castle Weekend', 19 April 1982, R78/2062/1; Leeds Castle Conference, 7–9 May 1982, Minutes, R78/2062/1. See also S. Barnett and A. Curry, *The Battle for the BBC: A British Broadcasting Conspiracy* (London: Aurum Press, 1994), 75.
62. 'Radio Programme Strategy' (Revised), 8 October 1982, BBC WAC R78/2062/1.
63. BBC WAC: Singer, 3 November 1981, Registry File B7-2; 'Programme Strategy', 9 June 1982, R92/2/1.
64. BBC WAC: 'Radio Programme Strategy' (Revised), 8 October 1982, R78/2062/1; 'BBC Radio for the Nineties: A Preliminary Appraisal', 15 September 1982, R78/2062/1.
65. *Daily Telegraph*, 15/16 October 1982, 30 November 1982; *Times*, 16 October 1982 and 30 November 1982; *Guardian*, 19/23 October 1982, 30 November 1982; *Sunday Times*, 17/24 October 1982, 5 December 1982; *Daily Mail*, 16 October 1982; *Financial Times*, 30 November 1982; *Evening Standard*, 25/28 October 1982; *Yorkshire Post*, 26 October 1982; *Scotsman*, 23 October 1982; *Sun*, 18 October 1982; *Daily Mirror*, 18 October 1982; *Broadcast*, 18 October 1982; *Television Today*, 2 December 1982. See also 'Summary of Public Reactions to the BBC', General Advisory Council Paper (GAC 641), *c.* February 1983, BBC WAC.

66. BBC WAC: Chief Press and Publicity Officer, BBC, 1 December 1982, R92/2/1; News and Current Affairs Meeting, 19 October 1982, R78/2062/1.
67. BBC WAC: Board of Governors' Programme Policy Committee, 21 October 1982, R1/143/2; Statement by Board of Governors, 21 October 1982, R78/2062/1.
68. *Daily Mail* and *Guardian*, 22 October 1982.
69. *Guardian*, 23 October 1982, *Daily Star*, 23 October 1982, *Daily Mail*, 23 October 1982, *Daily Express*, 23 October 1982, *Sunday Times*, 24 October 1982; Letter from BBC Secretariat, 20 October 1982, BBC WAC R78/2062/1.
70. 'Radio Development: The Next Stage', 17 December 1982, BBC WAC R92/2/1; *Broadcast*, 17 January 1983.
71. Broadcasting Research, 22 October 1982, BBC WAC R92/2/1.
72. Review Board, 25 October 1978, BBC WAC.
73. Review Board, 1 November 1978, BBC WAC.
74. Sims: 'Public Service Radio', 23 June 1980, BBC WAC R78/1176/1.
75. Wade: 'BBC Radio for the Nineties: A Preliminary Appraisal', and Sims's addendum, 15–16 September 1982, BBC WAC R78/2062/1.
76. 'Network Radio: Age and Class Profiles', 25 June 1980, BBC WAC R78/1176/1; Monica Sims, interview.
77. 'Radio Networks: Age/Class Programme Deviations from Network Norms', 23 June 1980, BBC WAC R78/1176/1.
78. Ibid. 'Comment on Draft GAC Paper', 27 November 1978, BBC WAC R92/69/1.
79. 'Draft Paper on Radio Programme Policy', 28 November 1978, BBC WAC R92/69/1.
80. Ibid. 'On Breaking Compromises', March, Hearst to Director-General Designate, 8 April 1982, BBC WAC R78/2062/1.
81. 'Radio's Development Plan: Listening Patterns', 6 September 1979, BBC WAC R78/1170/1.
82. Note of a weekend conference, High Wycombe, 28–30 September 1979, BBC WAC R78/1170/1.
83. *Listener*, 3 February 1983.
84. 'On Breaking Compromises', March 1982, BBC WAC R78/2062/1.
85. BBC WAC: 'Radio in the Late Eighties', 12 June 1979, R92/70/1; Review Board, 25 April 1979; *Times*, 20 October 1981.
86. Review Board, 6 June 1979, BBC WAC.
87. Monica Sims, interview.
88. Review Board, 30 December 1970, 5 January 1972, 4 January 1978, 1 October 1980, BBC WAC.
89. 'Radio Four, PM and the Six O'Clock News', 28 October 1983, BBC WAC Registry File B7-2.
90. Monica Sims, interview; BBC WAC: Review Board, 12 August 1980; 'BBC Radio for the Nineties: A Preliminary Appraisal', and 12-page addendum, 15–16 September 1982, R78/2062/1.
91. Review Board, 12 April 1978, 26 April 1978, 17 May 1978, BBC WAC; *Daily Telegraph*, 17 April 1978.
92. BBC WAC: Review Board, 28 January 1981; McIntyre, 19 April 1978, Registry File B7-2; 'Attitudes to News and Current Affairs', 24 April 1978, Registry File B7-2.

93. MOA Sussex: Directive 5, 1982: The Falklands Crisis: Men, A–Z. For other public opinion research, see: D. E. Morrison and H. Tumber, *Journalists at War: The Dynamics of News Reporting during the Falklands Conflict* (London: Sage, 1988), 284–344; G. M. Dillon, 'Public Opinion and the Falklands Conflict', *Bailrigg Paper on International Security Number 7* (University of Lancaster, 1984). For media coverage of the Falklands War in general, see: Milne, *DG*, 89–93, and D. Mercer, G. Mungham, and K. Williams, *The Fog of War: The Media on the Battlefield* (London: Heinemann, 1987), 17–211.

94. Private Papers of Monica Sims.

95. 'BBC Radio for the Nineties: A Preliminary Appraisal', and 12-page addendum, 15–16 September 1982, BBC WAC R78/2062/1.

96. Monica Sims, private communication with author, 12 March 2003; BBC WAC: 12-page addendum to 'BBC Radio for the Nineties: A Preliminary Appraisal', 15–16 September 1982, R78/2062/1; 'Public Service Radio', 23 June 1980, R78/1176/1; Monica Sims, interview.

97. The words are from Richard Hoggart writing in the *Guardian*, 13 September 1982, and quoted in 12-page addendum to 'BBC Radio for the Nineties: A Preliminary Appraisal', 15–16 September 1982, BBC WAC R78/2062/1.

98. Ibid; *Times*, 20 October 1981; 'Note of a Weekend Conference', High Wycombe, 28–30 September, BBC WAC R78/1170/1.

99. *Guardian*, 3 April 1975; BBC WAC Oral History Project: Clare Lawson Dick; George Fischer, interview with author, London, 30 June 2003; Ian McIntyre, interview with author, Radlett, Hertfordshire, 27 January 2003; Sims, interview; David Hatch, interview with author, London, 5 February 2003; BBC WAC: 'Draft Paper on Programme Strategy', 22 November 1978, R78/1170/1; 'BBC Radio for the Nineties: A Preliminary Appraisal', and addendum, 15–16 September 1982, R78/2062/1; Review Board, 6 October 1976, 29 August 1979; *Sunday Times*, 24 October 1982; *International Herald Tribune*, 10 September 1991.

100. On gardens and Englishness, I have drawn on: R. Colls, *Identity of England* (Oxford: Oxford University Press, 2002), 9, 69–73, 204–18, 292; S. Schama, *Landscape and Memory* (London: Harper Collins, 1995), 5–7, 153–75, 523–4, 530–9; J. Brown, *Eminent Gardeners: Some People of Influence and Their Gardens 1880–1980* (London: Viking, 1990), 139–60; J. Brown, *The Pursuit of Paradise: A Social History of Gardens and Gardening* (London: Harper Collins, 1999), 224–8.

101. A. Gordon, 'The Country Cottage', in P. Abercrombie (ed.), *The Book of the Modern House: A Panoramic Survey of Contemporary Domestic Design* (London: Hodder & Stoughton, 1939), 26–35.

102. Colls, *Identity of England*, 7, 204–18; Schama, *Landscape*, 538.

103. BBC WAC Oral History Project: Lawson Dick.

104. Board of Governors' Programme Policy Committee, 21 October 1982, BBC WAC R1/143/2.

105. Ibid.

106. *New Standard*, 21 October 1982.

107. Letter, private papers of Monica Sims.

108. *Times*, 23 October 1982.

109. *New Standard*, 21 October 1982.
110. Ibid.

CHAPTER 10.   YEARS ZERO

1. The first two sections of this chapter draw widely on the following: J. Birt, *The Harder Path* (London: Time Warner, 2002); J. Curran and J. Seaton, *Power without Responsibility: The Press and Broadcasting in Britain*, 5th edn. (London: Routledge, 1997), 201–34; S. Barnett and A. Curry, *The Battle for the BBC: A British Broadcasting Conspiracy* (London: Aurum Press, 1994); P. Goodwin, *Television under the Tories: Broadcasting Policy 1979–1997* (London: BFI, 1998); C. Horrie and S. Clarke, *Fuzzy Monsters: Fear and Loathing at the BBC* (London: Heinemann, 1994); T. O'Malley, *Closedown: The BBC and Government Broadcasting Policy 1979–92* (London: Pluto Press, 1994); M. Leapman, *The Last Days of the Beeb* (London: Allen & Unwin, 1986); G. Born, *Uncertain Vision: Birt, Dyke and the Reinvention of the BBC* (London: Vintage, 2005); P. Clarke, *Hope and Glory: Britain 1900–1990* (London: Penguin, 1996), 367–88. The Thatcher quote is in Clarke, *Hope and Glory*, 379.
2. Birt, *Harder Path*, 255, 299–300; Curran and Seaton, *Power*, 21–212.
3. Birt, *Harder Path*, 339.
4. Protheroe's popular epithet in the BBC was 'The Colonel', which alluded both to his known military background and to his widely suspected links with the intelligence services and the security vetting of staff.
5. Birt, *Harder Path*, 333–7; Barnett and Currie, *Battle*, 56–72.
6. Goodwin, *Television*, 69; A. Crisell, *An Introductory History of British Broadcasting*, 2nd edn. (London: Routledge, 2002), 220–41; Barnett and Currie, *Battle*, 211; P. Scannell, 'Public Service Broadcasting: The History of a Concept', in A. Goodwin and G. Whannell (eds.), *Understanding Television* (London: Routledge, 1990), 22.
7. Barnett and Currie, *Battle*, 19; Curran and Seaton, *Power*, 216–17; Birt, *Harder Path*, 250.
8. Barnett and Currie, *Battle*, 26, 76, 98–9, 155.
9. Birt, *Harder Path*; L. Purves, *Radio: A True Love Story* (London: Hodder & Stoughton, 2002), 35.
10. Birt, *Harder Path*, 248–9, 256–60; Horrie and Clarke, *Fuzzy Monsters*, 96–121.
11. Horrie and Clarke, *Fuzzy Monsters*, 96–7; Birt, *Harder Path*, 380, 384.
12. Barnett and Currie, *Battle*, 143–4.
13. Horrie and Clarke, *Fuzzy Monsters*, 10, 243; S. MacGregor, *Woman of Today: An Autobiography* (London: Headline, 2002), 253.
14. Members of the 'Black Spot' committee included David Hatch, Michael Checkland, Geraint Stanley Jones, and Geoff Buck, the BBC's Director of Finance: see Barnett and Currie, *Battle*, 26–7.
15. These policies can be traced in numerous memos in BBC WAC Registry File B7-2 and E2/RD4, and R78/2062/1. See also Barnett and Currie, *Battle*, 23–4, 26–7, 108–9.
16. Birt, *Harder Path*, 323.

17. Birt, *Harder Path*, 323–7, 349; Barnett and Currie, *Battle,* 180–7; Curran and Seaton, *Power*, 225–31. The voluntary move towards a goal of 10 per cent independent production for Radio was an initiative of David Hatch.

18. Birt, *Harder Path*, 323; 'New BBC Production Structure', BBC News Release, 6 November 1996; J. Abramsky, *Bi-Media: A Strategy for Radio?* Lecture, 6 February 2002, Green College, Oxford University.

19. Michael Green, interview with author, London, 13 December 2005; John Tydeman, interview with author, 30 June 2006; MacGregor, *Woman of Today,* 255; Barnett and Currie, *Battle,* 187–9.

20. Green, interview; Tydeman, interview; Caroline Millington, interview with author, 3 August 2006; Abramsky, *Bi-Media*; MacGregor, *Woman of Today,* 255; Purves, *Love Story,* 258.

21. C. Paling, *The Silent Sentry* (London: Vintage, 2000), 141.

22. Ibid. 3–10, 38, 53, 91–2, 137, 205, 207–9.

23. Barnett and Currie, *Battle,* 180–96, 206–7; Curran and Seaton, *Power,* 226–32; Horrie and Clarke, *Fuzzy Monsters,* 283–4; Born, *Uncertain Visions,* 109.

24. BBC WAC: 'The Audience for BBC Radio Services', 27 June 1986, R78/2062/1; 'Radio 4 Listeners and Their Use of Services', 1989, R9/1014/1.

25. *Radio: Choices and Opportunities*, Green Paper, Cm 92 (London: HMSO, February 1987); BBC WAC: 'Sound Thinking for the Next Decade', 15 April 1986, R78/2062/1; 'BBC Radio: Prospects for the 1990s', General Advisory Council Paper (GAC 694), 1987; *Today*, 11 May 1986 and 5 January 1987; *Daily Star*, 26 February 1987; *Guardian*, 18 June 1990; Crisell, *Introductory History*, 247–9.

26. BBC WAC: Review Board, 12 August 1980; Submission to Radio Network Working Party, 7 October 1980, R78/1176/1; *Guardian*, 15 July 1993.

27. 'Radio Four: Qualitative Research', December 1987, BBC WAC R9/388/1.

28. Ibid.

29. Papers of Monica Sims; Radio Four: Wavelength change/Listeners letters, 1982, BBC WAC R78/1905/1.

30. See: R. King and J. Rayner, *The Middle Class*, 2nd edn. (London: Longman, 1981); P. Hutber, *The Decline and Fall of the Middle Class—and How It Can Fight Back* (London: Associated Business Programmes, 1976); R. King and N. Nugent (eds.), *Respectable Rebels: Middle Class Campaigns in Britain in the 1970s* (London: Hodder & Stoughton, 1979); M. Veldman, *Fantasy, The Bomb, and the Greening of Britain: Romantic Protest, 1945–1980* (Cambridge: Cambridge University Press, 1994); M. Savage, J. Barlow, P. Dickens, and F. Fielding, *Property, Bureaucracy and Culture: Middle-Class Formation in Contemporary Britain* (London: Routledge, 1992); T. Butler and M. Savage (eds.), *Social Change and the Middle Classes* (London: UCL Press, 1995).

31. Note, 1 March 1983, Papers of Monica Sims.

32. *Guardian*, 15 July 1993; Birt, *Harder Path*; 'Radio Four: Qualitative Research', December 1987, BBC WAC R9/388/1.

CHAPTER 11.   PROVOCATIONS

1. David Hatch, interview with author, London, 5 February 2003; Hatch, 2 November 1983, BBC WAC Registry File B007-001; *Broadcast*, 18 April 1983; *Daily Telegraph*, 12 December 1983.

2. *Observer*, 23 January 1983; G. Priestland, *Something Understood: An Autobiography* (London: Andre Deutsch, 1986), 284; Richard Wade, interview with author, Oxford, 12 December 2005.

3. Hatch, interview; BBC WAC Registry File B7-2: 'R4 Annual General Meeting, 5 December 1986'; Hatch to Departmental Heads, 6 June 1983; Hatch, 'Features', 14 June 1983.

4. Hatch: 'Your Help Please', 12 May 1983, BBC WAC Registry File B7-2.

5. Hatch, 2 November 1983, BBC WAC Registry File B007-001; Hatch, interview.

6. Sims wrote of the need to achieve 'excellence in our bread and butter programming as well as in our outstanding prestige production': 'Future of Radio "The Three Network Proposal"', 21 March 1980, BBC WAC R92/125/1; Review Board, 31 January 1979, BBC WAC; Monica Sims, interview with author, London, 10 February 2003; Wade, interview.

7. 'Note of a Weekend Conference', 28–30 September 1979, BBC WAC R78/1170/1.

8. *Listener*, 17 May 1984.

9. Ibid.

10. In October 1983, the 8 a.m. news bulletin on Radio Four was attracting an audience share of between 3.4 and 3.7 per cent, while programmes that followed it on Thursdays were attracting only 0.8 per cent, and fell to around 0.7 per cent or less for the *Daily Service* and for some features. See: 'Rollercoaster: Radio Four: Background Research, 1983–85', Audience Research Report, BBC WAC R9/959/1; *Broadcast*, 13 January 1984.

11. *Times*, 25 October 1983; *Guardian*, 20 October 1983, 11 August 1983; *Standard*, 6 April 1984; *Sunday Telegraph*, 8 April 1984; *Daily Telegraph*, 10 April 1984; *Broadcast*, 13 April 1984; *Times*, 31 December 1983.

12. BBC WAC: Review Board, 18 April 1984; Milne: 'Radio 4', 26 October 1983, Registry B7-2; Protheroe, 1 November 1983, Registry File B007-001; Memo to Rogers, 23 November 1983, Registry File 10029277.

13. *Listener*, 17 May 1984.

14. BBC WAC: 'A Note on Rollercoaster', 7 December 1984, Registry File B007-001; 'Rollercoaster: An Overall Evaluation', 1985, R9/242/1; Minutes of Radio Four Current Affairs Magazine Meeting, 1 October 1984, Registry File B007-001; Board of Management, 15 October 1984, Registry File B007-001. A survey of those phoning in to Rollercoaster during the first week also revealed that opinion was roughly 60–40 against: *Sunday Telegraph*, 8 April 1984.

15. BBC WAC: Board of Management, 10 December 1984, Registry File B007-001; Board of Governors, 13 December 1984 and Board of Management, 17 December 1984, Registry File B007-001; Hatch, 30 May 1985, Registry File 100292277.

16. BBC WAC: 'Programme Strategy', 9 June 1982, R92/2/1; 'Radio Development: the Next Stage', 17 December 1982, R92/2/1; 'Sunday Morning—3 Hour Sequence', 12 November 1982, R92/2/1; Rogers to Sims, 9 August 1982, and Sims to Rogers, 17 December 1982, Registry File 100292277; *Broadcast*, 1 November 1982.

17. BBC WAC: 'BBC Network Radio: Presentation Practice and Related Matters', 26 July 1978, R92/69/1; 'The Sequences: Their Home', 6 April 1978, R92/69/1.

18. The 'host' scheme and creation of the 'Radio Four Department' can be traced through a large number of memos and reports in BBC WAC Registry File E2/RD4. See also: *Guardian*, 21 April 1981; *Sunday Telegraph*, 31 May 1981.

19. BBC WAC: 'Summary of Public Reactions to the BBC', General Advisory Council Papers (GAC 663 and 665), 1984. Details of Hatch's original conception of *Rollercoaster* can be traced in Registry File B7-2.

20. *Ariel*, 19 June 1985; *Broadcast*, 19 July 1985; *Daily Telegraph*, 21 August 1984; *Guardian*, 26 July 1985; *Radio Times*, 17 August 1985; Hatch, interview.

21. Green, July 1986, BBC WAC Registry File E2-RD4; *Sunday Telegraph*, 31 May 1987.

22. Michael Green, interview with author, London, 13 December 2005.

23. *Guardian*, 28 March 1994.

24. 'Radio Four: Qualitative Research', December 1987, BBC WAC R9/388/1; *Independent*, 3 August 1988.

25. *Sunday Telegraph*, 31 May 1987.

26. 'Radio Four: Qualitative Research', December 1987, BBC WAC R9/388/1.

27. Green, interview; *Times*, 19 November 1986; *Observer*, 23 November 1986.

28. *Observer*, 16 November 1986; Board of Management, 17 November 1986, BBC WAC Registry File B7-2; *Times*, 19 November 1986.

29. *Standard*, 5 May 1987; *Times*, 4 September 1987; P. Donovan, *The Radio Companion* (London: Grafton, 1992), 51; *Daily Telegraph*, 5 September 1987.

30. *Sunday Times*, 15 May 1988; Donovan, *Companion*, 51; *Mail on Sunday*, 14 February 1993.

31. *Sunday Times*, 15 May 1988.

32. *Guardian*, 16 January 1989; BBC WAC: 'Special Report: Citizens, February 1990', R9/587/1; Memo, 10 January 1989, Registry E40.

33. Green, interview; John Tydeman, interview with author, London, 30 June 2006; *Times*, 30 November 1990; *Sunday Times*, 15 September 1991.

34. *Guardian*, 28 March 1994; *Times*, 3 August 1994.

35. *Daily Telegraph*, 5 September 1987.

36. Green, interview; *Observer*, 16, 23 November 1986; *Sunday Telegraph*, 24 April 1994; *Sunday Mirror*, 14 April 1991; *Independent*, 26 March 1996; *Guardian*, 26 June 1996; 'Summary of Public Reactions, July–October 1988', BBC WAC General Advisory Council Paper (GAC 716).

37. *Guardian*, 11 November 1987; *Independent*, 3 August 1988; *Listener*, 18 August 1988 and 1 September 1988; *Sunday Times*, 5 February 1989; BBC, *Young Playwrights Festival 1988* (London: BBC, 1988); *Guardian*, 17 October 1988; *Independent*, 22 October 1988; *Daily Telegraph*, 28 October 1988.

38. Green, interview; *Independent*, 25 November 2005; *Observer*, 16 November 1986, 21 May 1989; *Independent*, 10 May 1988; M. Coward, *The Pocket Essential Classic Radio Comedy* (Harpenden: Pocket Essentials, 2003), 74–81.

39. 'Loose Ends/Desert Island Discs', 24 January 1986, BBC WAC Registry File B7-2; *Daily Telegraph*, 14 January 1986; *Observer*, 6 November 1988.

40. *Evening Standard*, 4 August 1993; *Mail on Sunday*, 14 February 1993; *Guardian*, 8 February 1993; *Sunday Telegraph*, 21 February 1993. See also: *Sunday Outing*, BBC Radio Four, 14 February 1993; S. Nye, N. Godwin, and B. Hollows, 'Twisting

the Dials: Lesbians on British Radio', in C. Mitchell (ed.), *Women and Radio: Airing Differences* (London: Routledge, 2000).

41. *Listener*, 15 October 1987 and 22 December 1988; *Observer*, 6 November 1988.
42. *Times*, 13 March 1987; *Guardian*, 17 and 18 March 1987, 15 July 1987; *Daily Telegraph*, 17 July 1987, 11 August 1987, 27 October 1987.
43. Green, interview; *Private Eye*, 24 June 1988; *Daily Mail*, 18 February 1991; *Daily Telegraph*, 23 February 1991; Donovan, *Companion*, 129.
44. *Daily Telegraph* and *Daily Express*, 9 February 1994; *Times* and *Guardian*, 11 February 1994; *Observer*, 13 February 1994; *Sunday Times*, 7 August 1994.
45. See for example: Val Arnold-Forster in the *Guardian*, 6 September 1991, Nigel Andrew in the *Listener*, 15 October 1987, Ian Bradley in the *Daily Telegraph*, 4 October 1989, and Gillian Reynolds in the *Daily Telegraph*, 17 July 1987, 11 August 1987, and 27 October 1987.
46. *Listener*, 22 December 1988.
47. Quoted in L. Purves, *Radio: A True Love Story* (London: Hodder & Stoughton, 2002), 140.
48. 'Public Reaction to the BBC', BBC WAC General Advisory Council Papers (GAC 708, 712, 716), 1988; *Daily Telegraph*, 22 August 1986, 3 July 1989.
49. S. MacGregor, *Woman of Today: An Autobiography* (London: Headline, 2002), 238.
50. *Daily Telegraph*, 22 August 1986.
51. 'Sex, Violence, Language and Taste', 20 February 1986, BBC WAC General Advisory Council Paper (GAC 683).
52. J. Tydeman, 'Bad Language and Radio Drama: A Personal View', in A. M. Hargrave (ed.), *A Matter of Manners? The Limits of Broadcast Language*, Broadcasting Standards Council Research Monograph Series 3 (London: Broadcasting Standards Council, 1991), 65–7. Both Richard Imison, from the Drama Department, and, notably, the head of Schools Broadcasting, had complained of the unnatural nature of 'clean' language in a play about a football team broadcast in 1980: Review Board, 10 September 1980, BBC WAC. See also: Review Board, 5 November 1980, BBC WAC; 'The Use of Language in Radio Drama', 31 July 1980, BBC WAC R78/2640/1; *Daily Telegraph*, 22 August 1986, 3 July 1989.
53. Green, interview; BBC WAC: 'The Language Seminar: A Report from Managing Director of Network Radio', 16 June 1988, R78/2640/1; Transcript of Language Seminar, 14 June 1988, R78/2640/1.
54. Ibid.
55. Ibid. By contrast, in 1994 the Broadcasting Standards Council revealed that only 6 per cent of people surveyed found 'bloody' offensive—compared with 90 per cent finding 'sexual four-letter words' offensive: *Broadcasting Standards Council, Annual Review, Radio & Audience Attitudes*, 1994; *Independent*, 8 December 1994.
56. *Daily Mail*, 15 June 1988.
57. Transcript of Language Seminar, 14 June 1988, and 'The Language Seminar: A Report from Managing Director, Network Radio', 16 June 1988, BBC WAC R78/2640/1; *Sunday Times*, 19 June 1988; Green, interview; Tydeman, interview. In 1994 the proportion of complaints about language on Radio Four actually upheld by the Broadcasting Standards Council was just 3 out of 110: *Broadcasting Standards Council, Annual Review, Radio & Audience Attitudes*, 1994.

58. Green, interview; *Daily Express*, 5 December 1989; *Observer*, 31 December 1989; *Observer*, 4 December 1994.
59. Green, interview; *Independent*, 2 August 1995; *Guardian*, 5 August 1995; *Daily Express*, 13 January 1995; Donovan, *Companion*, 34–5.
60. For the history of the *Today* programme in the 1980s and 1990s, and much of what follows, see: P. Donovan, *All Our Todays: Forty Years of the Today Programme* (London: Jonathan Cape, 1997); T. Luckhurst, *This is Today: A Biography of the Today Programme* (London: Aurum Press, 2001); MacGregor, *Woman of Today*; Purves, *Radio*, 128–39, 160–230; J. Humphrys, *Devil's Advocate*, (London: Arrow, 2000).
61. B. Ingham, *Kill the Messenger* (London: Fontana, 1991), 170.
62. 'Today and the Prime Minister', 4 September 1979, BBC WAC Registry File 10007679.
63. Donovan, *All Our Todays*, 102–3.
64. *Sunday Times*, 22 December 1991.
65. For the 1997 General Election see Luckhurst, *This is Today*, 135–41.
66. Humphrys, *Devil's Advocate*, 224.
67. *Sunday Times*, 7 March 1993.
68. MacGregor, *Woman of Today*, 307, 328.
69. Donovan, *All Our Todays*, 209–13.
70. 'Facing the Future: The BBC's Role in the Next Decade', 1985, BBC WAC General Advisory Council Paper (GAC 676).
71. Luckhurst, *This is Today*, 95–116; MacGregor, *Woman of Today*, 265–92.
72. See, for example: Paul Donovan in the *Sunday Times*, 7 March 1993; Anne Karpf in the *Guardian*, 23 October 1993; Joyce McMillan in the *Glasgow Herald*, 17 March 1984. The case for *Today*'s journalism is put in Luckhurst, *This is Today*, 96–107.
73. Anne Karpf, *Guardian*, 23 October 1993.
74. Purves, *Radio*, 134–5.
75. Humphrys, *Devil's Advocate*, 235.
76. The definition was provided by the Head of Religious Broadcasting Ernest Rea, in the *Church Times*, 19 October 1990.
77. Donovan, *All Our Todays*, 154; *New Statesman*, 30 March 1984; BBC WAC: Memo to Lawson Dick, 25 February 1976, R51/1297/3; Review Board, 30 June 1976.
78. Review Board, 12 August 1970, 31 March 1976, 30 June 1976, BBC WAC.
79. BBC WAC: Review Board, 19 September 1979, 27 February 1980; Board of Governors' Radio Programme Policy Committee, 20 December 1979, R1/144/1.
80. Review Board, 22 November 1972, 28 May 1975, 24 March 1976, 30 June 1976, BBC WAC.
81. D. Winter, *Winter's Tale: Living through an Age of Change in Church and Media* (Oxford: Lion, 2001),102–4; Donovan, *All Our Todays*, 160–1; Review Board, 3, 17, and 31 March 1971, BBC WAC; *Times*, 17 March 1971.
82. T. Benn, *Conflicts of Interest: Diaries 1977–80* (London: Arrow Books, 1991), 542–3, 346–7; Review Board, 3 and 10 October 1979, BBC WAC; *Daily Telegraph*, 29 October 1979.
83. Review Board, 17 March 1971, BBC WAC.

84. M. Brown and P. Ballard, *The Church and Economic Life—A Documentary Study: 1945 to the Present* (Peterborough: Epworth, 2006), 182. See also: G. Davie, *Religion in Britain since 1945* (Oxford: Blackwell, 1994), 152; D. Martin, 'The Churches: Pink Bishops and the Iron Lady', in D. Kavanagh and A. Seldon (eds.), *The Thatcher Effect* (Oxford: Clarendon Press, 1989), 330–41.

85. *Faith in the City: A Call for Action by Church and Nation* (London: Church House Publishing, 1985); David Jenkins' Enthronement Sermon, 21 September 1984, in D. Jenkins, *God, Politics and the Future* (London: SCM Press, 1988), 4–10.

86. Winter, *Winter's Tale*, 152–5.

87. The Managing Director of Radio told Review Board in 1981 of how *Thought for the Day* was 'a problem'. 'As social pressures built up because of unemployment, there was a tendency for it to become party-political': Review Board, 28 January 1981, BBC WAC. See also Donovan, *All Our Todays*, 162–4.

88. Winter, *Winter's Tale*, 152–3.

89. Ibid. 153–4.

90. Donovan, *All Our Todays*, 163; Donovan, *Companion*, 263–4; *Daily Telegraph*, 7 May 1996.

91. Luckhurst, *This is Today*, 121–2.

92. Ibid. 124; Donovan, *All Our Todays*, 164–5; *Daily Telegraph*, 24 and 25 April 1996, 7 May 1996; *Daily Express*, 7 May 1996.

93. Review Board, 12 August 1970, BBC WAC.

94. D. Childs, *Britain since 1939: Progress and Decline*, 2nd edn. (Basingstoke: Palgrave, 2002), 262.

95. The phrase was that submitted by the BBC to the Annan Committee. See also a wide-ranging discussion from 1976, in which Michael Mayne, the Head of Religious Programmes for BBC Radio described his department as 'not in any sense an arm of the Christian churches': Review Board, 30 June 1976, BBC WAC.

96. For details of the Buddhist contributions in 1975 see Review Board, 17 September 1975, BBC WAC. The producer quoted was David Coomes, in Luckhurst, *This is Today*, 124.

97. Review Board, 30 July 1975, BBC WAC; *Church Times*, 30 December 1994; Donovan, *All Our Todays*, 172.

98. Donovan, *All Our Todays*, 150–1.

99. Davie, *Religion in Britain*, 113.

100. L. Blue, *Bright Blue: Rabbi Lionel Blue's Thoughts for the Day* (London: BBC, 1985), 79–80.

101. L. Blue, *A Backdoor to Heaven: An Autobiography* (London: Fount, 1994); Donovan, *All Our Todays*, 152–5; Luckhurst, *This is Today*, 127.

102. Green, interview.

103. Ibid.; *Times*, 30 November 1990; *Guardian*, 30 November 1990; *Ariel*, 4 December 1990; *Sunday Times*, 15 September 1991.

104. The 'hot flushes' episode is told in MacGregor, *Woman of Today*, 150–1, and in S. Feldman, 'Twin Peaks', in C. Mitchell (ed.), *Women and Radio: Airing Differences* (London: Routledge, 2000), 67. Audience research in 1972 showed the number of its listeners who thought the programme 'too conservative' was three times as great

as the number who thought it 'too permissive': 'Woman's Hour Listeners' Attitudes', BBC WAC R9/858/1.

105. MacGregor, *Woman of Today*, 151; *Daily Telegraph*, 24 April 1974; BBC WAC: Woman's Hour, 29 March 1973, R51/1312/8; Review Board, 21 November 1973, 28 May 1975, 7 January 1976.

106. Feldman, 'Twin Peaks', 64–72; *Guardian*, 30 November 1990.

107. Feldman, 'Twin Peaks', 65. In November 1973, the Controller of Radio Four, Tony Whitby, told Review Board that 'The problem facing a magazine programme was that of knowing what its own identity was when there were many other programmes covering some of the same ground.' He, and others at the meeting, wondered whether *Woman's Hour* would survive into the Eighties: Review Board, 7 November 1973, BBC WAC.

108. Feldman, 'Twin Peaks', 64.

109. Ibid. 66.

110. *Times*, 1 December 1990.

111. Feldman, 'Twin Peaks', 66; MacGregor, *Woman of Today*, 174.

112. *Times*, 12 December 1990; *Independent*, 23 January 1991; Green, interview.

113. Green, interview; *Independent*, 23 January 1991; *Daily Telegraph*, 19 February 1991; Feldman, 'Twin Peaks', 68–9.

114. Feldman, 'Twin Peaks', 69–72; *Guardian*, 2 and 12 September 1991.

115. *Daily Mail*, 9 September 1991; Feldman, 'Twin Peaks', 70; Green, interview.

116. Green, interview; *Guardian*, 10 January 1994.

117. *Guardian*, 28 March 1994; *Independent*, 12 and 18 April 1994; *Sunday Telegraph*, 10 April 1994.

118. Green, interview; *Times*, 3 August 1994; *Sunday Times*, 7 August 1994; *Independent on Sunday*, 11 February 1996.

119. *Guardian*, 18 January 1995; *Times*, 3 August 1994; *Sunday Times*, 7 August 1994; *Independent on Sunday*, 11 February 1996; Green, interview.

120. *Radio Times*, 7–13 October 1995.

121. Green, interview.

122. Mark Lawson, *Independent*, n.d. (*c*.1994).

123. McIntyre, 17 April 1978, BBC WAC Records Management Registry File B7-2.

124. Quoted in R. Hewison, *Culture and Consensus: England, Art and Politics since 1940* (London: Methuen, 1995), 235–6.

125. John Grist, *Sunday Telegraph*, 17 April 1994.

126. Green, interview.

127. Libby Purves, *Radio*, 252.

128. 'Public Service Radio in the Cable Age', 15 March 1984, BBC WAC R78/2062/1.

129. 'The Glory of the Garden' in R. Kipling, *Selected Poems* (London: Penguin, 1993), 147–8.

CHAPTER 12.   A LONG WAVE GOODBYE?

1. *Meteorological Office Report: The Storm of 15/16 October 1987* (Bracknell: Meteorological Office, 1987); G. Hill, *Hurricane Force: The Story of the Storm of October 1987* (London: Collins, 1988), 169.

2. S. MacGregor, *Woman of Today: An Autobiography* (London: Headline, 2002), 232; J. Abramsky, *Sound Matters: Five Live—The War of Broadcasting House—A Morality Tale*, Lecture, 31 January 2002, Exeter College, Oxford University.

3. Michael Green, interview with author, London, 13 December 2005; Abramsky, *Sound Matters*.

4. 'BBC Radio: Possibilities for the Future', 30 October 1986, BBC WAC R78/2062/1.

5. *Sunday Times*, 19 July 1987.

6. J. Birt, *The Harder Path* (London: Time Warner, 2002), 251–2.

7. J. Abramsky, *Bi-Media: A Strategy for Radio?* Lecture, 6 February 2002, Green College, Oxford University.

8. BBC WAC: 'Splitting', 24 January 1986, Registry File B7-2; 'Public Reactions to the BBC', 1987, General Advisory Council Paper (GAC 705); BBC Chairman, 29 December 1987, Registry File B007-001; *Daily Telegraph*, 22 October 1987 and 2 November 1987; *Financial Times*, 1 December 1987; *Independent*, 19 January 1988.

9. Green, interview.

10. *Sunday Times*, 16 April 1989; Birt, *Harder Path*, 296–7; Abramsky, *Sound Matters*.

11. *Britain and the Gulf Crisis* (London: HMSO, 1993); *BBC World Service: Gulf Crisis Chronology* (London: Longman, 1991).

12. J. Simpson, *From the House of War: John Simpson in the Gulf* (London: Arrow Books, 1991), 281–7; J. Simpson, *Strange Places, Questionable People* (London: Pan, 1998), 385–412; S. Sackur, *On the Basra Road* (London: London Review of Books, 1991), 9–19; Abramsky, *Sound Matters*; T. Luckhurst, *This is Today: A Biography of the Today Programme* (London: Aurum Press, 2001), 153; S. L. Carruthers, *The Media at War: Communication and Conflict in the Twentieth Century* (Basingstoke: Palgrave, 2000), 133–5; R. Keeble, *Secret State, Silent Press: New Militarism, the Gulf and the Modern Image of Warfare* (Luton: University of Luton Press, 1997), 114–15.

13. Green, interview.

14. Ibid.; Abramsky, *Sound Matters*.

15. Carruthers, *Media at War*, 134–9; Simpson, *House of War*, 281, 287–329; Simpson, *Strange Places*, 404–12; Keeble, *Secret State*, 116; Sackur, *Basra Road*, 9, 10–19.

16. MacGregor, *Woman of Today*, 274.

17. Mass-Observation Archive, Sussex: Directive 33, Autumn/Winter 1990: 'Gulf Crisis', Women, A–C.

18. 'Gulf War on Radio 4: Listeners' Comments', February 1991, BBC WAC R9/545/1.

19. Sackur, *Basra Road*, 10, 24; Carruthers, *Media at War*, 135, 139; R. Fisk, *The Great War for Civilization: The Conquest of the Middle East* (London: Fourth Estate, 2005), 767; Simpson, *House of War*, 298; *Daily Telegraph*, 22 January 1991.

20. 'The Radio Four News FM Audience', June 1991, BBC WAC R9/677/1.

21. 'Special Report: News: Reactions to a Radio News Service', November 1991, BBC WAC R9/723/1; *Daily Telegraph*, 28 February 1991; *Times*, 14 January 1992, 13 October 1992, 9 September 1993.

22. Abramsky, *Sound Matters*; C. Horrie and S. Clarke, *Fuzzy Monsters: Fear and Loathing at the BBC* (London: Heinemann, 1994), 218; *Sunday Telegraph*, 3 March 1991.

23. Abramsky, *Sound Matters*; *Observer*, 28 April 1991; *Independent*, 18 June 1991; *Daily Telegraph*, 19 June 1991.

24. *Daily Telegraph*, 19 June 1991; Abramsky, *Sound Matters*.
25. Green, interview.
26. Abramsky, *Sound Matters*.
27. Green, interview; Abramsky, *Sound Matters*.
28. Sheena McDonald was writing in the *Guardian*, 17 August 1992; Charles Wheeler was speaking during a live debate held on Radio Four in January 1993, reported in the *Daily Telegraph*, 18 January 1993.
29. Abramsky, *Sound Matters*; *Daily Telegraph*, 19 June 1991; *Guardian*, 2 September 1991; *Sunday Times*, 8 September 1991; *Evening Standard*, 22 August 1991.
30. Green, interview. Abramsky, *Sound Matters,* quotes McKinsey and Company's finding that 'the existing radio news service would be insufficient to meet listeners' expectations and increasing competition'.
31. Green, interview; Birt, *Harder Path*, 302, 383; *Independent*, 15 July 1992; *International Herald Tribune*, 18 July 1992; *Guardian*, 16 July 1992; *Sunday Express*, 19 July 1992.
32. *Daily Telegraph*, 29 July 1992; Green, interview.
33. *Times*, 29 September 1992; *Observer*, 27 September 1992; letter, *Times*, 21 October 1992; *Daily Telegraph*, 19 March 1993.
34. Nick MacKinnon, interview with author, Winchester, 1 March 2006; *Daily Telegraph*, 29 July 1992, 14 October 1992; *Times*, 2 October 1992; *Sunday Times,* 11 and 18 October 1992.
35. MacKinnon, interview; *Observer*, 27 September 1992; *Daily Mail*, 28 September 1992; *Daily Telegraph*, 28 September 1992, 11 October 1992; *Times*, 29 September 1992; *Sunday Telegraph*, 18 October 1992; *European*, 22 April 1993; 'Radio Four Round-up', *British European* newsletter, December 1993.
36. *Daily Telegraph*, 8 August 1992, 7 November 1992, 2 January 1993; *Sunday Telegraph*, 4 October 1992.
37. *Daily Telegraph*, 21 January 1993, 14 and 17 August 1993; letter, *Times*, 17 September 1993.
38. *Times*, 13 October 1992. See also Daley's comments in *Times*, 14 January 1992 and 9 September 1993.
39. Abramsky, *Sound Matters*; Tony Hall, speech to Royal Television Society, 13 October 1992; quoted by Russell Twisk, *Observer,* 18 October 1992.
40. Green, interview; *Guardian*, 5 October 1992; *Observer*, 18 October 1992; *Sunday Times,* 18 October 1992; *Daily Telegraph*, 24 October 1992.
41. Hall, speech to Royal Television Society; Green, interview; *Times*, 29 September 1992, 14 October 1992; *Observer*, 11 October 1992; *Sunday Times*, 11 October 1992; *Independent*, 12, 13, and 14 October 1992; *Guardian*, 14 October 1992.
42. *Daily Telegraph*, 16 October 1992; *Guardian*, 16 and 19 October 1992; *Daily Mail*, 16 October 1992; *Evening Standard*, 16 October 1992; *Times,* 17 October 1992; *Independent on Sunday*, 18 October 1992; *Observer*, 18 October 1992; *Sunday Telegraph*, 18 October 1992.
43. Green, interview. See also: *Independent*, 13 October 1992, and *Guardian*, 19 October 1992.
44. Green, interview; M. Hussey, *Chance Governs All: A Memoir* (Basingstoke: Macmillan, 2001), 255.

45. Abramsky, *Sound Matters*; Birt, *Harder Path*, 383.
46. Birt, *Harder Path*, 358–9, 380; *Independent on Sunday*, 22 January 1995; *Independent*, 10 February 1993; MacGregor, *Woman of Today*, 278; Hussey, *Chance Governs All*, 264; Green, interview.
47. Abramsky, *Sound Matters*; *Guardian*, 10 February 1993; *Sunday Times*, 14 March 1993; *Ariel*, 16 March 1993.
48. Liz Forgan, letter to the author, 5 September 2006.
49. Abramsky, *Sound Matters*; Green, interview.
50. *Daily Telegraph*, 20 February 1991; *Independent*, 21 October 1992; Abramsky, *Sound Matters*; Green, interview.
51. Abramsky, *Sound Matters*; Green, interview.
52. Abramsky, *Sound Matters*.
53. *Daily Telegraph*, 27 March 1993; Hussey, *Chance Governs All*, 282–3; *Evening Standard*, 29 June 1993; *Guardian, Independent, Daily Mail, Times, Daily Express*, and *Daily Telegraph*, all 30 June 1993; *Guardian*, 30 August 1993; *Observer*, 5 September 1993; *Daily Mail*, 12 October 193; *Daily Telegraph*, 12 and 13 October 1993; Green, interview.
54. Hussey, *Chance Governs All*, 255.
55. Jocelyn Hay, letter in *Guardian*, 7 October 1992.
56. *The Citizen's Charter—Raising the Standard*, Cm 1599 (London: HMSO, July 1991). See also J. Willman, 'The Civil Service', in D. Kavanagh and A. Seldon, *The Major Effect* (London: Macmillan, 1994), 64–82.
57. *Independent*, 26 September 1994; *Daily Telegraph*, 18 August 1993; *Sunday Telegraph*, 4 October 1992; *Sunday Times*, 18 October 1992.
58. Lynne Truss, 20 October 1992.
59. Quoted in P. Donovan, *The Radio Companion* (London: Grafton, 1992), 261.
60. Luckhurst, *This is Today*, 154; Abramsky, *Sound Matters*; MacGregor, *Woman of Today*, 288; *Daily Telegraph*, 9 February 1994; *Guardian*, 28 March 1994.
61. MacGregor, *Woman of Today*, 314, 316; Hussey, *Chance Governs All*, 294–5.
62. W. Wyatt, *The Fun Factory: A Life in the BBC* (London: Aurum Press, 2003), 280.
63. Birt, *Harder Path*, 251–2, 380; Hussey, *Chance Governs All*, 301–2.
64. MacGregor, *Woman of Today*, 317.

CHAPTER 13. PLEASURES

1. M. Coward, *The Pocket Essential Classic Radio Comedy* (Harpenden: Pocket Essentials, 2003), 80.
2. Other writers included Richard Herring and Stewart Lee, Steven Wells, Andrew Glover, and David Quantick.
3. S. Coogan, P. Baynham, A. Iannucci, and P. Marber, *Alan Partridge: Every Ruddy Word: All the Scripts: From Radio to TV. And Back* (London: Penguin, 2004), 1.
4. Ibid. 29–30. See also *Radio Times*, 13 March 1993.
5. *People Like Us: The Hotel Manager*, June–July 1996, BBC Radio Four.
6. J. B. Priestley, *English Humour* (London: Longmans, Green & Co., 1929), 12.
7. M. Rose, *Parody: Ancient, Modern and Post-Modern* (Cambridge: Cambridge University Press, 1993); S. Dentith, *Parody* (London: Routledge, 2000).

8. On *Band Waggon*, see P. Scannell and D. Cardiff, *A Social History of British Broadcasting*, i: *1922–1939: Serving the Nation* (Oxford: Blackwell, 1991), 235, 244–5, 260–2, 269–71.

9. Priestley, *English Humour*, 19.

10. *The Adrian Mole Special*, 21 December 2003, BBC 7.

11. S. Townsend, *The Secret Diary of Adrian Mole Aged 13 3/4* (London: Methuen, 1982).

12. *Adrian Mole Special*; John Tydeman, interview with author, London, 30 June 2006.

13. *Adrian Mole Special*, BBC 7.

14. J. Eldridge, *King Street Junior* (London: BBC Books, 1988).

15. S. Brett, *After Henry* (London: Penguin, 1988); Gillian Reynolds in *Daily Telegraph*, 27 October 1987.

16. *Guardian*, 8 September 1988.

17. Green, interview with author, London, 13 December 2005.

18. D. Nobbs, *I Didn't Get Where I Am Today: An Autobiography* (London: Arrow Books, 2004), 139, 186–7, 230; *Daily Telegraph*, 27 October 1987.

19. *Evening Standard*, 13 March 1995.

20. For an interesting discussion of feature developments see T. Crook, *Radio Drama: Theory and Practice* (London: Routledge, 1999), 201–12.

21. *Soundtrack: A Lone Voice*, 2 March 1988, BBC Radio Four.

22. G. Worsnip, *Up the Down Escalator* (London: Coronet, 1991), 1–2, 93, 114, 124–5, 130, 148–72, 210, 219–20.

23. Ibid. 170.

24. J. Carey, 'Reportage, Literature and Willed Credulity', in J. Aitchison and D. M. Lewis (eds.), *New Media Language* (London: Routledge, 2003), 57–64; Crook, *Radio Drama*, 144–8.

25. Quoted in Crook, *Radio Drama*, 225.

26. *Independent*, 9 February 1988; *Guardian*, 2 September 1995.

27. *Touching the Elephant*, 16 March 1997, BBC Radio Four.

28. M. Thompson, *The Anatomy of a Radio Programme: The Making of Touching the Elephant* (unpublished manuscript, 2006), 14.

29. Worsnip, *Escalator*, 152. Worsnip wrote of the way in which BBC Radio, as an institution, 'was, and still is, good to me': ibid.154.

30. Crook, *Radio Drama*, 203.

31. C. Connelly, *Attention All Shipping: A Journey round the Shipping Forecast* (London: Little Brown, 2004), 20–6; P. Collyer, *Rain Later, Good: Illustrating the Shipping Forecast*, 2nd edn. (London: Adlard Coles Nautical, 2002), 10.

32. Radio Planning Committee, 8 November 1967 and 11 September 1968, BBC WAC.

33. Gerard Mansell writing in the *Daily Telegraph*, 26 June 1971. For criticisms from the public, see letters, 21 and 23 June 1971, *Daily Telegraph*, and reports on public correspondence in Review Board, 11 and 18 September 1974, 22 August 1979, and General Advisory Council, Minutes, 23 October 1974 (GAC 447)—all BBC WAC. On Fastnet, see: Review Board, 22 August 1979, BBC WAC, and Board of Governors' Radio Programme Policy Committee, 20 December 1979, BBC WAC R1/144/1.

34. Connelly, *Attention all Shipping*, 2–3. See also: D. Chandler, 'Foreword: Postcards from the Edge', in *The Shipping Forecast: Photographs by Mark Power*, 2nd edn. (London: Zelda Cheatle Press and Network Photographers, 1997); K. Fox, *Watching the English: The Hidden Rules of English Behaviour* (London: Hodder, 2005), 34–5.
35. S. Heaney, *New Selected Poems 1966–1987* (London: Faber & Faber, 1990), 115.
36. C. A. Duffy, *Mean Time*, 2nd edn. (London: Anvil Press Poetry, 1998), 52.
37. *Shipping Forecast, Donegal*, in S. Street, *Radio Waves: Poems Celebrating the Wireless* (London: Enitharmon Press, 2004), 64.
38. Connelly, *Attention All Shipping*, 27–31.
39. Street, *Radio Waves*, 11.
40. Chandler, 'Postcards', unnumbered page.
41. B. Cunliffe, *Facing the Ocean: The Atlantic and Its Peoples 8000 BC–1500 AD* (Oxford: Oxford University Press, 2001), 1, 554, 565.
42. Chandler, 'Postcards', unnumbered page.
43. Connelly, *Attention All Shipping*, 1.
44. *Independent*, 26 July 1993.
45. *Telegraph Magazine*, 26 March 1994.
46. A. R. Ekirch, *At Day's Close: A History of Nighttime* (London: Phoenix, 2006), xxvi–xxvii, 4–5, 263, 271–2.
47. *Daily Telegraph*, 6 April 1988; *Mail on Sunday*, 17 October 1993.
48. *Independent*, 26 July 1993; *Daily Telegraph Magazine*, 25 May 1991; *Broadcast*, 12 July 1985; L. Purves, *Radio: A True Love Story* (London: Hodder & Stoughton, 2002), 174; Charlotte Green, *The Archive Hour*, 18 March 2006, BBC Radio Four.
49. *Guardian*, 10 December 1982.
50. *Rushes: Undercoat*, 3 September 1993, BBC Radio Four.
51. *Mail on Sunday*, 17 October 1993. For a discussion of the importance of 'dailiness' to broadcasting in general, see P. Scannell, *Radio, Television and Modern Life* (Oxford: Blackwell, 1996),148–78.
52. Mass-Observation Archive, Sussex: Directive 40, Summer 1993: Pleasure.
53. Priestley, *English Humour*, 8–9.

EPILOGUE: 1997 AND SINCE

1. *The Death of Radio*, 18 October 1997, BBC Radio Four.
2. M. Thompson, *The Anatomy of a Radio Programme: The Making of 'Touching the Elephant'* (unpublished typescript, 2006), 99.
3. R. Sennett, *The Culture of the New Capitalism* (New Haven: Yale University Press, 2006), 7, 24, 40–99.
4. *Guardian*, 18 June 1990; *Independent*, 19 December 2005; *Independent on Sunday*, 6 July 2003; G. Dyke, *Inside Story* (London: Harper Collins, 2004), 176.
5. Sennett, *New Capitalism*, 181.
6. *Guardian*, 13 and 14 January 1997, 14 July 1997; *Broadcast*, 11 April 1997, 13 June 1997, 11 July 1997, 1 August 1997; *Evening Standard*, 13 June 1997; *Independent*, 29 July 1997, 28 February 1998, 17 March 1998; *Times*, 12 December 1997, 16 May 1998; BBC News Online, 3 April 1998, 21 October 1998; *Call Robin Lustig*, 17

March 1998, BBC Radio Four; BBC, *Annual Report and Accounts, 1997/8* (London: BBC, 1998).

7. *Guardian*, 13 January 1997; *Times*, 16 May 1998; BBC News Online, 16 September 1998, 22 October 1998, 4 February 1999, 10 June 1999, 16 January 2000; *Financial Times*, 23 October 1998; *Broadcast*, 13 June 1997, 26 February 1999, 2 April 1999, 25 June 1999, 21 January 2000; *Glasgow Herald*, 17 January 2000; BBC, *Annual Report and Accounts 1998–1999* (London: BBC, 1999); BBC, *Annual Report and Accounts 1999–2000* (London: BBC, 2000); J. Birt, *The Harder Path* (London: Time Warner, 2002), 384–6.

8. BBC News Online, 22 October 1998, 10 June 1999, 16 January 2000; *Financial Times*, 23 October 1998; *Glasgow Herald*, 17 January 2000; *BBC Annual Report and Accounts, 1998/9* (London: BBC, 1999); *BBC Annual Report and Accounts, 1999/ 2000* (London: BBC, 2000).

9. *Broadcast*, 26 May 2000, 23 March 2001; *Guardian*, 16 August 2000 and 27 September 2004.

10. Most discussion of the UK Theme referred to its '33 year' history on Radio Four: in fact, though the network had been running an opening theme tune since 1973, this particular arrangement had only been launched nationwide in 1978. For the key events, see: *Guardian*, 27 September 2004; *Broadcast*, 1 October 2004; *Guardian Unlimited*, 23, 24, and 25 January 2006, 31 March 2006; *Times*, 26 January 2006, 24 April 2006; *Belfast Telegraph*, 28 January 2006; BBC News Online, 29 September 2004 and 27 March 2006; *Hansard*, Column 1428, 25 January 2006.

11. 'Report of the Radio Network Working Party', 16 January 1981, Private Papers of Monica Sims.

12. *Independent on Sunday*, 7 March 2004; BBC News Online, 28 February 2006.

13. *Mail on Sunday*, 11 June 2000; *Independent on Sunday*, 11 February 2001; S. Collini, *Absent Minds: Intellectuals in Britain* (Oxford: Oxford University Press, 2006), 437–50, 489–90.

14. J. Peel, and S. Ravenscroft, *Margrave of the Marshes* (London: Corgi, 2006), 430–5; H. Chignell and J. Devlin, 'John Peel's Home Truths' (unpublished article, Bournemouth University, 2005); BBC News Online, 14 December 2005; *Independent on Sunday*, 26 February 2006.

15. Peel and Ravenscroft, *Margrave*, 432; *Daily Telegraph*, 25 October 2005; *Independent on Sunday*, 2 May 1999, 14 July 2002; *Guardian*, 30 April 2001; *Scotsman*, 29 October 2003; *Independent on Sunday*, 9 February 2003, 10 August 2003.

16. *Report of the Inquiry into the Circumstances Surrounding the Death of Dr David Kelly C.M.G., by Lord Hutton*, HC247 (London: HMSO, 28 January 2004), 319–25.

17. J. Lloyd, *What the Media Are Doing to Our Politics* (London: Constable, 2004), 2–24, 89, 187–95; Dyke, *Inside Story*, 1–4, 252–69.

18. J. Simpson, *Strange Places, Questionable People* (London: Pan, 1999), 367–8.

19. G. Born, *Uncertain Vision: Birt, Dyke and the Reinvention of the BBC* (London: Vintage, 2005), 54–5.

20. L. James, *The Middle Class: A History* (London: Little Brown, 2006), 5.

21. *Independent*, 1 June 2004.

22. Simon Blackburn in the *Guardian*, 5 August 2006. See also: S. Blackburn, *Plato's Republic: A Biography* (London: Atlantic Books, 2006).

23. *BBC Annual Report and Accounts, 2001–2* (London: BBC, 2002); *BBC Annual Report and Accounts, 2002–3* (London: BBC, 2003); *BBC Annual Report and Accounts, 2003–4* (London: BBC, 2004); *Guardian*, 15 September 2006; *Independent*, 19 December 2005.

24. S. Miller, *Conversation: A History of a Declining Art* (New Haven: Yale University Press, 2006), 267–304.

25. A. Sen, *Identity and Violence: The Illusion of Destiny* (London: Allen Lane, 2006), 156, 175–8, 186.

26. J. Carey, *What Good are the Arts?* (London: Faber & Faber, 2006), 195–209, 213–38, 252–8.

Select Bibliography

Newspapers and periodicals, radio programmes, regularly published BBC documents, sound archives, official documents, private papers, and websites are all cited in full in the endnotes. Here, apart from a brief explanation of the main archival sources, I list only published books, journal articles, and doctoral theses.

A NOTE ON ARCHIVAL SOURCES

At the BBC Written Archive Centre, Caversham, some records are kept on microfilm, and have been cited in the endnotes simply as 'BBC WAC' without a further file reference. These include the minutes of the Radio Planning Committee; the minutes of its successor from 1970, the Radio Weekly Programme Review Board; and General Advisory Council papers between 1955 and 1988. The Centre also holds on microfiche drama scripts and newspaper cuttings. Other files used belong to the following main series:

R1	Board of Governors
R2	Board of Management
R3	Internal Administrative Committees
R6	Advisory Committees
R9	Audience Research
R13	Departmental
R19	Entertainment
R28	News
R34	Policy
R41	Programme Correspondence
R51	Talks
R78	Management Registry
R92	Radio Management Registry
R101	Central Registry Management Section
R108	News and Current Affairs
R143	Oral History Project
M	Midlands Region/Birmingham
N	North Region/Manchester

Also consulted at the BBC Written Archives Centre were a number of files from the post-1979 period not normally open to researchers, grouped as 'Records Management Registry' or 'RAPIC' files. These included: B7-2, Radio Four, Part 1 1974–86; B007-001, Radio Four, Policy, Part 1, 1969–89; E2/RD4-2, Radio 4—Organization and Establishment, General, 1977–86; File 10007679: *Today*, General, File 1, 1974–84; File 10029277: *Rollercoaster*; File E40: *Citizens*.

At the Mass-Observation Archive, University of Sussex Library Special Collections, Brighton, research was drawn from post-1981 directives. These included:

Directive 5, Spring 1982: The Falklands Crisis: Men, A–Z.
Directive 33, Autumn/Winter 1990: Gulf Crisis, Women, A–C.
Directive 40, Summer 1993: Pleasure, Women, A–Z.
Directive 63, Summer 2001: Reality TV and Radio, Women, A–Z.
Directive 65, Autumn 2001: Media and Public Interest, Women, A–Z.

The Papers and Correspondence of Michael Meredith Swann, at Edinburgh University Library Special Collections, are arranged in several files series. Those concerned with Swann's role as BBC Chairman are concentrated in series 'E', which runs to nearly 1,000 files in total.

BOOKS AND ARTICLES

Abramsky, J., *Sound Matters: Soundtrack for the UK—How Did We Get Here?* Lecture, 30 January 2002, Green College, Oxford University.
—— *Sound Matters: Five Live—The War of Broadcasting House—A Morality Tale*, Lecture, 31 January 2002, Exeter College, Oxford University.
—— *Bi-Media: A Strategy for Radio?* Lecture, 6 February 2002, Green College, Oxford University.
Adams, D., *The Hitchhiker's Guide to the Galaxy: The Original Radio Scripts*, updated edn. (London: Pan, 2003).
Aitchison, J. 'The Media are Ruining English', in L. Bauer and P. Trudgill (eds.), *Language Myths* (London: Penguin, 1998).
Aldgate, A., *Censorship and the Permissive Society: British Cinema and Theatre, 1955–1965* (Oxford: Oxford University Press, 1995).
Amis, M., *The War against Cliché: Essays and Reviews 1971–2000* (London: Vintage, 2002).
Annan, N., *Our Age: The Generation that Made Post-War Britain* (London: Fontana, 1991).
Arnold, M., *Culture and Anarchy* (London: Smith, Elder, & Co., 1869).
Auden, W. H., 'The Guilty Vicarage', in *The Dyer's Hand and Other Essays* (London: Faber & Faber, 1963).
—— 'Introduction', in L. MacNeice, *Persons from Porlock and Other Plays for Radio* (London: BBC, 1969).
Bakewell, J., and Garnham, N., *The New Priesthood: British Television Today* (London: Allen Lane, 1970).
Bardon, J., *Beyond the Studio: A History of BBC Northern Ireland* (Belfast: Blackstaff Press, 2000).
Barnard, S., *On the Radio: Music Radio in Britain* (Milton Keynes: Open University Press, 1989).
Barnett, C., *The Audit of War: The Illusion and Reality of Britain as a Great Nation* (London: Macmillan, 1986).
Barnett, S., and Curry, A., *The Battle for the BBC: A British Broadcasting Conspiracy* (London: Aurum Press, 1994).
Barr, C. (ed.), *All Our Yesterdays: 90 Years of British Cinema* (London: BFI, 1986).
BBC, *Broadcast English: Recommendations to Announcers Regarding Certain Words of Doubtful Pronunciation, with an Introduction by A. Lloyd James*, 3rd edn. (London: BBC, 1935; originally 1928).

BBC, *Young Playwrights Festival 1988* (London: BBC, 1988).

Bell, D., *The Coming of Post-Industrial Society: A Venture in Social Forecasting* (London: Heinemann, 1974).

Benn, T., *Conflicts of Interest: Diaries 1977–80* (London: Arrow Books, 1991).

Bennett, A., *Untold Stories,* (London: Faber & Faber, 2005).

Bernstein, G. L., *The Myth of Decline: The Rise of Britain since 1945* (London: Pimlico, 2004).

Birt, J., *The Harder Path* (London: Time Warner, 2002).

Black, J., *Britain since the Seventies: Politics and Society in the Consumer Age* (London: Reaktion Books, 2004).

Blackburn, S., *Plato's Republic: A Biography* (London: Atlantic Books, 2006).

Blue, L., *Bright Blue: Rabbi Lionel Blue's Thoughts for the Day* (London: BBC, 1985).

—— *A Backdoor to Heaven: An Autobiography* (London: Fount, 1994).

Booker, C., *The Seventies: The Decade that Changed the Future* (New York: Stein & Day, 1981).

Born, G., *Uncertain Vision: Birt, Dyke and the Reinvention of the BBC* (London: Vintage, 2005).

Boyle, A., *Only the Wind Will Listen: Reith of the BBC* (London: Hutchinson, 1972).

Brett, S., *After Henry* (London: Penguin, 1988).

Bridson, D. G., *Prospero and Ariel: The Rise and Fall of Radio—A Personal Recollection* (London: Victor Gollancz, 1971).

Briggs, A., *The History of Broadcasting in the United Kingdom*, 5 vols. (Oxford: Oxford University Press, 1995).

Briscoe, D., and Curtis-Bramwell, R., *The BBC Radiophonic Workshop: The First 25 Years* (London: BBC, 1983).

Brown, J., *Eminent Gardeners: Some People of Influence and Their Gardens 1880–1980* (London: Viking, 1990).

—— *The Pursuit of Paradise: A Social History of Gardens and Gardening* (London: Harper Collins, 1999).

Brown, J. R., *A Short Guide to Modern British Drama* (London: Heinemann, 1982).

Brown, M., and Ballard, P., *The Church and Economic Life—A Documentary Study: 1945 to the Present* (Peterborough: Epworth, 2006).

Burchardt, J., *Paradise Lost: Rural Idyll and Social Change since 1800* (London: Tauris, 2002).

Burchfield, R., *The Spoken Word: A BBC Guide* (London: BBC, 1981).

—— 'Two Kinds of English? Jeffrey Archer and Anita Brookner', in C. Ricks and L. Michaels (eds.), *The State of the Language* (Los Angeles: University of California Press, 1990).

Burke, P., *What is Cultural History?* (Cambridge: Polity Press, 2004).

Burns, T., *The BBC: Public Institution and Private World* (London: Macmillan, 1977).

Butler, T., and Savage, M. (eds.), *Social Change and the Middle Classes* (London: UCL Press, 1995).

Callaghan, J., 'Industrial Militancy, 1945–79: The Failure of the British Road to Socialism', *Twentieth Century British History,* 15/4 (2004), 388–409.

Cameron, D., *Good to Talk? Living and Working in a Communication Culture* (London: Sage, 2000).

Cannadine, D., *Class in Britain* (New Haven: Yale University Press, 1998).

Carey, J., *The Intellectuals and the Masses: Pride and Prejudice among the Literary Intelligentsia, 1880–1939* (London: Faber & Faber, 1992).

—— 'Reportage, Literature and Willed Credulity', in J. Aitcheson and D. M. Lewis (eds.), *New Media Language* (London: Routledge, 2003).

—— *What Good Are the Arts?* (London: Faber & Faber, 2006).

Carpenter, H., *The Envy of the World: Fifty Years of the BBC Third Programme and Radio 3* (London: Weidenfeld & Nicolson, 1996).

—— *That Was Satire That Was* (London: Victor Gollancz, 2000).

—— *The Angry Young Men: A Literary Comedy of the 1950s* (London: Allen Lane, 2002).

Carruthers, S. L., *The Media at War: Communication and Conflict in the Twentieth Century* (Basingstoke: Palgrave, 2000).

Carver, R. (ed.), *Ariel at Bay: Reflections on Broadcasting and the Arts—Critics' Forum Festschrift for Philip French* (Manchester: Carcanet, 1990).

Chanan, M., *Repeated Takes: A Short History of Recording and Its Effects on Music* (London: Verso, 1995).

Chandler, D., 'Foreword: Postcards from the Edge', in *The Shipping Forecast: Photographs by Mark Power*, 2nd edn. (London: Zelda Cheatle Press and Network Photographers, 1997).

Chapman, R., *Selling the Sixties: The Pirates and Pop Music Radio* (London: Routledge, 1992).

Chignell, H., 'BBC Radio 4's "Analysis", 1970–1983: A Selective History and Case Study of BBC Current Affairs Radio', unpublished Ph.D. thesis (Bournemouth, 2004).

—— and Devlin, J., 'John Peel's Home Truths' (unpublished article, Bournemouth University, 2005).

Childs, D., *Britain since 1939: Progress and Decline*, 2nd edn. (Basingstoke: Palgrave, 2002).

Clare, A., *Psychiatry in Dissent: Controversial Issues in Thought and Practice* (London: Tavistock, 1976).

—— *In the Psychiatrist's Chair* (London: Mandarin, 1993).

—— and Thompson, S., *Let's Talk about Me: A Critical Examination of the New Psychotherapies* (London: BBC, 1981).

Clarke, P., *Hope and Glory: Britain 1900–1990* (London: Penguin, 1996).

Cleverdon, D., *The Growth of Milk Wood* (London: Dent, 1969).

Collini, S., *Absent Minds: Intellectuals in Britain* (Oxford: Oxford University Press, 2006).

Colls, R., *Identity of England* (Oxford: Oxford University Press, 2002).

Collyer, P., *Rain Later, Good: Illustrating the Shipping Forecast*, 2nd edn. (London: Adlard Coles Nautical, 2002).

Connelly, C., *Attention All Shipping: A Journey round the Shipping Forecast* (London: Little Brown, 2004).

Coogan, S., Baynham, P., Iannucci, A., and Marber, P., *Alan Partridge: Every Ruddy Word: All the Scripts: From Radio to TV. And Back* (London: Penguin, 2004).

Cooke, L., *British Television Drama: A History* (London: BFI, 2003).

Coward, M., *The Pocket Essential Classic Radio Comedy* (Harpenden: Pocket Essentials, 2003).

Cranston, D., 'From Portland Stone to the River Foyle: The Decentralising and Democratising of BBC Radio', in M. McLoone (ed.), *Broadcasting in a Divided Community: Seventy Years of the BBC in Northern Ireland* (Belfast: Institute of Irish Studies, 1996).

Crisell, A., *Understanding Radio*, 2nd edn. (London: Routledge, 1994).

—— *An Introductory History of British Broadcasting*, 2nd edn. (London: Routledge, 2002).

—— 'Look with Thine Ears: BBC Radio 4 and Its Significance in a Multi-Media Age', in A. Crisell (ed.), *More than a Music Box: Radio Cultures and Communities in a Multi-Media World* (Oxford: Berghahn, 2004).

Crook, T., *Radio Drama: Theory and Practice* (London: Routledge, 1999).

Crowley, T. (ed.), *Proper English? Readings in Language, History and Cultural Identity* (London: Routledge, 1991).

Crystal, D., *The English Language*, 2nd edn. (London: Penguin, 2002).

Cunliffe, B., *Facing the Ocean: The Atlantic and Its Peoples 8000 BC–1500 AD* (Oxford: Oxford University Press, 2001).

Curran, C., *A Seamless Robe: Broadcasting Philosophy and Practice* (London: Collins, 1979).

Curran, J., and Seaton, J., *Power without Responsibility: The Press and Broadcasting in Britain*, 5th edn. (London: Routledge, 1997).

Davie, G., *Religion in Britain since 1945* (Oxford: Blackwell, 1994).

Davies, J., *Broadcasting and the BBC in Wales* (Cardiff: University of Wales Press, 1994).

Day, R., *Grand Inquisitor: Memoirs* (London: Pan, 1990).

Dentith, S., *Parody* (London: Routledge, 2000).

Dewe Matthews, T., *Censored* (London: Chatto & Windus, 1994).

Dillon, G. M., 'Public Opinion and the Falklands Conflict', *Bailrigg Paper on International Security Number 7* (Lancaster: University of Lancaster, 1984).

Doherty, M., *Nazi Wireless Propaganda: Lord Haw-Haw and British Public Opinion in the Second World War* (Edinburgh: Edinburgh University Press, 2000).

Donovan, P., *The Radio Companion* (London: Grafton, 1992).

—— *All Our Todays: Forty Years of the Today Programme* (London: Jonathan Cape, 1997).

Douglas, S., *Listening In: Radio and the American Imagination, from Amos 'n' Andy and Edward R. Murrow to Wolfman Jack and Howard Stern* (New York: Times Books, 1999).

Drakakis, J. (ed.), *British Radio Drama* (Cambridge: Cambridge University Press, 1981).

Duffy, C. A., *Mean Time*, 2nd edn. (London: Anvil Press Poetry, 1998).

Dyke, G., *Inside Story* (London: Harper Collins, 2004).

Ekirch, R. A., *At Day's Close: A History of Nighttime* (London: Phoenix, 2006).

Eldridge, J., *King Street Junior* (London: BBC Books, 1988).

Eppel, E. M., and Eppel, M., *Adolescents and Morality: A Study of some Moral Values and Dilemmas of Working Adolescents in the Context of a Changing Climate of Opinion* (London: Routledge & Kegan Paul, 1966).

Esslin, M., *The Theatre of the Absurd*, 3rd edn. (London: Methuen, 2001).

Fairclough, N., *Media Discourse* (London: Arnold, 1995).

Feldman, S., 'Twin Peaks', in C. Mitchell (ed.), *Women and Radio: Airing Differences* (London: Routledge, 2000).

Fischer, T., *Under the Frog* (London: Penguin, 1992).

Fisk, R., *The Great War for Civilization: The Conquest of the Middle East* (London: Fourth Estate, 2005).

Foster, A., and Furst, S., *Radio Comedy, 1938–1968* (Virgin: London, 1996).

Fox, K., *Watching the English: The Hidden Rules of English Behaviour* (London: Hodder, 2005).

Fry, S., *Paperweight* (London: Arrow, 2004).

Gaiman, N., *Don't Panic: Douglas Adams and The Hitchhiker's Guide to the Galaxy* (London: Titan, 2003).

Gardiner, D., *Stereo and Hi-Fi as a Pastime* (London: Souvenir Press, 1959).

Garfield, S., *Our Hidden Lives: The Everyday Diaries of a Forgotten Britain 1945–1948* (London: Ebury Press, 2004).

Giddings, R., and Selby, K., *The Classic Serial on Television and Radio* (Basingstoke: Palgrave, 2001).

Gielgud, V., *Years of the Locust* (London: Nicholson & Watson, 1947).

Gilliam, L. (ed.), *BBC Features* (London: Evans, 1950).

Goodwin, P., *Television under the Tories: Broadcasting Policy 1979–1997* (London: BFI, 1998).

Gordon, A., 'The Country Cottage', in P. Abercrombie (ed.), *The Book of the Modern House: A Panoramic Survey of Contemporary Domestic Design* (London: Hodder & Stoughton, 1939).

Gosling, R., *Personal Copy: A Memoir of the Sixties* (London: Faber & Faber, 1980).

Gray, F., 'The Nature of Radio Drama', in P. Lewis (ed.), *Radio Drama* (London: Longman, 1981).

Gray, J., 'Broadcasting and Scottish Culture', in D. Daiches (ed.), *A Companion to Scottish Culture* (London: Edward Arnold, 1981).

Green, J., *All Dressed up: The Sixties and the Counter-Culture* (London: Pimlico, 1999).

Greenbaum, S., 'Whose English?', in C. Ricks and L. Michaels (eds.), *The State of the Language* (Berkeley and Los Angeles: University of California Press, 1990).

Greene, H., *The Third Floor Front: A View of Broadcasting in the Sixties* (London: The Bodley Head, 1969).

Grisewood, F., *The World Goes by: The Autobiography of Frederick Grisewood* (London: Secker & Warburg, 1952).

Grist, J., 'The Century before Yesterday: John Grist's BBC and Other Broadcasting Tales, Volume 2' (unpublished memoir, Private Collection, 2004).

Hall, L. A., *Sex, Gender and Social Change in Britain since 1880* (Basingstoke: Macmillan, 2000).

Hall, S., 'A World at One with Itself', *New Society*, 403 (18 June 1970), 1056–8.

Harris, J., 'Tradition and Transformation: Society and Civil Society in Britain, 1945–2001', in K. Burk (ed.), *The British Isles since 1945* (Oxford: Oxford University Press, 2003).

Harris, R., *Gotcha! The Media, the Government, and the Falklands Crisis* (London: Faber & Faber, 1983).

Hayes, N., and Hill, J. (eds.), *'Millions Like Us'? British Culture in the Second World War* (Liverpool: Liverpool University Press, 1999).

Heaney, S., *New Selected Poems 1966–1987* (London: Faber & Faber, 1990).

Hendy, D., 'Speaking to Middle England: Radio Four and its Listeners', in J. Aitchison and D. Lewis (eds.), *New Media Language* (London: Routledge, 2003).

—— 'Reality Radio: The Documentary', in A. Crisell (ed.), *More than a Music Box: Radio Cultures and Communities in a Multi-Media World* (London: Berghahn, 2004).

Hendy, D., 'Bad Language and BBC Radio Four in the 1960s and 1970s', *Twentieth Century British History*, 17/1 (2006), 74–102.

—— 'BBC Radio Four and Conflicts over Spoken English in the 1970s', *Media History*, 12/3 (2006), 273–89.

Heppenstall, R., *Portrait of the Artist as a Professional Man* (London: Peter Owen, 1969).

Hewison, R., *Culture and Consensus: England, Art and Politics since 1940* (London: Methuen, 1995).

Higson, A., '"Britain's Outstanding Contribution to the Film": The Documentary-Realist Tradition', in C. Barr (ed.), *All Our Yesterdays: 90 Years of British Cinema* (London: BFI, 1986).

Hill, G., *Hurricane Force: The Story of the Storm of October 1987* (London: Collins, 1988).

Hilmes, M., *Radio Voices: American Broadcasting, 1922–1952* (Minneapolis: University of Minnesota Press, 1997).

Hilton, M., *Consumerism in Twentieth Century Britain: The Search for a Historical Movement* (Cambridge: Cambridge University Press, 2003).

Hobsbawm, E., *The Age of Extremes: The Short Twentieth Century 1914–1991* (London: Abacus, 1994).

—— *Uncommon People: Resistance, Rebellion and Jazz* (London: Weidenfeld & Nicolson, 1998).

Hodges, A., and Hutter, D., *With Downcast Gays* (London: Pomegranate Press, 1974).

Hoggart, R., *The Uses of Literacy* (London: Penguin, 1958).

—— *Only Connect: On Culture and Communication. The BBC Reith Lectures 1971* (London: Chatto & Windus, 1972).

Horrie, C., and Clarke, S., *Fuzzy Monsters: Fear and Loathing at the BBC* (London: Heinemann, 1994).

Howkins, A., *The Death of Rural England: A Social History of the Countryside since 1900* (London: Routledge, 2003).

Hughes, G., *Swearing: A Social History of Foul Language, Oaths and Profanity in English* (London: Penguin, 1998).

Humble, N., *The Feminine Middlebrow Novel 1920s to 1950s* (Oxford: Oxford University Press, 2001).

Humphrys, J., *Devil's Advocate* (London: Arrow, 2000).

Hussey, M., *Chance Governs All: A Memoir* (Basingstoke: Macmillan, 2001).

Hutber, P., *The Decline and Fall of the Middle Class—and How It Can Fight Back* (London: Associated Business Programmes, 1976).

Ingham, B., *Kill the Messenger* (London: Fontana, 1991).

James, A. L., *The Broadcast Word* (London, 1935).

James, L., *The Middle Class: A History* (London: Little Brown, 2006).

Jenkins, D., *God, Politics and the Future* (London: SCM Press, 1988).

Jones, D., *Microphones and Muddy Boots: A Journey into Natural History Broadcasting* (London: David & Charles, 1987).

Judt, T., *Postwar: A History of Europe since 1945* (London: Heinemann, 2005).

Karpf, A., *The Human Voice: The Story of a Remarkable Talent* (London: Bloomsbury, 2006).

Keeble, R., *Secret State, Silent Press: New Militarism, the Gulf and the Modern Image of Warfare* (Luton: University of Luton Press, 1997).

King, R., and Nugent, N. (eds.), *Respectable Rebels: Middle Class Campaigns in Britain in the 1970s* (London: Hodder & Stoughton, 1979).

—— and Rayner, J., *The Middle Class*, 2nd edn. (London: Longman, 1981).

Kipling, R., *Selected Poems* (London: Penguin, 1993).

Knowles, W., and Evans, K. (eds.), *The Woman's Hour Book* (London: Sidgwick & Jackson and BBC, 1981).

Kumar, K., 'Holding the Middle Ground: The BBC, the Public and the Professional Broadcaster', in J. Curran, M. Gurevitch, and J. Woollacott (eds.), *Mass Communication and Society* (London: Edward Arnold, 1977).

—— *Utopia and Anti-Utopia in Modern Times* (Oxford: Blackwell, 1987).

Lahr, J., *Prick up Your Ears: The Biography of Joe Orton* (London: Bloomsbury, 2002).

Landau, C., *Growing up in the Sixties* (London: Optima, 1991).

Lasch, C., *The Culture of Narcissism: American Life in an Age of Diminishing Expectations* (New York: W. W. Norton & Co., 1978).

Lawley, S., *Sue Lawley's Desert Island Discs* (London: Mandarin, 1991).

Laybourn, K., *A History of British Trade Unionism, c.1770–1990* (Stroud: Alan Sutton, 1992).

Leapman, M., *The Last Days of the Beeb* (London: Allen & Unwin, 1986).

Lee, M. (ed.), *Woman's Hour: A Selection* (London: BBC, 1967).

Leitner, G., 'The Social Background of the Language of Radio', in H. Davis and P. Walton (eds.), *Language, Image, Media* (Oxford: Basil Blackwell, 1983).

LeMahieu, D. L., *A Culture for Democracy: Mass Communication and the Cultivated Mind in Britain between the Wars* (Oxford: Clarendon Press, 1988).

Lewis, P., 'Radio Drama and English Literature', in P. Lewis (ed.), *Radio Drama* (London: Longman, 1981).

Lewis, P. M., 'Referable Words in Radio Drama', in P. Scannell (ed.), *Broadcast Talk* (London: Sage, 1991).

Lesser, A., *Meet Me by Moonlight: A Play with Music in Three Acts* (London: Evan Brothers, 1958).

—— *Love by Appointment: A Comedy* (London: Samuel French, 1966).

—— *The Chicken Girl: A Comedy* (London: Samuel French, 1967).

Lesser, T., *The Bedwinner: A Comedy* (London: Samuel French, 1975).

Lloyd, J., *What the Media Are Doing to Our Politics* (London: Constable, 2004).

Long, P., 'British Radio and the Politics of Culture in Post-war Britain: The Work of Charles Parker', *The Radio Journal: International Studies in Broadcast and Audio Media*, 2/3 (2004), 131–52.

Low, D. A., 'Telling the Story: Susan Hill and Dorothy L. Sayers', in J. Drakakis (ed.), *British Radio Drama* (Cambridge: Cambridge University Press, 1981).

Luckhurst, T., *This is Today: A Biography of the Today Programme* (London: Aurum Press, 2001).

McDowell, W. H., *The History of BBC Broadcasting in Scotland, 1923–1983* (Edinburgh: Edinburgh University Press, 1992).

McFarlane, B., 'A Literary Cinema? British Films and British Novels', in C. Barr (ed.), *All Our Yesterdays: 90 Years of British Cinema* (London: BFI, 1986).

MacGregor, S., *Woman of Today: An Autobiography* (London: Headline, 2002).

McIntyre, I., *The Expense of Glory: A Life of John Reith* (London: Harper Collins, 1993).

McKibbin, R., *Classes and Cultures: England 1918–1951* (Oxford: Oxford University Press, 1998).

McLuhan, M., *The Medium is the Massage* (London: Penguin, 1967).

—— *Understanding Media: The Extensions of Man* (London: Sphere Books, 1967).

Madsen, V. M., 'Radio and the Documentary Imagination: Thirty Years of Experiment, Innovation and Revelation', *The Radio Journal: International Studies in Broadcast and Audio Media*, 3/3 (2006), 189–98.

Mandler, P., 'Two Cultures—One—or Many?', in K. Burk (ed.), *The British Isles since 1945* (Oxford: Oxford University Press, 2003).

Martin, D., 'The Churches: Pink Bishops and the Iron Lady', in D. Kavanagh and A. Seldon (eds.), *The Thatcher Effect* (Oxford: Clarendon Press, 1989).

Marwick, A., *The Sixties; Cultural Revolution in Britain, France, Italy, and the United States, c.1958–1974* (Oxford: Oxford University Press, 1998).

Matless, D., *Landscape and Englishness* (London: Reaktion, 1998).

Mercer, D., Mungham, G., and Williams, K., *The Fog of War: The Media on the Battlefield* (London: Heinemann, 1987).

Michelmore, C., and Metcalfe, J., *Two-Way Story* (London: Hamish Hamilton/Elm Tree Books, 1986).

Middlemas, K., *Power, Competition and the State*, ii: *Threats to the Postwar Settlement, Britain 1961–1974* (Basingstoke: Macmillan, 1990).

Miller, K. (ed.), *A Second Listener Anthology* (London: BBC 1973).

Miller, S., *Conversation: A History of a Declining Art* (New Haven: Yale University Press, 2006).

Milne, A., *DG: The Memoirs of a British Broadcaster* (London: Hodder & Stoughton, 1988).

Moncrieff, A., *Messages to the Future: The Story of the BBC Time Capsule* (London: Futura, 1984).

Moore, A., *The Beatles: Sergeant Pepper's Lonely Hearts Club Band* (Cambridge: Cambridge University Press, 1997).

Morris, N., 'US Voices on UK Radio', *European Journal of Communication*, 14/1 (1999), 37–59.

Morrison, D. E., and Tumber, H., *Journalists at War: The Dynamics of News Reporting during the Falklands Conflict* (London: Sage, 1988).

Mugglestone, L., *'Talking Proper': The Rise of Accent as Social Symbol* (Oxford: Clarendon Press, 1997).

Murdock, G., 'Organising the Imagination: Sociological Perspectives on Radio Drama', in P. Lewis (ed.), *Radio Drama* (London: Longman, 1981).

Nadel, I., *Double Act: A Life of Tom Stoppard* (London: Methuen, 2002).

Nicholas, S., *The Echo of War: Home Front Propaganda and the Wartime BBC 1939–45* (Manchester: Manchester University Press, 1996).

—— 'The People's Radio: The BBC and its Audience, 1939–1945', in N. Hayes and J. Hill (eds.), *'Millions Like Us?' British Culture in the Second World War* (Liverpool: Liverpool University Press, 1999).

Nobbs, D., *I Didn't Get Where I Am Today: An Autobiography* (London: Arrow, 2004).

Nye, S., Godwin, N., and Hollows, B., 'Twisting the Dials: Lesbians on British Radio', in C. Mitchell (ed.), *Women and Radio: Airing Differences* (London: Routledge, 2000).

O'Malley, T., *Closedown: The BBC and Government Broadcasting Policy 1979–92* (London: Pluto Press, 1994).

Painting, N., *Forever Ambridge: Twenty Five Years of The Archers* (London: Michael Joseph, 1975).

—— *Forever Ambridge: Thirty Years of The Archers*, rev. edn. (London: Michael Joseph, 1980).

Paling, C., *The Silent Sentry* (London: Vintage, 2000).

Peel, J., and Ravenscroft, S., *Margrave of the Marshes* (London: Corgi, 2006).

Perkin, H., *The Rise of Professional Society: England since 1880* (London: Routledge, 1989).

Perkins, G., 'Introduction to the First Edition', in D. Adams, *The Hitchhiker's Guide to the Galaxy: The Original Radio Scripts*, updated edn. (London: Pan, 2003).

Photofile, *Photographers of the American Depression* (Photofile, 1982).

Pimlott, B., *Harold Wilson* (London: Harper Collins, 1992).

Pinter, H., *Plays (3)* (London: Faber & Faber, 1997).

Plomley, R., *Plomley's Pick of Desert Island Discs* (London: Weidenfeld & Nicolson, 1982).

Priessnitz, H. P., 'British Radio Drama: A Survey', in P. Lewis (ed.), *Radio Drama* (London: Longman, 1981).

Priestland, G., *Something Understood: An Autobiography* (London: Andre Deutsch, 1986).

Priestley, J. B., *English Humour* (London: Longmans, Green & Co., 1929).

Purves, L., *Radio: A True Love Story* (London: Hodder & Stoughton, 2002).

Raban, J., 'Icon or Symbol: The Writer and the "Medium"', in P. Lewis (ed.), *Radio Drama* (London: Longman, 1981).

Rayner, C., *How Did I Get Here from There?* (London: Virago, 2003).

Rex, J., and Moore, R., *Race, Conflict and Community: A Study of Sparkbrook* (Oxford: Oxford University Press, 1967).

Robertson, J. C., *The Hidden Cinema: British Film Censorship in Action, 1913–1972* (London: Routledge, 1989).

Rodger, I., *Radio Drama* (London: Macmillan, 1982).

Rose, J., *The Intellectual Life of the British Working Classes* (New Haven: Yale University Press, 2001).

Rose, M., *Parody: Ancient, Modern and Post-Modern* (Cambridge: Cambridge University Press, 1993).

Sackur, S., *On the Basra Road* (London: London Review of Books, 1991).

Samuel, R., 'The Voice of Britain', in A. Light (ed.), *Island Stories: Unravelling Britain: Theatres of Memory*, ii (London: Verso, 1998).

Sandbrook, D., *Never Had It So Good: A History of Britain from Suez to the Beatles 1956–63* (London: Little Brown, 2005).

—— *White Heat: A History of Britain in the Swinging Sixties 1964–70* (London: Little Brown, 2006).

Savage, M., Barlow, J., Dickens, P., and Fielding, F., *Property, Bureaucracy and Culture: Middle-Class Formation in Contemporary Britain* (London: Routledge, 1992).

Scannell, P., *Radio, Television and Modern Life* (Oxford: Blackwell, 1996).

—— 'Public Service Broadcasting: The History of a Concept', in E. Buscombe (ed.), *British Television: A Reader* (Oxford: Oxford University Press, 2000).

Scannell, P.,'The *Brains Trust*: A Historical Study of the Management of Liveness on Radio', in S. Cottle (ed.), *Media Organisation and Production* (London: Sage, 2003).

—— and Cardiff, D., *A Social History of British Broadcasting*, i: *1922–1939: Serving the Nation* (Oxford: Blackwell, 1991).

Schama, S., *Landscape and Memory* (London: Harper Collins, 1995).

Schumacher, E. F., *Small is Beautiful: A Study of Economics as if People Mattered* (London: Blond & Briggs, 1973).

Seaton, J., 'Writing the History of Broadcasting', in D. Cannadine (ed.), *History and the Media* (London: Macmillan, 2004).

Sen, A., *Identity and Violence: The Illusion of Destiny* (London: Allen Lane, 2006).

Sennett, R., *The Culture of the New Capitalism* (New Haven: Yale University Press, 2006).

Shapley, O., *Broadcasting a Life* (London: Scarlet Press, 1996).

Sheldon, M., *Orwell: The Authorized Biography* (London: Heinemann, 1991).

Shellard, D., and Nicholson, S., with Handley, M. (eds.), *The Lord Chamberlain Regrets: A History of British Theatre Censorship* (London: British Library, 2004).

Shingler, M., 'Some Recurring Features of European Avant-Garde Radio', *Journal of Radio Studies*, 7/1 (2000), 196–212.

Simpson, J., *From the House of War: John Simpson in the Gulf* (London: Arrow Books, 1991).

—— *Strange Places, Questionable People* (London: Pan, 1998).

Simpson, M. J., *Hitchhiker: A Biography of Douglas Adams* (London: Hodder & Stoughton, 2003).

Skues, K., *Pop Went the Pirates* (Sheffield: Lamb's Meadow, 1994).

Smethurst, W., *The Archers: The History of Radio's Most Famous Programme* (London: Michael O'Mara, 1997).

Snowman, D., *The Hitler Émigrés: The Cultural Impact on Britain of Refugees from Nazism* (London: Pimlico, 2003).

Steiner, G., *Language and Silence: Essays 1958–1966* (London: Faber & Faber, 1967).

Stevenson, R., *The Oxford English Literary History*, xii: *1960–2000* (Oxford: Oxford University Press, 2004).

Storey, B., *The Way to Good Speech* (London: Nelson, 1937).

Street, S., *A Concise History of British Radio 1922–2002* (Tiverton: Kelly Publications, 2002).

—— *Radio Waves: Poems Celebrating the Wireless* (London: Enitharmon Press, 2004).

Stuart, C. (ed.), *The Reith Diaries* (London: Collins, 1975).

Sutherland, J., *Offensive Literature: Decensorship in Britain, 1960–1982* (London: Junction Books, 1982).

Swift, C., 'A Proteus at the Beeb: Acting with BBC Radio Rep', *Theatre Quarterly*, 4/13 (1974), 5–13.

Tennyson, H., *The Haunted Mind: An Autobiography* (London: Andre Deutsch, 1984).

Thomas, J., 'A History of the BBC Features Department, 1924–1964', unpublished D.Phil. thesis (Oxford, 1993).

Thompson, M., 'The Anatomy of a Radio Programme: The Making of Touching the Elephant' (author's unpublished typescript, 2006).

Timpson, J., *Today and Yesterday* (London: George Allen & Unwin, 1976).

Took, B., *Laughter in the Air: An Informal History of British Radio Comedy* (London: BBC, 1981).

—— *Round the Horne: The Complete and Utter History* (London: Boxtree, 1998).

—— and Feldman, M., *Round the Horne* (London: Futura, 1975).

Townsend, S., *The Secret Diary of Adrian Mole Aged 13¾* (London: Methuen, 1982).

Toye, J., *The Archers 1968–1986: Looking for Love* (London: BBC, 1999).

Trethowan, I., *The Development of Radio*, BBC Lunchtime Lectures Ninth Series, Number 4 (London: BBC, 1975).

—— *Split Screen* (London: Hamish Hamilton, 1984).

Trudgill, P., 'The Meanings of Words Should Not Be Allowed to Vary or Change', in L. Bauer and P. Trudgill (eds.), *Language Myths* (London: Penguin, 1998).

Tydeman, J., 'The Producer and Radio Drama: A Personal View', in P. Lewis (ed.), *Radio Drama* (London: Longman, 1981).

—— 'Bad Language and Radio Drama: A Personal View', in A. M. Hargrave (ed.), *A Matter of Manners? The Limits of Broadcast Language*, Broadcasting Standards Council Research Monograph Series 3 (London: Broadcasting Standards Council, 1991).

Veldman, M., *Fantasy, The Bomb, and the Greening of Britain: Romantic Protest, 1945–1980* (Cambridge: Cambridge University Press, 1994).

Vernon, T., *Fat Man on a Bicycle: A Discovery of France by Tom Vernon* (London: Michael Joseph, 1981).

—— *Fat Man on a Roman Road* (London: Michael Joseph, 1983).

Wade, D., 'British Radio Drama since 1960', in J. Drakakis (ed.), *British Radio Drama* (Cambridge: Cambridge University Press, 1981).

—— 'Popular Radio Drama', in P. Lewis (ed.), *Radio Drama* (London: Longman, 1981).

Watt, D., ' "The Maker and the Tool": Charles Parker, Documentary Performance, and the Search for a Popular Culture', *New Theatre Quarterly*, 19/1 (2003), 41–66.

Webb, N., *Wish You Were Here: The Official Biography of Douglas Adams* (London: Headline, 2004).

Weeks, J., *Sex, Politics and Society: The Regulation of Sexuality since 1800* (London: Longman, 1981).

Weight, R., *Patriots: National Identity in Britain, 1940–2000* (London: Pan, 2004).

Whitburn, V., *The Archers: The Official Inside Story* (London: Virgin, 1996).

Whitehead, K., *The Third Programme: A Literary History* (Oxford: Clarendon Press, 1989).

Wiener, M. J., *English Culture and the Decline of the Industrial Spirit 1850–1980*, 2nd edn. (Cambridge: Cambridge University Press, 2004).

Williams, R., *Culture and Society 1780–1950* (London: Chatto & Windus, 1958).

—— *Communications*, rev. edn. (London: Chatto & Windus, 1966).

Willman, J., 'The Civil Service', in D. Kavanagh and A. Seldon (eds.), *The Major Effect* (London: Macmillan, 1994).

Wilson, A., *No Laughing Matter* (London: Secker & Warburg, 1967).

Wilson, J., *Roger Cook's Checkpoint* (London: Ariel Books, 1983).

Winston, B., *Media, Technology and Society: A History from the Telegraph to the Internet* (London: Routledge, 1998).

Winter, D., *Winter's Tale: Living through an Age of Change in Church and Media* (Oxford: Lion, 2001).

Wolfe, T., *The New Journalism* (London: Picador, 1975).

—— 'The Me Decade and the Third Great Awakening', in T. Wolfe, *The Purple Decades* (London: Jonathan Cape, 1983).

Worsley, F., *ITMA 1939–1948* (London: Vox Mundi, 1948).

Worsnip, G., *Up the Down Escalator* (London: Coronet, 1991).

Wyatt, W., *The Fun Factory: A Life in the BBC* (London: Aurum Press, 2003).

Wyld, H. C., *A History of Modern Colloquial English* (London: Unwin, 1920).

—— 'The Best English: A Claim for the Superiority of Received Standard English' (first published 1934), in T. Crowley (ed.), *Proper English? Readings in Language, History and Cultural Identity* (London: Routledge, 1991).

Wyndham-Goldie, G., *Facing the Nation: Television and Politics 1936–1976* (London: Bodley Head, 1977).

Young, M., *The Rise of the Meritocracy 1870–2023: An Essay on Education and Equality* (London: Thames & Hudson, 1958).

Zeldin, T., *An Intimate History of Humanity* (London: Vintage, 1995).

Index